FIELDING'S
AUSTRALIA

Fielding Titles

FIELDING'S
AUSTRALIA

by
Zeke Wigglesworth
and
Joan Wigglesworth

Fielding Worldwide, Inc.
308 South Catalina Avenue
Redondo Beach, California 90277 U.S.A.

Fielding's Australia

Published by Fielding Worldwide, Inc.

Text Copyright ©1997 Zeke Wigglesworth and Joan Wigglesworth

Maps, Icons & Illustrations Copyright ©1997 FWI

Photo Copyrights ©1997 to Individual Photographers

FIELDING WORLDWIDE INC.

PUBLISHER AND CEO	**Robert Young Pelton**
GENERAL MANAGER	**John Guillebeaux**
OPERATIONS DIRECTOR	**George Posanke**
ELECTRONIC PUBLISHING DIRECTOR	**Larry E. Hart**
PUBLIC RELATIONS DIRECTOR	**Beverly Riess**
ACCOUNT SERVICES MANAGER	**Cindy Henrichon**
PROJECT MANAGER	**Chris Snyder**
MANAGING EDITOR	**Amanda K. Knoles**

PRODUCTION

Martin Mancha	**Rebecca Perry**
Ramses Reynoso	**Craig South**

COVER DESIGNED BY	**Digital Artists, Inc.**
COVER PHOTOGRAPHERS—Front Cover	**Doug Armand/Tony Stone Images**
Back Cover	**Chad Ehlers/Tony Stone Images**
INSIDE PHOTOS	**Courtesy of the Australian Tourism Commission**

Inquiries should be addressed to: Fielding Worldwide, Inc., 308 South Catalina Ave., Redondo Beach, California 90277 U.S.A., ☎ *(310) 372-4474*, Facsimile *(310) 376-8064*, 8:30 a.m.–5:30 p.m. Pacific Standard Time.
Website: http://www.fieldingtravel.com
e-mail: fielding@fieldingtravel.com

ISBN 1-56952-132-8

Printed in the United States of America

Letter from the Publisher

In 1946, Temple Fielding began the first of what would be a remarkable new series of well-written, highly personalized guidebooks for independent travelers. Temple's opinionated, witty, and oft-imitated books have now guided travelers straight to the heart of each country for more than a quarter century. More important to some was Fielding's humorous and direct method of steering travelers away from the dull and the insipid. Today, Fielding Travel Guides' status as the most researched and comprehensive travel guides— written by experienced travelers *for* experienced travelers—is being made even more *secure* through our lineup of seasoned travel writers. Our authors carry on Fielding's well-earned reputation for creating travel guides that deliver truly unique experiences with a sense of discovery and style.

Inspired by what was lacking in other guidebooks, Zeke and Joan Wigglesworth spent more than a decade researching the material for this book. They have condensed this wealth of knowledge and experience into what I believe is the most interesting, colorful and beneficial guide to Australia available today. The Wigglesworths have utilized their broad expertise in their location and attraction descriptions to bring to life this vast and varied continent. They've also been careful to guide you past the obvious and the overrated, while directing you to some of the country's most secret delights.

Today, the concept of independent travel has never been bigger. Our policy of *brutal honesty* and a highly personal point of view has never changed; it just seems the travel world has caught up with us.

Enjoy your Australian adventure with the Wigglesworths and Fielding.

R Y P

Robert Young Pelton
Publisher and CEO
Fielding Worldwide, Inc.

Dedication

For Carolyn, Paul and Tom: Russia will always have Leningrad.

Fielding Rating Icons

The Fielding Rating Icons are highly personal and awarded to help the besieged traveler choose from among the dizzying array of activities, attractions, hotels, restaurants and sights. The awarding of an icon denotes unusual or exceptional qualities in the relevant category.

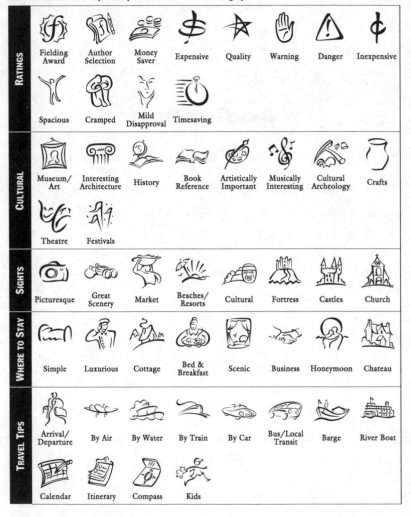

RATINGS

Fielding Award · Author Selection · Money Saver · Expensive · Quality · Warning · Danger · Inexpensive

Spacious · Cramped · Mild Disapproval · Timesaving

CULTURAL

Museum/Art · Interesting Architecture · History · Book Reference · Artistically Important · Musically Interesting · Cultural Archeology · Crafts

Theatre · Festivals

SIGHTS

Picturesque · Great Scenery · Market · Beaches/Resorts · Cultural · Fortress · Castles · Church

WHERE TO STAY

Simple · Luxurious · Cottage · Bed & Breakfast · Scenic · Business · Honeymoon · Chateau

TRAVEL TIPS

Arrival/Departure · By Air · By Water · By Train · By Car · Bus/Local Transit · Barge · River Boat

Calendar · Itinerary · Compass · Kids

ACTIVITIES

Downhill Skiing	X-country Skiing	Water Sports	Sailing	Scuba Diving	Snorkeling/ Diving	Deep-sea Fishing	Freshwater Fishing
Swimming	Hiking	Walking	Relaxing	Golf	Tennis	Horseback Riding	General Sports
Cycling	Workout	Spa	Camping	Off-Road	Boating	Rafting	Recreational Vehicle

SPECIAL INTEREST

| Nightlife | Singles | Romantic | Nude Beaches | Lecture | Spectacular Cuisine | Wine Tasting | Shopping |
| Cafe Stops | Gardening | Pro Sports | Mystery | Gambling | Wildlife | | |

Our Rating System

Apart from giving you information about what is available to see and do in Australia and background about its history and culture, the most valuable help we can provide is to evaluate sights, monuments, hotels and restaurants. For easy reference, we codify our opinions within a star system:

★★★★★   Outstanding anywhere in the world

★★★★   Exceptional, among the best in the country

★★★   Superior for a particular area of the country

★★   Good, a clear step above the average

★   Above average

For restaurants we provide $rating categories. This price is for a meal for two people.

$$$	Expensive	A$65+
$$	Moderate	A$40–$65
$	Inexpensive	Less than A$40

TABLE OF CONTENTS

LIST OF MAPS

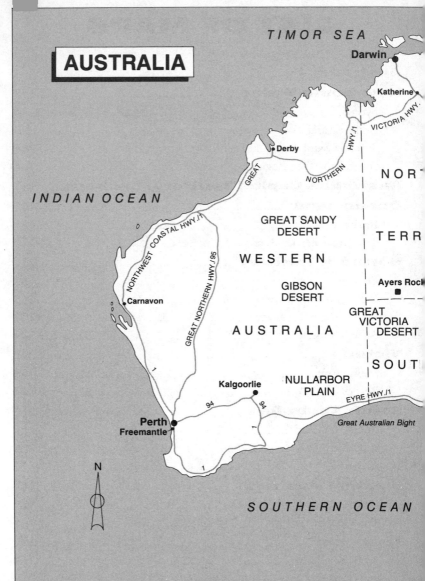

AUSTRALIA

TIMOR SEA

Darwin

Katherine

VICTORIA HWY.

Derby

HWY./1

NORTHERN

INDIAN OCEAN

NOR⁻

GREAT SANDY
DESERT

TERR

WESTERN

NORTHWEST COASTAL HWY./1

GREAT NORTHERN HWY./95

GIBSON
DESERT

Ayers Rock

Carnavon

GREAT
VICTORIA
DESERT

AUSTRALIA

SOUT

NULLARBOR
PLAIN

Kalgoorlie

EYRE HWY./1

94   94

Great Australian Bight

Perth
Freemantle

1

N

1

SOUTHERN OCEAN

| 0 | miles | 500 |
| 0 | kilometers | 800 |

ARAFURA SEA

Torres Strait

RNHEM
LAND

Gulf of Carpentaria

CORAL SEA

CAPE
YORK
PENINSULA

Cairns

GREAT DIVIDING RANGE

GREAT

BARRIER

REEF

ERN

BARKLY HWY. /66

Tennant
Creek

FLINDERS HWY. /78

Townsville

ORY

Mt. Isa

Mackay

Alice Springs

QUEENSLAND

Rockhampton

GREAT DIVIDING RANGE

SOUTH

SIMPSON
DESERT

PACIFIC

OCEAN

HWY. 87

USTRALIA

Brisbane

Gold
Coast

NEW SOUTH
WALES

GREAT DIVIDING RANGE

Spencer Gulf

Adelaide

Newcastle

Gulf St.
Vincent

Canberra

31

Sydney

Wollongong

VICTORIA

Geelong

Melbourne

TASMAN SEA

Bass Strait

TASMANIA

Launceston

Hobart

FOREWORD

The magic number in Australia today is 2000, as in the 2000 Summer Olympic Games being held in the Sydney area, and 2000, when the country might undergo a profound political change.

The end of the century marks the first time the Games have been Down Under since Melbourne was the host city way back in 1956. The international attention being focused on Sydney in particular and Australia in general comes at a time when the island nation is trying to decide who and what it will become as it enters the 21st century.

Since the end of World War II, Australia has gradually become less and less a creature of Europe and more and more a member of the Asian community of nations. It has not been an easy transition, but the once-tight ties that made Australia one of the most loyal of Commonwealth countries have been slipping constantly for 50 years.

As the country readies itself for the Games, there are serious moves afoot to change the nature of the Australian government itself. The former Aussie prime minister, Paul Keating, wanted to turn the country into a republic by 2000, and replace the queen, now the titular head of government, with an elected Australian. His party was defeated at the polls, mostly because of economic reasons, and the whole question of the queen's future is unclear. The new prime minister, John Howard, leans toward the monarchy and tradition. While the move toward an Australian republic is not universally popular in Australia, there seems to be enough support to keep the idea afloat. Keating's proposals included allowing Parliament to elect the head of state or having a general election for a president.

The games also caused the international Olympic community to focus on one of the major social problems facing Australia, the treatment of the indigenous Aboriginal peoples. The record of race relations in Australia, dating to white settlement in 1788, is not good, and while there have been major advances for black Australians, their living conditions and health standards are often a national disgrace.

For many Australians, the coming of the Games is a sign that the world is willing to accept the Land Down Under as a legitimate member of the international community. There is a thread of inferiority running throughout Australian history, caused by its beginnings as a penal colony and then almost two centuries spent as a lowly regarded satrap of the British Empire. Australia went crazy when the games were awarded to Sydney. There were wild celebrations in the city (one newspaper said it was the biggest party since the end of World War II), and the general reaction was one of pride and surprise. It was a lot like Sally Field at the Oscars: "You guys really do like me." One Sydney Olympic official put it this way: "This means, at last, that Sydney is becoming a true international city." Well, where's he been? Sydney *already* is a true international city, and the Olympics will prove it to the world.

For many people, Australia has an almost mythic attraction, based mostly on misconceptions and unachievable expectations. Because of time and distance, it's one of those places travelers put on a list of someday-places to visit, right up there with Nepal and Machu Picchu and the game parks of Tanzania. Part of the appeal is its location, far away in the South Seas, a remote island continent somewhere south of Hawaii and a bit north of Antarctica. And probably its biggest single lure is the incredible diversity and unique character of the animal life. Nature experimented in a big way Down Under, leaving an odd assortment of Doctor Seuss animals found almost nowhere else on earth. Add to that some striking photographs of the vast deserts, a video or two of an Aboriginal dance troupe complete with didgeridoo, and mix in the antics of a few of the more famous Australians wandering around on the public stage, and you might expect to suddenly end up on the other side of the rainbow when you get off your 747 in Sydney. The Australians know all about these myths, of course, and affectionately call their country "Oz."

One of the more famous Aussies around these days is Paul Hogan, universally recognized as Crocodile Dundee. (Other famous types include Mel Gibson, Greg Norman, Nicole Kidman and Elle McPherson, to name but a few). Hogan knew all about the world view of Australia when he decided to create his famous croc-hunting hero. During an interview on the ABC (Australian Broadcasting Commission) he was asked why he created the first immensely popular and immensely successful Dundee movie. Mostly, he said, he was just trying to make a buck. But also, he said, he did it because Australia has no heroes these days and he just wanted to create one. Like anyone else pondering such a task, Hogan drew on what he knew—the Aussie mystique—but he shook a little dust off it, took a look around at the 20th century and came up with Mick Dundee, an Australian hero unlike any before him, yet one so Australian you'd recognize him anywhere.

How successful Hogan was creating a modern Australian hero is best left to historians. But from this side of the Big Pond, we have to say that he builded better than he knew. On purpose, perhaps, or even without knowing it, *Crocodile Dundee* ended up being a pretty good example of what Australia is all about. (Other Australian movies, you will note, also hook deeply into the Aussie psyche: *The Man from Snowy River* and *Breaker Morant*, for example.) Few Australians actually live like Dundee, out in the bush, hunting crocs on the sly, but the attitudes Hogan gave his alter ego are plainly 20th-century Australian. The self-reliant spirit is there, as is the amazing ability Australians have of shedding social inhibitions. Within 10 minutes of hitting Heaven, Australians will be on a first-name basis with God. If they're ever awed by anybody, we haven't seen it happen yet.

You can't help liking Crocodile Dundee, partly because he is Paul Hogan (known to almost everyone in Oz as "Hoages") and the performing Paul Hogan is a totally likable person, but also because Dundee is everything we Americans like to see in our Australians. We like to think we're very much like the Aussies: honest, hard-working, independent, resourceful, frontier-minded, and we see in their lives a mirror of our own. And it's true, our two cultures share many things. It is only one of the reasons why an increasing number of Americans are heading Down Under for a look. What they will find is not a whole continent of Crocodile Dundees, any more than an Aussie visitor here would find the streets full of John Waynes.

What visitors to Australia *will* find are 18 million people living on one of the most peculiar and fascinating continents of the world. And as they drive through the Outback, or see the sunrise on the Coral Sea, or shop the stores of beautiful Sydney, perceptive travelers will also discover that like any great myth, there are big threads of truth in the saga of Crocodile Dundee.

But watch out for those myths. It's entirely possible to visit Australia and never see a kangaroo (it takes a little work, but it can be done), and if you ever meet somebody on the streets of Sydney wearing an Australian hat, he's probably from Cleveland. If you somehow miss meeting a kangaroo or a koala or a Tasmanian Devil, you still won't go home disappointed. What we've found over the years is that Australia's real treasure is its citizens. They're great folks and they seem to genuinely like their American cousins. They also make great beer—and they serve it ice cold. You're definitely not in London, Toto.

A Personal Note

Zeke and Joan Wigglesworth

We think it necessary, for you to judge this work in its approach and authenticity, to know a bit about us. Travel books, like any other form of journalism, carry within them the biases of their creators. Could there be, for instance, any more completely prejudiced view of the pitfalls of 19th-century continental life than the often nasty (and almost always accurate) views of the father of American travel writers, Samuel Clemens, in *Innocents Abroad*? We, too, are biased, because over the years and over the miles as we wandered around the world, we developed habits and patterns of enjoyment and methods of criticism that we apply to our travels, our selection of accommodations, our fancies in food, our methods of conveyance. There is nothing wrong with this, certainly, as long as the predilections are made plain.

So, first, we must tell you that we are in love with Australia, its people, its animals, its magnificent wastelands, its gum trees, its mountains, lakes, rain forests, reefs. At the same time, there are things in Australia we find less than lovable, including the current state of the Aboriginals there, as well as persistent wisps of latent sexism, racism, colonialism and what seems sometimes to be an almost casual governmental disregard for the natural resources of the continent. The Australians are not alone in this, of course, but then, this book is about Australia, not other nations. We have tried to take the Land Down Under as it comes, warts and all, and have found it, on balance, to be a society that ranks high as one of the world's most honest, most friendly and most successful.

Second, we should tell you that we are Americans, which carries with it hordes of prejudices concerning clean toilets, potable water supplies and legal rights.

The female half of this effort hails originally from the nation's capital, bringing with her the somewhat disgusting ability to devour a half-bushel of Chesapeake Bay crabs without pausing for air, but also bringing memories of Maryland forests and insect-thrumming ponds, animals and birds, clean air—and water singularly lacking in heavy metals. Given a choice between paying the rent and sending the monthly take to Greenpeace, there is to her mind little choice.

As for her partner in this affair, a Coloradoan by birth, he retains an almost religious regard for straight arrows. In some circles, a confession of regard for the works of John Wayne and Clint Eastwood might be met with scorn; still, he admits it freely, claiming that the Colorado blood in his veins makes him heir to all the rules and regulations that make up The Code of the West. (Always tip your hat to a lady, never rob a bank at night, don't draw first and never, ever kiss your horse with your eyes closed.) This love of Western mythology explains in part why he feels comfortable in Australia. The mythical credo of the American West lives Down Under with a vengeance, and the rules are basically the same. If you don't like songs about outlaws and truck drivers and also think that country western music is only for rednecks from Tennessee, stay out of Australia.

We have both spent a lot of time wandering around the Great Outback of the United States, the western deserts, which is fine basic training for anybody pondering a visit to anyplace in Australia more than a day's drive in from the coasts. We like isolation and wildernesses, and camped more than our share back when the kids were small and even a Motel 6 was a budgetary impossibility. But we also have explored cities, from New York to Casablanca, Oslo to Tehran, and we have real fondness for paved streets, room service and flush toilets.

Given a choice, we would be strangled by no timetables, hemmed in by no itinerary. Trains have their place, so do buses and guided tours. But for our tastes, the only way to travel is by personal vehicle, be it car or camper van— we are too lazy for bikes, too conventional for motorcycles. Monetary and time restraints often make such modes of independent travel impossible, of course, but whenever possible, we are on the road, enjoying the freedom of being able to stop where and when we want, of taking any back route that comes along, of making our days as long or as short as we choose. We fully realize that this approach is not for everybody, and in truth, is often simply unfeasible. There are those who backpack and those who like tours and those who prefer to train it or bus it or thumb it. We find no fault with these approaches, and indeed, have always tried to take disparate appetites into account.

If there is one message we want you to get from this book, it is that no matter how you get there, where you stay or how you decide to get around, Australia is necessary for your education, for your sense of humor, for your own good.

So, what's an Australian? That's a heavy question. We have some definite ideas and we have tried to make them plain. Don't worry about the Aussies being offended if we just go ahead and tell you what is right or wrong with their country, because they've never been reluctant to tell us what's wrong with ours. That's probably the most precious similarity we share with them: the gut-deep belief that unless you have the right to complain about your country—and anything else, for that matter—you aren't a free society. (We must be honest and say, however, that of all the democratic peoples, the Aussies are among the loudest complainers. They can deny it all they want, and they will. Loudly.)

Who are these people who live up to their ears in kangaroos and koalas and have sheep grazing from hell to breakfast? Who are these people who live on a great big island out in the middle of nowhere but somehow keep producing great movies and superstar rock groups? Who are these men and women who have so captured our imagination and admiration? Who are these people who claim, without so much as a blush, that they singlehandedly won World War II?

Who are these Aussies? Well, hang around, and we'll try to show you.

We have tried, throughout this project, to remember that the final word is up to those who will read what we have written. We are sure that if we have erred, either in fact or perception, we will shortly hear about it. And, we would have it no other way.

HISTORY

The Glasshouse Mountains, named by Captain Cook, are craggy volcanic remains and figure prominently in Aboriginal lore. The highest peak is 1800 ft.

For most of its history, Anglo-Saxon-Celtic Australia had clearly understood that should anything ugly or untoward arise to ripple the calm Caucasian-controlled waters of Southeast Asia, the mighty Royal Navy, operating from impregnable bases at Singapore and Hong Kong, would take care of matters in short order. This manifesto of the British Empire was noisily ignored by the Japanese, who sank two capital ships of the Royal Navy in December 1941, including the pride of the entire fleet, the 35,000-ton battleship *Prince of Wales.*

Soon after the *Prince of Wales* and the battle cruiser *Repulse* were sunk, Singapore fell. This, added to other Japanese advances—Hong Kong, Burma, the Philippines, Pearl Harbor—put an end to British control in Asia and the Pacific. Within months, Japanese armies were in the Solomon Islands, the Dutch East Indies and New Guinea, and Australian cities—notably Darwin in the Northern Territory—were being bombed by Japanese aircraft. It seemed that nothing could stop them from taking Australia. The British had their hands full in Europe and North Africa, and the United States Pacific fleet, it was believed, had died at Pearl Harbor. The notion that Great Britain was not immortal was to have a profound effect on the Land Down Under. As they stood on the shores of the Coral Sea and watched the skies above the Torres Strait and waited for invasion, the Australians abruptly entered the 20th century and began the final mental and emotional metamorphosis that made them what they are today.

> *Of course Australia is destined for greatness—its people have been*
> *chosen by the finest judges in England.*

> **—Old Aussie adage**

To appreciate why the humiliation of Great Britain at the hands of the Japanese in 1941 was such a rip in the national fabric of white Australia, you must understand the immense psychological bonds that have traditionally tied the two nations together. England, in its long and powerful reign, gave birth to many children. Australia was the bastard baby, born on the wrong side of the blanket, and more than any of the other children, has been the one who tried to please its parent most, to prove its place in the family, to somehow erase the shame of its birth. The English have, for the most part, treated Australia with a fair amount of disdain, as if it were a rather vulgar brat from the wrong side of the tracks who really shouldn't be let into any club frequented by gentlemen. (This never stopped Great Britain from using Australian troops whenever the Empire was at risk, however.) The result of all this has been a love-hate relationship between the two countries that has lasted to the present day. The story of Australia is an improbable saga in many ways, because few other nations can claim to have started so low and risen so high in such a short time.

The credit for the first thorough investigations of any part of Australia falls to the Dutch, who had, by the beginning of the 17th century, taken firm hold of Indonesia. Ships sailing southeast from Batavia—modern Jakarta—chanced upon the west and north coasts of Australia. Throughout the 1600s, Dutch traders and explorers flushed out the maps of western, northern and southern Australia.

In 1688, the English pirate ship *Cygnet* made landfall on the northwestern coast. The occasion was historic in two ways. First, William Dampier, one of the crew, became the first recorded Englishman to stand on Australian soil. Second, his account of the Australian natives set the tone for three centuries of racial bias:

"The inhabitants of this country are the miserablest people in the world...setting aside their humane shape, they differ little from brutes. They are tall, strait-bodied, and thin, with long limbs. They have great heads, round foreheads, and great brows. Their eyelids are always half-closed, to keep the flies out of their eyes...They are long-visaged, and of a very unpleasing aspect; having no one graceful feature in their faces."

In the summer of 1769, there was to be a transit of the planet Venus—Venus would pass between the earth and the sun—which was an astronomical event of major importance. The Royal Navy, at that time not occupied with any major wars, decided to send a spare ship off to take a look. It was the *Endeavor*, a sloop and former coal ship of 34 tons, under the command of Capt. James Cook, without doubt one of history's most successful and adventurous explorers, and at that time widely considered to be one of the most efficient navigators in the Royal Navy. While he was at it, the Admiralty said, he was to chart the coastline of New Zealand, earlier discovered by the Dutch.

The *Endeavor*, about 100 feet long, carried a crew of 94. In addition to Cook—who was a fellow of the most important scientific group in England, the Royal Society—there were several scientists, including an astronomer and two botanists. Cook left New Zealand on March 31, 1770. At about 6 a.m., Friday, April 19, 1770, he had his first glimpse of Australia, generally believed to be a rocky promontory in Victoria.

On April 28, he sailed into a bay northeast of the first sighting, "tolerably well shelter'd from all winds," and anchored two miles offshore. He first named the place Sting-Ray Harbour because of the large number of rays he and the crew supped on, but later in the voyage changed the name to Botany Bay to honor the accomplishments of his two young botanists. Having had his fill of Botany Bay, Cook sailed again, soon passing, 15 miles to the north, the entrance to a bay he called Port Jackson. He was in a hurry and made no effort to explore it. That would have to wait for 18 more years and another English sea captain.

A glance at a map of Australia will show you that in the south, near Botany Bay, there is nothing to the east but open water for a thousand miles. But as you go north, the Great Barrier Reef starts coming into shore. It's shaped like a large funnel, with the mouth to the south and the ever-narrowing neck to the north. In early June, Cook was well into the neck, near a group of large islands northeast of Mackay he named the Whitsunday Passage. A few days later, he was about 120 kilometers north of modern-day Cairns and at around 11 at night under a clear, moonlit sky, he met the reef.

"Before 10 o'clock we had 20 and 21 fathoms (of water beneath the keel)...until a few minutes before 11 when we had 17, and before the man at the lead could heave another cast, the ship struck and stuck fast." It was not immediately clear what damage, if any, the ship had sustained, and Cook did what he could to get the *Endeavor* off the reef, sending boats out to pull (no effect), then dropping an anchor off the starboard side in an effort to kedge it off the coral. He even tossed several tons of stuff overboard trying to lighten the ship: "Guns, iron and stone ballast, casks, hoop staves, oil jarrs, decay'd stores, etc.," which divers have been trying ever since to find. Nothing worked.

The next day, he managed to float the ship off the coral, but it was leaking badly. Some four days later, the *Endeavor* hove into a bay where a river flowed into the sea (now called the Endeavor River) and began repairs. The spot is the site of modern Cooktown. By Aug. 22, Cook and company, having gotten the *Endeavor* back into reasonable repair, sailed north past the tip of the Cape York Peninsula. On a small island, called Possession Island, Cook raised the British colors and claimed the entire east coast of Australia for England, naming it New Wales.

One of the major social concerns the English faced in the 18th and 19th centuries was what to do with their criminals. In the early 1700s, the English banishment laws were amended to allow minor offenders to be sent to the American colonies for seven years, major offenders for 14. This cozy relationship lasted for the better part of 70 years, with England getting rid of some of its undesirables, the colonies getting captive labor. The happy partnership ended abruptly in 1776 when the upstart Americans told George III to take a hike.

In 1786 the transportation of felons to the far-away shores of New Wales was approved by Prime Minister William Pitt. The plan was announced by Thomas Townshend, the Viscount Sydney, the home and colonial secretary. (Yes, that Sydney.) All that was needed now was somebody brave enough (or dumb enough) to go set up the new colony.

As heroes go, Capt. Arthur Phillip was reportedly about as dull as they come. He had been a good enough captain, as his 30-year service record starting in the late 1750s proved, but he seemed to be no Horatio Hornblower, just an average English naval officer competent enough to get the job done. One contemporary portrait shows a middle-aged man in cocked hat, with a prunish mouth, cow-brown eyes and a big nose—not the sort of guy you'd want to go buckle your swash with. Still, he was given orders that would make even the brave Capt. Hornblower blanch: sail from England in charge of a convoy of diddly little ships containing about 1500 felons, guards, administrators, officers and sailors, navigate his way down the South Atlantic through some of the worst seas in the world, cross vast stretches of the South Pacific, then proclaim himself governor of a colony that would jolly well become self-sufficient after two years—or else. By early May 1787, he was ready to go.

In all, Phillip had 11 ships. Two—including his flagship, the *Sirius*, were regular British Navy; the rest were private craft hired for the trip. The ships, of course, were inadequate for the job, being too small for the number of people they carried. The largest was a 114-foot transport that carried 195 male convicts plus crew, guards and officers. The smallest, H.M.S. *Supply*, the other navy ship, was 70 feet long and carried 50 people in all. On May 13, Phillip set sail from Portsmouth with his colonists: around 750 convicts (568 male, 191 female), 250 or so Marines, 20 officials, 210 Royal Navy seamen, 230 or so merchant seamen and 13 children, belonging to both convicts and guards. (The exact number of people on the first voyage is unclear; because of bad record-keeping, a variety of figures exist from a variety of sources.) The convicts ranged in age from over 80 (a woman) to under 10 (a boy).

The First Fleet, as it is called, is to Australians what the *Mayflower* is to Americans. And the myths are about the same, too. Every third Anglo-American would like to claim at least one relative on the *Mayflower*. Same thing in Australia, where they call it having "a ball and chain in the family." From all reports, you would think that everyone in Australia had at least one great-great-grandfather or great-great grandmother who was transported to Australia by the bloody English. In fact, only between 150,000 and 170,000 men, women and children were sent to Australia by English courts during the 80 years that transportation was in effect. Only about 25,000 of those transported were women, which had a long-lasting influence on the male-dominated society of Australia for many years afterward. The actual number of present-day Aussies who can lay claim to an ancestor with the First Fleet is tiny.

The trip took 252 days. From Portsmouth, the fleet sailed to Tenerife, then down the South Atlantic to Rio de Janeiro. Turning east, it sailed to the Cape of Good Hope, then due east again, 6500 miles without sight of land to Australia. The successful voyage was a miracle, beset as it was with terrible weather, bad food, overcrowding, poorly outfitted ships, disease and unsuccessful attempts at mutiny. Still, Phillip made it to Botany Bay on Jan. 20, 1788.

Armed as he was with only Cook's logs, Phillip was expecting a lot more than he found when he dropped anchor in Botany Bay. He took one look around at what was supposed to be a fertile continent and got so disgusted (and probably just a tad apprehensive) that he didn't even stay long enough to take possession of the new colony or declare himself governor. He gathered a troop of Marines and decided to explore about 15 miles farther north and take a look at Port Jackson, the bay Cook had noted in passing in 1770 but failed to explore. What they found was one of the finest anchorages in the world, big enough, Phillip later wrote joyfully to the Admiralty, to stash *"a thousand sail of the line."* It also turned out to be one of the most beautiful bodies of water in the world, the place we now call Sydney Harbour. Despite the fact that for many years, nobody even lived around Botany Bay, the name stuck in England and elsewhere and became synonymous with transportation and banishment.

Phillip ordered his 11 ships out of Botany Bay and into the new anchorage, and about 7 p.m., Jan. 26, 1788, the First Fleet entered the bay and landed near what is today downtown Sydney. He formally took possession of New South Wales (as all eastern Australia was now called) on Feb. 7, 1788.

The most famous animal in Australia is probably the kangaroo, followed closely by the duck-bill platypus. But there is another animal that has played such an enormous role in Australian history that it should probably be placed on the national coat of arms rather than the interesting but basically useless emu: the sheep.

Sheep helped make Australia a prosperous colony, and it is sheep that have made Australia a prosperous independent nation. The statistics are fairly impressive: the country has about 170 million sheep; something like two billion pounds of wool are shorn every year; the wool business employs about 300,000 people; and export earnings total well above U.S. $3.5 billion a year. Fully a third of the world's entire output of wool is produced in Australia.

At present, there are about 100,000 sheep farms and stations in Australia, and wool accounts for between 12 percent and 15 percent of the nation's total export earnings (it's the number one export) and has shown steady rises the past decade. Between 1985 and 1988, for example, wool export revenues doubled. The two largest customers are Japan and China. Australia is also the second-largest exporter, after New Zealand, of mutton and lamb in the world, something on the order of 300,000 tons a year.

One reason Canadians and Americans think like Australians is because we had a gold rush or two, all three of us. The Aussie version started in New South Wales and Victoria in 1851, then at Kalgoorlie in Western Australia in 1892-93. By 1860, the population of the country was around a million, a 10-year increase of 600,000, many drawn by gold fever. Included in that number, by some estimates, were 20,000 Americans. That trend has continued: the Australian government estimates that 80,000 Americans have migrated to Australia since the end of World War II.

In addition to boosting the population of the country, the early Australian gold strikes also hastened the end of transportation. The system was already being attacked in Australia and England, and the gold rush pretty much ended forever the idea that Australia was the Siberia of the South Seas. It was hard to threaten an English felon with prison Down Under when half the male population of England was already on its way to the gold fields.

Until the end of World War II, it seems to us outsiders, the Australians were well and truly trying to out-English the English. The early robber barons and wealthy sheep ranchers showed it by setting up lordly English-style estates every bit as ostentatious as those Back Home (or at least as ostentatious as the rugged frontier of the Outback would allow). English history was taught in Aussie schools. Things English were things good, and the bumpkin colony out in the southern thules knew it. For most of the 19th century, like Americans in the 18th century, many Australians felt themselves simply to be Englishmen living overseas. The Australians tried to prove their worth to beloved and haughty England by fighting on the worldwide battlefields of the Empire.

World War I came along, for reasons nobody in Australia really understood or cared about, and the Aussies were right there. Australian Prime Minister William Morris Hughes, the "Little Digger," promised to support England to Australia's last penny. Aussie forces during the Great War totaled about 416,000, or about half of all men of military age in 1914; of these, about 330,000 served overseas and incurred 226,000 casualties, including 60,000 killed—an astounding figure of 68.5 percent and the highest Allied casualty rate of the war. This from a population of less than 5 million. The first Australian troops were sent to Egypt for training. Joined with troops from New Zealand, they were known as ANZACs, and their first major participation in the war was in the spring of 1915 on the Turkish coast at a place called Gallipoli. The ANZAC troops, plus French, British and other imperial forces, were pinned to their landing areas from April 25, 1915 (now celebrated as ANZAC Day) to Dec. 20, when they finally withdrew. The Allied losses were bad at Gallipoli: 78,000 wounded, 35,000 dead. Of the dead, 8587 were ANZACs

By the time of Pearl Harbor, most of Australia's troops were already involved in the war far from home—four Australia divisions were either in the Near East or guarding Empire outposts in Singapore and Malaya. (When Singapore fell, 15,000 of the 130,000 captured troops were Australian.) The remaining Aussie troops back home, about 34,000 men, were incorporated into a combined command called ABDA (Australian, British, Dutch, American) and were about the only troops left to protect the Solomon Islands, the Dutch East Indies and Australia. Faced with a Japanese invasion, the Australian government decided to bring troops home from the Near East, a move that incensed the British—how dare the Aussies try to protect their own country when the Empire was at risk—but the Australians held fast and brought the Desert Rats home to fight in some of the dirtiest battles of the war defending their own shores.

As in World War I, the cost of Australian participation in a world war was high. About a million Australian men served in the Second World War, and half of those were either killed or wounded. Of those taken prisoner by the Japanese, more than 8000 died, a bitter statistic not forgotten in Australia.

In the 50-plus years since the sun went down on the British Empire, Australia has changed greatly. The nation is coming to grips with its location. It has forged strong ties with its Asian neighbors in trade, commerce and mutual cooperation, even again with the once-hated Japanese. It has changed its immigration policies to allow Asians to immigrate; it has looked less and less toward the Caucasian members of the Commonwealth and more toward its geographic brothers.

The ambivalent attitude the Aussies have toward Great Britain always seems to come into clear focus whenever the queen or her family visits Australia. On a trip to open Parliament in early 1992, her appearance was boycotted by several legislators who said *"Australians should be politically mature enough to have their own head of state and flag."* And it got worse. At one point, former Prime Minister Paul Keating, being Australian, showed his friendship to Her Highness by putting his arm around her shoulder—a very large no-no. (The queen is never, ever to be touched by mere mortals.) The British press, not known for its objectivity, went ballistic. *"Boring Boors Down Under,"* one headline read, with a story that said, in part: *"It's a question of manners—something, apparently, the Australians know little about."* To add a finishing touch, Keating's Dutch-born wife, Annita, refused to curtsy to the queen, a habit we Yanks got out of some time back. It all proved that the strained relationship continues, as does the traditional snobbery of the English toward the Australians.

It's not over yet. Keating's Labour Party is openly trying to change the way Aussies govern themselves, including removal of the queen as head of state. Plans to declare Australia a republic by the end of the century were put on the back burner after Keating was voted out of office, but the movement to form a republic is far from being dead. Before he left office, Keating, a realist, also said that if it came to a trade war between the United States and Japan, he'd go with Tokyo, no big surprise given the trade history of Japan and Australia. Despite their warts and their problems, the Australians are basically among the nicest people on earth. They are our cousins, black and white, and their future and their conflicts are, in many ways, the same future and the same conflicts we face in the United States.

PEOPLE

The Tjapukai Dance Theatre presents Aboriginal culture and dances.

Almost everyone in Australia claims at least one great-great-grandfather or great-great-grandmother who was transported in chains to Australia by the bloody English. A main part of the Aussie prisoner myth holds that most of those transported were just innocent victims of harsh and unfair English law. They were sent to the ends of the earth either for a minor crime they probably didn't commit or for political reasons, torn from the bosom of their poor-but-honest parents, fated to be the tool of a psychopathic prison guard whose major joy in life was lashing poor unfortunates with a cat-o'-nine-tails. To be sure, there were cases like that, but the vast majority of the felons sent to Australia were guilty as hell. It cannot be denied that Australia's penal beginnings have colored its people and contributed to their attitudes up to the present day.

It was not until the latter part of this century that Australian historians began looking at the convict days with any degree of professional detachment. One of the first and best was Manning Clark's *A History of Australia* series, which not only addressed the various myths of Australian history, but also dealt honestly for the first time with the two-century destruction of black Australian society. Another book, one that has probably laid more phantoms to rest than any other, is the exquisitely researched and written chronicle of the first days of Australia called *The Fatal Shore*, by Australian journalist Robert Hughes.

While the cow has not received as much publicity as the sheep in the agricultural affairs of Australia, it is a major industry: Australia is the world's biggest exporter of beef and veal, almost 630,000 tons a year. With that many cows around, you can't escape the fact that Australia had to evolve its own brand of cowboy.

In Australia, they call them drovers or stockmen, and they herd bullocks instead of cows and they use stockwhips instead of lariats, but aside from that, pard, they're just like the guys who hang out around Calgary or Miles City. Cowboys, y'all, cowboys. They look alike, they ride alike, they all have holes in their boots and cowpies on their Levis and they all think drinking beer and riding in rodeos is better than free air. Would you believe that country-western is the most popular music in Australia? Would you further believe that the most famous country-western singer in Australia is named Slim Dusty? (There was also a very popular Kiwi C&W artist in Australia, now dead, named Tex Morton.)

While we're talking about Western lore and such, you can also tell we're the Aussies' kissing cousins by taking a quick look at their road signs. Buckshot, rifle and pistol holes, a sure sign that the frontier mentality (dangerous as it might be) still lives. That's one thing Americans, Canadians and Australians share that most nations simply cannot understand: wide open spaces. If anything, the Aussies have an even more advanced sense of frontier freedom because not only are they completely surrounded by water, most of their wide open spaces are butt-busting, almost unlivable deserts. Plus on a land mass almost exactly the size of the continental United States, they have a population of only 18 million. That's elbow room, folks, but before you go thinking that every Aussie wears spurs and carries a stockwhip, just remember that the bulk of the population lives in urban areas.

By the mid-19th century, Australia had become a frontier nation, what with remittance men and gold strikes and drifters and gamblers and fallen doves and drovers, and you can't have a real-live frontier unless a bunch of the populace has been seduced by the dark side, so the escaped convicts were joined in their evil ways by men and women who figured holdups were more cost-effective than farming. In Australia, the guys in black hats are called bushrangers, and the stories and sagas about them are as popular—and probably as accurate—as the stories about Billy the Kid and Jesse James.

The most famous bushranger of all was Ned Kelly. When they're on the prod, the Aussies like to get us cornered in a pub and remind us that Jesse James only robbed a few trains and small banks, whereas Mr. Kelly and his bonny band captured whole towns. Ned was of Irish stock, as the saga goes, and being Irish, knew at birth that the English administration of Australia was out to get him—so he quite naturally started a life of crime just to get even. After becoming well known and carrying a price on his head, he hid out in the mountains of western Victoria for a while. Hearing that the gendarmes were coming by train to snuff them, he and his brother and two gang members kidnapped all the citizens of Glenrowan, Victoria, held them in a hotel pub, and tore up the tracks to stop the cops. The police just stopped the train outside of town, walked in bold as brass and started blasting away. Ned, a designing chap, had the foresight to make himself a suit of armor for just such an occasion.

The Kelly gang and the coppers went on discharging their firearms at each other for some hours when, apparently tiring of the fun, he put on the armor and attempted to escape. He was wounded and the cops torched the hotel, and the other three members of the gang died in the flames rather than surrender. Four months later, he was sentenced to hang on the gallows at the Old Melbourne Gaol, which he did on Nov. 11, 1880. The fable has Ned's mother coming to the hoosegow and telling him to *die like a Kelly,* and also reporting that his last words on the gallows were: *"Such is life."*

Until after World War II, the population of Australia was almost entirely Caucasian, partly because of its role as a British-settled colony, partly because a "Whites Only" immigration policy had been in place in the country since the beginning of the 20th century. Rampant racism in Australia, in fact, had been part of the European history of the country from the beginning, as the 200-year destruction of Aboriginal society shows. The surprise is not that the black Aboriginal people, sometimes called the "First Australians," live in less than ideal conditions in modern Australia—the surprise is that they are alive at all.

Anthropologists and archeologists are not precisely sure when the first humans arrived in Australia, with guesses ranging as far back at 176,000 years. Things got even more confused late in 1996 when anthropologists announced they had found rock carvings in the Northern Territory that are by far the oldest signs of artistic efforts on the entire planet. The carvings are at a secret site near Jinmium, on the border of the territory and Western Australia. The rock carvings are so old, in fact, there is speculation they were created by a group of pre-humans who inhabited the area before the Aboriginals arrived. Whatever the final result, there seems to be no doubt now that civilization on the Australian continent goes back—way, way back.

What is generally agreed is that the waves of later immigration to Australia which took place began in Southeast Asia and the Indian subcontinent and coincided with the world's ice ages. As the polar ice caps grew, the level of the oceans dropped, and ancient peoples were able to island-hop their way from Asia to Australia. It is now believed that the present Aboriginals descended from a group that arrived on the Australian mainland between 30,000 and 60,000 years ago when the oceans were about 500 feet lower than today. This period, also during an ice age, is about the same time that humans crossed the land bridge from Asia into North America.

The isolation, coupled with the environment, kept the human population low. It is estimated that in 1788, when the Europeans arrived, there were only about 300,000 Aboriginals on the continent, most of them living along the eastern and southern coasts and in Tasmania. Even by Stone Age standards, they were a primitive people, living a precarious life as hunter-gatherers. They were often unclothed, and knew nothing of elaborate shelters such as the kind made by North American plains Indians. They simply took pieces of tree bark, put them on the ground to act as windbreaks, and curled up. They had, of course, never seen a horse. Even with so few numbers, they were diverse, with perhaps 300 languages and between 500 and 1000 tribes. They seemed always to be at war with each other, and deaths from combat were common.

They had no written language. Instead they had an oral tradition, a complex and massive body of knowledge handed from generation to generation for thousands of years. Their creation myths begin in an era in the distant past called the Dreamtime. Before the Dreamtime, the universe was void, and without form. Then from the ocean came Warramurrungundji, whose human form was female. She created the land and the people, and other spirit animals created rocks and mountains and flowers. The people—the Aboriginals—were given the responsibility of guarding the land. They did not own the land, the land owned them.

It can be argued that it took a while for the guardianship to get straightened out. The Aboriginals brought wild dogs with them—the dingoes—which have been particularly hard over the centuries on native animals. And they brought with them the ability to hunt by fire. Aboriginal hunters, carrying fire sticks, set whole forests ablaze to scare out kangaroos and possums and other food, thinking nothing about the slaughter of the other animals and plants in the process.

It doesn't take a genius to figure out that the Australian people were just a disaster waiting to happen. It was a miracle a land mass the size of Australia had been sitting around for so long without being tied up in a ribbon and given to a king by some explorer type looking for gold and glory. But eventually it was, to good King George III. It was the Aboriginals' bad luck to be on the other end of the English convict trail. It is impossible to expect any group of humans (English or no) who have been brought up in an ignorant and prejudiced social system such as existed in 18th-century England to behave in any other manner than the settlers of Australia did.

In addition to outright violence, the Aboriginals also fell easy victims to European diseases, one of the little side effects of the colonial system that had occurred all over the world, from Hawaii to India. Thousands of Aboriginals died of smallpox and venereal diseases. The process of destruction was, for the most part, slow, urged on mainly by the ever-expanding need of the white Australians for more wheat acreage and sheep and cattle grazing areas. The fact that the woollies and the cattle were forcing the Aboriginals' food supply to disappear was of no great moment.

In modern Australia, the life of many Aboriginals is often dire, indeed. It is estimated that about two-thirds of them now live in urban environments. They are caught in the same terrible dilemma that faces Indians in the United States and Canada: how to live in two worlds at once. For many, it has become a struggle with alcohol and poverty. In the sandy stretches of the Todd River near Alice Springs in the Northern Territory, you see small enclaves of wretchedly poor Aboriginals, often drunk, always ill, living off the dole. The Alice Springs group is by no means an isolated case. Few Aboriginals anywhere in Australia return to the old ways of hunting and gathering in the vast stretches of the Outback, and many studies claim that many Aboriginals are living in less than Third World conditions. They have many diseases, such as tuberculosis, trachoma, leprosy and respiratory infections. They are often illiterate, they have a high infant mortality rate, their life expectancy is far lower than their white opposites and although they comprise only about one percent of the population—there are only about 125,000 Aboriginals left, of which 45,000 are pure-blooded—they account for 30 percent of the prison population.

There have been some advances. In 1967, the voters of Australia decided to give the power to deal with major Aboriginal problems to the federal government. Vast stretches of land have been deeded back to the Aboriginals— even Ayers Rock, Australia's most famous land mass, has been given back.

As for many white Australians, the problem simply remains. Many believe that the situation is hopeless because in the 200 years of English-Australian occupation, the Aboriginals have not learned the lessons they ought: to get jobs, to buy houses and tend gardens, to join the lawn bowling league, to go into the Outback only on camping trips. Others try to begin programs to teach Aboriginal history and ethics in schools. Some would not object to having the whole issue simply go away.

Former Prime Minister Malcolm Fraser: "We should not be guilty for our sins of 200 years ago," he said. "If that were so, there would not be a nation on earth that would not be guilty. When the English came from England, they behaved brutally. They were Englishmen. Not me, I'm Australian."

PEOPLE

The Aborigines are famous for their bark painting.

The condition and treatment of minority groups in Australia, especially blacks, became a topic of national discussion after Sydney put in a bid for the summer Olympic Games in 2000. The Australian Olympic Committee was obviously aware of the country's less than perfect racial record.

John Coates, president of the committee, told reporters soon after the bid was announced that the city had two large hurdles to overcome: the feeling that Australia is too far away from the rest of the world, and "we have to accept that there is a perception that the old 'Whites Only' policies persist. We must accept that some of the world's sports officials come to Australia and do not see many black/colored people competing and they wonder why."

How big a factor racial relations were in the final decision is not publicly known. At any rate, Sydney prevailed against some rugged competition—notably from the People's Republic of China—and was awarded the 2000 Games. The country went wild, not surprising given its lust for sporting events, and the events will give the world a chance to see just how friendly Australians can be. But, there will undoubtedly be more protests from the black community before and during the Olympic Games.

THE LAND DOWN UNDER

Geology

*Geological formations (weird domes, natural pyramids and shimmering rocks)
create a surreal landscape at Bungle Bungle National Park.*

Australia, like the other continents of the earth, traces its ancestry back to a
point millions of years ago when the proto-continent called Pangaea started
breaking up into two smaller land masses, Gondwana and Laurasia, from
which finally evolved today's seven continents.

Australia was part of Gondwana, a name given to the ancient land mass by
Eward Suess, a Swiss geologist. Around 130 million years ago, Gondwana it-

self started splitting apart, and around 65 million years ago, Australia and Antarctica separated. Tasmania and New Guinea were part of Australia during times of low sea levels—Sahul is the name given to the low-water land mass that included Australia and New Guinea during the Ice Age. When the last ice age ended and sea levels rose, New Guinea and Tasmania were cut off again. Although Australia was never covered by one of the polar ice formations, glaciation took place because of the extremely cold temperatures.

Geologically, Australia is considered the oldest continent. Here you can find rocks containing crystals formed 4.3 billion years ago—part of the earth's very first crust. Before the Permian Period and its widespread glaciation, Australia had already gone through most of the uplifting and shifts that were responsible for creating its alpine ranges. The continent had been flooded by seas, subjected to tidal forces and the effects of glaciation, rifting, fracturing, volcanic eruptions and finally, erosion. In fact, while the rest of the continents were changing and forming into what we know today, Australia was already in decline, its landscapes flattening out, its climate drying up.

The Western Plateau was once an island in the middle of a flooded Australia. It spreads across almost half the continent, taking in the Kimberley and Hamersley Ranges, the Great Sandy Desert, the Gibson Desert and the Great Victoria Desert. Though it was flooded many times, it was always the essential core of the continent.

Fossils of some of the earth's oldest creatures have been found on the plateau—3.5-billion-year-old stromatolites, layered rocks resembling cabbage heads that are produced by the activity of photosynthetic organisms. (These fossils are also found in southern Africa, along the shores of Lake Superior and in the Grand Canyon.)

In Shark Bay, on the northwest coast of Australia, are some modern cousins of those ancient life-forms: the blue-green pillars of the Hamelin Pool are living stromatolites. These pillars, standing on the sunlit shallow sea floor, give us some idea of what the scenery was like two billion years ago.

In Bitter Springs, in the Northern Territory, remains of green algae dated at about a billion years old have been found. Green algae are recognized as one of the first living organisms that contained genetic material. Just recently the oldest known fossil of a flowering plant found anywhere in the world was discovered in southwestern Australia. When first studied, it was thought to be a fern, but examination under a microscope revealed it to be a flowering angiosperm with fruit around its seed. It is only one inch tall but it is 120 million years old and may be the ancestor of all the world's seed-bearing plants.

Animals

Kangaroos range in size from nine inches to more than five feet tall.

Marsupials and Monotremes

The first time you see a platypus, kangaroo or frilled lizard, you figure the animals in Australia were designed by a committee. When descriptions of some of Australia's more peculiar lifeforms reached Britain after colonization began, they were simply not believed. Later, when specimens were taken back to England, they were written off as more evidence that things were totally screwy in His Britannic Majesty's colony Down Under—after all, harummph, what could you expect from a country that was, well, upside down?

The marsupials and monotremes of the Island Continent prove beyond a doubt that Mother Nature does have a sense of humor. When Australia drifted off by itself after the breakup of the ancient proto-continents, it took most of the world's supply of marsupials with it. Today, 13 of the 16 known families of marsupials are found in Australia. There are more than 180 species around the country, which have filled in almost every niche held in other parts of the world by placental animals. By a process called convergence evolution, many of the marsupials closely resemble their placental counterparts.

Marsupial comes from the Latin word, *marsupium*, meaning pouch, or purse. Marsupials are mammals, but differ from mammals in the way they reproduce. Depending on the species, the gestation period for a marsupial is from about a week to around 40 days. The young are born tiny and undeveloped, and by some unknown process—instinct, gravity, smell—must migrate from the birth canal to their mother's pouch to find the milk source. If they become disoriented and lose their way, they die. If everything goes well, the babies will be attached to their mother's teats within three minutes or so. It is in the pouch, permanently attached to the teats like an umbilical cord, that final development takes place.

The most successful of Australia's marsupials are vegetarians, and they are also among the most famous—koalas and kangaroos are both herbivores. But there are also carnivorous marsupials, the most famous of which is the Tasmanian devil. The devils, although wary of humans, are formidable scavengers and have jaws with chewing pressure equal to a shark. There are also marsupials that will eat anything, including bandicoots and the many species of tree-dwellers that like insects and small reptiles as much as they like fruit and nectar.

Not content with planting most of the world's marsupials in Australia, nature also decided to bestow monotremes on the continent, the only place in the world they are found. There are only two species: duck-bill platypuses and echidnas.

The term monotreme means the animals have only one passage for both waste and reproduction. Both species are egg layers but suckle their young and seem to be a link between reptiles and mammals. Monotremes have eye and bone structures similar to reptiles, and their young even have tooth-like structures resembling egg teeth when they are born. But they also have milk, are warm-blooded and have fur.

Both species of monotremes in Australia have filled a placental niche. The platypus is Australia's freshwater otter, and the echidna is Australia's hedgehog or porcupine.

Platypuses are shy aquatic feeders, normally under two feet long with fine, thick fur. When underwater, their eyes and ears are covered by flaps of skin and they find food using their very sensitive bills. They can eat their weight in grubs, worms and shrimp every day. Like muskrats and beavers, platypuses are diggers, living in extensive and winding burrows hollowed in river banks. They are normally solitary animals, coming together only for mating, which is done in the water. Because they are aquatic animals, evolution decided not to give them a pouch. Instead, the mother builds an elaborate burrow where she lays her eggs, then uses body heat to incubate them. In about two weeks, the eggs hatch and the babies begin suckling. The young might stay in the nesting chamber for as long as four months before they are allowed to hunt in the river or lake bottom with their mother. Like so many other things in Australia, platypuses are deceiving. The male, while normally a docile creature, does have poisonous spurs on his hind feet. Something is killing the platypuses in Tasmania. A fungus, which attaches itself to any sort of wound in the skin, infects the critters and eventually kills them. At present the fungus, which also attacks cane toads in Queensland, has no treatment. Platypuses on the mainland have not yet been infected.

Echidnas, about the size of a large house cat, have short quills. about two to three inches long. They are equipped with powerful digging claws, a long, tube-like snout and a sticky tongue. They feed on ants and termites, and are nomadic land-dwellers who can tolerate temperature extremes and are thus much more common than platypuses. Because they are constantly on the move foraging for food, they have adapted a marsupial-like method of reproduction. After about two weeks of gestation, the mother finds a temporary burrow to lay her eggs. In the meantime, she develops a temporary pouch where the eggs are placed after they are laid. She continues to move around while the eggs are incubated in the pouch for about 10 days. When the young are born with the aid of an egg tooth, they are about a half-inch long and feed from milk oozed from the mother's mammary glands. They stay in the pouch until they develop quills, then live in a temporary nest for about three months. They are able to live at least 50 years.

The results of convergence evolution in Australia will often astound you. The critters Down Under almost always remind you of something back home (the kangaroo is a definite exception). Where you look for a chipmunk or squirrel, you find the sugar glider. If you look for a small primate in a rain forest, you find a brush-tailed possum or a cuscus. There are marsupial moles, marsupial rats, marsupial mice. There are wombats, which are similar to the capybaras of South America and look like guinea pigs on steroids. Wombats are underrated—they have the largest brains of any marsupial, can grow to 80 pounds and are generally very good-natured. Finally, there was the Tasmanian tiger (thylacine) now believed to be extinct, and the spotted-tailed quoll, the present marsupial answer to a wild cat.

Probably our favorite animals in Australia are the Bennett's wallabies (small kangaroos) we met near Cradle Mountain-Lake St. Clair National Park in Tasmania. Bennett's are about three feet tall with black velvety noses and hands. You won't find it hard to meet and feed animals in Australia—but they have to have the right food or can develop diseases. The best thing is to try one of the animal reserves found all over the country where people are allowed to cuddle a koala or feed and pet the wallabies in controlled environments. (Most of these parks are regulated by the national park system, and are centers for breeding endangered species as well as treatment for orphaned or injured animals.)

There are 17 families of kangaroos, divided into 52 species and a multitude of subspecies. They range in size from nine inches tall to more than five feet, not counting tail. Kangaroo is normally used to describe the three largest species: reds, grays and the mountain kangaroo, also known as a wallaroo.

The other, smaller species are known as wallabies and the smallest of the lot are called pademelons. Since the arrival of Europeans in Australia, four species of kangaroos have been exterminated and 10 other species are on the verge of extinction.

The wallabies near Cradle Mountain National Park in Tasmania are about three ft. tall and gentle enough to feed.

The largest of the roos is the red, so named because the male acquires a bright red chest during mating season. Reds can run 60 miles an hour for short periods, can weigh as much as 160 pounds and can jump six feet standing still and 30 feet from a running start. Gray kangaroos are almost as large as the reds, but have black-tipped tails; the reds have pale tips. Wallaroos have black hands and feet and live in hilly locales. They can withstand heat and drought better than the other kangaroos.

Young kangaroos are still connected to the umbilical cord when they start the climb to the pouch. After about five months, when it weighs four to eight pounds, the young roo—called a joey—leaves the pouch for short periods. Eventually, Mama kicks the kid out and he or she joins the herd. Kangaroos often mate just after birth so there is a continuing supply of small roos, but during drought periods, the fertilized eggs will remain dormant until the rains come.

As the climatic conditions in Australia changed over the eons, so did the feeding habits of kangaroos. They were once forest tree-dwellers, but dwindling food supplies forced them onto the vast grasslands of the continent. They learned to eat and digest the tough grasses of the new climate, developing a new set of choppers to handle the job. Kangaroos normally go through four sets of cheek teeth in their lifetime, and roos who live beyond their normal 15 to 20 years face starvation because the supply of grinding teeth has run out.

The battle between pastoral animals and kangaroos has been going on since the first cows and sheep were introduced into Australia. Kangaroos, being native animals, are able to eat grasses sheep and cattle cannot, but they also compete with farm animals for pasture fodder. Ranchers get upset because roos are hard to contain. The fences they put up all around Australia to keep out dingoes and rabbits are no match for a big roo, who can jump over, or through, them. A serious overpopulation of roos near Canberra in late 1995 led one politician to suggest a major program of vasectomies for the boy roos. Ranchers are also concerned about an as-yet unidentified disease that is killing thousands of kangaroos in New South Wales, Victoria and South Australia. The disease, possibly carried by bush flies, started appearing in the late 1980s, and there is some suggestion that it could infect domestic animals.

The kangaroo (and the emu) is on the Australian coat of arms, and it seems a bit perplexing to realize that they routinely shoot one of their national symbols, make dog food and steaks out of it, turn its paws into ashtrays and tan its hide for leather. Not that shooting national symbols is a new thing to the world. The American bison was virtually wiped out but we still managed to put it on a nickel, anyway. One of the most promising export commodities these days is kangaroo skins, which are sent in large quantities to Italy, where they are made into high-fashion leather goods. If the Australians are, as they claim, smarter than we are, maybe they'll take better care of the kangaroo. Without kangaroos, why would anybody want to go see Australia, anyway? A China-Australia joint venture hopes to open a restaurant in Beijing soon where the menu will include good Aussie beer, damper and kangaroo. Opinion polls show most Aussies think culling the roo population is proper; a growing animal rights movement takes exception.

This brings us to that most photogenic of all Aussies, the koala. Its scientific name means "pouched bear," and the word koala is Aboriginal for "drink-not," which is inaccurate because they do. Also, you have to know right up front that the koala is probably the world's best example of a successful PR campaign. Thanks in part to Qantas airline ads, plus their cute little bods, everybody thinks koalas are slow-moving, sweet little animals just ready for adoption. (Qantas decided in late 1992 to drop the cuddly koala from its advertisements.)

Anyway, most Aussies will tell you that koalas are stinky, spaced out, mean-tempered little beasts. They spend their lives half-stoned on eucalyptus oil and come mating season, the males get very uptight and mean. An Aussie farmer told us about a randy koala that disemboweled a cat and a dog because they got in its way. They have evil-looking claws and are ready to use them to protect their harems, usually two or three fair damsel koalas. They also make gawd-awful grunting noises that sound like elephant seals with a bad cough.

One of the most popular places to see a koala up close is at the Lone Pine Sanctuary outside Brisbane. The sanctuary charges five bucks to have your photo taken with a koala, and this will prove several things to you: First, Aussies are capitalists. Second, koalas have big claws. Third, koalas stink. Fourth, they have been known to piddle on humans.

Note to Canadians: Not to worry. We were assured by the koala keepers that the little fellas only go toity on Japanese and American tourists. They figure about one out of every 1000 tourists gets his or her chemise dampened. We were 998 and 999. *Note:* The New South Wales government has passed legislation banning game parks and federal preserves from allowing visitors to cuddle koalas. As of Jan. 1, 1997, you'll be able to pet them at arm's length, but no hugging. Tourism officials in the state fear that many tourists, especially the 750,000 or so Japanese who visit Australia every year, will by-pass New South Wales and head for more user-friendly koala-cuddling states.

Koalas were hunted almost to extinction for their cute, cuddly little pelts, and are now protected by the federal government. Koalas reproduce slowly—maybe once every other year—and are in constant danger from fires because the eucalyptus trees they live in literally explode in bush fires. (Thousands perished in the 1994 bush fires around Sydney.) There are more than 30 species of eucalypts in Australia, and the koalas will feed on about 20 of them. Their favorite is the sugar eucalyptus. They have highly refined livers that filter out the bacterial cultures and poisons in their food supplies. Koalas must eat about 20 pounds of foliage a day, which is digested with the aid of an appendix four times the length of their bodies. The Australia Koala Foundation estimates there are only between 40,000 and 80,000 koalas remaining in the country, the lowest totals ever recorded. There are some fears that within 40 years, feral koalas will be extinct in Australia. Loss of habitat is usually blamed for the reduction in the koala population. In the Coff Harbour area of New South Wales, koalas are wearing pierced earrings that contain small transmitters to keep track of families. Our final note about koalas lurks in the windows of a gift store in the Rocks section of Sydney. There you will find small plastic koalas filled with, we kid you not, koala droppings. Called "poo-san," the dolls are supposed to bring luck. Money from the sale goes to koala preservation activities.

The Tasmanian devil, made famous in Bugs Bunny cartoons, is the largest known carnivorous marsupial in Australia. There are people who claim to have seen the extinct Tasmanian tiger (a dog-looking beast) from time to time, but until and if one is definitely spotted, the devil is the meat-eating champ. Once found all over Australia, they are now found only on the island of Tasmania. Some researchers speculate that the introduction of the dingo by migrating Aboriginals caused too much competition for the devils on the mainland and they died out. Dingoes never made it to Tasmania.

The devil's body shape is much like a badger with a bearlike head. They grow about two to three feet long, and are solitary animals, although they will congregate to share in a large chunk of carrion. The cartoon image of the devil is not far wrong—they will eat damned near anything. When presented with a half-carcass of a road-kill kangaroo, they start at the end of the tail and go forward, no thought about tender parts at all. Their incredible jaw pressure allows them to feast on bones, gristle, whatever.

Devils become sexually mature around two years old, and females never give birth to more than four babies—she has only four teats. The little devils stay in the pouch for about three months, and then move to a burrow, usually a tree trunk or an old wombat nest. The young are dependent on the mother for at least five months.

One of the most common groups of marsupials in Australia are phalangers, called possums by the Aussies. Possums form a large group of species, all tree-dwellers, whose second and third back digits have fused, creating a sort of two-pronged fork. They have apposing big toes and some species have prehensile tails. In size, they range from the dormouse possum at eight inches long to the four-foot-long, 15-pound cuscus. Among the many species are the gliders (four types), striped possums, ringtails, brawny brush-tails and the tiny honey possum, which feeds on nectar. Almost all are nocturnal. Hard to spot in the wild, many species are found in zoos all over the country. A cousin to the tree possums is the bandicoot, which also has the fused back digits that are used for digging rather than hanging onto branches.

Mammals

There are native mammals in Australia, as well, but only a few species, mostly rats or bats. The best known of these is the flying fox, a large fruit bat with a wing span of up to about five feet. They are nocturnal, but do not use sonar to find food. They can range as far as 30 miles or more foraging for food. The foxes are often spotted in northern Queensland and on many Barrier Reef islands.

Probably the most famous Australian mammal is the dingo, generally believed to have been brought to the continent by the Aboriginals. They are adaptable, sometimes hunting in loose packs for large prey such as kangaroos, or sometimes feeding on insects and road kills as a solitary hunter. They also prey on domestic livestock and are well and truly hated by ranchers. In addition to putting out poison meat for them, ranchers over the years built a fence to keep them out—the fence was 3000 kilometers long. Dingoes can howl but not bark, and are nocturnal hunters.

Birds

Emus can reach five feet tall and weigh 120 pounds.

The other animal that graces the Australian coat of arms with the kangaroo is the emu, Australia's answer to the ostrich and the rhea. There is only one species of emu left in Australia, and it can reach five feet tall and weigh 120 pounds. They are not well liked by ranchers, who see them as competitors for fodder, and who are not reluctant to crush their eggs when they are found, put out poison food or shoot them. As recently as 1964, Western Australia had a bounty on them, and the folks in South Australia, taking a page out of the dingo book, built a 500-kilometer-long fence to keep the big birds out of sheep pastures.

In 1992 and 1993, parts of Australia were having a bad drought, and emus started migrating in search of food. Herds of emus, 300 strong, were spotted in farm fields and they also started wandering down main highways. Body shops reported a substantial increase in damage from emu collisions. Emus are pretty stupid. It's hard to tell the sexes apart, females being slightly larger. Eggs are laid about 10 at a time and the incubation and hatching is left to the males. They seem to be fairly unaggressive and will eat out of your hand. They are popular zoo animals, but they're also becoming popular alternatives to red meat, and many progressive restaurants around the country offer emu specialties; the Aussies are actually consuming their coat of arms as we speak. Also, turning up in health food and specialty stores around the country these days are bottles of emu oil, said to be an old Aboriginal cure for damaged joints and muscles. The oil comes from farm-raised birds. A major growth industry in Australia these days is the raising of imported ostriches, which are starting to compete with domesticated emus.

Another of Australia's flightless birds is the cassowary, which can also hit five feet. You find them in the rain forests of Northern Queensland and New Guinea. They have distinctive heads, with a helmet of bone and bright purple, blue and yellow skin, with a red wattle. Males are again left in charge of hatching and raising the kids.

Australia also has three species of mound-building birds, the mallee fowl, the brush turkey and the scrub fowl. The birds spend 11 months a year preparing a nest, laying eggs and maintaining the nest. The females help dig the basic nest and lay down a compost layer. After the eggs are laid, they are covered up and the heat of the compost incubates the eggs. The males are in charge of opening and closing the nest hole to regulate the temperature, and when the chicks have hatched, they must dig themselves out. After the kids make it to the world, the parents take a month off, then start the whole thing all over again.

The kookaburra is famous for the insane laughing sound it makes.

Birds in Australia are just like the marsupials. You look at them and they sure seem familiar, but there's always something just a little out of whack. Swans? Sure, but they're black. Pelicans, all right, but with pink bills, gray feet and black and white feathers. A bird that is the spitting image of a red-winged blackbird, except the wing markings are white. The list goes on and on, making the 750-odd species of Australian birds a bird-watcher's dream come true.

Australia's best-known bird is probably the kookaburra, the laughing bird. There are two types of kooks in Australia; one makes the famous insane laugh, and the other one, while more colorful, is mostly silent. The birds, giant kingfishers, are sometimes very pesty around campfires, and a tree full of them can wake you out of a very sound sleep.

If you come from North America, where parrots and parakeets are in cages and cockatoos are in zoos, Australia will drive you crazy. How about a whole tree filled with parakeets or parrots, or the sky white with cockatoos? The cockatoos, as a matter of fact, are noisy, obnoxious and the bane of campers all over the country. In Australia, they're called *galahs*, which is also an uncomplimentary word for somebody who has a big mouth.

Many of the most colorful of the country's birds are found north of the Tropic of Capricorn. Here you find the dazzling little bee-eaters and finches, flycatchers, bowerbirds, ducks—something like 117 species. A favorite birding area is Kakadu National Park, whose flood plains and waterways are major nesting areas for such birds as the Australian stork, magpie geese, herons, fish eagles and sacred ibis. Australia's major aerial predator is the wedge-tailed eagle, which has been trapped and killed in large numbers because ranchers mistakenly assumed it was preying on livestock. The hawks are mostly carrion eaters and have been instrumental in keeping the rabbit population under control. Rabbits, one of the more destructive pests introduced into the country, at one time were as bad as locusts They are still considered to be a major pest today, so much so that in the fall of 1996, the government allowed scientists to use genetic engineering in an effort to kill off the bunnies. At about 280 sites around the country, a strain of genetically altered virus (rabbit calicivirus disease, or RCD) was released in the hope of making female rabbits sterile and thus wiping out at least 80 percent of the country's 170 million rabbits within two years. Farmers were elated, calling the first day of release "a national day of celebration." Farm groups estimate rabbits were causing losses in excess of US$600 million a year. There were protests from groups worried about the effects of genetically altered viruses, but theirs was a small voice in the crowd. Stay tuned.

The Australian bustard, a large, slow-flying bird, is endangered because the early settlers found it was quite tasty. Although it's now against the law to shoot them, they are still hunted. The prize for best hustle in the forest goes to the various species of bowerbirds. The males create elaborate bowers to entice lady friends. The bowers are decorated with anything colorful that can be found, and the birds are notorious camp robbers. Some species are so precise about the whole thing that if an article is put into the bower and doesn't suit his color scheme, he'll remove it. Once the lady has come calling, if she does, the bower is abandoned. This is the ultimate in bachelor pads, built with only one thing in mind.

The prize for best overall performance, however, has to go to the male lyre-bird, which woos the lasses with magnificent silvery tail feathers, aided by a courtship dance—plus a courtship structure along the lines of a bower. All the while that's going on, he is mimicking every bird call in the forest.

Reptiles, Amphibians, Fish and Snakes

When disturbed, the frill-necked lizard stands on its hind legs, expands its ruffled throat, and runs like The Roadrunner.

Just when you thought it was safe to go into the desert—meet the perentie goanna, a little number living near Ayers Rock that can grow to eight feet. The Australian goannas—a corruption of the word iguana—are monitors, one of about 500 species of nonvenomous lizards found in Australia. Most goannas are a foot or two in length. About 200 species of lizards live in arid areas, feeding on termites. The termites, called white ants in Australia, survive by eating the hardy and widespread spinifex plants. (Goannas can give you a nasty bite, however, so be wary.)

More bad news: Hiking in the rain forests of Queensland, you are urged to use lots of bug spray. Not only for the mosquitoes, but also for leeches. The Aussies suggest if they do attach themselves, get them off with an open flame or douse them with booze or salt. Even more bad news: Say hello to the bullrout, a freshwater stonefish. Yes, folks, stonefish, as in poisonous spines. Far as we know, you only find them in Northern Queensland. The locals recommend that when you're wading in fresh water up there, wear stout shoes; the spines are painful and potentially dangerous.

The most spectacular of the reptilian beasties is the frilled lizard, so named because when disturbed, it stands up on its skinny hind legs, opens parasol-like fans of skin along its throat and runs like hell. Australia has several species of skinks, both legged and legless varieties, and there are also several species of geckos.

Saltwater crocodiles grow to huge lengths and are highly dangerous. Supposedly, the freshwater crocs are a tad tamer.

Australia has two species of crocodiles, the saltwater and the freshwater. The saltwater, or estuarine crocodiles, live in fresh and saltwater coastal waters and grow to huge lengths. They are highly dangerous. The freshwater variety is *supposedly* no danger to humans.

There are no true toads native to Australia, but one of the ones that came calling is now a major problem. The cane toad was introduced from Hawaii in 1935 in an effort to control beetles eating the sugar cane. The toads—*bufo marinus*—come out at night, the beetles in the day; ergo, a useless but very lusty toad was loosed upon the land. Before they knew what was happening, Queensland farmers were up to their ears in semidangerous toads. The toads are large enough to eat small mammals and reptiles, and they also have poison glands behind each eye powerful enough to kill a dog or other animal which eats it. The Queenslanders are fighting back; one method being tried is broadcasting recordings of male cane toads in an effort to lure the females into traps. But it might be a losing battle. The toads are now found in more than 40 percent of Queensland and have started appearing in the Northern Territory and New South Wales. Females can produce up to 30,000 tadpoles a year. Actually, the toads do have a modicum of social redemption: they are becoming tourist attractions. Visitors who have heard about the dreaded amphibs are disappointed when they come to Queensland and discover that the toad population rises and falls with the seasons. Sometimes you're hard put to find even a single toad. Over on Dunk Island, a Barrier Reef resort, part of the week's entertainment is a series of toad races —if and when the staff (mumbling all the time) can go into the bush and round them up.

There are more than two dozen families of frogs in the world, four of which are found in Australia. Keeping with the usual way things work in the Aussie animal world, some of the local frogs are pretty weird. The female platypus frog carries her young in her stomach, while the male marsupial frog carries his young on pockets on his hips. The water-holding frog has been used by the Aboriginals as a water source for centuries.

Snakes? Yes, indeed, Australia has snakes, and the general rule is, if you see a snake, it's probably poisonous. There are no true vipers, but there are 70 species of elapids, or front-fanged snakes which Aussie herpetologists say are members of the cobra family. It's not clear how these snakes got to Australia because they are comparatively recent arrivals in the snake world. Even isolated Tasmania lays claim to three dangerous snakes. The two deadliest snakes on the mainland are the taipan and the tiger snake, found in Northern Queensland and the Northern Territory. Another one to watch out for is quaintly called the death adder. Others to avoid are the Australian copperhead, brown snakes and the red-bellied black snakes.

As long as we have your attention, you might as well know about two very nasty spiders that can cause major harm to humans: the red-back (black widow genus) and the funnel web. The red-back is mostly a desert spider found under old pieces of debris or in electrical junction boxes. The funnel web, according to popular lore, is found under toilet seats and only in the Sydney area. And let us not forget the bird-eating spider, about the size of a mouse and fond of noshing on frogs and rodents.

insects

The Cairns birdwing butterfly and the brilliant blue Ulysses butterfly are found in the rainforests of Queensland and a few other islands.

Australia has some of the most beautiful moths and butterflies in the world. The largest and most spectacular are the Cairns birdwing butterfly and the brilliant blue Ulysses. The female birdwing is huge, eight inches from wingtip to wingtip. Once she has mated, she can produce eggs for life, a fact often overlooked by the smaller but more colorful male who keeps trying to get another date. Both the birdwing and the Ulysses are found in rainforests in Queensland and some close-in islands. The largest moth in Australia, and one of the largest in the world, is the Hercules moth. The females have a wingspan of more than eight inches. The poor ladies have a sad story. They are born without mouths, so after they mate and lay eggs they starve to death.

The very worst insects in the whole country, as far as most people are concerned, are bush flies. They don't bite, but they get in your eyes, up your nose, down your blouse, up your shorts and have created what is widely known as the "Australian wave," a constant back-and-forth flutter of the hand to keep the damned flies away from your face. They are, by the way, just one of 6300 species of flies in the country. Bush flies, as far as we know, are impervious to anything short of an atomic bomb. Even Rid, the very powerful repellent sold in Australia, doesn't affect them.

Water Creatures

At Shark Bay you can stand in the surf and pet the famous Monkey Mia bottlenose dolphins.

Finally, because it is surrounded by water, Australia is the home of thousands of aquatic animals and plants, from world-class marlin to plankton that have drifted in from Antarctica and are in turn eaten by right whales who come to eat and mate. Australia even holds the record for the world's largest

THE LAND DOWN UNDER

bacterium. Most bacteria are so tiny, you need a microscope to see them. But in 1993, scientists at the James Cook University in Townsville found a beast they called *Epulopiscium fishelsoni*. The bacterium, about the size of a hyphen on this page, was discovered in fish living in the Great Barrier Reef. It's about a million times bigger than most bacteria. (See the Queensland section for words of warning about very dangerous jellyfish.) If you're crazy about animals, here are a few just to whet your appetite:

Fur seals along the coast of South Australia and Western Australia. Dugongs in submarine meadows on the east coast. Something like 2500 species of fish in the waters surrounding the continent. Sea horses off South Australia. The very poisonous and small blue-ringed octopus in the Barrier Reef, along with deadly cone shells. Crown of thorns starfish, which can strip a reef bare of coral in months. Hard corals. Soft corals. Three-foot-wide clams. Sharks. Salmon. The incredible edible barramundi. Prawns, oysters, crayfish. All you need is a marine guide and some drawn butter.

Flora

If you wonder what sort of tree you're looking at in Australia, the chances are it's a eucalypt—95 percent of the continent's 700 varieties of trees are eucalypts. Familiar to most people in the San Francisco Bay area (some freeways are lined with them), eucalyptus trees were first brought to California from Australia in 1856 and are used as wind-breaks and ornamental timber because of their rapid growth. There are whole generations of Californians who think they're native to the state. In the fall of 1991, many residents of Oakland, California learned first-hand what Australians have known for a long time eucalyptus trees literally explode in a fire. The terrible blaze that hit the Oakland hills was partially fueled by stands of blue-gum eucalypts, which cover many neighborhoods all over the state. The city of Oakland is thinking about banning eucalyptus trees, but they're difficult to get rid of and grow like weeds. The same thing happened two years later when horrendous bush fires burned thousands of acres around Sydney. The fires, fueled by high winds and eucalyptus trees, raged for weeks and destroyed at least one national park. In Australia, the various varieties of eucalypts that shed their bark are usually called gum trees. Aussie eucalypts can range in size from small shrubs, maybe 1.5 meters high, to giants that rise more than 200 feet into the air. •

Australian plants are just like Down Under animals—they all look familiar, but somehow, there's always something just a little different about them. Just to add to the confusion, the Aussie names for some plants vary from state to state. We made the mistake (several times) of asking the locals the name of a plant—it was like taking a poll. Also, forget Latin names. Why use dull nomenclature when you can deal with such things as "she-oaks" and "cathedral figs?" Anyway, from the rainforests of Eastern Australia and Tasmania to the hardy and often grotesque plants that inhabit the wastes of Central and Western Australia, the continent has wonderfully diverse plant life.

The forests of Northern Queensland are full of hiking trails and campgrounds, and here you find such dandy floral creations as the giant moss, which can have individual plants 20 inches in diameter. Australian rainforests are also home to some very beautiful orchids, many species of which can be shipped back to the United States if you want to grow them. You also find palms and some 30 species of mangroves. The mangrove roots often grow above ground because there is no oxygen in the swampy soil, and can be as tall as a man. In the Queensland highlands is red cedar that was highly valued in Victorian England—tons of the stuff was shipped off to build Old Bailey, the London courtroom complex. The Aboriginals made wide use of native plants. One, the so-called canary tree, supplied them with bark for canoes, poisons for fish, pain killers and dyes.

There are 16 species of fig trees in Australia, the most interesting being the strangler figs. In the Atherton Tablelands near Cairns are two superb examples of the strangler, the aforementioned Cathedral fig and an even more dramatic example, the Curtain Fig.

Nut cases will be interested to note that another native Australian plant has also been introduced into the United States besides eucalyptus trees—macadamia nuts. Rarely seen in their natural state any more in Australia, the nut trees have proven to be a boon to the Hawaiian economy—if the residents of the Big Island can keep the lava off their farms.

Also, Australia being Australia, there simply must be some nasties, one little gem being stinging shrubs, which have very painful hairlike stingers that can cause swelling, shock and breathing difficulty. Sometimes the symptoms last for months, and the plants usually grow in cleared areas, such as next to well-used trails; the plants have heart-shaped leaves. The poisonous hairs that cause the damage can sometimes be removed with depilatory wax or sticky tape. More bad news: As if the stinging shrubs weren't enough, you also have to contend with the so-called Lawyer Vine, also known as the Wait-a-While Vine. The crack about lawyers apparently originated because once the plant gets a hold of you, it won't let go. The spines on the vine must be drawn backwards in the opposite direction they grabbed you. It might comfort you to know the Aboriginals used the spines for fishhooks. Moral: if you wear shorts while hiking in a rainforest, don't touch anything.

The rainforests all over the country are noted for huge ferns, but in Tasmania the tiny backyard ferns we're used to in North America have run amok.

One species, called the man fern, is very ancient, with fossil records going back 300 million years.

Even in the vast arid center of Australia, all it takes is a little water and suddenly you have flora as far as you can see. Look for Sturt's desert pea, the state flower of the Northern Territory; rosy dock, an imported variety of hops that turns the desert floor near Ayers Rock a crimson in the spring; the yellow-stalked flowers of the mulga trees; the blues of the wild potato bush; and the bitter melons, whose seeds are so loved by cockatoos. In vast and arid Western Australia alone, there are more than 7000 varieties of wildflowers.

Australia also has varieties of some of the oldest plant species in the world. In a tiny gorge in the Northern Territory, for example, is a grove of cycad and cabbage palms. This type of plant (they have exposed seeds, much like pine cones) first appeared on earth about 350 million years ago. A close relative, the macrozamia cycads, are found in Western Australia. It's fascinating to note that one of the ways these cycads survive such a harsh environment is with a little help from an even older species. Blue-green algae live on their roots and help provide nourishment. In 1994, paleobotanists were delighted by the discovery of a stand of tall conifers that are the spitting image of fossil trees dating back to Cretaceous period, about 65–140 million years ago. The primitive plants, only 40 in number, were named Wollemi pines after Wollemi National Park west of Sydney. The trees were thought to have been extinct for more than 50 million years.

Throughout the arid regions of the country you find spinifex, which from a distance looks like sagebrush. There are blackboy trees that look from a distance like the strange Joshua trees of southeastern California. Up in the mountains of Victoria and New South Wales, you find alpine flowers. In national parks not far from Sydney you can find snow-gums (sub-alpine) and forests of Antarctic beeches. Near Melbourne are some remaining groves of the native mallee trees, a form of scrub eucalyptus that was a real pain to early farmers trying to clear the land.

The islands off the eastern coast, both coral and continental, have rainforests where you can find octopus bushes (they have long flowering arms) and dwarf poinsettias. Magnetic Island, off Townsville, has pine trees, banyans, she-oaks and the orange and scarlet blooms of the poincianas.

The country is also filled with food plants, everything from the banana and pineapple groves of Queensland to the grapes of Western Australia and the apple orchards of Tasmania. The country is one of the largest cotton producers in the world, and Australian rice is exported all over Asia. The national flower is the golden wattle, a yellow, bushy shrub that grows up to 15 feet and is only found in South Australia, Victoria and New South Wales.

There are so many plants in Australia that are found only in Australia that you could spend your whole vacation Down Under tracking them down. Because so many of the plants are alien to the Western Hemisphere, we strongly urge you to get a guidebook when you get to Australia, even if it's very basic. This will stop you from going mad when you wander across some strange Aussie fern that looks like something from the other side of the looking glass. One of the best sources of such books is at the various national park headquarters around the country. Park flora guides, usually priced below A$5, have the added advantage of concentrating on the plants in the immediate area.

Maintain an Even Strine

Australia's lifeguards go a little heavier on the sunscreen than their "Baywatch" equivalents.

Yes, most Australians do have a peculiar accent. Like North Americans, the width and complexity of that accent varies from city to city, state to state. Some Aussies speak English like the English, others are almost impossible for the North American ear to understand. Many New Zealanders feel it's a mortal sin if you confuse them with the Aussies, same for Australians similarly mistaken for Kiwis. We can't detect many differences between the two—but don't feel bad, because most Australians and New Zealanders can't tell Canadians and Americans apart either, eh? To prove something or other, there was a minor stink in New Zealand recently because a commercial for a

Kiwi breakfast cereal used Australian child actors. We couldn't detect a bit of difference, but the New Zealanders were slightly outraged.

Some observers like to make a big deal out of Australian "slanguage"—affectionately called "Strine" (from "Aus-strine," the way they say "Australian")—and make it sound like you're about to enter some sort of linguistic haunted house. But rest assured you will not, in most cases, need an interpreter. The Aussies will tell you, of course, that it's we who have the accent. Being polite and peaceful, we never bother telling them that when the first of Mel Gibson's Mad Max flicks (*Road Warrior*) was shown on American network TV, the whole thing was dubbed by American actors so us poor Yanks wouldn't have to contend with all that garble. In truth, and this sounds peculiar to Americans and Canadians who speak old-fashioned Midwest North American, it's probably going to be the Aussies who have trouble understanding you, not the other way around.

The scene is a general store in the Queensland Outback. Our hero, discovering he has failed to pack a towel, asks the matronly lady for help. "Need a towel," he says. Blank look. "You know," slowly, like he's talking to somebody in Hungary, "a tow-el?" Further blank look. So he tries charades, pulling an imaginary towel to and fro over his back. "Oh," she says, finally understanding, "you're wanting a tawl."

If you really get into it, Aussie slang is fascinating. The linguists will have you believe it's a combination of Irish and English cockney slang, added to and enhanced over the years by Aboriginal words and the peculiar lifestyle forced by the rigors of the Australian landscape. Whatever, it's a rich and bubbly stew. The only basic rule we know of is that if you give the Aussies a good, workable noun, they'll immediately put "ie" on the end of it. A truck driver is a "truckie." Morning sustenance is "brekkie." Your swimsuit is a "cossie," as in costume, and of course the Aussies always put their prawns on the "barbie." That's also why they call themselves "Aussies" (make sure you pronounce that "Ozzies"), and why that state south of the Bass Strait is called "Tassie," pronounced "Tazzie." A secondary diminutive form is to add an "o" to a noun, as in "going troppo" for somebody who's gone nuts in the tropics, "arvo," afternoon, or a favorite in these quarters, "journo" for members of the press.

There's only one way to describe the way a true Aussie speaks, and that's like an Australian. Take the expression: "Rise up, lides." A plea for insurrection? Nope, those are the things you shave with. This is another major Aussie trait: A's are like I's, which is why that most famous of all Aussie words, "mate," comes out sounding like "mite." You'll also find that the Australians, being an earthy lot, tend to have a fair number of earthy expressions wandering around. Like describing a tall, arrogant person as "a thin streak of pelican shit." Or like leaving in a hurry, "off like a bride's nightie," or extremely morose, as in "happy as a bastard on Father's Day." One of our particular favorites is the "technicolor yawn," which is what you do when you've had too much to drink. Bastard, by the way, is the universal Aussie word, used generally as a term of endearment, but also used to show derision, as in "pommie bastard," the standard description for any Englishman. "Bloody" comes in a close second, being the universal adjective, as in "my bloody oath," a common expression.

There are a few things you should know, just for self-preservation. For example, if some clot wearing an Outback hat asks you, as a gesture of Aussie-American harmony, to "shout the bar," tell him to get lost. When it's your shout, it's your turn to buy a round for your pals. If you shout the bar, you just bought one for the whole bloody pub, you poor bloody bastard.

A couple of phrases are all it takes to be a dinky-die (real, authentic) Aussie:

No worries—Everything's dandy, thanks.

She'll be right—The Aussie equivalent of "don't worry, be happy."

Dinkum, fair dinkum—honest, genuine.

Too right—Absolutely

You're right, she's right—No worries.

Galah—noisy clod, named after bird of the same name.

Seppo, septic—American, from septic tank. We're not sure how this one got here, but apparently it came about because of the influence of cockney rhyming slang, and tank rhymed with Yank, not because the Aussies hold us in, uh, low regard.

You'll find more useful words and phrases in the glossary on page 407.

The thing to do, if you're really crazy about Strine, is to find a good travel bookstore someplace that has an Aussie dictionary. Or wait until you get Down Under and find a little gem called *The Dinkum Aussie Dictionary*, by somebody called Crooked Mick of the Speewa, which has a nummy assortment of Australianisms with which to wow the crowd. (Child & Associates Publishers.)

Finally, if you really want to get in good with the blokes Down Under, learn The Song. For most of its history, white Australia managed to get along without an official national anthem, being content to let "Waltzing Matilda" do the job. But apparently some folks thought it was a bit demeaning to have a national tune based on a bum who steals a sheep, then commits suicide when the cops show up, so they picked up a new anthem, "Advance Australia Fair." The new number is pretty uninspired, and sounds like most of the national anthems in the world: very pompous and sort of English. But at heart the true Aussie national hymn remains "Waltzing Matilda," a tune that is almost universally associated with Australia. So here goes:

Once a jolly swagman camped by a billabong, under the shade of a coolabah tree. And he sang as he watched and waited 'till his billy boiled, "Who'll come a-waltzing Matilda with me?"

(The chorus throughout always repeats the last two lines of the previous stanza, so:)

Waltzing Matilda, waltzing Matilda, You'll come a-waltzing Matilda with me; And he sang as he watched and waited 'till his billy boiled, "Who'll come a-waltzing Matilda with me?"

(A swagman, or "swaggie," was a hobo, so called for his swag, or the tied-up bag or roll of personal belongings he carried around. A billabong is a pool of water that remains in a dry creek bed after the rainy season ends. A coolabah tree is a species of gum, or eucalyptus. A billy is a tin can or pot used to boil water for tea. "Waltzing Matilda" itself has many definitions inside the song; here it means to wander around with your pack, or matilda.)

Down came a jumbuck to drink at that billabong, Up jumped the swagman and grabbed him with glee; And he sang as he stowed that jumbuck in his tucker bag, "You'll come a-waltzing Matilda with me."

(Jumbuck is a lamb or young sheep. Tucker bag is a bag where the swaggie kept his food, or tucker. Waltzing Matilda here means the swaggie plans to nosh on the sheep.)

Up rode the squatter, mounted on his thoroughbred; Down came the troopers, one, two, three. "Where's that jolly jumbuck you've got in your tucker bag, "You'll come a-waltzing Matilda with me."

(Squatter was a wealthy rancher or farmer, troopers were probably the local cops. Here waltzing Matilda means they're going to incarcerate the poor swaggie.)

Up jumped the swagman, and sprang into the billabong; "You'll never catch me alive," says he. His ghost can be heard as you pass by the billabong, "You'll come a-waltzing Matilda with me."

The normal way to sing "Matilda" is loudly, with great feeling. The last chorus, about the swaggy's ghost, is often sung softly. Aussies will do Matilda at the drop of a hat, so memorize the words and join in. It's a lot easier to sing than the "Star-Spangled Banner" and has a lot more teeth than "Oh, Canada."

Driving

It was somewhere between Hughenden and Cloncurry, in north-central Queensland, no houses and no people for a million miles, when we decided to pull off the bitumen and take a break. That's what they call pavement in

Australia, bitumen, pronounced "bitch-oo-min." So we pulled off and parked under the shade of a big gum tree. That's when we discovered that there's more to driving in Australia than just being on the wrong side of the road.

See, you can't trust Aussies because they're outrageous kidders and love nothing more in the world than to slip one past some poor Yank tourist. So when we rented the pop-top VW camper, back in Townsville, the guys in the pub gave us all sorts of horse hockey about giant, man-eating kangaroos in the Outback, and 300-pound koalas, and herds of deadly snakes and, of course, bulldust.

"Struth, mate," one of the worst fibbers told us, "there's places out there where they've lost whole trucks in the dust. It's 30 feet deep and looks like solid rock, fair dinkum." Well, we did our research, and we knew there were no giant carnivorous roos in Queensland any more, let alone 300-pound koalas. So we just ignored all the stuff about treacherous pools of bulldust.

Bad mistake, very bad mistake.

It was nice and cool in the shade of the old gum tree after we pulled off and parked, and we had a cold beer and a hot sandwich and enjoyed the crows and the breeze. And when we started to back out, we knew we were well and truly in deep yogurt. Or in this case, deep dust.

Bulldust may not come in 30-foot-deep pools, but there's enough of it around to get novice Outback drivers in all sorts of trouble. Bulldust is fine, very fine dust, almost like baby powder and you can't get traction in it at all. It sits in the sun and gets a crust on it and looks just like solid ground. Eventually, some tourist pulls off the highway onto what looks like hard dirt and buries his or her car or camper up to the axles. It's not only Canadians, Germans and Americans who end up mired, either, because a fair number of slickers from Sydney and Canberra have met the same fate. Without four-wheel drive, bulldust can, like a disaster at sea, ruin an otherwise perfect day. (With some fancy back-and-forthing, rocking and popping the clutch, we finally managed to get out of the foot-deep dust and back on the main road. Not having four-wheel drive, we were very lucky.)

We raise the spectre of bulldust not to dissuade you from driving in Australia; indeed, it ends up being one of the little challenges of driving Down Under that makes a trip just that more memorable.

At the same time, bulldust and the other hazards of driving in Australia are not to be taken too lightly. Our little set-to with the dust was not serious—the biggest threat we faced was mortification if anybody ever found out. But there are some roads, in some places, that only a damned fool (or a damned fool with a good guide) should go. Note also that most Australian car/camper rental companies void insurance if vehicles are driven on unsealed roads. To do many places in the Outback or in remote national parks, you'll have to either go on a tour or rent a four-wheel-drive vehicle.

We have driven all over Australia, from the Kansas-flat stretches of cattle and sheep country in Queensland to the forests of Tasmania to the red-coated stretches of the Stuart Highway from Darwin to Ayers Rock. Seeing that we highly recommend that anybody serious about seeing Australia rent a car or camper and take off, it's only fair that we try to fill you in on some of the subtler forms of disaster you can run into tooling around Down Under. In addition to good old bulldust, try these:

The Basic Problem

This is, of course, the fact that we drive on the right and the Aussies drive on the left. Depending on your coordination and reaction times and common sense, this can be a very large deal, indeed, or no big thing. The most common mistake North Americans and continental European drivers make is looking the wrong way at the wrong time, usually at cross streets. The basic rule is the same that you see painted at every pedestrian crosswalk in London (where they lose an American at least once a day): LOOK RIGHT. This tendency to look the wrong way cuts both ways, of course. No less a light than Winston Churchill was hospitalized in 1931 after being knocked on his poopdeck by a New York City taxicab while he was trying to walk across Fifth Avenue. (He forgot to look left.) A sense of direction is particularly important in Australia when approaching that devilish English invention, the roundabout. We'd call it a traffic circle. Just remember to look right, because anybody coming from that direction has the right of way. Once on the roundabout, remember, clockwise, go clockwise. Once on the circle, you supposedly have the right of way, but we observe the California Freeway Right-of-Way Rule: if they want it, let 'em have it. (*Authors' note:* Be aware in Tasmania that drivers are taught to stay as close to the center line as possible, probably because the edges of the road are often jagged and the roads are narrow. They will stay on top of the white line until the last possible moment, then swerve to miss you. It can get a tad scary at times.)

You'll also notice that if you've rented a camper or car with a manual transmission, you have to shift left-handed (the foot controls are the same). This is no problem, and allows you to get a driver's tan on your right arm for once in your life. The bottom line is probably this: if you're a good driver in New York or Ottawa, with a little thought and concentration, you'll be a good driver in Australia.

The Roads

Around major population centers and between major cities along the coasts, Aussie highways are every bit as good as North American ones, perhaps just a tad narrower. They are well marked (make sure you're up on your international traffic signs) and well maintained. It's once you've gone past the Great Dividing Range (or in the case of Western Australia and the Northern Territory, when you get out of sight of the coast) that things get a little more challenging.

Rural roads all over the country tend to be either narrow and paved or wide and unpaved. The paved stretches, in addition to being narrow, sometimes have bad edges with jagged pavement and one-foot drops to the shoulders. The drier the country, the more bulldust you find on the shoulders. Sometimes even pulling off two or three feet will bury your axles. Road conditions seem to be at their least maintained in rural Queensland, as anybody in the state will tell you, blaming the potholes on politicians and other lowlifes.

Distances by Road (km)							
	Adelaide	Brisbane	Canberra	Darwin	Melbourne	Perth	Sydney
Adelaide		2130	1210	3215	745	2750	1430
Alice Springs	1690	3060	2755	1525	2435	3770	2930
Brisbane	2130		1295	3495	1735	4390	1030
Broome	4035	4320	5100	1965	4780	2415	4885
Cairns	2865	1840	3140	2795	3235	6015	2870
Canberra	1210	1295		4230	655	3815	305
Darwin	3215	3495	4230		3960	4345	4060
Melbourne	755	1735	655	3960		3495	895
Perth	2750	4390	3815	4345	3495		3990
Sydney	1430	1030	305	4060	895	3990	

The dirt roads are often in better shape than the pavement, particularly if a grader has been through recently. Note well, however, that nobody in the world makes washboard dirt roads like the Australians. There are some dirt roads so badly washboarded that you can lose tooth fillings from the shaking. The Aussie solution to this problem is to drive as fast as possible. This, they say, means the tires are only hitting the tops of the washboards and this reduces the shakes. We tried that once and immediately stopped before we either blew a tire or broke an axle.

The recognized rule on Outback dirt roads is to slow down when meeting another vehicle. This is so that you don't throw gravel or rock through each other's windshields. This is a nice theory, like everybody yielding to right-hand traffic, but we estimate about half the cars we've met on dirt roads passed us doing Mach 4 (to avoid the washboarding, no doubt). Even doing casual driving in Australia in the country can end you up on dirt roads. Unless you're in the middle of the great deserts, you should have no problems on dirt, aside from breathing dust and getting the stuffings rattled out of you. If uncertain, ask a local. Maybe he'll tell you the truth.

Bump in the Night

Once out of the cities, sometimes just by the time you get into the burbs, you start seeing cars and trucks with what look like aluminum roll bars attached to the front bumpers. These are often called bullbars, and they have one function in life—to stop kangaroos and other creatures of the night from going through the engine when you hit them at 80 miles an hour.

Most Aussies who live in rural areas have bullbars on their vehicles, despite strong evidence to suggest that if you hit a large roo, all the bars do is slide the beast up past the engine and through the windshield. "Oh, yay," says an Aussie friend of ours, "that's usually the way tourists see their first kangaroo—coming through the windscreen." He was not joking. You'll also see a fair number of vehicles with screen mesh over the windshields. This is supposed to stop rocks from hitting the glass (and has little or no effect on incoming marsupials). From all this, you probably think your basic Australian car looks like a Sherman tank. Not true. An armored personnel carrier, maybe.

You can get some idea of how sturdy your average Australian kangaroo is built from a tragic incident related by World War II historian Martin Caidin. A fully loaded American B-17 heavy bomber, weighing in the neighborhood of 40 or 50 tons, was taking off from an Australian airfield when a kangaroo hopped in front of the heavily-loaded plane. One of the B-17's tires hit the 'roo and the aircraft flipped onto its back and exploded, killing the crew.

Once out of the city lights and into the country, you should beware at all times of critters on the highway, especially at night. Back in the States and Canada, driving on country roads, you might see a rabbit or an armadillo once in a while (or now and then a moose or deer if you're in God's country—and as anybody from Alberta who's ever hit a moose will tell you, it ain't pretty.) In Australia, kangaroos love to park in the middle of the road or else jump in front of you, and there are any number of collisions involving emus, sheep and cattle. It's a jungle out there.

Probably the worst place for this is the Northern Territory. Fenced land in the Territory is infrequent so all manner of beasts wander around at will, and some of your basic animals, such as the occasional water buffalo, are built like a Brink's truck. The Stuart Highway is lined with carcasses. However, most of the damage to animals in the Territory is not from cars. Nosir, it's mostly caused by that peculiarly Australian threat to life, limb, tourists and stray animals—the road train.

Road trains are big, humping trucks, driven by insane Mad Max types who believe that all highways in the country are one-way—their way—and that anyone or anything that gets in their way has no right to live on this planet now or at any time in the future. The trains are really semi-trailer rigs, except higher and longer. Typically three units hooked together, these little wonders can reach 50 meters in total length, headlights to back bumper—that's half a football field, folks, and if you meet one on a narrow Outback stretch of bitumen, you have one of two choices, and we almost always head for the sidelines. The truckies (that's what they call the drivers) are so lost in their distant and powerful world, they never even see you disappearing into those 30-foot-deep pools of bulldust.

So we were renting a camper in Darwin, ready to head for Alice Springs, and the guy says: "Don't drive at night, under any circumstances, now or forever." Hawso, we figured, loose water buffaloes and kangaroos, sliding up over the bullbars into our laps, right? "No," he says, "road trains. They drive right down the middle of the bloody road 100 miles an hour and won't move over for anybody. It's worth your bloody life to drive in the bloody Territory at night." The funny thing is, you get those guys out of their half-football-field-long rigs, and they're among the nicest Aussies in the country. They do tell outrageous lies about bulldust, though.

Signs of the Times

Most Aussie road signs are straightforward, but there are some worth noting. They don't yield, they "Give Way," and when you come to a detour, the signs say "Sidetrack." That's where we get our expression for being sidetracked—country roads are called tracks, even some that are wide and in good shape. One of our favorites is a "jump-up," meaning a road that goes up onto a plateau or over a hill. Once you get into cow or sheep country, you'll probably see a sign now and then saying "Grid." That means cattle guard. Or maybe you'll see a sign: "Gladstone T/O 5km." That's the Gladstone turn-off. Driving here and there will give you proof positive that not all English is American. Take the sign that says "Refuse Tip." Should you now ignore folks who try to give you a gratuity for services rendered? No, it means you're approaching a garbage dump. And nothing stirs local pride more than being able to hang a sign out on the track that proclaims "Aussieberg-1998 Tidy Town Recipient," the Australian equivalent of the All-American City awards.

Rules of the Road

Wearing seatbelts in Australia is mandatory—get stopped, and you could earn a fine. The Australians are also serious about drinking and driving, and they pay no heed to the nationality of the driver. The legal level is .05 percent, which you can hit with a couple of rounds in a pub. The normal speed limit in cities and built-up areas is 60 kph and 100 to 110 kph on freeways and highways. (This rule does not apply to Sydney bus drivers, who go no

less than 60 miles an hour in any situation and are a greater hazard to life
than atomic bombs.)

Car Rentals

Americans and Canadians can rent cars or campers with a valid driver's license as long as they're 21—some companies have restrictions for drivers
under 25 or over 60.

The major rental agencies in Australia are familiar to North American drivers—Hertz, Avis, Budget and Thrifty. In addition, there are many other
local agencies that often have cut rates. One of the largest in the Northern
Territory, for example, is our old fave, the Cheapa Rent-a-Car Co., with
small cars going for as little as A$18 a day plus kilometerage. Most rental
contracts give you unlimited kilometerage and are on a per-day or per-week
basis. North American insurance is not valid in Australia, and all contracts
carry mandatory third-party insurance. A few things to know:

- The normal way to rent a car is by credit card, even if you intend to
  pay the bill in cash later. If you don't want to use a card, most companies require that you pay the total estimated costs of the car for
  the rental period plus an A$100 deposit. If you spend less than the
  estimate, you get a refund when you turn the car back in. Most
  agencies require you to add insurance to the rental agreement. You
  can either opt for a high deductible clause (usually A$500) or buy
  per-day coverage. The deductible normally does not cover windshield damage. The per-day insurance, in the A$10-15 range, usu-
  ally covers everything but tires. (These regulations can also vary
  from state to state.) Rental agencies also require you return the
  vehicle filled with gasoline or pay a high refill charge. One-way rentals must be arranged in advance and there is often a drop-off charge.

- Gasoline (called "petrol" Down There) varies widely in price, with
  city pumps running around A65 cents a liter. In the boonies, it can
  go for more than A70 cents a liter. This means gas prices of
  between $1.80 and $2.35 a gallon. Compact, manual transmission
  cars get about 30 miles to the gallon. Gas stations are common on
  major coastal highways and in cities, but tend to get scarce in rural
  areas. The major gasoline companies are BP, Shell, Caltex,
  AMPOL, Mobil and Amoco. Many gas stations will take Visa or
  MasterCard cards, bless them.

- Rates vary from company to company and depend on the rental
  period, but for cost estimating purposes, figure a small car goes for
  about A$50 a day; a compact, A$55; a medium, A$60; and a large,
  A$75. Most car companies in Australia offer fly/drive packages.

Also, good deals are sometimes offered through the various state travel offices.

Camper Rentals

Of all the ways to see Australia, this is probably the best all-around combination. A camper lets you go where you want, when you want, and you're carrying your hotel with you. While not everybody's cup of tea, a camper vacation is a great way to see the country and meet the natives. We guarantee, within five minutes of pulling in, you'll be on first-name basis with the Aussies parked on either side.

Caravaning—the word Aussies use for RVing—is one of the favorite Aussie ways to take a vacation, and the extensive system of caravan parks all over the country proves it. The basic parks have water, electricity and facilities (showers, toilets, a laundry) and can range in size from a mom-and-pop outfit to enormous parks such as the one at Ayers Rock that can accommodate hundreds of rigs. The normal one-night charge at an Aussie RV park, including electricity, averages around A$10-15. Most larger parks also have on-site campers that can be rented for a night or week and come equipped with bedding, kitchen equipment and other necessities of life. These units normally rent for between A$15 and A$40 a night for two persons. Insurance regulations for rental RVs are basically the same as for automobiles.

How good your mileage is in a camper depends on where you're driving— and how fast. In the flatlands of the Northern Territory, for example, driving a small, cab-over self-contained camper, we got between 17 and 22 miles per gallon. In Tasmania, hilly and curvy, it dropped as low as 10 or 11.

The rental cost of campers, as with cars, varies company to company depending on size and rental period. In Aussie nomenclature a campervan is usually a pop-top, and a motorhome is closer to the North American view of an RV. They range in size from cozy to huge, even some with inside plumbing. Approximate costs are about A$350-400 a week for a pop-top, A$450-600 for a small motorhome. Some companies offer unlimited kilometerage, others add a per-kilometer charge of around A15 cents after the first 1000 kilometers. Most RVs, regardless of size, come with pots, pans, dishes, propane, refrigerators, color TVs, radios with tape decks, and more and more, microwave ovens, which are the camper's savior. In some instances, there will be a charge of about A$20 for blankets, linens and some kitchen equipment. In spite of the number of caravan parks, it is sometimes essential to make reservations, particularly at high-volume places such as Kakadu National Park and Ayers Rock. Campers, like cars, are sometimes in short supply, especially around Christmas and school holidays, so advance bookings are a good idea.

In addition, most major camper agencies have fly/drive packages available, and state tourist agencies often have special rental packages.

Information on the major rental companies is available from a travel agent or by contacting these agencies:

Budget, ☎ *(800) 527-0700*, USA, or ☎ *(800) 268-8900*, Canada; **Thrifty**, ☎ *(800) 528-5808*, USA, or ☎ *(800) 367-2277*, Canada ☎ *(416) 532-9714*, Toronto); **Letz**, ☎ *(800) 445-0190*, California, ☎ *(800) 551-2012*, USA, and ☎ *(800) 235-8222*, Canada; **Explorer Motor Caravans**, ☎ *(800) 558-0872*, USA; **Horizon Holidays**, ☎ *(800) 423-2880* or ☎ *(800) 632-7915*, USA, or ☎ *(416) 863-0799*, Toronto; **Newman's Sunseeker Caravans**, ☎ *(800) 252-4616*, California, ☎ *(800) 421-3326*, USA, or ☎ *(800) 624-4349*, Canada; **Guthreys**, ☎ *(800) 854-3413*, USA, and **Holiday Motorhome Rentals**, ☎ *(800) 231-1468*, USA, ☎ *(714) 675-7306*, California and ☎ *(714) 675-2250*, (Canadians call collect). Another nation-wide agency is **Allaussie Campervans**, *20 Norwich Avenue, Thomastown, Melbourne VIC 3074,* ☎ *(03) 9469-2186.*

Four-Wheel Drive

If you're thinking about a four-wheel drive, you're probably thinking about an excursion into the incredibly rugged desert and mountain country of Australia. This means you're either crazy or an old Jeep hand. Unless you've had a fair amount of experience driving around southern Utah or the California desert, we strongly recommend that you avoid the true Aussie wilderness by yourself. In addition to Hertz and Avis, another company that has four-wheel-drive vehicles available is **Brits Rentals, Adventure Centre**, *5540 College Avenue, Oakland, Calif. 94618,* ☎ *(800) 228-8747*, California, or ☎ *(800) 227-8747*, USA.

Prices for four-wheelers will depend on where you are and how big a unit you're renting. As an example, we rented a small Suzuki to go to Cape Tribulation north of the Daintree River on the Cape York Peninsula in Queensland. The road wasn't that bad, but because it was dirt, washboarded and subject to flooding, we couldn't take a normal rental car. The rate was about A$90 a day, with 200 kilometers a day free. We had to give them a A$1000 security deposit, which usually has to be put on a credit card. You're responsible for any damage to the vehicle, including dings, broken windows, or undercarriage problems. This is a standard type of contract you'll run into all over the country. Like normal car rentals, you have to bring the four-wheelers back filled with gas.

This is not to say that you shouldn't try a four-wheel-drive adventure. But if you do, play it smart. Even old Aussie desert rats tend to travel in convoys, and there are a number of four-wheel-drive clubs in the country who welcome strangers along on trips—state automobile clubs have details.

The alternative is to take a guided trip with people who know what they're doing—you still get to see the incredible beauty and isolation of the Outback, but without the terror of breaking an axle all by yourself 5000 miles from the nearest mechanic. Many operators run safaris where you bring your own vehicle and they provide routes, mechanical help and planning.

A few agencies who do trips include **AAT King's**, **Australian Pacific Tours**, **Centralian**, **Desert-Trek Australia** and **Trekabout Expeditions**. The Australian Tourism Commission has further information about four-wheel-drive vacations. Call ☎ *(800) 753-0998* or *(708) 296-4900.*

SOS

The Australian equivalents of the AAA and CAA can be a big help for visiting drivers, offering map service, accommodations guides, national park information and brochures. The Aussies have reciprocal agreements with us, so take along your automobile club card.

Addresses

New South Wales: **National Roads and Motorists' Association** (NRMA), *151 Clarence Street, Sydney NSW 2000,* ☎ *(02) 9260-9222;* Queensland: **Royal Automobile Club of Queensland** (RACQ), *300 St. Paul's Terrace, Fortitude Valley, QLD 4006,* ☎ *(07) 361-2444;* Australian Capital Territory: **National Roads and Motorists' Association** (NRMA), *92 Northbourne Avenue, Braddon, ACT 2601,* ☎ *(06) 243-8800;* Victoria: **Royal Automobile Club of Victoria** (RACV), *230 Collins, VIC 3174,* ☎ *(03) 9650-1522;* South Australia: **Royal Automobile Association of South Australia** (RAA), *41 Hindmarsh Square, Adelaide, SA 5000,* ☎ *(08) 8202-4500;* Western Australia: **Royal Automobile Club of Western Australia** (RAC), *228 Adelaide Terrace, Perth WA 6000,* ☎ *(08) 9421-4444;* Northern Territory: **Automobile Association of the Northern Territory** (AANT), *79-81 Smith Street, Darwin NT 0800,* ☎ *(08) 8981-3837,* and Tasmania: the **Royal Automobile Club of Tasmania** (RACT), *corner Patrick and Murray Streets, Hobart TAS 7000,* ☎ *(03) 6326-300.*

Food

One of the ways the Aussies refer to themselves is as "The Lucky Country," which seems an apt name when it comes to Australia's abundance and variety of food. The Australians, despite many reports to the contrary, do eat other things besides ants, goannas, greasy mutton and stale pumpkin scones. They are blessed with many exotic fruits, more than 2500 species of edible fish, some of the best lamb in the world, lean beef and, thanks to the immigration rules that were changed after World War II, almost any sort of ethnic food you want.

The trend in many restaurants now is a combination of fresh, natural Australian meats and produce seasoned with Pacific Rim ingredients. So maybe because of the exotic food sources in the country, traditional Australian dishes generally tend to be more innovative and spicier than the usually dull colonial English fare they are based on. Still, there will not be many surprises for North American palates, which are already familiar with a number of diverse culinary styles. But the surprises, when they do come, are often strange, indeed. The first that always comes to mind is Vegemite, a dark-brown, gooey, salty vegetable yeast extract that Aussies use in much the same way we use peanut butter. They put the stuff on toast, over crackers and in sandwiches, and start eating the junk when they're toddlers—we opine that Vegemite is one of the few things the folks Down Under have that they can keep all to themselves. Yecccch.

Another example of Australian acquired taste must be the use of beets on hamburgers. You must be vigilant when ordering "the works" on your burger, because in addition to the beets (they call them beetroot and they're not pickled), they love to stick in shredded carrots, which while healthy, are a definite surprise for North American hamburger aficionados. They're learning, however (or being corrupted). Last time in Queensland, we went to a burger joint and the waiter, hearing the accent, said "You'll be wanting a hamburger without beets and some French fries, right, pardner?"

Also, you must use care when ordering the type of bread you want your burger wrapped in. Make sure you ask if it comes on a "roll" (hard) or a "bun" (soft). If it comes in a roll, get out your knife and fork, because the roll is so hard, all the meat slides out when you chomp. We thought it was very strange to see Australians eating hamburgers with a knife and fork—but now we know why.

There is a wonderful little inn/restaurant in South Australia that serves an occasional special meal using emu and kangaroo. In the kitchen, away from the guests, they call it the "Coat of Arms Delight," since both emu and roo are on the Australian coat of arms. They don't yet have courage to formally advertise it that way on the menu, fearing there are still those around who feel such treatment of the national symbols is a touch unpatriotic. Whatever, the dish is divine. Emu (in a red wine sauce) tastes like dark turkey, and kangaroo, if the proper cut (a rib loin) is used and it's prepared properly, is outstanding. There are some who think eating kangaroo is right up there with filleting the kids' kitten. We love kangaroos. But we also love them cooked. If this be hypocrisy, make the most of it.

For years, kangaroo was verboten in Australia, allowed only for pet food. But now it's generally available all over the country—butchers in Tasmania even sell packaged wallaby steaks and sausages. There are an estimated 900 restaurants in Sydney serving kangaroo. A few years back, the governor-general of Australia, Bill Hayden, said he was having a kangaroo over-population problem on his estate, and, ignoring appeals from animals rights groups, planned to not only kill them, but to have them for dinner. He told the press he "thoroughly enjoyed" eating not only roo but emu, and said that kangaroo was "low in cholesterol and very good for the diet." Let your conscience be your guide. Lest we forget, you can also sup on crocodile pies, water buffalo burgers and, as in New Zealand, domesticated venison. If it moves, eat it.

For the most part, you will recognize everything served up on your plate in Australia, but recognizing it on the menu can be a problem. It is easier than tackling a German, French or Italian menu, but still it helps to learn your way around Aussie food nomenclature. A few clues to help you with the fair d' jour:

When you see crayfish on the menu, do not order six dozen, as you might in New Orleans. Being huge fans of Lake Pontchartrain crawfish (or crayfish or crawdads), we were delighted to see crayfish offered on a menu, assuming they had discovered the little devils in Australia, and accordingly, ordered a couple of pounds. You can imagine the surprise when instead of a few dozen small crustacea, they wheeled in a spiny sea lobster weighing about a kilo. But it was no loss—Aussie "crayfish" have sweet, firm meat and you'll have trouble eating just one. The best ones come from along the eastern shore of Tasmania, or from the cool waters of the Bass Strait, which separates mainland Australia from Tasmania. We recommend stopping at a fish market and picking up a precooked, chilled crawfish. Add a bottle of Tasmanian Tamar Valley wine, some local cheese and bread and a quiet beach—well, you get the idea. Crays, as they're called, are also known in some places as Southern rock lobsters. Note: in the Aussie winter, crays are out of season and finding a fresh one can be tough—and expensive.

Queensland's mud crabs are very popular around Brisbane, but probably not as big a favorite as Morton Bay bugs. Before you reach for the Raid, realize that the bug is really a small crustacean, sort of a cross between a lobster and a crayfish. In restaurants around Brisbane, you can get bugs in almost any style you want, from curried to just plain with drawn butter. Remember, what Australians call prawns, we call shrimp—they only bait their hooks with shrimp. When ordering fish, we always find out what the local catch of the day is. With 2500 species to pick from, it's essential to find out which came from nearby waters. Some Australian species we can recommend are the John Dory, trumpeteer, barramundi, coral trout, redfish, gemfish and sole.

The Australians have a strange name for chickens: they call them *chooks*. Where the name comes from, nobody seems to know, but you'll see it here and there, as in signs offering *fish and chooks*. Chicken is just becoming an alternative to red meat in Australia. A standard we always found on the menu was *Maryland chicken*, which is chook covered in bread crumbs and then fried. (One of us grew up in Maryland and never heard of such a thing—maybe they decided that Maryland was close enough to the Confederacy to substitute for "Southern fried chicken".) Anyway, one of the more delicious ways to have your chook and eat it too is to try broasted (grilled on a spit) chicken, which can be found in fast-food places and makes for a great lunch.

If your steak or salad comes with *capsicums*, it means you'll be eating green or red bell peppers. On a salad, you might get "avos," or avocados; *pines*, or pineapples, or *paw-paws*, which are papayas. Queenslanders are fond of using pines and bananas as well as other fine fruits in everything. Do not be surprised if you find tropical fruit stuck into a steak. Also a horrid thing might happen if you order a Queensland pizza with all the trimmings—it'll come with pineapple. And—hello—in Victoria and New South Wales, you can get a kangaroo pizza.

In Australia, *scones* are the equivalent of our biscuits, but their biscuits are like English biscuits, meaning a cookie. Scones are often served with clotted cream as part of Devonshire teas. (They pronounce that "skawns.") Adding to the confusion, you should know that a *water biscuit* is a cracker, and an *Anzac biscuit* is a popular cookie. They are a chewy, oatmeal concoction made with brown sugar. *Damper* is a campfire bread and can usually be found in cafes and restaurants in touristy areas. Hot, with lots of fresh butter, damper makes a good breakfast or complement to an afternoon tea. Often, damper is cooked with fruits added, such as raisins. For a real treat, try an Australian pancake, which is thin like a crepe, then rolled and filled with sugar and fruit. With whipped cream on the side, they are heavenly and much less filling than Yankee flapjacks.

Aussies are also wild about cappuccino and espresso, and they actually make some of the best you'll ever taste (such as the big cups served up at the Jimmy's On the Mall in Brisbane), which means the country is eligible for entry into the Society of Civilized Nations. If it's a *brekkie* menu you are reading, you'll probably run across *snags*. Snags are sausages, and can be either fat and short (probably pork) or long and thin like hot dogs. Snags are not as spicy as North American sausage, and are made with bread filling—if you've ever had English or Scottish bangers, you'll know the taste. Pretty bland.

If you like your first meal of the day on the largish side, try an Australian *mixed grill*, a hearty dish of broiled meats, usually lamb chops, steak and snags, along with broiled tomatoes and maybe some mushrooms. For lunch, it would include chips—french fries.

Our next breakfast offering is *toad in the hole*, a dish that can also be served for lunch or dinner. The toad in question has no warts. It's composed of sausages cooked in an egg batter. If your server asks you if you want Vogel toast with breakfast, say yes—it's a tasty multi-grain bread. As for crisp bacon, forget it. Aussie bacon is very lean, like Canadian bacon only more so, and you can grill it all day without crisping it up. Most motels and hotels in Australia provide an electric kettle and tea and coffee makings. Also, you might find a packet of Milo, an instant chocolate-malt powder very popular in Southeast Asia. It was invented 60 years ago by an Aussie chemist for the Swiss chocolate giant, Nestle.

Now we come to desserts, foremost of which are the two that Australians are proud to call their own—the Pavlova and peach Melba. *Pavlova,* named after the famous Russian ballerina, Anna Pavlova, is a baked meringue filled with whipped cream mixed with fresh fruit. Done properly, it's yummy; done badly, or stale, it can be like eating a used truck tire. *Peach melba* is named after Dame Nellie Melba, a beloved Aussie soprano who supposedly had more affairs than Errol Flynn, which is saying something. You can find this dessert in many American restaurants, but if you've never had one, it's a piece of sponge cake placed in a glass dish or parfait glass, then topped with a peach half, sprinkled with sherry and covered with whipped cream and pureed raspberries or strawberries. Both desserts are exceedingly sweet.

For an afternoon snack, you might find a *Lord Lamington's* on the menu (he was the Queensland governor at the turn of the century). Again, a sponge cake, this time cut in squares, dipped in chocolate icing, then sprinkled with coconut. (How's your cholesterol these days?) Another popular type of dessert is a "slice," which as far as we can tell, is baked pastry sliced into strips and filled with cream custard, then iced. If you want a real cup of tea, find a tea room. You will know you're in the real thing when they bring a small tea strainer along with your pot of tea. Sorry to say, too many places simply bring a pot of hot water and a bag. The Empire, remember, has faded away.

As in England, a big Australian lunch favorite is fish and chips. The fish is usually whiting, although shark is also popular. If you're looking for ketchup for your chips (they call it *tomato sauce*), you might have a hard time; instead, they allow you to douse them in vinegar—which, as anyone knows, is the only way to eat French fries anyway. The chips, by the way, will probably not be crisp. The Aussies like them soggy (it brings out the flavor, they claim) and they are usually wrapped in with the fish. While we think this is a top take-out food, the Aussie favorite seems to be meat pies. The mass-produced ones we tried were not impressive; homemade ones are supposed to be better. There are many variations on the meat pie, such as sausage rolls, chicken and pork pies, egg and bacon pies (very much like a quiche). You can buy pies almost everywhere from sporting matches to supermarket freezers, corner stores to pubs. Pies, by the way, are supposed to be eaten with tomato sauce. Ketchup, that is.

In many places all over the country, you'll find pubs or restaurants that will sell you fresh meat or seafood and also have a *barbie* on the premises so you can cook things the way you like them. Everyone seems to enjoy the informal atmosphere, and the pubs also do a bang-up business. Barbie parties, by the way, are the single-most popular way to entertain in Australia. They think, you see, that they invented the barbecue, and we haven't had the courage to tell them the truth.

A word kept popping up at lunch counters that had us mystified for a long time—*jaffles*. These turned out to be grilled—not broiled—sandwiches, which come with a variety of fillings such as cheese, ham, baked beans, even spaghetti. And of course, unless you're quick, beetroot and carrots. Potted meats (a poor man's pate) are popular as a sandwich spread when they run out of Vegemite (or the smell drives them out of the house). Be advised, in Australia, the sandwiches are thin, and the bread is almost always spread with butter.

If you see a sign that says *Milk Bar*, you've found the neighborhood corner store. You can buy milk, of course, as well as ice cream bars and maybe a milk shake. But you can also buy small cooking items such as soup, newspapers or soft drinks and snacks. Never ask for a "soda" because they'll think you're after unsweetened carbonated water. If your palate hasn't been destroyed by too many Pavlovas, ask for a *lolly*, or candy. And if you want some potato chips, ask for *crisps*—if you order chips, they'll probably stick in some fish. One staple of the small corner store are *cordials*, and we don't mean the alcoholic kind you find in bartenders' books. Cordials are made of sweet, non-carbonated concentrates of various fruits, usually mixed with water to make hot-weather drinks. Lemon squash cordial is mixed with soda water and is an acceptable ladies' drink in pubs.

If you come from someplace that has a Chinatown, and the folks who live there are mostly from Canton, Aussie Chinese food might throw you a curve. What they call "dim sum" in Canton and San Francisco is called "dim sim" in Sydney and Melbourne. We thought it was a misspelling, but dim sim is the same stuff—which in Australia is quite good.

You can always eat cheaply in Australia, and in the many ethnic "food halls" in shopping centers and tourist areas, the choices are varied and often quite good. In some Australian cities, we found food halls only operating at lunch time. But in Brisbane, for example, they are open for dinner. The food hall solves the problem of satisfying a bunch of appetites at one time without moving the car. There are usually a dozen or more different ethnic foods to choose from, as well as the regular fish and chips and meat pie places. Italian, Chinese, Greek, Lebanese, Malaysian, even German fare is offered. In most food halls, there is also a central bar when you can get wine or beer. The drill is simple: pick out your food, pay for it (usually a central cash register) and find a table someplace in the hall. In some fancy food halls, you put a number on your table, go pick out the food and pay for it, and the staff brings it to the table. There are usually dessert places around, as well. Some halls even have piano players or other forms of live entertainment, and the prices are almost always reasonable.

Finally, in the "We don't get no respect" category, we should mention that a couple of years ago, two Queensland chefs were refused work permits in Japan because authorities declared that there was no such thing as Australian cuisine. The incensed chefs immediately produced platters of water buffalo salad, crocodile pie and Moreton Bay bugs and the Japanese relented. Yet another page in the curious history of Japanese-Australian relations.

ESSENTIAL AUSTRALIA

Sydney Opera House conducts tours of its 900 separate areas.

When to Go

Australia, being south of the equator, is all backwards. (Natives insist it's the other way around. But then, they also say we drive on the wrong side of the road.) Anyway, after 200 years, they're used to having Christmas when it's July-like outside and chilling out when it really is July. For example, Sydney in July averages between 8 and 16 degrees Celsius (46–60° F); in January, it's between 17 and 25 (62–77° F). Alice Springs, in the geographic center, averages between 4 and 19 in July (40–66° F), but between 22 and

37 in January (72–98° F). (Darwin is always easy to figure: it varies between hot and steamy and hotter and steamier.)

MONTHLY AVERAGE TEMPERATURES AND RAINFALL IN AUSTRALIA

CITY	Jan.	Feb.	Mar.	Apr.	May	Jun.	Jul.	Aug.	Sep.	Oct.	Nov.	Dec.
ADELAIDE (South Australia)												
Avg High (°C/°F)	30/ 86	30/ 86	27/ 81	23/ 73	19/ 66	16/ 61	15/ 59	17/ 62	19/ 66	23/ 73	26/ 79	28/ 83
Avg Low (°C/°F)	16/ 61	17/ 62	15/ 59	13/ 55	10/ 50	8/ 47	7/ 45	8/ 46	9/ 48	11/ 51	13/ 55	15/ 59
Rainfall (mm/in.)	20/ 0.8	18/ 0.7	25/ 1.0	46/ 1.8	69/ 2.7	76/ 3.0	66/ 2.6	66/ 2.6	53/ 2.1	43/ 1.7	28/ 1.1	25/ 1.0
BRISBANE (Queensland)												
Avg High (°C/°F)	29/ 85	29/ 85	28/ 82	26/ 79	23/ 74	21/ 69	20/ 68	22/ 71	24/ 76	27/ 80	28/ 82	29/ 85
Avg Low (°C/°F)	21/ 69	20/ 68	19/ 66	16/ 61	13/ 56	11/ 51	9/ 49	10/ 50	13/ 55	16/ 60	18/ 64	19/ 67
Rainfall (mm/in.)	163/ 6.4	160/ 6.3	145/ 5.7	94/ 3.7	71/ 2.8	66/ 2.6	56/ 2.2	48/ 1.9	48/ 1.9	64/ 2.5	94/ 3.7	127/ 5.0
DARWIN (Northern Territory)												
Avg High (°C/°F)	32/ 90	32/ 90	33/ 91	33/ 92	33/ 91	31/ 88	31/ 87	32/ 89	33/ 91	34/ 93	34/ 94	33/ 92
Avg Low (°C/°F)	25/ 77	25/ 77	25/ 77	24/ 76	23/ 73	21/ 69	19/ 67	21/ 70	23/ 74	25/ 69	26/ 69	26/ 69
Rainfall (mm/in.)	386/ 15.2	312/ 12.3	254/ 10.0	97/ 3.8	15/ 0.6	3/ 0.1	0/ 0	3/ 0.1	13/ 0.5	51/ 2.0	119/ 4.7	239/ 9.4
HOBART (Tasmania)												
Avg High (°C/°F)	22/ 71	22/ 71	20/ 68	17/ 63	14/ 58	12/ 53	11/ 52	13/ 55	15/ 59	17/ 63	19/ 66	21/ 69
Avg Low (°C/°F)	12/ 53	12/ 53	11/ 51	9/ 48	7/ 44	5/ 41	4/ 40	5/ 41	6/ 43	8/ 46	9/ 48	11/ 51
Rainfall (mm/in.)	48/ 1.9	38/ 1.5	46/ 1.8	48/ 1.9	46/ 1.8	56/ 2.2	53/ 2.1	48/ 1.9	53/ 2.1	58/ 2.3	61/ 2.4	53/ 2.1

MONTHLY AVERAGE TEMPERATURES AND RAINFALL IN AUSTRALIA

CITY	Jan.	Feb.	Mar.	Apr.	May	Jun.	Jul.	Aug.	Sep.	Oct.	Nov.	Dec.
MELBOURNE (Victoria)												
Avg High (°C/°F)	26/ 78	26/ 78	24/ 75	20/ 68	17/ 62	14/ 57	13/ 56	15/ 59	17/ 63	19/ 67	22/ 71	24/ 75
Avg Low (°C/°F)	14/ 57	14/ 57	13/ 55	11/ 51	8/ 47	7/ 44	6/ 42	6/ 43	8/ 46	9/ 48	11/ 51	12/ 54
Rainfall (mm/in.)	48/ 1.9	46/ 1.8	56/ 2.2	58/ 2.3	53/ 2.1	53/ 2.1	48/ 1.9	48/ 1.9	58/ 2.3	66/ 2.6	58/ 2.3	58/ 2.3
PERTH (Western Australia)												
Avg High (°C/°F)	29/ 85	29/ 85	27/ 81	24/ 76	21/ 69	18/ 64	17/ 63	18/ 64	19/ 67	21/ 70	24/ 76	27/ 81
Avg Low (°C/°F)	17/ 63	17/ 63	16/ 61	14/ 57	12/ 53	10/ 50	9/ 48	9/ 48	10/ 50	12/ 53	14/ 57	16/ 61
Rainfall (mm/in.)	8/ 0.3	10/ 0.4	20/ 0.8	43/ 1.7	130/ 5.1	180/ 7.1	170/ 6.7	145/ 5.7	86/ 3.4	56/ 2.2	20/ 0.8	13/ 0.5
SYDNEY (New South Wales)												
Avg High (°C/°F)	26/ 78	26/ 78	24/ 76	22/ 71	19/ 66	16/ 61	16/ 60	17/ 63	19/ 67	22/ 71	23/ 74	25/ 77
Avg Low (°C/°F)	18/ 65	18/ 65	17/ 63	14/ 58	11/ 52	9/ 48	8/ 46	9/ 48	11/ 51	13/ 56	10/ 60	17/ 63
Rainfall (mm/in.)	89/ 3.5	102/ 4.0	127/ 5.0	135/ 5.3	127/ 5.0	117/ 4.6	117/ 4.6	76/ 3.0	74/ 2.9	71/ 2.8	74/ 2.9	74/ 2.9

At first blush, this opposing climate would seem like a dandy arrangement for North American tourists. When we're freezing to death up here, all we have to do is hop down to Oz and it's summer. Or if one is a skier and wants to spend the whole year on the slopes, when the melt starts at Squaw Valley in May, it's just beginning to get frosty in the Snowy Mountains. Only problem is, the airlines and hotels on both continents know all about the temperature differences, so the most expensive time to go to Australia is in the North American winter. The best times to go, as a balance between climate and cost, are in the shoulder periods, basically North American spring and fall. North American summer is okay for a trip to Australia, too, as long as you stay north in Queensland, or go to Western Australia or the Northern Territory. Also, the kids Down Under get their summer off (our winter), and reservations start becoming necessary, especially around Christmas. There are also school holidays in May and in August–September.

Getting There

Any way you cut it, getting to Australia is a long haul, one of the reasons many otherwise eager explorers have given it a pass. From San Francisco, for example, it's about 15 hours to Australia, and if you're coming from the East Coast, add another five or six hours—if you're lucky and get a good connection. From Vancouver, the total trip time to Sydney is almost 17 hours, counting a layover in Honolulu. Even in a spacious 747, it's a long, hot, grueling trip down through the South Pacific.

It's also a fairly expensive trip, although the expansion of airline service in the past few years has helped keep things competitive. From the West Coast, during high season (November–March) an APEX economy round trip fare has recently been running around US $1000, although we've seen a lot of specials recently with fares under US$800. Airlines that currently have regular service from North America to Australia include **Canadian Airlines**, **Qantas** (the Australian national carrier), **United** and **Air New Zealand**. Check with United Vacations for the airline's packages: ☎ *(800) 328-6877;* or with Qantas Vacations, ☎ *(800) 252-6240* in the U.S. or ☎ *(800) 268-7525* in Canada. Our current favorite is Air New Zealand because of its service and relatively young fleet of aircraft. The airline has what it calls the Coral Route service, which flies to destinations all over the South Pacific on the way to Auckland or Sydney. For about US$1300, you get a ticket that lets you stop at several spots on the way Down Under. So you could break up your trip with a stay at the Cook Islands or Fiji, for example. Air New Zealand is an aggressive outfit and at the moment is probably the best South Pacific carrier. Qantas is planning to rapidly expand service in the area, however.

From the West Coast, flights either go nonstop from Los Angeles to Sydney or stop for refueling in Honolulu. Most airlines now offer service to Queensland after a stop in Sydney. As is the case with most South Pacific service, flights leave the West Coast at night and arrive in Australia the next morning. Some United nonstop flights leave San Francisco midday. The normal flying time is five hours from the West Coast to Honolulu, then 10 hours to Sydney. From Honolulu, a variety of carriers, including some of the smaller South Pacific airlines, fly to New Zealand and Australia.

Formalities

Australia requires anyone entering the country (aside from New Zealanders) to have a visa and a current passport plus proof of return airfare. Getting a visa in Canada or the United States is usually easy and free. Visas for tourists are usually issued for a year and are good for multiple entries. Processing fees are US$24 and $CAN30. Longer visas are also available. At most visa-issuing agencies, you can get the paperwork done the same day if you go in person; you can also have it done by mail—allow 21 working days for delivery.

Visas can be issued by the following offices in the United States:

Australian Embassy, *1601 Massachusetts Avenue N.W., Washington, D.C. 20036-2273,* ☎ *(202) 797-3000; FAX(202) 797-3100,* 8:30 a.m.–12:30 p.m.; **Australian Consulates General**, *630 Fifth Avenue, New York, N.Y. 10111,* ☎ *(212) 408-8400; FAX (212) 408-8485,* 9 a.m.–1 p.m.; *2049 Century Park East, Los Angeles, Calif. 90067,* ☎ *(310) 229-4840, FAX (310) 277-5620,* 10 a.m.–4 p.m.; *1990 Post Oak Boulevard., Suite 800, Houston, Texas 77056-9998,* ☎ *(713) 629-9131; FAX (713) 622-6924,* 8:30 a.m.–12:30 p.m.; *One Bush Street, San Francisco, Calif. 94104,* ☎ *(415) 362-6160; FAX (415) 956-9729,* 10 a.m.–4 p.m., and at *1000 Bishop Street, Penthouse Suite, Honolulu, Hawaii 96813,* ☎ *(808) 524-5050; FAX (808) 531-5142,* 8–11:30 a.m., 12:30 p.m.–4 p.m.

In Canada:

Australian High Commission, *50 O'Conner Street, Suite 710, Ottawa, Ontario K1P 6L2,* ☎ *(613) 783-7669; FAX (613) 236-4376,* 9 a.m.–noon and 2 p.m.–4 p.m.; **Australian Consulates General**, *175 Bloor Street East, Suite 314, Toronto, Ontario M4W 3R8,* ☎ *(416) 323-1155; FAX (416) 323-3910,* 9 a.m.–1 p.m. and 2–4 p.m., and at *World Trade Centre, 999 Canada Place, Suite 602, Vancouver, B.C. V6C 3E1,* ☎ *(604) 684-1177; FAX (604) 684-1856,* 8:30 a.m.–12:30 p.m.

Don't forget to get a visa, and don't just assume you can get one at the airport in Australia. The airline personnel of the carrier you're riding to Australia won't even let you on the plane without it. If you've purchased an APEX ticket and prepaid a tour or hotel and car costs, you're out the money, depending on the mercy of the airlines and other services, which often is nonexistent. Don't laugh; it's not unheard of for a passenger to show up at San Francisco or Los Angeles International airports without a visa, and it's not a pretty scene when they're not allowed on the aircraft.

Your passport must be current and not due to expire while you are in Australia; the authorities there recommend it expire at least three months after you leave Australia.

Australia is an island; as such, it has been spared many of the problem diseases found in other parts of the world—and its citizens want to keep it that way. They are very careful about allowing you to bring in fresh or packaged food, vegetables, seeds, animals or animal products (especially any internationally recognized endangered species) or birds—they are so careful, even the packaged nuts you get aboard the inbound aircraft are verboten. We once took in a jar of American instant coffee and declared it. We were told that technically, it was illegal, but the customs officer let it go. Others might not.

If you're over 18, you can bring in, duty-free, 250 cigarettes or 250 grams of tobacco products, one liter of alcoholic products and goods up to the value of A$400 carried in personal luggage. The country is rabies free, and if you plan to take a pet along, the quarantine process takes five months. **NOTE:** There is a A$27 per person departure tax, payable at the airport when you leave the country. It must be paid in Australian currency. However, airlines are now starting to include the tax on their ticket prices. Check with your travel agent before leaving for Australia.

Embassies and Consulates

If your passport is stolen or lost, it must be replaced before you can leave Australia. U.S. authorities are very good about replacing passports, providing you follow the correct procedures.

First, embassies do not issue passports; consulates do. There are consulates in most major Australian cities. Then, you must be able to prove you're an American citizen. This can be done with proper identification, such as a birth certificate, or, if you've lost everything, your traveling companion can swear to your citizenship—as long as he or she is carrying a U.S. passport. You'll also have to file a police report about the theft or loss, and supply two passport-sized photographs. In an emergency situation (your flight leaves the same day), the consular service can issue a passport in a matter of hours. In Australia, the **United States Embassy** (and consulate) is located at *State Circle and Perth Avenue in Canberra (Yarralumla)*, ☎ *(02) 6270-5000.* The **Canadian Embassy** is on *Commonwealth Avenue, Yarralumla* ☎ *(06) 6273-3844.*

Consulates are listed in telephone Yellow Pages under "consulates and legations." The **U.S. Consulate** in Sydney is at *29 Martin Place,* ☎ *(02) 9234-9200.* In Melbourne, the U.S. consulate is at *553 St. Kilda Road,* ☎ *(03) 9526-5900;* the Canadian at *Southbank Boulevard, South Melbourne* ☎ *(03) 9645-8643.*

Medicine

Health certificates are not required unless you're entering the country from an area where there has been an outbreak of yellow fever, smallpox, cholera or typhoid 14 days prior to your arrival.

The Australians become very displeased by people carrying unauthorized controlled substances. If you are carrying medications, declare them. You're allowed to take in a four-week supply of personal medicines. It is wise to take a prescription with you, not only to show customs, but in case you need a refill. After an Australian physician has signed your prescription, you can get it filled at a pharmacy (called a "chemist" in Australia). Australia does not have reciprocal health insurance schemes with the United States; you might want to investigate travelers' health and accident policies before your trip.

Money, Weights and Measures

Australia is yet another country that uses the dollar as its currency. The Aussies used to have the pound, with all its English holdovers (sovereigns, ha'pennies, tuppence) but got smart in 1963 and went metric. There was a little flap about what the name of the new money would be (was it a sign of weakness to adopt Yank names?) but in the end they finally settled on dollars and cents. Banknotes come in $5, $10, $20, $50 and $100 bills. Coins are 5, 10, 20, and 50 cents, plus $1 and $2. The $2 coin was first issued in 1988, and like the U.S. Susan B. Anthony $1 coin, immediately caused a flap—for the same reason. The problem is the Aussie $2 coin was almost the same size as the now-gone two-cent piece, and the amount of bitching rising from irritated Australians was enormous. It's a very pretty coin, however, gold-colored and the only coin not to have an animal on its obverse; instead, it features an Aboriginal man. H.R.H. the Queen is on the face of all Australian coins. At this writing, the Aussie dollar was worth between 70 and 80 U.S. cents.

Aussie weights and measures are officially metric, although you'll find many folks still hanging in with the old English measures. An Aussie friend of ours was measuring a length of board for a project and reckoned it was "two meters and about a quarter-inch." In some parts of the country, folks still figure beer in ounces and vow to never give in. Canadians, who have already gone metric, will supposedly have no problems. For Americans, mostly all you need to know is that gasoline comes in liters, distances are posted in kilometers, temperatures are in Celsius and things are weighed in kilograms.

Conversion is not that tough. If you're in a rental car, the speedometer is in kilometers, so if the limit is 60, just drive 60 and forget miles. (If you absolutely have to know, multiply the number of kilometers by .62 and you'll get the miles.) For temperatures, just remember water freezes at 0, 20 is mild, 30 is hot and if it's 40, you're probably in the desert country of the Northern Territory and should be headed for a cold pub. A kilogram is about 2.2 pounds. If you forget all these details, don't worry, just ask somebody. After all, they've only been at this metric business for about 20 years.

Electricity

Aussie current is 240-250 volts, 50 hertz. Just to be difficult, the usual European two-round-prong plug is not used. Instead, Australians use a three-pronged flat plug that looks like a smaller version of the plugs Americans employ with electric clothes dryers. Most international electrical travel kits have a plug that will work in Australia (two, rather than three prongs, but OK) and converter plugs can be found in some department stores and camping outlets in Australia. If you're going upscale, forget all the electricity differences because most high-grade hotels in the country have 110-volt outlets in the bathrooms, and the good ones have hair dryers and irons in the rooms. If not, loaner transformers will do the job. (Some hotel 110-outlets will not safely handle hair dryers and other high-wattage appliances, however.)

Time

Australia is the other side of the International Date Line from North America, so it's always ahead of us. The country has three time zones: Eastern Standard, Central Standard and Western Standard. These divisions are the easy part; from there time gets a little complicated, especially when either the U.S. or Australia goes on Daylight Savings Time.

Eastern Standard (Queensland, Australian Capital Territory, New South Wales, Victoria, Tasmania) is 18 hours ahead of San Francisco—when it's 4 in the afternoon in San Francisco, it's 10 in the morning, the next day, in Sydney. One way to make conversion a little easier is just forget the 18-hour bit and figure that Sydney is six hours behind San Francisco, but a day ahead. Make sense? If it's 10 a.m. Monday in Sydney, then it's six hours later in San Francisco, or 4 p.m., but a day earlier, or Sunday. The easy way around the whole thing is to buy a watch with two times zones.

Central Standard (South Australia and the Northern Territory) is 17.5 hours ahead of San Francisco, and Western Standard (Western Australia) is 16 hours ahead. In the Australian summer, all the states go on daylight time except Queensland, the Northern Territory and Western Australia.

Going to Australia, the 18-hour difference fries your brain. Coming back, because of the quirks of jet travel, you arrive on the West Coast the same day at almost the same time you left Australia. This experience also fries your brain, but after you tell your body that no time has passed, everything will be all right.

Hours

Most banks are open from 9:30 a.m.–4 p.m. Monday–Thursday and until 5 p.m. Fridays, and are closed on holidays and weekends. Airports in major cities have bank outlets for currency exchanges. Post offices are open from 9 a.m.–5 p.m. weekdays, closed on weekends. Most retail outlets are open from 9 to 5:30 weekdays. Many stores in the big cities stay open late at least one night a week.

Accommodations

Australia has a wide variety of places to stay, ranging from some of the finest ocean resorts in the South Pacific to stays in basic motels and rooms in local pubs. There are farm and ranch stays, fishing resorts, ski chalets, hiking huts and monolithic big-city hotels. Prices range from backpacker basic to incredibly expensive suites on Barrier Reef islands. Whatever your budget, the Aussies will find you a bed. Given their lust for in-country travel, you will also find a wide assortment of RV parks and national park facilities. Any state-run information office or local travel agency can guide you to accommodations designed for your needs and interests. In almost all cases, the quality of Australian facilities are on a par with any other modern country. There are a large number of passes available from various hotel groups that can be purchased before arriving in Australia; check with a travel agent.

Tipping

Generally not necessary. If the service is extra special in better restaurants, maybe 15 percent. Railway porters have set charges for carrying bags; ask ahead of time. Taxi drivers are happy if you round off the fare to the next highest dollar. Probably a good idea to tip luggage porters and concierges in big city hotels.

Phones

Most hotels and many motels have direct dial international and domestic capability, and it's also very easy to make international collect calls from pay phones. Local calls are 40 cents. Emergencies (police, fire, accident) can be reported by dialing 000, no coin required. If you do much calling in Australia, you'll soon run into the Aussie habit of doubling and tripling numbers when they talk. For instance, an American would read this phone number—544-1117—as "five four-four, one-one-one-seven." But the Aussies would say "five-double four, triple one-seven," which, when spoken rapidly and with an Australian accent, can be most confusing. They also double and triple street addresses.

For local calls, public phones are found all over in stores, malls and pubs. For long distance, you feed a number of coins into the phone and, as you talk, the coins drop. When you run out of coins, the conversation is ended unless you keep pumping them in. The same system is used for ISD (International Subscriber Dialing) calls. If you want to direct dial and not call collect, just have a handful of 50 cent pieces on hand. To call the United States or Canada, dial 0011 for overseas, then 1, then the area code and number. Public ISD phones are almost universal, but if you can't find one, check the general post offices or airports. Australia, like New Zealand, has also started using plastic phone cards which can be purchased in various denominations—stick the card in the proper phone, and the cost of the call is electronically deducted from the card. The cards are for sale at various stores. Also there are now many credit-card phones that will accept most major credit cards. *A caveat:* Australian states are in the process of changing phone numbers, in most instances going to an eight-digit system to increase the number of available numbers. The process is expected to take a couple of years. The phone numbers we list here are as current as we could make them, but there might be differences.

If you want to call Australia from North America, dial 011 (the international access code), then 61 (the Aussie code), then the city code, then the number. The major city codes in Australia are: Canberra, (06); Sydney (02); Melbourne, (03); Adelaide (08); Brisbane (07); Perth (08). If you're in the city calling a local number, drop the city code.

Getting Around

Shute Harbour is the busiest passenger port in Australia, handling 6000 people a day in high season.

Airlines

There are now only two major domestic airlines: **Ansett Australia** and **Qantas**. Qantas recently bought Australian Airlines from the government, and British Airways then purchased 25 percent of the new combined company. In essence, the Australian airline industry is now completely deregulated. What this will mean to internal air fares is anybody's guess, but hopefully it will mean prices will drop. But with Qantas buying up everything in sight, don't hold your breath. Traditionally, air travel inside the country has been expensive; but for foreign visitors, all sorts of special passes are available that drop the costs. In most cases, the **air passes** must be purchased in North America before you enter Australia and often must be part of an airline package that includes international flights; restrictions and costs are available from travel agents.

Many of the air passes are part of packages that include land transportation and accommodations. If you're planning any internal air travel, do check out deals with the individual airlines which are constantly changing—you can save a chunk of money.

Ansett has several alternatives, including a **Visit Australia Pass,** with fares about 40 percent off regular economy. Also available is the **See Australia** pass, with savings of about 25 percent. Qantas has a **Discover Australia** pass with savings of about 40 percent. Please note, there are often heavy restrictions on both carriers' passes.

In addition to the two major carriers, there are a number of smaller, regional air services, including such companies as **Kendell Airlines and Sunstate Airlines (part of the Qantas group).** Many of the local destinations served by regional carriers are also on schedules operated by subsidiaries of the major airlines.

Internal flights in Australia are closely regulated regarding carry-on luggage. The usual limit now is one piece, not including a briefcase or purse.

Buses

These are called *coaches* in Australia and offer substantial savings over air travel. Buses are, of course, a lot slower and Australia is a big country, so it's a trade-off. The major coach operator with national connections is **Greyhound-Pioneer**. In Tasmania, service is supplied by **Redline Coaches**, which is used by Greyhound-Pioneer in its pass networks. Australian buses are non-smoking, and most have on board toilets; some have TV and videos.

There are many bus **passes** and packages that provide a relatively inexpensive way of seeing the country without worrying about driving. These passes range from a week to three months; some even include accommodations. There are daily express routes between major cities, some of which are long hauls. Adelaide to Perth, for example, is 36 hours.

The Aussie Pass allows unlimited travel on the Greyhound Pioneer system for periods of one week to three months; the seven-day pass is about A$400 and must be used within a month; the three-month pass is A$2225 and must be used within six months. The pass can be purchased in Australia, but is normally cheaper out of the country. The **Down Under Pass** is designed for folks planning on hitting Australia and New Zealand on the same trip. It's offered by **Mt. Cook Lines**, the New Zealand-based company, and **Greyhound-Pioneer**. It allows unlimited bus travel inside both countries. The pass starts at about A$450 for a nine-day pass, up to A$1400 for a 45-day pass. The pass must be purchased outside Australia and New Zealand.

The **Kangaroo Road 'N Rail Pass** is a joint service of Greyhound-Pioneer and Rail Australia. The passes come in economy or first-class and are good for 14 to 28 days. A 14-day economy pass is about A$655; first-class is about A$1040. A month-long pass is economy A$1150 and first-class A$1530. The Kangaroo pass must be purchased outside Australia.

If you're going to Tasmania, **Tassie Passes** are available through **Redline Coaches** and can be purchased in Australia. The passes are good for between a week and 31 days and start at around A$110. There are Redline offices in most major Tasmanian cities. Information about Australian Coachlines, the umbrella agency for the country's various bus services, can be obtained through travel agents or by contacting one of the larger North American companies specializing in South Pacific travel.

Trains

It was, as an English friend of ours is wont to say when facing similar vistas, "400 miles of bugger-all." Since before dawn, the train had been chugging across the Nullarbor Plain in Western Australia, and the reports are accurate—there are no trees. About noon, the train stopped at some wide spot, and we piled out of the air conditioning and into the blast furnace of the Australian interior just to stretch our legs and get off the train. The name of the place was Cook, or Loongana or maybe Naretha.

Some place, at any rate, definitely what the Aussies call "back of Bourke," out in the middle of nowhere. We didn't get five feet before the bush flies attacked, and we were just spoiled enough to be very glad we didn't live in that godforsaken place. There are different ways of seeing the Australian Outback, neighbors, but driving from settlement to settlement across the Nullarbor is not a good choice. The best and most logical way to get across this vast sea of nothingness is to board one of the last great train trips in the world: the Indian-Pacific from Sydney to Perth. You get some idea of what you're dealing with by noting one stretch of tracks, between Watson and Ooldea, runs absolutely straight for 300 miles—supposedly the longest straight run of railroad tracks in the world.

The Sydney-Perth train gets its name because it goes all the way from the Indian Ocean at Perth to the Pacific in Sydney. It runs twice a week and takes three days (65 hours) to make the run. **The Indian-Pacific** has a long haul: 2700 miles, much of it through raw desert and bushlands. It was completely refurbished in 1996, adding ne themed lounge and restaurant cars.

It took a long time to get the line completed. Construction started in 1912 and Sydney was finally connected in 1982. By far the most fascinating part of the trip is the Nullarbor Plain, and if you don't want to spend the full three days on the train, you could still do the Nullarbor by taking the **Trans-Australian**, which runs twice weekly between Perth and Adelaide. It takes 37 hours to do the trip.

The basic amenities are the same for both trains. Sleepers include first-class twinettes (two sleeping berths) with toilet, washbasin, hot and cold water; first class roomettes (single bunk); Holiday Class twinettes (a la carte dining and access to a lounge), and economy-class coach seating. Coach-class passengers can buy meals at a cafeteria car; there is a dining car for sleeper passengers.

During normal schedules, the Indian-Pacific leaves Sydney Mondays and Thursdays at 1:30 p.m., arriving in Perth at 7 a.m. three days later; the train leaves Perth Mondays and Fridays at 9 p.m. and arrives in Sydney at 6 a.m. three days later. Fares are about A$950 per person first-class sleeper, including meals; A$600 Holiday Class and A$300 coach seating.

The **Trans-Australian** leaves Adelaide at 5 p.m. Tuesdays and Fridays, arriving in Perth at 7 a.m. two days later; it leaves Perth at 9 p.m. Mondays and Fridays and arrives in Adelaide at 1:30 p.m. two days later. A first-class sleeper is about A$800-900 per person including meals, depending on time of year; economy sleeper is about A$525-590; and coach seating is about A$300 all year.

The Indian-Pacific, like many other Australian trains, has rail car service. This is ideal if you're going one way and continuing your journey by car.

The cross-continent trains are popular with visitors, but the real star of the Australian rail network is the **Ghan**, which runs from Adelaide to Alice Springs. The Ghan follows a pioneer route up through the country's Red Centre, and is named after the Afghan camel drivers who carried supplies up and down the trail before the railroad was completed. It's so popular, it's often booked a year in advance.

The train that opened the Northern Territory was an adventure right from the beginning. The first trains had no air conditioning, and every so often, the wind would blow clouds of red sand into the cars. Flash floods washed out the tracks, white ants ate the cross ties, and, on one famous trip, the cook ran out of food and fed the passengers by shooting wild goats. The schedule was somewhat loose—it took anywhere from three days to a month to get to Alice Springs. The tracks between Port Augusta (north of Adelaide) and the Alice were begun in 1879, and the last stretch was completed in 1929.

The Ghan was recently renovated, a process that took three years and cost about A$2.5 million. The major work was done on first-class sleepers and the first-class bar cars. The economy coaches still need work and look rather bedraggled. The first-class bars and the restaurant are the showpieces of the train. The Oasis Bar, done in a jungly motif, is almost as long as two regular cars. The upholstery is meant to match the designs of the camel blankets used by the Afghan drivers. It's the smoking bar. The nonsmoker is the smaller but equally elegant Dreamtime Lounge, with an Aboriginal Dreamtime motif. The Stuart Restaurant is reddish Art Deco in tone, with etched glass dividers between booths. Going north, you get two meals, dinner and breakfast. Coming south, three meals. The menu offers such dainties as Liechardt's Lust (chicken schnitzel with potatoes Parisienne), grilled snapper in hollandaise sauce, and peaches with rum and creme—pretty fair bush tucker. Coach seating passengers have a buffet/bar car.

The train's sleepers are smallish, basically two bunk beds with fold-down washbasin and toilet. It takes about 22 hours to make the 908-mile run from Adelaide to Alice Springs. It leaves Adelaide at 2 p.m. twice a week all year, arriving around 11 a.m. the next day. Southbound, it leaves the Alice at 5:10 p.m. and arrives in Adelaide at 4:30 p.m. the next day. April–January, there are additional trains.

First-class sleeper and meals is about A$500; Holiday Class (economy sleeper) is about A$310, with access to a private dining car, and coach seating is about A$140. Rail car service is available.

The best tourist train on the East Coast is the **Queenslander**, which runs between Cairns and Brisbane. This is the sugarcane express, and if you get tired of seeing sugar cane fields after a few hours, you had better fly instead. The cars are new, but small, because it's a narrow-gauge train. The tiny single sleepers are worn like clothing, rather than lived in. It takes about 32 hours to make the 1680–kilometer trip, and the overwhelming memory is miles and miles of sugarcane and pineapple plantations. There are roomettes and twinettes available, as well as coach seating. The roomettes (singles) come with a toilet, sink and small hanging closet. The twinettes are spacious but have no toilets. There are showers and toilets at the end of the sleeping cars, no economy class sleepers. The first-class lounge is airy and pleasant, and the smallish dining car serves okay meals, not on a par with the Ghan.

The train leaves Cairns at 8:15 a.m. four times a week, arriving in Brisbane at 4:25 p.m.; northbound, it leaves at 9:10 a.m., arriving in Cairns at 5:20 p.m. First-class sleeper fare is about A$490 with meals. Cairns-Brisbane service is also available on the Sunlander, which does have economy sleepers.

For international visitors, the main rail pass is the **Australpass**, good for unlimited travel on Australian trains; the passes start at 14 days economy for about A$435, to first class 90 days, about A$1765. The passes do not cover sleeping berth or meal charges—these are payable in Australia and vary depending on route. In some cases, berth and meal charges are compulsory and must be prepaid. The **Flexipass** allows more stops and leeway if you plan a longer stay, but doesn't include the Ghan. The passes must be purchased before you arrive in Australia. The passes become valid starting the first day they're used.

Information about Australian bus and rail travel is available from **ATS Tours**, *2381 Rosecrans Avenue, Suite 325, El Segundo, Calif. 90245* ☎ *(310) 643-0044; FAX (310) 643-0032*, or in Canada, **Goway Travel** offices in Vancouver and Toronto. Once in Sydney, information on train travel is available from the **Countrylink office on the first floor of the Central Railway Station** at Eddy and Pitt streets ☎ *(02) 9213-2232*. Phone hours are 6:30 a.m.-10 p.m. daily; or **Railways of Australia**, which represents the five state-owned rail systems in the country, at *85 Queen Street, Melbourne;* ☎ *(03) 9608-0811*.

Aboriginal dancers perform in numerous Australian festivals.

Holidays

In addition to the various national holidays, all the Australian states have a slew of days off throughout the year that seem to be specifically designed to thwart tourists trying to find rooms or cash a traveler's check. Before making reservations Down Under, always check with either the Australian Tourist Commission or the office of the Aussie state you're planning to visit.

Major nationwide holidays include **New Year's Day**, **Good Friday**, **Easter Saturday**, **Easter Monday**, **Anzac Day** (April 25), **Christmas Day** and **Boxing Day** (Dec. 26). School holidays get very complicated because each state schedules them at a different time. Generally, the kids get off from late June or early July through the middle of July, then from the middle of September through the middle of October, and from the middle of December through late January or February.

Special Events

Every state and city in Australia seems to have an annual event or two, ranging from such biggies as the Australian Grand Prix in Melbourne to county fairs in rural Queensland. A few to keep in mind:

FESTIVALS AND HOLIDAYS		
January 1	New Year's Day	
January (last Monday)	Australia Day	
January	Cricket time	*Championship tourneys in Sydney, Brisbane, Melbourne, Adelaide and Perth.*
January	Life-Saving events	*On the Sunshine Coast in Queensland, the emphasis is on life-saving events, which Australians take very seriously; look for contests at the Alexandra Headlands Surf Club.*
January	Australian Tennis Open	*Grand Slam tennis in Melbourne.*
January	Schuetzenfest	*Hahndorf, South Australia. Happening time in German community.*
January	Jabiru Regatta	*Lake Jabiru, Northern Territory. Features offbeat games and races.*
February	Royal Hobart Regatta	*Tasmania*
February	Compass Cup Cow Races	*South of Adelaide*

FESTIVALS AND HOLIDAYS

February/March	Gay and Lesbian Mardi Gras Festival	*Sydney*
February	Kangaroo Island Racing Carnival	*Kingscote, South Australia. Two-day carnival.*
March (first or second Monday)	Labour Day	*Victoria*
March (second Monday)	Labour Day	*Western Australia*
March	Black Opal Stakes	*Horse race at the Canberra Racecourse*
March	Australian Indy Grand Prix	*Surfers Paradise in Queensland*
March (even numbered years)	Adelaide Arts Festival	*South Australia. Offers three weeks of premier theater, music, dance, arts exhibitions and fringe events.*
March (whole month)	Festival of Perth	*Western Australia. Similar to the Adelaide Arts Festival.*
April 25	Anzac Day	*Honors Australian war vets.*
April	National Boomerang Championship	*Perth*
April	Rugby Union Cup	*Northern Territory*
April	Royal Easter Show	*Sydney. Lasts about 14 days, opening the week before Easter.*
April (odd numbered years)	Barossa Valley Vintage Festival	*South Australia. A major "taste till you waste" week-long celebration in honor of the local grapes and vintners.*
April	Opal and Outback Festival	*Coober Pedy*
May 1	May Day	*Northern Territory. Signals the end of those treacherous box jellyfish and the beginning of beach parties.*
May (first Monday)	Labour Day	*Queensland*
May (third Monday)	Adelaide Cup	*South Australia*

FESTIVALS AND HOLIDAYS

May	Lions Foster Camel Cup	*Northern Territory. Camel racing and fireworks.*
May	Katherine Sky Diving Week	*Katherine, N.T.*
May	Bangtail Muster	*Alice Springs. Features a float parade and other events.*
June (first Monday)	Foundation Day	*Western Australia*
June (second Monday)	Queen's Birthday	*Queensland, Northern Territory, Victoria*
June	International Rugby League test series	*Brisbane*
June	Manly Food and Wine Festival	*Sydney*
June	Bougainvillaea Festival	*Darwin. Offers two weeks of horticultural events.*
June	Katherine Gorge Canoe Marathon	*Northern Territory. A 100 km race along the Katherine River, organized by the Red Cross.*
July	Kakadu Safari Ride	*From Darwin to Kakadu National Park.*
July	NT Royal Shows	*Agricultural shows in Darwin, Katherine, Tennent Creek and Alice Springs.*
July	Almond Blossom Festival	*Willunga, South Australia. Almond lovers will want to attend.*
August (first Monday)	Bank Holiday	*New South Wales*
August (first Monday)	Picnic Day	*Northern Territory*
August	Alice Springs Rodeo	*Alice Springs*
August	Beer Can Regatta	*Darwin. Boat races for boats constructed entirely out of beer cans, of which there are plenty in the world's beer-drinking capital.*
August	Darwin Rodeo	*Northern Territory. This includes international team events between Australia, the USA, Canada and New Zealand.*

FESTIVALS AND HOLIDAYS

August	Shinju Matsuri (Festival of the Pearl)	*Western Australia. Held in the old pearling port of Broome, this week-long festival is a great event and includes Asiatic celebrations.*
August	Sydney Marathon	*Sydney*
August	Mud Crab Tying Contest	*Darwin. Another must on the cultural calendar.*
September (first weekend)	Birdsville Cup	*New South Wales. The tiny town of Birdsville hosts the country's premier outback horseracing event.*
September	Tasmanian Tulip Festival	*Hobart*
September	Australian Rules AFL (footie) Final Series	*Melbourne Cricket Grounds. Followed almost religiously by everyone in the country. Akin to the U.S. Super Bowl.*
September	Henley-on-Todd Regatta	*Alice Springs. A series of races for leg-powered bottomless boats on the (usually) dry Todd River.*
October (first Monday)	Queen's Birthday	*Western Australia*
October (first Monday)	Labour Day	*New South Wales, Australian Capital Territory, Southern Australia*
October	Indoor Cricket World Cup	*Melbourne*
October	Australian Indoor Lawn Bowls Championships	*Tweed Heads, NSW*
October	McLaren Vale Bushing Festival	*South Australia. Commemorates the release of a new vintage with a variety of events including the crowning of a Bushing King and Queen.*
November	Fosters Australian Formula 1	*Melbourne*
November (first Tuesday)	Melbourne Cup	*The most prestigious horse race in Australia.*
November	The Australian Open	*Golf*
December 25	Christmas Day	

FESTIVALS AND HOLIDAYS

December 26	Boxing Day	*Christmas boxes presented to service workers.*
December	Snowy Mountain Trout Festival	*Lake Jindabyne and Lake Eucumbene, NSW*
December	Whitbread Round the World Yacht Race	*Freemantle/Hobart*

Information

A good first glance at Australia is provided by the *Australia Vacation Planner*, printed annually and available free by contacting the **Australian Tourist Commission**, *2049 Century Park East, Suite 1920, Los Angeles 90067; (310) 229-4870 or (800) DOWNUNDER.* In addition, the Australian Tourism Commission operates a travel inquiry service called **Aussie Helpline**, which operates from 8 a.m.–7 p.m. CST Monday–Friday ☎ *(847) 296-4900 (USA/CAN).* The web site is www.aussienet.au. Information is also available from **Tourism New South Wales** ☎ *(310) 301-1903; FAX: (310) 301-0913.*

Once in Australia, you will find individual state tourist offices in most major cities. These offices are excellent at providing information about tours, airfares and hotels, and can make reservations. Often, individual states will have special deals available that no one in North America has heard about yet; always worth a check, if for nothing more than brochures.

To Our Gay and Lesbian Readers

A major part of the Australian ethos over the years has been the so-called "mate mentality," a heavily male emphasis on masculine values of companionship and social behavior. It was probably inevitable, given the transportation system (almost all male prisoners), plus the remoteness of the country that forced small groups of men to depend and trust each other, that for most of its history, Australia has been a male-dominated society. Overt sexism is not officially tolerated any longer, but definitely still exists. But what has almost never been said publicly, of course, is that the prison system and isolation often led to homosexual relationships. But it was very definitely an in-the-closet arrangement, and gays and lesbians, when discovered, were social outcasts.

This has changed in the past two decades, although in some of the more frontier locales of Australia, such as Western Australia, alternative lifestyles are still anathema to many people. (Homosexuality is still officially illegal in Tasmania.) In Sydney, however, gay and lesbian lifestyles are well tolerated; this city is, in fact, much like San Francisco in that regard. The city's gay and lesbian population is openly active in the arts, in politics, in business and in general, is accepted with little overt persecution.

Evidence of this is the annual Gay and Lesbian Mardi Gras Festival held annually in Sydney in March. The festival, which includes parades and huge parties, was first held in 1978 as a counterpart to the famous Stonewall celebrations in New York. Like its American counterpart, the first years of the Mardi Gras were rocky. The first year it was held, there was a riot in Sydney with many injuries. Today, however, it's a much different scene. The police, according to Mardi Gras organizers, are the gay and lesbian community's best friends and recent galas have been almost devoid of violence or overt antagonism. In its 18-year history, as a matter of fact, the Mardi Gras has become politically correct, with all manner of local and national politicians praising its efforts. Part of the reason, no doubt, is practical. The Mardi Gras is one of the few civic events in Sydney that is not supported by tax dollars. The annual bash is self-supporting, and in fact, adds millions to the local economy. In recent years, it has been estimated that about a half-million people watch the parade in Sydney. The various parties and celebrations, combined with hotel and restaurant spending paid for by participants and spectators, drop about of A$10 million into the New South Wales coffers—it is, in fact, the biggest money-making event in the country.

There are gay and lesbian neighborhoods all over the city, with the main areas in Kings Cross and Darlinghurst. Two major sources of information about gay and lesbian activities can be found in the *G'Day Guide*, which covers Australia, New Zealand and other areas of the South Pacific, and the *Sydney Star Observer*, a gay and lesbian newspaper. The *G'Day Guide* can be ordered from the publisher at *P.O. Box 205, Fitzroy, Victoria 3065;* or try the Bookstore on Oxford Street. The Mardi Gras offices are at *15-19 Boundary Street, Rushcutters Bay in Sydney,* ☎ *(02) 9332-4088.* Ask for Richard Perram. In Melbourne, a good source of information is the *Melbourne Star Observer* (same publisher as the *G'Day Guide.*) In North America, check out a newsletter called *Out & About,* published 10 times a year. It costs about US$50 a year, and can be ordered from **Out and About Inc.**, *542 Chapel St., New Haven, Conn. 06511;* ☎ *(203) 789-8518.*

☉	**Fielding's Highest Rated Hotels in Australia**		
★★★★★	Lilianfels (Blue Mountains, NSW)	A$400–700	*page 132*
★★★★★	Lizard Island Lodge (Great Barrier Reef)	A$900–1000	*page 245*
★★★★★	Quay West, Sydney	A$260–1300	*page 118*
★★★★★	Sebel Town House, Sydney	A$200–450	*page 121*
★★★★★	Windsor Hotel, Melbourne	A$320–1500	*page 305*

ESSENTIAL AUSTRALIA

Fielding's Highest Rated Hotels in Australia

★★★★	Silky Oaks, Mossman, Queensland	A$350–500	*page 216*
★★★	Beaufort Heritage, Brisbane	A$300–1800	*page 181*
★★★	Cairns International, Queensland	A$225–1325	*page 206*
★★★	Cradle Mountain Lodge, Tasmania	$85–190	*page 401*
★★★	Dunk Island (Great Barrier Reef)	A$160–250	*page 243*
★★★	Radisson Observation City, Perth	A$200–2000	*page 351*

Fielding's Most Exclusive Hotels in Australia

★★★★★	Bedarra Island (Great Barrier Reef)	A$1065	*page 243*
★★★★★	Hayman Island (Great Barrier Reef)	A$375–1240	*page 239*
★★★★★	Kewarra Beach Resort, Cairns	A$213–440	*page 214*
★★★★★	Green Island Resort (Great Barrier Reef)	A$750–880	*page 244*
★★★★★	Seven Spirit Bay Resort (Arnhem Land)	A$1100	*page 264*

Fielding's Best Value Hotels in Australia

★★★	Coconut Beach Rainforest Resort, Cape Tribulation, Queensland	A$75–250	*page 216*
★★★	Daydream Island, Whitsundays, Queensland	A$175–275	*page 240*
★★★	Pepper's Hunter Valley, New South Wales	A$150–200	*page 148*
★★★	Salamanca Inn, Hobart	A$150–250	*page 379*
★★★	Thorn Park Country House, Clare Valley, South Australia	A$150–240	*page 335*
★★★	Welcome Inn, Melbourne	A$110–190	*page 306*
★★	Albert Park Motor Inn, Brisbane	A$125	*page 182*
★★	Gagudju Crocodile Hotel Kakadu, Jabiru, Northern Territory	A$100–200	*page 269*
★★	Russell Hotel, the Rocks, Sydney	A$105–230	*page 119*

ESSENTIAL AUSTRALIA

NEW SOUTH WALES

The coast east of Sydney is lined with good beaches for all tastes.

New South Wales, and especially Sydney, is the spiritual heart of Australia. Other cities and other states will proclaim their importance in the scheme of things Australian, to be sure, and there is a lot of the same sort of territorial rivalry you have between Texans and folks from Massachusetts, or between the farmers of Saskatchewan and the striped ties of Ottawa. But, at the bottom, Australians know Sydney is the core of the country.

As we have noted, Capt. Arthur Phillip and the first shipload of convicts from Merry Old England sailed into Sydney Harbour on Jan. 26, 1788, to begin the history of white Australia. Indeed, for most of its early history, mainland colonial Australia was known as New South Wales. The place where Phillip and his scruffy wards landed—Sydney Cove—remains today the heart of the city. The Rocks, the sandstone formations above the cove where the first halting steps at creating a city took place, still show signs of its colonial past, and a number of classic buildings from the transportation era still stand around the city.

Almost a third of Australia's 18 million people live in New South Wales, close to 4 million of them in Sydney. Once you get away from the harbor, you soon discover that metropolitan Sydney is huge (670 square miles), containing seven cities and four counties. New South Wales is large enough, about 300,000 square miles, that it goes all the way from the ocean to the Outback. In fact, the dusty regions of the Outback compose a full two-thirds of the state. Canberra, and the Australian Capital Territory, is completely surrounded by the state, stuck down about 180 miles southwest of Sydney. Sixty percent of the nation's coal comes from the Hunter Valley, Illawarra and the Blue Mountains, and the zinc, lead and silver deposits near Broken Hill gave start to the country's biggest corporate conglomerate, BHP, nicknamed the Big Australian. The state also is the nation's major wheat producer and has a third of the country's sheep.

The Hunter Valley northeast of Sydney also produces great wines. The Snowy Mountains are where many Aussies go to ski. The state offers caves to explore, houseboating, deep-sea fishing, take your pick; a vacation here allows you to see all the things Australia is famous for, from kangaroos to the Opera House to tons of sunny beaches to the cool green escapes of the Blue Mountains.

Essential New South Wales

Information

For information, contact the **Tourism Commission of New South Wales**, *2121 Avenue of the Stars, Suite 1230 Los Angeles, Calif. 90067;* ☎ *(310) 552-9566.* In Sydney, go to the **Travel Centre of New South Wales**, *19 Castlereagh Street*, or the **New South Wales Tourism Commission**, *140 Phillip Street.*

Getting There

Sydney's international airport is served by many major international carriers, including those flying from North America. Service to other major cities in the country is provided on **Qantas**, **Ansett**, **Eastwest** and other regional carriers. Flights are readily available to popular tourist spots such as Ayers Rock, Kakadu National Park and the Great Barrier Reef, as well as to other South Pacific destinations. When leaving the country, there is a A\$27 departure tax for passengers 12 years and older, payable at the airport in Australian currency only (credit cards accepted).

Many of the major settlements along the state's east coast and interior are served by bus and rail. Major rail routes, such as the Indian-Pacific to Adelaide and Perth, originate in Sydney. General information about **rail and bus service** is available from 6 a.m.–10

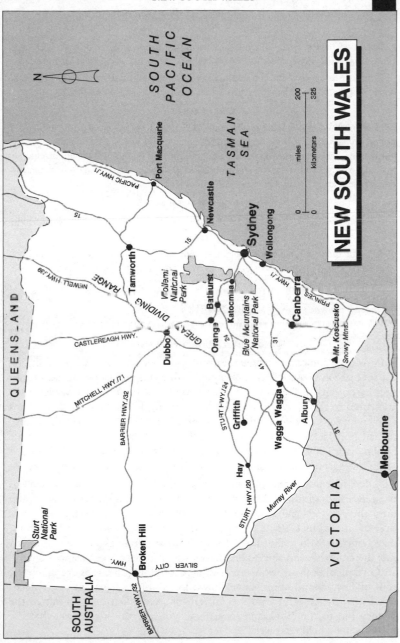

NEW SOUTH WALES

p.m. seven days from the information offices at major train stations or from the Countrylink hotline, which runs fro 6:30 a.m.–10 p.m. daily, ☎ *(02) 9213-2232*.

Bus service, unless you're heading for a major destination such as Melbourne or Canberra, can be slow. **The Sydney Coach Terminal** is at the corner of Riley and Oxford streets.

If you're **driving**, road and accommodations information is available from the **National Roads and Motorists Association**, *151 Clarence Street,* ☎ *(02) 9260-9222*.

Climate

New South Wales is far enough south of the equator to get nippy in places during the winter, but generally, the climate is warm. The Snowy Mountains are sub-alpine, and the northern beaches are mostly subtropical. Temperatures in Sydney will average around 70 to 80 degrees November-March, and around 45-60 degrees in the winter. It can rain any time of the year.

Telephones

The Sydney area code is (02). Free directory assistance is 013; emergency calls are 000.

Time

The state is on Eastern Standard Time, meaning it's 18 hours ahead of San Francisco. The state observes Daylight Savings Time from October through March; clocks go ahead one hour.

Sydney

The Harbour Area

It probably comes as outright treason for anyone who lives within shouting distance of San Francisco to suggest that Sydney might just be the most beautiful harbor city in the world, but it's definitely a thought. Sydney is always compared to the other great lovelies: Rio, Hong Kong, San Francisco, Vancouver, and it's a losing battle to pick the winner. The water part of Sydney, named Port Jackson by Captain Cook, is probably the most beautiful of the bunch, with 180 miles of shoreline and many picturesque coves and bays. It's seven miles from the headlands and the Tasman Sea to downtown Sydney.

Under the rules of the International Olympic Committee, a city that has been awarded a future Olympic games cannot advertise outside its country until the previous games are ended. Meaning that until the big party was over in Atlanta in 1996, Australia couldn't say much about the 2000 summer games in Sydney. But the rules don't say anything about advertising *inside* the country. And the Aussies have been at it with a vengeance. There's an Olympic flag flying from the Sydney City Hall, gift shops are up to the roof in T-shirts and other souvenirs with Olympic designs, buses are decorated with the colorful logo the Australians used when they submitted the Sydney bid to the IOC, and in general, you get the impression that the games will be held next week.

In reality, the games will run from Sept. 15-Oct. 1, 2000, and already there is a flurry of construction taking place at the Olympic site at Homebush Bay, about 14 kilometers west of the city center. About a dozen of the 25 sports scheduled for the games will take place there, and the Olympic Village, which will handle 15,000 officials and athletes, is also on the site. There has been a rash of major construction. The biggest stadium in town, for example, could only hold 40,000 people, so a new one will be ready for the summer games which will seat 110,000, the largest stadium in Olympic history. Organizers were telling the world that there would be no last-minute scrambles because most of the venues are already completed. The aquatic center, for example, was opened in 1995. One major concern is the ability of Sydney's international airport to handle a huge increase in traffic. And the folks who live near the airport, always making loud protests about the noise levels, are not especially keen on a lot more aircraft buzzing their houses.

The process, of course, has not been without its complications. The Sydney Games proposal promised to be a "Green Olympics," and was endorsed by the Greenpeace organization. A few months after the successful bid, environmentalists claimed the site of the Olympic Village was a contaminated military and industrial zone. Then, it was reported that the main site at Homebush Bay was the home of migrating waterfowl and the habitat of an endangered species of frog. Olympic organizers said all would be rectified, including building ponds for the frogs and birds.

The organizers have tried to make use of the lovely bayside setting of the city. Yachting events, for example, will be held in Sydney Harbour, and the marathon event will take competitors along the shoreline and up and over the Sydney Harbour Bridge. Even as construction continues for the next few years, visitors will be able to take tours of the Olympic site. The tours cost about A$5 and run from the Strathfield rail station near the site. Reservations and information: ☎ *(02) 9735-4800.* The Aussies, being Aussies, have already issued orders that hotels, restaurants and other businesses are not, repeat, not, allowed to gouge Olympic visitors. The Australian Hoteliers Association and the Motor Inn and Motel Association have agreed to limit accommodation prices, and the organizers are trying to keep event ticket prices as low as possible. If you want an overview of the 2000 Games, the city has created an Olympic information center aboard the "South Steyne," the oldest Manly city ferry. Included are interactive computers, background on the city's Olympic bid and a look at Australia's Olympic athletes during the past 100 years. The ferry is located in Darling Harbour and is open from 8 a.m.–7 p.m; admission is A$2 for adults.

Downtown Sydney is remarkably compact, making it one of the better walking cities in the world. Some of the major tourist sites are within blocks

SYDNEY

N

0 yards 550

0 meters 500

PORT JACKSON

■ **Opera House**

Sydney Cove

CIRCULAR QUAY EAST

Mrs. Macquaries Point

Farm Cove

Royal Botanic Gardens

Sydney Harbour Bridge

Dawes Point

To North Sydney

DAWES POINT

HICKSON RD.

LOWER FORT ST.

BRADFIELD HWY.

YORK ST. NORTH

THE ROCKS

MILLERS POINT

Walsh Bay

ARGYLE ST.

HARRINGTON ST.

KENT ST.

Circular Quay

LOFTUS ST.

BRIDGE ST.

PHILLIP ST.

BENT ST.

O'CONNELL ST.

HUNTER ST.

PITT ST.

PHILLIP ST.

MACQUARIE STREET

SPITAL RD.

CAHILL EXPWY.

CAHILL EXPWY.

CAHILL

YORK ST.

WESTERN DISTRIBUTOR

MARGARET ST.

GEORGE STREET

WYNARD

HICKSON RD.

Darling Harbour

Woolloomooloo Bay

BROADWAY

POTTS POINT

MRS. MACQUARIES RD.

MRS. MACQUARIES RD.

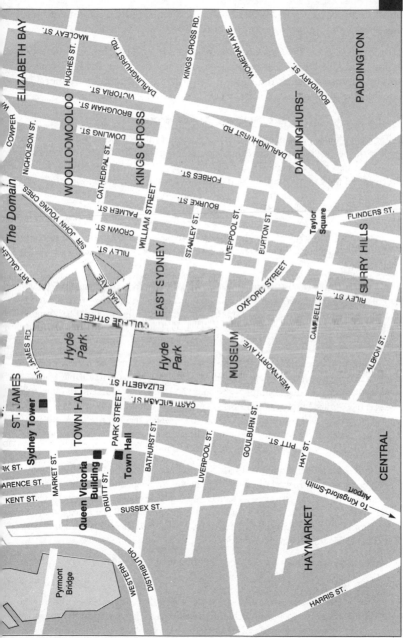

of each other, and the area is filled with restaurants, pubs, government buildings, boutiques, shopping arcades, hotels and department stores.

San Francisco has the Golden Gate Bridge, Hong Kong has Victoria Peak, Sydney has the Opera House and the Sydney Harbour Bridge. Walking around Circular Quay at night, with the Opera house and the Sydney Harbour Bridge all lit up, is a special treat. It's really gorgeous.

The Sydney Opera House

The **Opera House** is one of those edifices that seems to allow no middle ground. Some see it as the personification of the Australian spirit, soaring and vibrant. Others think it looks like a nest of giant mollusks mating—barnacles, maybe. Whatever, it is a striking structure and the harbor wouldn't be the same without it. Designed in the 1950s by a young Danish architect, Joern Utzon, its billowing form supposedly depicts sails. The cost went from A$7 million to the final completion figure of A$102 million and took a ridiculous 16 years to complete (1973). Utzon, apparently not keen about the noisy Australian politics and Mickey Mouse shenanigans that made his baby so late and so costly, left before it was completed and has reportedly never gone back to Australia to see the finished product.

The Opera House is more than one theater. There are, in fact, something like 900 separate areas contained under the mating mollusks, including five rehearsal studios, a reception hall, three restaurants, a library, six theater bars, 60 dressing rooms, a bar/canteen for the artists, administrative offices and large foyer/lounge areas. In addition to the Opera Theatre, there is also the 2700-seat Concert Hall.

The best way to see the Opera House is on a conducted tour, which takes visitors through the main performing halls and other public areas; tours are available from 9-4 seven days a week. The one-hour tours cost about A$10 for adults. On Sundays, there are also backstage tours, 90-minute treks that show you the behind-the-scenes areas and explain the workings of the theater areas. These tours, which also run from 9-4, are about A$15; kids under 12 not allowed. Tours might be curtailed or canceled if theater activities are scheduled. To book a tour, call ☎ *(02) 9250-7250*.

The box office is open from 9–8:30 Monday-Saturday. Note that tickets for most performances go on sale six weeks before. You can also do telephone bookings (there is a A$5 charge) and you can charge to a credit card. For phone bookings, call ☎ *(02) 9250-7111; FAX (02) 9221-8072.* For mail bookings, write to *Box Office Manager, Sydney Opera House, P.O. Box R239, Royal Exchange, NSW 2000.* Dinner/performance packages are available from Showbiz Bookings

The two major restaurants at the Opera House are:

Bennelong, The   **$$$**   ★ ★ ★

An à la carte, upscale eatery popular for pre-theater dinners, and the Forecourt. The Bennelong is also open for lunch Monday-Saturday. The view from the restaurant at night is fantastic. ☎ *(02) 9250-7578*.

Forecourt   **$$**   ★ ★

The very popular *Forecourt* is a brasserie-style restaurant that specializes in seafood and char-grilled meats. Hours are 9 a.m.–midnight, Monday-Saturday, and 11:30 a.m.–8 p.m. Sundays. ☎ *(02) 9250-7300.*

Reservations for both restaurants are advisable.

Cafe Mozart offers light meals before and after performances, and **The Harbour**, outside the Opera House, is open for lunch Monday–Saturday and dinner from 5 p.m. It also has take-away food. ☎ *(02) 9250-7191.*

For disabled information: ☎ *(008) 800-340.*

If you'd like to prebook a package before leaving North America, contact **ATS**, *2381 Rosecrans Ave., #325, #1 Segundo, Calif. 90245;* ☎ *(800) 423-2880; FAX (310) 643-0032.* The packages, called **"An Evening at the Opera House,"** can be booked 12 months in advance, but are not available on Sundays or public holidays. The festivities start around 4:45 p.m. with the tour, followed by dinner, then the performance. The cost of the package depends on what you will see and what time of year you're in town, but generally expect a tab of between A$140 and A$280 per person. Reservations should be made at least two months in advance; reservations made within 21 days of the tours are subject to a $US25 late booking fee. **Qantas** also has an Opera House booking service for its passengers.

You can get to the Opera House from anywhere in the city by taking a bus, train or ferry to Circular Quay. It's also a stop (No. 2) on the Sydney 111 Explorer Bus. There's no parking at the Opera House. If you're driving, park at the Domain parking ramp on Sir John Young Crescent at the south end of the Domain and then take the Opera House bus, which runs Monday-Saturday from 5:30 p.m. until five minutes after the start of the last performance; the last trip back to the Domain is at 11:45 p.m. Matinee bus service on Saturdays runs from noon until five minutes after the start of the last matinee.

Sydney Harbor is one of the most beautiful harbors in the world.

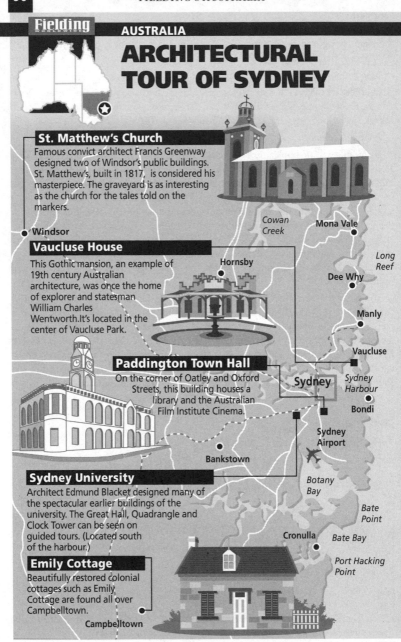

Fielding
WORLDWIDE

AUSTRALIA

ARCHITECTURAL TOUR OF SYDNEY

St. Matthew's Church

Famous convict architect Francis Greenway designed two of Windsor's public buildings. St. Matthew's, built in 1817, is considered his masterpiece. The graveyard is as interesting as the church for the tales told on the markers.

Windsor

Vaucluse House

This Gothic mansion, an example of 19th century Australian architecture, was once the home of explorer and statesman William Charles Wentworth. It's located in the center of Vaucluse Park.

Paddington Town Hall

On the corner of Oatley and Oxford Streets, this building houses a library and the Australian Film Institute Cinema.

Sydney University

Architect Edmund Blacket designed many of the spectacular earlier buildings of the university. The Great Hall, Quadrangle and Clock Tower can be seen on guided tours. (Located south of the harbour.)

Emily Cottage

Beautifully restored colonial cottages such as Emily Cottage are found all over Campbelltown.

Cowan Creek   Mona Vale

Long Reef

Hornsby   Dee Why

Manly

Vaucluse

Sydney   Sydney Harbour

Bondi

Sydney Airport

Bankstown

Botany Bay

Bate Point

Cronulla   Bate Bay

Port Hacking Point

Campbelltown

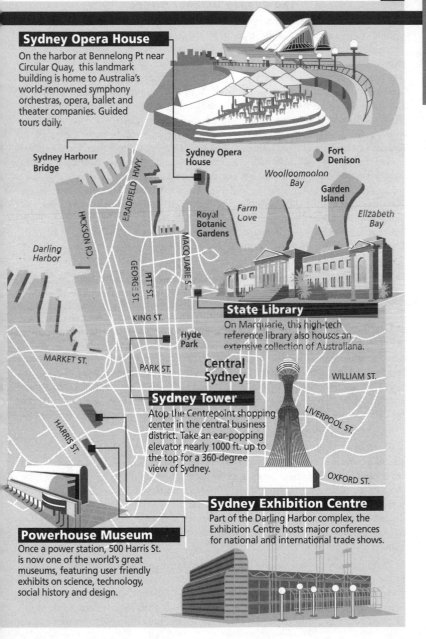

Sydney Opera House

On the harbor at Bennelong Pt near Circular Quay, this landmark building is home to Australia's world-renowned symphony orchestras, opera, ballet and theater companies. Guided tours daily.

Sydney Harbour Bridge

Sydney Opera House

Fort Denison

Woolloomooloo Bay

BRADFIELD HWY

Garden Island

Royal Botanic Gardens

Farm Cove

Elizabeth Bay

HICKSON RD.

Darling Harbor

MACQUARIE S.

GEORGE ST.

PITT ST.

KING ST.

State Library

On Macquarie, this high-tech reference library also houses an extensive collection of Australiana.

Hyde Park

MARKET ST.

Central Sydney

PARK ST.

WILLIAM ST.

Sydney Tower

Atop the Centrepoint shopping center in the central business district. Take an ear-popping elevator nearly 1000 ft. up to the top for a 360-degree view of Sydney.

LIVERPOOL ST.

HARRIS ST.

OXFORD ST.

Sydney Exhibition Centre

Part of the Darling Harbor complex, the Exhibition Centre hosts major conferences for national and international trade shows.

Powerhouse Museum

Once a power station, 500 Harris St. is now one of the world's great museums, featuring user friendly exhibits on science, technology, social history and design.

The Sydney Harbour Bridge

The **Harbour Bridge**, which spans one of the narrowest inlets in the harbor, was opened in 1932 and is one of the largest arch bridges in the world. It is 1650 feet across, contains somewhere around 52,000 tons of steel and carries eight traffic lanes and two railroad lines. (It is, of course, always crowded and a tunnel has been built to help out.) The bridge is called, with affection, the "Coathanger." You get a great view of the harbor and city from the pedestrian crosswalk on the bridge, or an even better idea is to climb to the top of the bridge's southeast pylon for a 360-degree view of the entire harbor area. To get to the top, you have to first get to the bridge deck, which is reached by walking through The Rocks. The easiest way is to walk up Argyle Street from the Orient Hotel (corner of George and Argyle streets). Just before you come to Argyle Cut, a tunnel hacked through the old rocks with convict labor beginning in 1843, you'll see a set of stairs going off to the right. Climb these, then cross Cumberland Street to a two-story bridge access building. Once on the bridge, go north to the pylon entrance. Climbing the 200 or so steps to the top takes you past art displays on the interior walls of the pylon and video programs about the construction of the bridge. Once on top, there are toilets, and a panoramic, if windy, view of the city. The pylon is open most of the year from 10 a.m.– 5 p.m. daily; hours change after mid-February. The entry fee to the pylon is about A$1.50. ☎ *(02) 9247-3408*.

On the north end is **Luna Park**, Sydney's largest amusement park. The park can also be reached by taking a ferry from Circular Quay. It's open Friday through Sunday.

The Quay

The anchor for the whole downtown area, as well as the transportation hub, is the dockside area of Sydney Cove, called Circular Quay (pronounced "key"). It has always been the major port facility for the city, and in the late 1980s a new cruise ship docking area was added. Behind the quay, toward downtown, are a number of fast-food joints, newspaper and film kiosks and usually a fair number of street entertainers, called "buskers" in Australia. The quay also has a major downtown railroad station and is the location for ticket offices for the city's extensive system of commuter ferries as well as the boats that take tours of the harbor.

The ferries, operated by the State Transit Authority, run from the quay to various locations around the harbor. The ferry docks are numbered 2 through 5. Among the ferries are ones to Manly, the resort area across the harbor north of the city, which leaves from Dock 3 (or hydrofoil service from Dock 2); the Taronga Zoo, from Dock 2; Darling Harbour from Dock 5; and Neutral Bay and Mosman, from Dock 4. The price of the ferries depends on the destination and whether it's a regular or high-speed service. The hydrofoil to Manly takes 15 minutes, and costs about A$10 one way; the regular ferry takes 35 minutes and costs about A$7.

There are a couple of dozen harbor cruise packages available from Circular Quay and Darling Harbour, everything from quickie tours to evening dinner and music cruises. If it's a general tour of Sydney Harbour you want, try one of the Explorer trips, which leave from Circular Quay and run out to the headlands with sidetrips to various scenic spots. The two-hour trips run all day and cost about $A20 per adult. Many of the harbour cruises offer either complimentary teas or meals not included in the ticket price. Speciality cruises include the **Sydney Showboat**, a paddle-wheeler with three trips a day including a cabaret dinner cruise which costs about A$100 per person (drinks not included). There is also a jazz luncheon cruise (about A$40 per person). ☎ *(02) 9552-2722.* A familiar sight on the harbor is the **Bounty**, a powered replica of William Bligh's ill-fated ship that was built for the Mel Gibson version of the movie saga. It now does duty as a floating restaurant, touring the harbor for coffee cruises in the daytime and a dinner cruise at night. The dinner price is about A$60 per person. ☎ *(02) 9247-1789.* **Matilda Cruises** operates trips from Darling Harbour, including sight-seeing and dinner cruises aboard a big catamaran or a lunch or dinner cruise on the sailing vessel **Solway Lass**. The catamaran sight-seeing tours are about A$20 per person; dinner cruises on both ships will run about A$45-60 per person. ☎ *(02) 9264-7377.*

For information about all the various Sydney-area cruises, check at the **Quayside Booking Centre** at *No. 2 Jetty* on the quay, ☎ *(02) 9247-5151.* There are also ticket offices for the various companies along the quay and at Darling Harbour. For information about ferry service around the harbor, stop at the ferry information center at Wharf 4 at the quay, or call ☎ *(02) 131-500.* In addition to the cruises and ferry services, you can also take tours by water taxi from both the quay and Darling Harbour. For information about taxi services, call ☎ *(02) 9955-3222.* There is an express taxi that runs every 15 or 20 minutes from the waterfront next to the Museum of Contemporary Arts in the Rocks to Darling Harbour; it costs A$3 per adults, and tickets can be bought aboard. One of our favorite spots to sup or sip on the quay is **Rossini's ★ ★**, with cafeteria-style food, good coffee and wine and beer. It's right across from the No. 3 wharf and is open until 11 p.m.

The Rocks

The Rocks, where Caucasian Australian history began, has had its ups and downs, mostly downs. But today, the area offers everything a visitor to the city would require, from top grade hotels and restaurants to activities that come close to explaining what the country is all about. In fact, the Rocks is such a good area, you could spend your entire vacation there and come away satisfied (not that we suggest you spend all your time in Sydney). Over the years, we have watched it grow and evolve to become a bouncy, interesting urban settlement which will satisfy most international visitor's needs. In its infancy, the area, which lies at the base of the Harbour Bridge above the waters of Sydney Cove across from Circular Quay, was not safe for man nor sheep. All the things that would later evolve into late 20th-century quaint—tiny alleys, stone walls, pubs, former houses of ill repute (they were called "harpies' dens")—made The Rocks famous the world around with sailors looking for rum and romance beneath the Southern Cross. The jolly tars have been replaced by visiting lubbers from Maine and Kansas, but a lot of the old spirit pervades the area. Restoration projects have helped preserve the historic buildings, although many were intentionally destroyed in 1900 when bubonic plague broke out in the city, and later when more fell to make way for the Harbour Bridge. Preservation began in the early 1970s.

The main drag through the area is George Street, named after Good King George III, lined with shops, pubs and many old historic buildings. You can explore the area by yourself or take one of the daily walking tours. In any event, your first stop should be at the

Rocks Heritage and Information Centre, at *106 George Street*, housed in an old white building built in 1864 as a sailors' home. There's a Sydney Explorer bus stop in front. Walking tours of the Rocks area begin here at 10:30 a.m. weekdays, 11:30 a.m. on weekends. The tours are about an hour and a half and cost A$9 (tours also start from the Argyle Centre). The visitors center is open every day of the year from 9 a.m.–5 p.m., and until 7 p.m. during the summer. There is a heap of information about shops, restaurants and other attractions. ☎ *(02) 9255-1788*. The Sydney Cove Authority, in charge of the Rocks, also operates an information number: ☎ *(02) 11606*. Another good bet for walking tours are those offered by Anne Sullivan. Her 2.5-hour tours are about A$25 per person and include morning tea at the **Hero of Waterloo**, our favorite pub in Sydney. Reservations: ☎ *(02) 9327-2954*. At the visitors center, you can purchase a Rocks Ticket, which for about A$32, you get admission to three of the Rocks attractions, a harbor cruise, a walking tour and a meal. Good deal.

In a small park at the corner of Argyle and George streets toward the quay is Sydney's oldest building, **Cadmans Cottage**, which dates from 1816. It is believed to have been built under the direction of the convict architect Francis Greenway. It now houses an information center and bookstore with materials about Sydney and New South Wales. Across the street at *77-85 George Street* are the old sandstone **Unwin Stores** (1844), and next to them the **Orient Hotel** (1843). Across Argyle Street from the Orient is The Rocks' police station, an old Victorian building. Playfair Street, between the Orient and the Argyle Centre, is worth a look with its groupings of 1870s-era terrace houses that have been restored and converted into shops. There's a McDonald's on the street, part of the Rocks Centre shopping mall.

If you go up Argyle Street, you come to the **Argyle Centre**, four old warehouses, the earliest dating from 1826. The buildings, clustered around a cobblestoned interior courtyard, are now being restored. The stores that were housed there have moved next door to the Rocks Centre, a modern two-story shopping mall with more than 40 stores. Continuing on Argyle, through Argyle Cut, you come to one of the city's oldest neighborhoods. To your left going up the hill is Observatory Point, the highest point in town. On this site in 1796 was built the fledgling colony's first windmill, used to grind flour. In 1858, the **Sydney Observatory** was built. Today, the facility has a regular program of exhibitions, films, lectures and night viewing. Daytime visiting hours are 2–5 p.m. weekdays; 10 a.m.–5 p.m. weekends. Free admission. The evening programs are open all year (closed Wednesdays). The programs include a short walk around the premises and telescope time. Admission is about A$5. ☎ *(02) 9217-0485*.

On up the hill to the right is **Holy Trinity Church**, also called the Garrison Church because it was used by the military in colonial days. The church, dating from 1848, is lovely inside. Nearby is Argyle Place, the oldest village green in Sydney, flanked on one side by cottages dating back to the 1830s. A couple of very nice old pubs are in the area: the **Lord Nelson Hotel** (1837) and the **Hero of Waterloo** (1845). We like the Hero of Waterloo because of the service but also because of its tawdry history. At one time, there was a trapdoor near the bar used to shanghai unsuspecting sailors. There is a room down below with manacles on the wall; ask the manager, John Gallagher, and he might give you a tour. The Hero claims to have the oldest liquor license in Sydney, and the last time we were there one of the most interesting pub bands in the city. The band members were all in their 80s, all former vaudevillians who played on weekends. They were a hoot and quite good. Our favorites, Naomi and Cyril, have gone to that great bandstand in the sky, but have been replaced; the new group, not as lively, still draws crowds. The pub, if you care, has 10 beers on tap. (For all we know the trapdoor is still in use.) The Hero is down Lower Fort Street from Observatory Hill; the Lord Nelson is at the end of Argyle Street. You can also get to Observatory Hill by taking a tunnel; it's next to the steps leading to the Harbour Bridge on Cumberland Street. Look for a sign saying Fort Street Tunnel.

The pubs along George Street are local hangouts, but they'll let polite tourists in. Our favorite is the **Fortune of War** *137 George Street* (also claims to have the oldest liquor license in town). Good service, good pub lunches. Go upstairs (door on the left of the George Street pub entrance) and you enter the pub's eating area, the First Fleet Lounge Bar. Lunch specials daily for about A$5, a great deal. Get there by 12:30 p.m. because the office crunch starts around 1 p.m.; open daily from noon–11 p.m. From the First Fleet, a door leads to **Nurses Walk**, site of Australia's first hospital (1788). Here, a noted Aussie artist, Ken Done, has opened a gallery. His works, popular on T-shirts and posters, are sold all over Australia as well as some places in North America. The gallery has original works, which aren't cheap. Ken and his designer wife, Judy, also have a number of other outlets around the city, including the Queen Victoria Building and Sydney International Airport.

On George Street near the information center is the Rocks' newest attraction, the **Museum of Contemporary Art**, housed in a large, ugly building next to the quay. It features modern Australia art, including TV and films, laser shows, sculptures, etc. It's an object of some civic pride, but we say it basically just blocks the view of the harbor. It does have a nice outdoor cafe and a gift shop. Hours are 11 a.m.–6 p.m. daily, guided tours Monday-Saturday noon and 2 p.m.; Sundays at 2 p.m. Information and bookings: ☎ *(02) 9252-4033*.

A great little place for a good meal is **Zia Pina** ★, at the corner of George and Argyle, a two-story, crowded, casual Italian place. The pasta is great, the prices decent, the service swift and friendly. ☎ *(02) 9247-2255*. For a snack or cheapo meal, try the **G'Day Cafe** ★ next to the Orient Hotel, which has deli food and Middle Eastern fare: tabuli, falafels, kabobs, Greek salads, all in the under-A$5 range. Open 5:30 a.m.–midnight for breakfast, lunch and dinner seven days. **The Ox on the Rocks** ★ bistro, *135 George*, serves crocodile and kangaroo. More upscale is one of Sydney's better-rated seafood restaurants, the **Rockpool** ★ ★ ★ ★, at *107 George Street*. This is a black-tied-waiter restaurant, with prices to match, but you can also try the oyster bar at the front where the menu is a bit more lower-class. The house wines are excellent. Lunch Monday–Friday from 2:30 p.m.; dinner Monday-Saturday 6:30–10 p.m., oyster bar open until 11 p.m.; ☎ *(02) 9252-1888*. You can also try the **Boulders** ★ ★, an Asian/Mediterranean style BYO restaurant housed on the bottom floor of the Russell Hotel, *143A George Street*. Very popular for lunch and dinner. Reservations: ☎ *(02) 9241-1447*.

Other places for a bite:

Orient Hotel, The $ ★

89 George Street; *(02) 9251-1255.*
Getting a little seedy but still does a good lunch business ; nice outdoor seating area.
The Orient, has live jazz on the weekends from 3–8:30 p.m. and live music Mon-
day-Saturday from 10 p.m.–3 a.m. Upstairs, there is a cook-your-own steak area.

If you haven't been to Australia before, you might try the:

Jolly Swagman Show $$$ ★★

18 Argyle Street; ☎ *(02) 9247-7782.*
A dinner performance housed in the Garrison Restaurant, an 1830-era building.
The Swagman show dwells heavily on raw colonial humor and history, with sheep
shearing, some didgeridoo music, a few bawdy waitresses and other tourist-style car-
rying-on. It's funny the first time. The show is given seven nights; the tab is about
A$60 per person, which includes a "typical" Australian dinner. The show can be
booked at the Argyle Centre ticket office. There is also an Australian buffet lunch
seven days.

Other Rocks attractions include:

The Earth Exchange   ★

18 Hickson Road.
It's open 10 a.m.–5 p.m. daily; admission about A$7.50.
A blend of simulated earthquakes, volcanoes, sulfur vents and other geologic activ-
ity, plus a look at an underground mine and a collection of valuable minerals.

Story of Sydney   ★★

100 George Street, next to the Visitors Centre.
Hour are 9 a.m.–6 p.m. daily; admission about A$10.
A one-hour multidimensional trip through the 200-year-old history of the city.
You'll see convicts and Aboriginals, refugees and brigands. There is also a book
store and terrace café.

Geological and Mining Museum   ★

36 George Street; ☎ *(02) 9251-2422.*
*Hours 9:30 a.m.–4 p.m. weekdays; 1–4 p.m. Saturday, 11 a.m.–4 p.m. Sundays and hol-
idays. About A$10.*
Displays of gold, gemstones and mining. It also sells jewelry and books on "fossick-
ing," the Strine word for prospecting.

Australian Wine Centre   ★★

Corner of George and Alfred streets next to the quay.
Hours are 10 a.m.–7 p.m. Monday-Saturday, 10 a.m.–5 Sunday.
A chance to taste a few of the 450 wines on hand, and you can ship them home from
here; it's in the basement of the Goldfields building.

Aboriginal arts

There are a couple of places in the Rocks offering art and souvenirs. Try the **Aborig-
inal & Tribal Art Centre**, *117 George Street*, and the **Dreamtime Gallery** *in the
Rocks Centre shopping mall.* The tribal art center is open 10 a.m.–5 p.m. Monday–

Sunday; the gallery 9:30 a.m.–5:30 p.m. Monday-Sunday. There is also an Aboriginal art shop on the upper concourse of the Sydney Opera House.

Shopping note: A few years ago, the **Rocks Weekend Market** was started, a street sale that takes place every weekend, rain or shine. It's located on upper George Street almost under the Harbour Bridge. Hours are 9 a.m.–5 p.m., 9 a.m.–6 p.m. in the summer. It's close to the **Mercantile Hotel**, which has pub lunches and cold drinks. Market information. ☎ *(02) 9255-1717.*

A washing note: One of the things that causes minor headaches on a trip longer than a week is laundry. You can wash a few things out in the shower, or submit to the often outrageous prices hotels charge—If you stay in one spot long enough to get your things washed and returned. In the Rocks, fortunately, there is a solution: a laundry that offers low-priced, one-day service. Drop off your duds in the morning, pick them up at night. The laundry, **Wash on the Rocks**, is up in the Observatory Hill area, on Argyle Street across from the Lord Nelson Hotel. A bag of clothing (say a week's worth) will run about A$8, washed and folded. If you want, for about A$6, they'll deliver the finished laundry to your hotel. We were amused to discover that our hotel was sending guest laundry to the same place—and of course, charging more. ☎ *(02) 9247-4917.*

Darling Harbour

Often, when cities get all lathered up for a world's fair or a major celebration, some good is actually accomplished. Two recent examples are the dreary and dilapidated dockside areas that were cleared and improved in Brisbane for the 1988 World's Fair and in Vancouver for a similar party in 1986.

New South Wales decided, as its major contribution to the bicentennial, to take Darling Harbour apart and put it back together. Once a prosperous cargo area to the west of Circular Quay, Darling Harbour decayed into an ugly area of ratty buildings. The ambitious, US$1.5 billion development for the harbor, named after Sir Ralph Darling, the colonial governor from 1825 to 1831, included the **National Aquarium**, the **Australian National Maritime Museum**, the **Powerhouse** (a huge science-technology museum), a seven-story **convention center**, a **Chinese garden** (designed and built by architects from Guangdong Province), the huge **Sydney Exhibition Centre** (25,000 square yards of column-free space), several parking garages and the **Harbourside** (a marketplace area to house 200 retail outlets, terrace cafés and restaurants). Also included is the **Darling Harbour Park**, which created a large green space along the harbor edge. It is adjacent to **Darling Walk**, set to be a major entertainment center. The first phases of the development, including the Chinese Garden, were completed in time for the 1988 bicentennial. Under construction now is a huge casino, part of the original plans but delayed for one reason or another; it is expected it will be operated by the Harrahs group, the American casino company.

The harbor project did not meet with unanimous enthusiasm, some more fiscally minded believing the project was a bit big for its britches, and there were also murmurs about the monorail built to connect the harbor area with downtown. The elevated track is pretty discordant in places where it crosses streets or wraps around buildings, and there are hints that it might be torn down: it's slow, expensive and underused. For Darling

Harbour generally, however, all seems well now, and the area has become one of the most popular spots in the city, not only for shopping, but for eating or taking in a show. One additional advantage is that the shops and some attractions at Darling Harbour stay open later than in the rest of the downtown area. For information about Darling Harbour transportation and events, call the hotline ☎ *(02) 0055 20261.*

Among the reasons to go to Darling Harbour:

The Sydney Aquarium   ★★

Aquarium Information: ☎ *(02) 9262-2300.*

As we have reminded you from time to time, when you dip your bod into the streams and harbors of Australia, you are entering the food chain. The aquarium gives you a chance to see all the local nasties up close without being asked to dinner—crocodiles, sharks, plus a very nice living reproduction of the Great Barrier Reef. It's a good bargain for the price, about A$15 per person. It's open from 9:30 a.m.–9 p.m. daily. The facility is located off King Street. If you're walking, there's a stairway down from King; if you're on the monorail, get off at the Harbourside station and walk back across Pyrmont Bridge to the aquarium. The old sandstone bridge, by the way, is another Sydney landmark, supposedly the oldest (1899) electrically operated swing bridge in the world.

Powerhouse Museum   ★★

Hours are 10 a.m.–5 daily. Information: ☎ *(02) 9217-0111; hotline number for current displays* ☎ *(02) 11-600.*

A close cousin to the Air and Space Museum at the Smithsonian in Washington, D.C., the Powerhouse also specializes in technological displays, everything from steam engines to replicas of the Space Shuttle. The city claims the museum is the number one attraction in all of New South Wales. Maybe. Anyway, it's free. The **Garden Restaurant ★** in the museum was decorated by Ken Done.

National Maritime Museum   ★★★

Open daily 10 a.m.–5 p.m.; admission about A$7. Take the monorail to the Harbourside depot. ☎ *(02) 9552-7777; hotline* ☎ *(02) 0055-62002.*

This is a special place for all of us around the world who cheered on the Aussies when they took the America's Cup away from the snotty Yanks. In the museum, in all its glory, is *Australia II*, the boat that did the deed. Also on hand is part of the only known remnant of the *Endeavor*, the ship Capt. James Cook sailed to explore Australia in 1770, the same one that almost sank on the Barrier Reef. After the momentous voyage, the old *Endeavor* was shipped off to the Falkland Islands as a supply ship, then turned into a whaler. Eventually, what was left of the ship ended up in a museum in Newport, R.I. Because of its importance to Australian history, the Newport museum gave a piece of the sternpost to the Maritime Museum. It's like having a piece of the Mayflower on view.

The museum displays cover the whole range of Australian oceanic history from the *Endeavor* to *Australia II* ships, Aboriginal canoes, explorers, naval history. In all, very much worth a few hours of your time. A permanent part of the museum is the United States of America Gallery, depicting U.S.-Australian naval history from early colonial days through the world wars.

Chinese Garden ★

Entry fee is about A$2; a cup of tea and a goodie will run about A$5. Hours are 9:30 a.m.–sunset weekdays, 9:30 a.m.–sunset weekends. ☎ (02) 9281-6863.

If you don't like Asian quaint, stay away. Here you have 10,000 square yards of Chinese art and architecture, fish-filled ponds, waterfalls, pagoda-buildings. It's awash in plant life, everything from flowering apricots and camellias to guava and bamboo. The site includes a teahouse and a store. It's a suitable place to haul in and rest your legs.

Harbourside

The shopping center is split into two pavilions. The north building tends to have upscale stores, the south has a lot of souvenir shops but also has a food hall on the second floor for snacking while you're shopping. Outside, the plaza is crawling with buskers (street entertainers) as well as wandering bands playing everything from Sousa to calypso. A couple of fun eateries are **Arnold's Diner ★** (you guessed it, right out of "Happy Days") and the **Craig Brewery ★ ★**. The Craig specializes in really good Aussie barbecue. Open from lunch on, seven days. At night, there's **Bobby McGees ★ ★** nightclub with dancing and dining until the wee hours. Take the monorail to Harbourside. Also a good bet is **Jordan's Seafood Restaurant ★ ★** near Harbourside; great seafood platter. ☎ (02) 9281-3711.

Another brew pub worth a shot is the **Pumphouse ★ ★**, contained in an old building on Pier Street at the south edge of the harbor complex. It has a wide variety of beers and some very good blackboard menu food. And its open seven days, 11 a.m.–late. ☎ (02) 9281-3967.

The Monorail

The monorail, completed in 1988, runs a circuit from the Centrepoint Sydney Tower, down Pitt Street to Liverpool, down Harbour Street past Chinatown and the Sydney Entertainment Centre, down the west edge of Darling Harbour to the Pyrmont Bridge, then back to the city center. It costs A$2.50 to make a circuit. There are depots at City Centre (near the tower), Park Plaza (near the Town Hall and the Queen Victoria Building), at World Square (a big office development at Pitt and Liverpool), Haymarket (the entertainment center), Convention (at the Convention Centre, which has a 3,500-seat auditorium and 25,000 square yards of column-free display space) and at Harbourside.

Turnstiles in the depots take either tokens or A$2 coins. The tokens can be purchased on the spot from vending machines that take paper money. Kiosks in the depots have souvenirs and film. *Operating hours are: summer (October-April) 7 a.m.–midnight Monday-Saturday, 8 a.m.–9 p.m. Sunday; winter 7 a.m.–9 p.m. Monday-Wednesday, 7 a.m.–midnight Thursday-Saturday, and 8 a.m.–9 p.m. Sunday. Information: ☎ (02) 9552-2288.*

If you're driving, Darling Harbour has four large parking facilities with space for about 6000 cars. They are located on the west side of the harbor. ☎ (02) 9281-3999.

A good bet is the:

Darling Harbour Super Ticket ★ ★

Darling Harbour information kiosks, Matilda Cruises or the aquarium. ☎ *(02) 9262-2300 or 9264-7377.*

For about A\$30 per person, you get a cruise on one of the Matilda catamarans, a free ride on the monorail, admission to the aquarium and Chinese Gardens, a 10-percent-off voucher from participating merchants at Harbourside, and a free lunch or dinner at the Craig Brewery.

Other Sydney Sights

Royal Botanic Gardens

Behind the Opera House and to the east of Circular Quay are the city's largest gardens, where the convicts planted their first vegetable plots. It has been a botanical garden and park since 1816. There are more than 400 varieties of plants from around the world in the park, which is free and open from 6:30 a.m. to sunset. Included among attractions are **The National Herbarium**, with an information desk open from 9 a.m.–5 p.m. weekdays; a visitors center and shop (open 9 a.m.–5 p.m. daily), and the **Sydney Tropical Centre**, with enclosed specimens of tropical plants, open from 10 a.m.–4 p.m. April–September, 10 a.m.–5 p.m. October-March. There is a A\$5 charge to enter the Tropical Centre buildings. ☎ *(02) 9231-8104.* Free guided tours of the main gardens starting from the park visitors center are available at 10 a.m. Wednesday and Friday and 1 p.m. Sunday. ☎ *(02) 9231-8111* or *(02) 9231-8125.*

Located within the confines of the park are **Government House** (not open to the public) and the **Conservatorium of Music**, designed by the famous convict-architect Francis Greenway in 1817 as the colonial horse stables. Lunchtime concerts are held periodically; ☎ *(02) 9230-1263.* At the harbor end of the park is **Farm Cove**, which got its name because of the early attempts at horticulture; the shores are now lined with shaded walkways.

Near the herbarium, on the east side of the park, is **Mrs. Macquarie's Road**, honoring the wife of Lachlan Macquarie, the most important of the early 19th-century colonial governors. At the end of the road is **Mrs. Macquarie's Chair**, a seat cut into a rock outcropping where legend has it that Herself sat, watching to make sure Hubby was hard at work.

Three blocks west of the park on Bridge Street (across from the conservatorium) is **Macquarie Place**, a tiny triangular park containing an obelisk from 1818 designed by Francis Greenway. At one time, all distances in the colony were measured from the stone. Also in the park is an anchor from Sirius, the flagship of the First Fleet, which was later sunk off Norfolk Island.

The Domain

South of the botanical gardens is another large green space, **The Domain**. On Sundays, the park is alive with soapbox orators who are met with enthusiasm by hecklers and supporters. In the center of The Domain is the **Art Gallery of New South Wales**, which houses an impressive collection of Australian art, including what is said to be the largest collection of Aboriginal works in the world, plus a selection of European pieces from the

Renaissance through the 20th century. The gallery is open daily from 10 a.m. to 5 p.m. Admission is free to the permanent exhibitions; a fee might be charged for special shows. *General information,* ☎ *(02) 9225-1744; exhibition information,* ☎ *(02) 9225-1790.* At the south end of The Domain is a parking ramp, strategically located for downtown area visitors.

Hyde Park

The park is split into two parts by Park Street. On the north side is the **Archibald Fountain**, commemorating the French-Australian alliance in World War I, featuring a statue of Apollo. To the northeast, between Hyde Park and The Domain, is **St. Mary's Cathedral**, a Gothic Revival Catholic church begun in 1831, opened in 1928 and still not finished. The interior is quite nice, and it's open for a look.

In the southern half of the park is the art deco **Anzac monument** honoring soldiers who served in World War I. To the east of the south section of the park is the Australian Museum, the nation's largest natural history museum, with an Aboriginal section, a re-created New Guinea village and examples of all the odd critters Down Under, including a dandy diorama on the Great Barrier Reef. The museum, located at the corner of William and College streets, is free and open from 10 a.m.–5 p.m. Tuesday-Sunday and public holidays; noon to 5 p.m. Mondays. ☎ *(02) 9339-8111.* There is a gift shop attached to the museum with Australiana and a lot of dinosaur stuff; all credit cards accepted.

Macquarie Street

The good governor was Sydney's first major mover and shaker, starting an energetic building program that changed the settlement from a rude colonial outpost into a city and in the process, naming almost everything in sight after himself. Sydney, up to his arrival in 1810, had grown haphazardly, a village of tiny, twisty streets, such as still can be seen in The Rocks. He envisioned a city with wide streets, parks and public areas, and much of what he built still stands.

Soon after he arrived, he laid out Macquarie Street himself, deciding that the major colonial buildings should be located along the east side, and the west should be the site of homes for the landed gentry. Several of the colonial buildings still standing along the road were designed by Francis Greenway.

Greenway was sentenced to death in England for fraud, but the sentence was commuted to 14 years' transportation to Australia. He made the acquaintance of Governor Macquarie, who knew talent when he saw it and named Greenway acting government architect.

In addition to the **Conservatorium** of Music in The Royal Botanic Gardens, Greenway also designed:

Hyde Park Barracks ★★

Admission is free; hours are 10 a.m.–5 p.m. daily. ☎ *(02) 9223-8922.*
Located just northeast of Hyde Park. The story goes that the governor was so pleased with the barracks (1819), which housed convicts, that he granted Greenway a full pardon. The barracks is now a museum, with displays of Australian history from colonial days to the 1950s. If you're hungry, the **Barracks Square Cafe** has lunches and teas.

The other Greenway building in the area is **St. James Church** (1819), the oldest church in town, located in Queens Square just off Macquarie next to the northwest corner of Hyde Park. He also designed **St. Matthew's Church**, now standing in the Sydney suburb of Windsor. It's the oldest Anglican church in the country, built in 1817.

Two other colonial buildings that still stand along Macquarie Street are part of what was once the first permanent hospital in the colony, the **Rum Hospital**. Built between 1811 and 1816, it got its name because Macquarie (finding the public coffers lacking) paid off the contractors by giving them a virtual monopoly in the rum trade, which in those days was a major force in New South Wales.

One wing of the former hospital houses the **Old Mint**, now the site of a free museum dedicated to the nation's decorative arts. It's open daily 10 a.m.–5 p.m.; Wednesdays noon to 5 p.m.; ☎ *(02) 9217-0333*. Another wing of the old hospital now serves as **Parliament House**. It was first used by the state legislature in 1829. Hours are 9:30 a.m.–4 p.m. Monday-Friday. When Parliament is sitting, visitors are admitted to the public gallery after 7:30 p.m.; reservations required. Daily tours are available; *Information from the sergeant-at-arms,* ☎ *(02) 9230-2111.* Next to Parliament House is the **Sydney Hospital**, a Victorian heap opened in 1879 to replace the old hospital.

Other buildings of interest along the street include the **State Library of New South Wales**, which maintains the early records of the colony (with computerized genealogical information) and holds periodic displays, open 9 a.m.–9 p.m. Monday–Friday; 11 a.m.–5 p.m. weekends. ☎ *(02) 9230-1414* or hotline ☎ *(02) 0055-21068*, and the **Royal Australian College of Surgeons**, *(145 Macquarie)*, housed in one of the last verandaed Georgian townhouses in the city.

Martin Place

All cities should have at least one fine pedestrian area amidst all the glass and concrete, and **Martin Place** fills the bill to a tee in Sydney. It cuts from George to Macquarie Streets in the heart of downtown. It's lined with shops and food outlets, and also has a band shell where noontime concerts are a favorite with the urban bees who work in the area. Between George and Pitt streets is the huge **General Post Office**, an impressive hulk of a building built in what is fondly called Venetian Renaissance style. It's a good place to pick up postcard stamps or mail stuff back home. Near the post office is a cenotaph honoring Australia's war dead, defaced with Aboriginal slogans during the Bicentennial, now clean again. Another nice pedestrian/shopping area is the Pitt Street Mall, which runs from Market to King streets.

Sydney Tower

The city dads decided you couldn't have a major-league metropolis without a tall tower (look at Seattle, Calgary or Chicago), so they flung up the 900-foot-high **Sydney Tower★**. Reaching into the heavens at the corner of Pitt and Market streets (it's also known as Centrepoint Tower). Up on top there is an observation deck where, on a non-smoggy day, you can see the Blue Mountains 60 miles away. *Information and hours,* ☎ *(02) 9229-7444.* The tower houses two revolving eateries; one a la carte, one cafeteria-style. To get to the ticket outlet to catch the elevator that whips you to the top, you have to take escalators up four floors from the street level, passing through **Centrepoint**

Arcade, full of 170-odd shops and fast-food emporia and one of the better places in town to grab a quick bite. The ride up to the observation desk costs about A$5. Being Australian, the tower also has to serve a sporting purpose and every June a bunch of crazies stage a race to the top up the 1500 or so stairs. This is just another excuse to have a beer when it's over, of course. Enter from Market Street, take the lift to Podium Level, then board one of three elevators to the observation level. Hours 9:30 a.m.–9:30 p.m. Sunday-Friday; 9:30 a.m.–11:30 p.m. Saturday. ☎ *(02) 9229-7444.*

Chinatown

Small by San Francisco or New York City standards, the Sydney **Chinatown** area is nonetheless a center of food, markets and culture well worth a stop if you like your diversions in the Asian manner. It's located about four long blocks up George Street from the Town Hall, essentially between Hay and Harbour streets. Dixon Street, which cuts through the heart of Chinatown, is closed to vehicles and has Chinese arches at either end. Across Harbour Street is the **Sydney Entertainment Centre**, where visiting rock groups and other entertainers of note hold forth.

The focal point of the Chinatown area is the Sussex Centre, located between Sussex and Dixon streets. It has more than 30 specialty shops, an Asian food hall, and the huge 500-seat **Yumsing Seafood Restaurant**, The entertainment center is open seven days from 10 a.m.–9 p.m. The area can be reached by taking the monorail to the Entertainment Centre depot.

Kings Cross

If a city has to have a 900-foot high tower in order to compete with other famous urban spots, it follows that it must also have a certain amount of sleaze. Enter **Kings Cross**, Sydney's answer to Market Street in San Francisco or Soho in London, located southeast of The Domain just north of William Street. But Kings Cross is Aussie sleaze, meaning it's not very serious, and amidst the neon-lit strip joints, sex shops and nightclubs are some good eateries and even a reputable shop or two. The future of The Cross looks gloomy if you're into porn. It's being slowly but surely yuppified as The Loo, the Woolloomooloo district of town to the north, starts to expand. The Cross is probably safe enough to walk around at night unless you're by yourself. If you like to wander around seedy areas of big cities at night, Kings Cross should keep you occupied. It ain't Kowloon, however. There are about 100 restaurants, 35 coffee shops and accommodations ranging from near-flop houses to five-star hotels.

Among the bouncier areas in the Cross area are:

Last Aussie Fishcaf   **$$**   ★★

24 Bayswater Road; ☎ *(02) 9356-2911.*
Open for dinner daily 6 p.m.–1 a.m.
A place that mixes '50s dance music (audience participation blatantly encouraged) with excellent seafood. Live entertainment in a decor that smacks of ocean-liner chic. Reservations essential on the weekends.

Hard Rock Cafe   **$$**   ★

121 Crown Street, Darlinghurst.; ☎ *(02) 9331-1116.*
Open noon–midnight seven days.

The Aussie member of the international Hard Rock Cafe group. Yankee food, rock n' roll, crowds, noise, confusion.

Studebakers   **$$**   ★

33 Bayswater Road; ☎ *(02) 9358-5656.*
Open seven nights until late.
Another rock house, also dealing in popular '50s and '60s dance music.

Cauldron, The   **$$**   ★

207 Darlinghurst Road, Darlinghurst.; ☎ *(02) 9331-1523.*
Open 7:30 p.m.–3 a.m.
Old and new, more stylish than some of the other places. Dancing to Oldies as well as the latest screaming.

Porky's   **$$**   ★

77 Darlinghurst Road; ☎ *(02) 9357-1180.*
Open from 10 a.m.–2 a.m. seven days.
If skin is your thing, they show a lot of it at this joint. You can't miss it—look for the big red neon sign and the piggy next to it.

For the more historically minded, plan a visit to the **Elizabeth Bay House**, a short walk from the Kings Cross train station. The house, with one of the dandiest staircases you'll ever see, was built for a colonial secretary in 1835. The two-story Regency house has free tours and an audio-visual presentation. It's Stop No. 9 on the Sydney Explorer bus. Hours are 10 a.m.–4:30 p.m. Tuesday-Sunday. ☎ *(02) 9356-2344.* Another spot is the **Sydney Jewish Museum** at *148 Darlinghurst Street.* The museum offers a look at the Jewish convicts who were part of the transportation history as well as displays on the Holocaust. It's open 10 a.m.–4 p.m. Monday-Thursday, 10 a.m.–3 p.m. Friday, and 11 a.m.–5 p.m. Sunday. Stop No. 8 on the Explorer bus. ☎ *(02) 9360-7999.*

There's a bureau de change next to the library at the corner of Darlinghurst and Macleay streets, open 8 a.m.–midnight seven days. And there's an information kiosk at the library itself. Walk a few blocks down Macleay to Potts Point and you'll find a post office. The shopping around the Cross is mixed, from souvenirs to garden hose and sex paraphernalia. One major shopping area is the **Kings Gate Shopping Centre**, underneath the Hyatt Kinsgate Hotel between Kings Cross and Bayswater roads. It also has a currency exchange and a post office. For more dining in the Cross, see the restaurant section.

Paddington

Southeast of the center city is this recovered Skid Row area, whose steep hills and twisted streets are now classed as one of the most desirable parts of the urban scene. Formerly crime-ridden, it now holds, as one observer noted, "large dogs and well-spoken children." Paddington's old Victorian terrace houses, once eyesores, have been lovingly restored a la New Orleans (they drip with iron filigree work) and the whole district is filled with ethnic restaurants, bistros, art dealers, antique shops and bookstores, the end result being very chi-chi. The heart of the area is **Oxford Street**, also reputed to be one of the gay centers of Sydney. A specialty of the shops along Oxford is **clothing**, offered by some of the country's leading designers. One of the best times to visit Paddo, as the area is called, is on Saturdays when the **Paddington Village Church Bazaar** fair is held. Held at the Uniting Church, *395 Oxford Street*. Crowded, food available, 10 a.m.–4 p.m. ☎ *(02) 9331-2646*.

One of the major draws in Paddo is the **Victoria Barracks**, a massive sandstone building erected between 1841 and 1848. Starting at 10 a.m. Thursdays, you can watch the changing of the colonial-uniformed guards in front of what is considered to be the finest Georgian edifice in the city. It was used as a barracks and later as a school for artillery and cavalry troops. After the changing of the guards, there is a guided tour where you can check out the military museum and the manicured grounds. *Bookings essential:* ☎ *(02) 9339-3543*.

Also near Paddington is **Centennial Park**, opened in 1888 to celebrate the centennial. It's a little worn around the edges these days, but kids like to fly kites there and bikes are for rent. It also has a horse track and plenty of ponds and places for a picnic.

Glebe and Balmain

These are the newest tony parts of the Sydney scene, small communities west of the city across from Darling Harbour. Glebe's main drag, **Glebe Point Road**, is lined with some of the best ethnic restaurants in the city, mostly found in little mom-and-pop-sized places. Glebe has a large student population, thanks to its proximity to the **University of Sydney**.

For its part, Balmain seeks to out-Bohemia its cross-town rival, Paddington. The lots are postage-stamp sized, the houses of stone, the populace heavily leavened with writers, publishers and other superior type humans. Some very nice little pubs are around, as well as a coffeehouse or two.

Beaches

Narrabeen Beach, New South Wales, attracts hundreds of sun worshippers.

Australians love the sun, as their very high rate of skin cancer attests, and take every opportunity to hit the beaches. The coast east of Sydney is lined with good beaches, with something for all tastes from nude bathing to surfing. The official beach season, when regular lifeguards are posted, begins in October and runs through March. It's pretty stupid to swim when and where guards are not around, because most of the beaches have dangerous riptides. The waters around Sydney also have sharks, and routine patrols are carried out on the water and in the air to warn swimmers. Shark attacks in the area are extremely rare, however.

One of the treats at many Australian beaches is a chance to watch the lifeguard squads practicing. The squads take their activity very seriously and go through their drills in precise military fashion, marching in step and perfecting the techniques used in life saving. Squad members are easily recognizable: they wear funny-looking caps, but don't tell them that. Lifeguarding is a national sport, as evidenced by the annual **National Surf Live Saving championships** held in March. In addition, there are frequent competitions among the squads. Information about these free events is available from the **New South Wales Surf Life Saving Association**, ☎ *(02) 9663-4298.*

The two most popular beaches in the Sydney area are **Bondi**, pronounced "Bond-eye," and **Manly**. Bondi is patrolled all year, and in the height of the Aussie summer, is up to the gills in oil-glistened bodies soaking up rays. Nearby are fast food places, dressing rooms and hotels. The area around Bondi is, quite frankly, a bit worn at the edges, but the sand is fine and the water is cool. Getting to the beach is easy: catch a 380 bus from downtown or take a Bondi Beach train from the Quay and catch a beach bus at Bondi Junction.

Competitors show their expertise in watersports at Sydney's Surf Festival.

Manly is a beach community northeast of Sydney across the harbor, also a bit creaky at the joints, but getting refurbished and modernized. It's abundant with fish and chips out-

The Rocks is Sydney's popular harbourside area.

Kuranda Scenic Railway offers great views of Stoney Creek Falls.

Lifeguards compete at Sydney's Surf Festival.

Boat trips to Great Barrier Reef often leave from Marlin Jetty, Cairns.

lets and surfers. Like Bondi, the beach at Manly is patrolled all year. It's an interesting walking-around area, particularly on weekends when droves of city dwellers hop the ferry for a day of sand and snacks (something like 7 million people a year visit Manly). You can get to Manly by slow ferryboat or fast hydrofoil from Circular Quay.

The Manly beachfront has a stand of very nice Norfolk pines, and there are some fast-food places dotted here and there. On the Sydney Harbour side is the Manly Oceanarium, built onto the ocean floor, which houses the requisite number of sharks, poisonous fish and colorful sea creatures. A moving walkway takes you through a transparent tunnel so the critters are all around you. Also on hand are some Australian and New Zealand fur seals, a touch pool, art gallery and an outdoor turtle pool. The facility is open from 10 a.m.–5:30 daily. Admission about A$12. ☎ *(02) 9949-2644.*

The Manly tourist information office is located on South Steyne on the beach side of town. Hours are 10 a.m.–4 p.m. daily. ☎ *(02) 9977-1088.*

You will notice a bit of sprucing up has taken place when you arrive on the ferry. The old 1940-era Manly wharves have been restored and stuffed full of more than 80 shops, four waterfront restaurants, a food hall and a small amusement park. A great place for bored teens: video games, bumper cars, shooting gallery and a McDonald's. The wharf is open daily 10 a.m.–6 p.m., later on Thursday. Food hall and bar open seven days 10 a.m.–9 p.m. ☎ *(02) 9976-2555.*

Beaches near Sydney are designated either as northern or southern, depending on which side of the harbor entrance they are located. The southern beaches are easier to reach by public transport than those north of Manly.

Other Southern Beaches

Coogee

Look for the Coogee Bay Hotel and beer gardens. To get to the beach take Coogee Buses No. 373 or 374.

Cronulla

Sydney's longest (two miles), quiet and calm. Take the Cronulla train.

Tamarama

Near Bondi, a lot quieter, but with often-dangerous riptides. Take the Bondi bus and walk south. Close by is **Bronte Beach**, wider and more open than Tamarama. Walking distance from Bondi.

Other Northern Beaches

Long Reef

Adjacent to the Long Reef Golf Club; can be quite dangerous. Nearby is Dee Why Beach, good surfing, two miles of sand.

Harbord

Between Manly and Dee Why, a favorite for body surfing, shops close by.

Curl Curl

To the north of Harbord, is another mile-long beach.

Most of the near-Sydney north-side beaches can be reached by bus; check with the Urban Transit Authority, ☎ *(02) 9954-9422.*

Fielding AUSTRALIA

SUN AND SAND TOUR

Sydney's northern beaches are more scenic while the beaches in the eastern suburbs attract larger numbers of beachgoers. Bus service connects beaches as far south as Maroubra with the city.

Palm Beach
Mona
Dee Why
Manly
Sydney
Bondi
Coogee
Bate Point
Bate Bay
Cronulla

Surfing

The best beaches for surfing are Bondi, Bronte and Coogee to the South and Manly, Collaroy and Palm Beach in the North.

Wollongong

Seven-Mile Beach National Park

Highlights of this area are the Kiama blowhole, banksia heaths and dunes. Hang-gliders are often seen catching the winds off Stanwell Park.

Kiama

Jervis Bay

The pristine waters of the South Coast give divers magnificent views of marine life.

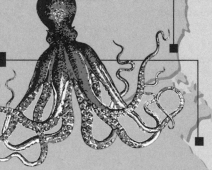

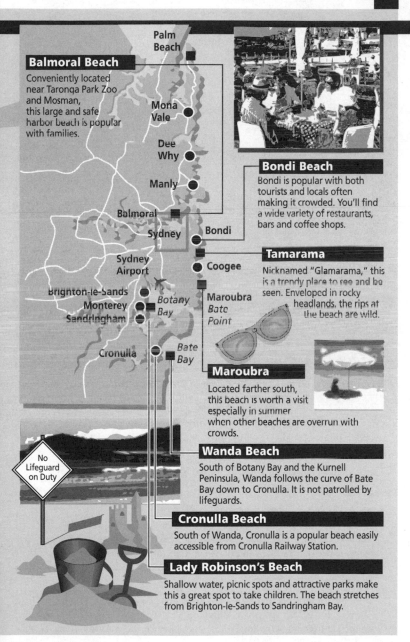

Balmoral Beach

Conveniently located near Taronga Park Zoo and Mosman, this large and safe harbor beach is popular with families.

Palm Beach

Mona Vale

Dee Why

Manly

Balmoral

Sydney

Bondi

Sydney Airport

Coogee

Brighton-le-Sands
Monterey
Sandringham

Botany Bay

Maroubra
Bate
Point

Cronulla

Bate Bay

Bondi Beach

Bondi is popular with both tourists and locals often making it crowded. You'll find a wide variety of restaurants, bars and coffee shops.

Tamarama

Nicknamed "Glamarama," this is a trendy place to see and be seen. Enveloped in rocky headlands, the rips at the beach are wild.

Maroubra

Located farther south, this beach is worth a visit especially in summer when other beaches are overrun with crowds.

Wanda Beach

South of Botany Bay and the Kurnell Peninsula, Wanda follows the curve of Bate Bay down to Cronulla. It is not patrolled by lifeguards.

Cronulla Beach

South of Wanda, Cronulla is a popular beach easily accessible from Cronulla Railway Station.

Lady Robinson's Beach

Shallow water, picnic spots and attractive parks make this a great spot to take children. The beach stretches from Brighton-le-Sands to Sandringham Bay.

No Lifeguard on Duty

You can feed kangaroos at Pebbly Beach in New South Wales.

Zoos

Coming to Sydney, but unable to head for the Outback and thus in danger of missing the wonders of Aussie wildlife? Not to worry, because you still have the chance to cuddle a koala or check out the kangaroos without even getting your feet dusty.

The prettiest and most convenient of the city's animal facilities:

Taronga Zoo

☎ *(02) 9969-2777. Open all week, 9 a.m.–5 p.m.*

A short ferry ride across the harbor from Circular Quay with great views of the city. The zoo has more than 4000 animals. One of the highlights is a seal pool, where there are free shows daily. You can also visit nocturnal critters, dingoes, lions, some of Australia's more lethal snakes and a children's zoo. Wheelchairs and baby strollers are available.

The easiest way to get to the zoo is to buy a zoo pass at Wharf 2 at Circular Quay. The pass, about A$20, gives you round trip ferry service, a pass on the bus that goes up the hill from the ferry dock to the zoo entrance, and zoo admission. Feeding time for the koalas is 3 p.m.; throughout the day there are talks at various locations by zoo staff members.

Featherdale Wildlife Park

Admission: about A$10 adults, A$5 for children; open 9 a.m.–5 p.m. daily. Coach tours from Sydney available: ☎ *(02) 9671-4984. Park information:* ☎ *(02) 9622-1644.*

About an hour from downtown, this park has some Aussie animal stars (a wombat named Fatso is a special treat), plus koalas and their wee families. There are also kangaroos, emus and other native animals. Here's your chance to feed or pose with a koala or a kangaroo.

Waratah Park Animal Reserve

Admission, about A$10 adults, A$5 children; open 10 a.m.–5 p.m. daily. ☎ *(02) 9450-2377.*

Another small sanctuary, about 30 miles north of downtown, where there are koalas and kangaroos to pet, as well as dingoes and wild fowl to examine.

The Arts Scene

Australia has a remarkable amount of activity in the arts, from movies to rock music, ballet to bush music, and you can take a large taste of what's current on the Australian scene at places all over the Sydney area.

A sampling of what's available:

Classical Music

Many events are held in the Concert Hall at the **Sydney Opera House** or at the **Sydney Town Hall**. Among the series to watch for are concerts and recitals presented throughout the year by the **Australian Broadcasting Commission**. Regular performances are made by the **Sydney Symphony Orchestra** in its subscription Recital Series. Also available is a series of programs on Sundays from 11.30 a.m.–12:30 p.m. which are broadcast on radio from the Opera House. *Information* on ABC activities is available by calling the ABC concert department, ☎ *(02) 9339-0211* or the Opera House box office.

Other classical performances by various groups are held at the Conservatorium of Music in the Royal Botanic Gardens; regular concerts are scheduled by students, as well as the conservatorium's own symphony orchestra. *Information: (02) 9230-1263.* Other student players can be heard at the University of Sydney's Music Department, which also offers a series of professional concerts; performances are held in the Great Hall of the university. *Information:* ☎ *(02) 9692-2923.*

Another popular group is the **Sydney Philharmonia Choir**, which performs with the Sydney Symphony as well as presenting its own series of programs during the year. There are actually two choirs, one for large works, one for a capella pieces. Many of the performances are at the Opera House. The local newspapers' music sections on Thursday or Friday carry information on what's playing around town; in all cases, reservations are probably necessary.

Opera

Many of the offerings are heavily booked by subscription, but some tickets are usually available. In January, the opera company gives an outdoor performance in The Domain.

Information is available from the Opera House Box Office; performances can be pre-booked before leaving North America (see above under Opera House).

Dance

The **Australian Ballet** performs in all of the country's major cities, and has two seasons: March–May and November–December, with frequent appearances at the Opera House. *Information:* ☎ *(02) 9357-1133* or the Opera House box office.

The **Sydney Dance Company** performs modern dance as well as classical ballet works, also in the Opera House. Information: ☎ *(02) 9358-4600* or the box office. For a real treat, try the Aboriginal works performed by the **Aboriginal and Islander Dance Theatre**. *Information:* ☎ *(02) 9660-2581.*

Theater

An evening of farce or tragedy is almost always available around Sydney, where more than 200 plays are presented every year. Tickets can be purchased by calling the individual theater box offices, or by contacting the **Mitchell's BASS agency** at ☎ *(02) 9266-4800.* Also, the **Sydney Convention and Visitors' Bureau** operates Halftix, through which you can buy half-priced tickets to theaters, Opera House performances and offerings at the Sydney Entertainment Centre. Tickets are available only on the day of the performance; the Halftix outlet is at the convention bureau's kiosk on Martin Street between Castlereagh and Elizabeth Streets. Hours are Monday–Saturday, noon–6 p.m.; ☎ *(02) 9235-1437.*

A few theaters include:

The Footbridge Theatre

Located at the edge of the University of Sydney campus in Glebe; ☎ *(02) 9692-9955.*
Concentrating on light fare and musicals; ticket price around A$30.

Her Majesty's Theatre

107 Quay Street downtown; ☎ *(02) 9212-3411.*
A favorite for staging touring Broadway and London offerings, but also dramas and one-person performances; tickets around A$30.

Ensemble Theatre

78 McDougall Street, Milson's Point; ☎ *(02) 9929-8877.*
Sydney's oldest professional theater company, light drama, comedic works; tickets about A$15-$30.

Sydney Opera House Drama Theatre

☎ *(02) 9250-1700.*
Where the Sydney Theatre Company holds forth, comedy, drama and musicals, often Australian works; tickets A$20-$30. Information: the Opera House box office. The Sydney Theatre Company also performs at the Wharf Theater at Pier 4, Walsh Bay, offering experimental and abstract works.

Seymour Centre

☎ *(02) 9692-3511.*
At Sydney University, three theaters in all, offering a variety including Aussie works.

Theatre Royal

☎ *(02) 9231-6111.*

One of the city's major sites for big-stage musicals and plays, seating around 1000, MLC Centre on King's Street downtown.

Have a Go, Sports

All the major forms of football Down Under can be found here and there in Sydney: **Rugby Union** (amateur), **Rugby League** (pro), **European football** (soccer) and **Aussie Rules Football** (madness). Matches are played during the Aussie winter. Papers carry times and locations of major matches.

The **Sydney Cricket Ground** is where the city hosts international matches during the season (October–March). Also held at the grounds are **Sheffield Shield** matches, which feature games between the Australian states. Ticket prices run from A$15-$30 for sheltered stands; around A$10 for open seating.

For golfers, there are around 40 public courses around Sydney, with greens fees running about A$20 for 18 holes. Among courses are the **New South Wales Golf Club**, ☎ *(02) 9661-4455*; **Castle Cove Country Club**, ☎ *(02) 9406-5444*, and the **Moore Park Golf Course**, ☎ *(02) 9663-3960*.

Tennis buffs also will find hundreds of public courts around the city, with court costs running around A$20. Some close-in courts are **Rushcutter's Bay Tennis Centre**, ☎ *(02) 9357-1675*; **Moore Park Tennis Centre**, ☎ *(02) 9662-7005*, and **Cooper Park Tennis Courts**, ☎ *(02) 9389-9259*.

Essential Sydney

Information

Maps, brochures and general information about the city and its environs are available from the **Travel Centre of New South Wales**, located at the *19 Castlereagh Street*. Open 9:30 a.m.–5 p.m. Monday–Friday; ☎ *(02) 9231-4444*.

The **Sydney Convention and Visitors' Bureau** operates a kiosk on the *Martin Place pedestrian mall between Castlereagh and Elizabeth Streets*, It has theater tickets as well as information. Hours are 9 a.m.–5 p.m. Monday-Friday; ☎ *(02) 9235-2424*. There is also a general information office at the Sydney Town Hall, corner of George and Druitt Streets, which has theater bills and bus schedules. Hours are 9 a.m.–5 p.m. Monday-Friday; ☎ *(02) 9265-9007*.

The city operates a general information line that gives information on a wide range of activities, from transportation to sightseeing and activities. ☎ *(02) 9875-4663, FAX (02) 9875-3516*.

Getting Around

Public Transportation

Public transportation is efficient and widespread in the Sydney metropolitan area. The international airport is about six miles from downtown, and is served by large yellow airporter buses (number 300) which run to Circular Quay and Kings Cross. A private company, **Kingsford Smith Transport**, picks up and drops off passengers at a number of hotels along the way. The one-way fare is about A$5; ☎ *(02) 9667-3221* or *(02) 9667-0663*. The company also has stretch limos for about A$50 one-way. Or try **Sydney Airporter**, with airport-hotel service; runs 5:30 a.m.–11 p.m. seven days, costs about A$6 one way. *(02) 9319-6600; FAX (02) 9699-8158.*

Once in town, several services are available to get you around. One bus, the 777, is free and runs in a loop through the city center; just hop on and ride. Another free bus, the 666, runs from the Art Gallery of New South Wales in The Domain along George and Macquarie streets to the Wynard Station near the Holiday Inn.

Sydney Explorer   ★★★

This bus has 22 strategic stops. Most of the major tourist attractions in the city are on the route. A one-day ticket costs about A$15 and can be purchased on board. With ticket in hand, you can get on and off at will. Special bus stop signs tell you where to pick up the buses. Included among the stops are The Rocks, the Town Hall, Kings Cross, Chinatown, and the Central Railway Station. The Explorer buses run every 17 minutes from 9:30 a.m.–5 p.m. all week except Christmas Day. The Explorer is one of the best ways to orient yourself to the city. Tickets and information can be obtained ahead of time at the Travel Centre of News South Wales; *(02) 9231-4444.*

Sydney Pass   ★★

A three-day pass which for about A$40 lets you travel on the **Sydney Explorer bus**, the **Airport Express**, the morning harbor history cruise and the afternoon **Harbour Lights** cruise; it also lets you have unlimited travel on the city's bus and ferry systems. All you do is hop on, show your pass and away you go. You can buy the pass at the international airport information office, from Ansett or Qantas Airlines ticket agents at the airport or from the NSW Travel Centre at Pitt and Spring streets. A good deal.

Cityhopper

A pass that allows unlimited one-day travel on the city's train system anytime after 9 a.m. and all day on weekends. The train system does a big loop around the city from Kings Cross to St. James (next to Hyde Park) to Town Hall, to the Quay and back. The pass is about A$3. *(02) 9954-4422.*

An invaluable source of information on buses, trains and ferries in the Sydney area is:

Metro Trips   ★★

Operates a telephone service from 7 a.m.–10 p.m. all week; ☎ *(02) 9954-4422.*

Taxis are plentiful (except when, as in all modern cities, it's raining). Meters start at about A$1 and then it's around A80 cents a kilometer. A trip in from the airport will run around A$15. Major cab companies are **Taxis Combined Services**, ☎ *(02) 9332-8888;* **ABC Taxis**, ☎ *(02) 9897-4000* and **RSL Cabs**, ☎ *(02) 9581-1111.*

The city's international and domestic airports are officially called Kingsford Smith, named for Australia's greatest early aviation pioneer. They are also lumped under the name of Mascot Airport, named for the suburb where they are located. The international airport is fully equipped with bars, restaurants, shops and travelers' information. From the domestic airport, you can catch flights to all locations in the country. Flight information is available from individual airlines.

Tours

Where do you want to go and what do you want to do in and around Sydney? Ask and ye shall receive. Some examples:

Australian Pacific Tours ★★★

In Sydney, takes you on a one-day trip that includes a stop at the Featherdale Wildlife Park outside the city (home to the more-or-less famous Qantas koala); a cruise on a Captain Cook luncheon excursion; a tour of all the city sights, including a stop at Bondi Beach, and a ride on the monorail followed by a tour of Darling Harbour. The tour (meals not included) is about A$70 per person. Or for about the same money, you can do the north beaches, The Rocks, Sydney sights, Bondi and Darling Harbour. Or you can sign up for a bunch of other options, including some tours that go to the Blue Mountains or the Hawkesbury River. For the racier, there's a night tour of the city, with dinner and admission to a strip club for about A$90 per person. To book tours or get information, stop in at any Sydney travel agency or call ☎ *(02) 9252-2988,* 24 hours a day.

Similar tours are offered by **Great Sights South Pacific**; see a travel agent or call ☎ *(02) 9241-2294.* If your time in Sydney is limited and you're not driving, one of these tours might be the thing.

Climate

Reversed, remember. Summer here is winter there. In the warm months (December-February), average high temperatures are normally around 70 to 75 degrees Fahrenheit. Fall (March-May), highs are around 60-70 degrees. Winter (June-August), highs around 50-60 degrees. Spring (September-November), highs around 60-70 degrees. Fall and winter tend to be rainy.

Services

Banks

There is a **Westpac Bank** bureau de change on the ground floor at Kingsford Smith International Airport that stays open until the last flight has arrived at night and opens at 6 in the morning. Major banks will cash foreign traveler's checks (mostly for a fee). Banks are normally open 9:30 a.m.–4 p.m. Monday–Thursday, 9:30 a.m.–5 p.m. Fridays. Some change bureaus are open longer.

Post Offices

The main post office in Sydney is located on Martin Place between Pitt and George Streets. You can buy stamps or make international telephone calls 24 hours a day, seven days a week. *Information:* ☎ *(02) 9230-7122* or *(02) 9230-7593.* A postcard to the United States or Canada is about A$1; a letter goes for around A$1.25.

Shopping

Stores in Sydney are generally open from 9 a.m. to 5:30 p.m. Monday-Friday; until 9 p.m. Thursday; Saturday 9 a.m.–4 p.m.

As befits a city of its size, Sydney has a store for every interest and every pocketbook. There are intimate boutiques, huge department stores, open markets and duty-free shops. The places that don't take major credit cards are rare; there are a few, however, that won't take American Express cards. With Visa or MasterCharge you won't have any problems. (Even some taxi drivers will take Visa.)

Most visitors would like a chance to pick up a piece of Australiana, and there are a number of stores specializing in Aussie works. There's also a fair amount of junk floating around. Aboriginal art is coming into its own, meaning the prices are going up. The moral is that if the price is cheap, the goods probably are, too. Aboriginal art, even in the Outback, is not inexpensive any more. In Sydney, in addition to the stores we mentioned in the Rocks section, try the **Hogarth Gallery Aboriginal & Tribal Art Centre** at *7 Walker Lane in Paddington.* Hours are 11 a.m.–5 p.m. Tuesday-Saturday (or special visits by appointment). *Information:* ☎ *(02) 9360-6839.*

Major Shopping Centers In The Downtown Area

Centrepoint

Corner of Market and Pitt Streets. ☎ *(02) 9229-7444.*
Site of the tower, jewelry, upscale fashions, about 200 shops.

MLC Centre

Corner of King and Castlereagh streets, next to Martin Place. ☎ *(02) 9231-6411.*
Leather goods, lots of fast food places. Open to 5 p.m. Saturdays.

Strand Arcade

George Street between King and Market streets.
A Victorian (1833) shopping complex. Lovingly restored with wrought iron and one of the nicest places in town to browse. Some of the city's top clothing designers hang their wares here.

Rocks Centre

18 Argyle Street.
The main shopping arcade in The Rocks. Knicks and knacks, glass, porcelain, lots of souvenirs. Also in the Rocks is Clocktower Square, part of a renewal area off Argyle Street. There are duty-free shops, restaurants and souvenir shops, including Everything Australian (wide selection of Australiana) and The Rocks Opal Mine.

Queen Victoria Building

The QVB is centrally located, occupying a whole city block on George Street across from the Hilton and near the Town Hall. ☎ *(02) 9264-1955.*
Probably the most picturesque shopping area in Sydney and one of the best in the world, for that matter. The QVB, as it's called, is a small miracle unto itself. It was built in 1893 to celebrate the diamond jubilee of Queen Victoria, and was designed to be a marketplace. Things didn't work out, and for years the old heap was boarded up and became a major downtown eyesore. The city dads decided to tear it down in the 1950s, but saner heads prevailed. The building, purchased and restored by a Malaysian company, is a wonder, complete with some of the nicest Victorian frippery you'll ever see. One of its most striking features is the central dome, which rises 200 feet from the ground floor. A major tourist attraction in the QVB is the Royal Clock, suspended from the ceiling, which marks the hours by showing scenes from English history: King Canute stopping the waves, the Battle of Hastings, Henry and his six wives, etc. The QVB contains about 200 stores, from Chinese restaurants to Aboriginal art dealers. Fast food available 24 hours.

Major Department Stores In Downtown Sydney Include:

DJL Limited (formerly David Jones)

Two locations, at the corner of Market and Elizabeth Streets and the corner of Market and Castlereagh Streets. ☎ *(02) 9265-5544.*

DJL is most often compared to London's Harrods; the Elizabeth Street store specializes in women's clothing. There are branch stores in Bankstown, Bondi Junction, Parramatta, Brookvale and Campbelltown.

Grace Brothers

436 George Street; ☎ *(02) 9238-9111.*

Not as prestigious as DJL, but still up to its cavern sized floors with goods; friendly staff. There are branches all over the Sydney metro area. The downtown store has entrances on George, Pitt and Market Streets.

Skygarden

77 Castlereagh, Pitt Street Mall; ☎ *(02) 9231-1811.*

Upscale designers housed in an award-winning shopping mall. Check out the Venetian glass tiles at the main door. Food on the premises. Open seven days.

Woolworth's

Corner of George and Park streets; ☎ *(02) 9264-1927.*

Just what you'd expect. Good place to replace stuff lost or broken on the trip.

Duty-Free Shops

Duty-free shops are available to tourists who have proof they are tourists. Officially, you're supposed to show them a return air ticket, but flashing a passport usually works as well. Some of the prices are about what you'd pay back home, but they do have tons of souvenirs of the stuffed-kangaroo variety and the normal booze-perfume-electronics-camera counters you'd expect. Among the stores are:

Downtown Duty Free

84 Pitt Street; ☎ *(02) 9221-4444.*

One of the largest, with a wide selection of Australian opals; camera equipment. Another outlet at the Sydney International Airport, ☎ *(008) 807-127.*

Orbit Duty Free

74 Pitt Street, ☎ *(02) 9233-8399 and 276 Pitt Street,* ☎ *(02) 9267-2159.*

Where to Stay

One of the best views of Sydney Harbour is also one of the most expensive: looking out the windows of one of the pie-shaped corner rooms high atop the **Regent of Sydney**—the Opera House on your right, the Harbour Bridge on your left, the wide expanse of the harbor on both sides and far, far below, the Rocks. It might be one of the best A$400-a-night vistas on the planet.

But the venerable Regent is having a lot of competition from some new kids on the block, one of which, the Quay West, arguably has even better views than the Regent. In fact, there are several new hotels in the Rocks and near-harbor area that have raised the level of Sydney hotels to true international standards. Add to that the smaller, so-called boutique hotels in the area, and there's a hotel for every taste and pocketbook. There are some very nice, relatively inexpensive inns scattered around the harbor for those on a

NEW SOUTH WALES

tighter budget. *Many of the area hotels, even the top-grade five-stars, often have special packages or weekend rates; always ask.* The number of first-class hotels makes it tough to pick a favorite, but among the Rocks-area five-stars, you can't go wrong trying Quay West, the Ana, the Regent or the Observatory, all excellent, all within walking distance of the harbor attractions. As for the more budget-priced hotels, we'd recommend the Russell Hotel, the Stafford or the Harbor Rocks.

Regent of Sydney   A$220–2000

199 George Street, ☎ *(02) 9238-0000; FAX (02) 9251-2851.*
City view rooms start around A$220; harbor views around A$350; suites up to A$2000.
Despite the competition, still the hotel in Sydney by which all others are measured. Impeccable service, delightful and decadent rooms. It's home to **Kables**, one of the best restaurants in the city. Health club, pool, business reference library, telex, fax, secretarial service.

Observatory, The   A$250–1200

89-113 Kent Street; ☎ *(02) 9256-2222.*
The basic room rate starts around A$250, with suites ranging between A$350 and A$1200.
One of Sydney's newest hotels, the Observatory is so named because it sits near Observatory Hill. It's operated by the Orient-Express Hotels group. It has 100 rooms plus more than 20 suites. It's awash with marble and wood paneling, modeled, they say, on an opulent 19th-century grand Australian home. The formal dining room is the Galileo, and Asian fare is offered up in The Orient Cafe. Rooms come with VCRs and CD players, opulent bathrooms and several phone lines. The decor, service and amenities make up for the lack of a decent harbor view. The health club, with a magnificent Roman-style indoor pool, is one of the best in the city.

Quay West   A$260–1300

98 Gloucester Street; ☎ *(02) 9240-6000.*
Harbour view, one-bedroom suites start at $A260; two-bedroom suites start at A$430, and penthouses (stunning) start at A$1300 for a harbor view.

The best hot-tub view in the South Pacific might be from the Pool Terrace at Quay West: sip a champagne, soak the bod and look out over the Harbour Bridge. In fact, the pool area is our favorite in Sydney, only rivaled by the Observatory. Quay West is simply splendid, all brass and glitter. The rooms, all suites, are truly opulent, with separate sitting rooms, washing machines and dryers (yahoo), entertainment centers and dishwashers in addition to mini-bars and gorgeous bathrooms.

Ana   A$300–510

176 Cumberland Street; ☎ *(02) 9250-6000.*
Harbor view rooms start at A$300; suites range from A$350-3000 and executive floor rooms range from A$350–510.
We think the Ana, splendid as it is, is just a step down from Quay West. The rooms, health club and service are easily five star, but compared to the dazzle of Quay West, the hotel is close, but no cigar. The Ana has 10 restaurants and bars, and several of these are housed in restored historic buildings joined to the hotel. **Lilyvale**, an 1845 residence, is one example. The hotel's executive floor is quite classy, with a very nice harbor view from the lounge, and the hotel has an excellent business center.

Old Sydney Park Royal   **A$270+**   ★★★★

55 George Street; ☎ *(02) 9252-0524; FAX (02) 9251-2093.*
Doubles start at A$270.
Excellent location in the Rocks, housed in a brick building, within walking distance
of the Harbour Bridge and the Opera House. A special delight is the eight-story-
tall, plant-shrouded atrium. There is an art-bedecked lobby, heated rooftop pool
garden with a tremendous view of the area; spa and sauna. The **Playfair** bar/brasse-
rie is a favorite local hangout.

Park Hyatt Sydney   **A$440–600**   ★★★★

7 Hickson Road; ☎ *(02) 9241-1234.*
Standard doubles (no balcony) from about A$440; harbor view with balcony, A$490;
suites from A$600.
A scenic location, set in a half curve at water's edge underneath the Sydney Harbour
Bridge. The decor is marble and air, with great views of the Opera House. The views
from the rooftop pool are nice, too (but the pool is often in the shade). Some rooms
have views of the city, the Opera House or the harbor. There's a health center, two
restaurants and popular harborside bar; butler service on every floor. It does tend to
be a tad noisy in the outside areas because of trains and traffic on the Harbor Bridge.

Russell, The   **A$105–230**   ★★

143a George Street, The Rocks, ☎ *(02) 9241-3543.*
There are 17 rooms with shared facilities. Shared bath from about A$105; doubles with
baths, depending on view, A$160–200; apartments and suites to around A$230.
One of the best locations in the Rocks—lean out your hotel window and watch the
world go by on George Street. The harbor view is partially blocked by the Museum
of Contemporary Art, but the central location is a plus. The Russell, delightful as it
is, has two drawbacks: it's on the second floor of the building (some rooms on the
third), so it's a long way to haul luggage; second, it sits above the Fortune of War
pub, which means it can be a tad noisy at night. If you don't absolutely require a
view, opt for one of the backside (Nurses Walk) rooms. Otherwise, one of the better
bargains in the area. Full continental breakfast included in the rates; have it in your
room or in the **Boulders** restaurant.

Harbour Rocks Hotel   **A$100–250**   ★★

34-52 Harrington Street; ☎ *(02) 9251-8944.*
Shared bathrooms from about A$100–125; doubles with private bath from A$165–185;
apartments and suites A$200–250.
Located a block up from George Street, the hotel is housed in a 100-year-old wool
store and workers cottages. It has had extensive renovation, and like the Russell, has
a range of facilities from shared baths to a luxurious penthouse. Very nice location,
away from the bustle of George Street. Two bars (one with live entertainment Fridays). It has handicapped facilities.

Stafford, The   **A$135–170**   ★★

75 Harrington Street; ☎ *(02) 9251-6711.*
Daily double rates start about A$170; one-bedroom penthouse, A$135.
Another restoration project, this one involving seven old terrace houses dating from
the 1870s and 1890s. The 50 or so units have been converted into studio and one-

bedroom apartments, most with balconies. They come with kitchens, TV and daily maid service. There is a guest laundry, pool, sauna, spa and mini-gym. Our only objection was the stale cigarette-smoke air in the lobby. Good bargain in a good location.

Mercantile, The   A$85–120   ★★

25 George Street; ☎ *(02) 9247-3570.*
Shared facilities are A$85 double; private baths for A$120.

This B&B hotel, built in 1914, has a stash of valuable green Art Nouveau tiles on its front, and was refurbished in the early 1990s. It's probably the best budget deal in the area. It has a bridal suite and an Irish pub, Molly Malone's, which is one of the best places in town to catch Irish music and Australian bush bands (the best groups play on weekends). Most of the rooms have shared facilities; four rooms have huge private bathrooms. There is a guest laundry.

Downtown

Sydney Hilton   A$330–500   ★★★

259 Pitt Street; ☎ *(02) 9266-0610.*
Doubles from about A$330; suites from A$500.

Probably the best central downtown location, right across from the QVB building, meaning next to major bus stops and shopping. On site is the famous **Marble Bar**, a restored Victorian saloon open at various hours and worth a look. The hotel normally has weekend packages that include dining and reduced room rates. The hotel is close to two monorail stops. Parking, restaurant, gym and sauna.

Sydney Renaissance   A$300–400   ★★★★

30 Pitt Street; ☎ *(02) 9259-7000.*
Doubles from A$300, suites from A$400.

Great location on Circular Quay with views overlooking the Opera House. The boxy building has been extensively renovated, one of the major jobs being a marble lobby with a three-story staircase and atrium. Among the hotel restaurants is **Raphael's**, with Asian-flavored offerings in a very nice venue. There is valet service, 24-hour room service, mini-bars, a gym, pool, sauna and nonsmoking floors.

Ritz-Carlton Sydney   A$200–485   ★★★★

93 Macquarie Street; ☎ *(02) 9252-4600; FAX (02) 9252-4286.*
Doubles begin at A$200–350; suites start at A$485.

Wood-paneled lobby, close to Botanic Gardens, the Opera House. Rooftop pool with fitness center and sauna, two restaurants, two bars. Marble bathrooms come with bathrobes; valet service and self-parking available.

Hotel Inter-Continental Sydney   A$230–450   ★★★★

117 Macquarie Street; ☎ *(02) 9230-0200; FAX (02) 9240-1240.*
Doubles from A$230; suites from $450.

(Pedestrian entrance at the corner of Phillip and Bridge streets). Part of the hotel is in the Old Treasury Building, built between 1899-1917. Large sandstone arches lead from the oval, tiled-floor lobby called the "Cortile" to a vaulted skylight. Rooms have views of the harbor, Opera House and Botanic Gardens. Pool, spa, gym, eight restaurants and bars, including one of our favorites eateries, **The Treasury**.

Holiday Inn Menzies   **A$180–350**   ★★★

14 Carrington Street; ☎ *(02) 9299-1000; FAX (02) 9290-3819.*
Room on the floor go for about A$300. Doubles A$180–300; suites from around
A$350.

Situated on Wynard Park near the Wynard rail station and close to a Sydney
Explorer stop. Five restaurants, four bars, pool, sauna, spa, valet parking, physician
on call. Weekend packages offer substantial savings on rooms and some include tickets to area attractions. The Executive Club floor offers concierge service with complimentary breakfast and evening cocktails and a private lounge.

Kings Cross Area

Landmark   **A$285–750**   ★★★

81 Macleay Street, Potts Point; ☎ *(02) 9368-3000.*
Doubles from about A$285; suites A$395–750.

Strategically located near The Cross. The hotel decor is pastels and washes, sterile
by some tastes, soothing to others. Good views of the harbor from the eastern side
of the Opera House. Two executive floors with private bar service and business
amenities. Great views from the Opera House suites. Swimming pool, underground
parking. Nonsmoking floor.

Sebel Town House of Sydney   **A$200–450**   ★★★★★

23 Elizabeth Bay Road, Elizabeth Bay; ☎ *(02) 9358-3244; FAX (02) 9357-1926*
Doubles A$200–235; junior suites A$450.

If you want to be near The Cross, or merely stay in one of the city's premier small
hotels, the Sebel is your best bet. It's a member of the Leading Hotels of the World
organization, and comes with views of both Elizabeth Bay and Rushcutters Bay.
Health club, elegant pool, parking. Larger-than-normal rooms. Courtesy limou-
sines to the central business district and North Sydney available Monday-Friday.
Several specials are normally offered, including one that includes a harbor view
room, English breakfast and dinner with Aussie wine for about A$300 double.

Gazebo Hotel Court   **A$130**   ★★★

2 Elizabeth Bay Road, Elizabeth Bay; ☎ *(02) 9358-1999.*
Doubles from A$130.

Another favorite, the Gazebo has some balcony rooms with views of the harbor.
The rooms are pastelish and airy; the suites large and well-appointed. The glass-
enclosed rooftop pool looks out over the harbor, as does the hotel bar. The hotel,
built in the form of a salt shaker, also has handicapped facilities, restaurant and parking. Close to the train station. A good bet.

Hyatt Kingsgate   **A$165–195**   ★★★

Kings Cross Road; ☎ *(02) 9356-1234, FAX (02) 9356-4150.*
Doubles from around A$165–195.

The hotel has undergone extensive remodeling, adding amenities to the rooms and
a new restaurant. The 10th-floor terrace and pool area offers good views of the harbor. Executive floor with breakfast and concierge service. Rooms are comfy. Good
location in the Cross.

Top of the Town   **A$160–200**   ★★

227 Victoria Street; ☎ *(02) 9361-0911; FAX (02) 9361-4972.*

NEW SOUTH WALES

Doubles A$160–200.
You can't get much more centrally located—the hotel is 200 yards from the Kings Cross train station. The rooftop pool has great views of the city and harbor, as do some of the balcony rooms. The deluxe rooms have private spas; special packages available during the holiday season. Parking, guest laundry.

Darling Harbour

Hotel Nikko   **A$165–1600**   ★★★

Sussex and Kings streets; ☎ *(02) 9299-1231.*
Doubles about A$165–185; suites A$245–1600.
With 645 rooms, the Darling Harbour Nikko claims to be the largest hotel in Australia, if you like large hotels. It's long on modern design, accompanied with great views of the harbor area. Available are underground parking and duty-free shops. It also has a nightclub, handicapped rooms and a good restaurant, the **Corn Exchange**. It's on the city side of Darling Harbour, not far from the Queen Victoria Building.

Parkroyal at Darling Harbour   **A$200–450**   ★★★

150 Day Street; ☎ *(02) 9261-4444; (02) 9261-8766.*
Doubles start about A$200; suites from A$450.
On the city side of the harbor, with good harbor and city views, close to Chinatown. The Parkroyal has some good weekend packages. Two restaurants, three bars. The emphasis is on business guests, and there is limited security parking available.

Furama Hotel Sydney (formerly the Metro Inn)A$115–165   ★★

64-76 Harbour Street; ☎ *(02) 9281-0400.*
Doubles start around $A115; suites from A$165.
Across from the Sydney Entertainment Centre and Chinatown, walking distance to Darling Harbour and next to a monorail station. The building is in an historic wool store. Nothing fancy, good comfortable, affordable hotel spaces in a good location; restaurant and undercover parking. (The staff speaks Cantonese.)

Novotel Sydney   **A$185**   ★★★

1 Darling Harbour; ☎ *(02) 9934-0000.*
Doubles start about A$185.
Located next to the exhibition centre with a well-stocked health area, free parking, tennis courts and good views of the harbor and the cityscape. The hotel, which looks like a truncated beehive, has become a Darling Harbour landmark. It's adjacent to a monorail station. Very good business center.

Airport Area

Sheraton Sydney Airport   **A$120–800**   ★★★

Corner of O'Riordan and Robey streets; ☎ *(02) 9317-2200.*
Doubles about $120–190; suites A$180–800.
Located close to both domestic and international terminals, with 24-hour room service, pool and sauna, health center and a variety of rooms from regular to royal suites. Flight details at the desk; regular airport shuttle service.

Sydney Airport Parkroyal   **A$120–300**   ★★

Corner of Bourke and O'Riordan; ☎ *(02) 9330-0600.*
Doubles from about A$120; suites from A$300.

Another good airport hotel also close to the terminal area with shuttle service as well as underground parking.

Manly

Manly Pacific Parkroyal   A$185–510   ★★★

55 North Steyne; ☎ *(02) 9977-7666; (02) 9977-7822.*
Doubles are A$220 ocean view, A$185 Manly view; suites A$395–510.
Down the Pacific Beach side of the Manly settlement, with great views of the ocean. Roof-top pool area as part of the health facilities. A lively nightclub, Dalley's, plus Nells Garden Restaurant. All rooms have balconies, some are Manly-city views. Many end-of-week packages.

Radisson Kestral   A$160–260   ★★★

8-13 South Steyne; ☎ *(02) 9977-8866.*
Normal doubles from A$160-260.
Another beachfront inn, this one a boutique hotel set in a grove of Norfolk pines. Two pools and health facilities, a nice beach dining area (Parasols on the Beach), free parking. Good weekend rates.

Manly Ocean Royal   A$110–215   ★★★

69-74 North Steyne; ☎ *(02) 9977-0099.*
Doubles in a two-bedroom range from A$110 to A$215. Weekly rates available.
Luxury furnished apartments on Manly Beach, probably the best of this type of lodging in Manly. Units are two- and three-bedrooms with kitchens, washer/dryers, balcony ocean views; parking, pool and some units with private spas. Price depends on either daily or weekly servicing.

Manly Waterfront Apartment Hotel   A$165–365   ★★★

1 Raglan Street; ☎ *(02) 9976-1000.*
Doubles A$165–365; weekly rates available.
Opposite the surfing beach, next to Ivanhoe Park. It has 25 rooms and 25 suites. Dinner and room service available. Swimming pool, parking, near a visitors center. Short walk to the wharf and Manly city center.

Furnished Apartments

An alternative to the hotel scene is to try a serviced apartment. These usually offer good prices, especially if you're going to be in town for a week or so. Basically what you get is a furnished apartment with hotel-style services. The best ones are located near downtown.

York Apartments   A$150   ★★★

5 York Street; ☎ *(02) 9210-5000.*
Daily doubles are about A$150; weekly rates A$850–950.
The York is pretty typical of the genre—you pick from one- and two-bedroom and studio units or a penthouse. The apartments are located about halfway between Darling Harbour and the downtown area. There is room service, a pool, restaurant/bar, handicapped access, parking; all units have balconies.

Some others worth a look are the **Savoy Apartments** on King Street ☎ *(02) 9267-9211* and the **Kingsleigh** apartments, also on King Street near the post office. ☎ *(02) 9299-1388.*

Where to Eat

One of the things that makes Sydney easy to take as an international destination is the wealth of restaurants and the wide variety of cuisines available courtesy of the open immigration that took place after World War II. Not surprisingly, given its location, many of the better places in town specialize in seafood, but there are also some really fine Aussie-style restaurants serving lamb, venison, buffalo and other national specialties, even kangaroo. Some of the best dining in the city is in the better hotels. But go ahead and explore; you're bound to find a few favorites of your own. You will find that as a general rule, prices in Sydney and Australia in general are good compared to the U.S. and Europe. You can eat very well in Sydney without spending a fortune, or you can go top drawer and drop a wad of money.

The Rocks Area

No 7. at the Park   **$$$**   ★★★

7 Hickson Road; ☎ *(02) 9241-1234.*
Lunch noon–3 p.m. Monday–Friday; dinner 6–10 p.m. Monday–Saturday.
In the Park Hyatt Sydney Hotel on the harbor below the Sydney Harbour Bridge. If you like stunning night views, accompanied by equally stunning food, this outdoor harborside terrace restaurant should do the trick. The food is described as "contemporary Sydney cuisine," which means there's a slight Pacific Rim flavor; but you can also order dishes with an Italian or South American influence—but the emphasis is really on seafood. Excellent Aussie wine cellar.

Kables, The   **$$$**   ★★★★

199 George Street; ☎ *(02) 9238-0000.*
Lunch noon–2:30 p.m. Monday–Friday; dinner 6:30–10:30 p.m. Tuesday–Saturday.
This is in the Regent of Sydney. Tasmanian rock lobster with caviar butter sauce? Grilled venison medallions with boneless quail? You get the idea. This always award-winning restaurant is one of the priciest in town, but if you want outstanding service, quality and decor, this is the place.

Waterfront Restaurant   **$$**   ★★★

27 Circular Quay; ☎ *(02) 9247-3666.*
Open for lunch and dinner seven nights.
The theme of this eatery is all maritime, from ships to wooden masts to overhead sails. Not far away, fishing boats unload fresh goodies for the restaurant, which is in sort of a contest with Sydney's most famous seafood restaurant, Doyle's. Try them both and you decide. The Waterfront has three floors of indoor and outdoor seating. The decor, depending on your tolerance for nautical motif, is maybe a bit gaudy but probably won't affect your appetite. Open for lunch and dinner seven days.

The Waterfront is one of three Sydney restaurants owned by the same company, the other one in The Rocks being the **Italian Village**, which, although just a bit heavy with Italiano motifs, is pretty good. There are lampposts and antiques strewn around, all imported from the Old Country. Good views of the harbor.

Lowenbrau Keller   **$**   ★★

18 Argyle Street; ☎ *(02) 9247-7785.*

Open early to late seven days.
A good place to haul in for a cold beer or German and Swiss style cuisine. Casual, full of tourists. Live oom-pah band on Friday and Saturday nights; Bavarian buffet at lunch daily.

Fish at the Rocks   **$$**   ★★★
29 Kent Street; ☎ *(02) 9252-4614.*
Lunch noon Monday–Friday; dinner from 6–9 p.m. Monday–Friday.
Near the Lord Nelson pub in the Observatory Hill neighborhood back of the Rocks. Small and intimate; nonsmoking, BYO (wine next door at the pub). Great seafood. Among the choices: calamari, barramundi, barbecued scallops with herb mayonnaise, good salads, excellent coffee.

Imperial Peking Harbourside   **$$**   ★★
15 Circular Quay West; ☎ *(02) 9247-7073.*
Lunch noon–3 p.m. seven days; dinner 6–11 p.m. Sunday–Thursday, 6 p.m.–midnight Friday and Saturday.
The Peking serves traditional northern Chinese food in standard Chinese surroundings, but being close to the waterfront, specializes in seafood. It has four tanks of live seafood on hand for the famished. Would you believe live abalones? Try the scallops and mud crabs with black bean sauce. Extensive wine list. And, here's a winner: the restaurant offers a courtesy bus from city hotels.

Bilson's   **$$$**   ★★★★
Upper level, Overseas Passenger Terminal; ☎ *(02) 9251-5600.*
Lunch noon–3 p.m. Sunday–Friday; dinner 6:30–10:30 p.m. seven days.
Sometime hangout for journos, great scenery, and always named as one of the better restaurants in Sydney, if not in the state. Game dishes are especially good, although the seafood ain't shabby; prices a tad high.

Doyle's at the Quay   **$$**   ★★★
Overseas Passenger Terminal, lower level, Circular Quay, ☎ *(02) 9252-3400.*
This is the younger brother of the original, internationally famous.

Doyle's   **$$**   ★★★
Over at Watsons Bay on South Head; ☎ *(02) 9337-2007.*
The Doyle family has been serving seafood for five generations. The Watsons Bay restaurant has been operating for more than a century. The Circular Quay restaurant is nowhere near as sexy as the one across the harbor, but it's still Doyle's, meaning platters of steamed shellfish, grilled John Dory, crabs and the famous Sydney rock oysters. Both restaurants are open for lunch and dinner seven days. To get to the Watsons Bay restaurant, call **Doyle's Water Taxi** at ☎ *(02) 9252-3400.* The taxis leave from the private dock (Number 6) starting at 11 a.m. and run until late at night. It's about A$10 for a round trip. The Circular Quay place (great scenery) is open for lunch from 11:30 a.m.–2:45 p.m. seven days; dinner 5:30–9:30 p.m. Monday–Saturday.

Downtown
Treasury, The   **$$$**   ★★★★
117 Macquarie Street; ☎ *(02) 9230-0200.*

Lunch noon–2:30 Tuesday–Friday; dinner 7–10:30 p.m. Tuesday–Saturday.
Located in the Intercontinental Hotel, the Treasury offers formal dining in an elegant Victorian-style dining room, complete with pianist and stately service. A specialty is an eight-course, fixed-menu lunch for those who wish to eat their way through an afternoon with oysters in sherry, clear quail soup and scallop salad. For dinner, you might try medallions of venison or maybe a lobster. The wine list matches the decor up to and including a bottle or two of Chateau Lafite-Rothschild 1900. Also has a wine bar, **Pierpont's**, with more moderate menus; daily specials plus wine by the glass. Reservations recommended.

Bridges   **$$**   ★★★★
4 Bridge Street; ☎ *(02) 9221-5862.*
Lunch noon–2:30 p.m. Monday–Friday; dinner 6–9 p.m. Monday–Friday.
Located in a classy old building, with Italian-flair cuisine with good veal and chicken dishes. Lot of pretheater business, good wine list.

Papillon   **$$$**   ★★★
71 York Street; ☎ *(02) 9262-2624.*
Lunch noon–3 p.m. Monday–Friday; dinner 6–9 p.m. Tuesday–Friday.
French cuisine using Australian seafood and fresh game. The restaurant is housed in a National Trust building, complete with high ceilings and a century-old cedar entrance. Especially noted for its fancy desserts; menu changes seasonally. Reservations recommended, even for lunch.

Sydney Tower Restaurants   **$$**   ★
Corner of Pitt and Market streets; ☎ *(02) 9233-3722.*
There are two revolving restaurants high above the city in the Sydney (or Centrepoint) Tower. The **Level 1** Restaurant is formal, with a la carte dining and full service. **Level 2** is cafeteria style. Neither one is especially economical, in fact, both come close to being a bit more than they're worth, but they are popular with tourists. You're paying for the view, of course.

Level 1 offers appetizers such as wild buffalo from the Northern Territory, scallops and prawns au vent, Sydney rock oysters and escargot. Main courses include rack of lamb, chicken cordon bleu and Queensland prawns. Counting appetizers, main course and dessert, look for a bill to run around A$60 per person, not counting wine. There's a A$20-per-person minimum and on Saturdays, a 10-percent surcharge for the increased labor costs, it says.

Level 1 is open for lunch from 11–3:30 Monday–Friday; dinner 5–11:45 p.m. Monday–Saturday; closed Sundays.

Level 2 offers fixed-price menus, normally three-course meals with coffee, tea or soft drink. The main courses are pretty basic fare: roasts, steaks, Asian food. The three-course menu runs between A$30 and A$40, wine extra. There is also a surcharge on weekends and holidays (those increased labor costs again).

Level 2 is open for lunch from 11 a.m.–3:30 p.m. Tuesday–Sunday; dinner 5–11:45 p.m., closed Mondays. Special rates for early dinner before 6 p.m.

Claudine's $$ ★★

Two locations, The Strand Arcade, 412 George Street, second floor, information *(02) 9233-3473; and Claudine's on Macquarie,* ☎ *(02) 9241-1749.*

Hours at both are the same: breakfast 7:30–11 a.m. Monday–Friday; lunch from noon Monday–Friday; dinner from 5:30 p.m. Monday–Friday.

These are both decent restaurants, specializing in such items as Snowy River trout, hot and cold seafood platters, racks of lamb, rich desserts. The Strand facility overlooks the Victorian opulence of the shopping arcade. Reservations needed for the Macquarie site, which is BYO wine only.

Corn Exchange $$ ★★★

In the Hotel Nikko Darling Harbour; *(02) 9299-1231.*

Open seven days, 6:30 a.m.–11 p.m.

Stylishly casual, skylight roof, seriously good food. Luncheon buffet, terrace seating.

Choys Jin Jiang $$ ★★

Level 2, QVB Building; ☎ *(02) 9261-3388.*

Lunch noon–3 p.m. daily; dinner 5:30–9:30 p.m. Sunday–Monday; 5:30–10:30 p.m. Tuesday–Thursday; 5:30–11:30 p.m. Friday–Saturday.

In 1899, there was a Chinese tearoom in the Queen Victoria Building. It went away, but has at long last been replaced by this Chinese offering. The decor is supposed to be a 1930s Shanghai dining hall. Great dumplings, drunken duck, prawns sauted in chiles. (Another Choys in the Haymarket area, same owner.)

Harry's Cafe de Wheels ℹ

1 Cowper Road, Woolloomooloo (no phone).

Open 7:30 a.m.–3 a.m. Monday–Thursday; 7:30 a.m.–5 a.m. Friday; 10 a.m.–5 a.m. Saturday; 10 a.m.–3 a.m. Sunday.

Gourmet Aussie meat pies? Hot dogs and pasties? First opened in 1945, this Sydney landmark is always busy; pie cart is a favorite with late-night Sydneysiders.

Jordan's Seafood Restaurant $$ ★★

197 Harbourside at Darling Harbour; *(02) 9281-3711.*

Lunch noon–3 p.m. Monday–Friday; dinner 6–10 p.m. Thursday; 6 p.m.–11 p.m. Friday; noon–11 p.m. weekends.

Inside or outside with views of the city skyline. All manner of seafood: bugs, rock oysters, barramundi, fresh catch of the day. Live jazz to help the digestion. Lunch and dinner seven days.

Sydney Cove Oyster Bar $

1 Circular Quay East; ☎ *(02) 9247-2937.*

A little spot down Writer's Walk near the Opera House. Fresh oysters and snacks, great harbor views. The Walk is worth a stroll. It honors such authors as Charles Darwin, Banjo Paterson, D.H. Lawrence, Jack London and Harry Lawson.

Kings Cross

Bayswater Brasserie $$ ★★

32 Bayswater Road; *(02) 9357-2749.*

Lunch noon–3 p.m. Monday–Friday; noon–5 p.m. weekends; dinner 3–11:15 p.m. Monday–Friday, 5–11:15 p.m. weekends. Sunday brunch 10 a.m.–noon.

The creation of well-known restaurateur Tony Pappas, the restaurant is known as a place for the local media to hang out. It's always busy, takes no reservations. The menu is unbelievably varied. Very popular and noted for its Sunday brunches.

Darley Street Thai $$

30 Bayswater Road.; ☎ *(02) 9358-6530.*
Lunch noon–2:30 p.m. Tuesday–Sunday; dinner 6:30–10:30 p.m. seven nights.
The second Thai restaurant opened by a noted Sydney chef, with Aussie goodies done up in the Thai manner: yabbies with lime and tamarind sauce, steamed snapper in lemon grass. Outdoor eating area.

Bombay Indian $$

33 Elizabeth Bay Road; ☎ *(02) 9358-3946.*
Mughlai and tandoori cuisine from the north of India—chicken, prawns, lamb. Vegetarian or meat curries as mild or hot as you like. One of several good Indian places in the Cross. Also try the **New Delhi Experience**, *229 Darlinghurst,* ☎ *(02) 9360-5623.* Or in Darlinghurst itself try the **Tandoori Palace**, *86 Oxford Street,* ☎ *(02) 331-7072.*

Around Town

Mulligans $$ ★★

137 Cleveland, Chippendale; ☎ *(02) 9699-5582.*
Dinner from 7 p.m. Tuesday-Sunday.
An Irish hangout, with meals served up with a background of fiddles and Ilian pipes. BYO. If you like Irish stuff, this does fine.

Lucio's Italian Restaurant $$ ★★★★

47 Windsor Street, Paddington; ☎ *(02) 9380-5996.*
Dinner Tuesday-Saturday 6:30–11 p.m.
As good as Northern Italian gets, with delightful offerings such as fish baked in a rock-salt mold, ravioli ranging from ricotta to ground veal. The restaurant is famous for its *fagioli* (prawns, beans and caviar) and homemade pastas.

Oasis Seros $$$ ★★★★

495 Oxford Street, Paddington; ☎ *(02) 9361-3377.*
Lunch Friday only, 12:30–2:30 p.m.; dinner Tuesday–Saturday 7–10 p.m.
Exquisite French food from an award-winning restaurant. Grilled, crumbled pig's trotters with shiitake mushrooms, glazed duckling with steamed ginger buns and a desert of grilled figs with ginger custard. Truly decadent.

Sails Harbourside $$$ ★★

McMahons Point, across the harbor from the Quay; ☎ *(02) 9955-5998 or (02) 9955-5793.*
Lunch daily; dinner Monday–Saturday.
Fabulous view of the bridge and downtown Sydney, inside or terrace dining. Pick live crayfish from a tank, nosh on John Dory, have some Aussie beef or lamb. You can drive over or take a ferry from the private dock (Number 6). Reservations recommended.

Manly

Armstrong's   **$$**   ★★

Manly Wharf shopping center; ☎ *(02) 9976-3835.*
Lunch noon–3 p.m. daily; afternoon teas 3–6 p.m. daily; dinner 6–10 p.m. daily.
Perched on a part of the wharf near the beach swimming area, Armstrongs has
inside and outside seating, and specializes in such dishes as roast lobster and ocean
trout in a creme freche sauce; great salads, daily specials.

Brazil Cafe   **$**   ★★

28 Belgrave Street; ☎ *(02) 9977-3825.*
Open for breakfast 9 a.m.–2 p m daily; dinner 6 11 p.m. daily.
Small but lively, with good food and fast service. Set menu for daily and seasonal
specials, with pastas, grilled foods and seafood the usual fare.

Belgrave Street, one of the main drags leading from the harbor area (go left as you
leave the wharf) is lined with many small and quite good ethnic restaurants. Try **Jerrys
Pizzeria**, **Cafe Tunis** and **Sahite's**.

Beyond Sydney

People, at least most sensitive people, cannot live by city alone and must,
from time to time, escape the noise and hydrocarbons for smaller and less
frantic scenes. New South Wales is filled with such oases of sanity, from the
vineyards of the Hunter Valley to the raw nothingness of the desert country
on the South Australia and Queensland borders.

If time is tight, however, there are many places of note outside the city
proper that can be done in a day or two.

The Blue Mountains

Before early explorers found a way across the Blues, these rolling mountains were a ter
rifying barrier to colonial expansion, part of the Great Dividing Range that runs along the
entire east coast of the continent. Even today, the steep mountains and heavily wooded
valleys in the Blues are not completely tamed. The mountains, mostly eroded sandstone,
get their name because, from a distance, minute oil droplets falling from the leaves in the
thick eucalyptus forests turn sunlight bluish-green.

The area became a popular summer retreat for Sydney's wealthy in the 1870s, and over
the years since, has become a major tourist spot served by daily train and bus service from
the city. (A train from the city to Katoomba is about A$20 round trip.) Driving, you take
the Great Western Highway (Parramatta Road in the city) or the Hume Highway, which
branches off Parramatta Road in the Sydney suburb of Ashfield.

Scenery

About 500,000 acres of the area are included in the Blue Mountains National Park,
which is filled with picnic spots, hiking trails and campgrounds. A gaggle of small resort
towns is scattered around, most of them on the rail line from Sydney to Bathurst. The
park abuts two other national parks, Wollemi and Kanangra Boyd, making the whole area

one of the largest protected areas in the country. Some of the once-grand housing is showing signs of wear, and some of the hotels and pubs are getting a tad grungy.

Still, the scenery and the cool air (crisp in the winter) are worth a day train trip or a longer visit. If you can't stay, just drive around and look at the scenery. If you're in the area in September and October, you're almost guaranteed a flower festival someplace. Try the *Leura Spring Garden Festival,* usually the second week in October; the annual *Spring Orchid Show* at Emu Plains the second week of September; the *Medlow Bath Bushfire Brigade Garden Festival* the first week of October; and the *Blackheath Rhododendron Festival* at Blackheath the last week of October.

Your first stop in the Blue Mountains should be **Katoomba**, the major town. If you're not averse to heights, check out the **Katoomba Scenic Skyway**, a cable car that dangles over the chasms of the Jamison Valley. The companion ride, almost as hairy, is the **Katoomba Scenic Railway**, a cog-rail beauty that drops at incredible angles into the valley. ☎ *(02) 4782-2699.*

At Katoomba is one of the Blue Mountains' most famous vistas, the **Three Sisters**, a set of sandstone columns stepping into the valley. If not driving, you can reach most of the scenic spots on the **Blue Mountains Explorer Bus**, which makes 18 stops on weekends and holidays. You can book the bus and pick it up at **Golden West Tours**, *283 Main Street, Katoomba;* ☎ *(02) 4782-1866.* Golden West Tours also runs special buses and four-wheel drive trips. In addition to the more staid excursions, a number of companies also offer rock-climbing, camping, horseback riding and other specialty trips in the park such as bike tours and photographic workshops.

Activities

The Blues are a hiker's paradise. Here you will find the so-called Six-Foot Track, the first recreational walking trail in Australia, dating from the 1880s. The whole trail is about 26 miles, and traverses forests and rivers. The trail runs from Katoomba to the Jenolan Caves. Probably the best way to do the trail is with **Walk Australia**, a company that has walking treks all over New South Wales. The Six-Foot Track trip takes three days, with stops at campgrounds. The normal cost is about A$300 per person; the company will arrange to pick you up at the train. Contact the company at ☎ *(02) 9555-7580.*

If you don't have time for a long trek, try these:

Three Sisters Walk—Starts at Echo Point in Katoomba, the place you definitely want to stand for a view of the Three Sisters. Takes about a half-hour, easy walk. Toilet facilities.

Boars Head Rock—Start at Cahill's Lookout on Cliff Drive in Katoomba. Just a kilometer round trip. Great views, picnic areas.

Round Walk—Start at the Katoomba information kiosk on Cliff Drive. About a kilometer round trip, with views of rainforest, waterfalls, birds. Toilet facilities.

Fairfax Heritage Track—Handicapped and wheelchair friendly trail about four kilometers round trip. It starts at the parks and wildlife center on Govetts Leap Road in Blackheath. The trail is lined with interpretive markers, designed for wheelchair users. Easy walk with birds, waterfalls, toilet facilities.

For the more strenuous and/or those with a bit more time:

Scenic Railway Track—Follow the path used by shale and coal miners a century ago. About 12 kilometers round trip. Super views, rainforest, moderate hike. Toilets. Or try the more strenuous **Furber Steps Trail**, a 14-kilometer trek into the gullet of the mountains past a rock formation called the Ruined Castle. Both trails start at the Scenic Railway office near Katoomba Falls.

Springwood Track—This medium-grade hike is about 10 kilometers around, with waterfalls, lots of birds, downs and ups near the Sassafras Reserve. The trail starts in Springwood, east of Katoomba.

Mount Victoria—Strenuous six-kilometer hike through open forest and past some really great waterfalls. Picnic and toilet facilities. Starts at the Victoria Falls lookout northeast of Katoomba. Near the trailhead is **One-Tree Hill**, the highest point in the Blue Mountains—3645 feet.

All the trails in the Blues are subject to sudden weather shifts, avalanches and trail blockages. Before taking off a long trail, check with the **National Park and Wildlife Service**. The NPWS main office in the mountains is at the *Heritage Centre on Govetts Leap Road, Blackheath* ☎ *(02) 4787-8877*.

Other interesting activities in the Blues include such diversions as:

Harley-Davidson cycle tours with **Cliff Edge Cruisers** in Leura; the package includes all riding equipment and clothes, pickup and returns and costs about A$40 per tour. ☎ *(02) 4782-4649*.

A cruise in the Nepean Gorge in the foothills of the Blue Mountain National Park on a paddlewheeler called the **Nepean Belle** ☎ *(02) 4733-1274*. A variety of cruises, some including meals. Prices range from about A$12 to about $A25 for a luncheon cruise or about A$30 at night when the boat becomes a floating restaurant. You board the boat at Tench Avenue in Penrith.

Lithgow, basically a coal-mining and industrial town, is the site of the famous **Zig Zag railway**, built in the late 1860s to allow trains to descend from the Blue Mountains to the Bathurst plains and, with its series of switchbacks and bridges, a real engineering marvel. The route has been restored and special steam trains run on weekends and periodically during school holidays. Information on times and fares is available from Golden West Tours in Katoomba. During the week, a diesel engine is used; on weekends and holidays, a steam engine is in operation. ☎ *(02) 6351-4826*.

Where to Stay

You will find the usual array of resort accommodations in the Blue Mountains communities, from motels to upscale hotels. The good people of the region, in a plan that should be adopted by all civilized nations, have set up a "duty motel" program: weekly, one Blue Mountains hotel or motel is designated to help visitors seeking accommodations. The name and number of the duty hotel is listed at the tourist information center at Echo Point in Katoomba.

One of the more famous Blue Mountain hangouts is an old yellow heap called the **Hydro Majestic ★ ★**, ☎ *(02) 4788-1002*, located in Medlow Bath just to the north of

Katoomba. The Majestic, built in 1904, was the queen in its day, and is a reminder of how the swells from Sydney used to hang. The hotel probably attracts as many sightseers as it does guests. It has good views of the Megalong Valley; package rates for all meals available. There are a pool and tennis courts, and three golf courses are nearby. It's a good place for Devonshire tea, a fixture in the area: tea, scones, jam, polite chats. Rates are around A$120 a night double including breakfast.

We think the absolute best and most genteel spot in the Blues is **Lilianfels** ★ ★ ★ ★ ★ ☎ *(02) 4780-1200; FAX (02) 4780-1300,* an 1890s estate in Katoomba overlooking the Jamison Valley. The hotel sits on two acres of English-style gardens, and offers great afternoon teas or a round or two of croquet. It comes with an indoor swimming pool (superlative views) and health center, tennis courts, plus a lovely bar, the Lobby Lounge, and two restaurants, including **Darleys** ★ ★ ★, one of the best in the mountains. Darleys leans toward European provincial, with offerings such as tartar of brook trout. Do ask for the famous chocolate marmalade souffle. Lunch and dinner, Wednesday-Sunday; fixed price menu available Sundays. Because it was once a private home, the resort's 86 rooms come in all sizes and shapes, up to and including suites. All suites have spas. The most exclusive digs are in the Cottage Suite, housed in the former servant quarters. It comes with a private spa, fireplace, antique furniture and a tremendous view. The Cottage Suite goes for A$700 a night. Standard doubles with breakfast and dinner midweek start at A$320; weekends with breakfast start at A$270 a night (minimum two nights). Suites without meals start at A$400. Meal service to units available. North America bookings, ☎ *(800) 525-4800.*

Katoomba is also home to another good choice, the **Mountain Heritage Country House Retreat** ★ ★ ★, ☎ *(02) 4782-2355; FAX (02) 4782-5323.* It's basically a cozy place with stained glass, stunning valley views and a licensed restaurant and piano bar. All rooms have private facilities; there are also one-bedroom suites with spa baths and fireplaces. Also available are a billiards room, swimming pool and gardens. Standard rooms with breakfast are A$70–90 Monday–Thursday, A$80–105 weekends; suites are A$150–175.

Worth a shot is the **Fairmont Resort** ★ ★ ★ ★, ☎ *(02) 4782-5222; FAX (02) 4784-1685.* It's located in Leura, just next to Katoomba. The Fairmont, also sitting above the Jamison Valley, has a wide range of athletic activities available, and is next to an 18-hole golf course. The resort, which looks like your average modern country club, is kid-friendly with weekend activities for the youngsters. There are two pools, tennis courts, squash courts, billiards room, aerobic classes, a massage center and a tour desk for bushwalking, horseback trips or other activities. There are several restaurants, a cocktail bar with great views and a weekend disco. Several of the suites have private spas. Package deals available. Midweek standard doubles start around A$155; weekends about A$200.

A very popular attraction in the Blue Mountains area is the **Jenolan Caves**, about 50 miles southwest of Katoomba, a large system of limestone caverns discovered in 1841 that were the home of Aboriginals for centuries. The most popular caves are lighted and have stairs for easy walking; others require a guide. The caves, open every day, cost about A$10; tours take about an hour and a half. ☎ *(02) 6359-3311; FAX (02) 6359-3307.*

You couldn't do any better from a quaint hotel point of view than by trying a night or two at the **Jenolan Caves House** ★★★ ☎ *(02) 6359-3304; FAX (02) 6359-3227.* Here we have a classy old Tudor-style resort hotel less than 50 yards from the cave entrances. The recently renovated lodge was begun in 1889 and built in stages. Today it offers 100 rooms, some with private facilities. Also on the grounds, surrounded by the 900-acre caves park, is a 28-unit lodge, all with private facilities. There is a large dining room in the Caves House, and in the afternoons, complimentary wine and cheeses. Room rates include breakfast and dinner (two-night minimum) Two-night doubles with private facilities in the main resort are A$300; weekends A$500; lodge rates, which also include breakfast and dinner, start around $A200 for two nights.

Information

General information about the Blue Mountains is available from the **Travel Centre of New South Wales** in Sydney at *19 Castlereagh;* ☎ *(02) 9231-4444.* There are two main tourist information centers in the mountains: **Glenbrook**, on the Great Western Highway ☎ *(02) 4739-6266, FAX (02) 4739-6787,* and **Echo Point** at Katoomba, ☎ *(02) 4782-0756.* The Katoomba facility is open 9 a.m.–5 p.m. daily; Glenbrook 8:30 a.m.–5 p.m. Monday-Saturday, 8:30 a.m.–4:30 p.m. Sunday. Brochures and general information are also available from the **Blue Mountains Tourism Authority**, *P.O. Box 273, Katoomba, New South Wales 2780;* ☎ *(02) 4739-6266.*

Among **bus companies** offering day tours are: **Fantastic Aussie Tours**, *323 Castlereagh Street, Sydney* ☎ *(02) 9281-7100;* **Great Sights South Pacific**, *Circular Quay West, Sydney,* ☎ *(02) 9241-2294;* **Clipper Tours**, *9 11 Alma Road, North Ryde, Sydney,* ☎ *(02) 9888-3144;* **Blue Mountains Sightseeing**, *283 Main Street, Katoomba,* ☎ *(02) 4782-1866;* and **Australian Pacific Tours**, *109 O'Riordan Street, Mascot,* ☎ *(02) 9252-2988.* To give you an idea what to expect, one of Great Sights trips leaves from Circular Quay around 9 a.m., tours most of the major spots in the mountains, and returns to the city by 5:30 p.m. The cost is about A$55. These companies normally offer a range of activities on their tours for an extra cost, including four-wheel-drive treks.

National Parks

There are 65 national parks in the state (including the **Blue Mountains**). Two others close in to Sydney are **Royal National Park** and **Ku-ring-gai Chase National Park**. Entry fees for most national parks is around A$8 per car. Information about parks in New South Wales, as well as any national parks in the country, is available from the National Parks and Wildlife Service, *189 Kent Street, Sydney;* ☎ *(02) 9237-6500.*

Royal National Park

Always a favorite, the 37,000-acre park was devastated in January 1994 when it was virtually destroyed in a bush fire. Thousands of animals, especially koalas, died in the blaze, which destroyed more than 90 percent of the park. A large colony of rare black-winged bats were also lost in the fire. More than 20,000 people fled their homes in the fire, which also heavily damaged one of the best hiking areas in New South Wales, Morton National Park. Most of the Royal Park is now open to visitors, and there are tours run by the National Park Service to show folks how the park is recovering—by some estimates, it will take 500 years before it's back to its pre-blaze status. The tours, run on Monday, Tuesday, Thursday and weekends, are A$10 per person; bookings available by calling ☎ *(02) 9542-0666*. Royal National Park became, in 1879, the second national park in the world (Yellowstone was created a year earlier). The park, about 20 miles south of Sydney, sits on a peninsula just below Botany Bay.

Ku-ring-gai Chase National Park offers many hiking trails.

Ku-ring-gai Chase National Park

A watery park about 25 miles north of Sydney in the Hawkesbury River delta. About 18 months before the great bush fires, park officials had a controlled burn in the park, a major koala habitat. Because of the burn, the park was not affected by the later fires. There are many hiking trails in the park, and boats can be hired by the day, no license required. You can also rent a houseboat for a week; rates range from around A$500 in the off-season to around A$1200 in the summer. Check with the Travel Centre of New South Wales for rental agencies. The park headquarters is reached by taking the Ku-ring-gai Chase Road turnoff from the Pacific Highway. The Pacific Highway starts in North Sydney across the Sydney Harbour Bridge. The park is also accessible by train.

A cushy way to check out the park area is to hop the mail boat tours run by **AAT King's Tours**. There are two one-day tours, which take passengers through the many inlets on the river with passing views of animal life; on some, you stop at a wildlife sanctuary. Tours depart Sydney and you board the mail boat, the last such service in Australia, at Brooklyn on the river. The cruises are two hours long. Depending on itinerary, the cost is about A$75 per person. The company is at the corner of Alfred Street and No. 6 Wharf at Circular Quay, ☎ *(02) 9252-2788, 24 hours*. **Float planes** can also fly you in for the day. Try **Vic Walten** at *Aquatic Airways Ltd., Berrenjoy Boathouse, Governor Phillip Park, Palm Beach*, ☎ *(02) 9919-5638*. The national park office: ☎ *(02) 9457-9853*.

The Coasts

The basic dividing line between the upper and lower coasts of New South Wales is Sydney Harbour, but you have to go a fair distance either direction to get out of the Sydney suburbs. The entire coastline is about 500 miles long. From the Hunter River north, it is basically semitropical. South of Sydney, Highway 1, the major coastal route, is known as Princes Highway; north of the city it's called the Pacific Highway. The highway system, usually called "Australia One," runs from northern Queensland around the continent to Western Australia.

Sydney to Tweed Heads

To the north, you are officially out of the Sydney metropolitan area once you pass the Hawkesbury River. Starting about 50 miles north of the city, the coastline encloses several large and popular lakes as it runs north, including **Tuggerah Lake**, **Lake Macquarie** and **Myall Lakes**.

An oceanside road runs up along the barrier islands separating Tuggerah from the sea. A long, narrow, and mostly deserted beach runs from the Entrance, a channel between the lake and the ocean, to Norah Head. You'll find **hotels** and **motels** all around the shores, with **cafes** and **restaurants** specializing in fresh seafood.

Lake Macquarie, the largest saltwater lake in the country, lies to the west of the Pacific Highway. The lake is four times larger than Sydney Harbour and is a major beach resort area for the central coast. One of the most famous spots on the lake is the village of **Wangi Wangi**, a mining village with dandy old architecture. Two major settlements on or near the lake, **Swansea** and **Newcastle**, offer accommodations and a wide variety of water activities including sailing, boat hires and fishing. The beaches in the area are very decent.

The sprawling industrial city of **Newcastle** is the seventh-largest city in Australia. It was here in early 1990 that Australia had a rare and very upsetting earthquake that leveled a number of buildings and killed several people. So rare are such incidents that locals thought a bomb had gone off or a plane had crashed. The city this century has basically been a company town for BHP, the giant Aussie conglomerate, which set up steel mills here. Despite this, there have been some comparisons between Newcastle and San Francisco because of hills with stately houses that run down to the harbor. The city is a gateway to the coal fields and vineyards of the Hunter Valley, which runs inland from the harbor along the Hunter River.

Just to the north of Newcastle is **Port Stephens**, one of the largest deepwater ports in Australia, known for great oysters, wildflowers, good fishing and pleasant beaches. The main settlement in the harbor is **Nelson Bay**. Cruises and fishing charters are available, and there is a golf course. A recommended hotel is the **Anchorage Port Stephens ★★**, a cozy nest on Corlette Point Road where every room has a sea view. The loft suites are especially nice, and on-site dining is very good at **Merrett's Restaurant**. All manner of beach and sea activities are available. Rates for doubles run between A$190 and $210 depending on season, with suites starting at A$260. ☎ *(02) 4984-2555; FAX (02) 4984-*

0300. The visitors center in Port Stephens is at Victoria Parade, Nelson Bay; ☎ *(02) 4981-1579.*

Just across the narrow harbor entrance from Nelson Bay is **Hawks Nest**, a small resort village with a golf course and several RV parks. Hawks Nest also marks the southern tip of a 25-mile-long beach that goes up the coast to **Seal Rocks**. There's a great beach at Seal Rocks, which is also a usually promising whale watch area. Right next door is the quaintly named settlement of **Tea Gardens**, which has accommodations.

The beach is part of **Myall Lakes National Park**, 77,000 acres in size and one of the best in the state. The shoreline areas of the park are lined with paperbark trees and palms, and the lakes and interior parklands are home to black swans, egrets and ducks, plus the usual assemblage of kangaroos, bandicoots and swamp wallabies. Unlike Lake Macquarie, Myall Lakes are freshwater, and stretches of the interior shore are rainforest. One way to enjoy the area is to take a **cruise** up the Myall River. **Boats** can be rented or booked at Tea Gardens or Bulahdelah, on the Pacific Highway. Canoe-camping trips are also available. A good bet for activities in Myall Lakes area is **Eco-Escapes**, a company that runs several bushwalking trips on the excellent Mungo Track, as well as canoe and offshore island trips. Two-day track trips are about A$220, including meals and equipment. *Information:* ☎ *(02) 4997-0573.* For general information about the area, contact *Superintendent, National Parks and Wildlife Service, 28 Sturgeon Street, Raymond Terrace 2324;* ☎ *(02) 4987-3108.*

The twin towns of **Forster** and **Tuncurry**, a few miles north of Myall Lakes, lie across Wallis Lake from each other. The area, popular for water sports, is also known for its seafood, especially prawns. **Taree**, a few miles farther north, is the agricultural center for the valley of the Manning River. For naturalists, there is a rainforest near town that is famous for its flying foxes, the huge Australian fruit bats that come out at night in masses to hunt.

About 45 miles north of Taree is the old penal settlement of **Port Macquarie**, which was set up in 1821 to take the worst felons from jails farther south, and had a reputation as one of the cruelest prisons in Australia. It's now a major tourist center with a fair amount of ticky-tacky amidst the old sandstone buildings of the colonial past; look for St. Thomas Church, built by the convicts. The beaches nearby are rated as excellent for surfing. Just south of town is **Sea Acres Sanctuary**, which has tropical rainforest displays, including 1000-year-old strangler figs. How popular a town it is you can judge by the fact that there are 18 RV parks and at least 40 motels.

By the time you get to **Macksville**, about 80 miles north of Port Macquarie, you know you've entered the tropics. The place is surrounded by banana plantations, and the houses are starting to take on Queensland attributes: they come with verandas and tinned roofs, and many are built on stilts, all developments designed to cool things off in the summer and stay dry in the winter rains.

The old timber port-gold rush town-dairy center of **Coffs Harbour** 40 miles north is a popular base for exploring this stretch of the coast and thus has a fair share of motels, pubs, and amusements. Tourist facilities are expanding rapidly as the area becomes more and more popular as a game fishing and water sports center. The visitors information center is located just off the Pacific Highway at the corner of Marcia and Rose streets; open 9 a.m.–5 p.m. seven days. ☎ *(02) 6652-1522; FAX: (02) 6652-5674*.

If you want to try a four-wheel-drive trek as we suggested in our driving section, with a guide and your own rental vehicle, contact **Coffs Harbour Mountain Trails 4WD Tours**. You just join one of the company's tours as a "tag-along." The route is not too hard and a good place for novice four-wheelers to practice. The tag-along cost is A\$70 per day per vehicle, meals included. You can also take a tour with one of the company's own vehicles and drivers. The cost is A\$60 per person and includes tea and a barbecue lunch. The company also runs less strenuous trips to the Dorrigo Plateau near Coffs Harbour, with an emphasis on forest walks and a trip to a deer farm and a gold mine; the price is about A\$55 per person. ☎ *(02) 6658-3333; FAX: (02) 6658-3299*. The nearby Nymboida River offers about 10 kilometers of good whitewater action. Try **Wildwater Adventures**, which has a one-day trip, including hotel pickup and meals, for about A\$110 per person. ☎ *(02) 6653-4469; FAX: (02) 6653-4469*.

Also, we should mention that it is not Americans alone who have carried the art of roadside attractions to the point of nausea. Consider, if you will, the Big Banana, a huge concrete thing stuck in the middle of a plantation as a monument to bad taste about three kilometers north of Coffs Harbour. Inside its startling form is a souvenir shop and here's the stopper: a display about the banana biz. Plantation tours and a look at a hydroponics farm are available. Not to be missed. ☎ *(02) 6652-4355*.

About 10 miles north is the **Coffs Harbour Zoo** where you can rent horses, look at 70 species of animals and try some bush tucker. There is local Aboriginal art, a rainforest aviary and a nocturnal house. Buses run regularly to the zoo. ☎ *(02) 6656-1330; FAX: (02) 6656-2155*.

One of the better places to stay in the Coffs Harbour area is the **Aanuka Beach Resort** ★★★★ at Diggers Beach just north of the city. The upscale suite bungalows are a la Fiji with spas in every unit, sundecks, a large outdoor pool with spa, two restaurants and the nearby beach. Doubles including breakfast start at \$A220. ☎ *(02) 6652-7555; FAX: (02) 6652-7053*.

Another good bet is the **Nautilus on-the-Beach** ★★, an upscale motel facility on the Pacific Highway near the town. Has a private beach and a nice pool area, plus a health facility and a restaurant/bar. Doubles A\$85; suites A\$135. ☎ *(02) 6653-6699; FAX: (02) 6653-7039*.

Inland, to the west of the Macksville-Coffs Harbour area, are several parks where you can see expanses of rainforest and the wee beasties that inhabit them. Included are **Dorrigo National Park**, a World Heritage subtropical rainforest with excellent hikes and many waterfalls and picnic areas, and **New England National Park**, which has the largest preserved area of rainforest in the state. Thirsty after a hike? Try the **Dorrigo Hotel** in Dorrigo, a National Trust building with food and icy beer. The best way to get to Dorrigo and both parks is by turning off at the Bellingen Road south of Coffs Harbour.

About 150 miles northwest of Coffs Harbour in the Outback is **Glen Innes**, a mountain foothill town, which was a bawdy bushranger town in the 19th century and is now a peaceful farming community. Glen Innes is due west of Grafton on Highway 38. Every

October there is a Bush Music Festival. Here you will also find one of our favorite tours in Australia, **Pub Crawls on Horseback**, a week-long riding trip that goes about 100 miles through the Glen Innes area, with overnight stays at pubs, plus cave exploring, bush barbecues and 4-by-4 treks. Perfect for the equestrian set—and those of us who like to explore Aussie pubs. The cost is about A$1000 per person. *Information: Bullock Mountain Homestead, Glen Innes,* ☎ *(02) 6732-1599.*

The **Clarence Valley**, 50 miles north of Coffs, is pasture country and its population center, **Grafton**, is a genteel old town famous for its late-Victorian architecture and streets lined with stands of jacaranda. Within driving distance are two coastal parks, the closest of which is **Yuragir National Park**, and a bit farther up, **Bundjalung National Park**, which has a fair population of emus, wallabies and koalas at the north end near Evans Head. Both parks have beaches, swimming and hiking.

The two main coastal towns north of Grafton are **Ballina** and **Byron Bay**. Ballina is situated at the mouth of the Richmond River and has a maritime museum. Byron Bay is the easternmost point of land on the continent, which is why there is an old lighthouse there, still working—and also the most powerful lighthouse in the country. It has one of the best surfing beaches in the nation.

The final stop on the coast before entering Queensland is the semitacky little settlement of **Tweed Heads**. Tweed Heads marks the beginning of one of the fastest growing tourist areas in the country, the so-called Gold Coast, that runs from Tweed Head's sister (and connected) city, Coolangatta, to Surfers Paradise near Brisbane.

South from Sydney

If you're heading south along the coast from Sydney, one place to stop, just for historical significance, is **Botany Bay**. It was here, you will recall, that Capt. James Cook landed in 1770 and so liked what he saw, that 20 years later, His Majesty's Government decided to send all of England's felons along to take a look, too. The only problem was when they arrived they discovered Botany Bay was worthless as a spot to start a colony and went north a few miles to what is now Sydney Harbour.

It might amuse the good captain to realize that Botany Bay is now the site of Sydney's international airport and its shores are lined by container ship docks. At any rate, there is a **park** on the spot where Cook and his party landed. It's on the south spit of land at the entrance to the bay in a suburb called Kurnell, reached from Princes Highway. To get there, go to Rocky Point Road, then to Captain Cook Drive. There are a museum, picnic area, and trails around the headland. The museum is open 10:30 a.m.–4:30 p.m. weekdays, 10:30 a.m.–5 p.m. weekends. The park actually contains two areas, the north and south headlands of the bay. North across the bay from the Captain Cook area is another part of the park containing a historical museum, an old fort site and an Aboriginal gallery. The park is open 7:30 a.m.–7 p.m., admission charge about A$5 per car. ☎ *(02) 9669-9923.*

The first major city south of Sydney is **Wollongong**, about 45 miles down, and the site of the state's largest steel plants. But there are also some fine beaches that draw Sydney-siders down by train on weekends. There are tours of the steel plants if you've a mind, and in **Mount Kembla Village**, an old coal-mining town west of the city, is a monument to the

1902 explosion that killed about 100 miners. The area's coal mines still produce millions of tons a year.

One of the most famous attractions in the area is the **Blowhole**, located at **Kiama**, 10 miles south of Wollongong. It was discovered by explorer George Bass in 1797, and if sea, surf, tide, and wind are right, it can spray a fountain almost 200 feet high.

Between Wollongong and Kiama, the Illawarra Highway (Route 48) runs west to **Morton National Park** in the highlands, a big park badly damaged in the Sydney bushfires. The park, 50,000 acres, is noted for deep gorges and waterfalls. Near the northwest corner of the park is Fitzroy Falls, which drops 250 feet. Nearby is the hamlet of **Kangaroo Valley**, which has a pioneer museum and tea rooms.

South of Kiama, the coast road heads inland to cross the Shoalhaven River estuary at **Nowra**. At **Berry**, a bit northeast of Nowra, a coastal access road runs east to **Seven Mile Beach National Park**.

To the southeast of Nowra on the coast are a group of **resort towns** centered around **Jervis Bay**, which has some of the best beaches on the whole New South Wales coast. For reasons that escape us, when the Australian Capital Territory was set up in 1911, it was decreed that the nation's capital had to have access to the sea, so about 18,000 acres around Jervis Bay were annexed to the ACT. The chunk of land is now home to the Royal Australian Naval College.

One good stop is the small settlement of **Huskisson**, famed for a colony of resident dolphins. If you want to see them up close, try a trip aboard the *Tekin*, which takes groups out a couple of times a day. It has a lunch and coffee cruise and a licensed bar aboard. Adults are about $A25–35 depending on the cruise. ☎ *(02) 4441-6311; FAX (02) 4441-5885*. At the small settlement of Jervis Bay is **Hyams Beach**, which claims to have the whitest sand in the world. It does have great scuba diving.

A group of coastal lakes and lagoons with white sandy beaches is centered around the town of **Ulladulla**, about 20 miles south of Jervis Bay. The town itself is a major fishing port, and the lakes offer water skiing, fishing and boating activities. From this point to Bega, about 100 miles south, there are dozens of coastal access roads that cut east from the Princes Highway. The beaches are almost uniformly white sand, and in several areas, the waters and islands offshore have been set aside as wildlife sanctuaries. The **Tollgate Islands** near Bateman's Bay, for example, are a haven for penguins. From Bateman's Bay, there are cruises up the Clyde River and a bit farther south, there is a bird sanctuary with tours.

About 20 miles south you find **Moruya**, a farming and seafood center whose major claim to fame is as the spot where the pylons for the Sydney Harbour Bridge were quarried.

From Moruya south, most of the coastal towns and villages are in the dairy-seafood-lumber business, although bits and snatches of tourism are rearing their heads. **Central Tilba**, just outside of Narooma, has been declared a national historical village and has several fine examples of mid-Victorian buildings. Just behind town is **Mount Dromedary**, the highest peak on the New South Wales coast (2700 feet/823 m), which has a trail to the top and attendant views.

This is also **cheese country**, and you'll find many places that offer tastings. **Bega**, south of Narooma, anchors an area known for its cheddars, and the **Bega Cooperative Society Cheese Factory** has tastings and tours. West of Bega is **Kameruka Estates**, an agricultural center begun in the 1830s and now listed in the National Trust. You want to see sheep, they have sheep.

Tuna fishing and tourism are the mainstays of **Merimbula** and its sister town, **Pambula**, back on the coast south of Bega. There are also oysters and prawns, and for *Wind in the Willows* fans, an old building called Toad Hall (apparently no connection).

The last community of any size before reaching the Victoria border is **Eden**, an old whaling port with museum to match. It's also a lumbering community, and the harbor of Twofold Bay is reputed to be one of the four or five deepest in the world. Every spring, humpback whales come to the bay, and local tour boats can take you out to meet them. On the coast north and south of the bay is **Ben Boyd National Park**, which has red sandstone cliffs and lots of wildlife.

The Mountains

Inland from the fertile coast, the land steps up into the peaks and high tablelands of the **Great Dividing Range**, then down again onto the ranch country of the range's western slopes, then lastly into the flat and arid western plains.

Of all the sections of the Great Dividing Range, perhaps the most famous and most popular is the **Snowy Mountains**, the "Alps of Australia." Some North Americans at least recognize the name because of the successful Aussie movie, *The Man From Snowy River*, a horse-and-rider saga based on the poem of the same name by Banjo Paterson, who also wrote "Waltzing Matilda."

By North American standards the highest peak in the range (and in Australia), **Mount Kosciusko**, is pretty small peanuts, only 7300 feet. The region nonetheless allows Australians to enjoy skiing and winter sports during the season, June-September. The total snowfalls can be iffy, however, and sometimes the skiing conditions are not very good. There are 10 peaks over 6800 feet, which, when you consider that most of Australia is flatter than a pool table, is geologically significant. The mountains are contained inside **Kosciusko National Park**, which sits at the state's southwest corner near the Victoria border. The park, at about 261,000 acres, is the largest in New South Wales and is the source of the Murray, Snowy and Murrumbidgee rivers.

The best way to get into the mountains is to drive to Cooma, either on the coast highway to Bega and then over, or down Highway 23 from Canberra. Once in Cooma, you can go northwest to Tumut or southwest to Jindabyne, Mount Kosciusko and the ski areas.

The two major downhill **ski areas** are located at **Thredbo** and **Perisher Valley**. Cross-country is allowed on almost all the snowfields. Most of the ski areas in the Snowies have accommodations, food, shops and pubs. Rental equipment is available at all.

Thredbo

The oldest and one of the most developed of the resorts, with new snow-making equipment and all three levels of runs; the resort's 500 acres are predominantly intermediate. It offers 12 chairlifts, 23 T-bars, and access T-bars near advanced runs. The highest lifted point is about 6,700 feet. The chairlifts also run in the summer for gawkers and hikers, and the resort reportedly does a fair amount of conference business. From the end of the top lift station, hikers can get to the crest of Mount Kosciusko, a popular foray. (That's pronounced "koz-ee-AWS-koe," by the way.) Lift tickets are running about A$60 a day. Contact the resort at *Thredbo Alpine Village, P.O. Box 92, Thredbo, New South Wales 2627;* ☎ *(064) 6457-6360.* The resort has year-round accommodations.

Perisher Valley

More than 75 miles of trails and the capability of lifting around 30,000 skiers an hour on the highest lift in the area, rising to more than 6600 feet. All three levels of difficulty are available, and new snowmaking equipment has been installed; 12 lifts operating. Lodges and luxury hotels are available. *Information:* **Perisher/Smiggins Resort Centre**, *Perisher Valley,* ☎ *(064) 59-4421.* Bookings also available in Sydney through **World Travel Headquarters**, *33 Blight Street, Sydney;* ☎ *(02) 2937-0300.*

Mt. Selwyn

Information: Mt. Selwyn Ski Resort, ☎ *(064) 54-9488 or (064) 52-1108.*
Mt. Selwyn, the northernmost resort, near Tumut, is an area that has concentrated on cross-country but does have some downhill. There are snack shops, 12 lifts, no overnight accommodations.

Major population centers in the mountains are **Jindabyne**, at the east center of the park; **Kiandra**, to the north, and **Tumut**, which is the northern gateway. Jindabyne is next to a lake of the same name, stocked with trout. A shuttle bus runs from here to the ski resorts in the winter.

The Aussies have come up with a novel way to get skiers and hikers around the mountains. It's called the **Skitube**, an electrically operated train that goes through and into several mountains. It runs from the Alpine Highway (the road between Jindabyne and Thredbo) to the Perisher ski area and on to Mt. Blue Cow, one of the highest and newest of the Australian Alpine resorts. The Skitube runs all year so hikers can also take advantage, and mountain bikes are also available for rent. The tube costs about A$20 for a round trip; a one-day bike hire plus round trip on the tube is about A$40. If you want to try Skitube, just stop at the terminal off Alpine Highway about 18 kilometers west of Jindabyne, or call ☎ *(064) 56-2010.*

The drive from Jindabyne to Thredbo is one of the loveliest in Australia. It follows a deep river valley most of the way, with the mountains on either side. Along the way are signs indicating "Wombat Crossings," and from the Skitube station on, the scenery gets even better. Thredbo is a raw tourist town, full of resorts and ski shops. Many of the resorts are perched on a hill above the valley; access is on a tiny road closed to buses and trucks. The chairlift running out of Thredbo is a wonder, steep, long and high, and lots of folks take it up to the top of the nearby peaks and then hike on to Mount Kosciusko.

The easiest way to get to the top of **Australia's highest mountain** is to drive from Jindabyne up the Kosciusko Road through the national park to a place called Charlotte's Pass. You can't miss the spot because the pavement ends. Park along the highway. You have two choices to get to the top, one goes right, one goes left. The easiest and shortest is to the left. At one time, you could drive to the top of the mountain, and this trail follows the old road. It's not at all hard, and it's not that far, maybe 8 or 9 kilometers, to the top. It gets a bit chilly, even in the summer, so wear a light jacket.

Once on top, you can go back the same way or complete a circle trip by taking the **Lake Albina/Club Lake trail**. It's a glorious hike, and the scenery rivals anything we've seen in Australia: hanging valleys, Alpine lakes, glaciated valleys, crisp air. The only problem is the last mile or so to Charlotte's Pass the idiots have paved the trail. First, it's very steep going down to a small river, then it's very steep going back up to the parking area. As any hiker can tell you, when it's steep like that, the last thing you want is pavement. We assume it was paved for wheelchairs, but it's so steep we don't see how anyone could push a chair up the slope. Still, it's worth it just to say you've been there. We estimate the complete circle trip at about 20 kilometers; we did it in six hours, including an hour lunch break at the top of the mountain. (Food always tastes especially good when you've packed it in.)

There are several national forest campgrounds in the area, as well as a very nice RV park at Sawpit, about 15 kilometers from Jindabyne. It also has chalets and on-site caravans. *Reservations and Information:* Alpine Accommodation Complex, ☎ *(064) 56-2224*. The headquarters for the national park is also at Sawpit.

Northwest of Kiandra on the Snowy Mountains Highway are the **Yarrangobilly Caves**, open all year. At **Cooma**, not really in the mountains, but the economic center of the area, there are food and beds. Museums in town have displays showing the work of the Snowy Mountains Scheme, a mammoth hydroelectric project that was built during World War II. During the ski season, Pioneer runs buses from the Cooma airport to the resorts.

Snowy Mountain **information centers** are located at various National Park Service locations in the area, including Jindabyne, Sawpit Creek, Bullocks Flat and Yarrangobilly Caves. General information is available from the **Snowy River Information Centre** in Jindabyne ☎ *(03) 656-2444*. You can also try the **New South Wales Ski Association**, *157 Gloucester Street, Sydney*; ☎ *(02) 24-1581*, or the **Sydney Snow Centre**, *74 Pitt Street, Sydney*; ☎ *(02) 9231-1444*.

The Hunter Valley

A day trip to the Hunter Valley's **vineyards** is possible but of course, if you've ever been in the wine country of France or the Napa Valley of California, you know that wine tasting is an endeavor best not rushed. The two important centers of the wine area are Maitland and Cessnock, which are also towns devoted to the huge coal industry that also exists in the valley. The largest shaft mine in the Southern Hemisphere is located in Cessnock, they claim. Some of the world's largest open pit mines (and a few of the ugliest power stations) are located in the Singleton area of the Upper Hunter. The Hunter Valley harvest, by the way, is usually in February.

Driving to the vineyards, about two hours north by car from Sydney, take the Pacific Highway to Newcastle, then hang a left onto the New England Highway, which parallels the Hunter River from Newcastle. The **State Rail Authority** runs a one-day trip to the vineyards from Sydney. Passengers ride to Newcastle, are bused around the valley and then hop a return train that afternoon.

The Hunter Valley, north of Sydney, is Australia's oldest commercial wine-producing area.

AUSTRALIA WINE REGIONS

Australia's famous wine region is the Riverlands of the Murray and Murrumbidgee river systems where New South Wales, Victoria and South Australia meet. The vine first arrived in Australia from the Cape of Good Hope in 1788. Irrigation of the near-desert region has produced high yielding, verdant vineyards and wines that are soft, fruity and flavorful.

◄ Merlot grape

Darwin

NORTHERN TERRITORY

TANAMI DESERT

KEY
● Wine producing regions

GIBSON DESERT

INDIAN OCEAN

1

SOUTH AUSTRALIA

GREAT VICTORIA DESERT

WESTERN AUSTRALIA

Perth

94 Great Eastern Hwy.

1 Eyre Hwy.

Bunbury

30 South Coast Hwy.

Chardonnay ► grape

Albany

WESTERN AUSTRALIA

The most exciting wines come from the Margaret River and Lower Great Southern regions. Famous as a region for reds and fortified wines, good dry whites are now more successful. Swan Valley, Perth Hills and the SW Coastal Plain were the first regions to produce wine.

GRAPE VARIETIES

RED WINES

CABERNET SAUVIGNON — The Bordeaux grape has been a success in Australia as a varietal wine and blended with Shiraz.

MERLOT — These grapes are used increasingly for blending with Cabernet Sauvignon.

SHIRAZ — The local name for the Rhone Valley's Syrah is also known as Hermitage. These grapes produce rich, deep red wines and blend well with Cabernet Sauvignon.

PINOT NOIR — These red burgundy grapes have been a success in some of Australia's cooler regions.

WHITE WINES

SEMILLON — A Bordeaux variety found especially in Hunter which makes a fine white wine.

CHARDONNAY — Extremely popular both for taste and ease of growing in many areas. Produce rich, buttery wines reminiscent of white burgundy.

RIESLING — These grapes produce good medium and sweet wines.

MUSCATS — Grapes of this variety are used increasingly for fortified and dessert wines.

SAUVIGNON BLANC, COLOMBARD, CHENIN BLANC Everyday wine varieties.

SOUTH AUSTRALIA

Clare Valley produces "cool climate" table wines. The Barossa Valley is where most of the larger wine companies are based. South of Adelaide are the Southern Vales, major producers of high quality reds and whites.

QUEENSLAND

The center of Queensland wine-making is in the high valleys of the Granite Belt, south of Stanthorpe on the New South Wales border. The Granite Belt is known as a table wine region. The Shiraz, the first classic variety planted in the region is the most successful.

NEW SOUTH WALES

Colonial Australia began in New South Wales and so did Australian wine. The Hunter Valley is less dominant than it once was, but the efforts of Hunter Valley and its Sydney supporters helped Aussie wine gain acceptance.

66

QUEENSLAND   Granite Belt   ● Brisbane

Lake Eyre

Lake Torrens

87

Lake Gairdner

32   NEW SOUTH WALES

Adelaide

Uxley

● Newcastle

39   32

20   Wagga Wagga   24   ● Sydney

Murray River   ○ Canberra

VICTORIA

8

Goulburn Valley

VICTORIA

Victoria's scattered vineyards followed the Gold Rush. In the late 19th century the phyllorexa louse devastated most vineyards in Victoria. Only in recent years has the region recaptured its position as a producer of a wide variety of wines.

Melbourne

TASMANIA

Vineyards were established in Tasmania in 1823 before either Victoria or South Australia but they were short-lived and not revived until the 1950s. Today the area is best known for sparkling wine grapes.

TASMAN SEA

Launceston

TASMANIA

Hobart

Several bus companies operate one- or two-day tours of the Hunter Valley from Sydney. **Australian Pacific Tours** has a one-day that leaves Circular Quay around 9 a.m. and returns about 7:30 p.m. The tour includes free hotel pickup and drop-off, lunch at a winery, a drive through the winegrowing areas and a chance to sample some wines and visit a wine museum. The fare is about A$70. The two-day tour visits six wineries, and includes accommodations, a wine appreciation course, champagne breakfast and two lunches. The fare is about A$200. Contact Australian Pacific at ☎ *(02) 9252-2988* in Sydney.

The one-day tour offered by **Great Sights South Pacific** visits four wineries, stops at a museum, includes lunch and tastings and stops at a farmers market. The fare is about A$70. The tour leaves around 9 a.m. from Sydney, returns at 7:30 p.m. Free hotel pickup and drop-off. Book by calling ☎ *(02) 9241-2294.*

If you can get to Newcastle, Maitland or Cessnock, you can hop a tour bus that drives around the valley stopping at a range of wineries. The bus, billed as the **Hunter Vineyard Tour**, costs about A$50 with lunch. It can be booked through travel agents or directly by calling ☎ *(02) 4991-1659* or *(02) 4938-1011.* The buses run daily.

Information about the vineyards, transportation, accommodations, restaurants and the wine biz in general is available from the **Australian Wine Centre**, in the Goldfields Building on Alfred Street near Circular Quay. Once in the area, there are tourist information offices at the **Hunter Valley Wine Society** in Cessnock ☎ *(02) 4990-6699*; the **Manning Valley Tourist Association** in Taree and the **Hunter Valley Tourist Association** in Hexham. Complete information about the valley, plus bookings for accommodations, is available at the **Cessnock Tourist Information Centre**, *Turner Park, Aberdare Road;* ☎ *(02) 4990-4477; FAX (02) 4990-6954.*

The wine area is divided in two: the **Upper Hunter** and the **Lower Hunter**. In any event, expect to find wines made from *semillon, shiraz* (known as syrah in France) and *cabernet sauvignon* grapes with others thrown in here and there. The valley is primarily respected for its reds, although its whites have won fame at competitions.

Tastings

At most Hunter Valley wineries tastings are very much in the California style, meaning low-pressure sales tactics, a liberal pouring policy, and no insistence that you be a wine snob. Some wineries charge for a tasting, but refund the money if you buy a bottle or two. Two good bets are Wyndham Estate cabernet sauvignon-shiraz blends and Rosemount shirazes. In addition, you might try the chardonnays from Rothbury Estate.

This should be your first stop in the area:

McGuigan Hunter Village ★★★

Broke Road, Pokolbin, ☎ *(049) 98-7466, or (049) 98-7600; FAX (049) 98-7710. The village is open 10 a.m.–5 p.m. daily.*

At Pokolbin, a village close to several of the more well known wineries. Hunter Cellars, located at the village, represents a number of wineries in the Upper and Lower Hunter Valley. Here you can see winemaking, do a tasting, eat at the **Cellar Restaurant**, and sleep at the **Vineyard Resort & Convention Centre,** Heated pool, tennis court, laundry. Doubles A$90–105; suites A$120–130. Plus there are extensive playgrounds and picnic areas.

Among wineries to check out in the Lower Hunter are:

Rothbury Estate

> Rothbury Estate, Broke Road, Pokolbin, ☎ (049) 98-7555 weekends (049) 98-7672; FAX (049) 98-7553.
> Open 9:30 a.m.–4:30 p.m.seven days.
> Has organized events all year.

McWilliams

> McWilliams Mount Pleasant Winery, Marrowbone Road, Pokolbin, ☎ (049) 98-7505; FAX (049) 98-7761.
> Open 9 a.m.–4:30 p.m. Monday–Friday; 10 a.m.–4 p.m. weekends; guided tours twice a day Monday–Friday.
> One of the oldest and largest.

Wyndham Estate

> Wyndham Estate, Government Road, Dalwood, ☎ (049) 38-3444; FAX (049) 38-3422.
> Open 9 a.m.–5 p.m. Monday–Saturday; 10 a.m.–5 p.m. Sunday.
> Wine buildings dating back to the 1830s, now under the National Trust. The winery also has a restaurant with hearty Aussie fare such as steaks stuffed with prawns.

Lindeman's

> Lindeman's Hunter Valley Winery, McDonald's Road, Pokolbin, ☎ (049) 98-7684; FAX (049) 98-7602.
> Open 9 a.m.–4:30 p.m. Monday–Friday; 10 a.m.–4:30 p.m. weekends.
> The Gallo of Australia, owned by Phillip Morris, comes with a wine museum.

Tyrrell's

> Tyrrell's Vineyards, Broke Road, Pokolbin, ☎ (049) 98-7509.
> Open 8 a.m.–5 p.m. Monday–Saturday.
> Where public tasting is done amidst furnishings both woody and quaint. This winery was one of the first to assert the excellence of Australian wines, winning against the best Continental wines in contests.

In the Upper Hunter Valley, try the **Arrowfield Winery** and **Rosemount Estate**, both just north of the town of Denman. This is white wine country, especially the chardonnays of Rosemount. *Arrowfield, Jerry's Plains.* Open 10 a.m.–4 p.m. seven days; restaurant open for lunch on weekends. ☎ (02) 6576-4041; FAX (02) 6576-4144. **Rosemount Estate,** *Rosemount Road.* Open 10 a.m.–4 p.m. Monday–Saturday; noon-4 p.m. Sunday. Brasserie open 10 a.m.–4 p.m. Tuesday–Sunday. ☎ (02) 6547-2467.

Finally, the way it goes these days, you aren't a reputable wine-growing area unless you have **balloon flights**, and there are several companies offering trips in the Hunter Valley; expect to pay around A$125 to A$150 for an hour-long flight, and demand a champagne breakfast. Try **Balloon Aloft**, Branxton Road, North Rothbury, open seven days. ☎ (02) (049) 38-1955, or toll free ☎ (008) 02-8568.

Where to Stay and Eat

Accommodations in the region, in addition to the resort at the Wine Village, include:

Peppers Guest House   **A$160–200**   ★★★★

Ekerts Road, Pokolbin, ☎ *(049) 98-7596; FAX (049) 98-7739.*
Doubles around A$160–200. (Two-night minimum on weekends; special packages all year.)

Probably the best in the area, a country-style building almost always booked on weekends, with pool, tennis, gym. The setting is very comfy, with 48 colonial-style rooms set in a landscaped garden. Also available is the self-contained, four-bedroom Homestead for small groups. The in-house restaurant, **Chez Pok**, is a favorite and widely regarded as one of the top in the valley; it's open seven days and has, not surprisingly, an extensive wine list, especially aged reds.

Hunter Resort, The   **A$100–130**   ★★★

Hermitage Road, Pokolbin, ☎ *(049) 98-7777; FAX (049) 98-7787.*
Doubles $A100–130.

The resort sits amid the 70 acres of vineyards that produce Hunter Estate Wines. In addition to wine tastings and a restaurant, the resort has tennis, pool, spa, mountain bikes and a playground. Rooms are timbered, with cathedral ceilings. The restaurant, **The Hermitage**, is open for dinner seven days; light lunches served on weekends. If you've bought wine at other wineries, bring it along; the restaurant allows BYO.

Convent Peppertree, The   **A$240**   ★★★★

Halls Road, Pokolbin, ☎ *(049) 98-7764; FAX (049) 98-7323.*
Bed and breakfast doubles start at $A240; higher on weekends.

Historic preservation at its finest: the Convent really was a convent, built in 1909, due for demolition in 1990, saved and turned into a spiffy guest house in 1991. They call it "chic Renaissance," but it looks more like a turn-of-the-century school. Whatever, the rooms are all suites, and the general decor is airy, woody and antiquated. Pool, spa, tennis court, lots of fireplaces. Breakfast on the terrace is a real treat. The restaurant, **Robert's**, is gaining a good reputation. It features French/ Italian cuisine, and a wood fire made of vine cuttings is used to flavor meats and bread. There is also a tasting barn and gift shop offering Pepper Tree wines.

Country Comfort Inn, The   **A$100**   ★★

Dwyer Street, Campbells Hill, Maitland, ☎ *(049) 32-5288; FAX (049) 32-6788.*
Doubles about A$100.

Once an oprhanage, the 125-year-old inn sits on 10 acres of landscaping with pool, tennis, gum, sauna, billiards and two restaurants. A good bet.

Kirkton Park Country Hotel   **A$175–285**   ★★★

Oakley Creek Road about a kilometer north of Pokolbin, ☎ *(049) 98-7680.*
Doubles A$175–230; suites A$285 and up.

All the comforts of home while in the wine country, set in a Victorian manor: saltwater pool, spa, tennis courts, laundry, gym, sauna, licensed restaurant, **Leith's** (vast wine list). The hotel has its own vineyards, where wine is produced solely for the guests. The restaurant will deliver dinner to your room on the weekend. Rooms have mini-bars and hair dryers. There are three suites.

Hunter Country Lodge and Restaurant   **A$100**   ★★

Branxton Road, Cessnock, ☎ *(049) 38-1744; FAX (049) 38-1983.*
Doubles start around A$100.

The lodge is located near the Wyndham Estate and Rothbury Estate vineyards north of Cessnock on Highway 82. There are 16 units, all with private facilities, a saltwater pool, mini-bars and a licensed restaurant, the **Vines**, that has a very good international menu; it also serves breakfast and lunch. A hot-air balloon company has offices across the road.

Casaurina   **A$160–450**   ★ ★

Hermitage Road in Pokolbin; ☎ *(049) 98-7888; FAX (049) 98-7692.*
Doubles from A$160; cottages A$250–450.

There is an upscale country lodge with saltwater swimming pool, tennis courts and sauna. There are fairly sumptuous suites (called "Fantasy Suites") decorated in varying degrees of decadence. Take a look at the "Bordello," for example. The resort restaurant, the **Casaurina**, has an Asian flair and is gaining attention as one of the valley's better eateries. It's open for dinner seven days, and for lunch weekends and holidays.

Some other restaurants worth a nod are:

Buttai Barn   **$$**   ★ ★

Off the John Renshaw Road in Buttai. ☎ *(049) 30-3153.*
This fun spot has a live bush band every Saturday night and good country tucker, moderate prices.

Braxton Inn, The   **$$**   ★ ★ ★

35 New England Highway, Braxton, ☎ *(049) 38-1225.*
Lunch noon-2 p.m. Wednesday-Sunday; dinner 6 p.m. Wednesday-Saturday.
Built in 1843, this is the oldest inn in the valley. The tables are fashioned from old sewing machines, and the menu is eclectic: crumbed brains to bush pies and scones.

The Interior

To many Australians, the Outback is a state of mind, a mythical place which, like the long-gone American Frontier, somehow encapsulates all the truths and myths that surround the pioneering spirit of the country. The difference is that in the United States, once you got past the desolation of the Great Plains and the deadly wastes of the western deserts, there was a reward: California, Oregon, Washington. The early white settlers of New South Wales soon discovered that once they started into the Outback, about the only thing they had to look forward to was a bunch more Outback.

If you're of an adventurous bent, a trip to the real Outback of New South Wales will give you a glimpse of Australia that many tourists, either too strapped for time or simply ill at ease about all that flat nothingness, never get a chance to experience. You can drive, without any real trouble, or you can take a quick tour from Sydney.

Our suggestion is to head northwest over the Great Dividing Range toward what is called Corner Country, the bleak area where New South Wales, Queensland and South Australia meet.

A driving tour will take you over the old explorer's route through the Blue Mountains to Bathurst, then along the Mitchell Highway to Dubbo. From Dubbo, you can turn north on the Castlereagh Highway toward the Queensland border, or go to Nyngan. At Nyngan, you then turn due north toward Bourke or take the Barrier Highway to Broken Hill. Any of these routes will get you into the arid deserts of the outback. Do not, however, attempt a drive without the proper precautions, and if you truly want to get off the beaten path, join a four-wheel-drive tour. Remember, check local conditions, availability of gasoline and stay home if it's raining. (See *Driving* section.)

After the first explorers pushed through the Blue Mountains and discovered good grazing on the other side, a road was built from Sydney to **Bathurst**, the country's oldest inland city. It was a pastoral center until 1851 when gold was discovered in the area and the rush was on. On **Mount Panorama** near town is the **Bathurst Gold Diggings**, a reconstructed mining village. Mount Panorama is also the location of the **Sir Joseph Banks Nature Reserve**, with native animals. Twice a year, the koalas are rudely awakened as bikers and race car drivers descend on the Mount Panorama race course. Easter is for motorcycles (often a fairly taut time, cops versus bikers), and in October, the Bathurst 1000 for production cars is held.

Famous for its fruits and livestock, **Orange** is also the birthplace of Australia's most famous poet, Banjo Paterson. About 20 miles north of town off the paved highway is **Ophir**, where the gold rush started. Farther up the Mitchell Highway is **Wellington**, where you'll see Burendong Dam and Lake, the last big body of water for several thousand square miles. Also near town are the **Wellington Caves**, which claim to have the world's largest stalactite. About 100 kilometers west of Orange is the city of **Parkes**, which is now the world's center for extraterrestrial research. When the SETI (Search for Extra-Terrestrial Intelligence) program was cut by NASA, scientists turned their attention to Australia, specifically the 210-foot radio telescope at Parkes, which can scan 28 million microwave channels at once. There is a visitors center open 8 a.m.–4 p.m. daily. ☎ *(02) 6861-1777.*

The area around Wellington and Mudgee, to the east, is becoming a fairly productive **wine area**, although the wineries are still small. Some of the best include *Platts, Huntington Estate and Miramar.* Information: **Montrose Winery**, *Henry Lawson Drive,* ☎ *(063) 73-3853;* **Platts**, *Gulgong Road,* ☎ *(063) 74-1700;* **Huntington Estate**, *Cassalis Road, Mudgee,* ☎ *(063) 73-3825;* and **Miramar**, *Henry Lawson Drive, Mudgee,* ☎ *(063) 73-3874.* The *Mudgee Tourist Information Centre* is at *84 Market Street;* ☎ *(063) 72-5874; FAX: (02) 6372-2853.*

Dubbo, about 260 miles northwest of Sydney (and about 125 miles from Bathurst) is in the heart of the wheat belt and is a main intersection for the interior part of the state. From Dubbo, you can keep going north and west into the harshlands, or head northeast or southeast on the Newell Highway, the fastest Brisbane-Melbourne route.

Just outside of town is what many Australians consider to be the finest wildlife park in the country, the **Western Plains Zoo**, about 700 acres of open range exhibits operated in conjunction with Sydney's Taronga Zoo. The zoo has more than 1000 animals, including many endangered species. Open daily 9 a.m.–5 p.m., admission charge about A$15. ☎ *(068) 82-5888; FAX: (068) 84-1722.* In town, check out the **Old Dubbo Gaol**, complete with gallows, a sure sign that Dubbo has been and continues to be the center of this part of Australia. Any colonial city worth its salt had at least one gaol and gallows to match. Open 9 a.m.–4:30 p.m. daily. *Information:* the **Dubbo Visitors Centre**, *232 Macquarie Street;* ☎ *(068) 84-1422.* Dubbo has a half-dozen RV parks and about 30 motels.

Lightning Ridge is in the middle of nowhere or almost. It's about 250 miles north of Dubbo on the Castlereagh Highway, sitting next to the huge Lightning Ridge opal mines, said to be the only place in the world where you can find black opals. The remoteness of the town does not stop the city dads from cashing in on tourism, of course. There are opal showrooms, opal mine tours, and artesian baths. You can tell how far out you are: the nearest landmark marked on the highway map is a water tank. One thing you'll soon find out about the Outback towns, no matter where you are: the beer is ice cold. In this case, check out the **Diggers Rest Hotel**, where anybody who is anybody will be found.

Driving between Dubbo and Lightning Ridge takes you through only two towns of any interest, **Coonamble** and **Walgett**. Coonamble is where things really start getting vacant, although not far to the west are the huge Macquarie Marshes, a major bird breeding area. Walgett, about 175 miles up the Castlereagh from Dubbo, is in the heart of a major opal mining area. In nearby **Grawin**, an opal weighing almost 500 grams was pulled from the ground in 1928. Walgett has an RV park, hotels and motels.

Going up the Mitchell Highway from Dubbo is a big citrus and cotton-growing area. At **Nyngan**, the Mitchell runs northwest toward Bourke and the Queensland border. **Bourke** has lent its name to an Aussie expression: Back of Bourke. If you're "back of Bourke," you're well and truly in the thules. This is sheep country, and from November to March, it's hotter than an old pistol and full of bush flies.

From Nyngan west, you're on the Barrier Highway for a long and lonesome 370 miles to Broken Hill. About 80 miles west of Nyngan is **Cobar**, a copper-mining town with one of the best examples of a grand bush hotel in the country: the Great Western Hotel. The old heap, now protected by the National Trust, has the longest iron-lace verandah in New South Wales, and its rooms have been modernized. The bar is large and friendly.

About 25 miles west of Cobar are the Grenfell **Aboriginal cave paintings**, a group of very good animal and human figures. If you want to visit the caves, you'll have to turn off the Barrier Highway and drive about 20 miles north to the Grenfell station; the turnoff is marked.

At **Wilcannia**, the highway crosses the Darling River and there are remains of an old wharf and buildings that were once part of a lively riverboat business when the town was the third-largest river port in the country. It boggles your mind that paddlewheelers could come this far north, but the Darling runs into the Murray, and the Murray is the Mississippi of Australia. At one time, there were several hundred boats working the Murray-Darling rivershed.

Broken Hill is the mining center that gave rise to Australia's biggest conglomerate, **Broken Hill Proprietary**, or BHP, often called "the Big Australian." The hill that gave the town its name is the world's largest known deposit of silver, lead and zinc, a chunk estimated to be five miles in length, 500 feet wide, and 2000 feet deep. That's one hell of a nugget.

One of the most striking things about Broken Hill (aside from its mines and the somewhat quaint idea of naming all the streets after minerals) is the abundance of greenery, supplied by water from Darling River dams. There is also an office of the **Flying Doctor Service**, which has airborne emergency medical service for the Outback, and the School of the Air, which provides shortwave classes for isolated school children. There is a Flying Doctor film museum and a souvenir shop. *Tours 10:30 a.m. and 3:30 p.m. Monday–Friday; 10:30 a.m. weekends.* ☎ *(080) 88-0777.*

Underground tours of an abandoned mine are available through **Delprat's Mines**; ☎ *(080) 88-1604. General information is available at the Tourist Information Centre, corner of Bromide and Blende streets;* ☎ *(080) 88-6077.* The town is run by labor unions (the Barrier Industrial Council) and is actually closer to Adelaide (315 miles) than Sydney (725 miles). Just to prove something, the city runs on South Australia time, which is 30 minutes behind New South Wales.

Bus service is available from Adelaide and Melbourne. Smart travelers, however, will take the opportunity to go to Broken Hill on the Indian-Pacific, one of Australia's great train routes. It goes through Broken Hill on its way to Perth. The journey is about 18 hours and is made easier because the train has sleepers, dining cars and a lounge car. *Information: Rail Travel Centre of New South Wales, Transport House, 11-31 York Street; or Railways of Australia, which represents the five state-owned rail systems in the country, at 85 Queen Street, Melbourne* ☎ *(03) 9608-0811.*

About 15 miles west of Broken Hill is **Silverton**, a once-thriving silver boom town which is becoming a feature in Aussie movies including being a set for a *Mad Max* film and *A Town Like Alice.*

Two national parks lie north of Broken Hill. The smallest is **Mootwingee National Park**, where there are Aboriginal paintings believed to date back 25,000 years, many badly defaced by vandals. Farther up the Silver City track about 200 miles is a wide spot called **Tibooburra**, which is at the entrance to Sturt National Park. Tibooburra has some fine old period sandstone buildings dating from its heyday as a gold rush town. There is an RV park and one hotel, The Albert.

Sturt National Park is 465,000 acres of flood plains, rocks, sandhills, and lots of animals and birds. It's about five hours from Broken Hill. At Cameron's Corner, the northwest point where the three states come together, there is a monument proclaiming that fact, a dandy target to add to your personal accomplishment list. Also in the Broken Hill area is **Kinchega National Park**, about 60 miles southeast. The park is noted for its large flocks of waterbirds and is also a habitat for the big red kangaroos. *Information about the parks is available from the Broken Hill district office of the National Parks & Wildlife Service, 5 Oxide Street, Broken Hill,* ☎ *(080) 88-5933.*

If you're uncomfortable driving yourself, try the five-day four-wheel-drive excursions that leave Broken Hill, go to the national parks, and also stop off at the White Cliff opal fields north of Wilcannia. The price of about A$700 includes meals, accommodations, and guides. The trips can be booked through **Bill King's Australian Experience**, which uses ATS/Sprint in Los Angeles as its North American broker.

If you're in a hurry, go with the mailman in this case, the **Barrier Air Taxi Service**, which allows paying passengers on two flights, one to White Cliffs and one on its 25-ranch postal route. *Contact the service in Broken Hill;* ☎ *(080) 88-4307.*

AUSTRALIAN CAPITAL TERRITORY

War Memorial, Canberra, is the second most-visited spot in Australia.

The Australian Capital Territory, the Aussie equivalent of the District of Columbia, is a very nice place to live and work, and if you have time on your Australian jaunt, a nice place to visit. It is a planned area, born in the early part of this century, and as national capitals go, refreshingly clean and well-managed. But, and this is of course a biased view, you can visit Australia without going to Canberra and not feel a sense of loss. It's very much like going to Brazil and missing Brasilia. Comfortable and calm, that's Canberra.

Having said that, however, it remains that if you want to put the entire Australian experience in order, the tree-lined boulevards and stately federal buildings of the ACT are essential. Besides, as is said of many other places in the world, it's close to a lot of great stuff.

Being Australians, it was impossible for them to pick the national capital without a lot of shouting and carrying on, so when Australia decided to become an independent nation in 1901, the bickering started immediately. The loudest protagonists were Sydney and Melbourne, the new nation's economic and political centers, but it seemed as if every village on the continent wanted the honor of having the capital, as well. It took until 1908 for all the hoo-haw to die down enough to pick the spot, which turned out to be a grazing area in the Monaro Tablelands about 200 miles southwest of Sydney, 400 miles northeast of Melbourne. You could say that both sides won—more or less. Melbourne got its way because the capital didn't end up in Sydney. On the other hand Sydney won because it's twice as close to the ACT as Melbourne. Ain't democracy grand?

When it came time to design the new capital city, a competition was held with a prize of $3500 for the winner. British architects, reportedly in a snit because of the way the bumpkin colonials had resolved the issue of location, opted not to enter designs, leaving the way open for one Walter Burley Griffin to snatch the honors. Griffin was, of course, an American.

What he had in mind was a city of around 75,000, but federal bureaucracies being federal bureaucracies, the present population hovers around 300,000. It is also worth noting that Griffin's grand scheme fell afoul of this and that (including World War I), and it wasn't until 1927 that Parliament first met in the new city. Between 1901 and the first session, the nation's leaders assembled in Melbourne. The Depression and the next war also took their toll, and it wasn't until the 1950s and 1960s that major attention was paid to starting construction of the necessary facilities for the government. The first major building, Parliament House, was completed in 1927 as a temporary site, to be replaced at a later date—the later date, as it turned out, was 1988, when the new Parliament building was opened.

There was also a fairly strenuous debate about what the new capital should be called, and after a couple of years of pondering, the boys decided to use the name that had been there all along: Canberra (pronounced CAN-braw). One of the first settlers in the area started a station on the nearby Murrumbidgee River and named it Canberra, a form of the Aboriginal word for "meeting place," a fitting name for a seat of government.

The Founding Fathers of the United States, when they had their chance, chose to put the national capital in a swamp that, to this day, draws quite nasty and thoroughly justified comments about its lousy climate, especially during one of the hot, muggy summers that so often descend on the White House and other centers of national enlightenment. Canberra, while not

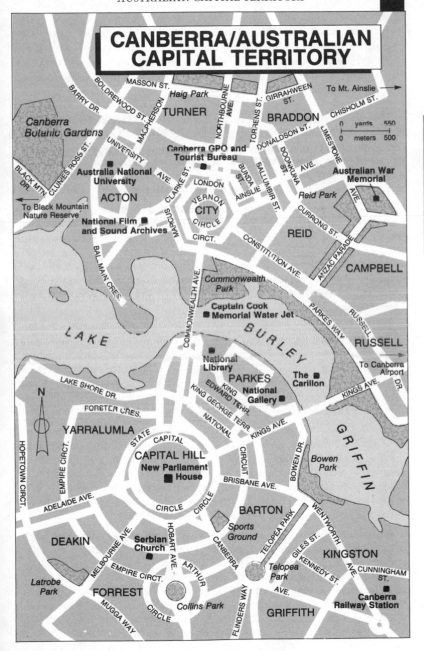

nearly as bad, does have a reputation for being uncomfortably hot in the summer and uncomfortably cold in the winter. Unlike the other major cities in Australia, it is not on the coast and is unable to cash in on the calming climatic influences of the ocean. The time to visit Canberra is in the spring and fall. Autumn, with its change of colors and pleasant weather, is probably best.

Sights

The most striking feature of the city, and its centerpoint, is **Lake Burley Griffin**, completed in 1964 by damming the Molonglo River. The lake, which created more than 20 miles of shoreline, lies just to the north of the major federal buildings, including the new **Parliament House**, the **National Library**, the **National Art Gallery** and the **High Court of Australia**. With Parliament House as the center, a series of circular streets then radiates south into the suburbs, and that's where you find foreign embassies.

In the center of the lake, near the **Commonwealth Bridge**—which runs from Capital Circle and Parliament House to the downtown area—is the **Captain Cook Memorial Water Jet** (we'd call it a fountain) that spurts water 450 feet into the air and is reminiscent of the fountain in Lake Geneva. On Aspen Island, next to another bridge (Kings Avenue) is the **Canberra Carillon**—given to the city to mark its 50th anniversary in 1963, but officially opened by Queen Elizabeth in 1970. A footbridge connects the mainland to the island. The carillon bells are played Sundays from 2:45–3:30 p.m. and Wednesdays from 12:45-1:30 p.m.

The one place in Canberra that should be high on your list is the **Australian War Memorial and Museum**, the second-most-visited spot in Australia after the **Sydney Opera House**. It's a moving display of Australia's participation in wars and conflicts from the 19th century Maori wars in New Zealand to Vietnam, with emphasis on World Wars I and II. It shows clearly the out-of-proportion sacrifices the Aussies made to help out Great Britain and the United States on some of the worst battlefields of both wars including Gallipoli and New Guinea.

Some Americans think the idea of inscribing a wall with the names of war dead originated with the Vietnam Memorial in Washington, D.C., but the Aussies were there long before us. The **War Memorial** was completed in 1941, with the intention of placing all the names of the country's war dead on bronze plaques around the outside corridors of the building. By the time it was finished, Australia was at war again, so after World War II, and also after Vietnam and Korea, more names were added. A guide told us that, in all, there are 102,000 names on the plaques—most from World War I.

The memorial also has some interesting exhibits, such as the **Aeroplane Hall**, which contains a number of historic aircraft including a Lancaster bomber. There is also a display about the 96 Australians who have thus far won the Victoria Cross, the Commonwealth equivalent to the Congressional Medal of Honor. The view for the memorial, across Lake Burley Griffin to Capital Hill, reminds us of the view from the Washington Monument to the Capitol. Guided tours of the memorial are available at 10:30 a.m. and 1:30 p.m. weekdays. The memorial, at the end of Anzac Parade east of the city center, is open daily from 10 a.m. to 5 p.m.; no admission charge. ☎ *(06) 6243-4211.*

Other buildings worth a look include:

The Australian National Gallery

☎ *(06) 6271-2502.*

The gallery, opened in 1982, has more than 75,000 square feet of exhibition space and houses, and on the second floor, an excellent collection of Australian art going back 200 years. One of the most popular displays is the collection of Ned Kelly paintings by Sir Sidney Nolan. There is also a fine display of Aboriginal art and some famous sculptures by such artists as Rodin and Modigliani. The gallery sits on the south side of the lake next to the High Court, and is open daily from 10 a.m.–5 p.m; admission A$3. Guided one-hour tours leave from the lobby. It has a restaurant overlooking the lake and a gift shop.

The National Library

The public areas of the library are open from 9 a.m.–9 p.m. Monday-Thursday and 9 a.m.–4:45 p.m. Friday-Saturday, 1:30-4:45 p.m. Sunday. ☎ *(06) 6262-1111.*

The library houses at least one copy of every book printed in Australia and in addition, has a wonderful collection of Capt. Cook's papers, including his diaries from the epic journey between 1768-1771 when he explored New Zealand and the east coast of Australia. In the foyer of the library is one of the cannons Cook threw overboard to lighten ship after *Endeavor* struck the Great Barrier Reef in 1770.

New Parliament House

Like the Opera House, the new edifice is not without its detractors, many of whom think the size—and the cost—were a tad much just to house a bunch of low-life politicians. The size is impressive—1600 foot long granite walls—and so was the cost, somewhere in the neighborhood of a billion Australian dollars. The structure is carved into Capital Hill behind the old Parliament building, and was officially opened by Queen Elizabeth during the Bicentennial. One of its major features—and points of artistic dispute—is a gigantic flagpole that rises almost 300 feet above the site.

We would be unpatriotic if we failed to mention that the building was designed by—who else—an American. The overwhelming feeling you get walking into the entry hall is air and marble—it has 48 greenish marble columns and two marble staircases going to the Senate and the House of Representatives. Past the foyer is the Great Hall, the centerpoint of which is a huge hanging tapestry created by Australian artist Arthur Boyd. Of particular interest in the Members Hall just past the Great Hall is an original copy of the *Inspeximus Issue* of the *Magna Carta*, dating from 1297 and one of only three such copies in existence.

The building took 300,000 cubic meters of concrete—enough, we were told, to build 25 Sydney Opera Houses. Part of the total cost of the project went into artwork—the government commissioned 70 original pieces and purchased more than 3000 paintings and other works.

The building is open 9 a.m.–5 p.m. seven days. Guided tours are available when the houses are not in session; they start at 9:30 a.m. in the Great Hall. When Parliament is in session, visitors are welcome in galleries at both houses. The most popular time to be at the House of Representatives is at "question time," when members, usually the opposition party, get to hack and chew on the prime minister and his cabinet. There is also a self-guided audio-visual tour available. The building has handicapped access and a cafeteria open from 9 a.m.–5 p.m. There is a huge underground parking ramp with space for 6000 vehicles (campers will fit). ☎ *(06) 6277-5399.*

Black Mountain

> *The tower is open daily 9 a.m.–10 p.m; A$3 admission.* ☎ *(06) 6248-1911.*

West of the city center, is the site of the Telstra Tower, which rises about 640 feet above the ground and has viewing platforms and a revolving restaurant for the best views of the capital area.

Also at Black Mountain is the **National Botanic Gardens**, a display of native flora envisioned by Burley Griffin in his original design. The 100-acre site contains more than 6000 species, and includes an Aboriginal trail showing how they used native plants. The gardens are open daily 9 a.m.–5 p.m. with guided tours on Sundays. There is an outdoor restaurant, bookstore and visitors center, all open daily 9:30 a.m.–4:30 p.m. ☎ *(06) 6250-9540.* Another good view is available from the top of Mount Ainslie, which rises 2700 feet above the city northeast of the city center. Both Black Mountain and Mount Ainslie can be reached by car.

Other sites include the **Royal Australian Mint** on Denison Street, west of Capital Hill. It's open seven days, Monday–Friday 9 a.m.–4 p.m. and weekends 10 a.m.–3 p.m., no charge. There's a public coin press where you can mint your own dollar. ☎ *(06) 6250-9540.* The **Australian High Court**, below Capital Hill, has 50-foot-high courtroom walls and oak panels, and is open daily 9:45 a.m.–4:30 p.m. It has a cafe. **Blundell's Cottage** on Parkes Way across the lake from Capital Hill, built in 1858 and kept around as an example of the sort of building that existed in Canberra before the Yank architects got going, is open daily 10 a.m.–4 p.m. Nearby is the 260 foot-high aluminum spire of the **Australian-American Memorial** honoring U.S. efforts to help Australia in World War II.

Since every other major city in Australia has one, the ACT added a **casino**. It's located at *21 Binara Street,* next to Glebe Park and the Capital Parkroyal Hotel. The casino, European in design, has 50 gaming tables and a bunch of "pokies," coin-operated poker machines and electronic slot machines. It's open 24 hours on weekends, noon–6 a.m. weekdays. ☎ *(06) 6257-7074; FAX (06) 6257-7079.*

Essential Canberra

Information

In Sydney, the tourist bureau for the ACT and Canberra is located at *64 Castlereagh Street;* ☎ *(02) 9233-3666.* In Canberra, the tourist bureau offices are in the Jolimont Centre, *61-65 Northbourne Avenue;* ☎ *(06) 6245-6464; toll free 1-(800) 026-166.*

If you need them, the United States embassy (and consulate) is located at *State Circle and Perth Avenue in Canberra, Yarralumla,* ☎ *(06) 6270-5000,* and the Canadian embassy is on *Commonwealth Avenue, Yarralumla* ☎ *(06) 6273-3844.*

Telephones

The Australian Capital Territory area code is (06).

Getting There

Canberra is one of the few national capitals in the world not served by an international airport, but it does have **air service** to and from major Australian cities. The nonstop, one-way flights from Sydney on most airlines cost around A$100. The airport is about five miles outside of town. Bus service downtown is infrequent; a taxi ride will be around A$10.

There is a daily **express train** from Sydney that leaves about 6:30 p.m. and arrives in Canberra around 11 p.m. The return express leaves at 7:10 a.m. and arrives at 11:20 a.m. The one-way economy cost is about A$30. **Regular service** departs Sydney at 7:30 a.m., arriving in Canberra around noon and costs about the same. Return service leaves Canberra at 12:30 p.m., arriving Sydney around 5 p.m.

Getting to and from Melbourne is a bothersome job by train. There are several departures a day both directions, but a chunk of the trip is by **bus** and takes most of the day— the 10:45 a.m. from Canberra, for example, arrives in Melbourne at 8:30 that night. Cost of the train/bus trips is around A$50. A one-way flight, by contrast, is about A$150.

The capital is also served by regular buses from Sydney and Melbourne on the Hume Highway, priced around A$20 (Sydney) to A$40 (Melbourne). It takes about 9.5 hours from Melbourne, 4.5 from Sydney.

Getting Around

Public transportation is casual in Canberra, and if you're serious about seeing the sights, renting a car is probably your best bet. There are four agencies at the airport: **Avis**, ☎ *(06) 6249-6088*; **Hertz**, ☎ *(06) 6257-4877*; **Thrifty**, ☎ *(06) 6247-7422*; and **Budget**, ☎ *(06) 6248-9788*. For maps and other information, contact the *National Roads & Motorists Association, 92 Northbourne Avenue;* ☎ *(06) 6243-8800.*

If you must have a taxi and can't flag one, call ☎ *13-1008.* Public bus information is available from *ACTION*, the municipal transportation authority, by calling ☎ *(06) 6207-7611.*

The city proper has about 70 miles of paved bike paths, a popular way to get around and generally regarded as the best urban bike facilities in Australia. If you feel inspired, you can rent bikes at the local youth hostel or at **Mr. Spokes Bike Hire** near the Ferry Terminal at West Basin on the lake. The cost will be around A$10 a day. The tourist office has special biking maps showing the network of paths. ☎ *(06) 6257-1188.*

Tours

The Canberra Explorer

Buses run every hour from 10:15 a.m.–4:15 p.m. starting from the Jolimont Tourist Centre at the corner of Northbourne Avenue and Alinga Street. The buses stop at 19 locations, hitting all the high spots from Parliament to the war memorial. With ticket in hand you can get on and off at any stop. A day ticket is about A$18. Free hotel pickup is available. *Information:* ☎ *(06) 6295-3611.* Or check with the **Murrays Coachline** desk at the Jolimont Centre.

Monarch Tours

Tours that take in the usual sites, but also go to some sites outside the city such as Tidbinbilla Nature Reserve. The city highlights tour, including admissions and lunch, is about A$70 per person. A wildlife tour, with admissions and lunch, is about the same, as is a city tour coupled with a barbecue at a local sheep station (complete with shearing demonstration.) There are also half-day tours. *Information:* ☎ *(06) 6259-1686 or any local travel agent.*

Shopping

The main shopping area in Canberra is around Vernon Circle, straight across the Commonwealth Bridge from Capital Hill. Here you will find a pair of pedestrian malls, movie theaters, retail stores and David Jones, the department store. You're probably better off buying souvenirs and such in Sydney—you have to go back there anyway.

Where to Stay

Many hotels in Canberra have weekend specials. Among the best in town:

Hyatt Hotel Canberra   **A$290–350**   ★★★

Commonwealth Avenue, Yarralumla; ☎ *(06) 6270-1234.*
Doubles from A$290–350.
Close to Parliament. The hotel restaurant—the ★★★**Oak Room** is a national tourism award winner. The Hyatt is a businessmen/politicians hotel, one of the most expensive in town.

Lakeside International   **A$115–500**   ★★

London Circuit; ☎ *(06) 6247-6244.*
Doubles with breakfast A$115–265; suites A$170–500.
Located close to downtown on Lake Burley Griffin. Airy white marble lobby, rooms with a view of Parliament and the lake. The rooftop dining room—the ★★★**Burley Griffin Room**—offers upscale dining with nice scenery. Indoor heated pool, business facilities, mini-bars. Six suites.

The Pavilion   **A$195–250**   ★★★★

Canberra Avenue and National Circuit, Forrest; ☎ *(06) 6295-3144.*
Doubles from A$195; suites from A$250.
This is the closest hotel to Parliament. It's neo-Art Deco in style, with lots of glass and a big atrium. Indoor heated pool, gym, business center. Many suites have private spas.

Canberra Travelodge   **A$120–220**   ★★★

150 Northbourne Avenue, Braddon; ☎ *(06) 6248-5311; FAX (06) 6248-8357.*
Doubles from A$120; suites from A$220.
About a kilometer from the lake, recently renovated. Fairly standard rooms, but with cable TV and mini-bars. Indoor pool, sauna, gym, valet service, guest laundry. Restaurant and 24-hour bistro, tour desk.

Capital Parkroyal   **A$50–280**   ★★★

1 Binara Street; ☎ *(06) 6247-8999; FAX (06) 6257-4903.*
Doubles from A$50; suites from $A280.

Heart of downtown, close to the National Convention Centre in Glebe Park and adjacent to the Canberra Casino. Pool, sauna, seven suites, four dining areas, two bars.

Olims   A$80–100   ★★

Corner of Limestone and Ainslie avenues, Braddon; ☎ *(06) 6248-5511; FAX (06) 6295 2119.*
Doubles from around A$80; suites from A$100.

Northeast of the city center, not far from the war memorial. Refurbished in 1994, now a Mediterranean-style facility with large courtyard, balconies, nice lounge, beer garden and some quite nice split-level executive suites. Restaurant, bar/bistro.

Canberra International   A$120   ★★

242 Northbourne Avenue, Braddon; ☎ *(06) 6247-6966; FAX (06) 6248-7823.*
Doubles from A$120.

The best part of this hotel is the palm-bedecked atrium, with a bar and restaurant. Good location, close to the city center. Guest laundry.

Where to Eat

Almost all non-hotel restaurants in Canberra close Sunday, and some are closed when Parliament is not in session. But there are several hundred places to eat around town, so you shouldn't starve. A few suggestions.

John Pierre le Carrousel $$$ ★★★★

Redhill Lookout, Redhill; ☎ *(06) 6273-1808.*
Lunch noon–2 p.m. Monday–Friday; dinner 6:30–10 p.m. Monday–Friday, 6–midnight Saturday.

Award winner with great views of the city. French, as the name suggests, always crowded. It serves the national symbol: kangaroo filets with pink peppercorn and berry sauce; or veal scallopini with mango and wine sauce. Reservations a must.

Fringe Benefits $$ ★★★

54 Marcus Clarke Street, near Vernon Circle; ☎ *(06) 6247-4042.*
Dinner from 6 p.m. Reservations a good idea.

Mediterranean cuisine, always popular, wins a lot of prizes, political hangout. Located in the heart of the city center and always worth a try.

Hill Station $$ ★★★

Sheppard Street, Hume; ☎ *(06) 6260-1393.*
Lunch Thursday–Friday; dinner Wednesday–Saturday. Call for hours and reservations.

A National Trust homestead, with an art gallery and antiques. A popular watering hole, with five lounge and dining areas with open fires and a verandah for outdoor service. Fancy teas on weekends and traditional roast lunches on Sundays. Big wine list.

Imperial Court $

40 Northbourne Avenue; ☎ *(06) 6248-5547.*
Open seven days for lunch and dinner; also has takeaway food.

The best Chinese tucker in town, open late. Live music Friday and Saturday night.

Outside Canberra

The diplomatic corps—at least those who can ski—must love being stationed in Canberra in the winter because it's next door to the Snowy Mountains, a major skiing center in Australia. The ski resorts, located in Kosciusko National Park, Australia's largest, are about 100 miles from the capital, and offer full services and ski equipment. The national park is also a summer playground with many miles of fine hiking trails. *Park information*: ☎ *(06) 6456-2102*. (See skiing information in *New South Wales* section.)

Other sites to check out around the Canberra area:

Tidbinbilla Deep Space Tracking Center
☎ *(06) 6201-7800.*
The hills west of Canberra used to be almost filled with U.S.-owned tracking stations, several of which were run by NASA. The only one still going is this station, operated for NASA by the Australian Department of Science. The station has spacecraft models, audio-visual displays and radio telescopes. The visitors' center and gift shop is open 9 a.m.–5 p.m. and is located 25 miles southwest of the city. Admission and parking free.

Tidbinbilla Nature Reserve
☎ *(06) 6237-5120.*
Next to the space station, this 12,000-acre park offers hidden picnic areas and miles of trails through virgin bush. There's a special pen where you can ogle emus, roos and wallabies. The reserve information center is open daily from 9 a.m.

Lanyon

☎ *(06) 6237-5136.*
Here's your chance to see how gentlemen squatters lived in the Victorian Age. Lanyon is an old farmhouse begun in the 1850s and is set in a green and tree-surrounded area in the middle of rich pastureland. It's filled with period furnishings and farm equipment. You reach it by taking the Monaro Highway south from Canberra (the road to Cooma) and turn off to Tharwa. Lanyon Homestead is open 10 a.m.–4 p.m. Tuesday-Sunday and holidays. There's a coffee shop with artwork by contemporary Aussie artists.

QUEENSLAND AND THE GREAT BARRIER REEF

Great Barrier Reef Island features unmatched beauty above and below the sea.

If you had time only for one stop in Australia, and were thus forced to make a truly horrible decision, we think your time would be best spent in Queensland. We do not say this lightly, because it is not easy to dismiss Sydney and the other great cities of Australia, nor is it easy to ignore the other great experiences to be found around the country.

But Queensland? Well, Queensland is the California of Australia, the perfect one-stop vacation destination. It has more going for it than any other single Aussie state, with a menu of activities that ranges from the singular beauties of the Great Barrier Reef, to the crocodile-infested jungles of the Cape York Peninsula, to the sunny sandboxes along the coast, to the raw and lonely Outback.

They call Queensland the Sunshine State, partly because of its subtropical and tropical climate, but also because of the string of glorious beaches stretching from the Queensland-New South Wales border north. The beaches have given rise to a series of resort communities where the air is filled with the smell of coconut oil, and thousands of Australian families make an annual pilgrimage to spend a fortnight or two seeking fun and sun.

Queensland is huge—at about 667,000 square miles, the second largest state (Western Australia is the biggest), more than twice the size of Texas. It takes up about a quarter of the Australian continent. There are about 2.9 million people living in the state, which is split almost in half by the Tropic of Capricorn. Taking the Cape York Peninsula and the Gulf of Carpentaria into account, Queensland has an enormous coastline, something like 3200 miles, but only about half of that, from Coolangatta to Mossman, is readily accessible by motor vehicle.

Queensland started out as a penal colony set up as part of New South Wales in 1824. An influx of free settlers, many who entered illegally, changed its face from prison to agricultural center. In 1842, it was officially opened to free settlement, and by 1859, the population was large enough to justify its status as a separate colony. The settlers made their way with sheep, cattle, wheat, an abundance of natural resources and cash crops—including bananas, which gave rise to the rather derisive name the rest of Australia sometimes uses for Queensland natives: "Banana-benders."

The state is also a major producer of ores (bauxite, tin, coal) and produces almost 100 percent of Australia's pineapple crop as well as peanuts and sugar cane. But the allure of the climate and the semi-South Seas life style of the Queensland tropics (the Aussies call it "going troppo") was just too much to ignore, and now tourism is the state's second-largest industry, raking in nearly A$10 billion a year. By some estimates, more than half of all tourists heading for Australia have Queensland as their major destination—much of the reason being, of course, the Great Barrier Reef. Brisbane only gets about a tenth of all the tourist business that comes to the state.

Finally, it is at least a poetic necessity to remember that two of the country's most recognizable symbols were born in Queensland. *"Waltzing Matilda"* was written and first performed here, and Qantas Airlines first flew from Queensland's Outback airfields—the name stands for Queensland and Northern Territory Air Services.

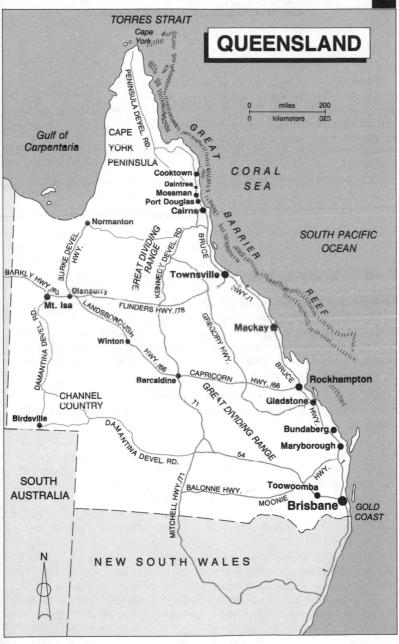

TORRES STRAIT

Cape
York

PENINSULA DEVEL. RD.

QUEENSLAND

0   miles   200
0   kilometers   025

*Gulf of
Carpentaria*

CAPE
YORK
PENINSULA

GREAT BARRIER REEF

*CORAL
SEA*

Cooktown
Daintree
Mossman
Port Douglas
Cairns

*SOUTH PACIFIC
OCEAN*

Normanton

GREAT DIVIDING RANGE

KENNEDY DEVEL. RD.

BRUCE

BURKE DEVEL. HWY.

BARKLY HWY.

Cloncurry

Mt. Isa

LANDSBOROUGH

FLINDERS HWY. /78

Townsville

HWY. /1

GREGORY HWY.

Winton

HWY. /66

Mackay

DAMANTINA DEVEL. RD.

Barcaldine

CAPRICORN

HWY. /66

BRUCE

Rockhampton

GREAT DIVIDING RANGE

Gladstone

HWY.

CHANNEL
COUNTRY

Birdsville

/1

DAMANTINA DEVEL. RD.

Bundaberg

Maryborough

/1

**SOUTH
AUSTRALIA**

MITCHELL HWY. /71

BALONNE HWY.

54

HWY.

Toowoomba

MOONIE

Brisbane

*GOLD
COAST*

N

NEW SOUTH WALES

Essential Queensland

Information

Queensland has **tourism offices** in all the major cities of Australia. These offices can supply information as well as make reservations and recommend tours. The various offices are:

Sydney, *75 Castlereagh Street;* ☎ *(02) 9232-1788*; **Melbourne**, *257 Collins Street,* ☎ *(03) 9654-3866*; **Adelaide**, *10 Grenfell Street,* ☎ *(08) 212-2399*; **Brisbane**, *Level 36 Riverside Centre, 123 Eagle Street,* ☎ *(07) 3833-5400*; **Canberra**, *25 Garema Place,* ☎ *(06) 6248-8411*; **Perth**, *55 St. George's Terrace,* ☎ *(09) 9325-1600*. The main information center in the city is at the City Hall on Elizabeth Street. Hours are 8:30 a.m.–5 p.m. Monday-Friday and 9:30 a.m.–12:30 p.m. Saturdays. ☎ *(07) 3221-4811; FAX (07) 3229-5126.*

For information about national parks around the state, contact the **Queensland National Parks and Wildlife Service**, *P.O. Box 190, North Quay, Brisbane;* ☎ *(07) 3224-0414.*

Getting There

Queensland has three international airports capable of handling wide-body aircraft: Cairns, Townsville and Brisbane—it's the only state with more than one **international airport**. For those planning a visit to the Great Barrier Reef, Cairns is the recommended destination, being close to the Reef and many of the Reef island resorts. The Townsville airport, developed and planned as the first international gateway to northern Queensland, has largely been bypassed in favor of Cairns, but still receives a fair amount of international service, mostly from Southeast Asia and the Pacific.

Normally, from North America, you reach the major Queensland cities by flying first to Sydney, then taking either an international or domestic airline to Cairns or Brisbane. **Qantas**, with its subsidiaries, flies all over Queensland, and **United** has service to Brisbane. **Air New Zealand** has stops in Brisbane and Cairns.

Getting Around

Among internal **air carriers** with service to major Queensland cities are **Ansett**, **Australian** and **Sunstate**.

Traveling around the state by **rail** is a tedious process, with long hours involved between major population centers—speeds averaging less than 30 miles an hour are not unusual on many runs. The government has tried to speed things up with trains such as the daily **Sydney-Brisbane XPT** (for express passenger train.) It leaves Sydney late in the afternoon and arrives in Brisbane the next morning. This is not a sleeper train, just reclining seats. The return leaves early in the morning and arrives late that night in Sydney. The one-way fare is about A$130 first class; $100 economy. The train has a buffet car; the trip takes about 14.5 hours.

From Brisbane, a number of trains provide service to outlying communities. These include the **Westlander**, which runs to Cunnamulla in the Outback, west via Charleville with connections to Quilpie; the **Inlander**, which runs between Townsville and Mt. Isa, and the **Midlander**, which has service between Rockhampton and Winton. These trains have sleeping cars and dining cars. One-way fares on all three are about A$170 first class, about A$90 economy.

There is regular **daily service** between Brisbane and Coolangatta, the south end of the Gold Coast. The service is a combined bus/rail trip taking about 2.5 hours. A popular service to the Gold Coast from Sydney is the **Pacific Coast Motorail**, an overnight (17 hours) that lets the natives ship their cars up to the Gold Coast on the same trip. The train goes to Murwillumbah, leaving Sydney at 6:30 p.m. and arriving the next morning at 11. The return trip leaves Murwillumbah at 4:30 p.m. and arrives Sydney the next morning at 9 a.m. A one-way first-class berth is about A$125 per person; first-class sitting, about A$90, economy sitting, about A$60.

Another Gold Coast train from Sydney goes to Surfers Paradise, also about 17 hours. It leaves Sydney at 6 p.m., arriving in Surfers at 11 a.m. the next morning; return service leaves Surfers at 1:30 p.m., arriving Sydney at 7 a.m. The one-way costs are comparable to the Pacific Coast Motorail.

Three trains go north along the coast from Brisbane, all of which are equipped with berths, dining cars and bars: The **Spirit of Capricorn** takes a bit more than nine hours to make the run between Brisbane and Rockhampton. Trains leave Brisbane around 8 a.m. and arrive in Rockhampton at 6 p.m.; same return schedule. An economy one-way ticket is about A$60.

The **Queenslander** and the **Sunlander** both go from Brisbane to Cairns with stops in Townsville and other cities along the way; the trip takes around 33 hours. (For a description of the Sunlander, see the TRAIN section.)

The Sunlander offers service to Cairns Monday–Thursday and Saturdays. It leaves Brisbane around 9 a.m. and arrives in Cairns about 6:30 p.m the day after. A first-class berth is about $220 per person; economy berth, A$140; economy sitting, A$120.

From Rockhampton, the Midlander runs inland to Winton, with stops at Barcaldine and Longreach. The train leaves Rocky about 6:30 p.m. and arrives in Winton around 1:15 the next afternoon. The return train leaves Winton about 4 p.m. and arrives in Rockhampton at 9:50 a.m. the next day. A first-class berth runs about A$170 per person; economy-class berths A$100.

From Townsville, the Inlander runs to Mount Isa in Queensland's Outback. The train leaves Townsville Wednesdays and Sundays at 4 p.m., arriving in Mount Isa the next morning at 9:45 a.m. The return leaves Mount Isa Mondays and Thursdays at 2 p.m. and arrives in Townsville at 7 a.m. the next morning. A first-class berth is about A$170; economy sleeper about A$100.

For information on railroad service in Queensland, contact the **City Booking Office**, *Queensland Railways, 208 Adelaide Street;* ☎ *(07) 3235-1122. Information is also available from* **Railways of Australia**, *85 Queen Street, Melbourne;* ☎ *(03) 9608-0811. Intrastate trains leave the city from the* **Brisbane Transport Centre** *on Roma Street beneath the Brisbane Travelodge. The centre is also the main bus station, and tickets for both rail and bus trips can be purchased there; Information:* ☎ *(07) 3225-0211 or* **Queensland Rail Traveltrain Network,** ☎ *13-2232.*

Two other sources of information about railroads, as well as other services, are the **Public Transportation Information Centre**, *Brisbane City Council, Brisbane Administration Centre, 69 Ann Street,* ☎ *(07) 3225-4444, open Monday–Friday 8:15 a.m.–4:45* p.m.; and the **Public Transport Information Centre** at the Central Station in Ann Street, open Monday–Friday 8:15 a.m.–5 p.m.

Express bus service from Brisbane to outlying cities is regular, fairly inexpensive, and sometimes faster than the trains. The trip from Sydney to Brisbane takes about 17 hours by bus, and costs around A$60. Brisbane-Cairns takes about 25 hours and costs about A$125. There is also service from Brisbane to Mt. Isa through Longreach and also from Rockhampton and Townsville to Mt. Isa. There is also regular bus service between Brisbane and the nearby resort coasts.

For RV fans, there are a couple of hundred **caravan parks** around the state, with rates generally in the A$10 to A$20 per-vehicle, per night range. For a guide to many of them, look for the *Caravan Parks & Regional Tourist Guide* issued by the Caravan Parks Association of Queensland, available through government tourist offices. It's also handy for auto drivers because it contains gasoline station locations and tourist site information.

Driving in Queensland can be boring or dangerous, depending on where you are and what you're driving. Generally, the 600-mile-long coast road between Brisbane and Cairns is adequate, but once you turn inland, roads tend to get narrow and shoulders tend to disappear. Rental car agencies are normally available anywhere there is air service—but watch out for drop-off charges if you're not planning to return to the city where you rented the car.

For general road information and other help—particularly if you're a member of the CAA or AAA—contact the **Royal Automobile Club of Queensland**, *300 St. Paul's Terrace in Fortitude Valley;* ☎ *(07) 3361-2444; FAX (07) 3257-1863*. There is also a RACQ office in the General Post Office at *261 Queen Street* in downtown Brisbane ☎ *(07) 3361-2444*. Or get a guide to the state's highways, complete with a list of rest stops, from the *Main Roads Department, Boundary Street, Spring Hill, Brisbane;* ☎ *(07) 3834-2011*.

Climate

As befits a subtropical/tropical state, annual temperature ranges tend to be generally kind to humans, with highs along the coast ranging from 70°F in the winter to 90°F in the summer. Inland, it gets a bit beastlier: Mount Isa, way out in the Outback, gets about 30 days a year in the 100-degree range. Rainfall is also varied, with Cairns receiving between 80 and 100 inches a year and Longreach getting under two inches—farther west is even dryer. In the wet (December-March), it can get pretty swampy north of Cairns in the Cape York area, but it might make you feel better knowing that the Queensland tourism folks assure us that a lot of the rainfall comes during the night. Reef resorts and islands offshore tend to be cooler than the mainland, with steady sea breezes. The sea can get so rough at times, however, that it's impossible to visit the Reef in safety.

ONE VERY SERIOUS NOTE ABOUT THE NORTH QUEENSLAND COAST: Swimming. Australia has several species of deadly coelenterates, such as physalia and chironex—what we'd call jellyfish and the Aussies call box jellyfish, sea wasps or stingers. Every year when the jellyfish come out (November–March), it seems there's at least one death from these creatures, although most beaches are clearly marked. Forget about being eaten by sharks—more people have died in Australia from contact with jellyfish than any other creature. Even though there are some anti-venoms for some species, the chances of a fatality due to anaphylactic reaction or pulmonary edema is very strong, even in healthy adults. The problem is that some of the deadliest species are tiny, almost invisible. Some resort areas try to use special nets to keep the critters out, but uninhabited beaches and even some freshwater rivers rely solely on a swimmer's common sense. Some swimmers, male and female, claim pantyhose will protect them, but our advice is if you're not totally sure, don't go swimming. Watch where you're walking on the beach because even the stingers of a dead jellyfish can harm you. You will notice that many beaches have warning signs about the jellyfish, often accompanied by gallon bottles of vinegar, which is the normal emergency first-aid treatment for tentacle stings.

Time

Queensland is on Australian Eastern Time, meaning it's 17 or 18 hours ahead of Pacific Standard Time on the U.S. West Coast; when it's noon Saturday in San Francisco, it's 6 p.m. Sunday in Brisbane. Queensland does not go on daylight savings time, and probably won't. In the spring of 1992, there was a very expensive, often rancorous referendum on the question, which saw the pro-daylight savings forces go down to a resounding defeat. This, despite predictions that the populous and powerful Brisbane/Gold Coast business factions would carry the day.

Brisbane

Brisbane's climate is one of its greatest assets.

Flowers, gardens, palm trees and the river—that's what you mostly remember about Brisbane. The city has a manageable population, about 1.5 million, and sits about 20 miles up the Brisbane River from Moreton Bay on the coast.

The climate, Brisbane's greatest asset, is mostly pleasant, normally ranging from highs of about 85 Fahrenheit in the summer (December-January) to lows in July of around 50. The highest point of land in town is about 135 feet above sea level.

The city center is nicely placed, sitting on a peninsula carved by the meandering river, with several large parkland areas to break up the urban skyscape. The city's external appearance is not much to get excited about, being mostly efficiently designed banks and high-rises. The city got a major shot in the arm from the 1988 Expo, which saw the development of several new hotel and office areas around town, but more importantly, the development of the Expo site itself. The area, on the river directly across from the city center, had been an old and ugly warehouse district. After Expo moved out, the city started developing the area as part of a larger scheme to enhance the riverfront, which until recent years had been mostly overlooked.

Several projects were completed along the river, including the **Heritage Beaufort Hotel** and the **Eagle Street** complex, a shopping/business/restaurant area on the river off Market Street. Another water-directed project was the **Gateway Marine Centre**, located near Fisherman Islands at the mouth of the river. The major effort was on the Expo site itself, which became a major park/amusement center called **South Bank Parklands**.

In addition, expansion of the city's international airport runways and facilities was undertaken. Some planning estimates see an annual increase in passenger loads of around 13.5 percent, with about 7 million passengers a year clearing the airport by the year 2000.

The housing areas spreading out from the city center are basically just comfortable suburbs. Driving around will give you a chance to study classic Queensland architecture—verandas, houses up on stilts, iron grillwork, tinned roofs, yards filled with flowers and palm trees. The urban area goes on forever—the city limits contain about 470 square miles of country.

Brisbane cannot rival watery Sydney or stately Melbourne in beauty or attractions, but it is one of the most comfortable of the large Australian cities. The city showed off its friendly ways and vitality well enough in 1988 when it held the Expo, and judging from the amount of development already begun and what is planned, it seems there will be no keeping the city down. The name, by the way, is pronounced "BRIZ-bun." Or, if you're feeling Australian, you could call it Brissie (that's Brizzie).

Downtown

Queen Street Mall

The best part of the city is its heart, which centers on the **Queen Street Mall**. Almost every city of any size in Australia has a pedestrian mall, and this is one of the best in the country. It's casual and easy, a place where you can get a coke and a hamburger or a suite

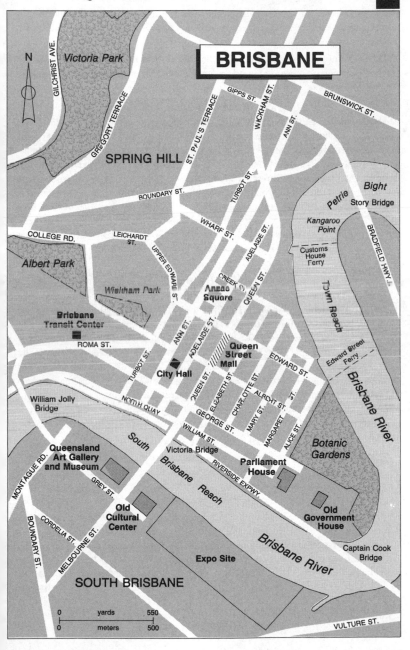

BRISBANE

N

Victoria Park

GILCHRIST AVE.

GREGORY TERRACE

SPRING HILL

ST. PAUL'S TERRACE

GIPPS ST.

WICKHAM ST.

BRUNSWICK ST.

ANN ST.

BOUNDARY ST.

TURBOT ST.

WHARF ST.

Bight

Petrie

Story Bridge

COLLEGE RD.

LEICHARDT ST.

ADELAIDE ST.

Kangaroo Point

BRADFIELD HWY J.

Albert Park

UPPER EDWARD ST.

CREEK ST.

Customs House Ferry

Wickham Park

Anzac Square

QUEEN ST.

Brisbane Transit Center

ANN ST.

ADELAIDE ST.

Town Reach

ROMA ST.

Queen Street Mall

EDWARD ST.

City Hall

TURBOT ST.

QUEEN ST.

ELIZABETH ST.

CHARLOTTE ST.

ALBERT ST.

Edward Street Ferry

Brisbane River

William Jolly Bridge

NORTH QUAY

GEORGE ST.

MARY ST.

MARGARET ST.

ALICE ST.

Botanic Gardens

MONTAGUE RD.

South

WILLIAM ST.

Victoria Bridge

Brisbane Reach

RIVERSIDE EXPWY.

Parliament House

Queensland Art Gallery and Museum

GREY ST.

Old Government House

CORDELIA ST.

Old Cultural Center

MELBOURNE ST.

BOUNDARY ST.

Expo Site

Captain Cook Bridge

Brisbane River

SOUTH BRISBANE

| 0 | yards | 550 |
| 0 | meters | 500 |

VULTURE ST.

in a five-star hotel. The mall was begun in 1982 to show off for the Commonwealth Games, and was expanded and gussied-up again in time for Expo 88. Part of the 1988 expansion was an underground bus station.

The mall runs for two long blocks from near the river to Edward Street. Many of the best hotels, important offices and good restaurants are either on the mall or within a short walking distance of it.

Anzac Square

The Australians are thorough when it comes to remembering their war dead, and Anzac Square is Brisbane's chief monument to the fallen. Located at the northeast end of Ann and Adelaide streets, the monument has an eternal flame and bronze tablets to commemorate European battlegrounds where Anzac forces were involved, and in a vault underneath the flame is the **Shrine of Memories**, which has soil from countries where Australian armed forces fought. Directly across Adelaide Street from the war memorial is Post Office Square, which contains one of Brisbane's prides and joys, the **General Post Office**. The old stone hulk was built in the late 1870s on the site of what had once been the quarters for female convicts, and has been restored to its Victorian excellence. Inside is a museum with displays of 175 years of Aussie postal history. It's open 10 a.m.–5 p.m. Monday-Friday, Saturday until noon. ☎ *(07) 3224-1215.*

The City Hall

This is probably the public building that Brisbaners prize the most. Construction of the massive stone structure began in 1920 and took 10 years to complete. Its centerpoint has always been the 300-foot-high clock tower, for its early years the tallest structure in the city. The tower has an observation platform and is included on conducted tours of the facility. The building also houses a concert hall and what is considered to be one of the finest pipe organs in the Southern Hemisphere. Inside are the **City Hall Art Gallery and Museum**. The building faces King George Square, which is highlighted by small gardens and a fountain—and as befits its latitude, (27 degrees, 28.3 minutes south), there are

palm trees all over. The building is open 9:30 a.m.–4 p.m. Monday-Friday. Tours Monday, Wednesday, Friday, Saturday. *City Hall information:* ☎ *(07) 3403-4890.*

The Convict Past

Most of the convict-labor buildings from Brisbane's penal past are long gone. One which does remain is the **Old Windmill**, also called the Observatory, located on Wickham Terrace, a quiet residential street on a hill above the city. The tower dates to 1828 and was built as a windmill under the orders of Capt. Patrick Logan, the infamous prison master who was slain by an Aboriginal. In this century, the building was used in the 1930s to broadcast some of the world's first television signals. It's not open to the public.

The oldest general-use structure in town is the **Old Commissariat Store**, *115 William Street*, which sits on what was once the town's original wharf. It was built in 1829 and now houses the offices of the **Royal Historical Society of Queensland**. *Information:*

☎ *(07) 3221-4198.* An interesting collection of century-old buildings called **Earlystreet Historical Village** is located in the suburb of Norman Park, east of downtown. Included in the buildings are a pub, general store, slab hut and a cottage, all sitting on two acres of native bush. *Information:* ☎ *(07) 3398-6866.*

Two other old buildings are now being put to modern use. The **Treasury Building**, built in the 1890s to house the colony's winnings from the gold fields, is now the home of the **Conrad Treasury Casino** between George and William streets near the river. The classy old sandstone building has a six-story atrium, three restaurants, seven bars and more than 100 gaming tables and a stash of coin machines. It's open 24 hours.

The **Customs House** at the north end of Queen Street has been turned into a gallery by the University of Queensland. The building, easy to spot with its copper dome, also has a brasserie and bookstore.

Other Brisbane Sights

Parliament House

Queensland's Parliament House dates from 1868, and is done in a style called French Renaissance. It sits next to the river on the city center's peninsula, adjacent to the Botanic Gardens. The building, copper-topped and built of stone, contrasts nicely to the groves of palm trees surrounding the site. Tours of the building, at the corner of George and Alice streets, are available Monday-Friday from 9:15 a.m.–2:45 p.m. *Information:* ☎ *(07) 3226-7111.*

Botanic Gardens

The Botanic Gardens are a favorite spot for picnics and weekend concerts. The gardens date from 1865, and while not spectacular, are still a breath of green in the increasingly urban nature of the downtown area. The concerts are part of the city's **FREEPS** programs—Free Recreation and Entertainment for Everyone in the Parks. The gardens are open sunrise to sunset. *Information:* ☎ *(07) 3221-4528.*

Near the gardens and Parliament House is **The Mansions**, a set of restored townhouses now used as a shopping center. The buildings are some of the best examples of 1890s colonial architecture in the city. One of the better stores in the complex is the **National Trust gift shop**. *Information for The Mansions:* ☎ *(07) 3221-4965.*

Queensland Cultural Centre

If you're an art or science fan, the center of things in Brisbane is the Queensland Cultural Centre, located directly across the river from downtown and adjacent to the Expo site. The centre houses the **Queensland Art Gallery**, the **Performing Arts Complex**, a museum and a state library. The gallery has an impressive collection, including works by Picasso, Toulouse-Lautrec and Renoir, plus a number of works by Australian artists. The museum has a fine display on the exploits of aviation pioneer Sir Charles Kingsford Smith. The performing arts area has three theaters, and is home to the **Queensland Symphony Orchestra**. Tours of all the facilities in the cultural centre are available. ☎ *(07) 3844-8800.*

Queensland Maritime Museum

The museum is located next to the old Expo site and adjacent to the Cultural Centre. On hand are an historic dry dock, a steam tug and even a World War II frigate. It's open 10 a.m.–5 p.m.; small admissions charge. ☎ *(07) 3844-5361.*

If you want to do the city historical sites up proper, stop in at a city information office and get a free copy of **Heritage Trails**, a guide that takes you point to point through the city.

South Bank Parklands

At about eight acres, the Parklands area, adjacent to the Brisbane Cultural Centre on the river across from the city center, is a complex of nature attractions, a beach, outdoor concert area, shops and eateries—probably the best thing that's happened to the Brisbane River in a century. Included in the sights are the **Gondwana Rainforest Sanctuary**, with crocodiles, parrots and pythons; the **Butterfly and Insect House** and the **Suncorp Piazza** entertainment area. The area is nicely landscaped with 4000 trees and more than 175,000 other plants; there are barbecue areas and picnic tables. Included among the cafes is the **Plough Inn**, an old inn built in the 1880s and saved during the Expo festivities. Access to the area is by ferry from North Quay or by bus from the city. ☎ *(07) 3867-2051.*

Close to the City

Lone Pine

The most famous attraction in the Brisbane area is probably the **Lone Pine Koala Sanctuary**, the largest such private reserve in the country—and we think the best. Here's your chance to have your photo taken with a koala. There is strong evidence to suggest that the eucalyptus-leaf diet they exist on keeps them stoned out of their minds most of the time, leading one Australian travel writer to describe them as "grotty little dope fiends." Well, you decide for yourself.

What Lone Pine does offer—and this is one of the best-kept secrets of Australian animal life—is a chance to meet kangaroos up close and personal and to discover that they, unlike koalas, are intelligent, friendly creatures with great personalities. The Lone Pine roos have life made. All they do is lie around in the shade all day and let tourists feed them. To give you an idea of what you're dealing with in a tame kangaroo, just watch them with children—even when the little monsters pull their ears and walk on their tails, they just get up and walk away. If they wanted, they could open the kids up like a tin of sardines—they have claws like a saber-tooth tiger's tooth. The park also has emu, platypuses, dingoes, Tasmanian devils and deer.

Lone Pine makes for a pleasant day in the country. You can get there either by bus or by boat, or a combination of both. There is a **Lone Pine express** (BCC 518) that leaves from a bus stop at the Koala Platform in the underground bus station at the Myer Centre. It starts running at 7:35 a.m. and costs about A$4 per person one-way. One boat, run by **Mirimar Cruises**, leaves downtown around 1 p.m. and arrives at Lone Pine around 2:15 p.m. The boat returns to the city at 3:50 p.m. Tickets for the boat back to the city can be bought at Lone Pine. The one-way trip is about A$15 per person. The boat has a bar and snacks. The company offers a transfer service from downtown hotels to the quay for some trips. *Information: Mirimar Cruises, Queens Wharf Road, North Quay, Brisbane;* ☎ *(07) 3221-0300.*

Lone Pine is open from 7:30 a.m.–5 p.m. The platypus tanks are open for view from 11:30 a.m.–noon and 2:45–4 p.m. There is a souvenir shop, cafe and refreshment kiosk. Ticket costs are about A$10 per person. *Information: Lone Pine Koala Sanctuary, Jesmond Road, Fig Tree Pocket, Brisbane;* ☎ *(07) 3378-1366.*

Lone Pine Koala Sanctuary near Brisbane is the place to get up close and personal with the furry critters.

Mount Coot-Tha

The Brisbane City Council has developed this bush area about four miles west of downtown into what is expected to be Australia's largest subtropical gardens. A winding road leads to the top where excellent views of the city are available. In the park are the botanical gardens, the **Sir Thomas Brisbane Planetarium** and the **J.C. Slaughter Falls**. The gardens are open 8 a.m.–5 p.m. daily; free admission. *Information about the park*: ☎ *(07) 3403-2533*. On the road to the top is the **Mount Coot-tha Summit Restaurant**, a licensed place that serves light meals and Devonshire teas, as well as lunches and dinners. ☎ *(07) 3369-9922*.

The planetarium (the largest in Australia) honors the city's namesake, who was governor of Australia in the 1820s. It offers shows twice a day Wednesday-Sunday. The planetarium has an information number for hours and activities: ☎ *(07) 3377-8896*. The BCC runs its Gardens 39 bus from Ann Street on King George Square hourly to the park.

Newstead House

The oldest residential building in the city is Newstead House, which was built in 1846 as the home of pioneer squatter Patrick Leslie. The carefully restored and furnished house sits on a hill above a bend on the Brisbane River about 2.5 miles north of the city center in the Newstead area. Sunday is a good day to take a look and have a Devonshire tea at the same time. Admission to the house is A$1; children free. It's open Monday-Friday 11 a.m.–4 p.m. and Sundays 2 p.m.–5 p.m. Buses run from downtown. *Information: Newstead House, Breakfast Creek Road, Newstead;* ☎ *(07) 3252-7373*.

Chinatown and Fortitude Valley

Northeast of the city center is Fortitude Valley, a modest shopping and eating area with a few department stores and the renovated Chinatown that serves as the city's center of Asian cuisine—there are something like 50 ethnic restaurants in the area. The main shopping/eating area is centered around Brunswick Street between Wickham and Ann streets. The valley keeps the same store hours as downtown Brisbane, and is serviced regularly by BCC buses.

Australian Woolshed

This is Brisbane's answer to tourists who want to see the sheep culture at work. Located in Ferny Hills close to downtown, the Shed has working sheepdogs, shearing demonstrations and a clutch of kangaroos and koalas. Shows daily at 10 a.m., 11 a.m. and 2 p.m. It comes with a gift shop and two restaurants, souvenir koala photographs and "bush dancing dinners." Very popular with bus tours. Admission A$12 adults. ☎ *(07) 3351-5366; FAX (07) 3351-5575*.

On the Water

In addition to the cruise upriver to Lone Pine, there are several other tours available on the Brisbane River, as well as trips to Moreton Bay and some of its vacation islands.

Kookaburra Queen

☎ *(07) 3221-1300; FAX (07) 3229-6334*.

This paddlewheeler has restaurant facilities and offers morning and afternoon teas, lunches and dinners. The teas are in the A$15 range; lunch from A$15-40 and dinner from A$20–50. Dinner cruises are about four hours long. It leaves from a dock at the Eagle Street Pier at Waterfront Place.

Brisbane Paddlewheeler II

Information: ☎ (07) 3846-1713.
Another popular excursion that runs a variety of trips on the river in the downtown area. Sundays, there is a chicken and champagne jazz trip (live band, lunch) for about A$25 per person. There are also party nights with live dance music and a smorgasbord for about A$30 per person.

Golden Mile Ferry Service

Information: Golden Mile Ferry, Riverside Centre, 123 Eagle Street, Brisbane; ☎ (07) 3399-5054.
Offers daily trips up and down the river, starting at the Botanic Gardens. It's the best bargain on the river, costing about A$5 for a round trip that takes about an hour. Sundays, the ferry goes all the way to Moreton Bay on a three-hour trip that costs about A$10.

Brisbane City Ferries

Information: Brisbane City Ferries, ☎ (07) 3399-4768 or the **Transinfo** number, ☎ 13-1230.
The way a lot of folks spend a weekend afternoon in Brisbane, also offers a chance to see the city from the river. Ferries stop along the way to inspect some of the sights, including Newstead House (Saturdays) and the Queensland Cultural Centre (Sundays). Reservations necessary.

Moreton Bay

Bay tourism information: ☎ (07) 260-7823.
Twenty miles from downtown, is a large (410 square miles) protected ocean area with several hundred islands, the largest of which are **North Stradbroke**, **South Stradbroke** and **Moreton**. At the south end of the bay is the beginning of the Gold Coast and its resorts and long sandy beaches.

Bribie Island

At the north end of the bay is a wildlife sanctuary with several small settlements and a permanent population of several thousand. The island, about 20 miles long, is connected to the mainland by a bridge to Bellara, near the main town on the island, Bongaree. Campgrounds and RV facilities are available on the island.

Moreton Island

Twenty-four miles long and six miles wide, Moreton Island forms the northeastern part of the bay. Its chief geological feature is **Mount Tempest**, at 920 feet one of the highest stable sand dunes in the world. The island is home to 125 species of birds and has several freshwater lakes in its interior. Most of the island is a national park, although there is a hotel on the west side of the island, the **Tangalooma Moreton Island Resort ★★★**. It has space for about 250 guests, with rooms running around A$150 double. The resort is a deep-sea fishing center. Every night, there's a wild dolphin feeding excursion from the resort. There's a courtesy bus to the resort from the Brisbane Transit Centre every Tuesday–Saturday. *Information: Tangalooma Resort;* ☎ (07) 268-6333. The national park ranger can be contacted in care of the resort or by calling ☎ (07) 408-2710. The beach is about 25 miles long, and there is a lighthouse at the north end of the island that is still in use. Only four-wheel-drive vehicles can drive on the island. Also, there is high-speed catamaran service to the island from Brisbane; information from the resort. A passenger launch for day trips runs from the Holt Street Wharf at Pinkenba near the airport. It leaves at 9:30 a.m. Tuesday–Friday, 9 a.m. weekends. The cost is about A$45 for a round-trip ticket.

Passenger launches

Leave regularly for the island from the wharf at **Hamilton**; from **Redcliffe**, north of town, and from **Bribie Island** and **North Stradbroke Island**. The one-way cost, depending on port, ranges between A$20 and A$30. There are also two small airstrips on the island. Campsites must be reserved, and supplies are available on the island.

North Stradbroke

The largest of the Moreton Bay islands, North Stradbroke is also a sandy barrier island, with freshwater lakes and several impressive headlands. There are three settlements on the island, which is a popular fishing and surfing destination for city dwellers. There are camping areas at all three locations.

Anchorage Village Beach Resort   A$80–150   ★★★

At Point Lookout, on the ocean side of the island: ☎ *(07) 409-8266.*
Offers a variety of accommodations from small units to suites. There is a pool, tennis courts and a licensed restaurant. Courtesy transportation available, and fishing gear and surfing equipment included in the room charge. Price range for the rooms runs between A$80 and A$150 for a double.

There is regular **barge and water taxi service** to Dunwich, on the island's west side, from Cleveland and Redland Bay. *Information in Cleveland,* ☎ *(07) 286-2666; in Redland Bay,* ☎ *(07) 358-2122.* There is also **helicopter** service from the Brisbane airport.

A plusher way to see the sights of Moreton Bay and the Gold Coast area is aboard the **M.V. Brisbane Explorer**, a 170-passenger, four-deck cruise ship that runs two-night and four-night cruises around the area. Cost of the four-night cruise in high season (September–April) is between A$550–A$650 per person; all meals and teas included. *Information: Captain Sturt Marine,* ☎ *(07) 844-3533.* The ship leaves from downtown Brisbane Mondays and Fridays.

Essential Brisbane

Information

For general help and brochures about activities around the state, contact the Queensland Government Travel Centre at Edward and Adelaide streets, ☎ *(07) 3221-6111.*

There are several offices that offer information about the city itself, including the **Greater Brisbane Regional Tourist Association**, which is located on the pedestrian mall at the Brisbane Transit Centre on Roma Street near downtown; ☎ *(07) 3236-2020.* If you're downtown, try the **Brisbane Visitors and Convention Bureau**, with offices in the City Hall, open Monday-Friday 8:30 a.m.–5 p.m.; ☎ *(07) 3221-4811.* You can also make use of the **Brisbane City Council information booth** located on the Queen Street Mall, just northeast of Albert Street, open Monday-Friday 8:30 a.m.–5 p.m. and 8:30-11:30 a.m. Saturdays ☎ *(07) 3229-5918.*

Getting Around

The **Brisbane City Council bus system** (BCC) serves the city and suburbs, running up and down both sides of the river as well as crossing back and forth. Buses normally run from 5:30 a.m.–11 p.m. daily. Normal fares within a zone are about 60 cents. The BCC, however, offers a Day Rover Pass that allows unlimited travel on BCC facilities for A$5. Also available is a **City Sights bus**, which lets you stop at 18 places of interest around the city for about A$12. *Information and timetables can be obtained from the Brisbane City Council Transport Information Counter at the Brisbane Administration Centre, 69 Ann Street;* ☎ *(07) 3225-4444.* The city's information offices also have bus and ferry information available on a hotline ☎ *13-1230.*

There is regular **ferry service** at more than a half-dozen spots along the river. The two main routes in the downtown area are between Edward Street (next to the Botanic Gardens) and Kangaroo Point, and the Customs House Ferry, which also runs to Kangaroo Point. Fares are the same as buses. *Information: Brisbane City Ferry Cruises, located at the transport information centre, 69 Ann Street;* ☎ *(07) 3399-4768 or* **Transinfo** ☎ *13-1230.*

There are several radio-operated **taxi services** in the city, the largest of which is **Black and White**. Fares start around $1, and meters rack up fees at a rate of about 60 cents a kilometer; no charge for luggage. *Information:* ☎ *3229-1000.*

Getting into the city, seven miles from the airport, is possible by **airporter bus** for about A$6.50, or by taxi for around A$17. A major site at the airport is the Southern Cross, the Fokker tri-motor that made the first crossing of the Pacific under the control of Australian aviation pioneer Sir Charles Kingsford Smith. (The Sydney airport is named in his honor.) The Brisbane airport, located in the suburb of Eagle Farm, is in the process of being updated, but currently has all expected amenities; *General Information:* ☎ *(07) 3268-9511.*

Post Office

The General Post Office in Brisbane is at *261 Queen Street* and is open, as is the case for most Queensland post offices, from 7 a.m.–7 p.m. Monday–Friday. The GPO does have 24-hour vending machines; suburban offices open normally 9 a.m.–5 p.m Monday–Friday. *Information:* ☎ *(07) 3224-1215.*

Telephones

The area code for Brisbane is *(07).*

Banks

Normal banking hours are 9:30 a.m.–4 p.m. Monday–Thursday and until 5 p.m. Fridays. There are foreign currency exchanges at all banks as well as the airport.

Consulates

In Brisbane, the U.S. consulate is at *383 Wickham Terrace,* ☎ *(07) 3831–3340.*

Shopping

Normal hours are 8:30 a.m.–5:30 p.m. Monday-Thursday; 8:30 a.m.–9 p.m., Friday, 8:30 a.m.–9 p.m., Saturdays; 9 a.m.–4 p.m. optional on Sundays with city center stores usually open 10:30 a.m.–4 p.m.

Downtown shopping is primarily centered around the **Queen Street Mall**, where you will find three large department stores: David Jones, Myer and C.J. Coles. **David Jones**, the most upscale, is at *194 Queen Street*. The **Broadway** mall area next to Jones has 50 specialty shops and a dozen or so eateries; open seven days. **Meyer**, which has just undergone a major renovation, and in the process created a shopping center with movie theaters, parking and 200 specialty shops, now takes up a city block along the Mall. **Coles** is a supermarket/variety store at *210 Queen Street*. There are several shopping centers in the area, including the **Wintergarden**, on the mall; **Post Office Square**, and the **City Plaza**, next to City Hall. **The Rowes Arcade**, *235 Edward Street*, follows in the footsteps of Sydney's Queen Victoria Building and lets shoppers glory in Victorian ambiance, complete with native woods and lots of glass. It houses about two dozen shops. Another place to shop in period architecture is at **The Mansions** next to the Botanic Gardens.

Unfortunately, there are few places around the city where you can get good Aboriginal artwork. About the best is **Queensland Aboriginal Creations**, *135 George Street*. Amidst the hokey stuff for tourists (do you really wanna buy a boomerang?), there are also some authentic pieces. *Information:* ☎ *(07) 3224-5730.*

The city's duty-free shops, like those in Sydney, offer the usual array of electronic and photographic goods, along with souvenirs and booze. Among the several are **City International Duty Free**, *86 Queen Street*, ☎ *(07) 3229-2556;* **Downtown Duty Free**, *corner Edward and Queen streets*, ☎ *3221-5666;* **Orbit Duty Free**, *136 Queen Street*, ☎ *(07) 3229-2922* and two **Alder's**, *78 Queen Street Mall and the airport*. These stores usually require proof that you're a tourist; a passport works, and sometimes even a driver's license.

If you're a compulsive flea market fanatic, check out mounds of used Aussie junk at **Paddy's Market** in New Farm, east of the city center across from Kangaroo Point. The market, corner of Macquarie and Florence streets, is open daily from 9 a.m.–3 p.m. You can find produce and milk in addition to the oddments. Admission is free Monday-Friday; weekends there's a A$5 entry charge. *Information:* ☎ *(07) 3252-7211.*

In addition, there are two Sunday markets. One, the **Closeburn County Markets**, is about 15 miles north of the city in the community of Petrie. Craft items are a specialty. It's open from 9 a.m.–2 p.m. A more urban scene is the open air **Eagle Street Markets**, *123 Eagle Street* in the city (near the wharf area), where you can see artisans at work— glassblowers, painters, potters. It's open Sunday 8 a.m.–3 p.m. At South Bank Parklands, there are two markets, **Lantern,** open 5–10:30 p.m. Fridays, and the **Craft Village**, open 11 a.m.–5 p.m. Saturday and 9 a.m.–5 p.m. Sunday.

Outside of the city center, in the western suburbs, is **Paddington Circle**, a five-mile stretch of antiques and bookshops, restaurants and small art galleries housed in restored Queensland houses. It's worth a drive, and is about two miles from downtown. Most of the shops are located along Given Terrace and Latrobe Terrace.

Where to Stay

One thing to always check in Brisbane is weekend specials at many hotels. Sometimes they can offer great bargains; some are advertised, some are not, so always ask.

Hilton International Brisbane   A$200–500   ★★★★

190 Elizabeth Street; ☎ *(07) 3231-3131; FAX (07) 3231-3199.*
Doubles start around A$200; executive floor, A$300; suites start around A$500.
Faces onto the Queen Street Mall. The lobby has a 35-story atrium, and there are three floors of shops. Pool, sauna, spa, tennis courts, gym, nightclub, handicapped facilities. **Victoria's Fine Dining Room** is the hotel's white napkin eatery; more relaxed is the Tropicana pool deck restaurant. One of our favorite budget/quickie places in town is here, the **New Orleans Restaurant** in the Wintergarden Shopping Centre inside the hotel. Also try the **America's Cup Bar** in the hotel.

Sheraton Brisbane Hotel and Towers   A$225–500   ★★★

249 Turbot Street; ☎ *(07) 3835-3535; FAX (07) 3835-4960.*
Doubles A$225–350; suites A$500 and up.
The hotel sits in the middle of the city's financial center with nice views overlooking the river and downtown. Sauna, squash courts, parking, pool, two restaurants, five bars, nightclub, fitness center. The top two floors are executive: private lounge, butler service, business facilities, separate registration.

Heritage, The (a Beaufort Hotel)   A$300–1800   ★★★★

Corner of Margaret and Edward streets; ☎ *(07) 3221-1999, FAX (07) 3221-6895.*
Doubles from around A$300, suites A$450–1800.
Here's one of the best locations in the city, part of the aforementioned post-Expo redevelopment. It sits on the river next to Waterfront Place, and all 250 or so rooms have river views. What sets the hotel apart is its use of the Port Office, a 19th-century building renovated during Expo and now housing the main restaurant, a wine cellar and a shopping arcade. The restaurant—**Siggi's**—is supposed to recall images of the places where you might meet erudite folks such as Somerset Maugham, and it comes close. It's all marble and dark wood, very good and very expensive. The main hotel has a heated pool and views plus a fitness center. Two nonsmoking floors.

Mayfair Crest International   A$150–250   ★★

Corner of Ann and Roma streets; ☎ *(07) 3229-9111; FAX (07) 3229-9618.*
Doubles around A$150; suites from A$250.
Right across from the Roma Street transportation center, this has been our Brisbane base several times. Large, airy lobby with coffee shop; two other restaurants, six bars. **Spillane's**, a nightclub, is popular. Two nonsmoking floors. Heated pool, sauna, gym.

Brisbane City Travelodge   A$150–350   ★★

Roma Street; ☎ *(07) 3238-2222; FAX (07) 3238-2288.*
Doubles from A$150; suites from A$350.
Sits atop the city transit centre a short walk from the Queen Street Mall. There are two nonsmoking floors, handicapped access and the pretty-good **Drawing Room** restaurant. Rooftop spa.

Brisbane Parkroyal   A$195–300   ★★

Corner Alice and Albert streets; ☎ *(07) 3221-3411; FAX (07) 3229-9817.*
Doubles start around A$195; suites from A$300.

Located next to the Botanic Gardens, four blocks from the Queen Street Mall. Bar, restaurant (overlooking the gardens), pool, sauna.

Bellevue Hotel   A$75   ★★

103 George Street (opposite Treasury Casino); ☎ *(07) 3221-6044; FAX (07) 3221-7474.*
Doubles from A$75.

The lobby sets the tone: very Queenslandish, with plants and wooden shutters, gold tones and tile. Undercover parking, pool, spa, cooking facilities, a good value in a decent location.

Lennons Hotel Brisbane   A$100–250   ★★★

66-76 Queen Street; ☎ *(07) 3222-3222; FAX (07) 3221-9389.*
Doubles from A$100; suites from A$250.

Lennons—the name—has been around Brisbane since 1880. That's when John Lennon (no relation, we think) built the first Lennons Hotel. The 1880 version was demolished in 1940, and a new one rose in 1941—just in time to become the wartime headquarters for Gen. Douglas MacArthur and his staff. The hotel moved out of that building in 1972 and opened at its present location. Just before Expo, the hotel company spent around A$5 million refurbishing the rooms and public area. Over the years, everybody has stayed in the hotel (wherever it was): Lyndon Johnson, Diana Dors, Prince Charles, Louis Armstrong...us. Pool, sauna, spa, barbecue area, parking, two restaurants—the **Hibiscus Room**, famous for luncheon seafood smorgasbords—and the Traditions Restaurant, which is French. Check out the picture of Dugout Doug in the cocktail bar.

Hilltop Hotels

Above the city center to the north is the Albert Park area of Spring Hill, a leafy, quiet residential oasis dotted with several small, but pretty good hotels. Nice area if you like things a little less hectic and urban. Our choices:

Gazebo, The   A$115–120   ★★

345 Wickham Terrace; ☎ *(07) 3831-6177; FAX (07) 3832-5919.*
Doubles from A$115; suites from A$120.

Down the street from the famous Old Windmill. Some rooms have balconies with views; some have cooking facilities. Free underground parking, pool, three nonsmoking floors, restaurant/cocktail lounge with good views, 24-hour brasserie.

Albert Park Motor Inn   A$125   ★★★

551 Wickham Terrace; ☎ *(07) 3831-3111; FAX (07) 3832-1290.*
Doubles from about A$125.

The hotel underwent major surgery in the early 90s, refurbishing and expanding. It, like the Gazebo, has city views and, to our mind, one of the better small restaurants in the city, Short walk to the city center. Great eatery, **Aldo's on the Park** (closed Sundays). Pool, parking.

Chancellor on the Park   **A$130**   ★ ★ ★

Corner of Leichhardt Street and Wickham Terrace; ☎ *(07) 3831-4055; FAX (07) 3831-5031.*

Probably the best of the hilltop hotels. The Chancellor has a rooftop pool with the usual stunning views, 24-hour reception, a business center, bottle shop, guest laundry, five bars, four restaurants, barbershop, sun deck and barbecue areas. The rooms are all suites with business folks in mind, and have FAX lines, separate dining areas and minibars. It also offers some of the best weekend deals in town; once it charged 90 bucks a night for a suite that regularly went for around A$170. We like this one a bunch. Suites (in four categories) start at about A$130.

Where to Eat

This is Brisbane, remember, and that means seafood, especially a wonderful little sea critter called the Moreton Bay Bug, which is downed in immense quantities by the locals. Before you start running for the door (Eat bugs—Me?), relax. The bug is really a crustacean; some call it a lobster, some a crayfish. Whatever, it's delicious and served in hundreds of different ways, from curried bug to bug with drawn butter.

They also serve up mud crabs (big hummers) and a wide variety of fresh catches from the bay and the ocean, including Australia's answer to fancy European fish, the barramundi. Add that to the list of tropical fruits available, and the Brisbane eating scene can be fun—and fattening. You won't find as wide an ethnic mix as Sydney or Melbourne, but there are enough choices to keep you busy.

The city also has its share of food halls if you like your dining less formal and less expensive—one of the best is in the Hilton Hotel. As is the case elsewhere in Australia, many restaurants are closed Sundays, so call ahead to make sure. In addition to the hotel restaurants we've mentioned, some other ideas:

Michael's Riverside   **$$$**   ★ ★ ★ ★

Waterfront Place, 123 Eagle Street; ☎ *(07) 3832-5522.*
Open for lunch and dinner; closed Sundays.

One of the best locations in Brisbane, right on the river, especially at night. It's actually two restaurants. The Garden Room is more formal Continental-style dining; the popular Waterfront Cafe is more casual and serves homemade pastas and other Italian dishes. The whole layout has already won several dining awards.

Daniel's Steakhouse   **$$$**   ★ ★

145 Eagle Street; ☎ *(07) 3832-3444.*
Open lunch and dinner Monday–Friday.
Also part of the Waterfront Place complex. The decor features Aboriginal paintings and carvings. It's famous for grain-fed steaks, but also has fresh lobster, seafood and chook.

Breakfast Creek Hotel   **$$$**   ★ ★ ★ ★

2 Kingsford Smith Drive, Albion; ☎ *(07) 3262-5988.*
Open seven days for lunch; dinner from 5:30 p.m.

There are several restaurants in the Breakfast Creek area near the airport, and this is the most famous of the lot. The building was erected in 1889 and the restaurant over the years has won many awards for its barbecued steaks. You get to pick your own cow before grilling, but if beef is not your bag, it also serves chicken, lamb and fish. It also has a beer garden.

Il Centro   **$$**   ★★★
1 Eagle Street Pier; ☎ *(07) 3221-6090.*
Saucy Italian restaurant winning heaps of awards for its offerings. Sidewalk seating in the summer is a delight. Close to the shops and activities of the Eagle Street area. Lunch from noon Sunday–Friday; dinner seven days from 6 p.m. Worth a stop.

Jimmy's   **$**   ★★
Three locations on the Queen Street Mall.
They started life as Jimmy's on the Mall, one of our favorite inner-city lunch or snack shops. It got so popular, more facilities were, including one at the Edward Street end of the mall—Jimmy's Uptown. All locations feature good cafe food— burgers, steak and chips, soup and the biggest cappuccinos in town. Prices are good; so's the food.

Jo-Jo's   **$**   ★★
Queen and Albert streets; ☎ *(07) 3221-2113.*
Our first love in Brisbane (the first place we ate in town), and Aussie ambiance in its basic form. It's a small food hall with a mix of cuisines and a friendly bar. It's on the breezy second floor with open windows; always crowded, a good place to catch lunch after walking around the mall. There's a happy hour from 4–6 p.m. Monday– Thursday.

Friday's   **$**   ★
123 Eagle Street; ☎ *(07) 3832-2122.*
Another waterfront area facility, a bit like Jo-Jo's but more modern. It's a large complex with three restaurants, four bars and a nightclub. Watch the paddlewheel- ers chug by and get your chow from a buffet or an a la carte menu. There's live music at night, plus it's open seven days until late.

Oshin   **$$**   ★★
256 Adelaide Street; ☎ *(07) 3229-0410.*
Lunch noon–2:30 Monday–Friday; dinner 6:30–10:30 p.m. Monday–Saturday.
The Oshin is on the second floor of Koala House, corner of Adelaide and Creek streets near Anzac Square. It specializes in barbecues at your table and high-quality beef dishes.

Two popular places for noshing among the city crowd are the South Bank Parklands across from the city center in the old Expo site, and Fortitude Valley, Brisbane's Asian center. The parklands has 20 cafes, restaurants and fast-food places. Among the group is **Ned Kelly's** ★★ ☎ *(07) 3846-1880.* It serves a variety of fare, including, we kid you not, witchetty grubs, a famous bit of yucky Aboriginal bush tucker. It's open for break- fast. lunch and dinner.

Fortitude Valley, northeast of the city center, has 50 ethnic restaurants and cafes. There are village markets every Saturday and sidewalk jazz performances every Sunday. The valley business association has an information number, ☎ *(07) 3252-5999.*

A bit out of town is:

Mount Coot-tha Summit Restaurant $$$ ★★★★

Sir Samuel Griffith Dr.; ☎ *(07) 3369-9922.*

Probably the best view in the city, and arguably some of the finest food. The decor is tans and blacks, and the menu offers a wide range of Queensland goodies from Moreton Bay bugs to vegetarian specialties, plus some we try to forget: lamb's brains. Anyway, the bugs are maybe the best in Australia, butterflied with garlic, tarragon and wine. Mushroom caps with cheese and crab, quail, rabbit. It's open early to late seven days. If you're out touring, try a morning or afternoon tea. The drive out is only about 10 kilometers. Worth a try.

The Gold Coast

Gold Coast, Queensland is Australia's surfer's paradise.

The Gold Coast is Australia's answer to California, Atlantic City and Miami Beach rolled into one. It's a 30-mile stretch of beach from Southport (about 50 miles southeast of downtown Brisbane) to the New South Wales border. In many parts, unfortunately, it has become tacky, beach-front ugly, a prime example of everything bad that can happen to a quiet, beautiful resort area: high-rise apartments, hokey attractions, bikini emporia, fast-food joints, water slides—you get the idea. It was probably inevitable when you realize that the center of things on the coast is a place called Surfers Paradise. (And if you get homesick, drop in at three of the other communities: Miami, North Palm Beach and Palm Beach. We do not lie.)

But one critic's tourist disaster is another's delight, and more than three million souls annually flock to the Gold Coast to drink in the sun and fun—and donate something like A$600 million a year to the local coffers in the process. It's popular with families from all over the country, as well as becoming a growing mecca for Japanese honeymoon couples. We are, quite frankly, not sure why North Americans would come this far to do what they could do just as easily in Florida, California, Mexico, Hawaii or the Bahamas.

The Gold Coast, at least for us, is not a major Queensland attraction. Given the delights of other parts of the state, we would go to the coast only if we were in the Brisbane area and were dying from beach withdrawal. There is another side to this part of the coast, however: not far inland, there are some very nice rainforests and watery areas far removed from the beach madness. More of this later.

But if you're a surfer or a true beach freak—or perhaps just a sociologist looking for new forms of tribal behavior—the Gold Coast will probably draw you like a moth to a bug zapper. And in all honesty, the beaches themselves are really excellent, and there are more golf courses than you can shake a four-iron at. Green fees here, even though it's a resort area, are a steal by American standards, mostly around A$50 for 18 holes.

Our favorite memory of the coast is the beach outside the old Grundy's entertainment center in Surfers Paradise. Here, tanned the color of old horsehide, stood a gent operating a paint sprayer on a much paler gent (obviously a tourist). The sprayer was full of Coppertone, 50 cents a spray. Somehow it all made sense, because the whole atmosphere of the coast is that way—you will, by God, have fun, as efficiently as possible.

On the way to the Gold Coast, you run across the first of the many popular theme-park-type attractions in the area, **Movie World** ★ ★ ★ ★, a Warner Bros. complex with working studios and all sorts of rides, displays, shows and tours highlighting Hollywood's contributions to world culture. It's near Oxenford on the Pacific Highway about an hour's drive from the Brisbane airport. A few of the attractions: a Batman adventure ride, Looney Toons studio tour, the Blazing Saddles Shooting Gallery, a Superman video studio, the Dirty Harry Bar—it goes on forever. Stashed amid the film and video projection theaters and attractions are stores, cafes and boutiques. Great for the kids or movie freaks. We're not high on theme parks, but this one ain't bad. It costs about $A35 adults, A$22 for kids. It's open daily 10 a.m.–5 p.m. ☎ *(07) 5573-3999; information hotline, (07) 5573-3891; FAX (07) 5573-3666.*

Southport, the original settlement in the area, is at the northern end of the coastal strip. It's a lot more citylike than the rest of the strip, and doesn't actually sit on the coast—a sand spit separates it from the ocean. It is the commercial and administrative center of the coast.

Across from Southport on The Spit (in what is called Main Beach) is the **Fisherman's Wharf tourist development** with shops, fishing fleet, bars, restaurants—supposedly modeled after its namesake in San Francisco (which, depending on how you look at it, is either a good idea or purgatory).

Diehard surfers refer to grommets on boogie boards as "shark biscuits."

QUEENSLAND AND
THE GREAT BARRIER REEF

Nearby is **Seaworld**, another big draw park, this one with marine animal attractions and shows, said to be the largest such in Australia. There are also some killer water slides, fast-food joints and a bar or two. ☎ *(07) 5588-2222.* Next to the wharf is a place for "Jaws" fans, the **Great White Shark Expo ★**. The admission charge to Sea World is around A$35; open 10 a.m.–5 p.m. daily.

On the spit, fronting both the ocean and the Broadwater (the inlet between the Spit and the mainland), is one of the coast's snazziest resort hotels, the **Sheraton Mirage ★ ★ ★ ★** ☎ *(07) 5591-1488; FAX (07) 5591-2299.* It has shopping, a marina, butler-service, restaurants and hovercraft service to and from the Brisbane airport. It has 300 rooms, with doubles starting around A$300. Southport is also a popular camping spot—it's full of **caravan parks**, many with rental units. Most of them also allow tent campers.

Surfers Paradise, where it's happening on the Gold Coast, is the most crowded stretch of beach on the coast; the place to see and be seen. It rocks and rolls with the best of the world's beach resorts, and it always reminds us more of Fort Lauderdale than anything else.

Whatever; you can do just about anything in the Surfers area that humans have devised to amuse other humans.

One of the most popular spots on the Gold Coast is the **Conrad International Hotel ★ ★ ★** and its glass-enclosed **Jupiters Casino**. The hotel, part of the Hilton chain, sits on its own island in the Nerang River, 15 acres of park and resort where you can sleep in style and lose the family fortune any night of the week at the 24-hour casino. Next door is the **Pacific Fair Shopping Centre** with restaurants. The hotel has 600 rooms, four licensed restaurants and a 1000-seat showroom for Las Vegas-style revues. There's a short monorail that connects the hotel/casino area to the beachfront. Double rooms start at around A$180 and suites A$650–2100. ☎ *(07) 5592-1133.*

Probably the most upscale development along the coast is the posh **Sanctuary Cove area**, situated on Hope Island in the Coomera River north of Southport, about 20 minutes by car from Surfers Paradise. It was developed by Shinko Australia, the Australian arm of Shinko Limited, one of Japan's major golf course and resort companies. The resort includes expensive single-family homes for a population of about 1500, a marina, the Marine Shopping Village with 80 stores, two golf courses (including one designed by Arnold Palmer), harbor front restaurants, nine tennis courts, three swimming pools and a recreation center. The anchor for the development is the **Hyatt Regency resort ★ ★ ★ ★**, modeled in classic Outback mansion style. Doubles begin at around A$230; suites A$300–1800. ☎ *(07) 5530-1234; FAX (07) 5577-8234.*

Two other choices for hotels are the **Pan Pacific ★ ★ ★** and the **Marriott Surfers Paradise ★ ★ ★ ★**. The Pan Pacific, *81 Surf Parade in Broadbeach*, is on the beach and sits next to the Oasis Shopping Centre and is on the monorail line to Jupiters Casino. It has a pool, sauna, gym, tennis, parking, restaurant and bar. Prices, including a light breakfast, begin at A$140 double; suites from A$400. ☎ *(07) 5592-1133; FAX (07) 5592-3747.* The Marriott, *158 Ferny Avenue* in Surfer's Paradise, is a short walk from the beach and has a definite South Seas feel. It comes with a heated saltwater lagoon (complete with coral reef), tennis and health club, balcony views, handicapped facilities, free shuttles to area attractions, restaurant and bar. Doubles run about A$170–350; suites A$400–2,000. ☎ *(07) 5592-9800; FAX (07) 5592-9888.*

Not far from Sanctuary Cove, on the Pacific Highway just inland from the coast, is another major attraction, **Dreamworld**, Australia's answer to Disneyland. There are about 30 rides, including the Thunderbolt, claimed to be the world's largest double-loop roller coaster. For the kids, in lieu of the Mouse family, are Kenny Koala, his mate Belinda Brown and Coo-ee, the Gum Nut Fairy. The park has a number of theme areas based on Australiana—Gold Rush Country, Koala Land, etc. There is a six-story IMAX theater. Entry fees are about A$30, which lets you ride everything; open 9 a.m.–5 p.m. daily. ☎ *(07) 5573-1133.*

For the naturalists in the crowd, the Gold Coast does have two quiet areas away from the sandy bustle. **Burleigh Heads National Park** has walking trails and views of the coast, and the **Currumbin Sanctuary** has an aviary with daily feedings of Aussie birds as well as koalas and kangaroos. Sanctuary hours are 8 a.m.–5.m. daily; tickets are A$13. Information about the national park—as well as other regional parks, is available at the National Parks and Wildlife kiosk at Tallebudgera. ☎ *(07) 5535-3032. For information about the sanctuary,* ☎ *(07) 5534-1266.*

The Gold Coast has one thing going for it: plenty of places to stay, from tent sites to the Hyatt and its ilk. During the high season, it might be hard to find a place, but there are so many between Southport and Coolangatta that something is always available. It helps, of course, to book in advance. The area code on the Gold Coast is (07). *Information is available from the* **Gold Coast Tourism Bureau**, *second floor, 64 Ferny Avenue, Surfers Paradise;* ☎ *(07) 5592-2699; FAX (07) 5570-3144.* Or by mail *to P.O. Box 7091, Gold Coast Mail Centre, Bundall, Queensland 4217.* **The Royal Automobile Club of Queensland** *is located at the Pacific Fair Shopping Centre in Broadbeach;* ☎ *5572-4066.* On the coast, there are information centers at the *Cavill Mall in Surfers Paradise,* ☎ *(07) 5538-4419; or at the Beach House, Coolangatta,* ☎ *(07) 5536-7765.*

Getting to and around the Gold Coast is easy, either by driving yourself, taking a bus or going on a tour. There is also a small airport at Coolangatta. From Brisbane, buses run about A$20 one way and leave from the city transit center on Roma Street in Brisbane. Buses also run from the Coolangatta and Brisbane airports. Train service from Brisbane is also in the works. On the beach itself, the Gold Coast Tourist Shuttle makes regular trips between major tourist attractions and hotel areas; A$10 for an all-day ticket. There is also a five-day bus ticket that can be used to visit the various attractions on the coast, as well as Tamborine Mountain and Movie World. The pass is A$50 for adults. Information: **Gold Coast Explorer** ☎ *(07) 591-3131; FAX (07) 591-3145.*

Near the Coast

Within easy driving distance of the surf madness and the high rises are several bush areas well worth a visit if you like rainforests and green calm. They are generally situated in the string of low mountains that begin to rise about 10 miles inland. Some are getting cluttered with boutiques and galleries, but there are still plenty of places to take a walk by yourself in the silence.

One of the most popular areas is **Tamborine Mountain**, an area about 15 miles west of Coomera. In a 10-square-mile area are seven small national parks, filled with waterfalls, ancient stands of palms (they claim some are 15,000 years old) and hiking trails. *Information on the area is available at the Tamborine Mountain Visitors Centre in Doughty Park, North Tamborine* ☎ *(07) 545-1171,* Monday–Friday 7 a.m.–3:30 p.m. The center is open daily 10:30 a.m.–3:30 p.m. except in "very wet weather."

Farther south is the **Springbrook** area, about 25 miles west of Coolangatta. Near the small town are two national parks, **Gwongorella** and **Warrie**. In Gwongorella is the famous **Purlingbrook Falls**, with many trails, including one that goes behind the falls. In the area also are stands of 3000-year-old Antarctic beech trees, which grow in only four places in the world. A good drive is the **Lyrebird Ridge Road** near town, with great views of the coast. The ranger number for the parks is ☎ *(07) 533-5147.*

To the northwest of Springbrook is **Lamington National Park**, about 30 miles from Southport. The 50,000-acre park is in an area formed by volcanic activity, and the result is a wild mix of deep canyons and waterfalls (500 by estimate), and a dense jungle filled with ferns, mosses and 700 species of orchids. The streams are home to platypuses (count yourself very lucky if you spot one), and the skies to rare Australian lyrebirds and hordes of rosellas. You will also see bowerbirds, as well as ring-tailed possums. There are several excellent bushwalks, one in the Green Mountains section of the park, the other in the Binna Burra area. There is a camping area at the Green Mountains. There are two ranger stations in the area—the easiest of which to reach from the Gold Coast is at Beachmont on the main road into the area. ☎ *(07) 545-1734.*

There are two resort facilities in the park. **O'Reilly's Mountain Resort** ★ ★ in the Green Mountains has wheelchair trails, four-wheel drive excursions, a licensed restaurant and 30 units. Rates, including all meals, run around A$135 per person; budget rooms with no meals are about A$100. Camping available. Check road conditions before driving to the resort. *Information:* ☎ *(07) 544-0644; FAX (07) 544-0638.* The second facility is the **Binna Burra Mountain Lodge and Campsite** ★ ★, 10 kilometers south of Beachmont. The resort has tent sites, on-site tents and cabins, plus a licensed restaurant, and hot showers and a supplies kiosk. There are packages available that include transportation from Brisbane, two nights in a shared facility cabin, all meals and guided activities for A$180 per person. Without transport, the cabins, including all meals, are about A$145 per person. ☎ *(07) 533-3758*.

Up the Coast

It is about 1100 miles from Brisbane up the coast to Cairns, and much of the highway is rural boring—long stretches of sugar cane fields, small towns, farms. The coastal road, which north of Brisbane changes names from the Pacific Highway to the Bruce Highway, is in really nasty condition in places (holes, no shoulders), and farm vehicles and heavy trucks add to the fun. Still, if you have the time, a drive along the coast will at least let you see how Queensland got its start as an agricultural and mining area. Also, many of the major towns along the way have services out to offshore islands or the Great Barrier Reef.

Just north of Brisbane is the state's next major beachy playground, the **Sunshine Coast**, probably fated to end up looking just like its ugly stepsister, the Gold Coast. The Sunshine Coast runs roughly 45 miles, from Caloundra to Noosa Heads. The attraction here is fine beaches with things not yet as hectic as Surfers Paradise. The Queensland government says the Sunshine Coast is the fastest-growing area in the state, but at present, there is relative calm available. You get a feel for the future, however, by looking at the solid residential and tourist developments that have sprung up along the beaches from Maroochydore to Mooloolaba. One good bet in the area is the **Novotel Twin Waters** ★★★ resort near Maroochydore; ☎ *(07) 448-8000*. The hotel, on Mudjimba Beach, sits on a four-acre area of lagoons, beaches and the Maroochy River. Pool, spa, tennis, golf, restaurant and bar. Doubles A$150-310; suites start at A$210.

At Coolum Beach, about 20 kilometers north of Maroochydore, is the **Hyatt Regency Coolum** ★★★★, *Warran Road* ☎ *(07) 446-1234*. Set among 300 acres of littoral rainforest, the hotel is primarily a villa complex, but has studio units as well. There are pools, spa, sauna, gym, squash courts, Robert Trent Jones 18-hole golf course, driving range and beach sports. The Ambassadors villas, the most upscale, are two- and three-bedroom units with spa baths, kitchenettes, laundries and mini-bars. They range from A$830-1300. Presidents Club villas start at A$400. Studio units start at A$240 (no kitchens). It's popular among the spa set, offering special diet programs, exercise regimens and the requisite number of herbal body wraps.

The Sunshine Coast is as close to Brisbane as the Gold Coast, and is served by a number of buses, trains and tour companies. Driving up from Brisbane is about an hour's effort—turn off for the coast at the Caloundra road, then follow a small coast road all the way to Noosa. Coaches run daily trips from the Roma Street transit center in Brisbane. Train service is available by catching either the **Queenslander** or **Capricornian**, which run to Nambour. There is direct air service from Brisbane, Sydney and Melbourne to the Sunshine Coast airport at Maroochydore.

The major population centers, going north, are Caloundra, Maroochydore, Nambour (inland a ways and the largest), Tewantin and Noosa Heads. Noosa started life as a tiny fishing village and Aboriginal preserve; now it's pretty yuppified. The **Heads** are internationally known among surfers as the site of some of the world's most perfect waves, and it's also an area of lush private retreats as well as the rainforest quiet of **Noosa Heads National Park**. The city beach is called Main Beach, and is protected from the wind and is very crowded in the summer. All the action in town (i.e. food, bars, shopping) is on Hastings Street. Noosa claims to average seven hours of sunshine daily. Information is available from **Tourism Noosa**, ☎ *(07) 447-4988; FAX (07) 447-9494*. General information about the area is available from **Tourism Sunshine Coast**, *P.O. Box 246, Mooloolaba, Queensland 4557;* ☎ *(07) 443-6400; FAX (07) 443-6160*.

There is a wide range of **accommodations** on the Sunshine Coast, from motels and RV parks to resorts. Many of the best are at Noosa. One of the finest is the **Sheraton Noosa Resort** ★★★, *Hastings Street* ☎ *(07) 449-4888; FAX (07) 449-2230*. The hotel is six stories of pinks and blues. All suites have spa baths, balconies and kitchenettes. Heated pool, spa, sauna, gym, rec room, nonsmoking floors, boats for hire, restaurant and bar. Close to the beach. Doubles A$225–320; suites A$305–630. Another good bet is the **Noosa International** ★★, *Edgar Bennett Avenue* ☎ *(07) 447-4822; FAX (07) 447-2025*. The hotel has one- and two-bedroom apartments with two pools, spas, saunas, bar and restaurant, courtesy coaches, tour desk and parking. Prices range from A$100–160. Right on the beach is the **Netanya Resort Hotel** ★★, *75 Hastings Street*, which sits on the beach and has about 50 suites. Each suite has its own spa, kitchenettes and furnished balconies. Heated pool, common spa, sauna, gym, security parking and a cafe. Rates A$160–420. ☎ *(07) 447-4722*.

Also worth a try is **Accom Noosa**, a rental agency that handles several properties in the area and can make bookings; information: *P.O. Box 694, Noosa, Queensland 4567;* ☎ *(07) 447-3444; FAX (07) 447-2224*.

Two of the more popular tourist attractions in the area back of the coast are the Glasshouse Mountains, southeast of Caloundra, and the Sunshine Plantation. The **Glasshouse Mountains**, so named by Capt. Cook on his 1770 exploration because they reminded him of the glass furnaces of his native Yorkshire, are craggy volcanic remains and figure prominently in Aboriginal lore. The highest of the 13 volcanic peaks is about 1800 feet. You get to the mountains, and three national parks in the area, by turning off the Bruce Highway near Beerburrum. The area around the peaks is mostly pineapple plantations.

The Sunshine Plantation is another one of those roadside tourist spots so beloved by "tacky places" collectors. The main feature of the facility (in addition to a collection of Aussie fauna) is the Big Pineapple, a two-story fruit-cum-souvenir stand. There is also a train available to take you around the sugar cane fields of the area. Admission to the plantation, at Woombye just south of Nambour, is free; hours are 9 a.m.–5 p.m. every day; charge for the train and tour. *Information:* ☎ *(07) 442-1333*. We probably should not overlook the Big Cow, a giant bossie in the same spirit as the pineapple, which celebrates the dairy industry with farm animal displays and hiking trails. It's near Nambour; *information:* ☎ *(07) 446-7144*.

From Nambour, the Bruce Highway cuts inland past Gympie to Maryborough and Hervey Bay; the main population centers near Fraser Island. **Gympie**, an old Gold Rush town, is the gateway to **Cooloola National Park**, for our money one of the most scenic stretches of the whole coast. The park, a 97,000-acre mixture of deserted sandy beaches, freshwater lakes, swamps, rainforest and stands of eucalypts, is a popular hiking and four-wheel-drive area. It is criss-crossed by numerous tracks and trails, and there are several campgrounds with toilets, fresh water, fireplaces and showers. Advance booking for all campsites is required. Mainland hotel and motel accommodations are available at Rainbow Beach, Pomona and Boreen Point. Gympie has a week-long **Gold Rush Festival** every October.

One of the most famous spots in the park is the ***Cherry Venture***, a 3000-ton freighter that was blown high on the beach during a hurricane in 1973. It's a fairly easy stroll from Rainbow Beach southeast along the coast to Double Island Point, where the beached ship slowly rusts in the Queensland sun. Another popular destination is **Teewah Coloured Sands**, a stretch of beach at the far southern edge of the park, noted for 650-foot-high cliffs composed of earth toned deposits. The easiest way to get to the area is by renting a boat at Boreen Point, crossing Lake Cootharaba and hiking over to Teewah. Although the park itself is closed to non-four-wheel-drive vehicles, you can drive from the Bruce Highway to Tin Can Bay, Rainbow Beach and Boreen Point near the park. Tin Can Bay Inlet, a popular fishing and prawning area, marks the southern edge of the range of one of Australia's most dangerous animals, the saltwater crocodile. Several companies in Brisbane and Noosa offer four-wheel-drive rentals or tours to Cooloola National Park as well as Fraser Island. Check with **Suncoast Safaris** ☎ *(07) 447-2617; FAX (07) 447-2060*, or **Everglades Cruises** ☎ *(07) 449-9177. For information and reservations in Cooloola National Park, contact the Kinaba Information Centre* ☎ *(07) 449-7364.*

Fraser Island features 800 ft.-high sand dunes, thick forests, 40 freshwater lakes, ancient Aboriginal sites, and more than 250 species of birds.

Fraser Island, north of Cooloola National Park and due east of Maryborough, is said to be the largest sand island in the world. The island is a naturalist's feast, offering everything from 800-foot-high sand dunes to thick forests and 40-odd freshwater lakes nurtured by an annual rainfall of around 60 inches. The island is large enough (about 75 miles long, nine miles wide) to sustain small herds of brumbies (wild horses), and packs of what are believed to be the purest strains of dingos in Australia, about 200 to 300 animals in all. There are also 250 species of birds, and large stands of satinay trees that reach 250 feet in height. It also has a number of ancient Aboriginal sites and relics. The island was the scene of a bitter and successful environmental fight in the 1970s when sand mining was damaging the fragile island ecology. The island is now managed by the national government, and permits are required to visit and camp on the island. Most of the northern end of the island is taken up by **Great Sandy National Park**, which is about 26 square miles in area. In 1993, the island was named a World Heritage site.

Access to the island is by boat or small aircraft. **Charter planes** leave from Hervey Bay, Maryborough and Bundaberg, and cost about A$85 per person one way. Travel on the island is by four-wheel drive vehicle or by foot. Car ferries run from Inskip Point near Rainbow Beach to the only paved road on the island, which heads north toward the Eurong Beach Resort (only four-wheel vehicles allowed, permits required). Bus service is available from Rainbow Beach to the island for A$25 per person round trip. Security parking is available at Rainbow Beach. Boat service also is available from Urangan and from North Head, south of Urangan. In addition to campgrounds, there are several resorts and tourist centers on the island.

Accommodation information, as well as general information about the island and tour operators, is available from the **Hervey Bay Tourist & Visitors Centre**, *63 Old Maryborough Road, Pialba,* ☎ *(07) 124-4050.* **Kingfisher Bay and Resort Village** ★ ★ ★ is located near Lake McKenzie and overlooking the Great Sandy Strait, with three restaurants and bars, pool, two- and three-bedroom villas (some with spas), plus regular rooms, each with a deck. In the village, there is a bakery, general store, pizza parlor, bottle shop and gas station. There are four-wheel-drive vehicles for rent. Resort rates are around A$175 per person, which includes transportation to the island; villas require a three-night minimum, and range from A$580–$1150 a night. Activities include whale watching (August-October), four-wheel-drive tours, bushwalks and watersports. To get to the Kingfisher, take the resort's catamaran or car/passenger ferry from Urangan Harbour/Kingfisher Bay northeast of Maryborough. The round-trip fares on the boats run between A$20 (pedestrian) to A$40 for a car, plus A$3 per person in the car. *Kingfisher Resort information:* ☎ *(07) 125-5155; toll free 1-(800) 072-555.*

Information about Great Sandy National Park is available from the **Queensland National Parks and Wildlife Service**, *Rainbow Beach Road, Rainbow Beach;* ☎ *(07) 186-3160. Island permits are available at the* **Hervey Bay Council Office** *or the district forestry office in Maryborough;* ☎ *(07) 122-2455.*

Maryborough, the major port for the area's Gold Rush, was built on the backs of "blackbirds," black slaves imported to work in the cane fields. It still shows some vestiges of the golden past, including the city's pride and joy, an iron lacework bandstand. **Hervey Bay**, about 10 miles from Maryborough, is a middle-class seaside community that is sometimes called the "caravan capital of Australia"—there are at least a dozen RV parks in the area. The park service is trying to create a marine environmental area off Hervey Bay to protect humpback whales that swim through during their annual migration along the Queensland coast.

Bundaberg, the next major community up the coast, is a sugarcane processing center and home to the most famous rum in Australia, named after the city. Once, in the Northern Territory, we stopped at a bottle shop to pick up a case of XXXX beer for ourselves and a bottle of Bundaberg for the mem-sahib's cuba libras. The clerk accused us of being Queenslanders who, he said, are notorious for combining XXXX and Bundaberg to make incredibly wicked boilermakers. We decided not to even think about trying one. *Information: Bundaberg District Tourism and Development Board, corner Mulgrave and Bourbong streets;* ☎ *(07) 152-2333.* **RACQ** *in Bundy: 92 Bourbong Street;* ☎ *(07) 152-3377.*

From Bundaberg north, you start getting into **Great Barrier Reef country**. The first chunk of the reef, now set aside as part of the **Great Barrier Reef Marine Park**, is due east of Gladstone and Rockhampton. Gladstone, once a quiet rural town, is now a major seaport and mining center, and has paid the price in smokestacks and industrial sprawl. The world's largest bauxite processing plant is here, as well as coal-handling facilities.

Rockhampton, about 60 miles north, is the capital of what is called the Capricornia area, so named because it sits astride the tropic of Capricorn. The tropic, in fact, goes right through the city's tourist information center on the Bruce Highway at the south entrance to town. Rocky is a major beef-shipping center, with an estimated 2.5 million cattle feeding on ranges within 150 miles of the city. It has some fine old pioneer buildings preserved along the Fitzroy River, including some pubs. The Capricorn Highway, a major route to the Outback via Winton and beyond, starts in Rockhampton.

Upscale digs are absent in Rocky, but worth a shot is the **Country Comfort Inn** ★★, *86 Victoria Parade* ☎ *(07) 927-9933.* It overlooks the Fitzroy River, and has a small pool, restaurant, bar and two nonsmoking floors. Doubles from A$90; suites A$155.

Near Rockport, at Yeppoon, a Japanese industrialist, Yohichiro Iwasaki, has been in the process of creating a huge resort supposedly catering to Japanese tourists. The resort, at first called the **Capricorn Iwasaki Resort**, now more than a decade in the building, has been embroiled in controversy from the start. Some Australians objected to cattle being raised on the resort property, seeing them as a threat to the Australian beef business, and others, still remembering World War II, were less than enthused at having a huge Japanese settlement on the Queensland coast. The project has been in and out of courts, and construction delays put the whole affair in hot water. It also changed names since the first phase was opened in 1987: it's now the **Capricorn International Resort** ★★★. The change was made, hotel spokesmen said, because the bulk of the resort's clients are Australians and Europeans. The present 400 units are one- and two-bedroom apartments plus motel rooms. The resort has 22 kilometers of beaches and sits amid 22,000 acres of wildlife sanctuary. There are three licensed restaurants, two golf courses and it also boasts the largest freshwater swimming pool in the Southern Hemisphere. Rooms range from hotel units to apartments. Rates are in the A$110–A$200 range. *Information:* ☎ *(07) 939-5111.*

Mackay (pronounced muck-Eye), about 190 miles north of Rockhampton, is the sugar capital of Australia and the southern end of the Whitsunday Coast. The buildings in town are relatively new, courtesy of a cyclone that destroyed everything in 1918. *Mackay information center, Nebo Road* ☎ *(07) 952-2677.* **Mackay RACQ**, *214 Victoria Street;* ☎ *(07) 957-2918.* About 50 miles west of Mackay is **Eungella National Park**, one of the largest undeveloped parks in the state. It's a vast expanse of rainforests and low mountains, with no roads but plenty of trails. *Information: Queensland National Parks and Wildlife Service, corner Wood and River streets;* ☎ *(07) 951-8788.*

The small cities between Mackay and Townsville—Proserpine, Bowen, Ayr—are basically agricultural centers that are also jumping off places for visits to the Whitsunday Islands and the Reef itself. On the coast near Proserpine is a peninsula extending into **Repulse Bay**, where resort and tourist development is on the increase because of its close proximity to the Whitsundays. Here you will find boat charters, small airlines and tour companies servicing the islands. The main departure point for day trips is **Shute Harbour**, next to Circular Quay in Sydney, the busiest passenger port in Australia—currently Shute Harbour sees 6000 people a day in the high season. Five miles away is **Airlie Beach**, a growing resort community with accommodations, RV parks, restaurants and a growing assortment of T-shirt and souvenir shops.

At **Cannonvale**, just west of Airlie Beach, is the **Club Crocodile** ★★, a sprawling resort development sitting on a lagoon next to the Whitsunday Passage. The resort has a coffee shop and restaurant, bar, squash courts, pool, spa, health club, nightly entertainment, tour desk and kids activities. Rooms range from deluxe to budget, and most water sports are included in the price. Superior rooms start at A$100; deluxe about A$120; budget about A$65. ☎ *(07) 946-7155, FAX (07) 946-6007.*

The passenger and cargo facilities at Shute Harbour have been upgraded, an undertaking estimated to cost around A$100 million. Also at Shute Harbour, Seair Pacific has opened a new airport terminal for service to Mackay as well as reef trips and charter flights. Of interest to bushwalkers is **Conway National Park**, on the end of the peninsula, with hiking trails and some small beaches. A new national park just north of Airlie, **Dryander**, includes six prominent headlands and 11 islands.

About 10 miles south of Townsville is the **Billabong Sanctuary** ★★, a wildlife park where you can catch koalas, pythons, crocodiles, fruit bats and other animals. The animals are fed at various times a day—koalas at 10:30 a.m., crocs at noon. There is a snack bar and swimming pool. The facility is open daily 9 a.m.–5 p.m.; admission is A$12 adult.

Townsville

Townsville, the first of the northern Queensland coastal cities to start into the tourist business in a big way, has a present population of more than 100,000, making it the state's second-largest city. The first international airport in Northern Queensland capable of handling jumbos was built in Townsville, and for some years the city got a major share of the Great Barrier Reef tourism business from North America. The international airport at Cairns has changed that, and Townsville now handles mostly Asian traffic. This does not mean the city is fading away, however. Townsville is a more or less typical coastal Queensland city, with wide streets, a prosperous pedestrian mall downtown, good restaurants and a casual tropical lifestyle.

One of the major tourist attractions near the city is **Magnetic Island**, a tall island about seven miles offshore that is increasingly being developed into a resort area. Fortunately, more than half of the island has been turned into a national park, and at **Horseshoe Bay** a small area has been designated as a waterfowl refuge. *Information for the park is avail-*

able from **The Queensland National Parks and Wildlife Service**, *Northern Regional Centre,* ☎ *(07) 774-1411.*

Included among the accommodations on the island are **The Latitude 19 Resort★★** at Nelly Bay, presently the largest on the island, which offers rooms ranging from lodges in the A$90 double category to suites in the A$100 and up range. There is a pool, restaurant and cocktail lounge, tennis, gym. Multi-day packages include transport to the island. ☎ *(07) 778-5200; FAX (07) 778-5806.* Another major lodge is the **Arcadia Resort Hotel ★★** ☎ *(07) 778-5177.* Rooms at the Arcadia are in the A$90 to A$110 range, and there are shops, two pools, two bars and a restaurant. The newest Aussie resort sport has come to Magnetic. Cane toad races. Catch them at the Arcadia Wednesday nights.

Magnetic Island Ferries runs about a dozen trips a day to and from the island. There are packages available that give island tours and meals. A round-trip ticket for normal passenger service is about A$10 per person. Information and sailing times: ☎ *(07) 772-7122 or (07) 721-1913.* Both resorts listed above will arrange a pickup at the island dock if notified ahead of time. There is also air service from the city airport to the island and a car ferry. Once on the island, you can rent mokes (the Aussie cross-breed of a dune buggy and golf cart) or motorbikes for getting around on the paved roads between the residential and shopping areas on the island. *The island has an information centre at the Picnic Bay Mall at the island wharf;* ☎ *(07) 778 5155.*

Offshore island resort areas served by Townsville transportation services include: **Orpheus**, **Hinchinbrook**, **Dunk** and **Bedarra** islands. Townsville was also the jumping-off place for guests heading for the now-defunct Four Seasons Barrier Reef Floating Hotel, anchored on the John Brewer Reef about 50 miles offshore—it was sold and towed off to Vietnam. Townsville is also a major transportation hub, connecting with a major Outback-bound route, the Flinders Highway, as well as the rail line that runs to Mount Isa. Although many international-grade hotels and tour operators have located in the Cairns area, Townsville has its share, including several diving outlets and some very good hotels.

Townsville is a center for marine research, with major studies of coral life being done by **James Cook University** as well as the **Australian Institute of Marine Science**, both located in the city. Of major interest to Townsville scientists has been the decimation of the reef near the city by crown-of-thorns starfish, a major threat to the entire reef because they eat huge chunks out of the living coral. James Cook also has the National Centre for Studies in Travel and Tourism, which says something about the popularity of the Queensland coast. The university is also planning a A$100 million tropical medicine research facility.

A quite good introduction to the Great Barrier Reef is available at the **Great Barrier Reef Wonderland ★★**, where an artificial section of reef has been created, complete with tides and spectacular examples of the animals that inhabit the reef. The facility, near the Flinders Mall pedestrian shopping area, has a 70-foot-long transparent underwater tunnel to see the marine displays up close, as well as an Omnimax theater, museum, a food arcade and a gift shop. It's open weekly from 9 a.m.–5 p.m., entry fee for all attractions is about A$20. ☎ *(07) 772-4249; Omnimax information* ☎ *(07) 721-1481.*

Townsville also has one of the best-equipped dive shops near the Reef, **Mike Ball Watersports ★★**. The shop has a diving tower where you can learn deep diving, and offers

Scuba certification as well as bookings on reef-bound dive and snorkeling boats working out of Townsville. *Information: (07) 252-256 Walker Street, Townsville;* ☎ *(07) 772-3022.*

If you want to see some wildlife near Townsville, try the environmental park at the **Common**, about 10 minutes from downtown. The park is a wetlands area and during the rainy season is filled with water fowl. You can either drive through the park or take one of the trails; the park has several blinds set up for birdwatching.

As befits its role as a growing tourist center, Townsville during the past decade has acquired some first-rate hotels, including the **Sheraton Breakwater**, which opened the first casino in Northern Queensland. Next to the casino on the waterfront is the new conference center, the largest such facility in Northern Queensland, which also serves as an entertainment center offering major-league international stars and concert events. Information about the city, the surrounding area and the state in general is available from the **Magnetic North Tourism Authority**, located in the center of the Flinders Mall. For an overview, either drive, bus or taxi to the top of **Castle Hill**, the 950-foot peak that sits behind the city. Once there, you can also chow down at **Panorama House** ★★, which has seafood dinners and snacks. *Information:* ☎ *(07) 772-4555.* There are a group of eateries at Fisherman's Wharf, a block south of the mall: sidewalk cafes and restaurants, live entertainment most nights. There are also restaurants at the Casino Entertainment Centre.

The main tourist information office is on the Bruce Highway eight kilometers south of town. ☎*(07) 778-3555.* There is also an information kiosk on the Flinders Street Mall downtown. The **RACQ** office in Townsville is at 202 Ross River Road, in the suburb of Aitkenvale ☎*(07) 775-3999.*

Where to Stay

Sheraton Breakwater Casino-Hotel   A$200–850   ★★★
Sir Leslie Thiess Drive; ☎ *(07) 722-2333.*
Doubles about A$200; suites from A$300–850.
In addition to the casino, the hotel has a pool, tennis courts, laundry facilities, handicapped services, nonsmoking floors, health club and two licensed restaurants. There is also a tour desk.

Townsville Travelodge   A$90–250   ★★
Flinders Mall; ☎ *(07) 772-2477.*
Doubles start around A$90; suites about A$250.
This cylindrical structure, hated and loved, and sometimes called the "Sugar Shaker," is in the heart of downtown Townsville. It features a roof-top pool, two restaurants and three bars, gym, nonsmoking floors, rooms with minibars.

Aquarius on the Beach   A$125–175   ★★★
75 The Strand; ☎ *22-9777; FAX (07) 721-1316.*
Doubles about A$125 beachfront; seaview suites around A$175.
One of the first and best of the city's hotels, it has recently been refurbished and renamed (formerly the Ambassador). It's now all suites, with ocean views, balconies and kitchenettes. There is a pool and a licensed restaurant, cafe and bar. Nonsmoking and executive suites available.

Reef International   **A$100–120**   ★★

63 The Strand; ☎ *(07) 721-1777.*
Doubles around A$100 depending on view; suites from A$120.
Situated on the waterfront, the Reef has airy rooms with good views of the ocean.
There is a licensed restaurant and bar, parking garage and pool, spa and tour desk.

A few hours' drive inland from Townsville you start running into cattle country, and old towns that were created by the gold rush in the 1870s. The two major tourist spots are **Charters Towers** and **Ravenswood**. The diggings around Charters Towers, about 90 miles southwest of Townsville on the Mount Isa highway, produced millions of ounces of gold before they went dry in the 1920s. With those proceeds, the locals built some very fine residences, many of which still stand, and also erected the Stock Exchange, the Queensland National Bank, and other historic buildings that have been restored. **Ravenswood**, due south of Townsville, is more ghost town than Charters Towers, with lots of old mining equipment and slowly collapsing Boomtown buildings scattered around. You can still find gold in the creek beds around town. To get there, take a turn at Mingela on the Mount Isa highway.

Continuing up the coast from Townsville are huge areas of rainforest, sugarcane fields, small coastal cities and many access points to the Great Barrier Reef.

About 30 miles inland from Ingham, 60 miles north of Townsville, is **Wallaman Falls**★ ★, which has the longest drop in Australia: 911 feet. Offshore between Ingham and Cardwell are several island resort areas, including **Orpheus** and **Dunk** islands and a favorite naturalist's destination, **Hinchinbrook Island**. **Cardwell** is the last town on the Bruce Highway that's on the coast until you reach Cairns. The highway south of Cardwell climbs through a small coastal range offering great views of the offshore islands and the reef.

Tully, about 60 miles north of Ingham, is the wettest spot in Australia, receiving something in excess of 10 feet of rain a year. The area around town is dense rainforests, and the Tully River is a popular white-water canoeing spot.

Near **Innisfail**, an important sugar center, is **Mt. Bartle Frere**, at 5300 feet the highest peak in Queensland. Also close to town is Australia's only tea plantation, about 20 miles west at the small settlement of **Nerada**; open daily except Mondays. For nine days, starting the last Saturday in August, Innisfail is home to a large sugar festival. The town is also a deep-sea fishing center and is on the Palmerston Highway, which connects to the Kennedy Highway to the west and thus allows a back-door approach to the Atherton Tablelands.

About nine miles north of Innisfail is the turnoff to the headquarters of **Bellenden Ker National Park**, which contains **Mt. Bartle Frere**. The park, largely undeveloped, is a hiker's feast. Here and there, you'll see huge gaps in the forest. These were not caused by loggers, but by the cyclones which frequently hit the coast here and cause widespread damage. A popular track goes from the ranger's offices to the summit of the peak. Another popular hike, nowhere near as strenuous as the peak trek, is a half-mile jaunt to **Josephine Falls**, a popular swimming spot where the fun is sliding down slippery rocks in Josephine Creek. Another approach to the park is from **Babinda**, about five miles north of the headquarters turnoff. From Babinda, there's a road that goes about six miles into the park to **The Boulders**, a popular swimming and picnic area. Camping is allowed in the park, but permits must be obtained. *Information is available at the ranger office at the Josephine Falls trailhead or from Bellenden Ker National Park, P.O. Box 93. Mirriwinni, Queensland 4871;* ☎ *(07) 067-6304.*

From **Gordonvale**, about 20 miles north of Babinda, the Gillies Highway runs west into the **Tablelands**. The road is a piece of work, with almost 300 tight curves along the way. It's a scenic drive through the rainforests and volcanic crater lakes.

Cairns

Cairns, Queensland is a fast-growing tourist area.

Cairns, with a new, privately owned international airport, new hotels and millions in developments taking place, is rapidly becoming the capital of the Great Barrier Reef, and the center of one of the fastest-growing tourist areas in Australia. This is one of those Aussie cities you'd better pronounce as they do, or no one will understand what you're saying: it's Cans, with no "r." The city area code is (07).

The city, like some other coastal Queensland communities, started life as a Gold Rush settlement, followed by emergence as a remote sugar port. It was an ore-shipping terminus and is the last stop on the railroad north from Brisbane. The present population of about 75,000 is expected to double by the early 2000s as the coast from Cairns north to Cape York continues to expand as a major vacation destination. At this writing, the city dads estimate that something like 1.5 million people pass through Cairns every year, about

200,000 from overseas. *(For information about the offshore islands near Cairns, see the Great Barrier Reef section.)*

Cairns is a pleasant enough city, and we like it a bunch, but in and of itself, it's not very exciting. What makes it special is its proximity to the Reef and the Cape York Peninsula, as well as being a gateway to Papua New Guinea. Its group of high-quality hotels and restaurants are a definite plus, and it offers just about any travel or tourist service you will ever need to explore one of Australia's premier vacation areas. Cairns really got into the air business in a big way in 1988 when the Australian and U.S. governments, which have been sniping at each other for some years, finally agreed to allow Continental and United Airlines to fly to Cairns (Continental has since suspended service to Australia); in return, Qantas was allowed to expand its service to interior U.S. cities. About 50 flights from all over the world arrive in Cairns each week. The city also is an internationally recognized fishing center, sitting next to what is considered to be one of the best marlin areas in the world. It is also close to all the new resort settlements being built at Port Douglas and other spots north along the coast, and is near the splendid Atherton Tablelands, a farming/forest area with some of the prettiest scenery in the country. We encourage anyone coming to Australia, even those connecting to Sydney or other places in the country, to take two or three days at least and check out some of the wonderful experiences to be had on day trips from Cairns.

It is a city of wide, wide streets, palm trees, tin-roofed houses, marinas, new high-rise hotels and many shops. It is also an orchid-growing center, and the bulbs are so packed and purified that they can be taken back with you to the United States. Try **Lonne's Nursery**, *15 Hoad Street, Earlville, about four miles from the city center,* ☎ *(07) 054-1746.*

Around Town

Cairns is flat and wide, sitting with its north end facing the **Coral Sea** and the center and south of the city facing **Trinity Bay** and **Trinity Inlet**, where mangrove swamps abound. One of the main centers of activity in town is at **Marlin Jetty**, where the large fleet of sports fishing boats are based. The jetty is also the base for several of the larger boats that run trips to the reef and resort islands. (For reef and island trips, see the Reef Adventures entries in the Barrier Reef section later in the book).

Just to the side of the jetty is **The Pier**, a shopping center anchored by the Radisson Plaza Hotel. The shops range from pushcarts filled with knickknacks to upscale clothing stores and opal dealers. The center is open 9 a.m.–9 p.m. seven days. Farther down the harbor, past the Hilton Hotel, is another shopping center, **Trinity Wharf**, with 35 specialty shops, bars, restaurants and an entertainment centre. Try the **Trinity Wharf Bar** ★ ★ for a cold XXXX and some pub food; good views. Next to the shopping center is the cruise ship dock.

A long waterfront stretch along the center of the city, the **Esplanade**, is the location of many restaurants and hotels. If you're looking for beaches, you'll have to go north of Cairns. Off the Esplanade you have high tides and mostly ugly mudflats.

If you know your Australian history, you'll know about the **Royal Flying Doctor Service** ★ ★, and there's a branch in Cairns. There are tours of the facility every day, including a video show and museum. The RFDS station here also serves (for a price) as a radio, telegram and radio-telephone communications service. The service is located in the Edge Hill section of the city, not far from the international airport. Open 9 a.m.–4:30 p.m. daily; admission charge is A$5. *Information: Royal Flying Doctor Service, 1 Junction Street, Edge Hill, Cairns;* ☎ *(07) 053-5687; FAX (07) 053-7971.*

Cairns City Place, at the intersection of Shields and Lake streets, is the central downtown square of the city, where people-watching is in full flower, and toward dusk you'll think every bird in Queensland has come to call. Situated in an old art school on City Place is the **Cairns Museum**, which has displays on the early history of the city as well as a good section on the Aboriginal people who lived in the nearby rainforests.

The new **Reef Hotel Casino**, due to open early in 1996, is located between the Hilton and Cairns International hotels. The casino building tries to match the architectural style of the Old Customs House, which is incorporated into the sire. The centerpoint of the casino/hotel complex is a huge glass dome, which will be a venue for entertainment and cultural shows. There will be an Aboriginal theater, art displays and a covey of eating and drinking establishments. *Information:* ☎ *(07) 030-8888; FAX (07) 030-8788.*

In North Cairns, on the way to the Flying Doctor offices, is the **Flecker Botanical Gardens**, where you can see Queensland's tropical flora up close. There are lakes, walking trails and gardens. There is a restaurant at the gardens that specializes in Devonshire teas.

Shopping hours in the city are generally 8:30 a.m.–8 p.m. Monday–Thursday; 8:30 a.m.–9 p.m. Fridays; 8:30–5 p.m. Saturday and 3–8 p.m. Sunday.

Among the many shops in Cairns, you might try **Fred Jones Mens and Boy's Wear** at the corner of Shields and Sheridan Streets downtown. The store has a good selection of Australian wear, including Akubra hats, Speedo swimwear and a variety of luggage. We finally found an Akubra here that would fit: the Snowy River model, for about US$60.

Gem shopping is a big deal in Cairns, and a place to check out Australian opals is **Shiray Gems** at *26 Abbott Street*. The family owned store is open from 9 a.m.–late Monday-Saturday and 1 p.m.–late on Sundays; ☎ *(07) 051-2576*. Or try the **Diamond Gallery**, down the street at *42 Abbott Street* ☎ *(07) 051-4460*.

For New Guinea and Indonesian artifacts, try the **Asian Connections Emporiums** ★ ★, *51 Abbott Street;* ☎ *(07) 051-7392*. Or the **New Guinea Adventure Centre**, which has some artifacts for sale, and is also a major travel agency handling adventure travel to New Guinea—four-wheel-drive, dugout canoe, rafting, you name it. *The centre is located at 44B Aplin Street;* ☎ *(07) 051-0622.*

Aboriginal and New Guinea artworks can be found at **Gallery Primitive**, *26 Abbott Street downtown;* ☎ *(07) 031-1641*. **Anuaka Arts & Crafts**, in Portsmith, south of the city center, is an art store managed and staffed by Aboriginals. *The store is at the corner of Palmer and Toohey Streets in Portsmith;* ☎ *(07) 051-7786.*

Adelaide's old Victorian buildings are best viewed on foot.

Some kangaroos can run 60 mph and jump 30 ft. from a running start.

Sailboats and black swans are fixtures on Perth's Swan River.

The Opera House is Sydney's distinctive landmark and cultural center.

Port Arthur's historic prison is Tasmania's most famous attraction.

Melbourne's Yarra River meanders through the heart of the city.

There are a couple of duty-free shops in the city: **City International Duty Free**, *29B Shields Street*, ☎ *(07) 051-2338*, and **Downtown Duty Free**, *18 Abbott Street*, ☎ *(07) 051-0211*.

A popular shopping area weekdays as well as Saturday and Sunday mornings is **Rusty's Bazaar**, a group of specialty shops located in the block between Grafton and Sheridan streets and Shield and Spence streets. There's a Mexican restaurant there as well as shell, opal and T-shirt places. If you're looking for camping or hiking gear, try the **Outdoor Equipment Centre** at Rusty's. **Ken Done**, Australia's best known and most successful contemporary artist, has a gallery on Lake Street. ☎ *(07) 031-5592*.

Fishing

The average cost for hiring a boat to go pursue the wily black marlin (best done between September and December) is around A$100 to A$300 per person per day depending on season, tackle and niceties, but can be lower or much higher. The marlin grounds are between 50 and 60 kilometers offshore, and if you're lucky, you might hook into a 1000-pounder. But the reef and the open ocean areas around Cairns offer far more than just marlin. If you're a fisherman, this is Heaven. Know, however, that the marlin boats are so popular, many are reserved years ahead of time. If you're thinking about going fishing, try to book your boat from North America in advance of your trip.

Any of the Queensland Tourist & Travel Corporation offices in North America or Australia should be able to supply information on companies that handle fishing vacations or individual fishing outfits all along the coast. One company that can arrange charters out of Cairns from North America is **So/Pac**, which also handles hotel reservations all over Australia. *Information, So/Pac 1448 15th Street, Suite 105, Santa Monica, Calif. 90404;* ☎ *(800) 551-2012 USA;* ☎ *(800) 445-0190 California;* ☎ *(800) 235-8222 Canada*. A Cairns outfit to try is **John and Barry Cross Fishing Safaris**, *P.O. Box 84, Earlville, Cairns 4870;* ☎ *(07) 055-1641*. Or Peter Bristow at ☎ *(07) 031-1744*.

In Cairns, one way to try for a marlin trip is just to walk down to the jetty and check the boats; many will have chalkboards out listing prices and availability. If you like to fish, but don't like oceans, try **Dolphin Boat Hire**, in front of the Hilton, which hires aluminum outboards and tackle for fishing the inlet and mangrove areas for perch, snapper and coral trout. If you want tackle, deep-sea or otherwise (and even if you don't), go to **Jack Erskine's tackle shop** at *51 Mulgrave Road;* ☎ *(07) 051-6099*. You have to see if Big Momma, which they claim is the world's largest captive barramundi, is still around, or whether they finally decided to eat her. Feeding times for the big fish were: 4 p.m. Monday–Thursday, and 7 p.m. Friday. *For general Cairns-area fishing information, contact Blackboard Travel and Charters,* ☎ *(07) 031-4444* or ☎ *(07) 053-4803. Or contact the Cairns Professional Game Fishing Association at* ☎ *(07) 031-4742.*

For information about reef diving and snorkeling, as well as services to the resort islands off the coast of Cairns, please refer to our section on the Great Barrier Reef.

Activities

In addition to all the reef-centered activities you can book in Cairns are many speciality trips, one of the reasons the city is becoming a popular tourist mecca. For your enjoyment:

A.J. Hackett, the mad New Zealander who perfected bungy jumping, has invaded North Queensland. One bungy tower is set up in the rainforest north of the city. A first-time jump (it's about 145 feet) goes for about A$90. You get a T-shirt, a certificate of valor and transfers from the city. Basic jumps are around A$60. The company also has trips that include whitewater rafting followed by a bungy jump. If all you want to do is watch the crazies jump, there's a bungy jump bus tour that picks you up in Cairns, lets you climb to the top of the bungy tower and do a rainforest walk, all for A$10. If you are overcome by a need to jump, they'll knock off five bucks from the jump price. The company also has a bungy jump at Kuranda in the Tablelands. ☎ *(07) 031-1119 or (07) 093-8772; FAX (07) 031-3803.*

The **S.S. Louisa**, a paddlewheeler, runs 2.5-hour jaunts through Trinity Inlet, a marshy area the Aussies call the Everglades. Depending on time of year and tides, you can expect to see flocks of water fowl and, if you're lucky, a saltwater croc or two. The boat has a licensed bar and offers complimentary Devonshire teas. The fare is A$15 per person; it departs from the Marlin Jetty. ☎ *(07) 031-3065.*

Another bet for a waterborne tour of the Cairns area is a half-day excursion aboard the **Teri-Too**, which goes around the harbor and down the inlet into the mangrove swamps and around Admiralty Island. There are three trips a day. The fare, which includes coffee or tea, is about A$15 per person. The 2 p.m. cruise offers a prawn lunch for A$20. ☎ *(07) 031-4007.*

Several companies offer **rainforest treks** near Cairns. For example, *AWT Adventure Travel* has an afternoon/night trip which goes in search of rock wallabies and the elusive platypus, capped off by an evening Aussie barbecue. Trips start at 2:30 p.m., return to Cairns at 10:30 p.m. The price is about A$80 per person. ☎ *(07) 031-5058.* More intimate (six persons max) are the tours by *Wait-a-While Rainforest Tours.* These tours also pursue wily forest creatures, and come with afternoon tea and a candlelight dinner. The cost is about A$100 per person. ☎ *33-1153.*

Essential Cairns

Getting Around

The best way to do the Cairns area is by car, and there are plenty of rental agencies to pick from, with prices as low as about A$30 a day at **Leisure Wheels**, *196A Sheridan Street*, ☎ *(07) 051-8988.* Other rental agencies include **Hertz**, *corner Sheridan and Shields streets;* ☎ *(07) 053-6701;* **National**, *143 Abbott Street*, ☎ *(07) 051-4600;* **Budget**, *153 Lake Street*, ☎ *(07) 051-9222;* and **Cairns Rent-a-Car**, *137 Lake Street*, ☎ *(07) 051-6077.* The big names have offices at the airport. RVs can be rented at Budget, Maui, Koala and Brits Australia. One to avoid, at least from our experience, is Apollo. Note that these rental agencies do not want you going any farther north than Daintree without four-wheel-drive because the roads get rotten, and your insurance is worthless.

There is **airport bus service** to most downtown hotels for about A$5; ☎ *(07) 053-4162;* check with the airport shuttle desk at the terminal. **Coral Coaches** also provides airport-hotel service for about A$10; ☎ *(07) 031-7577.* The main **taxi service** is **Black & White,** ☎ *(07) 051-5333;* about A$8-10.

Direct internal **airline** service from Sydney and other major Australian cities is provided by **Australian** and **Ansett** airlines. **Sunstate,** a Qantas subsidiary, has daily service from Brisbane, with stops along the coast. **Rail service** is provided by the two major Queensland coast routes, the **Sunlander** and the **Queenslander**.

Tourist information about Cairns and the area is available at Far North Queensland Promotion Bureau, corner of Grafton and Hartley streets; *P.O. Box 865 Cairns 4870;* ☎ *(07) 051-3588, 3371* or *3392; FAX (07) 051-0127.* Also available is the Welcome North Australia office at *105 W. Lake Street in City Place;* ☎ *(07) 051-8177.* The offices of the **National Park and Wildlife Service** are on McLeod Street; ☎ *(07) 051-3096.* For international money transfers and currency exchange, there are two Travelex offices, one at the airport, one downtown on Lake Street. The company is associated with Western Union. The **RACQ** office is at *112 Sheridan Street;* ☎ *(07) 051-4788.*

A good place for **maps** of the area (as well as the whole state) is the Sunmap Centre, 36 Shields Street; ☎ *(07) 052-3221.*

Where to Stay

High internal air fares or long driving distances usually mean that when many Australians take a vacation, they tend to stay put in the same spot and rent an apartment-type unit for a week or two. Which is why, all over the country, you have villas, apartments and long-term motels available. If you're planning on a lengthy stay in the Cairns area, you might want to give it a try. Any travel agent in town can fix you up; some of the nicer units are in small beach settlements between Cairns and Port Douglas. Depending on the unit and how fancy your tastes, look to pay something around A$500 a week for a moderate two-bedroom unit with a kitchen. As for the short term:

Hilton International　　　　　**A$220–1050**　　　　★★★
Wharf Road; ☎ *(07) 052-1599; FAX (07) 052-1370.*
Doubles with city view A$220; ocean view A$260; suites A$750–1050.
On the waterfront, halfway between Marlin Jetty and Trinity Wharf. Some parts of the Hilton are showing some signs of age, but we still think the service is the best in town. The concierge desk is manned by young, eager types who seem to know everyone in Queensland—you want a tour, a restaurant idea, shopping tips—they can arrange it. The lobby bar is airy, the pool has a good sandwich/bar facility, the restaurants are perfectly adequate. A case where service and detail overcome lack of glitter.

Pacific International　　　　　**A$195**　　　　★★
Corner of the Esplanade and Spence streets; ☎ *(07) 051-7888; FAX (07) 031-1445.*
Doubles from A$195.
The Pacific, like the Hilton, it's a bit long in the tooth, but the service makes up for the decor. The parking lot is a bit small, and you might end up on the street. The second-floor bar is a popular watering hole, as is the rooftop pool. Lee Marvin *(The*

Dirty Dozen) used to come to these parts to fish for marlin. So, no surprise, there's the Lee Marvin suite, available for about A$550.

Radisson Plaza   A$200–800   ★★

At the Pier; ☎ *(07) 031-1411; FAX (07) 031-3226.*
Doubles from about A$200; suites from about A$325–800.

Ideal location, right next to the water. The hotel design and furnishings are a bit pedestrian, but the suites are adequate and the shops in the Pier Marketplace are close. It has handicapped access and a pool, two restaurants and a bar.

Cairns International   A$225–1325   ★★★

17 Abbott Street; ☎ *(07) 031-1300; FAX (07) 031-1801.*
Doubles, depending on view, start at A$225; suites from A$385–1325.

The International is one of the city's newest elegant hotels, noted especially for its lobby, which utilizes native marbles and what seems like acres of native Queensland timbers, including kolantis wood. It's near the city center and next to a small shopping arcade. It has a 3/4-acre garden area with three swimming pools and poolside restaurant and bar. Parking, business center and health facility.

Harbourside Quality Inn   A$135–150   ★

209 the Esplanade; ☎ *(07) 051-8999.*
Doubles from A$135; suites A$150.

The hotel, which has a pool, licensed restaurant and bar, is about a mile along the Esplanade from the city center. Pool, spa. Rooms come with mini-bars and refrigerators.

Cairns Colonial Club Resort   A$100–150   ★★★

18-26 Cannon Street, Manunda, Cairns; ☎ *(07) 053-5111; FAX (07) 053-7072.*
Doubles in a standard rooms are about A$100–150; one-bedroom suites with cooking facilities, A$150; weekly rates less.

This one's a ways out of the city center, but is a real treasure. It has a tropical garden feel, with three large palm-fringed swimming pools, extensive health center, large outside restaurant and a decor set in classic Troppo Queensland. The hotel verandah is gorgeous, the perfect place for a dusk aperitif. Tennis courts, gym, restaurant. Rooms are furnished in South Seas style with balconies or patios. Shuttle service from the airport plus free shuttles to the city center and back. An excellent bet.

Tradewinds Esplanade   A$170–230   ★★

137 The Esplanade; ☎ *(07) 052-1111.*
Doubles, depending on view, from about A$170; suites from $A230.

Set in a tropical area with very nice pool and outside barbecue area. The hotel has light and airy rooms, a huge tropical lobby and a couple of very decent restaurants. Live entertainment nightly and good standby rates (check at the desk). Pool and spa.

Outrigger Country Comfort Inn   A$120–175   ★★

Corner Florence and Abbott streets; ☎ *(07) 051-6188.*
Doubles around A$120; suites around A$145–175.

The Outrigger is awash in jungle growth; it almost takes a machete to get to the saltwater pool. Good bar/restaurant, the **Raffles Room**. The rooms are also tropical, with rattan furnishings and sliding louvered doors. More than half the rooms are suites; good digs for the price.

Holiday Inn Cairns　　　　　　　**A$175–320**　　　　★★★

Corner The Esplanade and Florence streets; ☎ *(07) 031-3757; FAX (07) 031-3770.*
Doubles, depending on view, from around A$175; suites from A$320.
On the waterfront overlooking Trinity Inlet. Rooms open onto a landscaped atrium with mountain or harbor views. Pool, spa, restaurant/bar, bottle shop. Parking, guest laundry.

Rainbow Inn　　　　　　　　　**A$60–85**　　　　　★★

179 Sheridan; ☎ *(07) 051-1022.*
Doubles start at A$60 (very basic); better units are about A$85.
One of the better bargain motels in the area, with a very nice pool, friendly bar and moderate prices. The Coral Gardens Restaurant is worth a try, or you can barbecue your own next to the pool.

Matson Plaza　　　　　　　　　**A$130–250**　　　★★★

Corner of The Esplanade and Aplin streets; ☎ *(07) 031-2211; FAX (07) 031-2704.*
Doubles from around A$130–260; suites A$150–250; apartments from A$200.
One good thing about this hotel (owned by the same company as the International) is the lobby-bar/cafe, open from 10 a.m.–10 p.m. seven days; plus the Coral Hedge Brasserie, open 6 a.m.–10 p.m. Rooms have mini-bars, suites have kitchens. Pool, BBQ, handicapped access, tennis.

All Seasons Sunshine Tower　　　　**A$110–165**　　　★★

136-140 Sheridan Street; ☎ *(07) 051-5288; FAX (07) 031-2483.*
Units start at about A$110–165.
Good range of apartment accommodations available, plus two swimming pools, heated spa and outdoor BBQ areas. Good location not far from the city center. Restaurant, bar.

Acacia Court　　　　　　　　　　　　　　　　　★★

223-227 The Esplanade; ☎ *(07) 051-5011.*
Ocean-view units about A$90; sea view, about A$100.
Despite the architecture (sort of Iron Curtain blocky), this is a nice place, with views of the mountains or the sea. It's a bit away from the action, two kilometers from downtown, but it has tennis, sauna, pool and a tour desk. It also has ★★★ **Charlie's**, maybe the best little cafe in town. The seafood buffet is a killer—bugs, barra, reef fish, prawns—and the price is only about A$15. Cowabunga.

For general information about accommodations in the Cairns area, plus the beach areas to the north, try the **Cairns Reservations Centre**, *36 Aplin Street,* ☎ *(07) 051-4066; FAX (07) 052-1090; toll free (1-800) 80-7730; FAX (1-800) 06-2774.*

Where to Eat

A number of restaurants in Cairns are BYO. Thus you might want to check out the **Liquor Barn** in the Barrier Reef Hotel, which is one of the largest discount liquor outlets north of Brisbane. There's a large wine cellar (tax-free if you're from overseas) and seven-day-a-week hours. The store is at the corner of Abbott and Wharf streets.

As befits a port city, many of its restaurants specialize in seafood, but Cairns also has a large number of ethnic restaurants. In addition to Charlie's (see above), try these:

Breezes   **$$**   ★★★

Wharf Road; ☎ *(07) 052-1599.*

In the Hilton Hotel, one of the better hotel restaurants in town. Open and airy, overlooking Trinity Wharf and the hotel gardens. Seafood buffet Friday and Saturday nights starting at 6 p.m.; the tab, including dessert and coffee, is around A$40. There's also a Sunday champagne brunch.

Damari's   **$$**   ★★

171 Lake Street; ☎ *(07) 031-2155.*
Lunch noon–2 p.m. Monday–Friday; dinner nightly from 6 p.m.

This is another good bet, serving pizza and pastas plus steaks and seafood. Indoor or outdoor dining.

Dundee's   **$$**   ★★

Corner Aplin and Sheridan streets; ☎ *(07) 051-0399.*
Dinner from 6 p.m. seven nights.

Great place for the greenhorns to come in and try some food they can brag about later, what the restaurant bills as "the flavors of Australia." To wit, seafood, crocodile, buffalo, emu, beef and pasta. Casual and usually crowded.

Cooee Pizza and Pasta   **$**   ★

153 Sheridan Street; ☎ *(07) 031-2800.*

Stuck in your room, all the restaurants closed, maybe just too tired to go out? This friendly pizza joint delivers free within the city limits. Or you can go to the cafe itself for fast service. Good basic pizza fare at decent price.

Taste of China   **$**   ★

36 Abbott Street; ☎ *(07) 031-3668.*

Contemporary Chinese cuisine using local Aussie produce and meats. Good lunch specials seven days; dinner also seven days.

Beyond Cairns

Your traveling choices from Cairns include going up the last stretch of paved highway along the coast to Mossman or hanging a left and heading inland to the Atherton Tablelands. Either choice leads to some great Aussie adventures. The area code for all phones in the Far North is the same as Cairns, (07).

About 16 kilometers north of Cairns is the intersection of the Cook and Kennedy highways. The Kennedy angles up into the Tablelands to Kuranda, the Cook goes on to Mossman. At the intersection is a large shopping mall, the **Smithfield Shopping Centre**, which has a major grocery store, bottle shop, clothing stores, fast-food outlets and the Smithfield Tavern (live music Fridays and Saturdays). Just the spot to stock up on sandwich materials or traveling needs. One attraction here that should not be missed is the **Tjapukai Dance Theatre** ★★★★★, a group formed to show the public the dances, music and ceremonies of the Aboriginal people of the Tablelands. This might be the only chance you have in Australia to see authentic Aboriginal dances—and listen to a didgeridoo played as it should be. The performances are held daily at 11 a.m. and 1:30 p.m. daily, plus a 12:15 p.m. show on Wednesday, Friday and Saturday. The dancers are a real success story, the brainchild of Don Freeman and David Hudson. Freeman's background is theater; Hudson, an Aboriginal from Cairns, has a degree in recreation and is also one of Australia's premier didgeridoo players. Hudson (tribal name Dwura) was once part of the act; now he's so busy he doesn't get many chances to dance or play. After we first saw them in 1988, the dancers became so successful Hudson was able to build a new theater for the performances, plus a visitors center and audio-visual displays. The group has done a world tour, performed all over Australia and won many tourism awards. The dancers—the name is pronounced JAPU-guy—are easily one of the most popular attractions in Northern Queensland.

Try to book in advance, because the troupe is very, very popular with tour operators. Tickets are about A$16 per person all credit cards and most foreign currencies accepted. A gift shop at the theater building features Aboriginal art, including Hudson's own hand-made didgeridoos. He'll custom-make one for you—just tell him what key you want it in. *Information:* ☎ *(07) 093-7544.*

The Atherton Tablelands

Because of its proximity to Cairns, the northern part of the Atherton Tablelands is probably the best explored and most popular part of the huge rainforest and timberland area that rises a few miles inland from the coast. There are those—and we're getting there—who think the area is so popular it has become too touristy. The Tablelands runs south from Mossman, all the way past Innisfail, and from just west of the coast to the center of the Great Dividing Range. The forests get wetter and wetter as you travel from the Range east to the ocean, with rainfall ranging from 30 inches a year in the west to more than twice that on the eastern edge.

The Tablelands rise about 2300 feet above sea level, hence the rainfall, and the area's granite valleys and hills are filled with animals and plants seen nowhere else on the planet. Here you can find most of Queensland's huge butterflies. Birds are all over the place, but because of the high forest canopy, sometimes difficult to spot. One of our favorites is Victoria's riflebird, which makes a loud cracking noise and which we have heard many times—but never seen. One of the more interesting animals is the tree kangaroo, two species of which inhabit Queensland rainforests. The major mammals in the Tablelands are possums, including several ring-tailed species. The other major mammal family is rats, which range all the way north to the tip of the Cape York Peninsula. Of all the vegetation, among the most impressive are strangler figs, which in some cases grow hundreds of feet high. Pine trees also reach high into the air, and there are big ferns everywhere—not as large as the monsters you find in Tasmania, but impressive nonetheless.

There are several national parks in the Tablelands, the largest of which is **Bellenden Ker** (see description under Innisfail notes). Another is **Palmerston National Park**, at the south end of the area, reached by taking the Palmerston Highway west from Innisfail. Here is a chance (slight) to see platypuses in the wild (near the Henrietta Creek campground) and something like 500 species of trees and more orchids than you can believe. Especially interesting are the trees that have giant buttress roots, some big enough to stand behind. *Information about the park is available from the ranger at Palmerston National Park, P.O. Box 800, Innisfail 4860;* ☎ *(07) 064-5115.*

The most pleasant way to see the Atherton Tablelands is by private car, although many companies run day trips. The drive from Cairns into the Tablelands is remarkably short;

from the Smithfield turnoff, you can be in Kuranda in less than an hour. You will be able to see many of the highlights of the area in one day if you hustle a bit. If you dawdle, there are places to stay and restaurants to explore at one of the many settlements in the area. If you have time and interest, try renting an RV and exploring.

We suggest a **circle trip** starting in Cairns up to Kuranda, north to Mareeba, then along the route to Atherton, Ravenshoe, Millaa Millaa, Malanda, Yungaburra and back to the coast south of Cairns. This does not include everything, of course, but it will show you why the Tablelands is so popular.

Kuranda is one of the more touristed villages in the area, one reason being the famous **Kuranda Scenic Railway**, an engineering marvel and one of the prettier rail trips around Australia. The line is only about 20 miles long, but has 15 hand-cut tunnels and almost 100 curves, a route which took 1500 men four years to build in the late 1880s. Along its climb toward Kuranda, the train passes many waterfalls, including **Stoney Creek** with its impressive bridge, and **Barron Gorge**, where the train stops for photographs of **Barron Falls**. How great a vista that is depends on the season—sometimes almost no water comes over the falls. (Sit on the right side going up). A one-way trip takes about an hour and a half, counting waterfall stops. At the end of the line is the almost too-quaint **Kuranda Train Station**, a restored Victorian edifice festooned with hundreds of orchids and other plants.

There are several **rail trips** a day starting from Cairns, including non-tourist trains that regularly serve the highlands. Several tourist ticket choices are available; some include breakfast at the Kuranda train station. Straight fare is about A$25 one way; round trip about A$40 when the Kuranda markets are open, A$35 when they're closed. Also available are cars that have guides giving commentary on the route. These seats, reserved, run about A$20 one-way and A$30 round trip. *Ticket information is available from Queensland Railways, McLeod Street, Cairns;* ☎ *(07) 051-0531.* **Freshwater Connection**, a tourist company that runs a restaurant in a reconstructed railway station about six miles from Cairns, and is a stop on the journey, has several choices available including reserved commentary seats or "royale service," which offers drinks, souvenirs and commentary in a special coach, for around A$30 round trip. *Information: Freshwater Connection, Kamerunga Road, Freshwater, Cairns;* ☎ *(07) 055-2222.*

In addition, there are several companies that run Tableland trips by bus that include riding the railroad one way. Try **Australian Pacific Tours**, ☎ *(07) 051-9299*, which offers a full-day trip for about A$45, or **Down Under Tours**, ☎ *(07) 031-1355*, which has a tour that includes the train, the Tjapukai Aboriginal dance company which now operates in Smithville, and free hotel pickup for about A$65 per person. One of the largest outfits running trips around the area, including the Reef and the Cape York Peninsula, is **Tropic Wings**, *54 Lake Street, Cairns;* ☎ *(07) 035-3555; FAX (07) 035-3535.* The company's Tablelands trip runs about A$50.

The newest attraction in the Tablelands area, and one that has Greenies up in arms, is the 7.5-kilometer gondola line operated by the **Skyrail Rainforest Cableway**. The developers claim the skyway blends in with the World Heritage rainforest it glides over, and actually protects the environment because it doesn't require roads or trails and keeps the tourists off the shrubbery. Lots of folks think it just doesn't belong in a rainforest, period.

Anyway, the gondola line is said to be the longest in the world, running from near the Smithfield Shopping Centre northwest of Cairns to Kuranda.

The six-passenger gondolas travel about 10 miles an hour, and stop at two spots on the way to Kuranda: **Red Peak Station** and **Barron Falls**. Red Peak has a rainforest interpretive center, toilets and a boardwalk trail into the forest. Barron Falls is next to the Kuranda railroad and has views of the falls. Eventually, developers hope the Skyrail will carry about 700 passengers an hour; printed guides will be available in several languages, including Mandarin and Korean. Riding time if you don't get off at the two intermediate stations is about a half-hour.

A one-way adult ticket, Smithfield-Kuranda, is A$23; round trip is A$39. Hotel pickup from Cairns and northern beach areas is available for an additional A$10. You can also ride the gondolas one way, the Scenic Railway the other; adults A$56 including hotel transfers. Or there is a package with transfers, rail and gondola rides plus tickets to the Tjapukai dancers for A$72 per person. Information: Skyrail Rainforest Cableway, corner Kamerunga Road and Cook Highway, Smithfield; ☎ *(07) 038-1555; FAX (07) 038-1888.*

Kuranda, as small as it is, has several interesting attractions.

Another interesting stop is the **Australian Butterfly Sanctuary ★ ★**, where you can see Australia's largest butterfly—the female birdwing—as well as the country's most beautiful species, the brilliant blue Ulysses butterfly. On a guided tour of the small facility you'll see the insects being fed and tenderly cared for. If you want a few memorable photos, wear a red shirt—the critters love red, and you might end up with a half dozen nesting on your chest. Tickets to the sanctuary are about A$10 per person; tours are run from 10 a.m.–3 p.m. daily. ☎ *(07) 093-7575.*

Another major draw in Kuranda are the open markets held every Wednesday, Thursday, Friday and Sunday. You can buy everything from worthless trinkets to food to good clothing. The markets are in an area just across the road from the village centre. Next to the market is **Kuranda Settlement**, a pseudo historic group of small shops and eateries. Another attraction is the **Kuranda Wildlife Noctarium and Zoo ★ ★**, located at the top of the main street. Among the animals are bats, flying foxes, echidnas, bandicoots, wallabies and rat kangaroos. It's open 10 a.m.–4 p.m. daily. Feedings are 10:30 and 11:30 a.m. and 1:15 and 2:30 p.m. Admission A$8. ☎ *(07) 093-7334.*

There are several places to sup or sip in Kuranda. Just up from the train station as you make your way into town is the **Bottom Pub**, with a garden bar and good pub lunches; live music at night. In the center of town, look for **Frogs**, where you can get a beer or great Devonshire teas (A$3.50). The **Trading Post Restaurant** has good dampers and excellent cappuccino. Good Italian food is available at **Monkey's**, a BYO that has an outside deck and a fine example of a fish-tail palm tree.

Kuranda is short on accommodations, but a good bet is the **Kuranda Rainforest Resort ★ ★ ★**, a bit out of town on the Greenhills Road. It has a wide range of accommodations from rustic log lodges to dormitory-style backpacker units. It has a nice natural rock swimming pool, spa, tennis courts, a guest laundry, rental cars, scuba hire, shops and baby sitting. Free pickup from Cairns is available. The lodge restaurant, popular with bus tours, has decent moderately priced food and a terrific fruit-laden Queensland breakfast.

The bar is friendly, as well. Doubles in the better digs go for around A$195; the bunkhouse section for about A$15 per person. ☎ *(07) 093-7555; FAX (07) 093-7567.*

Mareeba, up the road from Kuranda, is the largest commercial center in the area. In July, the town goes nuts with one of Australia's biggest rodeos. Around town are tobacco fields and south of town, the remains of a U.S. Army Air Force base built during World War II. About six miles west of town is **Granite Gorge Park**, with swimming, camping and picnic areas.

Down the Kennedy Highway between Mareeba and Atherton is the tiny village of **Tolga**, where there is a good restaurant and bar at the **Corn Cob Motel**, which also has rooms. Or you can scarf down pub meals and icy beer at the elderly but nice **Tolga Hotel**. At Tolga, you can take the Tinaroo Road, which heads for Lake Tinaroo.

Lake Tinaroo was created by damming the Barron River for hydroelectric power, and is a popular sailing and fishing hole, especially for Australia's favorite fish, the barramundi. If you want to haul in, the **Lake Tinaroo Pines RV Park ★** has cabins; doubles are about A$45. ☎ *(07) 095-8232.* Seafood is available at the **Tinaroo Licensed Restaurant**, open seven days a week.

Next to the dam wall, for flower lovers, is yet another orchid garden. At the north side of the dam begins the 20-mile-long **Danbulla Forest Drive**, a scenic woodsy trip that passes some nice overlooks with picnic areas and also takes you past one of the two Big Figs. The fig in question here is the rare **Cathedral Fig**, a parasitic plant *(ficus virens)* that frows some striking forms as it drops long tendrils from the top of its host tree. This is also riflebird country—once you hear one, you'll never forget. Much of the road is narrow, dirt or gravel, and can be a pain during The Wet. In dry conditions, a normal car can make it with no problem (but remember your insurance might prohibit dirt-road travel; ask before you go). The road joins the Gillies Highway southeast of Malanda.

Just west of Tolga is **Atherton**, the center of a peanut and maize-growing area. It has five motels and five campground/RV parks. If you're hungry, there is the **Fu Wah Chinese restaurant** and the **Continental Pizza House**, both open seven days. There's a market day in Atherton the first Saturday of each month. Between Mareeba and Atherton is a spot called the Big Peanut, yet another giant veggie. You can, of course, buy peanuts. From here, you can either keep on the Kennedy Highway to **Ravenshoe** or cut down to Yungaburra. Ravenshoe is significant for two reasons. First, it's in the heart of a controversy about logging in the Tablelands, and you'll see signs here and there saying "Greenies Suck." It's probably not a topic you want to raise in a local pub. Secondly, if you know how to pronounce it, the locals will figure you're a straight bloke: it's Ravenshoe, not Raven-shoe, as we tried it the first time.

If you keep going southeast on the Kennedy Highway, you pass through the tablelands and start entering what is called the Gulf Savannah. Near the town of Mt. Surprise, about 450 kilometers northwest of Townsville, are the **Undara Lava Tubes ★ ★**, created about 200,000 years ago, well worth a visit. The area is also rich in bird and animal life. The spot to haul in is the **Undara Lava Lodge ★ ★ ★**, which boasts compartments in turn-of-the-century railroad coaches, plus a tent village (electric lights, cots) and a campground. The lodge also has a rail car dining room and bar. There are guided tours daily for residents or day-trippers. The tours are A$70 for the full-day package which includes meals. Daily bed and breakfast rates in the lodge are about A$200 double; tent cabins are about A$30 double. ☎ *(07) 097-1411; FAX (07) 097-1450.* Cairns office ☎ *(07) 031-7933.*

Just before reaching Yungaburra, you come to the other Big Fig, this one the **Curtain Fig**, so named because it has toppled its host tree and dropped vines like a curtain to the forest floor. In **Yungaburra**, you'll find our favorite Tablelands pub, the **Town and Country** ★ ★ ★ in the **Lake Eacham Hotel** ★, which also has reasonably priced rooms. Doubles about A$45. ☎ *(07) 095-3515.* Downtown 'Burra has been listed by the National Trust, and has a number of oldies and goodies to look at. Being close to Lake Tinaroo, there is water sports equipment for rent. Also, there is a growing artists' colony in town. One oddity in town is a Swiss chalet building that bills itself as the Black Forest Cuckoo Clock Centre. It's next to Nick's Restaurant.

West of Yungaburra is **Malanda**, which has a few of what pass as upscale digs in the Tablelands. Try the **Malanda Lodge** ★, with pool and licensed restaurant, rooms in the A$60 range; ☎ *(07) 096-5555.* If you like traditional Aussie ambiance, try the **Malanda Hotel**, which they say is the largest wooden hotel in Australia. It has a nice bar and rooms in the A$25–A$40 range; ☎ *(07) 096-5101.*

A bit farther west is **Millaa Millaa** (mill-AH mill-AH), the waterfall capital of the area, with at least a half-dozen worth a look. The best is probably **Millaa Millaa Falls**, which looks like it was imported from Hawaii. Others of note are **Zillie Falls, Elinjaa Falls** and **Mungali Falls**. While you're in the area, try to find a store and pick up some Millaa Millaa cheese, which (you must forgive them) is touted as The Great Australian Bite.

Heading toward the coast on the Gillies Highway from Yungaburra, you come to two of the more popular lakes in the area, **Barrine** and **Eacham**. Both are in the remains of an-cient volcanic craters, now surrounded by pleasant walking paths and picnic areas. Eacham has a place set aside for small kiddies to swim. At **Barrine**, the larger of the two, there is a boat that takes folks on excursions around the shoreline to look for platypuses, pythons, herons and tortoises. Around the edge of either lake, you can also spot cassowaries and bush turkeys. At Barrine is the **Lakeshore Restaurant**, which has Devonshire teas and shops, and on the shore below it, a mostly tame herd of Australian pelicans, whose bright colors make American brown pelicans look like ugly stepsisters.

Farther down the Gillies Highway at the Mulgrave River, just a few miles from the coastal road at Gordonvale, you'll find a nice spot for lunch or a beer at the **Mountain View Hotel**.

The Marlin Coast

The other major onshore touring area near Cairns runs north along the Cook Highway to Mossman and Daintree. Just north of the city you begin to run into some nice beaches which have a wide range of accommodations ranging from RV parks and tenting grounds to super-deluxe resorts. The stretch between Cairns and Port Douglas is virtually one long beach and the area is referred to as the **Marlin Coast**.

Within an hour north, there are the small communities of **Holloways Beach**, **Yorkey's Knob**, **Trinity Beach**, **Kewarra Beach**, **Clifton Beach** and **Palm Cove**. Almost all the beach areas have protected swimming areas (but don't forget the dangerous jellyfish), and most have picnic areas. At each settlement, there are also a number of apartment and condominium units for rent, usually by the week, but also by the day. There are also a slew of small resorts.

First off, there is the **Kewarra Beach Resort** ★★★★★, about five miles north of Cairns, one of the best spots in all Australia. The resort, a member of the Relais & Chateaux group of upscale properties, has rainforest accommodations in South Pacific styles including bungalows and suites. There are 60 acres of gardens, excellent beaches and a very away-from-it-all ambience. Courtesy transport available. There are two restaurants, a pool and tennis plus water sports. All sports activities are included in the room rates. NB: **There are no ocean activities May–October (those box jellyfish, remember.)** Reef trips, rainforest walks, nearby island excursions. Room rates in the bungalows, meals not included, start about A$215 double; better units start at A$300; suites go for A$380–440. ☎ *(07) 057-6666; FAX (07) 057-7525.*

Down a few notches but a good bet anyway is the **Ramada Reef Resort** ★★★ at Palm Cove, with big pool, bars, barbecues, tennis courts and tons of palm trees, courtesy transport, with doubles running between A$155–220; suites A$255–345. ☎ *(07) 055-3999; FAX (07) 055-3902.* Another very good spot is the **Jewel of the Reef** ★★★, right on the beach in Palm Cove, a white, almost-Moorish suites-only resort with three glistening pools, a restaurant and courtesy buses to Cairns. The units are one, two or three bedrooms with two bathrooms, fully equipped kitchens, air conditioning, courtesy transport and private laundries. Doubles range from A$200–450. ☎ *(07) 055-3000.*

Almost all the resort units can be booked in Cairns or through the Queensland Tourist and Travel Corporation offices in North America. Ask for a copy of the *North Queensland Sunlover Holidays* book, which has booking information and details.

If you don't mind a fairly heavy dose of gee-whiz tourist stuff, there are a couple of animal farms along the route to the Port Douglas-Mossman area where you can see birds and snakes and flowers and things, including "crocodile attack shows," which, while pretty hokey, do give you some idea of how big a saltwater croc can grow. There's **Wild World**, just north of Palm Cove, and **Hartley's Creek Zoo**, north of Ellis Beach. Hartley's is open from 8 a.m.–5 p.m. daily. For the more scenery-minded, the 35-mile drive from Palm Cove, about five miles north of Smithfield, to Mossman is one of the better beach drives in Australia. It's lined with white-sand beaches, mostly deserted, and the highway folks have built some overlooks with great views. Be sure to stop at the Rex Lookout, about halfway up, where you'll get your first really good look at the Coral Sea.

Port Douglas

The Port Douglas area is one of the fastest-growing tourists spots in Queensland, with an emphasis so far on rather upscale resorts and hotels. To reach Port Douglas, you have to take a cutoff just south of Mossman that goes about five miles to the ocean. South of town is **Four Mile Beach**, a perfect tropical paradise. If they take care, developers might not destroy its charm, but there are already bites being taken here and there, including the very posh **Sheraton Mirage Hotel** ★★★★. It's a low-rise, expansive place, complete with an 18-hole golf course, tennis courts, rooms for the disabled, jogging tracks, a marina (home of the hovercraft that makes daily runs to Cairns), shops, restaurants, bars—all the goodies you'd expect at a high-quality resort, including butler service and courtesy transportation. There are 300 rooms and suites, with prices starting at around A$400–580 for hotel-style rooms; villas are A$650–850, and suites are A$1800–2000. ☎ *(07) 099-5888.*

Across the road from the Sheraton is the **Radisson Royal Palms** ★★★. The resort has a waterfall-bedecked pool, golf courses, restaurants and bars. Rooms start from A$145; suites A$260–480. ☎ *(07) 099-5577; FAX (07) 099-5559.*

Near the Sheraton is **Habitat** ★, a three acre enclosed zoo/aviary with many Aussie animals on view. Ever seen a fruit bat up close? There's usually one or two hanging around the guides—literally. There are roos, koalas, crocks, emus—the whole range. At 8 a.m. Wednesday and Sunday, you can have "Breakfast with the Birds," a champagne and orange juice affair for about A$20, which includes admission to the facility, which charges A$10 for regular tickets. As these things go, it's OK; if you haven't seen native animals anywhere else, give it a shot. To get to Habitat, drive north on Captain Cook Highway to Port Douglas and then turn at the Sheraton road. Hours are 8 a.m.–5 p.m. daily. ☎ *(07) 099-3235.*

For the cost-conscious, there are a number of other places around Port Douglas that will let you soak up the sun and sand without pecuniary strangulation. In the A$80 to A$150 range, these include self-contained units such as the **Coral Sea Villas**, 60 Macrossan Street, Port Douglas, ☎ *(07) 098-5511;* the **Mango Tree**, 91 Davidson Street, ☎ *(07) 098-5677;* the **Rusty Pelican Inn**, 123 Davidson Street, Port Douglas, ☎ *(07) 099-5266,* **Whispering Palms**, Langley Road, Four Mile Beach, Port Douglas, ☎ *(07) 098-5128;* and the *Outer Reef Beachfront Apartments* on Four Mile Beach, ☎ *(07) 099-5169.* So far the developments around town haven't destroyed its South Seas, small-town charm. But hurry.

Information about the Port Douglas area is available from the **Port Douglas-Cooktown Tourist Information Office**, 23 Macrossan Street, Port Douglas 4871; ☎ *(07) 099-5599; FAX (07) 099-5070.* The office can make hotel or lodge bookings, and has information about fishing, reef trips, jungle excursions and other activities. Another good resource is the **Port Douglas Accom-Holiday Rentals** office across from the Post Office downtown at 1-50 Macrossan Street. The office, open seven days, is privately operated and can be used to reserve resorts or other accommodations direct from North America. ☎ *(07) 099-4488; FAX (07) 099-4455.*

One of the big shopping draws in the area is the **Marina Mirage Shopping Center**, on the waterfront next to downtown. It's a shopping-mall area with upscale and medium scale stores, some fast food places, a few bars and the dock where you catch Quicksilver reef trips. There is another shopping center adjacent to the Sheraton.

A good idea to get a sense of the Port Douglas area is to try a cruise on the *Lady Douglas*, a paddlewheeler that plies the inland and coastal waterways near the city, with views of sugar cane fields, mangrove forests and some sleeping saltwater crocs. Part of the trip is aboard a popular sugarcane train, the Bally Hooley. The tours depart four times a day from the train station at the Marina Mirage, and cost about A$20 per person.

If you want to see the oldest cattle ranch in Northern Queensland, try a trip to the **Wetherby Station** ★★ about 40 miles northwest of Port Douglas. The 120-year-old homestead offers visitors a cattle herding show, damper and tea, cold beer and Aussie wines and a barbecue. Tours run Tuesday-Friday from Port Douglas or Cairns. The price is about A$80 for adults. The Lady Douglas and Wetherby tours can be booked at travel agencies in both Cairns and Port Douglas.

To feed your shopping frenzy, try the Port Douglas Sunday Market on Wharf Street. It's a smallish flea market featuring local artists, fruit and veggies and knick-knacks. To chow down in Port Douglas, try the **Courthouse** ★★ in the downtown area across from Anzac Park (near the Sunday Market). The Courthouse is a thoroughly typical Aussie pub/restaurant, housed in an old white wooden building with outdoor or indoor seating and very friendly service (the guy who owns it is a Texan). Good Yankee hamburgers and fries, cold beer.

The **Belmont** ★★★, on the main drag, is a BYO upscale French restaurant with set three-course meals for A$25. Opens at 6:30 p.m. for dinner. ☎ *(07) 099-4229.*

Danny's ★★, a seafood restaurant with a great menu, is located on Wharf Street, not far from the Marina Mirage center. Open for lunch and dinner; reservations recommended. ☎ *(07) 099-5535.*

Or try the **Cafe Macrossan** ★★ on Macrossan Street, a BYO leaning toward Greek and Italian fare, with seafood and red meat tossed in. Prices are very reasonable, service very friendly. It's open for breakfast, lunch and dinner. ☎ *(07) 099-4372.*

Around Mossman

Mossman, about nine miles north of the Port Douglas turnoff, is the gateway to **Daintree National Park** and has, as yet, escaped any major developments. The 140,000-acre park is a splendid way to examine the vegetation and wildlife of the Main Coast Range that rises west of town. Among its more spectacular attributes is **Mossman Gorge**, a deep, 10-mile long canyon carved through the granite by the Mossman River. The trails through the rainforest are some of the best in the state, and getting to the lower reaches of the gorge is an easy hike. To get to the parking lot, take the park road which starts near the post office in Mossman. It's a three-mile drive. There are swimming holes in the river, and one short loop trail takes you over a suspension bridge, then past some huge fig trees. All in all, a great place for a hike. Serious back-country hikers must register with the rangers. *Information: Ranger, Daintree National Park, Cairns Regional Office, P.O. Box 2066, Cairns 4078;* ☎ *51-9811. Or if you're in Cairns, stop off at the office at the Far Northern Regional Centre, 41 Esplanade.*

We confess to not much appreciating the mega-resort look of the hotel developments around Port Douglas, which come close to matching the overwhelming glitter of some of the new resorts in Hawaii. So if you're looking for a place that is almost completely rainforest in its look and feel—but has excellent food, a wonderful staff and very tidy accommodations—we urge you to try **Silky Oaks** ★★★★, a P&O resort a few miles inland from Mossman. The lodge is surrounded by World Heritage rainforest, and has won several environmental awards for the way it has been integrated into the natural surroundings. Silky Oaks, along with the **Coconut Beach Resort** ★★★★ north of the Daintree

River near Cape Tribulation, is showing others how you can have first-class resort complexes and still not destroy the environment or end up looking like the Kauai Lagoons.

Silky Oaks sits on a hill above the Mossman River, which is a great place to swim or sunbathe. The river, by the way, is croc-free. The sleeping units are separated, surrounded by forest growth, and the large dining room is open air with a view into the river gorge below. **The Tree House** restaurant, an award winner, is open to non-guests. If you don't want to spend the night, you can still come up for lunch or dinner. A booking for meals lets you use the resort facilities—including the river.

Lunch courses run around A$10–20, and include such items as prawn and buffalo brochettes, country-style pate or just burgers and open-face sandwiches. Dinners are in the A$20-30 range. Try the fresh barramundi or a rack of lamb. Breakfast is from 7–10:30 a.m.; lunch from noon–2:30 p.m. and dinner from 6:30–9:30 p.m. Bring a towel and swimming suit.

The resort has hiking trails, a pool and a wallaby nursery. To get to the lodge, drive north from Mossman to the Foxston Bridge over the Mossman River; from the bridge go 2.4 kilometers and watch for a small blue sign on the left side of the road. If you don't want the hassle, you can take a limo (max four people) from the Cairns airport to Silky Oaks for about A$220 round trip. The lodge goes for about A$350 a night double, not including food. **Note**: kids under six are not allowed. *Resort information:* ☎ *(07) 098-1666; FAX (07) 098-1983.* To book from North America, contact P&O, *(800) 225-9849.* (P&O also operates the Cradle Mountain Lodge in Tasmania and Heron Island on the Great Barrier Reef.)

North of Mossman

North of Mossman, the road becomes a dirt track running to the tiny settlement of **Daintree**; after that, it's four-wheel-drive all the way. But it's an easy drive to the Daintree River ferry crossing, where there is a parking lot and a small restaurant. Here is where the Daintree River trips begin. A number of outfits run river trips and can be booked either in Cairns or Port Douglas. The most popular, and our favorite, is **Daintree Rainforest River Trains** ★ ★ ★ which operates a "river train" that carries passengers along the river for views of the forests—and close-up looks at saltwater crocodiles that inhabit the river. Please note the "no swimming-crocodile" signs and pay heed. There are 27 species of mangrove on the river and 250 species of fish. It's also the spawning grounds of box jellyfish, which then float out to sea to grow up. After spawning, it takes them about two weeks to grow to adult size; each one has enough poison to kill 200 people. There are also feral pigs, left over from the original porkers put ashore by Capt. Cook. The trip, with great guides (the boats are quite safe, as well), is about A$20 per person; there are two daily, at 10:30 a.m. and 1:30 p.m. You can book the trip at any of the information offices, or the manager of the lodge or hotel where you're staying will give them a call. You can also arrange to be bused to the Daintree dock; a total package costs about A$80 per person from Cairns, or A$70 from Port Douglas. *Information:* ☎ *(07) 090-7676; FAX (07) 090-7660.*

Beyond Daintree, there is only one more sizable spot of civilization on the coast near Port Douglas: **Cooktown**, the place where Capt. James Cook repaired his crippled *En-*

deavor during the 1770 exploration of Australia. During a gold rush in the 1870s, the town reportedly had more than 90 pubs and 30,000 people. Today, there are under 1000 living here, and the last time the pubs were counted, the total was down to four. One of the highlights in town is the **James Cook Museum**, an old convent building now housing the anchor and some cannons Cook dropped overboard trying to get the *Endeavor* off the Barrier Reef. The building was occupied by American forces during the Battle of the Coral Sea.

Getting to Cooktown can be fairly easy or a pain, depending on weather conditions. Indeed, the only time to do any exploring on your own in the Cape York Peninsula is during the Dry, between June and December. The trek to Cooktown can be made in a normal car or small RV (with difficulty) but that's not recommended—and your insurance is likely to be no good, either. The road, mostly a gravel track, runs out of Mossman, through Mt. Molloy and crosses several river beds and flood plains. An easier way is to call the **Quicksilver** people, who run an excellent Barrier Reef trip from Port Douglas, and who also offer regular service from Port Douglas to Cooktown. *Information: Quicksilver Connections, Port Douglas,* ☎ *(07) 098-5373; Cairns,* ☎ *(07) 051-8311; and Cooktown,* ☎ *(07) 069-5555.* **Coral Coaches** also runs daily bus service from Cairns to Cooktown via Ellis Beach; ☎ *(07) 098-2600 in Mossman;* ☎ *(07) 031-7557 in Cairns;* ☎ *(07) 099-5351 in Port Douglas.* The one-way fare is in the A$50 range. If you want to hang around Cooktown, check out the **Sovereign Hotel** ★★ on Charlotte Street, Doubles go for A$40-115. It also has budget rooms, large pool, guest laundry and a licensed restaurant. *Information:* ☎ *(07) 069-5400; FAX (07) 069-5582.*

A popular day trip from Daintree is to **Cape Tribulation National Park**, on the coast about 16 miles from Daintree. The 42,000-acre park has the state's third-highest peak, **Mt. Thornton** (4500 feet) and a wide array of flora and fauna, including strangler figs, tree kangaroos, ferns, orchids, pythons, forest dragons (a species of lizard) and saltwater crocodiles in the Daintree and Bloomfield rivers, which flow into the ocean in the park. Camping is allowed in the park, with permits available from the parks and wildlife service in Cairns; ☎ *(07) 051-9811.* There are also private developed campgrounds at Thorntons Beach.

A number of companies run four-wheel-drive bus or truck trips up to Cape Trib and Cooktown—or farther. One of the best is **Australian Wilderness Safaris** ★★★ in Mossman Gorge. Like most of the tour operators, the company offers a one-day tour that hits it all: a trip on a Quicksilver boat from Cairns to Port Douglas; morning tea and hikes at Silky Oaks; and a barbecue lunch and tour around Cape Tribulation National Park. The daily tours will pick you up at your Cairns hotel; you can, if you wish, stay overnight in the Cape Trib area and take a later return bus. Fares are about A$120 per person. *Information:* ☎ *(07) 098-1766.*

Kangoala Australian Safaris ★★★—Here's another best bet. For example, a one-day trip to the Hartley's Creek Crocodile Farm, a Daintree cruise, an Aussie barbecue with wine and a tour around the national park, will run about A$100 per person. Tours go every day starting at 7:30 a.m., and are aboard air-conditioned Mercedes-Benz buses. There are optional overnight stays at the Coconut Beach Resort or the Heritage Lodge north of the Daintree crossing. A good outfit, it's part owner of the Habitat attraction at Port Douglas.

Strikie's Safaris has rainforest hikes, a Daintree River cruise, Bloomfield Falls and kangaroo feeding trips. One-day from Cairns, about A$90; from Port Douglas, about A$80; two-day trip with overnight at Cooktown, A$190, food and accommodation not included. Cairns ☎ *(07) 017-9090* or Port Douglas, ☎ *(07) 099-5599*.

Daintree-Bloomfield Explorer, a family owned operation, will pick you up in Port Douglas and Cairns or at your accommodation in the Mossman area, then take the ferry across the river with several stops on the way to Cape Tribulation, including a small-boat cruise on the Daintree River. The all-day excursion, limited to 11 people, includes teas and lunch, with swimming, four-wheel-drive treks, and a stop at Mossman Gorge. From Cairns, the fare is A$105; from Port Douglas, A$100; can be booked at your accommodation. ☎ *(07) 098-2720*.

Reef and Rainforest Coast Connections provides rainforest walks, lunch at the Coconut Beach Resort, swimming hole in the heart of the forest, beach stop at Cape Tribulation, and Daintree River cruise. One-day trips start around A$60, food not included. *Information:* **Port Douglas & Cooktown Tourist Information Centre,** ☎ *(07) 099-5599*.

Or you can do it yourself. We rented a four-wheeler in Cairns for about A$100 a day (plus a credit card deposit charge of A$1000, redeemable if you come back alive with the vehicle.) You can make it from Cairns to Daintree in plenty of time for the first river cruise at 10:30 a.m. After the 2.5-hour cruise, you take the ferry across the river (A$2 per person) and head up the bumpy dirt path of the Cape Tribulation Road. It's rutted and dusty, but we've seen worse in the Outback. Note it's subject to flooding during the January–June rainy season. The first thing you notice is that the southern environs of the Cape York Peninsula are not all lonely jungle—all along the way from the river to Cooktown there are motels, resorts, restaurants and pubs, a few of the reasons environmentalists tried so hard to stop the road from being built. Still, the small businesses are mostly lost in the vastness of the rainforest. Development is very restricted, and the world's oldest rainforest is still pretty virgin.

By mid-afternoon, you can haul in at your selected accommodation or, depending on how far you've gone, head back to Cairns or Port Douglas. One accommodation north of the river is the **Heritage Lodge** ★★, about 20 kilometers north of the crossing. There are individual bungalows with private facilities, plus a bar/restaurant, guided hikes, horseback riding, reef trips and swimming in a pool or a freshwater creek. The resort is next to the national park near a 530-foot waterfall. Doubles around A$100. ☎ *(07) 098-9138; FAX (07) 098-9004*.

About 30 kilometers north of the crossing is **Coconut Beach** ★★★★, our favorite digs north of the Daintree. The resort, as noted before, is one of the more progressive environmental lodges in the Cape Trib area, and has won several national and international awards. It sits on 50 acres of land in the middle of the national forest and next to a lovely beach. You can't spot the resort from the road, and units are built in and around the rainforest vegetation. The rooms are in tree houses and bungalow blocks with verandahs. Rooms are not air-conditioned because the noise of machines at night would intrude on the feel of the place. In the place of compressor sounds, there are ceiling fans overhead and some incredibly loud frogs out back. The main restaurant is housed in a beamy, wooden building next to a pool and close to the beach. It's a great place to sip a cold one and try one of the excellent luncheon buffets—this is definitely worth the drive up from the river.

Or if you don't want to drive, you can take the Quicksilver to Port Douglas and be bused to the resort from there. There is also light-plane service into Cow Bay south of the lodge. Current room rates at the resort are about A$230 double, including breakfast and a guided bushwalk. *Information:* ☎ *(07) 098-0033; FAX (07) 098-0047.*

Another popular spot still farther north is the **Bloomfield Wilderness Lodge** ★ ★ ★ at the northern end of the national park. A favorite spot for serious fishers or just those who want to get some (expensive) peace and quiet in the depths of the rainforest, the lodge is isolated and the only way to get there is by terrible road or airplane from Cairns. The lodge has 16 rooms: eight are suite units, seven with shared facilities and a honeymoon suite. There is a pool, and the evening meal is often what has been caught during the day. The bar has an extensive wine list. The fare, depending on what sort of package you want, includes transport and all meals. Room rates begin around A$250 per person, per day and go higher. *Information: Bloomfield Administration Office, 29 Shields Street, Cairns 4078;* ☎ *(07) 051-9687.*

On the south shore of the river near Daintree is the **Daintree Eco Lodge** ★ ★ ★ , another resort trying to be politically correct. The upscale resort's 15 individual lodges are mounted on stilts set in the rainforest with enclosed balconies (mosquitoes by the gazillions). The sewer system uses natural chemicals, and the menu does not include crocodile or kangaroo (not ecologically ethical, you see). The lodge resort is near many walking trails, and has Aboriginal guides to do bushwalking tours. And, so you'll be comfortable in your ecologically correct digs, all the lodges have air conditioning, satellite TV and direct-dial phones. It's a very pretty spot, close to the Daintree River cruises; pool, bar/restaurant. NB: Kids under 10 not accepted. Doubles with breakfast start at A$285 a night. ☎ *(07) 098-6100.*

Cape York Peninsula

Most of the Cape York Peninsula, until recently, was the least-disturbed natural area in Australia, a huge tongue of forests and rivers and crocodiles and marsupials left untouched since the days of Captain Cook. It is also a land of natural resources, including timber and the world's largest deposits of bauxite. There have been several skirmishes between environmentalists and those less inclined, notably a battle over putting a road through the Daintree forest, which was a defeat for the Greens. As yet, the development of major tourist areas in the cape has been very slow, but there are many in Australia who see the increasing numbers of people hopping four-wheel-drive buses and trucks on safaris to the top of the peninsula as just the first drops in an eventual flood. Would you believe there are even plans afoot to build a spaceport on the peninsula's west coast? True. Australia has created the **Cape York Space Agency** to develop a facility at Weipa, which is also the site of those huge deposits of bauxite. But it's far away from the rainforests, so no one has complained yet. The space folks tell us, by the way, that a geo-stationary satellite launched into orbit from Cape York would require less fuel than one from Cape Canaveral and thus be able to stay up longer—and also be cheaper to put up.

The peninsula is divided into two basic climatic zones, created by the **Great Dividing Range**, which starts in Cape York and runs along the Australian coast all the way to New South Wales. From the mountains east, there are the huge expanses of rainforests, subject to monsoon rains. To the west of the range, things are a great deal drier, with stands of eucalypts. There are two seasons on the peninsula: wet and dry. In the wet, creeks and rivers flood and the roads often disappear under water, and about the only way anyone gets around is by air. In the dry, the roads north are dusty, rock-strewn and often filled with safari vehicles. The east coast areas get something like 60 to 80 inches of rain a year.

You could, if you wish, drive north from the relative civilization of the Cape Tribulation area all the way to The Top by yourself, and many hardy adventurers do. But if you're not an experienced bush traveler, we suggest you don't try. Even in The Dry, things along the route can get very dicey in-deed, and a busted axle in the middle of nowhere is not conducive to a good vacation.

Instead, grab a place with one of the outfits that regularly run trips up the peninsula. These safaris can range from pretty basic to cushy, depending on how much time and money you are willing to invest. But if you are even a bit audacious, this is one of the great adventure trips in Australia, not to be missed.

Most **safaris** leave from Cairns, go up through Cape Tribulation, then back down through Mossman, then up the Peninsula Developmental Road to Lakeland, then Laura, then to Coen (about halfway up), then to a fork in the road where they either go to the Gulf of Carpentaria coast at Weipa or on north to Bamaga and Thursday Island. Along the way, there are several na-tional parks to explore, including Lakefield, one of Queensland's largest, plus ample opportunities to check out the things that go bump (or hiss) in the night. The number of people on the trip can vary from a half-dozen or so to 30 or 40, and vehicles range from air-conditioned buses to Land Rovers. The average length of a round trip is two weeks, but some of the safaris are only one-way—you fly back to Cairns. In most, the cost of the trip includes food, camping equipment (not including sleeping bags, which are usually for rent) and air fares. Trips can be booked in major cities in Australia, or in Cairns. But if you're smart, you'll book ahead from North America.

Several examples:

New Look Adventures, *129A Lake Street, Cairns 4870*, ☎ *(07) 051-7934*, runs a variety of trips including a 16-day round-trip for about A$1300 per person, which includes touring Thursday Island and the Barrier Reef; group size six to 18. A 10-day, one-way trip is about $1200, including air back to Cairns; group size four to 10.

Aussie Airways, *based at the Cairns airport;* ☎ *(07) 053-3980*, runs a variety of flights to Cooktown, Lizard Island and Cape York. The Top of Australia trip is a two-day flight that goes to the tip of the peninsula and on to the Torres Strait settlements. The price, including accommodation and meals, is about A$700 per person.

The founding father of adventure travel in Australia is **Bill King**, who runs wild and woolly trips all over the country. His company, **The Australian Experience**, has several Cape York trips, including a 14-day safari for about A$1700; group size four to 12. An eight-day trek is about A$1300 including air fare to Cairns; group size four to 12. *King's trips can be booked through ATS/Sprint, 1101 E. Broadway, Glendale, Calif. 91205;* ☎ *(800) 232-2121* California, USA ☎ *(800) 423-2880.* In Australia, call toll-free ☎ *(008) 33-1373.*

It might be that all that bouncing around over rocky tracks and creeping through sodden rainforests is not your bag. Not to worry. You can hop a plane and fly up to Bamaga, and then hop a bus for the 15-mile trip to the very tip of Australia where you will find the **Pajinka** ★★, a lodge about 400 meters from the tip of the peninsula. The lodge, owned by the Injinoo tribe of Aboriginals, has a pool, restaurant/bar and guided tours. Double rates including all meals run between A$190-380. Food and transfer fees from the Bamaga airstrip are extra. ☎ *(008) 802-968 toll free; FAX (07) 031-3966.* Sunstate has a direct flight from Cairns to Bamaga on Mondays 8 a.m. and 2:40 p.m.; Tuesdays and Thursdays at 2:45 p.m. The round-trip price is about A$400 per person.

The Queensland Outback

Well, there's Outback, and then there's Outback. In eastern Queensland, the Outback more or less starts when you leave the lush coastal plain and pass over the Great Dividing Range going west. In western and southern Queensland, the whole country is Outback. And then, there's the Channel Country of southwest Queensland, which is about as far as you can get from somewhere and still find a cold beer—down in that corner is one of the most famous out-in-the-middle-of-nowhere places in Australia, **Birdsville**, and brother, to drive far enough to drink a beer at the **Birdsville Hotel**, you really have to want to be away from it all.

The vast chunks of Queensland beyond the coast are not all sandy desert. Some of the Outback is cattle country, some is rock outcroppings, some is miles of flat scrub with no trees, and some is, indeed, sandy wastes. Because even a harsh land must have some compensation, a huge section of western Queensland sits atop mammoth deposits of artesian water, and annual rains can turn parched mud flats into lush pastures overnight. Sometimes, though, the rains don't come, and cattle die and fields burn up. Being a rancher or sheepman in Queensland can be a painful occupation. As we speak, rural Queensland has had almost a decade of drought conditions, and things are looking pretty bleak for the ranchers and farmers in the Outback.

There are several major highways that serve the towns and cities of the Outback, but many of the tracks *Out There* are dry-season only, and even then, not to be undertaken lightly. The country out around Birdsville is what caused the famous Australian explorers, Burke and Wills, to lose their lives in 1861.

Rural Queensland is friendly country because people are few and far between, and the spirit is very reminiscent of northern Arizona or southern Utah, where a harsh environment seems often to create gentle people. Much of the area is also cowboy country. At Longreach, on the Capricorn Highway west of Rockhampton, is the **Stockman's Hall of Fame**, a very popular museum and national monument to the Aussie cowboy (drover, that is).

Outback Queensland also gave birth to two of Australia's national symbols: Qantas airlines and *"Waltzing Matilda."* If you like to camp by yourself and get away from it all, or simply would like to meet a breed of Australian a bit less complex and more down to earth than the sophisticated mob down in Sydney, the Queensland Outback will be just your ticket.

How far you go into the Outback depends on your frame of mind—and the frame of your four-wheel drive. Many of the more interesting spots can be reached by passenger car, but it gets hot and dusty—lordy, does it get dusty—and getting off the main tracks is for the adventurous. (See our section on driving in Australia, with particular attention to bulldust.) Your best bet is to do the Outback between April and October.

The major highways from the coast run west from Brisbane, Rockhampton, Gladstone and Townsville, and of these, the **Flinders Highway**, which cuts across the country from Townsville, is probably the most traveled. The Flinders Highway makes its way from the lushest of rainforests to the driest of deserts, ending up at the isolated mining community of **Mount Isa**. From there the highway changes names (becoming the Barkly) and goes another 520 miles to **Tennant Creek**, half-way between Darwin and Alice Springs in the Northern Territory.

About 250 kilometers west of Gladstone is the tiny settlement of Planet Downs, where you can find an increasingly popular Outback getaway, the

Gunyah Lodge, part of the Planet Downs cattle ranch, a 250,000-acre working spread now catering to city slickers who want to muster cattle, learn to boil a billy and pack a swag, try a campout in the bush, or go horseback riding or hiking. The lodge, a member of the Select Hotels International group, has a pool, tennis court, air conditioning and a restaurant/bar. There are bush dances, and on the site is a 400-acre wildlife sanctuary (camels have been spotted). You can get there by flying from Brisbane or by driving from Gladstone (check that insurance). Doubles, including all meals and activities, are about A$360 per person a night. Vehicle transfer from Gladstone or Rockhampton is A$95 per person one way; a three-night package from Brisbane, including meals, activities and round trip air, is A$2200 per person; in Brisbane call ☎ *265-5022.*

Even farther afield and more Outback is the **Oasis Lodge** at Carnarvon Gorge National Park, to hell and gone from anywhere, way west of Gladstone. The gorge, cut into rugged sandstone, is a refuge for platypus and is home to some of the oldest and rarest plants in the world, including angiopteris ferns and cycads. Accommodation is in tent cabins equipped with private bath and verandahs. The central lodge building has a bar and restaurant, a lounge for movies and dances and a barbecue area. There is also a gift shop and general store, a library and activities for children. Getting to the lodge is half the fun, maybe. By road, you go from Gladstone to Biloela and Rolleston then to the park, about 510 kilometers, some of it through some very rugged territory. Even worse is to take the bus from Brisbane to Roma, where the lodge will pick you up in air-conditioned coaches and rattle your bones going north for almost 300 kilometers over some terrible roads (there are also flights to Roma from Brisbane). The easy way is to fly from Brisbane or the Gladstone coast to the lodge in a private airplane (the lodge can arrange that). Doubles start at A$125 per person a day, including meals, activities and entertainment (but not transportation). A week-long stay goes for about A$800 per person. ☎ *(07) 984-4503; Booking information in Brisbane:* ☎ *(07) 533-3758.*

Between Townsville and the old Gold Rush settlement of Charters Towers is an area called the **Anthill Plains**. The reason will become clear as you start passing mile after mile of termite mounds along the road—in Australia, termites are called white ants. You'll also see herds of cattle, big groves of eucalypts and rocky hills. Going down into the plains west of **Charters Towers**, you start running into grasslands, where you can spot wild kangaroo and bustards and, now and then, a windmill next to a stock pond. Cars and towns are few and far between. The road basically follows the tracks of the Townsville-Mount Isa railroad, the Inlander.

Hughenden, about 150 miles west of the Towers, is a major intersection. From there, you can go southwest to Winton or continue on west to Cloncurry. Hughenden has about 1800 people and is the nearest town to **Porcupine Gorge National Park**, about the only national park for several thousand square miles and sometimes called the Grand Canyon of Australia—but a lot smaller than the real thing. To get to the park, which has camping areas and some rugged trails, take the **Kennedy Developmental Road** (dirt and washboarded) about 30 miles north. **Porcupine Gorge** lies at the extreme southern tip of the mountain range that runs north through the Atherton Tablelands to the Cape York Peninsula. There are four motels and several pubs in Hughenden, which also has gasoline.

From Hughenden, you can either keep on the Mount Isa road or head down the Kennedy to Winton. Toward Mount Isa, there are three settlements of note, Richmond, Julia Creek and Cloncurry. Around **Richmond**, a small agricultural center, are some of the richest grasslands in Australia. At **Julia Creek**, another 100 miles west, there are several motels and hotels. From the town north runs a paved highway to Normanton and Karumba, fishing and agricultural towns on the Gulf of Carpentaria. **Cloncurry**, 80 miles more, was once a copper boomtown, but now gets along quietly as an agricultural center. Of interest is **Scarr Street Museum**, which has relics from the Burke-Wills expedition, as well as artifacts from the fierce Aboriginal tribe that once ruled here. Cloncurry also has the honor of being the site of the first Flying Doctor service base. Another paved road runs north to Normanton.

Mount Isa is a mining town, plain and simple, sitting atop some of the world's richest deposits of silver and lead, as well as major veins of copper and zinc. The population is around 30,000, a fifth of whom work directly for Mount Isa Mines, and everybody else depends on the miners for a livelihood. The city is in the *Guinness Book of Records* as the largest city in the world in area—about the size of Switzerland. Tours of the mines are available, either above or underground. North of town are two man-made lakes, including **Lake Moondarra**, about 12 miles away, which is a popular boating and recreational area. **Lake Julius**, the town's main water supply, is about 60 miles out. Tours are also available at the **Royal Flying Doctor Base** on the road to the airport (the Barkly Highway, also known as Camooweal Road). With the flying doctor is the **School of the Air**, which runs short-wave classes for children isolated all over the Outback.

The **Winton-Longreach** area, to the south of Hughenden, is one of the most interesting parts of the Outback. In the bush about halfway between Cloncurry and Winton (bad road) is a place called the **Combo Waterhole**, where Banjo Paterson supposedly wrote "Waltzing Matilda." However, we have it on good authority that at least three other billabongs in the region were the true site of the deed. Whatever, Winton has adopted the anthem as its own, and in the middle of town, there is a statue of the Swaggie made famous in the song. Winton also has the distinction of being the birthplace of Qantas

Airlines—which stands for Queensland and Northern Territory Air Service. Qantas rose to fame and power from its base at Longreach, however. For *Crocodile Dundee* fans, it should be noted that the tiny settlement of McKinley served as Mick Dundee's Walkabout Hotel in the film. McKinley is southeast of Cloncurry on the way to Winton.

The Great Barrier Reef

Australians call the Great Barrier Reef the Eighth Wonder of the World.

If you have ever dived on the Great Barrier Reef, or at least snorkeled it, you know that written descriptions of its incredible allure are hopelessly inadequate. In the whole world, there are few places so singularly beautiful as the Reef. The Australians call it the Eighth Wonder of the World, and that's an understatement. Of all Australia's attractions, the Great Barrier Reef is probably the most famous—and one of the most visited. It makes Queensland the important tourist destination it has become, although despite this, we have to say in all honesty that over the years, the Australians have been pretty cavalier about protecting the reef. All manner of ecologically damaging schemes have managed to become reality, including actually anchoring a floating hotel above the living reef. (This dumb development, we are delighted to say, was a failure; a Japanese company bought the hotel and towed it to Ho Chi Minh City.) Many of the islands of the reef system have been exploited, and it seemed in the past that only the constant hue and cry of environmentalists kept the Queensland government from doing something new to despoil the reef. In addition, there have always been natural threats, such as cyclones and coral-eating predators. Despite it all, however, the reef today seems to be holding its own.

The reef is often called the largest living organism on earth, a vast group of interrelated marine creatures living in an oceanic community that runs more than 1400 miles down the east coast of Australia, from the Torres Strait southeast of Papua New Guinea to a spot east of Gladstone on the Queensland coast. There are more than 700 islands involved in the system, which also includes some 2000 individual reefs. Nowhere does the reef make contact with the shore. The Great Barrier Reef, as Capt. James Cook discovered in 1770 (see the History section), generally resembles a funnel, with its wide mouth to the south and its ever-narrowing spout at the far north. Some parts of the reef are more than 200 miles offshore; near the tip of the Cape York Peninsula, you can almost throw a stone and hit the reef.

The reef is not a single type of coral structure, but rather several main groups, including what are called "ribbons," the long narrow strips of barrier reef that caused Capt. Cook so much trouble on his voyage. Farther south, coral is often found in circular formations, often surrounding a continental island. One thing about coral makes it great for us tourists: it has trouble growing much below 100 feet, and large chunks of it are in the 20- to 30-foot-deep range, making it ideal for diving and snorkeling. There are more than 400 separate species of coral in the reef, the largest such grouping on the planet. The reef supports an abundance of life, including something like 1600 species of fish and hundreds of other reef dwellers, such as crustaceans, mollusks, marine worms and algae—all of which come in every hue of the palette. The reef is so colorful, as a matter of fact, you will not believe it's real even when you're looking at it. The scores of uninhabited reef islands in the system are important nesting areas for many species of sea birds and amphibians. Reef waters, as well as the deeper waters that surround them, provide some of the richest sport fishing in the world. The best fishing is on the outer reefs, where the coral formations sit next to deep drop-offs and the big gamefish come to play—marlin, tuna, billfish. The combination of warm water and high visibility makes the reef and its lovely islands a perfect destination for stressed-out tourists. The scuba diver of our duo, just as an example, decided he'd finally reached Heaven the day he was able to stick his bare hand out and stroke the soft and gentle lip of a three-foot-wide giant clam, sitting on the bottom of a coral formation in warm, quiet water with at least 150-foot visibility.

Fielding **AUSTRALIA**

THE GREAT BARRIER REEF

The Aussies call it the Eighth Wonder of the World. The reef is often called the largest living organism on earth. It stretches for 1400 miles down the coast of Australia. The islands have interesting vegetation and some offer resorts, camping and hiking. But the true excitement lies in the waters around the islands where divers and snorkelers find a plethora of exotic marine life including more than 2000 species of tropical fish. The reef is an important habitat for sea turtles with many of them nesting on Heron, Lady Elliot and Raine. The cheapest way to get a good look at the reef is to book a day trip from Cairns. Some islands like Lady Elliot and Lizard are far out and have to be flown to. Check the tour listings for diving and day tours.

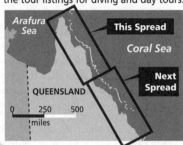

Arafura Sea Coral Sea **This Spread** **Next Spread** QUEENSLAND 0   250   500 miles

Lizard Island National park is noted for its profusion of wildlife including goannas and dugongs, huge sea mammals. Lizard Island Lodge is a first class resort. Excellent snorkeling and diving plus a marine research station.

Great Barrier Reef Marine Park

Dugong

Cape York
Bamaga

Cape Grenville

Thursday Island

CAPE YORK PENINSULA

Cape Weymouth Cape Direction

Cape Melville

Weipa

Peninsular Devil Road

GULF OF CARPENTARIA

QUEENSLAND

Lizard Island Lodge

LIZARD ISLAND NATIONAL PARK

Cook's Look

Lighthouse

0   1   2
km

LIZARD ISLAND

QUEENSLAND AND THE GREAT BARRIER REEF

Continued on next page ☞

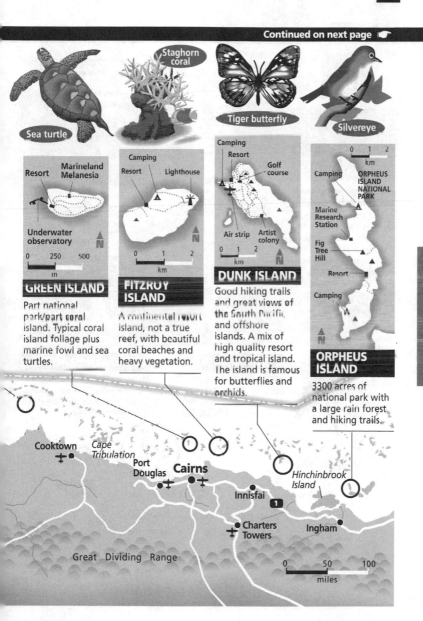

Sea turtle

Staghorn coral

Tiger butterfly

Silvereye

GREEN ISLAND

Resort — Marineland Melanesia

Underwater observatory

0   250   500
m

Part national park/part coral island. Typical coral island foliage plus marine fowl and sea turtles.

FITZROY ISLAND

Camping — Resort — Lighthouse

0   1   2
km

A continental resort island, not a true reef, with beautiful coral beaches and heavy vegetation.

DUNK ISLAND

Camping — Resort — Golf course

Air strip — Artist colony

0   1   2
km

Good hiking trails and great views of the South Pacific and offshore islands. A mix of high quality resort and tropical island. The island is famous for butterflies and orchids.

ORPHEUS ISLAND

0   1   2
km

Camping — ORPHEUS ISLAND NATIONAL PARK

Marine Research Station

Fig Tree Hill

Resort

Camping

3300 acres of national park with a large rain forest and hiking trails.

Cooktown

Cape Tribulation

Port Douglas

Cairns

Innisfail

1

Hinchinbrook Island

Charters Towers

Ingham

Great Dividing Range

0   50   100
miles

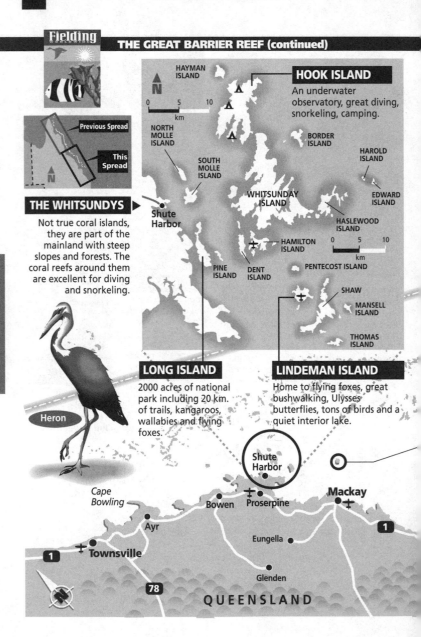

HAYMAN ISLAND

N

0   5   10
km

NORTH MOLLE ISLAND

SOUTH MOLLE ISLAND

HOOK ISLAND

An underwater observatory, great diving, snorkeling, camping.

BORDER ISLAND

HAROLD ISLAND

WHITSUNDAY ISLAND

EDWARD ISLAND

HASLEWOOD ISLAND

THE WHITSUNDYS ▶

Not true coral islands, they are part of the mainland with steep slopes and forests. The coral reefs around them are excellent for diving and snorkeling.

Shute Harbor

HAMILTON ISLAND

0   5   10
km

PINE ISLAND

DENT ISLAND

PENTECOST ISLAND

SHAW

MANSELL ISLAND

THOMAS ISLAND

Heron

LONG ISLAND

2000 acres of national park including 20 km. of trails, kangaroos, wallabies and flying foxes.

LINDEMAN ISLAND

Home to flying foxes, great bushwalking, Ulysses butterflies, tons of birds and a quiet interior lake.

Shute Harbor

Cape Bowling

Bowen   Proserpine

Mackay

Ayr

Eungella

1

Townsville

78

Glenden

QUEENSLAND

Previous Spread

This Spread

N

QUEENSLAND AND THE GREAT BARRIER REEF

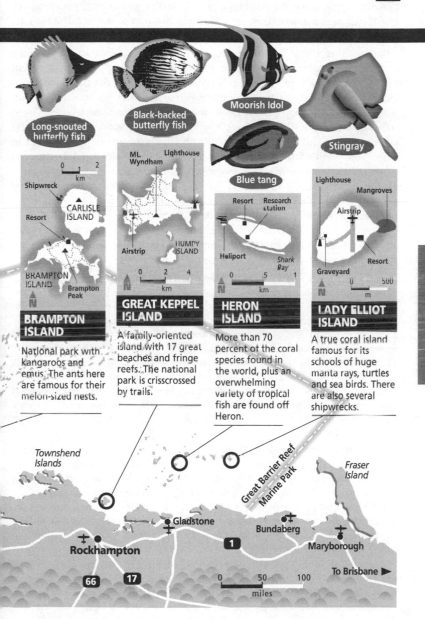

Long-snouted butterfly fish

Black-backed butterfly fish

Moorish Idol

Stingray

Blue tang

BRAMPTON ISLAND

National park with kangaroos and emus. The ants here are famous for their melon-sized nests.

GREAT KEPPEL ISLAND

A family-oriented island with 17 great beaches and fringe reefs. The national park is crisscrossed by trails.

HERON ISLAND

More than 70 percent of the coral species found in the world, plus an overwhelming variety of tropical fish are found off Heron.

LADY ELLIOT ISLAND

A true coral island famous for its schools of huge manta rays, turtles and sea birds. There are also several shipwrecks.

Townshend Islands

Great Barrier Reef Marine Park

Fraser Island

Gladstone

Bundaberg

Rockhampton

Maryborough

To Brisbane ▶

66 17

1

0   50   100
miles

In this section, we list the major island resorts and attractions along the coast, although many of them are technically not part of the reef. But they are all off the Queensland coast and generally offer the same sort of adventures.

Barrier Reef island accommodations vary in price and amenities from camping to ultra-swank five-star international resorts, but most of the decent ones are in the high to medium price area. Our very favorite upscale resort is **Lizard Island**, about as far north on the reef as you can go. In the medium-priced range, we recommend **Dunk**, **Brampton** and **Hamilton islands**. Good bargain stays are available at **Long Island, Fitzroy** and **South Molle**. How you get to the reef and the resorts depends on which group you're heading for. The main Barrier Reef centers are in the north, at Cairns and Townsville, while the gateways to the Capricorn section of the reef (including popular Heron Island) are Gladstone and Rockhampton. The major reef and island gateways on the mainland can be reached by train, plane or bus. If your stay in Australia is brief, we suggest you make some arrangement to fly to Cairns or Townsville and do your reef explorations from there. Cairns is especially attractive because it's closer to the reef than Townsville and is also close to some other fascinating rainforest areas.

The Great Barrier Reef Park

In 1983, the Australian government created the Great Barrier Reef Marine Park, the largest marine preservation area in the world. Run by an agency based in Townsville, the park extends the entire length of the reef (plus some non-reef areas), and is divided into a number of parts, including the **southern section**, which takes in the far-offshore reef running from east of Mackay to east of Bowen; the **Capricornia section**, which is off Gladstone and Rockhampton; the **inshore southern section**, which contains the close-in islands and reef from Gladstone to Cairns; the **central section**, which takes in the far off-shore formations from roughly east of Bowen to Innisfail; the **Cairns and Cormorant Pass** section, from Innisfail to Lizard Island; and the **northern section**, which runs from Lizard Island to the tip of the Cape York Peninsula. In all, something like 98 percent of the reef is in the park.

The **Great Barrier Reef Authority** has the unenviable job of trying to oversee all the possible uses of the reef, from tent camping on deserted islands to commercial fishing. One of its toughest jobs is trying to gauge the effect coastal development might have on coral growth, and also of balancing tourist dollars against overuse—when do many people become too many people? Working with the authority are other agencies, including the Queensland government and a number of private and public agencies. James Cook University also pioneered studies of the crown of thorns starfish, which has denuded big chunks of the reef off Townsville.

Another sign of the increased attention being paid to the reef came along in 1989 when the National Parks and Wildlife Service announced plans to increase aerial inspections of the park. The flights cover the Dunk Island-to-Whitsundays section of the reef. The area around Cairns and the Capricorn section were already being patrolled. The flights look for park rules violations, including illegal fishing and oil spills.

Any Australian tourism office, especially the **Queensland Tourist and Travel Corpora-tion**, can supply information about the Great Barrier Reef. The reef authority in Towns-ville has a number of publications available, including an excellent overview of the reef called the *World Heritage Nomination Book*, which has history and science information, as well as management policy and strategy. *For information, contact the Great Barrier Reef Marine Park Authority, 2-68 Flinders Street, P.O. Box 1379, Townsville, Queen-sland 4810;* ☎ *(07) 781-8811.* Another general information source is the **Queensland National Parks and Wildlife Service**, *MLC Centre, corner of George and Adelaide streets, Brisbane 4000;* ☎ *(07) 224-0414. For information about fishing licenses and regulations for coastal areas as well as inland, contact the* **Queensland Fish Management Authority**, *P.O. Box 344, Fortitude Valley (Brisbane) 4006;* ☎ *(07) 224-4335.*

Finally, before you start out on a reef adventure, a few words of caution. First and fore-most, do not go scuba diving unless you've had the proper training. We know of no dive shop or training center in Australia that is not reputable, but we haven't seen them all. We are suspicious of hotels in some tropical ports around the world that offer to teach you to scuba dive in two hours. The mechanics of using scuba gear can be deceptively simple, but there are enough things involved that proper training is essential. You can get into some serious—and possibly fatal—situations if you haven't had proper scuba training, even in shallow water. You can easily get your scuba card in Canada or the United States through dive shops or often the local YMCA. If you have time, you could take the train-ing in Australia. But you should have a card from either **PADI** (the Professional Associa-tion of Dive Instructors) or **NAUI** (National Association of Underwater Instructors) certifying that you have had the requisite hours of training. The Great Barrier Reef is not a place to learn things the hard way. If you ever go into a dive shop in Australia—or any-where else in the world—and they offer to sell you air without asking for your dive card, just walk on by.

Secondly, and we are not trying to make a big deal about this, the Great Barrier Reef, with all its beauty, has some very nasty critters, some perfectly capable of killing you. So, even if you're an experienced diver, the first time out on the reef should be with an Aus-tralian buddy, or with a local group. Sharks are probably the least of your worries, but among the evil cast of characters, there's a small seashell that is deadly, and there's a dandy species of poisonous octopus as well as fire coral and sea snakes. Snorkelers proba-bly won't get into too much trouble floating above the reef—but again, if you're inexpe-rienced or new to the reef, go with a local group or agency—and don't leave home without a pair of old tennis shoes. Walking around a coral head barefooted is just asking for major league problems. Having said all that, we now insist that you move heaven and earth to get underwater on the reef. Otherwise you will have missed one of the greatest sights in this or any other solar system.

The Southern Islands (Capricornia Section)

North of **Fraser Island** (the world's largest sand island) is the Capricornia section of the Great Barrier Reef Marine Park, a group of coral reefs and islands about 340 miles up the coast from Brisbane. The area is divided into two parts, the Capricorn group and the Bunker group. (Bunker was a Yankee whaler who passed by in the early 1800s.)

*More than 70 percent of the coral species in the world are found off Heron
Island in the Great Barrier Reef.*

The most popular of the islands in the group is **Heron ★ ★ ★**, which is a true coral
island about 50 miles offshore. The island, only about 30 acres in size, is the home of a
resort hotel and a marine biology station, and more than half of it is a national park—
more than 70 percent of the coral species found in the world are off Heron, plus an overwhelming variety of tropical fish. In addition to being close to some excellent diving, the
island is also filled with birds, is a breeding spot for green sea turtles, and is one of the
most heavily forested keys on the reef. There are usually daily lectures from staff members
of the research station and reef walks. The fastest way to get to the island is by helicopter
from Gladstone, (**Lloyds Air Services**) which costs about A$375 per person round trip;

half price for kids. There are also daily launches from Gladstone, which cost about A$70 per person one way and take about 90 minutes. **Author's note:** Weight restrictions are tight on the choppers: 10 kilograms (about 22 pounds) per person. The launches allow the island to be done on a day trip. They leave the mainland at 11 a.m. and arrive at the island at 1:15 p.m.; return leaves the island at 1:30 p.m. and arrives back at the mainland at 33:30 p.m. There are no camping facilities on the island.

The **resort** itself is built into the forest and offers accommodations for about 300 guests in several ranges from beach houses to lodges. There are no TV or room phones. There are two pools, a dive shop, scuba instruction, tennis and nightly entertainment. The lodges go for A$140 per person including meals; suites are from A$205 260 per person, meals included. Kids 3–14 are half-fare. The rates also include some activities. *Reservation information is available from* **Heron Island Reservations** *at 160 Sussex Street in Sydney;* ☎ *(02) 364-8800; or from* **P&O Resorts**, *520 Monterey Drive, Rio Del Mar, Calif. 95003;* ☎ *(408) 685-8902; fax (408) 685-8903; or toll free (800) 225-9849.* Resort phones: ☎ *(07) 978-1488; FAX (07) 978-1457.*

Information about the island and its flora and fauna is available from the **Queensland National Park and Wildlife Service**, *P.O. Box 1395, Rockhampton 4700;* ☎ *(07) 927-6511,* and there is an office on the island. There is regular air service from Brisbane to Gladstone, as well as regular train service.

Another popular island in the Capricorn section of the reef is **Lady Elliot Island** ★ ★ ★, which marks the southern tip of the reef. The island has an airstrip and reasonably priced accommodations, and is a major target for divers. The reef formations at Lady Elliott are widely regarded as being some of the best in the whole system, and there are also turtles and sea birds to enjoy. The island is about 100 acres in size, and like Heron, is a true coral island. It is famous for schools of huge manta rays, and for divers, there are a number of shipwrecks. The accommodations come in several styles: beachfront and garden cabins, suites and safari tents. There are also limited bunkhouse spaces available. There are no room phones, one restaurant, bistro, two bars, a general store, pool, dive shop, guided eco-tours. The resort operates a glass-bottomed boat, and scuba lessons are available; there are child-care services. Air service to the island is included in the room rates. For day-trippers, flights from Bundaberg on Sunstate are about A$120 per person round trip; half fare for kids 3-14. **NB:** Weight restrictions require passengers, including resort guests, to carry no more than 10 kilos (22 pounds) of luggage per person. There is also catamaran service from Bundaberg. *Information: Lady Elliott Island Resort, LMB 6, Post Office, Bundaberg 4670;* ☎ *(07) 171-53-2485.*

Also in the Capricornia group are several small islands, including **Lady Musgrave**, **Northwest Island** and **Tryon Island**, which are available for campers. None have water or firewood, and transportation is up to you, available from services in Gladstone and Rockhampton. There are package tours available to Lady Musgrave through Lady Musgrave Cruises and Lloyd Aviation and can be booked in Bundaberg, Brisbane, the Gold Coast and Sydney. A day trip by boat is about A$70 per person; a seaplane day trip runs about A$150. Permits and information are available from the Queensland National Park and Wildlife Service offices. Cruise packages to the trio of islands can be booked through Lady Musgrave Cruises in Bundaberg ☎ *(07) 152-9011.*

Great Keppel Island, formerly a sheep ranch, is now a national park offering great beaches, fringe reefs, camping, freshwater pools, tennis and a nightclub.

Opposite Yeppoon, northeast of Rockhampton, is **Great Keppel Island** ★★, only eight miles offshore and a long boat ride from the reef, but popular because of its great beaches and fringe reefs. Most of the island, about 3000 acres, is a national park criss-crossed by trails. At one time, the island was a sheep ranch, and the old ranch house still stands. The island, one of the five owned by a subsidiary of Qantas (Australian Resorts, based in Brisbane), traditionally catered to a young, hard-drinking clientele, and has room for about 400 guests. The official motto of the island used to be: "It's a great place to get wrecked." But these days, it's become more of a family oriented resort, with baby-sitting service and children's activities. The resort claims to be jellyfish and shark free—still, use care.

In addition to the 17 beaches on the island, the resort has four freshwater pools, a nightclub with cabaret shows, tennis courts, scuba activities. There is an underwater observatory for coral viewing. Access to the island is either by a thrice-daily launch from Rosslyn Bay (about A$24 per person round trip) or by air from Rockhampton for about A$75 round trip. The accommodations were renovated in the late 1980s, and are either beachfront motel units, ocean-view villas or garden units. There are also small cabins and camping available. The villas go for A$190–345 double, meals not included; the beachfront units are A$170–290; garden units are A$150–250. Cabins are A$75 double; tent sites are A$15 a day. ☎ 1-(800) 81-2525 *toll free in Australia, or in Brisbane,* ☎ *(07) 3360-2400; FAX (07) 3360-2436.. Australian Resorts booking in North America:* ☎ *(800) 227-4411.*

The other island of the group, **North Keppel**, is an uninhabited national park. It has camping facilities with limited water supplies and some firewood in designated sites with toilets. *Information is available from the parks and wildlife service in Rockhampton* ☎ *(07) 936-0511.*

General information about the area is available from the **Queensland Tourist and Travel Centre**, *119 East Street, Rockhampton 4700*, ☎ *(07) 927-8611;* the **Capricorn Tourism and Development Organisation Inc.**, *Curtis Park, Gladstone Road, Rockhampton 4700*, ☎ *(07) 927-2055,* and **Reef Adventureland Information**, *56 Goondoon Street, Gladstone 4680*, ☎ *(07) 972-4000.*

The Whitsundays

The Whitsundy Islands offer dozens of resorts and lodges, plus excellent opportunities for diving and snorkeling.

This group of islands, opposite the cities of Mackay, Proserpine and Bowen, is probably the singlemost popular destination on the whole reef, as the dozens of resorts and lodges strewn about prove. The Whitsundays, so named by Captain Cook, are not true coral islands; rather they are part of the mainland, with steep slopes and forests. Most of the 74 islands in the group do have coral reefs around them, however, and are excellent for diving and snorkeling. The islands offer just about any style vacation you want, from the five-star plush palaces on Hayman and Hamilton islands to beach camping on uninhabited islets. One thing to keep in mind is that most of the resorts have **stand-by rates**; if they have cancellations, you might be able to sneak in at a reduced rate, so give them a call if you're in the neighborhood. *For general information, contact the Whitsunday Tourism Association, P.O. Box 83, Airlie Beach 4802;* ☎ *(07) 946-6673.*

The main access point for trips to the islands is **Shute Harbour**, the developing tourist area near Proserpine. In addition, air service is available to the larger settlements. Some of the island resorts, in fact, are owned by airlines. A rare treat would be to hire a bareboat yacht and do the islands at your own speed. (If you're interested, contact **Australian Bareboat Charters** ★★★, *P.O. Box 357, Airlie Beach, Queensland 4802;* ☎ *(07)*

946-9381, or **Queensland Yacht Charters**, *16 McLachlan Avenue, Rushcutters Bay, Sydney, NSW 2011;* ☎ *(02) 331-1211.*

If you're ecologically minded, the development of **Hamilton Island** ★ ★ ★ will make you grind your teeth. The 1500-acre island looks a bit like a clone of Waikiki and got that way with what seems to be little or no regard for nature. The island was unique because it was owned outright by one man—Keith Williams—rather than being in the public domain as is most of the barrier reef. Williams is infamous in Queensland for the way he built the resort. First, he dynamited the top off a mountain to put in a helipad, dredged the harbor and dynamited another peak to extend the island's jet landing strip. In early 1994, the Holiday Inn group bought the island and is in the process of changing things, hopefully for the better. Hamilton is ground zero for the Whitsundays because it provides almost the only access to several other Barrier Reef islands including Hayman, Daydream, Lindeman (Club Med) and South Molle. The airport, equipped to handle big jets, is an international facility with flights coming in from Japan and Singapore and is linked directly to major eastern Australian cities including Sydney. There is also daily air service from Proserpine, Cairns, Brisbane and Mackay, and two daily launches from Shute Harbour.

The resort has everything from Mexican fast food to exclusive penthouse apartments. You can rent VCRs, hire a motor buggy, cook your own food in a kitchenette, or drop a foot in one of the resort's eight swimming pools. It's enough like a Hawaiian resort to leave us wondering why anyone from North America would bother coming this far when the beaches are better and much closer on Maui. There is the reef, of course, but there are less populous and more attractive places to hang your hat on a reef trip. Having said that, we do acknowledge that Hamilton does make life easy with all the activities it offers, as well as the range of accommodations and food outlets. There is 24-hour medical service and a health center.

One of the delights of the island is being visited by birds on your balconies (cockatoos are especially pushy) and at dusk, watching large streams of flying foxes come out to feed. Getting around the island is either by foot (strenuous) or by taking an island taxi. Or you can rent golf-cart-type vehicles for a couple of hours or your whole stay. The main business area of the island is centered around the marina area at Hamilton Harbour. You'll find a laundromat, post office, pharmacy, bank, barber shop, deli/bakery, several restaurants and boat/fishing charters. At Catseye Beach on the other side of the island, you can rent almost any form of water vehicle, including bareboats or canoes. If you've a mind, you could also visit the Fauna Park, home to kangaroos and koalas (A$5 a head), or hike on several trails in the mountains. The resort offers all manner of activities, including boat trips to the reef, with snorkeling and reef walks, lunches, bar service, all for about A$70 per person for a half-day. The island is popular with day-trippers, who take a launch from Shute Harbour for about A$15 each way.

The island has space for about 1100 guests. One of the main venues is **Hamilton Towers**. There are 411 rooms in the 20-story tower, which has a 24-hour coffee shop and a 2000-seat tennis stadium. Daily double room rates are from A$195–300; suites A$600 and up. The **Whitsunday Towers** has one-bedroom units for A$295 a night or two-bedroom units for A$295–375. There are also beachfront units at the **Bougainvillea Lodge** starting at A$295, or Polynesian-style bures starting at A$195. The motel-style **Allaman-**

da Lodge rooms go for $A200 double. Most of the accommodation groups have coin laundry facilities scattered about. **Holiday Inn** is offering a three-night package including breakfast, transfers from the airport or launch dock, scuba, snorkeling, and the resort's choice of your accommodations depending on availability, for A$260 double.

Reservation information in North America for Hamilton Island is available by calling ☎ *(800) 465-4329* or in Queensland, Hamilton Island Holiday Inn Crowne Plaza Resort, ☎ *(07) 946-9999*.

Remote **Lindeman Island** is home to flying foxes, great bushwalking, Ulysses butterflies, tons of birds and a quiet interior lake. It is almost all a national park with sandy beaches, mangrove swamps and stands of eucalypts. Once out-of-the-way Lindeman Island is now home to the first **Club Med** ★ ★ in Australia. So now, along with the scenery, you have an 18-hole golf course and room for 300 guests and an international clientele. If the Club Med scene is to your taste, you can get to the resort by taking a one-way, A$40-per-person launch trip from Hamilton Island, or by air from Shute Harbour or Mackay. The resort has three stories of bungalow-style accommodations, with prices running from A$400–500 double, including all meals and some beverages and transfers. Some activities are included, others are extra. You have to join Club Med to use the island: pay $US30 per family for a lifetime membership. There are free activities for kids four and up. A five-day stay including air fare from Cairns and transfers, depending on season, runs between A$995 and A$1300 per person. ☎ *(800) 258-2633 USA, or in Australia (07) 946-9333; FAX (07) 946-9598*.

The northernmost resort island in the Whitsundays is **Hayman Island** ★ ★ ★ ★ ★, which was closed down for two years in the late 1980s for a A$260-million facelift. The upgrade included a waste treatment plant, a desalinization plant, six generators, solar heating and 30 acres of gardens. The gardens include a group of lovely Phoenix palms, an Oriental garden with a teahouse, and a swan pond featuring two lovlies named Siegfried and Odette. The resort's saltwater pool is enormous, seven times the size of an olympic pool, and is just one of several pools in the complex. The resort is generally regarded as the snazziest in the Whitsundays, and has about 200 rooms and suites and 11 penthouses. The place is stunning, awash in marble and antiques, with separate reception areas in each wing of the facility. Here is the land of dress codes for dinner, a huge wine cellar and underground service tunnels so you can't see the gnomes who provide the first-class service. There are five restaurants, including an elegant French abode where prices are on a par with Sydney's best. Once a week there is a **chef's table special**, a five-course silver service gala with five different wines. Included is a tour of the kitchen, where you can watch your chow being prepared. Only 20 guests at a time, so make reservations. The price is A$150 per person. There is also a weekly Aussie barbecue for A$60 per person. There are nightly cabaret shows and a late-night disco. If you get tired of all the fluff, you can take advantage of the resort's tennis facilities or water sports. Complimentary activities include snorkeling, catamaran boats, tennis, a putting green, weekly screened movies and a huge billiard table. Pay-for activities include almost anything that requires gasoline. There are trips to the reef, for example, in a glass-bottomed boat for A$50 per person. There is a health club, and if you're in the mood, some spectacular hiking trails. The best trail on the island is up to **Cook's Lookout** with splendid views (he was never up there, by the way). Along with all this is other normal big-money resort hotel stuff you'd expect such as a hairdressers, pharmacy and an art gallery.

For our taste, the major problem we have with Hayman is that it could be a five-star island resort almost anywhere in the world. The level of services and accommodations are such that you're tempted never to leave your rooms. For this reason, we fancy smaller and much more intimate Lizard Island, more of which later.

Access to the island is by helicopter or charter planes from Proserpine or Shute Harbour, or aboard the elegant *Sea Goddess* launch from Hamilton Island, which connects to flights from Brisbane and other mainland cities. Aboard the *Goddess*, you can snack on champagne and canapés and watch the ocean go by. Service is also provided aboard the *Sun Paradise*, a second boat. Round trip fare on the boats is about A$100 per person. Standard rooms start at $A375 per room per night and can go as high as A$630; suites are about A$1000–1300 and the penthouses range from A$1500 to A$2900. The rates include a very good breakfast. Standby rates, often much lower, are available through Airlie Beach travel agents. *Booking information:* ☎ *(800) 223-6800* USA and Canada; in Australia, ☎ *(07) 940-1234; 6-9100 or 1-(800) 075-175; FAX (07) 940-1567.*

At the south end of the Whitsunday Passage is **Brampton Island** ★★★, another spot owned by Australian Resorts. The emphasis here is on couples, but like many island resorts, it also has activities and facilities for kids. The island is almost all national park and has kangaroos and emus, as well as two special local inhabitants to watch out for, scrub hens and green tree ants. The birds are one of Australia's mound-building species; the ants are famous for their huge melon-sized nests. The resort offers the usual water sports and has nightly parties and frequent barbecues. There's a six-hole golf course, a laundry, two pools, tennis courts and a coral reef right off the beach. There are a restaurant, several bars and a boutique. There are two grades of accommodations: beachfront and garden view. All units have air conditioning, TVs, in-house movies, separate laundry facilities and two beds. The island is a 20-minute flight from Mackay or 50 minutes by launch. The rate for the beachfront units, five nights or less, is A$136 per person, meals not included; garden units are $A122 per person. Meals are A$65 per person a day for full board; A$47 per person for American plan. *Booking information is available through Australian Resorts* ☎ *(800) 227-4411; in Australia* ☎ *1-(800) 81-2525.*

Another resort worth a stop is **Daydream Island Travelodge** ★★, a revitalized island getaway just three miles from Shute Harbour. There has been a resort of one form or another on the tiny island since the 1930s; the newest A$100 million version is a Travelodge with four eateries and pools, saunas, live entertainment and some great standby rates, one of the best deals on the Barrier Reef. The resort units are in a complex of wings with a central atrium, all nestled next to the marina and backed by bushland. The island is compact enough—a kilometer long, half a kilometer wide—that you can get to all the activities easily. The resort emphasizes kid care, with baby sitting and activities provided. A boat to the island from Shute Harbour is about A$25. There are three grades of accommodations. Garden units are A$180; the Daydreamer section (ocean view) goes for A$200, and the Sunlover units (private spa baths, great ocean views) $A260. Meals are extra; expect to pay about A$40 a day per person and up for food. *Booking information:*

Southern Pacific Hotels, ☎ *(800) 441-3847 in the USA; in Australia* ☎ *(008) 075-040 or (07) 948-8488; FAX (07) 948-8499.*

Other Whitsundays worth a look include Hook, Long Island and South Molle. **Hook** is close to some of the best diving and snorkeling areas in the area and has an underwater observatory where, for A$5, you can peek through one of the three dozen or so windows at the fish. Camping is available nearby, and there is a place to get food and beer.

On **Long Island**, eight kilometers from Shute Harbour, are two resorts built among the 2000 acres of national park, 20 kilometers of trails, and wildlife including kangaroos, wallabies and flying foxes. The **Long Island Palm Bay Hideaway** ★ ★ sits on the western side of the island, and has tropical bures and cabins. They offer a restaurant, bar, pool and spa, ceiling fans, no TVs or phones. Bure room rates start at A$285; cabins at $A190. Meals are extra; full board is about A$55 per person. ☎ *(07) 946-9233 or (03) 9274-7422; FAX (03) 9274-7400.*

The second resort is the **Long Island Resort** ★ ★, a bit north of the Palm Bay Hideaway. There are two pools, spa, sauna, a pool bar/grill, restaurant, health center, day and night tennis courts, dance floor and water sports. Wallabies and kangaroos wander the area, and fruit bats come out at night. There are garden view (no air conditioning) and beachfront (with air conditioning) units. Garden view doubles are $A140; beachfront units are A$170 double. Meal options include full board for about A$50 per person per day. Access to the island is by launch or water taxi from Shute Harbour, about A$25. Or you can take a launch from Hamilton Island. *Booking information:* ☎ *(008) 075-125 or (07) 946-9400; FAX (07) 946-9555.*

South Molle ★ ★ ★ another Ansett Airlines property, has a casual air, with bungalows and motel-style units stuck in tropical gardens. One of the best views of the island group is available from the top of the island's peaks. The resort can hold around 500 guests, and has two restaurants, tennis, a very nice golf course, scuba equipment, lawn bowling and a health center and kids club. There are reef and fishing trips as well as day trips to other spots in the Whitsundays, including Hook Island, now owned by the airline. All activities except scuba and motorized sports are included in the room rates. Daily launch service for resort guests only is A$25 round trip from Shute Harbour; half price for children. There are six classes of accommodation, starting at A$280 double a day including all meals and going to the top in the Whitsunday units for about A$350 a day double, including all meals. *Booking information:* ☎ *(800) 366-1300; in Australia* ☎ *(008) 075-080, or (07) 946-9433; FAX (07) 946-9580.*

Campers should take note of these Whitsunday islands, which are among the 100 or so uninhabited islands in the group: **Saddleback**, **North Molle**, **Shute**, **Tancred**, **Rabbit** and **Outer Newry**. Most have toilets, picnic areas, firewood and camping areas. The islands are all within 10 miles of Shute Harbour and are administered by the **Queensland National Parks and Wildlife Service**, *P.O. Box 582, Mackay 4740;* ☎ *(07) 957-6292.*

North of the Whitsundays, the barrier reef starts coming closer and closer to shore, and the resort islands gets fewer and farther apart. In their place, however, are the numerous resort hotels and restaurants on the mainland at Cairns and Townsville, plus the dozens of tour operators that run day trips or longer excursions out to the reef.

About 15 miles offshore from Ingham, on the coast north of Townsville, is the upscale **Orpheus Island** ★★★★, part of the Palm Island group. The island is a mix of exclusivity (only 74 guests at a time) and low-key, with camping available in the national park areas of the island. The park portion of the island (about 3300 acres) has a large rainforest and hiking trails. *Camping by permit is available through the Cairns office of the park service, P.O. Box 2066, Cairns 4870;* ☎ *(07) 053-4533.* James Cook University has a facility on the island, and the snorkeling is excellent right in front of the resort. The island is a kilometer wide and 11 kilometers long.

Rooms are in bungalows and studios with terra-cotta tile floors and South Seas furniture. Some rooms have enclosed gardens with sunken tubs; no TVs or phones in the rooms, and no kids under 15 allowed. There are two swimming pools and a spa, tennis court, recreation room. Rates, including all meals and nonmotorized water activities, range between A$600-940 double a day. Special dive and honeymoon packages are available. Access to the island is by air from Cairns (about A$210 one way) and Townsville (about A$140 one way). *Information:* ☎ *(07) 777-7377; FAX (07) 777-7533; USA (800) 227-9246;* toll free in Australia ☎ *(008) 07-7167.*

Near Cardwell, north of Ingham, is the largest island national park in the world and one of the largest islands on the Queensland coast—**Hinchinbrook** ★★★, which is something like 145 square miles in area. It is one of Australia's premier wild and scenic areas, with volcanic peaks, dense rainforests, mangrove swamps and important breeding areas for a wide variety of waterfowl. The tallest peak on the island is **Mt. Bowen** at about 3650 feet. There is only one resort on the island, with only 23 units. The island is hard to get to, and the plans are to keep it that way. The facilities at the resort are water-oriented. Although there are several well-maintained trails (including a boardwalk through the mangroves) most of the island is rugged and fit only for experienced bushwalkers. The treks are worth it, however, because the bush is filled with pools, waterfalls and hardwood forests. There are secluded beaches and giant sea turtle nesting areas. All in all, for a camper, Hinchinbrook is ground zero. Camping is allowed (for 14 days at a time) at two spots with permits from an on-duty ranger.

The **resort**, at **Cape Richards** on the northern tip of the island, has rustic units set into the forest, a pool, lending library, water sports and a dining room with great food and a bar. A tribe of tame wallabies and some large goannas run around nearby. The beach is fantastic, and not far away you can spot Ulysses butterflies and orchids. Rooms range from one-room cabins to two-bedroom treehouses; no TVs or phones. Treehouse rates are around A$260 a day per person, meals included; cabins are A$200 per person, meals included. Access to the resort (and the camping areas) is by launch from Cardwell (about A$40 per person round trip). Information on the resort: ☎ *(07) 066-8585; (07) 66-8742. Information on the national park is available from Queensland wildlife service offices in Cairns or Townsville.*

Next in line are two more Australian Resorts properties, **Dunk** and **Bedarra** islands. Of the two, Dunk is the most traditional, a nicely meshed mix of high-quality resort and tropical island laziness. Bedarra is designed for very rich or famous folks trying to get away from the rest of us slobs.

The advertising logo for **Dunk** ★★★ is a Ulysses butterfly, not surprising because the island is full of butterflies and orchids (it's tough spotting the Ulysses, but the best time is June and July). The Aboriginal name for the island, which is coming into popular use, is *Coonanglebah*, meaning Isle of Peace and Plenty, and it is. The bulk of the island is a national park, with limited camping facilities. There are some excellent beaches, and the sports activities at the resort are abundant. You can, if you wish, shoot skeet with a $3000 shotgun (you pay for the shells and the skeet), or play golf or tennis, go walkabout, water ski or go sniff orchids. It's only three miles from the mainland, so there is a chance of jellyfish; always ask. There are some very nice hiking trails that go into the highlands for great views of the South Pacific or offshore islands. The immense main bar/dining area is one of the most attractive we've seen, and the food comes in prodigious quantities. The more intimate **Rainforest Brasserie** is one of the reef's best restaurants, but always crowded; the minute you land, make a reservation.

The resort can handle about 300 guests at a time in several grades of rooms, including bayview villas (very nice, and furnished so you don't feel bad about tracking in sand) for about A$250 per person, double, meals not included. Standard beachfront units are A$240 per person double, no meals. Garden cabanas are about A$185 per person double, no meals, and rooms in two-story units go for about A$160 per person. Rates for stays longer than four days are less. Two meal packages are available, full board and half board; full board is A$70 per person a day, half board is A$55 a day.

Day-long trips to the reef are available for about A$70 per person, which includes lunch.

Camping on the island is limited to three-day stays, and facilities include toilets but no water. Permits are required and are available from the Cairns parks and wildlife service. Access to the island is by air; from Cairns A$195 round trip, from Townsville A$215 round trip. There is a launch from Clump Point Beach near Tully (about A$20 round trip); water taxi from South Mission Beach, A$18 round trip. *Booking information: Australian Resorts* ☎ *(800) 227-4411; in Australia,* ☎ *1-(800) 81-2525.*

Dunk's sister island, **Bedarra** ★★★★, is the home of a small and exclusive resort whose sole aim seems to be pampering a maximum of 32 gilt-edged guests (about 35 percent are Americans). Accommodations in the resort are in apartment-like units (small treehouse villas, they say) set into the foliage, with great views and airy space. Everything here is taken care of—including an open bar and a resident gourmet chef—and total isolation is the key—no children are allowed and members of the press are shot on sight. You halfway expect to see Joan Collins or Marlon Brando wander by, and the resort, unlike almost anywhere we have been in Australia, has a jacuzzi that actually gets to a decent temperature (Aussies like 'em cold). The rainforest on the island is home to a covey of flying foxes and other smaller critters. Rates reflect the exclusivity: about A$1065 a day double, everything, and we mean everything, included; packages for more than three nights are somewhat lower. Reservations needed three months in advance. Sports activities for Bedarra guests are available at Dunk, and a free launch is available for guests. Getting to Bedarra is via Dunk. *Reservation information is available through Australian Resorts (see above); in Australia* ☎ *(07) 3360-2400; FAX (07) 3360-2436.*

Bedarra is an exclusive resort island catering to those who like isolation with a gourmet chef nearby.

Two island resorts near Cairns are **Fitzroy** and **Green** islands. Fitzroy is a continental island, not a true reef structure, but it has beautiful coral beaches and heavy vegetation. The **Fitzroy Island Resort** ★ has space for about 160 guests in villa units and also operates a hostel area where you can share cooking facilities; there is a dive shop. The villas go for about A$195 per person, some meals included; the hostel bungalows are A$25 per person shared; sole use A$68. Campsites are $A10. ☎ *(07) 051-9588; FAX (07) 052-1335.*

The island is a popular day-trip destination, and is on a catamaran route that runs from Cairns to Green Island. It's possible to hit both islands the same day, and there is late service on weekends. **Big Cat Tour Services** in Cairns runs daily trips to the two islands on several itineraries, including several that give you a chance to snorkel on the reef. The price, no meals, no equipment, runs about A$30 per person for a four- to five-hour trip. *Information: Big Cat Tour Services, 111 Lake Street, Cairns 4870;* ☎ *51-0444.* The catamaran leaves Cairns at 8:30 a.m. and 10:30 a.m. daily and takes about 45 minutes to get to Fitzroy. Day-trip service to Fitzroy, no extras, is A$20 round trip. It then leaves for Green at about 1 p.m. Fitzroy offers trips to the close-by reef and also excursions in a semi-submersible submarine for reef viewing.

Nearby **Green Island**, which is partly a national park, is a true coral island which sits on the inner part of the reef system and has typical coral island foliage such as casuarina and dune plants. It's a marine fowl nesting area, and sea turtles are often seen. No camping is allowed. Green Island is the site of the new Japanese-developed property, the **Green Island Resort** ★★★★, yet another "environmentally friendly" set-up, which is going for big bucks. There are a couple of large pools, the very good Emeralds Restaurant, water sports, guest library, underwater observatory, fish feeding. Reef suites start at

A$880 double, all meals and transfers from Cairns included; deluxe units start at A$750, meals and transfers included. ☎ *(07) 031-3300.*

Finally, opposite Cooktown north of Cairns, there is **Lizard Island ★★★★**, where Captain Cook climbed a peak and spotted a path through the reef after his unfortunate experiences—although the staff at Lizard says that's all a myth and Old Cookie never made the climb. There is a trail you can follow to the exact spot where he supposedly stood; it's a great trek and the view from the top is great (yes, you can see holes in the reefs). The island is a national park, noted for a profusion of wildlife including three-foot-long goannas and dugongs, huge sea mammals that look like giant pigs and which were almost hunted to extinction for their oil. The goannas, by the way, have adapted nicely to the resort. If you take a picnic lunch to a secluded spot, they'll likely show up to mooch. They probably will only hiss and demand food, maybe. The resort staff will be glad to give you some tidbits of raw meat to assuage their hunger (just don't feed them by hand). Camping by permit is allowed for one-week stays: *Information available from the Cairns parks and wildlife service.*

We have mentioned that **Lizard Island Lodge** is our favorite first-class resort on the reef, and the reason is the service, the great food and the almost tree-sloth relaxed atmosphere. David Irvine, the assistant manager, is a jewel, and his boss, Robyn Pontynen, is one of the most respected resort managers in Queensland. The guys running the lodge are the first to admit that the rooms are not up to Hayman or Bedarra standards, and in truth are not much fancier than a medium-grade motel in the U.S.; the two deluxe units are a bit better. But the staff, the great white-sand beaches (two dozen in all) and the climate make it a real treasure. Unlike other Barrier Reef islands, Lizard is not covered with rainforest; it is, in fact, very desertlike, and the island, even as close as it is to the Cape York Peninsula, has much less humidity than other islands. Within a half-hour of the front door are several excellent snorkeling and diving spots (including the famous Cod Hole) and the Clam Garden, where you can pet centuries-old giant clams. Included in the room rate are most water activities; game fishing and scuba are extra. Near the resort is a marine research station where you can enjoy lectures on reef life and tours for A$15 per person. There's room for 64 guests, and unlike Bedarra, there seems to be no overwhelming urge to put on dark glasses and mumble "I vant to be alone." As a sign of something, none of the rooms have keys (lock up your goodies at the front desk). Upon arrival, rather than a glass of champagne and a hearty handshake, guests are given a sumptuous afternoon tea.

It is, of course, expensive, with double rooms including all meals starting around A$900–1000 a night; package rates for five nights or more are A$800–900 a night; no children under six allowed. **A note**: the waters around Lizard are internationally famous for huge marlin, and during the marlin run (a two-week period in early October), the place is full of fishermen, and your chances of getting a reservation then are not good—book now for 2010. The staff says the best time to come down, given weather conditions and availability, is May, June, July or November; even so, reservations at least three months in advance are recommended. Access to the island is by Sunstate from Cairns (about A$250 round trip) and the scenic flight takes you over great chunks of the reef at 8000 or so feet. *Information: Australian Resorts (see above); in Australia* ☎ *(07) 3360-2400; FAX (07) 3360-2436.*

Reef Adventures

Day cruises to the Great Barrier Reef are a great way to see exotic sea life.

It would take a whole book just to list all the companies that provide reef trips. Almost any community of any size along the Queensland coast has a tour operator or boat/diving service available, and the range of options available is immense, from helicopter overflights to two-week long camping excursions. Here are a few to consider:

One of the best ways to get a quick, comfortable and satisfying first look at the reef is aboard one of the **Quicksilver catamarans** that run from Port Douglas to Agincourt Reef, a ribbon formation about 90 minutes offshore. The boats offer huge smorgasbord lunches with a licensed bar, free snorkeling equipment, lectures by reef biologists, a stop at an underwater observatory and, for an extra cost, snorkeling trips guided by a marine biologist, or divemasters and scuba equipment. The one-day trip costs A$115 per person from Port Douglas; coach transfers are available from Cairns to Port Douglas for A$10. Sample dive prices are A$185 for an introductory trip; or A$190 for already certified divers. The price for the already certified trips includes two 40-minute dives and all equipment; there are 20 dive sites to choose from. If you only have time for one trip to the reef, this might be your best bet. *In Port Douglas, information is available from* **Quicksilver Connections**, *Marina Mirage shopping center;* ☎ *(07) 099-5500.*

Another good guided snorkeling trip is available from Port Douglas with **Wavelength**. The 20-passenger boats visit three spots on the outer reef, and the price of A$80 per person includes all equipment, guides. lunch and morning teas. *Information:* ☎ *(07) 099-5031.*

Or try **Great Adventures** based in Cairns, which has trips to the reef and Green and Fitzroy islands. For instance, the Fitzroy trip includes a catamaran to the island, snorkeling on the outer reef, use of the resort facilities, and a tropical lunch; all for about A$85 per person with pickup from most Cairns hotels. Great Adventures also has helicopter trips to Fitzroy and the reef; a full-day trip with stops at the island reef snorkeling is A$130. *Information* ☎ *(07) 051-0455.*

A comparable trip is offered by the **Ocean Spirit**, which has two sailing catamarans and offers day trips from Cairns with a stop at Michaelmas Cay for about A$115 per person, including lunch, teas, lectures, snorkeling equipment and live entertainment. *Information* ☎ *(07) 031-2920.* Or for a longer jaunt, try **Coral Princess Cruises** in Cairns, which has three-or seven-night cruises for between A$650 and A$860 per person double. The ship has two lounges, sun deck and a spa, plus water equipment. *Information: Adventure Center, Emeryville, Calif.* ☎ *(800) 227-8747.*

If you're a dedicated diver and want to see the reef area around Lizard Island, try the **Taka II**, a 72-foot dive boat with trips from Cairns to the Cod Hole and other ribbon reef sites. It's one of the best dive boats on the reef. The price for a four-night voyage includes transfers, meals, tanks and weights, additional gear for hire. A four-share cabin goes for A$650 per person, a suite for A$850 per person. *Information: 132 Lake Street,* ☎ *(07) 051-8722.*

QUEENSLAND AND
THE GREAT BARRIER REEF

NORTHERN TERRITORY

Uluru (Ayers Rock) is Australia's most celebrated, most visited hunk of stone.

Red, as far as you can see, red. Flat, hot, desolate—and magnificent. One-sixth of the land mass of Australia, 480,000 square miles in all, twice as big as Texas. You could stick most of Europe in here and still have room left over. A huge chunk, some 95,000 square miles, is all sand dunes and claypan desert. But the Northern Territory is more than just desert—it's also a land of monsoons, with heavy rains, tropical vegetation, deep river gorges, and crocodile-infested coastal wetlands. All in all, you're faced with a vast and empty place with a total population of only about 200,000.

If you travel around the Northern Territory, that's what you remember, the seeming lack of human life, a land where nature, at least for now, seems to be in charge. The Territory is for those who like their views unobstructed, their pleasures at a leisurely pace, and their adventures on the peculiar side. Where else, for example, can you ride a camel to a wine tasting? Or watch a boat regatta down a dry stream bed? Or see an emu getting a shampoo? Or take a drive on a highway infested with trucks measuring a half-football field in length?

The Territory, which got self-government in 1978, is split geographically (and philosophically) into two parts: the **Top End** and the **Red Centre**. Each area has one of the Territory's major attractions. In the Red Centre is the nation's most celebrated hunk of stone—**Ayers Rock**—and in the Top End are the wonders of **Kakadu National Park**, which has one of the richest storehouses of ancient human art in the world. The Red Centre is the home of **Alice Springs**, the settlement made famous in the Neville Shute novel *A Town Like Alice*, and the Top End is the home of one of the seasonally most humid cities around, **Darwin**, the territorial capital—which gets something like 300 inches of rain during the rainy season. For all its red desert and general lack of water, the Territory is amazingly lush with animal and plant life, clinging to oases and river banks and coastal rainforests and eco-zones. There are at least 400 species of birds, 100 species of butterflies, and more reptiles and frogs than you can throw a textbook at. The rangers at Kakadu claim there are at least 250 species of birds in the park alone.

The original inhabitants of the Territory were Aboriginals who came to Australia on an island-hopping expedition at least 40,000 years ago. They first settled around Kakadu, and over the course of about 30,000 years, made their way to Uluru, the Aboriginal word for **Ayers Rock**. One of the first Europeans to pass by was Dutch sea captain Jan Carstensz, who came calling in a ship named the Arnhem, after which the huge Aboriginal land mass called **Arnhem Land**, at the northeastern tip of the Territory, was named. The bay where Darwin sits was named after Charles Darwin in 1839. The early 19th-century explorations of the Territory were the stuff of legends, with the doomed Burke and Wills expedition passing by, as well as Capt. Charles Sturt, who went from Adelaide to the Tropic of Capricorn near Alice Springs before he was forced to give it up. In 1862, a member of Sturt's original party, John McDouall Stuart, tried it on his own and became the first white Australian to traverse the continent north to south. The early telegraph line and the present Adelaide-Darwin highway follow his route. Indeed, it's even called the **Stuart Highway**.

Construction of the 1760-mile-long telegraph line, itself a daring undertaking, was begun in 1871 under the direction of Charles Todd, the South Australian superintendent of telegraphs. The Todd River was named after

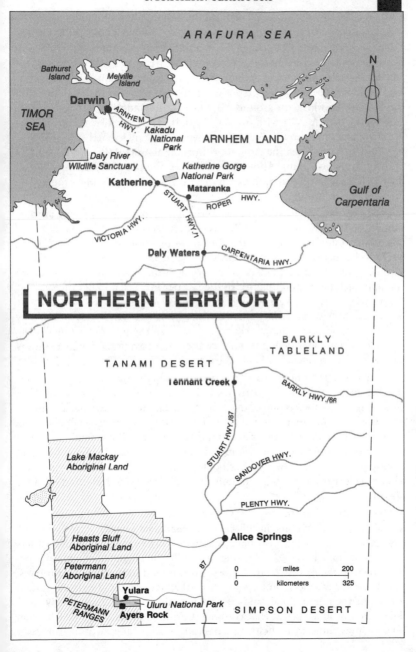

him, and the site of a telegraph station and watering hole along the route was named after his wife: Alice Springs (not to be confused with the present city).

The Territory was first part of New South Wales, became part of South Australia in 1863, then became a federal territory in 1911. Self-government allows Territorians to control their own finances, but Canberra retains control of uranium mining and Aboriginal affairs. The two major population centers are **Darwin**, with around 80,000 people, and **Alice Springs** (widely known as "the Alice") with around 25,000. They are two of the fastest-growing cities in Australia. Any other towns of size are located along the Stuart Highway, although the large tourist center at **Ayers Rock** could qualify as a town in its own right. About 25 percent of the population is Aboriginal, living either in small communities in the Outback or—often unfortunately—in poor conditions in the Alice and Darwin.

The long-standing isolation of the Territory is rapidly disappearing as tourism raises its ugly head—now the Territory's second-largest source of income after mining. Visitors to the area, most of whom head for Ayers Rock, seem to be increasing geometrically every year, with international traffic accounting for about 25 percent of the total. Annual revenues from tourism are approaching A$500 million. In the last decade, the number of guest accommodation spaces has risen something like 150 percent. Darwin's airport is a true international facility, and the Alice and Ayers Rock are reachable by either air-conditioned motor coach or regional airline service. One of the most important developments, long awaited, was paving the Stuart Highway all the way from Adelaide, 1700 miles north to Darwin.

Many foreign visitors to the Territory see only the tourist village at Ayers Rock, which is a shame. The drive from Darwin down the Stuart to the Alice and then to the Rock is one of the most rewarding in all Australia. Towns are nicely spaced, and there are scenic spots along the route that will blow you away. You haven't really experienced the Territory until you stand in a village pub, covered from cheek to toe in red dust, scarfing down an icy beer and telling tall tales about the rigors of the Outback. If time is short, our suggestion is to forget the Rock—although climbing it is a big deal—and head for **Kakadu**.

The Northern Territory might well be the first place you'll encounter Australia's oldest inhabitants, in this case, the **Aboriginal peoples** of the Top End and Red Centre. Their lives have changed enormously since white settlers came, and some have not been able to handle the pressures of a lifestyle totally alien to their own. White history was not kind to the First Territorians. Gold rushes, ranchers, and cattle drives throughout the Territory pushed them off their traditional lands, and when they fought back, many were killed in a protracted war that continued on into the late 1920s. Christian missionaries came in to help, but basically made things worse—this time causing mostly psychological problems—and the tribal patterns that had ruled Aboriginal lives for thousands of years started to disappear.

Many Aboriginal leaders think the best way to solve many of their people's problems—alcoholism, crime, poverty and illiteracy—is to move back into the bush and leave the white world alone, and there are a number of tiny, isolated Aboriginal communities all over the territory. Access to Aboriginal lands is restricted, with permits from the owners required to enter. Permits are rarely given to casual tourists, although arrangements have been worked out with some white tour operators. (This is true all over Australia.) Entering Aboriginal land without a permit can result in a fine of A$1000. It is possible to drive across Aboriginal lands if the highway is public, but before taking off, check with the land councils.

Three **land councils** are in charge of Aboriginal holdings in the Territory, under provisions of the Aboriginal Lands Act of 1976. If you want to try for a permit, you must fill out a proper application form, either in person or by writing (enclose a SASE). The three councils are:

Darwin, Nhuulunbuy, and Katherine regions: *Permits Officer, Northern Land Council, P.O. Box 42921, Casaurina 0811 3; ☎ (08) 20-5100; FAX (08) 8945-2633.*

Alice Springs and Tennant Creek: *Permits Officer, Central Land Council, P.O. Box 3321, Alice Springs 5750; 33 Stuart Highway, Alice Springs; ☎ (08) 8951-6211; FAX (08) 8953-4343.*

Melville and Bathurst islands: *Permits officer, Tiwi Land Council, Nguiu, Bathurst Island, via Darwin 5791; ☎ (08) 8978-3957 or (08) 8981-4111.*

One of the provisions of the 1976 law created methods of returning Aboriginal lands to their traditional owners. A very symbolic return took place in 1985, when Ayers Rock and the Olgas were returned to tribal land councils. The federal government, of course, was not about to let the highly profitable Rock get too far away, and it was immediately leased back to the commonwealth for 99 years.

Some Aboriginal efforts, however, are very mainstream, such as the Aboriginal-owned hotel at Kakadu National Park, a radio/TV station in Alice Springs, plus a number of Aboriginal owned or operated tour companies offering walkabouts, guided tours into Arnhem Land, or *corroborees* (tribal get-togethers, complete with food, music, and story-telling). In 1984, the Northern Territory Tourist Commission created a position for an Aboriginal liaison officer, and since then tribal tourism activities have expanded greatly.

Among the **Aboriginal-oriented tours** available in the Territory are these:

Ipolera tour—This tour departs Alice Springs on a one-day trek that visits the Ipolera Aboriginal outstation, about 75 miles west of the Alice, where community leaders Herman and Mavis Malbunka give you a cuppa and a chunk of damper and then take you off to learn—men in one group, women in another—and to study sites of significance and discuss Aboriginal lore. Don't feel like it's sex discrimination: some traditional knowledge is only for women, some only for men. Cost is about A$100 per person. *Information: ☎ (08) 8952-2350 in Alice Springs; at Hermannsburg (08) 8956-7466; FAX (08) 8956-7316.*

7-Day Top End Adventure—Offered by Australian Kakadu Tours, this trip goes to Kakadu and winds up with a stay on Bathurst Island. The cost is about A$1200 including meals and transportation. The company also offers shorter and longer trips around the Territory. The company will also fly you from Darwin to Putjamirra, at the tip of Melville Island, for two- or three-day tours and stays with the Tiwis. The cost, including airfare, is around A$700 per person double for the three-day trip. Accommodations are in an African-style safari camp. *Information: Australian Kakadu Tours, Smith Street Mall, Darwin 0800; ☎ (08) 8981-5144; toll-free, ☎ (008) 89-1121. North American bookings and information: ☎ (800) 551-2012.*

Melville and Bathurst islands—A trip to these islands in the Timor Sea about 30 miles north of Darwin is becoming very popular. The islands, the traditional home of the *Tiwi* people, cannot be visited by individuals, but are open to tour groups. Tiwi, by the way, means either "People, we the people" or "the chosen people." The major population center is Nguiu on Bathurst, where you can watch islanders make pottery, clothing and silk screens. Day or half-day tours are available, which include air transportation and visits to one or both islands. The major company offering island trips is **Tiwi Tours**, *Smith Street, Darwin,* ☎ *(08) 8981-5115; FAX (08) 8981-5391*—full day, about A$200 per person. Longer stays can be arranged. Three days for example, is A$560. All rates include air, meals, guides and accommodation.

The Dreamtime Tour—One of the best quickie Aboriginal tours in Australia, this comes highly recommended by Burnum (he wrote the definitive book on Aboriginal Australia). The tour is run by Rod Steinert, and goes near Alice Springs to hear Aboriginal people explain how life was before the Europeans came. They even feed you bush tucker. On other Steinert tours, the Aboriginals will explain the magic meaning of an ancient ceremonial ground and rock paintings. On Wednesdays, there is a *corroboree* (Aborigine festival). The Dreamtime cost is about A$60 in the summer, less in the winter. The trip takes a half-day, leaving the Alice around 8 a.m. every day. There is also a one-day trip that will teach you rudimentary bush survival skills, using Aboriginal teachers—here's a chance to try snacking on a witchetty grub (a big caterpillar that is a favorite canape of the bush folks). *Information: Rod Steinert Tours, P.O. Box 2058. Alice Springs N.T., 0871;* ☎ *(08) 8955-5000; FAX (08) 8955-5111.*

One of the few people allowed to come and go into Arnhem Land is a wonderful guy named **Max Davidson**, who runs tours to a private lodge at a place called Mt. Borradaile. You get a safari-tent experience at Max's place, which is near to Aboriginal rock art and has fishing, bird watching or just lying in the sun. It's a very special place, but it's no Hilton. It's mosquito nets at night, strange noises in the dark, *Out of Africa* sort of stuff. There's a close-on billabong infested with birds, and there's always a chance to see a croc, a dingo or a wild pig. The fee of A$300 per person includes payments to the Aboriginal land owners, all meals, accommodation, guides tours and fishing. A tremendous experience. You can often find Max at the Gagudju Lodge in Cooinda, where he takes folks out for fishing trips. Otherwise, contact him at ☎ *(08) 8927-5240 or (08) 8941-1394.*

Another outfit to contact in the United States, which has information on a number of companies that offer Aboriginal tours, is Australia's Aboriginal and Torres Strait Islander Tourism, ☎ *(408) 685-8901; FAX (408) 685-8903.*

The Essential Northern Territory

Information

NOTE: Tour companies and services without North American contact numbers can often be booked through a travel agent. Or, if you're playing it by ear, book when you get to the Territory. There is almost always space available today—or tomorrow. The NT tourist office in Sydney is at *89 King Street, Sydney 2000;* ☎ *(02) 9235-2822.* In the Territory, the headquarters are in the *Ford Plaza Building, Todd Mall, Alice Springs 5750;* ☎ *8951-1299.* Other bureaus are located at *31 Smith Street Mall, Darwin 5790,* ☎ *(08) 8981-6611; corner of Stuart Highway and Lindsay Avenue, Katherine 5780,* ☎ *(08) 8972-2650, and corner Paterson and Davidson streets, Tennant Creek 5760,* ☎ *(08) 8962-3388.*

Telephones

The area code for the Territory is *(08).*

Getting There

Unless you have lots of time—and patience—driving to the Territory is probably just not worth it. There are three major interstate roads into the area: the **Stuart from Adelaide**; the **Barkly Highway** from Tennant Creek to Mt. Isa in Queensland, and the **Victoria Highway** from Katherine to Western Australia. They're all long and arduous. The best way is to fly in.

There are no direct flights from North America to the Territory, but there is regular interstate service to Darwin, Alice Springs and Ayers Rock. The two major national carriers going to Darwin and the Alice are **Ansett** and **Qantas**. In addition, a number of tour companies operate small plane services. Within the Territory, there is service between the major settlements on a subsidiary of Ansett, **Ansett NT**. Probably your best bet is to buy one of the **air passes** available that will allow you to include the Territory on a tour of Australia. **Eastwest**, for example, has two passes starting at US$525 that allow flights either from Sydney to Ayers Rock, and Alice to Brisbane, or from Brisbane back around. Once you're in Australia, you'll find that booking internal flights between cities is quite expensive, although most airlines offer standby fares if you have the time. Without a pass, expect to pay in the neighborhood of $450 for a one-way ticket from Sydney or Brisbane.

One of the most popular ways to get to Alice Springs is on the **Ghan**, a weekly 23-hour run from Adelaide. The train is equipped to take automobiles, so you can avoid those long stretches on the Stuart but still have a car when you get to the Red Centre. First-class sleepers go for around $300 per person one way; taking a car is about A$200 extra. There is a dining car and a bar and—would you believe—an entertainment car with video games, a bookstore and poker machines.

There is also **bus service** into the Territory, but guys, it's a long haul. The **Greyhound** bus from Brisbane to the Alice takes about 44 hours; Brisbane-Darwin is about 50 hours; Adelaide-Alice, 20 hours; and Adelaide-Ayers Rock around 22 hours. If you want to try the bus bit, we urge you to get a pass on one of the major carriers so you can get off once in a while and relax. **Deluxe** has several passes, including the **Great Divide**, which lets you do the Stuart Highway (plus the Queensland coast) for around A$600 per person, good for 12 months. A similar pass, **Aussie Highlights**, is offered by **Greyhound** for about the same money.

Once in the Territory, there are a slew of **charter companies** that can either fly you or drive you around to the sights. **Deluxe**, for example, has a number of tours from the Alice to Ayers Rock and the Olgas, or from Darwin to Kakadu. Prices vary according to itinerary, but a week trip around the Alice Springs area, including accommodations, can be as little as A$500 per person.

Renting a car in the Territory is a snap, with at least a dozen rental agencies on hand, including the biggies. Almost all allow one-way hires, allowing you to fly into Darwin, say, then drive to Ayers Rock and fly out. Many have special weekly rates, with the tariff, depending on size of car, going for around A$50 to A$70 a day. There are also campers and mokes (the little dune-buggy-sized cars) for hire. You can get cars in Darwin, Katherine, Ayers Rock Resort, Tennant Creek, Jabiru (Kakadu National Park) or Alice Springs. (See the DRIVING section for a few cautionary notes on Outback motoring.)

Climate

If you don't time it right, the Northern Territory can bake your buns or give you a terminal case of mildew. Maximum temperatures in the Top End in the summer (Nov.-March) are in the 90s. In the Red Centre, it gets ghastly, with highs above 110 degrees. A couple of years ago, a German Boy Scout wandered off by himself near Ayers Rock and died within a few hours from exposure to temperatures reported to be around 140 degrees, so it's not something to take lightly. In the winter, high temperatures around Darwin are in the 80s, around 65 degrees in the Ayers Rock area. Spring, with its incredible bloom of wild desert plants, is the best time to see the Red Centre. You should know, also, that Alice Springs gets cold in June or July, with temperatures sometimes below freezing.

Darwinians take a certain perverse pride in their lousy climate. "Nobody ever drowns here," a local told us, "they just rust." The Aussies have succinctly described the climatic conditions near the Timor Sea as "the Wet" and "the Dry," and when it's wet, it's very wet. The Red Centre, by contrast, gets around 90 inches a year, a lot of that during torrential downpours. The monsoon Wet is generally from October through April, the Dry is from May through September. During the Wet, rivers overflow, waterfalls get humongous, and road conditions can get very dicey. The Todd River through Alice is normally dry, but recently has overflowed its banks and flooded the downtown part of the city.

Time

The Northern Territory is on Central Standard Time, meaning it's a half-hour behind Queensland and New South Wales.

The Top End

Gone troppo—the Aussie expression for becoming a lotus eater—is a fair description of the whole area around Darwin. The whole town is about as uptight as a rock lizard, and pretense and big-city running around is met with quiet derision. Detractors would have you believe that Darwinians are as relaxed as they are because the heat has melted their brains, but the good folks around town seem bright enough. Part of their personality results from being so far away from what passes as civilization in Australia—Darwin is closer to Asia than Sydney. As the crow flies, Sydney is about 1800 miles; Jakarta is 1500, Manila, 1700, Singapore, 1900. Even other places in the Territory are a fair jaunt there; the Alice is 700 miles away, for example. Darwin has a population of about 80,000.

The Top End's proximity to Asia has not been without its perils. Darwin was the first Australian city to be bombed by Japanese aircraft in World War II. Between February and November 1942, it was bombed 64 times; 243 people were killed, including the postmaster and his family. They have a saying around town: "Darwin: blown up and blown away"—(because of Cyclone Tracy, which roared into Darwin on Christmas Eve 1974 and virtually flattened the city). The hurricane's 140-mile-an-hour winds destroyed more than 5000 buildings in a four-hour period. More than 60 people died in what has been recorded as Australia's worst natural disaster. As a result, Darwin is a brand-new city. Only a few colonial buildings managed to survive both the Japanese and the cyclone.

The modern result is a wide-avenued, tropical settlement where shade is found beneath bamboo and mango trees. This is not to suggest that visitors are forced to rack out in palm-thatched hovels on the beach, because, in fact, there are some nicely upscale digs. But the combination of palm trees and wet air, and sun and clear skies (when it's not raining) is a balm to a frazzled mind. In truth, the weather between May and October can be very pleasant, with sunny days and cool nights. But Darwin's greatest lure, to be honest, is as a base to check out the other delights of the Top End.

Darwin

Darwin holds numerous ethnic festivals.

If the kids are getting out of hand (or you have a thing for fish), direct yourself to **Doctor's Gully** where, at high tide, a swarm of finny devils come in to snatch a free meal from all the tourists. For A$4 an adult (A$1.50 for kids) they give you free bread and you can feed the critters. It's a pleasant enough way to kill an hour, and you'll get to see, among others, milkfish, mullet, toad fish, catfish and gar. Feeding times vary according to the tide. The feeding grounds are in the Aquascene on the city's waterfront Esplanade. ☎ *(08) 8981-7837.* If you're a World War II buff, or just curious, the city has set aside an old military bunker area at **East Point**, northeast of the city center, with displays of old tanks and other equipment, plus photographs of the bomb damage. Admission is A$2. There is also a park at the point with walking paths and BBQs.

For colonial buildings, check out **Government House**, a house of seven gables built in 1869 (and rebuilt every time a cyclone comes through). The administrator of the Northern Territory, what passes as a governor in the USA, lives in the old relic, built on a point of land on the southeast corner of the Esplanade. Open to the public July-August.

At **Indo Pacific Marine**, next to Cullen Beach near Myilly Point, you'll find large seawater tanks filled with coral animals. Small by some aquarium standards, it is nonetheless a dandy place to check out some of the sea denizens that inhabit Australia's oceans. It's open all week. *Admission A$10 for adults.*

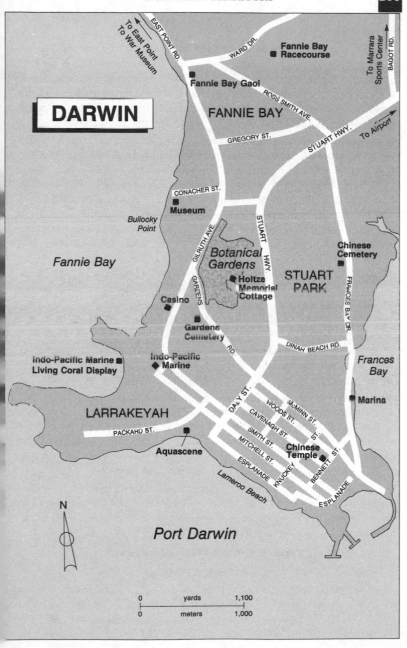

DARWIN

To East Point
To War Museum

EAST POINT RD.

WARD DR.

Fannie Bay
Racecourse

To Marrara
Sports Center

BAGOT RD.

Fannie Bay Gaol

ROSS SMITH AVE.

FANNIE BAY

GREGORY ST.

STUART HWY.

To Airport

CONACHER ST.

Museum

Bullocky
Point

GILRUTH AVE.

Botanical
Gardens

STUART HWY.

Chinese
Cemetery

Fannie Bay

Holtze
Memorial
Cottage

STUART
PARK

FRANCES BAY DR.

Casino

GARDENS

Gardens
Cemetery

RD.

DINAH BEACH RD.

Indo-Pacific Marine
Living Coral Display

Indo-Pacific
Marine

Frances
Bay

Marina

LARRAKEYAH

PACKARD ST.

DALY ST.

WOODS ST.

McMINN ST.

ST.

CAVENAGH ST.

SMITH ST.

Aquascene

MITCHELL ST.

KNUCKEY

Chinese
Temple

BENNETT ST.

ESPLANADE

Lameroo Beach

ESPLANADE

N

Port Darwin

0   yards   1,100
0   meters   1,000

NORTHERN TERRITORY

Open 9 a.m.–5 p.m. May–October, 10 a.m.–5 p.m. November–April. Guided tours available. ☎ *(08) 8981-1294.*

Not far away is the **Diamond Beach Hotel and Casino**, where you can play 10- or 20-cent slots or go after bigger game. Shoreward of the casino is the city's botanical gardens, started in 1891, but, like Government House, rebuilt every time a big blow comes along. It has 1400 species of tropical and sub-tropical plants. Every Sunday afternoon May-September, there is a free jazz concert on the casino grounds.

A good display of Aboriginal and Southeast Asian art and history is available at the **Northern Territory Museum of Arts and Natural Sciences** near Bullocky Point north of the gardens. There's a restaurant and art gallery as well. A memorial worth a look honors the completion of the telegraph line (finished Aug. 22, 1872), located in a small area just to the north of Government House. The free museum is open 9 a.m.–5 p.m. Monday–Friday; 10 a.m.–5 p.m. weekends. ☎ *(08) 8989-8211.* Because Australians seem fascinated with jails and executions, you can visit the **Fannie Bay Gaol** in the Fannie Bay area of the city, where the National Trust has preserved a 100-year-old prison, complete with gallows. The jail was last occupied in 1979. Free admission; open daily 10 a.m.–5 p.m.; ☎ *(08) 8989-8290.*

Darwin claims to have at least 40 ethnic groups living in town, including a healthy number of Greeks and newly arrived Southeast Asians. This leads to a good variety of food in the city, and the best time and place to check it out is Thursday nights along **Mindil Beach**, when local cooks offer their wares—everything from grilled lamb and pita bread to hot satays from Indonesia. Things get hopping around 5 p.m. and the party—very popular with Darwinians—lasts past 9 p.m.; April through October.

Darwin holds several festivals every year, the most outrageous of which is the **Beer Can Regatta**, a wet affair requiring all entrants to make boats out of beer cans, held every summer. There is also the August **Mud Crab Tying Championships**, another blast of frivolity, which sees contestants tying up huge mud crabs with their bare hands. The **Bougainvillea Festival** is August.

Finally, a note about swimming. Darwin's excellent white sand beaches are plagued by deadly box jellyfish (called stingers) between October and May, and swimming on most beaches is prohibited. In one area off Nightcliff, there is supposedly a stinger-free net, but use care.

The Essential Darwin
Getting Around

Darwin Radio **Taxis** can be contacted at ☎ *(08) 8981-8777.* The main downtown taxi rank is on the Knuckey Street end of the mall; a trip is about A$12. The main city bus terminal is in Harry Chan Avenue near the Bennett Street end of the city mall. **Buses** run throughout the city except on Sundays. *Information:* ☎ *(08) 8989-6540*; there is also airport bus service; ☎ *(08) 8981-2000.* For **highway conditions** (in case you're heading someplace and it's been raining heavily, contact either the **AANT (Automobile Association of the Northern Territory)**, *81 Smith Street;* ☎ *(08) 8981-3837;* or the **NT Emergency Service** ☎ *(08) 8984-4455.*

Every major rental car company is represented in Darwin. The rates are pretty good, often in the A$25-a-day range (plus insurance and a kilometerage charge). Our favorite used to be **Cheapa Rent-A-Car**, but the company changed its name to the more distinguished **Territory Rent-A-Car**. The rates are still good, however, and the company now has agencies all over the territory. In Darwin, the office is at *64 Stuart Highway;* ☎ *(08) 8981-8400.*

If you're going to do the territory or Kakadu National Park in a camper, in our opinion the only way to fly, there are several RV outlets in Darwin and Alice Springs. You can rent everything from a VW pop-top to a rig able to handle six adults. Pop-tops go for around A$80 a day plus insurance and taxes; the big rigs go for around A$200 a day plus insurance and tax. Note that insurance does not cover you on unpaved roads unless you get prior approval from the company.

Campers are very popular in the Territory, so you're advised to book them in advance from North America through a travel agent. Or if you wait until you arrive, we suggest either **Koala Campers** or **Budget Campervans**. Budget has been great to work with, including one terrible day when the generator went out on our RV in the middle of the nowhere in above-100-degree temperatures—they rescued us, gave us a cold beer, fixed us up with another vehicle and were totally professional. The office is on Mitchell Street in Darwin ☎ *(08) 8981-9800; FAX (08) 8981-1777.*

Koala has an office in Darwin at *39 Cavenagh Street* ☎ *(08) 8941-0877; FAX (08) 8941-3009;* or in Alice Springs at the *Melanka Lodge, 94 Todd Street* ☎ *(08) 8952-2233.* Another good choice for RVs is **Sunseeker Campervans**, *64 Stuart Highway;* ☎ *(08) 8981-0911; FAX (08) 8981-0912.*

Darwin is served internationally by **Qantas**, **Royal Brunei**, **Garuda**, **Merpati** and **Singapore Airlines**; internal air is available with **Ansett**, **Qantas**, **Ansett Airlines WA** and **Ansett NT**. There are also commuter and charter flights all over the territory and to nearby islands.

Shopping

Many stores in Darwin are open weekdays from 9 a.m.–5 p.m., but stay open to 9 p.m. Thursdays; Saturday hours 9 a.m.–1 p.m. The major shopping area in the central city is the mall, which is situated on Smith Street between Bennett and Knuckey streets. If you're looking for Aboriginal art, try the **Raintree Aboriginal Art Gallery** *on Knuckey Street;* ☎ *(08) 8981-2732;* for Australiana, try **It's Australian** in the mall, open seven days; ☎ *(08) 8981-5246.*

Information

The **Darwin Region Tourism Association** *is at 33 Smith Street Mall;* ☎ *(08) 8981-4300; FAX (08) 8981-7346.* More regional information is available from the **Australian Nature Conservation Agency**, *81 Smith Street;* ☎ *(08) 8981-5299.*

NORTHERN TERRITORY

Banks

Banking hours are Mon.–Thurs. 9:30 a.m.–4 p.m.; Fri. until 5 p.m.

Where to Stay

Beaufort Hotel, The A$225–1000 ★★★

The Esplanade; ☎ *(08) 8982-9911; FAX (08) 8981-5332.*
Rooms, most of which have harbor views, start at A$225 double; suites A$350–1000.
The city's premier hotel, not an architectural gem, but done in pleasant pinks and blues with two restaurants, several bars, a pool, spa, health club and business facilities.

Plaza Hotel Darwin A$195–1100 ★★★★

32 Mitchell Street; ☎ *(08) 8982-0000; FAX (08) 8981-1765.*
Doubles A$195; suites A$450–1100.
Located downtown near the mall, with Flinders and Mitchell's restaurants, both licensed. Pool, spa. Nonsmoking floors.

Diamond Beach Hotel/Casino A$180–220 ★★★

Gilruth Avenue, Mindil Beach, the Gardens; ☎ *(08) 8946-2666; (08) 8981-9186.*
Doubles A$180; suites A$220.
Next to tennis courts and golf course, across from botanical gardens. The large white building, a hallmark of the city, contains a casino with disco Friday-Saturday. Hotel has a lounge, recreation room, sauna, pool, spa, handicapped facilities and some cooking facilities. The casino is open from midday to around 3 a.m.

Darwin Travel Lodge A$165–190 ★★

122 Esplanade; ☎ *(08) 8981-5388; FAX (08) 8981-5701.*
Doubles A$165; suites A$190.
Close to shopping and the beaches. Licensed restaurant, pool, barbecue area, good city views from one of the few tall buildings that survived Tracy.

Atrium Hotel Darwin A$150–200 ★★

Corner of Peel and the Esplanade; ☎ *(08) 8941-0755; FAX (08) 8981-9025.*
Doubles A$150; suites from A$200.
One of the newest in town, with a seven-story atrium. Suites have kitchens. Mini-bars, licensed restaurant, pool, barbecue area, laundry, garden pool, spa, parking.

Marrakai Luxury Apartments A$200 ★★★

93 Smith Street; ☎ *(08) 8982-3711; FAX (08) 8981-9283.*
Doubles A$200 a day; weekly rates available.
The facility has 25 two-bedroom suites, all of which have kitchens with dishwashers; two bathrooms, daily maid service, private laundries, pool, spa, BBQ area, disabled facilities.

Poinciana Inn A$105 ★★

Corner McLachlan and Mitchell streets; ☎ *(08) 8981-8111; FAX (08) 8941-2440.*
Doubles A$105.
Motel-style units, with doubles and family rooms. Licensed restaurant, pool, tour desk, rental cars, parking.

Frontier Darwin Hotel A$135 ★★

3 Buffalo Court; ☎ *(08) 8981-5333; (08) 8941-0909.*
Doubles A$135.

Harbor view close to a golf course and casino. Pool and tropical garden setting. Rooftop licensed restaurant, in-house movies. April-September, there are Aboriginal corroborees.

Top End Hotel   **A$105–115**   ★

Corner Daly Street and the Esplanade; ☎ (08) 8981-6511; FAX (08) 8941-1253. Doubles A$105–115.

Disco Wednesday-Saturday; pool, laundry, kitchens, licensed restaurant.

Tops Boulevarde   **A$80**   ★

38 Gardens Road; ☎ (08) 8981-1544. Motel units A$80 double.

In the botanical garden-casino area. Has apartments or motel units. Licensed restaurant, indoor/outdoor bar, laundry, pool, barbecue area, tennis courts.

City Gardens   **A$110**   ★★

93 Woods Street; ☎ (08) 8941-2888; FAX (08) 8981-2934. Doubles A$110.

Another apartment complex, this one with 15 two-bedroom units with laundry and kitchen facilities in the rooms. Pool, barbecue, baby-sitting.

Darwin Transit   **A$15–40**   ★

69 Mitchell Street; ☎ (08) 8981-9733. Singles A$15–30; doubles A$30–40.

A hostel-like facility located at the bus depot; some rooms air-conditioned, some with fans. TV lounge, kitchen, laundry, barbecue area, pool, sauna, game room, luggage storage, parking; more than 200 rooms, some with private baths.

KOA and Malak Caravan Park   **A$17**   ★

McMillan's Road south of town; ☎ (08) 8927-2651 or (08) 8927-3500. A$17 per person; A$10 bathroom key deposit.

Next to shopping plaza and a golf course. All 327 sites are paved; laundry, store, barbecue area.

Where to Eat

Beagle, The   **$$**   ★★★

In the Northern Territory Museum of Arts and Sciences at Fannie Bay; ☎ (08) 8981-7791. Lunch from noon Monday–Friday and Sunday; dinner from 6:30 Monday–Saturday.

Eighteenth century atmosphere, named after Charles Darwin's ship which called here in the 1830s. If you like sunset views with your food, here's the spot. Specializes in seafood, also popular smorgasbord lunches. Reservations.

Peppi's   **$$**   ★★

84 Mitchell Street; ☎ (08) 8981-3762. Lunch from noon Monday–Friday; dinner from 6:30 p.m. seven nights.

Opposite the Beaufort Hotel, specializing in international cuisine. Special business lunches (three courses, A$20), good wine list.

Orchid Room   **$$**   ★★

First floor at the casino; ☎ (08) 8981-1190. Lunch noon–2:20 p.m. Monday–Friday; dinner 6:30–11 p.m. seven nights.

Cantonese cuisine, with à la carte For buffet. Seafood a specialty. Has won several dining awards.

Jessie's Family Bistro   **$$**   ★★

Casaurina Tavern, Trower Road, Casaurina (south of town); ☎ *(08) 8927-9155.*
Lunch Monday–Friday; dinner from 6 p.m. seven days.

Award-winning steak house also serving seafood. A blackboard menu offers daily specials.

Victoria Hotel   **$**   ★★

Smith Street Mall; ☎ *(08) 8981-4011.*
Open from midday–2 a.m. Monday–Saturday.

More lives than a cat, this old wreck was built in 1890, and was damaged in cyclones in 1897, 1937 and 1974 and was damned near burned to the ground by rioting soldiers in 1942. Rebuilt after Tracy, the Vic is probably the closest Darwin has to an authentic old-style Aussie pub. Buffalo burgers are a luncheon special; basic pub and family food.

Finally, for those who want to do the Top End experience in real style, there is the **Seven Spirit Bay resort** ★★★★★ on the Cobourg Peninsula in Arnhem Land, part of the Gurig National Park. The lodge has 24 cottages with louvers and screens to keep the mozzies out. Each cottage has a private garden and private bathroom. They come with two double beds, ceiling fans, hair dryers and bathrobes. The lounge is air-conditioned, with a restaurant and bar, outdoor decks overlooking the pool. The resort area is near the ocean, and the emphasis is on getting close to the remoteness of the area. There are naturalist-led bush walks, and the resort has its own photo lab to process film you shoot on treks. There are boats, bikes, four-wheel-drive vehicles. Note: no ocean swimming: crocs, sharks, stonefish, etc.

This is definitely off the path, and there has been some grumbling about it having been built in the area at all. The resort has a small airstrip for light aircraft flights from Darwin. Doubles are about A$1100 a night, which includes meals, activities and round-trip flights from Darwin. *Information: Seven Spirit Bay, P.O. Box 4721, Darwin 0801;* ☎ *(08) 8979-0277; FAX 8979-0284. Booking information in the U.S.: (800) 745-8545.*

Toward Kakadu

The main route to Kakadu National Park is the Arnhem Highway, which runs for about 120 miles, ending at the park's boundary at East Jabiru. You catch the Arnhem by taking the Stuart south of Darwin about 20 miles.

About 10 kilometers south of town on the Stuart Highway you'll come to the Big Pink Buffalo, which houses a souvenir shop and, more importantly, a Northern Territory information office that's open seven days. The buff is really ugly; the folks inside are friendly and can book tours. Along the way to the park on the good pavement of the Arnhem road, you come to one of the friendlier spots in the Territory, the **Humpty-Doo Hotel**. The pub comes with a bull that drinks beer, barramundi and buffalo meals, and a very popular Sunday barbecue. *Information:* ☎ *88-1372.* A few miles on past the Humpty-Doo is the turnoff to **Fogg Dam**, a waterfowl nesting area. Thirty miles from the Stuart turnoff, you come to the **Bark Hut Inn**, which has rooms, meals, gasoline, and an RV park. *Information:* ☎ *(08) 8978-8988.* As you drive between the two pubs, you'll come alongside some enormous termite nests, which provide a dandy photo op.

The yam figure at Nourlangie Rock in Kakadu National Park is believed to be 25,000 years old.

Kakadu

If you've seen the first *Crocodile Dundee* movie, you've seen a lot of Kakadu National Park. The park, about 20,000 square kilometers in area, is a mixed bag of ecosystems and land forms, composed chiefly of flood plains highlighted by the dramatic cliff edges of the vast Arnhem Land escarpment, which runs for about 250 miles through the Territory. Its wetland, billabongs, streams, gorges, grassland, and eucalypt forests are home to a huge variety of animals: 250 species of birds, 1000 different plants, 75 reptiles, 50 mammals, 25 frogs, and 55 fish, plus 16 different vegetation zones. Its popularity is increasing by the minute: in 1980, about 40,000 visitors came through, but by the end of the decade, the number was in excess of 200,000 a year.

The park is named after the traditional owners of the land, the Gagudju, who leased the park area to the federal parks and wildlife service in 1978. Tribe members still have a voice in the park operation, and a number of them

Fielding

KAKADU NATIONAL PARK

Kakadu National Park's 20,000 square kilometers of wetland, billabongs, streams, gorges, grassland and eucalyptus forests are home to a huge variety of flora and fauna. There are 250 species of birds, 1000 different plants, 75 reptiles, 50 mammals, 25 frogs and 55 fish, 4500 insects, plus 16 different vegetation zones. Many of the plants are still used by Aborigines for food, medicine and other purposes. The park i named after the traditional owners of the land, the Gagudju, who leased the park are to the federal parks and wildlife service i 1978. It became a national park in 1979 an is on the World Heritage list. Kakadu ha one of the most impressive rock ar collections in the world with Aboriginal roc paintings dating from 20,000 years ag

KAKADU NATIONAL PARK

WESTERN AUSTRALIA

NORTH AUSTRALIA

QUEENSLAND

SOUTH AUSTRALIA

Frilled lizard

FISH

The most amazing fish is th silver barramundi which changes sex from male to female at age five. It is eas to spot due to the unique swirl it creates near the surface of the water.

OTHER REPTILES

Interesting reptiles include the frilled lizard and the northern snake necked turtle. The Oenpelli python was not discovered until 1977.

Wallaby

Black-necked stork

Kangar

BIRDS

Kakadu is home to several bird species including the green pygmy goose, the magpie goose, the black-necked stork, rainbow bee-eaters, barking owls, red-tailed black cockatoos, and bustards, among others.

MAMMALS

Several types of kangaroo and walla are found in Kakad Twenty-five species bat are also found i the park. The black wallaroo is rarely se outside of Kakadu.

NORTHERN TERRITORY

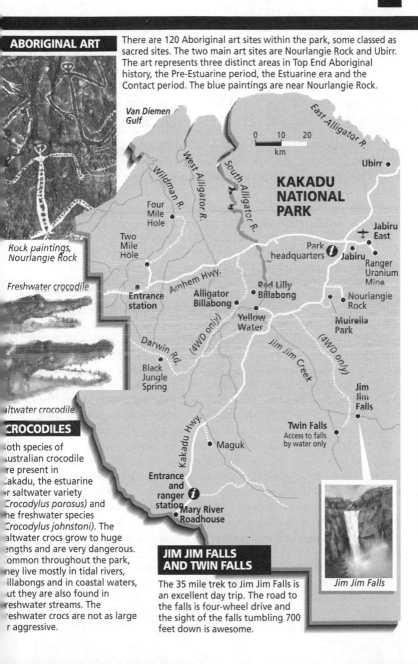

ABORIGINAL ART

There are 120 Aboriginal art sites within the park, some classed as sacred sites. The two main art sites are Nourlangie Rock and Ubirr. The art represents three distinct areas in Top End Aboriginal history, the Pre-Estuarine period, the Estuarine era and the Contact period. The blue paintings are near Nourlangie Rock.

Rock paintings, Nourlangie Rock

Freshwater crocodile

Saltwater crocodile

CROCODILES

Both species of Australian crocodile are present in Kakadu, the estuarine or saltwater variety (*Crocodylus porosus*) and the freshwater species (*Crocodylus johnstoni*). The saltwater crocs grow to huge lengths and are very dangerous. Common throughout the park, they live mostly in tidal rivers, billabongs and in coastal waters, but they are also found in freshwater streams. The freshwater crocs are not as large or aggressive.

Map labels

Van Diemen Gulf

East Alligator R.

Wildman R.

West Alligator R.

South Alligator R.

0   10   20
km

Ubirr

KAKADU NATIONAL PARK

Four Mile Hole

Two Mile Hole

Jabiru East

Park headquarters

Jabiru

Ranger Uranium Mine

Arnhem Hwy.

Entrance station

Alligator Billabong

Red Lilly Billabong

Nourlangie Rock

Yellow Water

Muirella Park

Darwin Rd.

(4WD only)

Jim Jim Creek

(4WD only)

Black Jungle Spring

Jim Jim Falls

Kakadu Hwy.

Twin Falls
Access to falls by water only

Maguk

Entrance and ranger station

Mary River Roadhouse

JIM JIM FALLS AND TWIN FALLS

The 35 mile trek to Jim Jim Falls is an excellent day trip. The road to the falls is four-wheel drive and the sight of the falls tumbling 700 feet down is awesome.

Jim Jim Falls

are park rangers. It became a national park in 1979 and is on the World Heritage list. The rocks in the park are very old, dating in some cases back 2 billion years. Indeed, a full third of the park area is rock, but the annual monsoon rainfall allows wild orchids and other exotic plants to flourish. The whole area is alive with flowering plants between December and March.

The park very nearly never came to be. When Frank Woerle, the park's first ranger, arrived in 1970, he found the area overrun by water buffalo. In the 1830s, a herd of 150 of the voracious critters were introduced into the area; by the time Frank and his wife arrived, there were more than a quarter of a million, and the delicate environment of the Kakadu area was in deep trouble. Water buffalo remain a problem in the Territory even today. He was able to cull out the herd at Kakadu and begin the slow task of bringing the park to the condition it enjoys today.

Here, we think it prudent to discuss the mightiest of Kakadu's inhabitants: crocodiles. Around the park, and on the roads leading to it, you will see signs warning people not to swim because of crocodiles. This is not a publicity stunt based on Paul Hogan's movie—it's deadly serious. Both species of Australian crocodiles are present in the park: the estuarine, or saltwater variety (*Crocodylus porosus*, called "salties"), and the freshwater species, (*Crocodylus johnstoni* or "freshies"). The saltwater species grows to huge lengths and is very dangerous. Common throughout the park, these crocodiles live mostly in tidal rivers, billabongs on the floodplains, and in coastal waters. But they are also found in freshwater streams, so the basic rule is, don't swim. It's not even safe to get close to the water in some places, because the big reptiles are not averse to coming ashore to grab a meal, and they can move incredibly fast. The freshwater variety, not as large or as hungry, is generally regarded as safe to be around, but why take a chance on being the first exception to the rule? The various tours around Kakadu provide plenty of chances to see the crocs in safety, so try to avoid meeting them on your own.

The park has provision for campers, RVers, or folks who want to stay in upgrade hotels. You can tour by yourself or go with one of the many excellent adventure tour groups offering Kakadu trips. From June through October, the park ranger staff offers a number of free guided tours and evening programs. The tours include Aboriginal painting sites, wetlands hikes, and forest walks.

There are two **park information offices** at Kakadu. The **Bowali Visitors Centre** is located in Jabiru at the intersection of the Arnhem Highway and the road that cuts off to Yellow Water. In addition to park information, the center has an excellent slide and sound show with a general overview of the park, well worth a look. Library, craft gallery, cafe. Hours are 8 a.m.–5 p.m. daily. *P.O. Box 71, Jabiru 0886,* ☎ *(08) 8938-1121; FAX (08) 8938-1115.* The **Warradjan Cultural Centre** is on Cooinda Road in Yellow Waters. The center is built in the shape of a pig-nosed turtle (hence the Aboriginal name for the beast) and has videos, a craft gallery and park displays. Available at both centers is a general visitors guide to the park which has good information. The park entry fee is A$15, good for two weeks. If you're not in a car or RV, there is bus service to the park, or you can fly to Jabiru. For air service and fares, contact Kakadu Air Services in Jabiru ☎ *(08) 8979-2411; FAX (08) 8979-2303.*

There are more than a dozen designated **camping** areas in the park, which are free and range from the very primitive to sites with showers and flush toilets. The biggest private RV/hotel complex is the **Frontier Kakadu Village** ★ ★ , a large settlement on the Arnhem Highway at the South Alligator River west of Jabiru. There are 200 RV sites—100 with power—plus a pool, general store, tennis, barbecues, laundry and a tour desk. Powered sites are A$20 for two people. The motel has about 140 units, with air conditioning, refrigerators and a restaurant. Doubles run A$125–145. ☎ *(08) 8979-0166; FAX (08) 8979-0147.*

At the **Frontier Kakadu Lodge and Caravan Park** in Jabiru, there are 186 RV sites, about 100 with power. The park has a pool, laundry, store, restaurant and BBQs. Powered sites are A$20 for two persons. The lodge is designed for families and backpackers, with shared facilities. Dormitory beds are available May-April and start about A$22 per person. ☎ *(08) 8979-2422; FAX (08) 8979-2254.* There is also a small RV park at the Kakadu Highway intersection with the Stuart Highway at **Pine Creek**; powered sites A$15 two persons; bunkhouse accommodation A$35.50 double. ☎ *(08) 8976-1288.* And there are RV facilities at **Point Stuart Wilderness Lodge** *at Mary River Park* ☎ *(08) 8978-8914; FAX (08) 8981-3720.*

Bush camping is allowed in the park, but permits are required from the park ranger's office. Many of the camp areas are closed during the Wet.

The major accommodations in the park are the 48-room **Gagudju Lodge Cooinda** ★ ★ and the **Gagudju Crocodile Hotel** ★ ★ ★ . The Gagudju Lodge, centrally located at Yellow Waters, has rooms going for about A$130 double. The motelish lodge has airport transfers from Jabiru, baby-sitting, restaurant, guest laundry, air conditioning, pool. There is also an RV park with 150 sites, 40 of them with power; A$15 for two persons. The backpacker bunkhouse units are A$12 per person. ☎ *(08) 8979-0145; FAX (08) 8979-0148.*

The most popular facility in the park is the **Crocodile Hotel**, probably because of its unusual shape: the 110-room hotel in Jabiru is built in the shape of a crocodile. The rooms have air conditioning, mini-bars, fridges. There are Jabiru airport transfers, handicapped facilities, restaurant, bar, guest laundry. with doubles at A$110-190. ☎ *(08) 8979-2800; FAX (08) 8979-2707.*

The small village of Jabiru has food, gasoline, supplies and a shopping center. Gasoline and water are also available at the **Frontier Kakadu Village** and the **Border Store** near Ubirr at the northeast boundary of the park. There is also a **youth hostel** just past the Border Store. Rates are about A$10 per person. ☎ *(08) 8979-2333.* It's subject to closure during the rainy season.

High on your list of things to do at Kakadu must be a visit to the **Aboriginal art sites** that are open to the public. There are at least 120 artwork locations in the park, some of which are classed as sacred sites. As part of the Aboriginal land rights legislation in 1976, a law was passed creating the Aboriginal Sacred Sites Protection Authority, which is empowered to keep a record of such sites around the country and to handle Aboriginal claims about sacred tribal places. Disturbing sites under protection of the authority can result in heavy fines, as you will see on signs here and there in Kakadu. *For information about the sites, contact the Aboriginal Sacred Sites Protection Authority, P.O. Box 1890, Darwin 5794;* ☎ *(08) 8981-4700.*

The **artwork** you see at Kakadu represents three distinct areas in Top End Aboriginal history. First, there was **pre-estuarine**, a period that lasted until the sea level rose to flood the present-day tidal area of the park, which took place about 7000 to 8000 years ago. One famous painting, the *yam figure* at Nourlangie Rock, is believed to be about 25,000 years old. The second period, or **estuarine era**, lasted from the sea level rise until the arrival of European settlers. From this era is the famous painting of a thylacine—the *Tasmanian tiger*—believed to have become extinct on the Australian mainland about 4000 years ago. Some of Australia's most famous Aboriginal artworks, the so-called *X-ray paintings*, were created during this era. The unique style of art shows the inner organs and bones of animals and is quite striking. The most common animal in the paintings is a barramundi. The third era is called the **contact period**, because artwork reflects the results of association with the white colonists. Here you see paintings showing rifles and steel axes.

The two main visitor sites at Kakadu are at Nourlangie Rock and Ubirr. Near **Nourlangie** are the so-called **Blue Paintings**, the only ones in the park in that color—the ancient Aboriginals had no blue pigments. These paintings are modern, completed in 1964 using laundry bluing.

Ubirr is the most popular and accessible site, with part of the trail able to accommodate wheelchairs. Among the paintings on view are the X-rays, the thylacine, and the early monochromes done in red ochre. The trail past the major galleries is about a kilometer long. At the end is a moderately steep path to the top of Obiri Rock for another great view of the escarpment.

The "other" must in the park is to take a **water trip** to check out the birds and beauties of the wetlands and see a few crocodiles in the process. We recommend the two-hour **Yellow Waters boat cruise** at about A$25 per person. Among the beasties on view is the jabiru, also known as the black-necked stork, which is the Northern Territory symbol. There are normally six trips a day, starting at 6:45 a.m. From January-March during the floods, there's a 3.5-hour wetlands tour. Probably the best of the year if you're there in the rainy season. The tours can be booked at the **Gagudju Lodge Cooinda** or by calling ☎ *(08) 8979-0111; FAX (08) 8979-0148.*

Another boat trip takes visitors on a five-hour **tour of the East Alligator River** with **Guluyambi River Cruises**. These trips are about A$25 per person and can be booked in Jabiru ☎ *(08) 8979-2411; FAX (08) 8979-2303; toll free in Australia 1-(800) 089-113.*

There are also some excellent **day trips**, the best of which is the 35-mile trek to **Jim Jim Falls**, which tumbles 700 feet down the edge of the escarpment, truly awesome when the streams are running high. The road to the falls is strictly four-wheel drive. Tours can be booked either in Darwin or at the hotels in the park.

If you're **driving** yourself—even in a regular car—and are heading south on your stay, try taking the Kakadu Highway out of the park. It's in the process of being paved, but long stretches are still dirt and you might have to ford a couple of streams along the way—don't try it between November and March without checking with the park rangers—also check with your rental agency to see if this stretch is verboten. There's a **gasoline station** at the Mary River crossing, and the road is paved at least 50 kilometers west from Pine Creek, where it meets the Stuart Highway.

There are scads of Kakadu **tours** available, everything from a one-day jaunt to canoe trips or tent camping expeditions. A couple of companies you might check are **Kakadu Gorge and Waterfall Tours** in Jabiru or **AAT King's Australian Experience** in Darwin. The gorge and waterfall folks do an all day trip to the various falls and sights in the park for about A$115 per adult, including lunch. ☎ *(08) 8979-0111; FAX (08) 8979-0148.* King's offers several four-wheel drive treks around the park, anything from three to nine days, staying either in tents or in one of the park hotels. The seven-day trip, for example, includes Jim Jim Falls, Yellow Waters, and a trip down to Katherine for a boat trip through Katherine Gorge. The cost is about A$1500 per person, including lunches and accommodations. The one-day tour of Kakadu with King's runs about $A135. ☎ *(08) 8979-47-1207; FAX (08) 8947-1324.*

Another company, one of the largest, is **Australian Kakadu Tours**, which has a wide variety of Kakadu experiences, from one-day trips from Darwin to 10-day treks that do Kakadu, Melville Island and the Katherine area. The one-days run around A$90, and include the Yellow Waters cruise and other Kakadu highlights; the 10-day Melville Island excursion goes for about A$1850, which includes airfare and accommodations. *Australian Kakadu*

Tours, Smith Street Mall, Darwin ☎ *(08) 8981-5144; toll-free in Australia* ☎ *(008) 89-1121; North America:* ☎ *(800) 551-2012.*

Down the Stuart

As you drive down the Stuart, gathering up red dust in every pore and counting the number of kangaroos and water buffalos left dead in the wake of lumbering road trains, the last thing you'd ever expect to encounter is a spectacular river gorge able to handle large tour boats. But there it is, **Katherine Gorge**, a miniature Grand Canyon and one of the Territory's more photogenic spots.

The city of **Katherine** is about 200 miles south of Darwin, in what is called the "Land of the Never-Never," so named because once you live here, you'll never, never leave it. But the name is more often associated with *We of the Never-Never*, a book written by a pioneer woman named Mrs. Aeneas Gunn who set up life on a station near Mataranka, south of Katherine, in 1902. It's a great book for capturing the spirit of the white Australians who settled the desolate lands of the Territory. Katherine, named after the daughter of one of the men who financed Stuart's expedition, is the third largest city in the Territory, with about 7000 population. The region languished for many years, but the enlargement of a Royal Australian Air Force base near the city, plus the general increase in Territory tourism, has created a mini-boom that will probably double Katherine's population by the turn of the century.

The **gorge** is actually a series of canyons cut over a period of 25 million years by the Katherine River, which starts in Arnhem Land, flows south to Katherine, then joins the Daly River, which turns northwest and empties into the Timor Sea southwest of Darwin. The whole gorge area is now a large **national park**, situated 20 miles north of town on a paved highway (hang a left at the police station in downtown Katherine). The gorges, 13 in all, sprawl along a 10-kilometer system and in some spots are more than 200 feet deep. In places, high on the canyon walls, are large Aboriginal paintings, some dating back 10,000 years. Most visitors take a boat trip into the gorges, which start from a landing located near the RV campground in the park. (It was next to the camp headquarters where we watched a guy give his pet emu a bath, a truly remarkable sight. The bird ate it up.)

The **boat tours** are for two hours, a half day, or a full day. The trip is a ride-and-walk arrangement because the gorges are entered through a series of waterfalls, exposed down to bare rocks during the dry season. The two-hour trip goes to the first two gorges; the longer ones will go back to the seventh or eighth gorges. The cost of the half-day trip is about A\$30 per person. In the Wet, the water level in the gorge system can rise 40 feet. If you're lucky on your trip, you might spot freshwater crocodiles, who share the river with

40 species of fish. **Nitmiluk (Katherine) Gorge Cruises** ☎ *(08) 8972-1253; FAX (08) 8971-0715; toll free 1-(800) 089-103.* The gorge area is also a favorite bushwalking area, with more than 60 miles of trails. Canoeing is also popular, although there is a lot of portaging involved. If you're interested, contact **Kookaburra Canoe Hire** at the park near the boat dock; a full day's rental starts at A$20. ☎ *(08) 8972-3604 or (08) 8972-3301.*

Information on the park is available from Katherine Gorge National Park, Katherine 5780, ☎ *(08) 8972-1886, or from the Conservation Commission of the Northern Territory, Katherine Terrace* ☎ *(08) 8972-1799.*

Among the **accommodations** available in Katherine are the **Katherine Hotel-Motel** ★, with bar, restaurant, and pool ☎ *(08) 8972-1622; FAX (08) 8972-3213;* the nice **Paraway Motel** ★, also with bar, restaurant, and pool ☎ *(08) 8972-2644 FAX (08) 8972-2720;* and the **Katherine Frontier Motor Inn** ★ ★ outside of town with pool, tennis courts, restaurant and bar ☎ *(08) 8972-1744; FAX (08) 8972-2790.* Rates for all three are in the A$75-A$115 double range, depending on season. For information about the city and area, including other lodging and food, contact the **Katherine Region Tourist Association**, *corner Stuart Highway and Lindsay Street* ☎ *(08) 8972-2650; FAX (08) 8972-2969.* **Note**: there's a **coin laundry** in Katherine on Kintore Street.

Sixty miles down the pike from Katherine, put there because God took pity on the heat-stroke victims passing by, is **Mataranka Homestead**, where you will find one of the truly fine watering holes on the continent, the **Mataranka thermal pool** ★ ★ ★. The pool, a Territory park, is located behind a privately owned caravan park, and is always a pleasant 93 degrees, with a daily flow of 5 million gallons. Words fail us remembering the glorious feeling of dipping bodies into the pool after a rugged day wandering around in the heat. (If you go, get on the down-flow side of the footbridge and sit in one of the deep pools. It almost beats sex.) **Accommodations** at Mataranka include a motel, caravan park, and campgrounds at the **Mataranka Homestead Tourist Park** ★ ★, with licensed bar and cafe, and a youth hostel (right next to the thermal pool). Most nights, there is a live country-western music show. Rooms at the Homestead with air conditioning are A$60–75. Cabins are A$55 double; powered RV sites are A$20 double. ☎ *(08) 8975-4544; FAX (08) 8975-4580.* There is also the **Territory Manor Motel** ★, which also has RV and tent sites. There's a laundry, pool and spa. Air-conditioned rooms go for A$75 double; powered RV sites are A$20 double; tent sites are A$10. ☎ *(08) 8975-4516; FAX (08) 8975-4612.* Next to the Homestead campground is a replica of the Gunn family house, complete with verandah and some furniture. Then, about seven kilometers south of Mataranka is a turnoff that goes another seven kilometers to the graveyard where Jeannie Gunn and her husband are buried at the Never-Never homestead.

NORTHERN TERRITORY

AUSTRALIA'S NORTHERN TERRITORY

DOWN STUART HIGHWAY

KATHERINE GORGE

Thirteen gorges sprawl along a 10km. system and some are more than 200 ft. deep. Large Aboriginal paintings on the canyon walls date back 10,000 years. Bushwalking, boating, and canoeing are popular around the gorge. The scenery includes waterfalls and a stunning variety of flora and fauna.

KATHERINE

Katherine is a booming tourist center best known for nearby Katherine Gorge and the Cutta Caves. It's the third largest city in the Northern Territory.

MATARANKA

Mataranka Homestead is a popular watering hole, and the thermal pools are a relaxing respite for worn-out tourists. Nearby Elsey Station Homestead was the set of the 1981 film *We of the Never Never*.

DALY WATERS

Founded by Stuart on his trip north, this historic place has served as a pony express stop, telegraph station and World War II base. It also boasts a pub.

TENNANT CREEK

A modern Outback cattle and tourist town with a colorful past as a gold, silver and copper mining center. It is home to Warumungu Aborigines. Devil's Pebbles, 11 km. north is a granite formation with spectacular sunsets.

DEVIL'S MARBLES

Located 104 km. south of Tennant Creek, these granite boulders spread across a wide valley were created from a single granite mass. Aborigine legend says they are eggs laid by a rainbow serpent. Sunrise and sunset are the best viewing times.

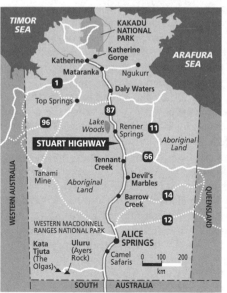

NORTHERN TERRITORY

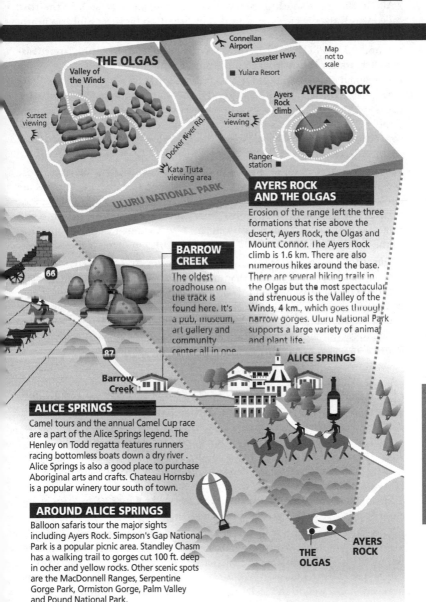

THE OLGAS

Valley of
the Winds

Sunset
viewing

Docker River Rd.

Kata Tjuta
viewing area

ULURU NATIONAL PARK

Connellan
Airport

Lasseter Hwy.

Yulara Resort

Map
not to
scale

AYERS ROCK

Ayers
Rock
climb

Sunset
viewing

Ranger
station

AYERS ROCK AND THE OLGAS

Erosion of the range left the three formations that rise above the desert, Ayers Rock, the Olgas and Mount Connor. The Ayers Rock climb is 1.6 km. There are also numerous hikes around the base. There are several hiking trails in the Olgas but the most spectacular and strenuous is the Valley of the Winds, 4 km., which goes through narrow gorges. Uluru National Park supports a large variety of animal and plant life.

BARROW CREEK

The oldest roadhouse on the track is found here. It's a pub, museum, art gallery and community center all in one

66

87

Barrow
Creek

ALICE SPRINGS

ALICE SPRINGS

Camel tours and the annual Camel Cup race are a part of the Alice Springs legend. The Henley on Todd regatta features runners racing bottomless boats down a dry river . Alice Springs is also a good place to purchase Aboriginal arts and crafts. Chateau Hornsby is a popular winery tour south of town.

AROUND ALICE SPRINGS

Balloon safaris tour the major sights including Ayers Rock. Simpson's Gap National Park is a popular picnic area. Standley Chasm has a walking trail to gorges cut 100 ft. deep in ocher and yellow rocks. Other scenic spots are the MacDonnell Ranges, Serpentine Gorge Park, Ormiston Gorge, Palm Valley and Pound National Park.

THE OLGAS

AYERS ROCK

NORTHERN TERRITORY

About 100 miles south of Mataranka is an historic wide spot in the road called **Daly Waters**, which was founded by Stuart on his successful trip north, and has served over the years as a drover station, pony express stop, telegraph station, and World War II base. It's also the home of the self-proclaimed **Historic Daly Waters Pub ★ ★**, which features, among other things, a Taffy Special—named after a barkeep. Don't ask what's in it; just make sure you have a designated driver. The pub has good lunches for a buck and a night barbecue for A$8.50. There is a moldy but serviceable motel for A$35 a night double. There's also a gasoline station. In September is the **Daly Waters Rodeo, Campdraft and Gymkhana**, with a rodeo, wild goings-on and a big dance at the pub. ☎ *(08) 8975-9927.*

From Daly Waters south, the country gets drier and drier, the vistas more and more bleak. This is the north end of the Red Centre, and humans are few and far apart. Between Daly Waters and Tennant Creek, 250 miles away, there are two villages, **Elliott** and **Renner Springs**, which have gasoline and motels. About 10 miles north of Tennant Creek is **Three Ways**, the junction of the Barkly Highway that runs east to Mount Isa in Queensland.

This is the land where many of the Big Myths of Australia were born: tiny towns, wild and woolly one-horse pubs, huge cattle ranches, and hopeful prospectors. The area around is known as the **Barkly Tablelands**, and is desert in climate (freezing at night in the winter, 110 degrees in the shade in the summer). **Tennant Creek** (about 4000 population) is the largest town between Katherine and Alice Springs, and word has it the smallest settlement is **Rabbit Flat**, population two, out in the Tanami Desert near the Western Australia border.

Myth? Well, legend has it that Tennant Creek was founded by the drivers of a beer wagon that broke down, who then decided to stay put and drink up all their cargo. Tennant Creek is a place to stop only if you have to, being basically a sleepy village. But it does have three motels (check the **Eldorado ★**, named after a nearby gold mine). Doubles go for A$65. ☎ *(08) 8962-2402; FAX (08) 8962-3034.* There are a couple of RV parks in Tennant; try the **Tennant Creek Caravan Park** on Paterson Street. Powered sites are A$15 double. ☎ *(08) 8962-2325.* If you want to call the whole thing off and go home, Tennant Creek does have an **airport**, with service by **Ansett NT** to Darwin and Alice Springs. It's also a stop for bus companies.

Between Tennant Creek and Alice Springs, distances are calculated, not in kilometers, but in beer stops. At **Wauchope** there is the colorful **Wauchope Hotel**, which has an annual cricket match taking on the rest of the world—called, you have to know—*Wimbledon at Wauchope*, a charity event. The hotel also has gasoline and lodgings. Just north of town is a strange rock formation called the **Devil's Marbles**, a bunch of huge granite boulders strewn about, worth a photo or two. Next along comes **Barrow Creek**, with another great Outback pit stop, the wide-verandahed **Barrow Creek Pub**. (Population, around 10; gasoline and lodging available.) **Ti Tri**, a bit farther on, also has gas and rooms.

Alice Springs

So, after 700 miles of noble trek, you have now arrived in Alice Springs, where, as you will immediately discover, there ain't no town like Alice.

Alice Springs, because of Neville Shute's book (and a certain amount of hot air from the local tourism people), has an international reputation as the original wild and colorful Outback town, full of hard-drinking drovers, a pub every 10 feet, sand and bulldust and fallen women, camels in the streets, cattle in the bathrooms. Tain't so, folks. The Alice looks like just what it is: a rapidly growing, quite successful commercial center, the gateway to both Kakadu National Park and Ayers Rock, a place with libraries, churches, supermarkets, nice hotels, and even a car wash. There are bits and snatches of the old Alice here and there, but if you came here hoping to see raw Australia at its best, you're about 60 years too late. The city dads estimate that more than 400,000 tourists a year going through town and not a stampede or lynching to be seen.

The Alice, population about 25,000, started life at a small springs about three kilometers north of the present town, where a repeater station for the overland telegraph station was built in 1871. The waterhole was discovered by William Mills, one of the surveyors pushing the telegraph line north to Darwin from Adelaide. But the village that grew up near the waterhole in this century (at first named Stuart) was mostly isolated until the late 1920s, when a rail link finally arrived from Adelaide. The train was called "the Ghan" to honor the Afghan cameleers who had been the main source of supplies and transportation for years. Camels were first introduced into Australia in the 1830s; the Burke and Wills expedition, for example, relied heavily on the beasts to carry supplies—not that it helped. Camels played a big role in many early pioneering efforts, including hauling supplies to gold fields all over the country as well as working on railroads.

Camels are still a big part of the myths about Alice Springs. The Australians say they have the only wild herds of dromedary (one-humped) camels left in the world, and the folks around the Alice say half of all the wild camels in Australia are in the Territory. As a matter of fact, Australia is now exporting camels back to places in the Near East where the beasties have become almost extinct. One of the groups most interested in the export business is the Aboriginal Central Lands Council. So the local camels won't feel lonely, there is even an outfit in Alice Springs growing date palms, and the Territory is thinking about expanding the industry. Although camel activities are a major tourist attraction around Alice Springs, the Territory has not cornered the market on dromedary tourism. There are camel tour operators in at least three other Australian states, all eager to get you humping. In Alice Springs every year, there is the **Camel Cup**, a hell-for-leather race right out of *Lawrence of Arabia*. If all these dates, palms and camels make things around town sound like you're in East Fez, Morocco, not to worry. Alice Springs is about as Australian as it gets.

The heart of Alice Springs is the **Todd River**, a usually dry watercourse that fronts the downtown area. But in March 1988, a huge storm dumped so much water, the Todd overflowed its banks and flooded the city. The sandy riverbed is famous as the site of the annual **Henley-on-Todd Regatta ★★★**, where every October, bottomless boats propelled by runners gallop down the Todd for money and glory. Apparently, nobody was paying attention to the flood waters, because two of the city's premier hotels were built—and expanded—on the Todd River floodplain south of the business district.

One of the things to take a look at in Alice Springs is the **Royal Flying Doctor Service ★★**, the legendary outfit that was begun to provide free emergency medical care to folks in trouble in the Outback. During the day, the service is used as a telephone system, patching in calls all over the area. Two hours a day are set aside for emergency medical communications. Tours of the base are available every half-hour during the day for A$2 per person. The base is located at the corner of Stuart Terrace and Hartley Street. Hours are 9 a.m.–4 p.m. Monday–Friday. ☎ *(08) 8952-1129.*

That other great Outback invention—the **School of the Air**—is also open for inspections; admission fee. The school, which has taught generations of Outback kids via shortwave classes, is located on Head Street, west of Stuart Highway near the Telegraph Road turnoff. The school is open for visits 8 a.m.–noon Monday–Friday, February-November–February. ☎ *(08) 8951-6800.*

To get to Alice Springs—the real Alice Springs—you head back up the Stuart Highway at the north edge of town to Telegraph Road and drive east to the springs and restored repeater station and its outbuildings. Entry to the station, now a national park, is free. The area near the springs is great for picnics, and there are emu, wallabies, and peacocks wandering around. The park, called the **Alice Springs Telegraph Station Historical Reserve**, is open 8 a.m.–9 p.m., October–April, and 8 a.m.–7 p.m., May–September. Daily tours. ☎ *(08) 8952-1013.*

South of town near the Ross Road turnoff to the MacDonnell Ranges is the **Pitchi Richi Sanctuary**, a large outdoor museum and botanical garden that displays the wonderful sculptures of Aboriginals by Victorian artist William Rickets (whose works are also on display near Melbourne). Admission to the park, which is open 9 a.m.–7 p.m. all week, is A$2. ☎ *(08) 8952-1931.*

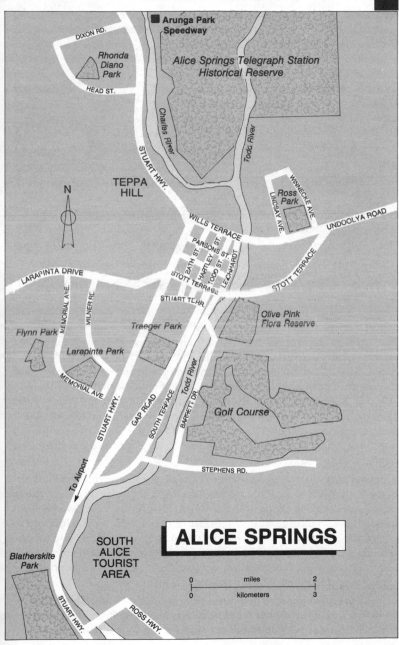

ALICE SPRINGS

Authentic Aboriginal art can be bought at numerous galleries and shops.

If you are at all interested in *Aboriginal art*, Alice Springs is one of the best places in Australia to pick some up, particularly paintings. The area has a long tradition of art. One of Australia's most famous artists, the Aboriginal Albert Namatjira, lived at the Hermannsburg Mission about 90 miles west of Alice Springs. He painted the Outback in European-style watercolors, and his works sold all over the country. The Alice is now a magnet for Aboriginal artists living throughout the Red Centre, who create works in traditional tribal style. The best place to acquaint yourself with Namatjira's works, plus other Aboriginal artists, is at the **Araluen Centre** on Larapinta Drive in Alice Springs. In addition to two major galleries displaying Central Aboriginal art, there is a 500-seat theater, bar and restaurant, gift shop and self-guided tours. The center is open 10 a.m.–5 p.m. Monday–Saturday, February–November; A$2 admission. ☎ *(08) 8952-5022.*

Around Alice you will find a number of small galleries offering regional Aboriginal art. While most of the stock is paintings, you'll also see jewelry, purses, bags, and carvings done in mulga wood. One of the artists to look for is named (honest) George Bush, a member of the Walpiru tribe. He is said to be the first man to take tribal sand paintings, created on the ground for ceremonial use much like the Navajo sand paintings of the Southwestern United States, and reproduce them on canvas. Bush (tribal name Tjanpala) has works on display in the National gallery in Melbourne.

If you're really interested in a camel trek, go to the **Frontier Camel Farm** ★ on Ross Highway about five kilometers east of the Stuart Highway intersection. There's a camel ride for all tastes, from a five-minute jaunt around a corral to full-day safaris. Also at the farm is **Reptile World**, where you can eyeball some of Australia's deadliest snakes. There are guided tours daily at 10:30 a.m. that include all the beasts, including a camel ride, for about A$10 per person. The admission charge also lets you use the farm's barbecue and picnic area. Open daily 9 a.m.–5 p.m. ☎ *(08) 8953-0444.*

By far the most popular camel excursions are the rides to **the Winery ★★**, the home of Australia's most unlikely vintages. A full-day trek to the winery, which goes down the dry Todd River bed, is A$50, including a barbecue lunch and a wine tasting. The price includes a gander at the snakes, plus pickup at your hotel or RV camp. Also available is a dinner trip to the winery, with wine tasting and a dinner of Territory buffalo or fish. It also includes pickup at your hotel. Overnight treks in the area are also available. *Bookings and information; Frontier Camel Tours, P.O. Box 2836, Alice Springs 5750;* ☎ *(08) 8953-0444 FAX (08) 8955-5015.*

You can avoid the camels and still do the tasting bit, of course. The Winery is reached by taking the Stuart Highway south of town toward the airport, then turning east on Colonel Rose Drive. About five kilometers along Rose Road, turn left on Petrick Road to the winery. The place is open air, sunny, and schedules lunches and dinners on request. The winery produces shiraz, moselle, and riesling-semillon wines. A couple of bottles of shiraz (they're really not bad) will run you around A$25. ☎ *(08) 8955-5133.*

If you want to get into the camel thing a lot more intensively, there are a number of tour operators around the Territory who offer week or longer treks. Among these are **Alice Springs Camel Outback Safari,** ☎ *(08) 8956-0925;* **Central Australian Camel Treks,** ☎ *(08) 8952-7611; or* **Camel-Time Walking** ☎ *(08) 8952-8466.* These tours normally can be booked through AAT King's Australian Experience office in the Alice at ☎ *(08) 8952-1700; FAX (08) 8952-8028.* For these long trips, including meals, camping equipment, guides and of course, the camel, you can expect a price of around A$100 a day per person, twin share.

Essential Alice Springs

Information

The **Central Australian Tourism Industry Association** is located at the corner of Gregory Terrace and Hartley Street ☎ *(08) 8952-5199; FAX (08) 8953-0295.* The **Automobile Association of the Northern Territory** is on Gregory Terrace ☎ *(08) 8953-1322.*

Getting Around

Taxis

Alice Springs Taxis, ☎ *(08) 8952-1877;* 24 hours, seven days.

Airport shuttle

Alice Springs Airport Shuttle Service, *113 Todd Street,* ☎ *(08) 8953-1011 or (08) 8953-0310;* pickup at hotels, motels, and caravan parks, about A$7 per person, reservations required. The airport, by the way, is too small for the number of flights going in and out, and there's often a mob scene, so be prepared.

Where to Stay

Plaza Alice Springs   **A$210–400**   ★★★

Barrett Drive, ☎ *(08) 8952-8000; FAX (08) 8952-3822.*
Doubles from A$210; suites from A$400.
On the Todd River about 1.5 miles from downtown adjacent to Lassiters Casino. Also next door is the 18-hole Alice Springs Golf Club. The hotel has tennis, heated pool, health club, several bars, coffee shop and two restaurants; handicapped facilities, nonsmoking rooms.

Lasseters Hotel Casino   **A$110–150**   ★★★

93 Barrett Drive; ☎ *(08) 8952-5066; FAX (08) 8953-1680.*
Doubles from A$110; suites from A$150.
Gambling from midday to early in the morning; the disco runs from 11 p.m. Sunday-Wednesday; from 9 p.m. Thursday–Saturday. Pool, tennis, restaurants, night club, three bars.

Red Centre Resort   **A$100–120**   ★★

North Stuart Highway, about four kilometers from town; ☎ *(08) 8952-8955; FAX (08) 8952-8300.*
Doubles A$100–120.
About a third of the rooms have kitchens. Pool, spa, restaurant/bar, laundry, photo service, courtesy van, volleyball courts. Cook-your-own meat in the barbecue area.

Frontier Oasis Resort   **A$100**   ★★

10 Gap Road; ☎ *(08) 8952-1444; FAX (08) 8952-3776.*
Doubles A$100. A good bet.
Near downtown with restaurant/bar, pool, sauna, spa, squash courts, tour desk. Barbecue dinners several times a week. Try Galah's Bar.

Alice Springs Pacific Resort   **A$150**   ★★

34 Stott Terrace; ☎ *(08) 8952-6699; FAX (08) 8953-0995.*
Doubles from A$150.
On the banks of the Todd River downtown. Pool, laundry, recreation room, minibars, licensed restaurant.

Vista Hotel   **A$130**   ★★★

Stephens Road; ☎ *(08) 8952-6100; FAX (08) 8952-1988.*
Doubles A$130.
Opposite the casino. Pool, tennis courts, barbecue, licensed restaurant, handicapped facilities.

Elkira Motel   **A$75**   ★

65 Bath Street; ☎ *(08) 8952-1222; FAX (08) 8953-1370.*
Doubles A$75.
Restaurant, pool, barbecue, laundry, handicapped access.

Desert Palms Resort   **A$65**   ★

Barrett Drive; ☎ *(08) 8952-5977; FAX (08) 8953-4176.*
Doubles A$65.
Near the casino and golf course. Kitchenettes, laundry, pool, barbecue, tennis.

Alice Tourist Apartments　　　　　　**A$60–100**　　　　　★★
Corner of Gap Road and Gnoilya Street; ☎ *(08) 8952-2788; FAX (08) 8953-2950.*
Doubles A$60–100.
One- and two-bedroom units with kitchens. Pool, barbecue, laundry, parking.

Swagman's Rest, The　　　　　　**A$70**　　　　　★
67 Gap Road; ☎ *(08) 8953-1333; FAX (08) 8953-0404.*
Doubles A$70.
Self-contained units with kitchens. Pool, barbecue, laundry, handicapped facilities.

Melanka Lodge　　　　　　**A$12–65**　　　　　★
94 Todd Street; ☎ *(08) 8952-2233; FAX (08) 8952-3819.*
Motel doubles A$50–65; guest house doubles A$40; backpackers dorms A$12 per person.
Pool, restaurant/bar, TV lounge, recreation room, barbecue, laundry.

Toddy's Backpackers　　　　　　**A$15–40**　　　　　★
41 Gap Road; ☎ *(08) 8952-1322; FAX (08) 8952-1767.*
Dorms start at A$15 per person; cabins daily A$40.
Free pickup, air conditioned rooms, pool, store, barbecue, laundry, two kitchens, bike hire, tour desk. Must rent crockery and linens.

Where to Eat

Alice is not generous in its variety of eating establishments. What you basically have to choose from, outside the good but not yet great hotel restaurants, is family-style food with a traditional Australian approach—Territory meats, fried fish, Italian, sandwiches. It's not a culinary desert, exactly, but if you're looking for five-star food, fly back to Sydney. Still, it's the Territory, meaning good value for the money and generous portions. To name a few:

Melanka Steak House　　　　　　**$$**　　　　　★
94 Todd Street; ☎ *(08) 8952-2233.*
Dinner 6–9 p.m. seven nights.
Part of the Melanka Lodge; good pub food. Salad bar, buffalo steaks, regular beef steaks and burgers, schnitzels and some seafood. Most items are fried, unfortunately, but the servings are often enormous.

Terrace　　　　　　**$$**　　　　　★★
134 Bath Street; ☎ *(08) 8952-1222.*
Dinner from 6:30 p.m., seven nights a week.
In the Elkira Motel. A mixed menu: French, Italian and Asian. Nice cocktail bar for pre-dinner drinks.

Golden Inn　　　　　　**$**　　　　　★★
9 Undoolya Road; ☎ *(08) 8952-6910.*
Lunch noon–2 p.m. Monday–Saturday; dinner 5–midnight seven days.
Wide range of Chinese and some other Asian dishes. Take-aways.

La Casalinga　　　　　　**$**　　　　　★★
105 Gregory Terrace; ☎ *(08) 8952-4508.*
Dinner 6–10 p.m. seven days; the pizza parlor open from 5 p.m.–1 a.m. seven days.
Italian fare and pizza.

In the Alice Area

There are dozens of tour operators offering trips in the Alice Springs area, everything from tours of town to flights over Ayers Rock and extended safaris in the bush. If you haven't booked ahead, one place to stop is the **Alice Springs Tour Booking Centre** at *74 Todd Street;* ☎ *(08) 8952-6266.* The company has a 24-hour tour booking service for a group of companies offering trips all over the Red Centre. The service includes free hotel pickup.

Ansett Trailways, which offers a number of Red Centre fly/coach packages in the Red Centre, has a couple of Alice Springs-area tours that can be booked in town. The two-day package takes you through some Outback cattle stations, and includes a trip to the Olgas and a sunset stop at The Rock. The next morning, you have enough time to climb Ayers before heading back to the Alice. Rates, depending on where you stay at Ayers Rock Resort, are around A$200 per person, including accommodations and food. *Information: Ansett Trailways, Todd Mall;* ☎ *(08) 8952-2422.* Deluxe Coaches runs a day tour to Ayers Rock and the Olgas for around A$100. The Deluxe office in the Alice is *on Gap Road;* ☎ *(08) 8952-4444.*

If you're more adventurous (and more laden with gilders) you could fly to and over Ayers Rock and the desert. **Alice Springs Air Charter** will fly to Ayers via Palm Valley and Kings Canyon for around A$300-400 per person, including lunch and some ground touring. *Information:* ☎ *(08) 8952-1250 or* ☎ *(08) 8952-5086.* **Skyport** takes the same route for about the same money. *Information;* ☎ *(08) 8952-3059 or* ☎ *(08) 8952-3105.*

You can look down on it all at a slower pace from one of the balloons available in the Alice. Check with **Toddy's Balloon Safaris**, *41 Gap Road, Alice Springs 0870;* ☎ *(08) 8952-1322 or* ☎ *(08) 8952-5999.* A sunrise champagne flight will run you about A$150 for an hour. Toddy's also has week-long trips, ballooning at Ayers Rock and visiting tourist areas near the Alice. The safaris or sunrise trips can be booked ahead through ATS/Sprint.

Two highways going east and west out of town get you to a number of historic sites and territorial or national parks. The **Ross Highway**, going east, is paved almost all the way to the hamlet of Ross River. You pick it up south of town on the way to the airport. Along the route are **Trephina Gorge Nature Park**, with good MacDonnell Ranges scenery, and **Corroboree Rock Conservation Reserve**, an area of significance to the Aboriginals in the area; overnight camping allowed. **N'Dhala Gorge Nature Park**, with Aboriginal rock carvings in the two gorges, requires four-wheel drive.

West of the Alice, on Larapinta Drive, are some of the more popular spots around town. Catch the road by turning west at the intersection of Stott Terrace and the Stuart Highway (look for the K mart). The first biggy is **Simpson's Gap National Park**, an area eroded over 60 million years by river action with a dramatic but small gorge in the cliffs. There are rock wallabies about and the area is filled with ghost gums. It's a popular picnic area. The park (free entry) is open 8 a.m.–8 p.m.

One of the more dramatic places in the Red Centre is about 24 kilometers farther west from the gap: **Standley Chasm**, also carved by river action, has a wonderful walking trail back to gorges cut 100 feet deep into the ocher and yellow rocks. The chasm is owned by the Iwupataka Aboriginal Land Trust. There's a $3 per person entry fee. It has a food kiosk and picnic area. The best time to do the chasm is around noon, when the light is at its best in the gorges; it's mostly shady all the way. The park is open 8 a.m.–5 p.m. A bit farther along are **Serpentine Gorge Nature Park**, more of the same only less, and **Ormiston Gorge and Pound National Park**, a dramatic waterhole where you can cool off with a swim. Overnight camping allowed at both parks. Finally, you come to the end of the non-four-wheel drive road about 80 miles west of the Alice at **Glen Helen Gorge Nature Park**, more river-cut topography with majestic red cliffs. Nearby is the **Glen Helen Homestead**, which has rooms and a pleasant RV park. Doubles are A$70; backpackers, A$10. If interested, you can book through the NT tourism office or by writing the lodge at *P.O. Box 3020, Alice Springs 5750;* ☎ *(08) 8956-7489.*

Other scenic spots, such as **Kings Canyon**, **Finke Gorge National Park** (in which you find the famous **Palm Valley**, where palm trees bloom in the middle of a furnace-blast desert), and the **Redbank Gorge Nature Park**, are for four-wheel drive when things are dry. If you're interested, contact **Brits Rentals** on the Stuart Highway in town. *Information:* ☎ *(08) 8952-8814; toll free 1(800) 331-454.* Again, it's probably a good idea to book them ahead from North America.

Information about all the Alice-area parks, as well as Ayers Rock and the Olgas, is available from the Conservation Commission of Australia offices on Gap Road in town; ☎ *(08) 8950-8211.*

Uluru (Ayers Rock) and Kata Tjuta (The Olgas)

Uluru (Ayers Rock), in Kata Tjuta National Park, is the world's largest monolith and an Aboriginal sacred site.

Make sure you top off with gasoline before you head south toward Ayers Rock—there's no gas for 125 miles between the Alice and Erldunda, where the Lasseter Highway cuts west from the Stuart. There are a couple of stations along the 150-mile stretch between Erldunda and the Rock, but there are lots of other drivers with the same idea. We stopped at a station on the Lasseter once and they were out of gas.

Your first look at the famous rock shows that it's a strange pebble, indeed, sticking up a thousand feet and more into the air, looking like a huge red-orange bagel. The minerals the rock is made of act like an artist's palette, changing colors throughout the day from a light tan to a deep orange as the sun sets. The Olgas and Ayers are made of a sandstone with a rich iron content, so rich the rocks actually rust when they get wet. Because the surrounding landscape is so flat, both formations are striking, and Ayers, particularly, is so strangely beautiful it's easy to understand why people come from around the world to stare.

The rock got its Christian name in 1873 when William Gosse, the first European to see the rock, named it in honor of Sir Henry Ayers, then chief secretary of South Australia and later premier of the state. The Aboriginal people have inhabited the area around the rock for at least 10,000 years. The traditional owners, the Pitjantjantjara, Yunkantjatjara and Ngaanyatjara peoples, call it Uluru, which means "giant pebble," and it has great spiritual significance for them. Several areas of the rock are sacred sites and off-limits to tourists.

Ayers, and the Olga Mountains, about 20 miles west, are basically part of the same geologic formation. They are conglomerate, part of a sandstone formation between 600 million and 700 million years old that was folded and pushed up as part of a mountain chain. Erosion of the range left the three formations that now rise above the desert: Ayers Rock, the Olgas, and nearby Mount Connor. Some geologists say Ayers took the form it has now about 40 million years ago. It is thought that the Olgas, a system of 36 domes spread over an area of about 15 square miles, were once a giant single dome, much larger than Ayers, that eroded into its present form. Ayers is believed to be the tip of a formation that extends at least 6000 meters below ground. There is a slight difference in texture between the Olgas and Ayers, because Ayers is arkosic sandstone, a finer grain than the Olgas. The rangers at the park say the top of Ayers is 348 meters above the surrounding landscape, or 1141 feet.

At first blush, especially from a distance, it looks impossible to climb the thing. From some angles, the cliff faces look vertical. But there is a trail, and it's well used. Between 1931 and 1946, when just getting to the area was an adventure, only 22 people climbed the rock. Now about 300,000 people a year visit, and many of them make the 1.6-kilometer climb.

The route up is on the west face of the rock, a short drive from the ranger station. The first 200 yards are very steep, and for most of that distance, a chain and metal posts have been set into the sandstone so you can pull your-self up. Toward the top, the trail becomes a series of ups and downs as it wanders through the wind-and water-cut mini-canyons. At the end of the trail there is a cairn that has a guest book to record your epic. The trail, while not technically difficult, is very strenuous. In hot weather, you should do the climb early in the morning, and when it's raining, stay off. The normal time for the trip to the top and back down is around two hours, but a crazy New Zealander made it to the top once in 12 minutes. **A word of caution:** a number of people have died climbing Ayers Rock, many from heart attacks, but a few by slipping off the sheer sides. Stick to the trail, and if you have kids along, watch them like a hawk.

The prehistoric looking goanna, found near Uluru (Ayers Rock) can grow to eight feet in length.

In addition to the climb, there are several hikes along or around the base of the rock. Ayers Rock is about six miles in circumference at the base, and a four-hour walk should get you around. The rock itself is about 1.3 square miles in area. There is also a paved road that circles the rock if you want to see it from all sides. If you turn left at the intersection with this road and the road past the ranger station, you'll come to **Mutitjulu**, also known as Maggie Springs, where a trail takes you back to an area at the base of Ayers Rock where there are Aboriginal paintings.

There are daily **ranger walks** around parts of the base. The schedule for these is located on a bulletin board at the parking lot at the base of the climbing trail, or available at the ranger headquarters on the road into Ayers Rock. The rangers operate a small museum at the station with information about the area. Next door is an Aboriginal display area and museum which also has artworks for sale.

NOTE: Taking photographs of the Aboriginals, anywhere in the park, is not allowed. The rangers also stage dune walks around the Ayers area, and a 2.5 hour jaunt across the desert from the ranger station to the rock is escorted by Aboriginal guides.

The most popular spot in the whole park to watch the sun set on Ayers Rock is on the paved road that runs from the resort to the ranger station. You'll see a sign about seven kilometers past the Olgas turnoff that says: *"sunset viewing,"* and near it is a parking lot, usually filled with tour buses and camper vans. Find a spot, get out about 30 rolls of film, and have at it. If you're feeling like a swell, you can hire a limo and liveried chauffeur to get you to the rock on time, complete with champagne and canapes. The price is about A$75 an hour. Call **VIP Chauffeur Cars** ☎ *(08) 8956-2388; FAX (08) 8956-2150* in the resort for details. If you're not the limousine type, but still want to see your rock and eat too, try the bus-dinner trip, which parks you at the sunset viewing area and serves Aussie meals for around A$50 per person. It leaves the Ayers Rock resort around 4:30 p.m. and gets back two hours after sunset. Information: ☎ *(08) 8956-2171*. If you want to fly around the area, you can take a half-hour helicopter tour of the Olgas and Ayers Rock for about A$130 per person.

Kata Tjuta (Olgas) in Northern Territory features 36 domelike rock formations, spectacular scenery and many Aboriginal sacred sites.

The Olgas are higher (some peaks are about 1800 feet high) and spread out. They were discovered by explorer Ernest Giles, who spotted them in 1872 and named them after the then-Queen of Spain. Together with Ayers Rock, the Olgas comprise **Uluru-Kata Tjuta National Park**, about 500 square miles in area. The Aboriginal name for the Olgas is Kata Tjuta, or "Many Heads." The road from the resort to the Olgas is terrible, and unless you're keen on busting the springs of your rental car, take a bus. A number of tours are available.

There are several **hiking trails** in the Olgas, relatively easy but potentially dangerous in hot weather without proper precautions. The most popular trail goes from a parking lot up past Mt. Olga into Olga Gorge; it's about two kilometers to the trail end. A bit more strenuous, but an emotional high is the **Valley of the Winds** walk, about four kilometers, which goes through narrow gorges. In hot weather, the rangers suggest you have a pint of water for every hour you plan to hike. Detailed hiking maps are available at the ranger station.

In addition to its rocky lures, the national park is also recognized as a fine example of an arid-zone Australian ecosystem, which despite a low annual rainfall (7 to 12 inches), supports a large variety of plant and animal life. Some of the animals—70 reptiles, 42 mammals, and some amphibians—are the usual strange critters you expect in Australia. On the one hand, there are *perenties*, the largest lizard in Australia, which can grow to eight feet long. On the other hand, in depressions worn into the top of Ayers Rock, you find shield shrimp, which lay eggs that can lie around for years in the sun waiting for rain so they can hatch.

A valuable lesson for Australians was learned in 1976, when lightning storms started fires that burned more than 75 percent of the vegetation around the park. The ancient Aboriginal practice of starting small fires to burn out brush and other tinder had been stopped at Ayers Rock, but after the fires, it was begun again.

In spring, after the rains, the desert around the area is full of wildflowers, particularly rose dock, a non-Australian plant introduced as ground cover, which is slowly killing off many native species. Old Ayers Rock hands say that one of the best times to visit is during a rainstorm when the waterfalls are full and Ayers is covered with huge streams falling down the sheer sides of the rock.

The Northern Territory Tourist Commission alleges that the Ayers Rock area has the clearest skies in the world, and offers a chance to prove it. The Southern Skies Observatory, operated by the Sydney Observatory, allows day and night use of its facilities, which include three telescopes, video screens and adaptors that allow some models of 35mm cameras to take photos of both the sun and the night sky. During the day, the charge is a modest A$2; evening sessions are about A$10. Check with the Visitors Information Centre adjacent to the Sails in the Desert Hotel. It's open 8 a.m.-9 p.lm. daily. ☎ *(08) 8956-2240.*

NORTHERN TERRITORY

Ayers Rock Resort

Large questions of morality are still being discussed about this A$160-million resort complex near Ayers Rock, the same sort of questions you get discussing the Black Hills with a member of the Oglalla Sioux. But, for better or worse, the resort complex is there and it's an oasis for tourists who want to sweat and strain hiking up the rock or through the Olgas and then come home to a hot shower, tennis or a swim. Counting all the hotel and lodge rooms, plus camper spaces and tent sites, Ayers Rock can accommodate around 5000 tourists at any one time. The resort, which also includes a school, police station, fast-food joints, restaurants, bars and an interpretive center, is laid out in a sand dune area about 18 kilometers from the base of Ayers Rock. There is an airport, served by **Ansett**, **Qantas**, **Kendall** and others, as well as car and moped rentals and a service station.

There are six accommodation choices available:

Sails in the Desert   A$275–450   ★★★★
☎ *(08) 8956-2200; FAX (08) 8956-2018.*
A$275–295 double; suites from A$360–450.
All amenities, including a licensed restaurant, tennis, minibars and a pool, with a range of 235 rooms.

Desert Gardens Hotel   A$225   ★★★
☎ *(08) 8956-2100; FAX (08) 8956-2156.*
Rooms begin around A$225 double.
Around 100 rooms, with a licensed restaurant, pool and the Oasis Bar.

Outback Pioneer Hotel and Lodge   A$20–185   ★
☎ *(08) 8956-2170; FAX (08) 8956-2320.*
Motel units start at A$185 double; lodge cabins start at A$80, dormitory spaces are A$20 per person.
Budget and moderate units in cabins or rooms with fridges, guest laundry, TVs and private baths.

Spinifex Lodge   A$85   ★★
☎ *(08) 8956-2131; FAX (08) 8956-2163.*
Doubles from around A$85.
One-bedroom units with cooking facilities, common laundry.

Emu Walk Apartments   A$200–250   ★★★
☎ *(08) 8956-2100; FAX (08) 8956-2156.*
One-bedrooms from A$200 per room, two-bedrooms from A$250.
One- and two-bedroom units, use of facilities at the Desert Garden, cooking facilities, minimum of three nights.

Ayers Rock Campground   A$10–60   ★★★
Lasseter Highway, ☎ *(08) 8956-2055; FAX (08) 8956-2260.*
Rates start at around A$10 for a tent site; rental RVs around A$60 a night double; powered sites A$25 for two persons.
There is space for 3600 campers, including powered sites, tent sites and areas for bus tour groups. There are also permanent RV units for rent. Five amenity blocks, with showers and laundries.

General information about the resort is available by calling ☎ *(08) 8956-2240.*

VICTORIA

A windsurfing speed record was set at Victoria's Sandy Point.

Victoria had a tough time getting started. Somebody back in the Foreign Office in London, taking note that the French were sniffing around, tried to start a convict colony in 1803 on the Mornington Peninsula at the outlet of Port Phillip Bay, but bad soil and lack of support stopped the effort within a year. Another quarter-century passed before another attempt at colonization was made, this time in 1835 at a spot far inside Port Phillip where John Bateman, a land speculator, found acreage more adaptable to grazing and agriculture. Like the Dutch in Manhattan, he came laden with trinkets and baubles and conned the local aborigines out of 600,000 acres of prime real estate. In 1836, the tiny settlement was named after Lord Melbourne, the English prime minister at the time. It should be noted that the first successful attempts at founding settlements in what would become Victoria were not a result of the penal system. Meanwhile, enterprising explorers and graziers had succeeded in crossing the Blue Mountains in New South Wales and discovered the vast and gentle pastures of what would become northern Victoria. It was the great Gold Rush of 1851, however, that established Victoria and Melbourne as permanent Australian fixtures. The strikes began in New South Wales and worked their way along the topography into what is now Victoria. In September 1851, the biggest field of all was found at Ballarat, a mere 75 miles northwest of Melbourne, and, within seconds, the area was flooded with diggers from all over the world, including a bunch of 49ers fresh from the gold fields in California. While all this activity was going on, the leaders of the Melbourne area had been agitating to create a separate colony from New South Wales, with emphasis on making transportation of prisoners illegal, and, that same year, separation was granted and the new colony named after the Empress Queen back in London. The gold strikes faded, depressions came and went, but the colony had received instant population. By 1860, Melbourne was a city of 600,000 and had become the largest city in the country.

Today, in addition to farming, manufacturing, and industry (Victoria accounts for a full third of the nation's GNP), the state is a popular domestic tourist target, especially the Murray River basin and the ski areas in the Victorian Alps. Victoria is also outlaw country, the Deadwood and Whitehorse of Australia, where bad guys roamed up and down the Hume Highway, which runs across the state and then north to Sydney. The most famous of the bushrangers, of course, was Ned Kelly, Australia's Jesse James. Whole towns up in the northeast part of the state thrive on Kelly-based tourism. Northeast Victoria is also the heart of Victoria's growing wine industry. The Rutherglen area, particularly, is well known for its reds, and the Milawa-Glenrowan district is a major producer of table wines. Some of the country's major producers are in this part of the state, including Lindeman's, Brown Brothers and Seppelt's. *Information about the wine areas all around the state is available from the Victoria Wine Industry Association in Melbourne,* ☎ *(03) 9614-5811.*

Victoria's compact size—only about 85,000 square miles, the smallest of the mainland states—makes for easy touring. Despite its small area, it has some of the most diversified topography in Australia. In the east, along the border with New South Wales, are the rugged Snowy Mountains, and, for

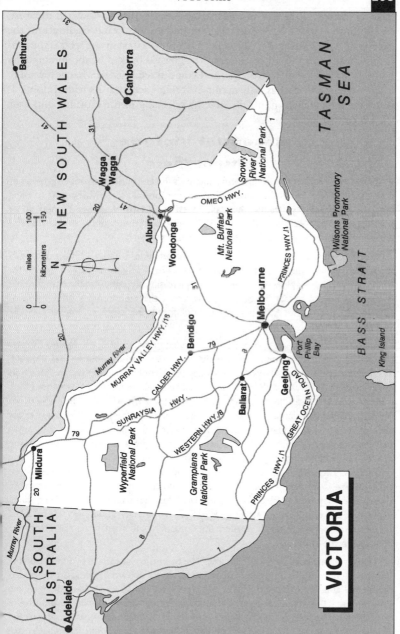

most of the way along that boundary, the mighty Murray flows. In the west, on the border with South Australia, are flat and dry plains leading into the deserts of central Australia. Along the Bass Strait coast in the west is the dramatic Great Ocean Road; in the east, the coast is backed by mountains. The highway system is easy to manage, and you can see most of what you want in a short while; the state is only about 500 miles across at its widest point. If you have the inclination, it's possible to go skiing in the morning and walk the beach that afternoon.

Essential Victoria

Getting There

Air service to Melbourne from North America is direct, usually with one stop either in Queensland or Sydney. All the major airlines serving Australia fly to Melbourne. In addition, the city is served by **Qantas, Kendall**, **Ansett** and **Eastwest** airlines. Without an air pass, expect to pay between A$150 and A$200 one-way from Sydney, around A$225–A$300 from Brisbane, and A$350–A$450 from Cairns.

Melbourne International Airport, located in **Tullamarine**, is about 12 miles outside of town, and cab fares into the city average about A$25. In the latter part of the 1990s, major expansions took place to handle the ever-increasing air traffic into the city (currently about 12 million a year). There is a shuttle service that will drop you off downtown: **Skybus**. The fare is about A$10 per person. Look for the bus every half-hour outside the domestic section of the terminal.

Rail service into Victoria from Sydney is provided on two routes, the **Sydney Express** (which becomes the Melbourne Express the other way) and the **Intercapital Daylight**. The Express operates seven days, leaves Sydney (or Melbourne) at 8 p.m., and arrives in Melbourne (or Sydney) at 8 the next morning. The trains are parked at the stations by 7 p.m., so you can have dinner aboard before you leave if you wish. The Express has sleepers, a buffet car, dining car, and lounge. Without an Austrailpass, the one-way fare is about A$110 plus sleeper fare. The *Daylight* runs through some great scenery on its way between the two rival state capitals. It leaves Sydney at 7:45 a.m., arriving in Melbourne at 8:20 p.m. Fares are about the same as the Express; note that the *Daylight* doesn't run on Sundays. There is also rail service to Canberra and Adelaide. Trains within the state are run by **V/Line**. *Information on interstate service is available from Railways of Australia, 85 Queen Street, ☎ (03) 9608-0811. For service within the state, contact V/Line Travel, Transport House, 589 Collins Street ☎ (03) 9619-1500; reservations, ☎ (03) 13-2232.* Interstate trains leave from the Spencer Street Station; suburban trains leave from the Flinders Street Station.

A variety of **bus lines** service Melbourne. The two main routes from Sydney are on the Princes Highway, which hugs the coast as it turns a circle toward Victoria; the other uses the Newell and Great Western Highways to cut over the Great Dividing Range. The Princes route takes about 18 hours; the mountain route about 16 hours. A third route goes through Canberra on its way between the cities. Without a bus pass, expect to pay around A$50 one way. *Information*: **Greyhound Australia**, *Greyhound Terminal, corner* of Franklin and Swanston streets; ☎ *(03) 9668-2666.* **Deluxe**, *58 Franklin Street;* ☎ *(03) 9663-6144.* **Pioneer Express**, *465 Swanston Street;* ☎ *(03) 9668-2422.* For automobile information, contact the *Royal Automobile Club of Victoria, 230 Collins Street* ☎ *(03) 9650-1522.*

Climate

Outside of the much-maligned Darwin up in the Top End, Melbourne arguably often has the worst weather in urban Australia. Weather wags—probably from Sydney—say the city has four seasons; the only trouble is, they all come the same day. It's usually cooler in the winter (Apr.–Sept.) than Sydney, and hotter in the summer. Statistically, the city receives less rainfall than Sydney, but the problem is, it can come at any moment—few Melbournians leave home without an umbrella, even when the dawn is clear. Summer highs are around 75°; winter lows can get down to near freezing.

Time

Victoria is on Eastern Standard Time, the same as Queensland, Tasmania and New South Wales, putting it 18 hours ahead of San Francisco.

Melbourne

Melbourne is the commercial and manufacturing center of Australia as well as the country's busiest port.

The easiest way to get into a fight in Melbourne is to suggest, however marginally, that Sydney really is the Number One city in Australia. The debate about which of the two Australian biggies is best has been going on almost as long as white Australia has been around, and it's not likely to be settled soon. Sydneysiders look upon their cousins in Melbourne as stuffy, conservative and dull, and caustically point out that the reason the streets in Melbourne are so wide is because they were designed so herds of sheep could pass freely. The folks in Melbourne, on the other hand, think all the citizens of Sydney are flaky extroverts with big mouths and no sense of propriety. Melbourne is also a tad bent out of shape because it remembers when it served as the capital of Australia between 1901 and 1927, before political compromises forced all the bureaucrats to move to Canberra. For visitors, the differences in the two cities are great enough that you miss a big chunk of what makes Australia unique by not seeing them both.

Melbourne (pronounced MEL-burn) is a city of diverse ethnic backgrounds. It has, for example, the third-largest urban Greek population in the world after Athens and Thessaloniki. It's a place of wide-wide avenues, rich stands of Victorian architecture, and a streak of madness when it comes to any form of sport. This is, after all, the home of that most Australian form of athletic insanity, footy-Australian Rules Football. But it is also the home of the richest and most prestigious horse race in the country, the Melbourne Cup. The city's new, international-grade tennis facilities are the site of the Australian Open. Across the Yarra River is the Melbourne Cricket Ground, which also serves as the footy stadium, and is the largest cricket facility in the world, capable of holding 120,000 fans. It served as the main stadium for the 1956 Olympics and every year is the site of a variety of international cricket matches. In 1994, the city became home to the Australian Grand Prix, an international race that was for years held in Adelaide. Adelaide let the race slip through its fingers, and now the noise and big money are seen at Albert Park in Melbourne.

Melbourne, with about 4.1 million people, is also the commercial and manufacturing center of the country, sometimes called the Detroit of Australia because of its motor vehicle plants, refineries and industrial parks, and the city's port is the busiest in the nation. It's also called the Garden City because parks account for about a fifth of the city's acreage. Like San Francisco, it is famous for maintaining a fleet of historic public transit vehicles—in this case, the famous Melbourne trams, which flit like green insects around the downtown area. The city is also home to the company that brews Australia's most famous beer, Foster's.

Around Melbourne

The heart of the city and target of much derision from nondwellers, is the Yarra River, which splits the city in half and flows into Port Phillip Bay. Because of its silt-laden waters, the Yarra is sometimes referred to as the "river which flows upside down," but its muddy waters don't look any worse than the Brisbane River up in Queensland. Most of the city's downtown business district and shopping area are laid out in a grid system north of the river. To the south are the arts complexes and large garden areas. Most of the major hotels are in a 16-square-block area near Parliament House. *It's sometimes almost impossi-*

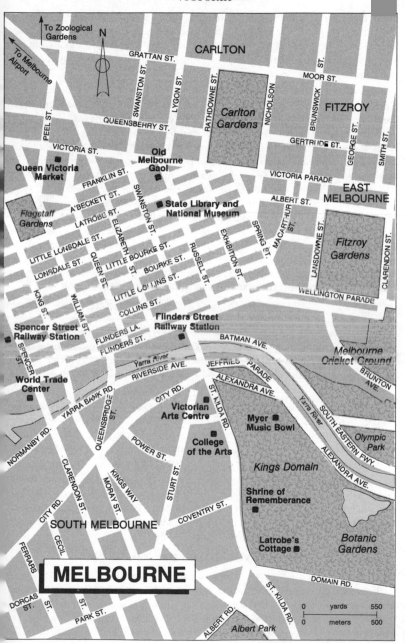

To Zoological Gardens

N

To Melbourne Airport

CARLTON

GRATTAN ST.

SWANSTON ST.

LYGON ST.

RATHDOWNE ST.

NICHOLSON ST.

MOOR ST.

BRUNSWICK ST.

FITZROY

GEORGE ST.

SMITH ST.

Carlton Gardens

PEEL ST.

QUEENSBERRY ST.

GERTRUDE ST.

VICTORIA ST.

Old Melbourne Gaol

VICTORIA PARADE

Queen Victoria Market

FRANKLIN ST.

ALBERT ST.

EAST MELBOURNE

A'BECKETT ST.

SWANSTON ST.

State Library and National Museum

MACARTHUR ST.

LANSDOWNE ST.

Flagstaff Gardens

LATROBE ST.

ELIZABETH ST.

SPRING ST.

Fitzroy Gardens

CLARENDON ST.

LITTLE LONSDALE ST.

QUEEN ST.

LITTLE BOURKE ST.

BOURKE ST.

RUSSELL ST.

EXHIBITION ST.

LONSDALE ST.

KING ST.

WILLIAM ST.

LITTLE COLLINS ST.

WELLINGTON PARADE

COLLINS ST.

SPENCER ST.

Flinders Street Railway Station

FLINDERS LA.

Spencer Street Railway Station

FLINDERS ST.

BATMAN AVE.

Melbourne Cricket Ground

Yarra River

RIVERSIDE AVE.

JEFFRIES PARADE

BRUNTON AVE.

World Trade Center

YARRA BANK RD.

CITY RD.

ALEXANDRA AVE.

Yarra River

SOUTH EASTERN FWY.

NORMANBY RD.

QUEENSBRIDGE ST.

ST. KILDA RD.

Victorian Arts Centre

Myer Music Bowl

Olympic Park

POWER ST.

College of the Arts

ALEXANDRA AVE.

CLARENDON ST.

KINGS WAY

MORAY ST.

STURT ST.

Kings Domain

Shrine of Rememberance

SOUTH MELBOURNE

COVENTRY ST.

Botanic Gardens

FERRARS ST.

CECIL ST.

Latrobe's Cottage

MELBOURNE

DOMAIN RD.

DORCAS ST.

ST.

ST. KILDA RD.

PARK ST.

ALBERT RD.

Albert Park

0   yards   550
0   meters   500

ble to find a place to hang your hat in town during the annual Melbourne Cup race in November; plan ahead. The downtown area is a combination of high-rises and Victorian relics. There is supposed to be a pedestrian mall, like every other city in Australia, but the one in Melbourne (on Bourke Street) is open to trams and if you don't pay attention, you'll get nailed proper.

Many of the finest old Victorians around the city are the result of the Gold Rush, and include such noble works as the carefully restored **Windsor Hotel** (1883), the gaudy **Royal Exhibition Buildings** (1880) and the biggest and best, **Parliament House** (1854). Most of the important old buildings are now protected by the National Trust. The city's two main shopping strands are Collins Street and Bourke Street. **Collins**, once likened to a boulevard in Paris, runs up and down on hills between Spring and Swanston streets and is the site for many of the city's—and the nation's—major financial houses. The northeast end of the street, near Parliament House, was once an area of small exclusive shops; a few remain, but skyscrapers have taken over. **Town Hall** and the **City Square** are at the intersection of Collins and Swanston. Aside from **St. Paul's Cathedral** at the south side of the square, the square is worth a miss, but nearby is the city's most infamous pub, **Young and Jackson's Hotel**, at Number One Swanston Street. The bar is home to one of Australia's most beloved paintings, the naked but demure form of lovely *Chloe*, a work that caused a national uproar when stiff-necks arrived in the city for the 1880 Melbourne Exhibition and just happened to wander by in herds to gawk and then protest. She's upstairs in Chloe's, a bar/cafe in the old hotel. Pretty tame by Playboy standards, but still the center of it all.

Along Collins there are several old buildings of note, including the massive **ANZ Bank Building**, *386 Collins;* the **Melbourne Stock Exchange**, *351 Collins*, open Mon.–Fri. for visitors, and the **Commonwealth Banking Association Building**, *335 Collins*. At the top of the street is the sandstone mass of the **Old Treasury**, built in the 1850s, where most of the gold from the Ballarat fields was stored during the Rush.

Bourke Street, containing the aforementioned mall, is the site of the city's major department stores, including **David Jones, G.J Coles** and **Myer**. The Myer building is reputed to be the largest department store building in the Southern Hemisphere. The mall, which runs between Swanston and Elizabeth streets, is awash with small boutiques as well as big stores. At the Elizabeth Street end is the Melbourne General Post Office.

In addition, there are hundreds of shops and stores along side streets, many of which, just to add to the confusion, are named after the bigger lanes: Little Bourke, Little Collins, Little Russell, etc. Here you can find at least a dozen small shopping arcades including the **Royal Arcade**, (built in the 1870s), where small shops bask in restored elegance in a smaller version of Sydney's Queen Victoria Building.

Other Melbourne Sights

Museums

The Aussies have a peculiar fascination with jails and executions, caused, no doubt, by their colorful penal past. You find restored jails and gallows all over the country, and none finer or more grisly than the **Old Melbourne Gaol**, which has a particularly revolting display of death masks from just-hanged prisoners. In its day (1841–1929), more than 100

The Great Australian Bight

Melbourne's Princess Theatre has been beautifully restored.

prisoners were executed in the jail. The star of the show is Ned Kelly, who was hanged here in November 1880. The immortal bushranger's famous bullet-dented suit of armor is here, as are the gallows they used to send him to his reward. There are also a few restored cells so you can see how prisoners were housed. The museum, at the corner of Franklin and Russell streets, is open daily 9:30 a.m.–4:30 p.m., admission charge about A$6.50. ☎ *(03) 9663-7228; FAX (03) 9639-0119.*

Downtown, the **Museum of Victoria** and **State Library** complex stretches about a block between Swanston and Russell streets facing La Trobe Street. Access to the museum, *328 Swanston Street Walk,* is from Russell Street, the **Science Museum Section** from Swanston. The complex houses a rich stew of Australiana, from Aboriginal weapons to a stuffed racehorse. The complex is open 10 a.m. 5 p.m. daily; no admission charge. ☎ *(03) 9669-9888.*

The Chinese who came to Australia to work or to hunt for gold had about the same experience as their brothers and sisters who went to North America at about the same time, and the persecution, racial bigotry and brutality shown to them in Australia are displayed with no holds barred at the **Museum of Chinese Australian History** in the heart of Melbourne's Chinatown. The museum is open Sunday–Friday 10 a.m. 4:30 p.m.; noon–5 p.m. Saturdays. The museum is at *22 Cohen Place off Little Bourke Street* ☎ *(03) 9662-2888.*

The Arts Scene

The cultural heart of the city is a complex of three buildings on South Kilda Road on the south side of the Yarra River. Here are found the **Melbourne Concert Hall**, the **National Gallery**, a **theater complex** and the **Performing Arts Museum**. The gallery houses some of the finest Australian art in the country, everything from Victorian landscapes to Aboriginal works less than a decade old. It also has a formidable display of foreign works, including Picasso and Durer and a good selection of pre-Colombian and Asian art. The gallery is open daily, admission about A$6; free on Mondays. Guided tours of the whole complex, called the **Victorian Arts Centre**, are available daily for A$8; backstage tours on Sundays are A$12. In the complex are several restaurants, gift shops, facilities for those with disabilities and ticketing information. ☎ *(03) 9281-8152 or (03) 9281-8000.*

The theaters in the complex offer performances by the **Australian Ballet**, the **Australian Opera**, the **Victorian State Opera** and the **Melbourne Theatre Company**. The concert hall is the home of the **Melbourne Symphony Orchestra**. The arts complex is immediately recognizable because of the tall spire that sits on top of the theater building. Detractors say it looks like a TV tower; admirers, that it soars into the air as a symbol of artistic freedom. Whatever. Ticketing information: the Theatres Box Office, located in the theater complex between the National Gallery and the Concert Hall, is open 9 a.m.–9 p.m. Monday–Saturday. ☎ *(03) 9684-8484 or (03) 11-566; FAX (03) 9682-8282.*

Gardens

As noted, a big chunk of Melbourne is green, with large and well-tended parks on both sides of the Yarra. On the north side near downtown, are the **Carlton Gardens**, the **Flagstaff Gardens**, the **Fitzroy Gardens** and the **Treasury Gardens**.

Fielding

AUSTRALIA

BEST OF MELBOURNE

To Bendigo and Swan Hill

Hanging Rock

Mt. Macedon

Melbourne is a city bursting at the seams with myriad attractions. Within a two hour drive of the city are majestic ranges, wineries, forests, islands, bays and peninsulas.

Ballarat

This gold-rush city built in the 1850's offers a fun look back at a chapter in Australia's history.

Yarra River

The Yarra's meandering course takes it many miles to the northeast into the valley. Bicycle and hiking tracks, parks and reserves are found all along its course.

Macedon Ranges

Mt. Macedon has been a summer retreat since the 19th century. At Hanging Rock you can climb a 300-million year old rock .

VICTORIA ST.

ST. KILDA RD.

LA TROBE STREET

FINDERS ST.

Performing Arts Center

Melbourne is the performing arts capital of Australia whose acclaimed Arts Centre has a spectacular interior.

YARRA RIVER

SWAN ST.

Cario Bay

Geelong

Royal Botanic Gardens

These world-renowned gardens contain more than 60,000 plant species spread over 100 acres.

Point Nepean National Park

Torquay

Great Ocean Road

Stretching from Torquay to Warrnambool and beyond to Victoria's western border, this scenic drive is steeped in history and dotted with villages, forests, lighthouses and other attractions.

Lorne

GREAT OCEAN ROAD

The Surf Coast

Geelong is the gateway to the Surf Coast and a spectacular coastal drive. Surfing, swimming, sailboarding, and a national surfing museum are just a few of the attractions here. Anglesea's golf course has kangaroos and wallabies bounding around the golfers.

VICTORIA

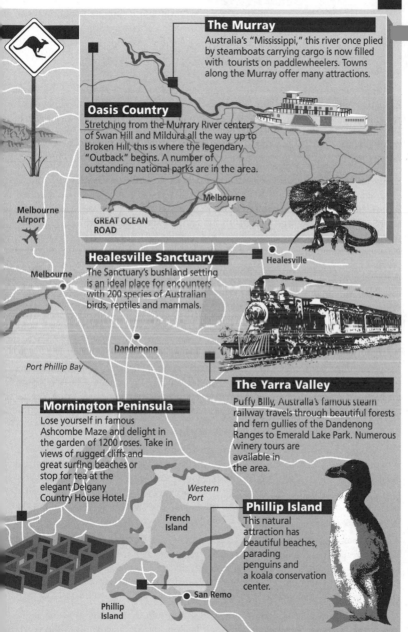

The Murray

Australia's "Mississippi," this river once plied by steamboats carrying cargo is now filled with tourists on paddlewheelers. Towns along the Murray offer many attractions.

Oasis Country

Stretching from the Murrary River centers of Swan Hill and Mildura all the way up to Broken Hill, this is where the legendary "Outback" begins. A number of outstanding national parks are in the area.

Melbourne

GREAT OCEAN ROAD

Melbourne Airport

Melbourne

Healesville Sanctuary

The Sanctuary's bushland setting is an ideal place for encounters with 200 species of Australian birds, reptiles and mammals.

Healesville

Dandenong

Port Phillip Bay

The Yarra Valley

Puffy Billy, Australia's famous steam railway travels through beautiful forests and fern gullies of the Dandenong Ranges to Emerald Lake Park. Numerous winery tours are available in the area.

Mornington Peninsula

Lose yourself in famous Ashcombe Maze and delight in the garden of 1200 roses. Take in views of rugged cliffs and great surfing beaches or stop for tea at the elegant Delgany Country House Hotel.

Western Port

French Island

Phillip Island

This natural attraction has beautiful beaches, parading penguins and a koala conservation center.

Phillip Island

San Remo

In the Fitzroy Gardens northeast of the downtown grid is **Captain Cook's Cottage**, hauled board by board from its home in Yorkshire by a public-spirited Melbournian in 1934. Take a look, but know that it was the home of the bold explorer's parents and he apparently never lived in it. The house is open 9 a.m.–5 p.m. daily; admission about A$2; ☎ *(03) 9419-4677.*

At the center of the Carlton Gardens, northwest of Parliament House, are the **Royal Exhibition Buildings**, a huge fluffy Victorian complex opened in 1880 and still used as a convention and trade show area. Part of the complex was used by the Victorian Parliament after it moved out when its quarters were taken over by the federal government before the capital was moved to Canberra. Tours by appointment. Information: ☎ *(03) 9270-5000.*

The major parkland in the city is the **Kings Domain-Royal Botanic Gardens** area on the south shore of the river. In all, the area is about 600 acres of huge lawns, flowerbeds, and recreation facilities. You can rent a **bicycle** near the Botanic Gardens and check out the six-mile **Yarra River Bikeway**. There is also an outdoor **amphitheater**, which is used as an ice rink in the winter. In the center of the Domain is the **La Trobe Cottage**, the state's first government building. ☎ *(03) 9654-5528.* The Botanic Gardens have around 12,000 species of plants, plus gardens and lakes with at least 50 species of birds. The gardens are open from sunrise to sunset daily; free guided tours are available leaving from the Herbarium Building (corner Birdwood and Dallas Brooks Drive) at 11 a.m. and 1 p.m. Tuesday–Friday and Sunday. ☎ *(03) 9655-2300.*

The major **sports activity** in Melbourne takes place in two parks on the north bank of the river opposite the Kings Domain: **Yarra Park**, which houses several cricket fields including the immense **Melbourne Cricket Ground**, and **Olympic Park**, with the **Melbourne Indoor Sports and Entertainment Centre**, and the **National Tennis Centre**. There are a couple of **sports museums** at the cricket grounds, open from 10 a.m.–4 p.m. daily. The field is open for a look if no games are on; tours available for A$7 every hour staring at 10 a.m.–3 p.m. non-event days. ☎ *(03) 9654-8922 or (03) 9657-8864; FAX (03) 9654-1387.*

More Sights

The largest bazaar in town (and maybe the country) is the **Queen Victoria Market** at the corner of Elizabeth and Victoria streets. It's awash in food and fish vendors, clothing stalls, antiques. The markets open at 6 a.m. Monday–Saturday, at 9 a.m. Sundays. Closing hours vary; late night is Friday until 6 p.m. It's worth a stroll just to see half of Victoria walking around. There are a few coffee houses and small cafes scattered around the periphery. ☎ *(03) 9658-9600 or (03) 9658-9601.*

The **Greek area** of town is centered around Lonsdale Street between Swanston and Russell streets. In the summer, it's outdoor eating time at a variety of cafes and restaurants with typical Greek fare. **Chinatown**, as mentioned, is on Little Bourke Street and is connected to the Greek quarter at Heffernan Lane. In addition to lots of first-class restaurants, there are also a number of Chinese grocers and artisans doing business.

The Polly Woodside, an 1885 commercial sailing ship, is the main attraction at the **Melbourne Maritime Museum** on the south bank of the Yarra across from the World

Trade Centre. The ship and museum are open weekdays 10 a.m.–4 p.m., weekends 10 a.m.–5 p.m. Admission is A$6. ☎ *(03) 9699-9760.*

Melbourne maintains a fleet of trams that help residents and tourists get around the city.

The largest casino in Australia is being completed in Melbourne. It started life in the World Trade Centre complex on the city side of the Yarra, and is in the process of occupying new digs in a large complex across the river. Eventually, the new casino complex will operate 24 hours and will have a large hotel. ☎ *(03) 9685-4200.*

The Essential Melbourne

Information

In Melbourne, the **Victoria Tourism Commission's** offices (it's called Victours in Australia) are located in *Building D of the World Trade Centre, corner of Flinders and Spencer streets;* ☎ *(03) 9619-9444.* Also check the **Melbourne Tourism Authority**, with an office on the 5th floor, *114 Flinders Street* ☎ *(03) 9654-2288.* Tourist information booths are located in **City Square**, corner Swanston Walk and Collins, open 9 a.m.–5 p.m. Monday-Thursday, 9 a.m.–7 p.m. Friday, 10 a.m.–4 p.m. Saturday, 11 a.m.–4 p.m. Sunday; **Bourke Street Mall**, corner Bourke Street and Swanston Walk, same hours; and in the **Rialto Towers Plaza**, *525 Collins Street*, weekly 11 a.m.–6 p.m. There is another booth at the international arrival hall at the airport. Budget travelers can check with the **Youth Hostels Association of Victoria**, *122 Flinders Street* ☎ *(03) 9654-5422.* There are several offices of the **Royal Automobile Club of Victoria** in the city, including one at *230 Collins.*

Getting Around

The historic **trams** really are the best way to get around Melbourne, and the ticket cost of around A$2.10 (depending on destination and how many zones you pass) also lets you ride trains, subways and buses operated by the city's transport service, the Met. The basic fare applies for a two-hour period; other tickets are available for longer periods. If you plan to ride a lot, buy a daily ticket for A$4.10 that allows travel on any Met service within the city center and near environs. Met information maps are available from the Metropolitan Transit Authority bus terminals, train stations and tram depots. The City Met Shop is at *103 Elizabeth Street. Information on transportation schedules is available by calling* ☎ *(03) 9613-1638.* Handicapped services are available on the Met; information ☎ *(03) 9610-7482 or (03) 9619-2300.*

There are two ways to get a quick tour of the city. By bus, the **Melbourne City Explorer** leaves the Flinders Street Railway Station every hour with stops at 18 major sites around town, including the Old Gaol, Captain Cook's Cottage, the Polly Woodside and the Victorian Arts Centre. A day ticket is A$15 per adult; purchase it from the driver. Hours 10 a.m.–3 p.m.

Free, and a chance to try out the city's famous trams, is the **City Circle**, a tram service going both ways around the city in a big circle. The trams interconnect with other Met services, and run about every 10 minutes. Most of the major city center attractions are within walking distance of a City Circle stop. The trams (some dating back to 1936) run daily 10 a.m.–6 p.m. Information available at the Met Shop (see above) or from the public transport information number: ☎ *(03) 13-1638.*

Telephones

The area code for the Melbourne area is *(03).*

Shopping

Normal shopping hours in the city are 8:30 a.m.–5:30 p.m. Monday–Wednesday; 8:30 a.m.–9 p.m. Thursday and Friday; and 8:30 a.m.–5 p.m. Saturday.

In addition to the large department stores and arcades already mentioned, you might want to look at these shops:

The **Opal Mine**, *121 Bourke Street*, for jewelry made from opals and other Aussie gems, prices moderate to astounding; the **Aboriginal Artists Gallery**, *12 Liverpool Street*; the **Meat Market Craft Centre**, *42 Courtney Street, North Melbourne*, for crafts in progress (also has a store at the departure lounge of the international airport), and the **Victorian Tapestry Workshop**, *260 South Melbourne*, for internationally recognized weavings. (Some of the works have sold for A$400,000.)

Some of the city's more upscale fashion outlets are in South Yarra, where prices are high and so is quality. Toorak Road, which runs through South Yarra and Toorak (also on tram lines) is sort of an antipodean Rodeo Drive in spots, a lot longer but with the right mix of fancy stores and expensive cars. Elegant restaurants are on hand, as well.

Where to Stay

Our favorite hotel in all Australia is located in Melbourne, the grand and elegant **Windsor**. The Victorian style and grace of this hotel, especially the excruciating elegance of the Grand Dining Room, puts the Windsor in a class all by itself. (There are those who think the Old Lady fell a few grades in 1995 when the Hard Rock Cafe was created on the ground floor of one corner of the old building.) Anyway, the Windsor is not the only great hotel in town; we put the **Le Meridien** second. They are worlds apart in tone and atmosphere, but each in its own way is a wonderful experience.

Part of the charm of the city's central hotel district is the tree-lined sidewalks and broad boulevards, always compared to Paris (close, but no cigar), but offering a more genteel atmosphere than most of Sydney and all of Adelaide. If you don't feel like plunking down $A800 a night for a butler-serviced suite at the Windsor, there are digs for all pocket-books.

Windsor, The   **A$320–1500**   ★★★★★

103 Spring Street; ☎ *(03) 9653-0653; FAX (03) 9654-5183.*
Regular doubles start at $A320; small suites $A600; or the Royal Suite (private dining room with butler service, separate lounge, festooned with works of art), about $A1500.
The Grand Old Lady of Spring Street, as it's known, was built in 1883 and has been completely refurbished and gussied up, from the top of its twin towers to its elegant lobby. You are greeted by a top-hatted doorman (last time it was James of the Windsor), and the service goes uphill from there. It's near parks and Parliament House, and the whole thing is part of the National Trust. The pride of the hotel is its suites (there are 20), furnished in Victorian style and fitted with antiques. The other rooms, more modern, are still excellent. The Grand Dining Hall is right out of a movie, all chandeliers and thick carpeting, orchestral trio, silver service and tuxedo-attired waiters. It is, of course, very expensive. There are also a more casual cafe and the Windsor Lounge where you can have morning or afternoon tea (cucumber sandwiches and such). Truly one of the premier hotels in the world.

Le Meridien   A$275–440   ★★★★

495 Collins Street; *(03) 9620-9111; FAX (03) 9614-1219.*
Doubles at the hotel from A$275; suites from A$440.

The hotel complex is an excellent example of what a good architect can do. Half of it is an old Victorian building; half is modern, but blended in so you can't really tell them apart. Between the old and new wings is a vast, 10-story atrium, overlooked by the hotel room balconies. The atrium holds **Cafe Rialto**, a popular garden-like dining and bar area. The **Chandelier Room**, which is one of the best restaurants in the city, has a business lunch from noon–3 p.m. Monday–Friday (about A$50); dinner from 7–10:30 p.m. Monday–Saturday (jacket and tie required).

Hilton on the Park   A$245–1125   ★★★★

192 Wellington Parade, East Melbourne; *(03) 9419-3311.*
Doubles A$245–395; suites A$555–1125.

East of downtown near the Fitzroy Gardens and the cricket grounds. Glass and marble, antiques everywhere. Several restaurants, including the Gallery Cafe, which has a nifty Sunday brunch. Pool, sauna, spa, handicapped facilities, parking.

Grand Hyatt on Collins   A$330–1800   ★★★★

123 Collins Street; *(03) 9657-1234.*
Doubles from A$330; Regency Club from A$400; suites from A$620–1800.

Huge marble foyer, lots of art, to us a discordant art deco-flavor, pink lit ceilings, sterile feel. Collins Chase is an atrium-like complex of bars and international food outlets. The rooms have marble-top desks, mini bars and the bathrooms are all marble and mirrors; great views. The Regency Club floor has guest lounge, free breakfast, evening cocktails and snacks; comes with a butler and concierge. The hotel has two restaurants, bar, nightclub, health center including a golf driving range, tennis courts, sauna, pool, business center, kosher kitchen, and parking.

Regent of Melbourne, The   A$240–1500   ★★★★

25 Collins Street; *(03) 9653-0000; FAX (03) 9650-4261.*
Doubles A$240–285; suites A$295–1500.

North end of Collins near Parliament, occupying part of the 50-story Collins Tower—soaring interior, atrium lounge. Health center, two restaurants including **Le Restaurant**, one of the best in town, and the **Black Swan** bar. Rooms have original art, great views, fresh fruit and flowers, marble bathrooms. Pool, tennis, business center.

Rockman's Regency   A$300–850   ★★★

Corner of Exhibition and Lonsdale streets; 🕾 *(03) 9662-3900; FAX (03) 9663-4297.*
Doubles A$300–315; suites A$400–850.

Smaller luxury hotel; spacious rooms with separate dressing rooms, movie library, mini-bars, umbrellas (it's Melbourne, remember). Also one- and two-bedroom apartments and suites with spas. The restaurant—**Kabels**—has won awards as one of the city's best. Pool, spa, sauna, health center, free valet parking.

Welcome Inn   A$110–190   ★★★

265-281 Little Bourke Street; 🕾 *(03) 9639-0555; FAX (03) 9639-1179.*
Rooms at the Welcome go for A$110–130 double; at the Swanston, A$125–150; suites A$190.

We like this one because of its location, almost on top of Chinatown and several major shopping centers. The rooms are pretty standard, and the tour groups going through turn the lobby into a zoo, but it makes getting around downtown very easy. It's connected to another All Seasons hotel, the **Swanston**, which acts like a twin sister and has facilities such as a swimming pool that are used by guests in both hotels. Between the two, there are two restaurants, two bars, a cafe and an Asian food court.

Centra Melbourne on the Yarra   A$110–580   ★★★

Corner of Flinders and Spencer Sts.; ☎ *(03) 9629-5111; FAX (03) 9629-5624.*
Doubles A$110–205; suites A$250–580.

Situated in the World Trade Centre, the city's new and ponderous convention complex that is also the temporary location of the Crown Casino. The hotel is modernistic, sterile, about as far from the grace of the Windsor as possible; still it's popular. Two restaurants, two bars, business facilities, outdoor heated pool, gym and three nonsmoking floors. Rooms have minibars, hair dryers, irons.

Country Comfort Old Melbourne Hotel   A$110–250   ★★

5-17 Flemington Road, North Melbourne; ☎ *(03) 9329 9344.*
Doubles A$110–135; suites A$200–250.

Mock-English building near the University of Melbourne. Restaurant and bistro bar; pool, parking, mini bars.

Melbourne Airport Travelodge   A$100–375   ★★

1 Centre Road; ☎ *(03) 9338-2322.*
Doubles A$100–175; suites $A375.

Opposite the international terminal, 20 kilometers northwest of the city. Restaurant, pool, courtesy airport van.

St. Kilda Road Travelodge   A$80–200   ★★

Corner of Park Street and Kilda Road, South Melbourne; ☎ *(03) 9699-4833; FAX (03) 9690-1603.*
Doubles A$80–200.

Near Kings Domain and a tram ride to downtown. Restaurant/bar, pool.

New Chateau Hotel   A$105   ★★

131 Lonsdale Street, Melbourne 3000; ☎ *(03) 9663-3161; FAX (03) 9662-3479.*
Rates start around $A105.

Near the Greek-Lebanese restaurant quarter and Chinatown. Restaurant, bar, pool, sauna, mini-bars, parking.

Magnolia Court Boutique Hotel   A$100–200   ★★

101 Powlett Street, East Melbourne 3002; ☎ *(03) 6419-4222.*
Rates start around $A100–200 double; suites A$145.

Another boutique hotel, not far from Fitzroy Gardens. Spa, cooking facilities.

Townhouse, The   A$130–200   ★★

701 Swanston Street, Carlton; ☎ *(03) 9347-7811.*
Doubles A$130–150; suites from A$200.

Close to the university, green and leafy residential area northwest of the city center; on tram lines. Sauna, pool, barbecue, handicapped facilities.

VICTORIA

Astoria City Travel Inn   **A$80**   ★

288 Spencer Street; *(03) 9670-6801.*
Doubles A$80.

Near the Spencer Street railway station. Restaurant, pool, sauna, barbecue area, limited parking.

Where to Eat

Stephanie's   **$$$**   ★★★★★

405 Tooranga Road Hawthorn East; ☎ *(03) 9822-8944; FAX (03) 9822-6352.*
Lunch Tuesday, Friday and Sunday; dinner Tuesday–Saturday.

Housed in a National Trust building east of the city center, this is probably the best place in town. The changing menu concentrates on fresh Australian foods cooked in a French style. Elegant dining room, good service.

Mietta's of Melbourne   **$$$**   ★★★★

7 Alfred Place; ☎ *(03) 9654-2366.*
Lunch and dinner seven days.

Always one of the city's finest, with the emphasis on French-style fish and native game. Excellent service. Downstairs in the two-story facility you can get a two-course set lunch for a reasonable price.

Colonial Tram Car Restaurant   **$$$**   ★★★

Level One, 319 Clarendon Street, South Melbourne. ☎ *(03) 9696-4000; FAX (03) 9696-3787.*
Lunch 1–3 p.m.; early dinner, 5:45–7:15 p.m., dinner 8:35–11:30 p.m. Dinners run about A$50 per person, higher on weekends.

In a city of tram cars, the best of the lot because it's a restaurant. The tram, built in 1927, is burgundy on the outside, gleaming brass and velvet on the interior. It's white tablecloth, silver-setting evening dining, with one-way glass so the slobs can't watch you eat your seafood en cocotte Matthew Flinders or tenderloin of beef Sherwood. All food is prepared aboard the tram by the chef. Reservations are necessary to book times and days. The whole thing is stabilized, so your wine doesn't end up in your lap.

Vivaldi   **$$**   ★★★

45 Collins Street; ☎ *(03) 9650-3630.*
Lunch 11:30–3 p.m. Monday–Friday; dinner 6–11 p.m. Monday–Saturday.

Dandy little Italian cafe, specializing in fresh pasta seafood dishes. Casual atmosphere, located near the Treasury Gardens.

Fortuna Village   **$$**   ★★★

235 Little Bourke Street; ☎ *(03) 9663-3044.*
Lunch noon–3, Sunday–Friday; dinner 5:30–11 p.m. seven days.

Award winner offering Chinese specialties. Popular at lunch with dim sum offerings.

Westlake   **$$**   ★★

189 Little Bourke ☎ *(03) 9663-4265.*

Another good choice. Right next door to the Fortuna Village.

Sawasdee Restaurant   **$$**   ★★

139 Little Bourke Street; ☎ *(03) 9663-4052.*

Lunch noon–2:30 Monday–Friday; dinner from 6 p.m.; seven nights. Music Wednesday–Sunday nights.

Thai cuisine, winner of best ethnic restaurant awards. Some seating in small booths with Thai-style roofs. Chili prawns, noodles, seafood. Thai-style buffet from noon-3 p.m. Sundays.

Charles Dickens Tavern $$ ★★★

290 Collins Street (between Swanston Walk and Elizabeth Street). *(03) 9654-1821. Open seven days; lunch at the Pickwick Room from noon–3 p.m., dinner from 5:30 p.m. The pub portion opens at 10 a.m., stays open late.*

Everybody's favorite watering hole in downtown Melbourne; it's one of the few eateries marked on the official tour maps of the city. The pub itself has daily specials in addition to standard blackboard offerings, and the Pickwick Room restaurant has an extensive menu with daily specials. Make sure you get into the place before 12:30 p.m., otherwise you'll be hip deep in suits as the offices nearby empty.

Tsindos $$ ★★

197 Lonsdale Street; *(03) 9663-3194. Lunch Monday-Friday; dinner from 6 p.m. Monday–Saturday.*

Greek fare, specializing in fresh fish. Live Greek music Friday and Saturday nights. Two floors, BYO and licensed. Very good food, friendly service, a good bet.

Copperwood $$ ★★

318 Lygon Street, Carlton; *(03) 9347-1799. Lunch and dinner seven days.*

Restaurant or bistro-style dining. Restaurant is seafood and steaks; bistro Italian and French. Dancing on Friday and Saturday nights.

Pancake Parlor $ ★

Three locations, including Centrepoint basement of the Bourke Street Mall; *(03) 9654-1893. BYO. Open early to late, seven days a week.*

Family restaurant. Pancakes and crepes, excellent coffee.

Stalactities $ ★

Corner of Lonsdale and Russell Sts.; ☎ *(03) 9663-3316.*

Open 24 hours; specializes in Greek and Mediterranean food. Take-aways. BYO and licensed.

Beyond Melbourne

The Blue Dandenongs

When Sidneysiders want to get away from it all and breathe some fresh air, they head for the Blue Mountains, which can be seen from the city's skyscrapers on a clear day. When Melbournians have the same urge, they turn to the Dandenong Ranges, a long hop and a short skip from the city center. The low, forested ranges, the highest of which is Mt. Dandenong at around 2000 feet, are only about 30 miles southeast of the city. The area is easily reached by getting onto Toorak Road, which in turn becomes Burwood Road and leads up into the forests.

There are several sections of public lands in the area, including **Ferntree Gully National Park**, the **Mt. Dandenong Forest Reserve**, and several state forests. The mountains were a retreat for Melbourne's rich, and many of their old mansions and cottages have been converted into restaurants and guest houses. One of the more popular spots is at the top of Mt. Dandenong, where there is a **restaurant** with splendid nighttime views of the metropolitan area. Another popular attraction is **Puffing Billy**, a restored narrow gauge steam train that runs from Belgrave to Emerald through about eight miles of thick forest. A complete round trip takes about two hours and costs about A$15. ☎ *(03) 9754-6800.*

Other spots to see in the Dandenongs are the **National Rhododendron Gardens** in Olinda, part of the Olinda State Forest, admission about A$5, and the **Healesville Sanctuary**, which has an excellent collection of Aussie animals including wombats, platypuses, kangaroos, wallabies and the elusive lyrebird. In 1944, the staff at the reserve was able to breed platypuses in captivity for the first time. If your visit to Australia and Melbourne is brief, make this a definite stop. Open daily 9 a.m.–5 p.m. Admission charge about A$12. *Information:* ☎ *(03) 5962-4022.*

The Mornington Peninsula

The beaches around Melbourne cannot really compare to those in Sydney or the coast of Queensland, but they are very popular with city folks. The most popular seaside area is the Mornington Peninsula, which forms the eastern cusp of Port Phillip Bay starting about 25 miles from the city. From Frankston, a series of small resort areas and beaches run along the bay to the tip of the peninsula at Portsea. The beaches are mostly calm water and are very crowded in the summer; at Portsea, there is a surfing beach. Of note on the bay side is Sorrento, where the 1803 expedition settled. There are more beaches, rockier and wilder, on the ocean side of the peninsula along Cape Schanck Coastal Park. The oceanside beaches can be dangerous—it was at Cheviot Beach, on the tip of the peninsula, where Prime Minister Harold Holt was drowned in 1967. A series of small roads lead from the bay coastal road (the Nepean Highway) to the park. There are also a number of beaches on the northeastern side of the peninsula. It is from Westernport, on the Westernport Bay side of the peninsula, that you catch a ferry to go to Phillip Island.

The Fairy Penguins

Undeniably one of the major tourist attractions in the Melbourne area is the nightly parade of foot-high fairy penguins that live on Phillip Island. The birds *(Eudyptula minor)* spend their days fishing in the Bass Strait, then come home nightly to their colony at **Summerland Beach** on the island's southwest tip. You can watch the penguins struggle out of the surf at dusk from a fenced-off area for about A$5 per person. The penguin parade is included on many bus tours run from Melbourne; an average cost of the trip out from the city is around A$60 per person. Information is available from the Victours office in the city or call ☎ *(03) 5956-8691; FAX (03) 5956-8394.* The island also has a large colony of seals, and there are koalas snoozing in trees at the **Koala Conservation Centre** at Fiveways on Philip Island Tourist Road; open 10 a.m.–sunset, admission A$2.50. The seal colony is at a spot called the Nobbies, an area of huge cliffs and enormous swells coming in from the ocean. In fact, the entire island is a hiking paradise and worth more than a penguin visit. Note, however, that it's very popular, with daytrippers by the thousands cramming in on summer weekends. The ferry trip across to the island is about A$5 one way. *Information:* ☎ *(03) 5952-1014.*

Phillip Island's foot-high Fairy Penguins fish the Bass Strait during the day and parade at dusk on Summerland Beach.

Around Victoria

The Great Ocean Highway

One of the most photogenic stretches of ocean highway in the world—for us Northern Californians, this is tough to admit—runs for 180 gorgeous miles along Victoria's south-west coast. Called the Great Ocean Highway, it begins at Torquay, runs southwest to Cape Otway, and then northeast to Peterborough. Torquay is near Victoria's second largest city, Geelong, which sits on the western edge of Port Phillip Bay about 50 miles southwest of Melbourne.

Between Torqay and Cape Otway, the coast is backed by the Otway Ranges and the road passes through miles of Bass Strait surfing beaches. The **Australian Surfing Championships**, for example, are held each year at Bell Beach next to Torquay. There are a number of small resort villages along this stretch, many with old seaside buildings and safe swimming beaches. **Lorne** is the largest of the resort towns and was a popular watering hole even before the road was completed in 1932. Lorne was almost destroyed in the Ash Wednesday bushfire in 1983. As you come into town from the north, you can still see evidence of the monster fire, which destroyed at least 2000 homes in the area and forced Lorne to be evacuated. Past Lorne, the road starts making its way along steep cliffs and the scenery is poetry-inspiring. At **Kennett River**, there is a turnoff to a trail that takes you on a 1.5-kilometer hike into a gorge with magnificent Victorian blue gums.

Australia's surfing championships are held each year at Bell Beach next to Torquay in Victoria.

The last of the good beaches is at the resort town of **Apollo Bay**. Here the road leaves the sea and goes inland through the lush, fern-ridden forests of **Otway National Park**. The park, filled with ringtail possums, black-tailed wallabies, and satin bowerbirds, is also a treasure house of plant species, including many orchid varieties and huge tree ferns. There is an eight-mile unpaved road that leads to a lighthouse perched on 300-foot cliffs. The lighthouse has been there since 1848 in an attempt (often vain) to keep ships from the hostile shore. The stretch of shore from the lighthouse northwest is known as the **Shipwreck Coast**; more than 1000 vessels have met their doom there. The lighthouse is open Tues. and Thurs. 10 a.m.–noon and 2 p.m.–4 p.m; A$5 admission. *Information:* ☎ *(03) 5237-9240.* The park has several camping areas, 60 kilometers of towering coastline, and many hiking trails. *Information about the park: National Parks Service, Geelong-Otway District, 28 Murray Street, Colac, Victoria 3250;* ☎ *(03) 5231-3833. Or ranger in charge, Apollo Bay,* ☎ *(03) 5231-3833.*

As the road turns northwest, it comes to some of the most dramatic scenery on the entire continent, a stretch of seastacks and arches and rugged cliffs carved by ocean waves smashing into the limestone formations after roaring unimpeded 15,000 miles from Cape Horn. Australia's second-most famous rock formation (after Ayers Rock) is here: the **12 Apostles**, just one group of sea sculptures among many. The Apostles are contained in **Port Campbell National Park**, a 20-mile strip along the coast that is slowly disappearing as the waves wear away the limestone. In the park is the site of the 1878 wreck of the immigrant ship Loch Ard, which sank with the loss of 52 lives. There are a number of turn-offs that take you to the more breathtaking vistas. There is camping in the park. The road leaves the coast soon after the park. At Warrnambool, about 40 miles from the park, is the **Flagstaff Hill Maritime Museum**, a recreated 19th-century port that has a museum with displays on the dangers of the Shipwreck Coast, including artifacts salvaged from the Loch Ard. It's open 9:30 a.m.–4:30 p.m.; admission A$9.

Wilson's Promontory National Park

The Prom, as it's known, is as far south as you can go on the Australian mainland, and is the most popular national park in Victoria and one of the top draws in the nation. More than 100,000 people a year come to enjoy the park's bushwalking trails, camping facilities, huge flocks of birds, and good beaches. The park is basically 360 square miles of granite peaks and eucalypt forests, and lies about 150 miles southeast of Melbourne. The park area once was part of the land bridge across the Bass Strait to Tasmania. The park has several tall peaks, the highest being **Mt. Latrobe** at about 2500 feet.

Among the most popular of the park's animals are rainbow lorikeets and the noisy rosellas. Also, you'll find wombats, laughing kookaburras, gray kangaroos and emus. In parts of the park, trees grow 200 feet tall, but there are also mangroves and ferns. There are a number of hiking trails, but access is limited as rangers try to keep the environmental impact of the annual summer tourist invasion to a minimum. Some parts of the park are off-limits completely and camping is by permit only to prevent overcrowding. The park is so popular that space in the park's rental cabins is decided by a lottery. There are camping fees and a day-use fee of A$6.

Gold Country

Victoria's gold fields, site of the 1851 gold madness, lie northwest of Melbourne, centered between the two boomtowns of Ballarat and Bendigo. The rush saw a flood of prospectors wash into the area, and by 1854, there were 100,000 people looking for gold. It was from this experience that one of the nicknames for Australians arose: diggers. **Ballarat** was also to earn an unending place in Australian political history when it became the site of the miner's strike and of the famous **Eureka Stockade** incident. (See the *History* section.) After a time, the easy gold was all taken and the mines became large, company-owned operations. The gold fields returned to their pastoral beginnings, and Melbourne, which had become a ghost town during the boom, grew back to normal size.

In its wake, just like its 1848 counterpart in California, the 1851 Victoria Gold Rush left the residues of sudden wealth: mansions, ornate public buildings, fine hotels and large churches. It was the peak of the Victorian Age, remember, and, when the newly rich diggers built, they modeled their efforts after England's finest. Ballarat is worth a visit if for nothing else than a look (and a jar) at the incredible wooden bar at **Craigs Royal Hotel** ★★. You can also get a room (nothing fancy) for about A$60–140. *Information:* ☎ *(03) 5331-1377*. The whole town is a rich stew of Italianate, Gothic, Romanesque and French Renaissance touches, all highlighted by intricate wrought iron grilles. Nearby Creswick has a wonderfully ornate **town hall**, and Clunes, a nearby town where the first strike was made, is famous for its **verandas** and **elegant banks**. **Bendigo**, where some of the richest lodes of gold in the world were discovered, is noted not only for its Victorian architectural excesses but also for its history of racial tension, when thousands of Chinese flocked into the area to look for gold.

Ballarat is the usual destination in the area because of **Sovereign Hill**, a touristy re-creation of a working gold field and boomtown, complete with stagecoach rides, gold panning, costumed residents, and shops and businesses from the era of the Rush, including a small **Chinatown** and more steam-age machinery than you can imagine. Needless to say, it's often packed with people. The Hill is open daily 10 a.m.–5 p.m., admission charge about A\$20. *Information:* ☎ *(03) 5331-1944.* Nearby is the **Gold Museum**, open 10 a.m.–5 p.m. with displays of Gold Rush and Aboriginal history of the area; A\$5 admission. Also in Ballarat is the **Eureka Stockade**, which has a memorial to the uprising and an historical display; open 9 a.m.–5 p.m.

One of the main draws in Bendigo is the **Central Deborah Mine**, restored to working order and open to daily tours above and below ground, and the **"Talking Trams"** which start at the mine and give a taped commentary as they wind around the town. They run hourly, starting at 9:30 a.m.; the fare is A\$6. The charge for above-ground mine tours is A\$5.50 and A\$11.50 for underground. Worth a look in town are the tall spire of **Sacred Heart Cathedral**, the impressive **Victorian Post Office** and nearby, **Sandhurst**, a smaller re-created mining community. Northeast of Ballarat on the Western Highway is a **wine-growing region** centered around Great Western, known for its white table wines and sparkling wines.

The Victorian Age

Victoria says it has the largest ski resort in the Southern Hemisphere, **Mt. Buller**, just three hours from Melbourne in that part of the Great Dividing Range known as the Victorian Alps. The mountains are the highest in the state, leading up to the border of New South Wales and **Snowy River National Park**. The entire area is becoming increasingly popular both for downhill and cross-country skiing in the winter and for bushwalkers and trout fishers in the summer. There are a half-dozen major ski resorts in the state, with runs for all skills and ages. In addition, there are several national parks. **Accommodations** at the ski resorts run from motels to fancy lodges. In addition to Mt. Buller, which is served by V/Line buses from Melbourne, other resorts include **Falls Creek**, with 22 lifts and more than 50 runs; **Mt. Buffalo**, with one lift; **Mt. Hotham**, the highest in the state, with three lifts; **Bogong High Plains**, a mecca for cross-country skiers; **Mt. Baw Baw**, the southernmost of the resorts; and **Lake Mountain**, only 1.5 hours from Melbourne and popular with novice skiers. *Information about the resorts and accommodations is available from the Victorian Ski Association, P.O. Box 210, South Melbourne, Vic. 3205;* ☎ *(03) 9699-3292. Or the Ski Touring Association of Victoria, GPO Box 20A, Melbourne 3001;* ☎ *(03) 9329-2262.*

National parks in the area include **Bogong**, which contains the 10 highest peaks in Victoria. *Information: National Parks and Wildlife Service, North East District Office, P.O. Box 456, Wangaratta 3677,* ☎ *(03) 5721-5557.* Also **Mt. Buffalo National Park**, has camping, hiking, skiing and 140 kilometers of trails. *Information: Mt. Buffalo National Park, Mt. Buffalo 3745,* ☎ *(03) 5755-1466.*

The Mighty Murray

Australia's Mississippi, complete with paddlewheelers, drove early explorers crazy—it was believed that after it started flowing from its source near Mt. Kosciusko in New South Wales, it flowed inland to a great central lake. It doesn't, of course; it goes almost due west and dumps into the ocean in South Australia after a run of about 1200 miles. After it gets serious east of Albury and creates the watery recreation area at **Lake Hume**, the Murray meanders through the dry country of north-central Victoria, now green thanks to irrigation schemes, and along the way passes some old steamboat towns that recall the days when boats came all the way up from Adelaide. Taking a cruise on the Murray is a popular vacation, although most of the fleet operates on the South Australia stretch of the river.

Taking a paddlewheeler cruise on the Murray River is a popular activity.

The most famous of the river towns is **Echuca**, which sits at the confluence of three rivers and still has a wooden pier to mark its days of glory. The old **Star Hotel**, dating from the 1860s, serves as the city's information center. Several paddlewheelers are available for cruises in Echuca, including the *P.S. Canberra*, with a one hour trip going for about A$8. Tickets are available at the **Bond Store**; ☎ *(03) 5482-2141*. The Bond Store is an old building where goods were stored until customs duties were paid to all three states on the river, a complicated procedure.

Another famous river town was **Swan Hill**, about 100 miles downstream from Echuca. The spot was named by an irate explorer who was kept up all night by black swans honking on the river. The **Swan Hill Pioneer Settlement** is a reconstruction of a 19th-century river town, along lines of Sovereign Hill in Ballarat. On hand are a blacksmith forge, a Cobb and Co. coach, shops, and the *Gem*, the Murray's largest paddlewheeler, preserved and open to tours. Admission to the village, open from 8:30 a.m.–5 p.m. daily, is about A$10 per person. At night, there's a light and sound show, also about A$10. *Information: ☎ (03) 5032-1093.*

Mildura, near the three corners where New South Wales, South Australia and Victoria meet, is the heart of the state's citrus industry, made possible in this dry and dusty area by Murray irrigation waters. Also in the area are **vineyards** of two of Australia's giant winemakers, Lindeman's and Mildara, as well as other wineries. Mildura also claims to have the largest bar in the world—about 300 feet, housed in the **Workingman's Club**. You can take a five-day-long excursion aboard the P.S. *Coonawarra*, which goes from Mildura downstream, and includes a side trip up the Darling River, and enters the Murray at Wentworth, a few miles away. The cost, including meals, is about A$620 per person for a cabin with private facilities. Book it through Ron's Tourist Centre in Mildura; ☎ *(03) 5021-1166*. Another boat to try is the P.S. *Emmylou*, which departs from Echuca and, depending on river conditions, goes upstream or down about 70 kilometers. A two-day, two-night cruise, including most meals, is A$350 per person. *Information: Emmylou Enterprises in Moama, NSW;* ☎ *(03) 5482-3801*.

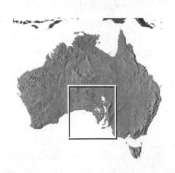

SOUTH AUSTRALIA

Adelaide's layout makes it a perfect city for a walking tour.

Much of the island continent of Australia is a contrast between the often-lush and very livable verges around the coastlines and the dry and often un-livable central deserts. Perhaps nowhere is that contrast as obvious as in South Australia, the driest of the nation's states, yet a state also known for its graceful, almost-English farmlands and rich bounties of wine, fruits and wheat. But it is also the state where you find the town of Coober Pedy, on the southern edge of the Great Red Centre, where temperatures are so beastly, most of the population lives underground. A full two-thirds of the state is either desert or near desert, and because of this, almost 75 percent of all South Australians live in Adelaide, making it the most urbanized state in Australia. The city itself averages less than 25 inches of rain a year.

South Australia has long had a reputation as one of the most conservative states, a tradition begun when the colony was founded in 1836. It was thought, by the men suggesting the colony be started, that many of the things that gave Australia such a bad image in those days could be avoided with a little fiscal responsibility. Looking at the brash crop of colonists over in New South Wales, especially in Sydney, the founders of South Australia ordained that land in their new colony would be sold for a high price, thus assuring that those who came to settle were neither riff nor raff, but solid citizens. Starting with such a base, it is no surprise that South Australia came to be a tad conservative, but the brush that painted that picture has been a little too broad. South Australia, for example, was the first state to give women the vote and to allow women into universities, and more recently it ruled that homosexuality between consenting adults was legal, a quite interesting step given Australia's long history of macho male ethic.

South Australia is called the festival state, so-named because of the many ethnic, artistic and harvest festivals held there, especially the **Festival of the Arts**, Australia's premier gathering of performers and artists, held in even-numbered years. It is also the home of diversified industries producing automobiles, chemicals and steel along with a host of other commodities. It has one of the world's largest **copper mines** (a copper boom in the 1840s assured the success of the fledgling colony) and also boasts one of the world's largest **uranium mines**. The country's **rocket and nuclear research station** is located at the top-secret Woomera Prohibited Area off the Stuart Highway in the north.

It's not all desert, as is witnessed by the fact that there are about 15 million sheep in the state. To protect them (sort of) there is a 1000-mile long, six-foot-high dingo fence. South Australia also produces some of the best wines on the continent. The state has more than 150 wineries, the most famous of which are in the **Barossa Valley** near Adelaide. The valley, in addition to the vines, has some really excellent restaurants and some of the best inns in Australia. A trip to the Barossa is very similar to the sort of experience you might have in the Napa Valley of California—only not quite as crowded. South Australian vines produce almost 60 percent of all Australian wine, and most of the tourists who come to the state do so because of wine—and to visit the green velvet tables of the very spiffy **Adelaide Casino**.

Essential South Australia

Getting There

Adelaide is served by the major national airlines, including **Ansett** and **Qantas**. Air fares from Sydney will cost between A$300 and A$350 one way. It's about an hour and a half flight from Sydney. The airport is about four miles west of the city. Taxi fares into town are about A$12; the airport shuttle bus downtown, with stops at some hotels, is about A$5.

SOUTH AUSTRALIA

Adelaide is a major rail transportation hub. The **Indian-Pacific**, which runs from Sydney to Perth, passes through Adelaide, and the **Ghan**, which runs north to Alice Springs, starts here. The trip from Sydney on the Indian-Pacific takes about 27 hours and costs about A$350 first class. There is also a daily speedlink service between the two capitals, which takes about 20 hours. There is also Monday-Saturday service to Melbourne and service to Perth five times a week. *Information is available from ATS/tourPacific or from the Australian National Travel Centre, 132 North Terrace, Adelaide 5000,* ☎ *(08) 8217-4455; mailing address GPO Box 1743.*

Telephones

The area code for South Australia is (08).

Time

South Australia, like the Northern Territory, is on Central Standard, which puts it a half-hour behind Sydney. From October–March, the state goes on Daylight Savings Time.

Climate

As noted, it ranges from Mediterranean in and around Adelaide to forbidding desert north and west. Adelaide averages around 85 degrees in the summer, around 60 in the winter. Up north, it can get well above 130 degrees in the summer and freezing during a winter night.

Adelaide

Downtown

Adelaide, compared to the vitality of Sydney and the gentility of Melbourne, is pretty tame. It's not unattractive, nor is it overly appealing. It lies in a coastal plain between the gentle rolls of the Mount Lofty Ranges and Gulf St. Vincent, a city of churches and parks, modern hotels and old Victorians. Once upon a time, the city streets were filled with noise and excitement every October or November when world-class drivers roared around town during the Australian Grand Prix. In 1994, somebody somehow screwed up and decided the city no longer wanted the hassle, and the race was moved to Melbourne, leaving a lot of local merchants and travel agencies wondering how it all happened. The city is sort of a reverse of Melbourne: it, too, is cut by a river, in this case, the Torrens, but the parks are to the north and the business district to the south. It was designed and laid out by William Light, the surveyor-general of the infant colony, who named it in honor of Queen Adelaide, the consort of King William IV (he preceded Victoria as sovereign). Light's grand, very symmetrical designs have made downtown Adelaide a perfect walking city, with Victoria Square at the heart, four other squares at each corner, and beyond, green parks everywhere. The outside boundaries of the downtown are delineated by four streets, East, West, North and South terraces. The urbanites of Adelaide, if they're smart, live in the Loftys and commute the 20 or so miles to work.

A logical place to start a walk around Adelaide is on **North Terrace**, four lanes wide with shady trees, where you find many of the city's major buildings. On **King William**

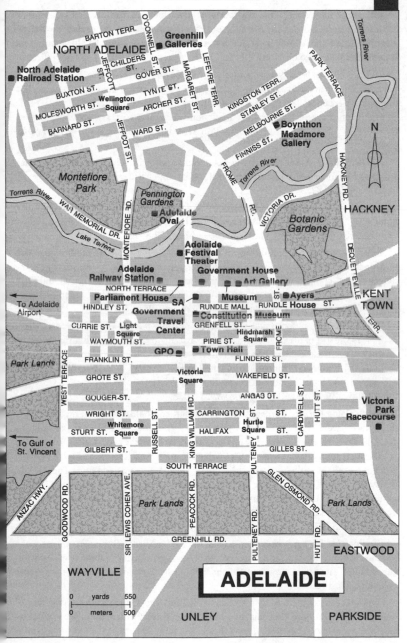

SOUTH AUSTRALIA

BARTON TERR.

NORTH ADELAIDE

CHILDERS ST.

O'CONNELL ST.

Greenhill Galleries

North Adelaide Railroad Station

JEFFCOTT ST.

GOVER ST.

MARGARET ST.

LEFEVRE TERR.

KINGSTON TERR.

Torrens River

PARK TERRACE

BUXTON ST.

TYNTE ST.

STANLEY ST.

MOLESWORTH ST.

Wellington Square

ARCHER ST.

MELBOURNE ST.

Boynthon Meadmore Gallery

BARNARD ST.

JEFFCOTT ST.

WARD ST.

FINNISS ST.

HACKNEY RD.

N

Montefiore Park

MONTEFIORE RD.

Pennington Gardens

FROME RD.

Torrens River

VICTORIA DR.

HACKNEY

Torrens River

WAR MEMORIAL DR.

Adelaide Oval

Botanic Gardens

DEQUETTEVILLE TERR.

Lake Torrens

Adelaide Festival Theater

Government House

Art Gallery

To Adelaide Airport

Adelaide Railway Station

NORTH TERRACE

Museum

Ayers House

ST.

ST.

KENT TOWN

Parliament House

SA Government Travel Center

HINDLEY ST.

RUNDLE MALL

RUNDLE

Constitution Museum

FROME ST.

CURRIE ST.

Light Square

GRENFELL ST.

Hindmarsh Square

WEST TERRACE

WAYMOUTH ST.

PIRIE ST.

GPO

Town Hall

FLINDERS ST.

Park Lands

FRANKLIN ST.

GROTE ST.

Victoria Square

WAKEFIELD ST.

GOUGER ST.

ANGAS ST.

HUTT ST.

CARDWELL ST.

Victoria Park Racecourse

WRIGHT ST.

RUSSELL ST.

KING WILLIAM RD.

CARRINGTON

ST.

ST.

Whitemore Square

Hurtle Square

To Gulf of St. Vincent

STURT ST.

HALIFAX

PULTENEY ST.

ST.

GILBERT ST.

GILLES ST.

SOUTH TERRACE

ANZAC HWY.

GOODWOOD RD.

SIR LEWIS COHEN AVE.

Park Lands

PEACOCK RD.

GLEN OSMOND RD.

PULTENEY RD.

HUTT RD.

Park Lands

GREENHILL RD.

EASTWOOD

WAYVILLE

ADELAIDE

0 yards 550

0 meters 500

UNLEY

PARKSIDE

Street, just off the terrace, is the **city tourist office**, which has maps. Within a short walking distance along North Terrace are the **old Parliament building**, the **casino**, the **University of Adelaide**, the **Art Gallery of South Australia**, the **South Australia Museum** and the **Botanic Gardens**. Also on North Terrace are the Ansett and Australian airlines offices.

Up King William from North Terrace is the **Adelaide Festival Centre**, home every two years to the Adelaide Festival of the Arts. It looks like a series of huge tents, and sits in a lovely grassy area near Torrens Lake (part of the river). It has four theaters, a concert hall, an experimental theater and an open-air amphitheater. Tours are available Monday-Friday from 10 a.m.–4 p.m., and four times on Saturday; cost about A$3. ☎ *(08) 8216-8600.*

The **Art Gallery of South Australia** has a mixture of Asian, European and Australian art, including some displays of early colonial history. Open daily, 10 a.m.–5 p.m., free admission. ☎ *(08) 8223-7200.*

Next door is one of the best displays of Aboriginal art and anthropology in Australia, housed in the **South Australian Museum**. It also boasts one of the world's largest displays of meteorites. Open daily 10 a.m.–5 p.m. ☎ *(08) 8223-8911.*

Another good place to see Aboriginal art and music is at the **Tandanya Aboriginal Cultural Institute**. The institute, at *253 Grenfell Street*, not far from North Terrace, is the only multi-arts complex in Australia owned and operated by Aboriginals. In addition to a museum, there is a performing arts area, workshops and a visual gallery. Open Monday–Friday 10:30 a.m.–5 p.m.; weekends, noon–5 p.m. ☎ *(08) 8223-2467.*

Ayers House, on the south side of the terrace near the Botanic Gardens, is an excellent example of the sort of place the early colonial patriciate hung their hats. Built as the home of Sir Henry Ayers, the premier of South Australia, the building now houses the offices of the National Trust and a pair of restaurants. (The famous Rock in the Northern Territory was named after him.) The house is open Tuesday–Friday 10 a.m.–4 p.m. and weekends from 2–4 p.m.; admission A$2. ☎ *(08) 8223-1655.*

The **Adelaide Botanic Garden, State Herbarium and Conservatory** at the east end of the terrace have a huge collection of plants from Australasia and Malaysia, including a good display of rainforest trees. The conservatory, said to be the largest such facility in the Southern Hemisphere, has two levels of walkways, both wheelchair accessible. There is a licensed restaurant in the center of the garden. There are free guided tours Tuesday and Friday starting at 10:30 a.m. The gardens are open daily from 7 a.m. to sunset; 9 a.m.–sunset weekends; the conservatory is open daily from 10 a.m.–4 p.m. The gardens are free; small admission charge to the conservatory. ☎ *(08) 8228-2311; restaurant information,* ☎ *(08) 8223-3526.*

The **Adelaide Casino** is housed in half of the city's old central train station, part of a restoration project that included the Adelaide Convention Centre and the new Hyatt Regency Hotel. The casino is a popular night spot, plush, lively and visited by more than 2 million people a year.

Here's the perfect place to try your hand at two-up, the Aussie addition to the various ways it's possible to lose your shirt in a casino. (See Robert Mitchum do the two-up bit in *The Sundowners*. Great scene, great flick.)

Anyway, it's all binary, just like computers. Two coins are used. On one side they're marked with an X. The coins are then carefully tossed into the air. Just before the toss, you bet whether they will come down with both sides showing Xs or both sides showing no Xs. If they come down one of each, they get tossed again. If they come down so mixed five times in a row, the house automatically wins. As an added lure, they try to entice players to walk down into the pit and toss the coins. It's hard to toss them properly, and a couple of bad throws will get the crowd restless. But the whole scene is great fun, not too expensive and very contagious.

The casino is owned by the same company that owns Burswood in Western Australia and other casinos in Malaysia and the Bahamas. It's open 11 a.m.–4 a.m. Monday-Thursday and from 11 a.m. Friday to 4 a.m. Monday. It also has a number of bars and a popular restaurant. There is a limited dress code. It's easy to find; just off King William at North Terrace. ☎ *(08) 8218-4100.*

Other Adelaide Sights

On the south bank of the Torrens northeast of the Botanic Gardens is the **Adelaide Zoological Gardens**, considered by many to be among the best breeding zoos in the world, particularly well-known for being able to breed and raise rare and endangered wild animals in captivity. The collection ranges from polar bears to probably the best display of Australian birds in the country. Open 9:30 5 p.m. daily and during January, until 9 p.m. certain evenings. Free tours by calling ahead; also has a licensed restaurant. Admission A$6; ☎ *(08) 8267 3255.*

Glenelg, southeast of the city, is a fine beach area, offering an ocean escape from the fairly routine style of downtown Adelaide. South Australia began here when the province was proclaimed by Gov. Hindmarsh and the first settlers on Dec. 28, 1836. The actual proclamation site is at the corner of MacFarlane Street near the beach. At the beach you will also find the **Buffalo**, a replica of the ship that brought the first colonists to South Australia. In addition to the various historical displays, the ship (built in 1980-82) has a restaurant and an aquarium; it's open Monday–Friday 9 a.m.–noon, 2:30–5 p.m., weekends 10 a.m.–5 p.m. ☎ *(08) 8294-7000.* (See "Where to Eat," for restaurant specifics.)

The Essential Adelaide

Information

The **South Australia Travel Centre** offers city information as well as information about the entire state, *1 King William Street,* ☎ *(08) 8212-1505.* From other parts of Australia, you can call toll free ☎ *(800) 882-0920.* It's open Monday, Wednesday, Thursday and Friday from 8:45 a.m.–5 p.m.; Tuesdays from 9 a.m.–5 p.m.; weekends and holidays, 9 a.m.–2 p.m. The general post office is at the corner of King William and Franklin streets.

Getting Around

The city has free bus service around the downtown area on the **Beeline** and **Loop** buses, which run every 10 minutes 8 a.m.–6 p.m. Monday-Saturday. *Information about the city and suburban bus services, run by the State Transport Authority, is available from the STA Centre, 79 King William Street,* ☎ *(08) 8210-1000.* It also has train schedules.

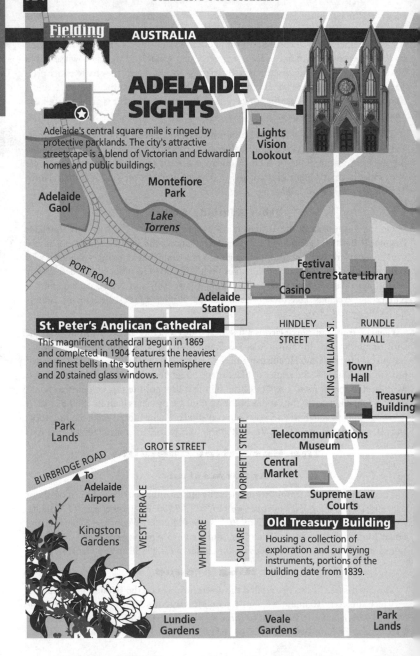

Fielding

AUSTRALIA

ADELAIDE SIGHTS

Adelaide's central square mile is ringed by protective parklands. The city's attractive streetscape is a blend of Victorian and Edwardian homes and public buildings.

Lights Vision Lookout

Montefiore Park

Adelaide Gaol

Lake Torrens

PORT ROAD

Festival Centre State Library

Casino

Adelaide Station

St. Peter's Anglican Cathedral

This magnificent cathedral begun in 1869 and completed in 1904 features the heaviest and finest bells in the southern hemisphere and 20 stained glass windows.

HINDLEY STREET

RUNDLE MALL

KING WILLIAM ST.

Town Hall

Treasury Building

Park Lands

GROTE STREET

MORPHETT STREET

Telecommunications Museum

BURBRIDGE ROAD

▲ To Adelaide Airport

Central Market

WEST TERRACE

Kingston Gardens

WHITMORE

SQUARE

Supreme Law Courts

Old Treasury Building

Housing a collection of exploration and surveying instruments, portions of the building date from 1839.

Lundie Gardens

Veale Gardens

Park Lands

Torrens River

Zoological Gardens

This zoo breeds rare species like the red panda and Persian leopard as well as Australian mammals such as the yellow-footed rock wallaby.

To Morialta Conservation Park

Art Gallery of South Australia

Works of South Austrailian, European and Asian artists are on display in this gallery first opened in 1881.

NORTH TERRACE

Botanic Gardens

Hackney

Royal Adelaide Hospital

South Australian Museum

SAM is recognized internationally for its Aboriginal collections and many of its cultural history collections.

THE PARADE

Kent Town

DEQUETTEVILLE TERRACE

FULLARTON ROAD

Tandanya National Aboriginal Cultural Institute

Rymill Park

WAKEFIELD STREET

WAKEFIELD ROAD

PULTELEY STREET

HUTT STREET

SOUTH TERRACE

To Hahndorf

Victoria Park Racecourse

The **Adelaide Explorer**, a tourist bus disguised as a tram, runs to many of the important sights around town, with service every 90 minutes or so; tickets are about A$20. You can catch it at the government travel centre on King William Street. *(08) 8231-4144.*

For taxis, contact United Yellow Cab, *(08) 8223-3111.*

Shopping

Shopping hours are generally 9 a.m.–5:30 p.m. Monday-Friday, and 9 a.m. to noon Saturday. Many stores stay open either Thursday or Friday nights.

 The major shopping spot in Adelaide is the **Rundle Mall**, the first enclosed shopping mall built in Australia, which is situated on a pedestrian-only stretch of Rundle Street east of King William Street. The mall has the big Aussie department stores—**DJL, Meyer**—plus scads of smaller stores, flower stalls, street musicians, brick streets and outdoor cafes. Here you'll find such innovative brands as Dryzabone foul-weather gear, Akubra hats and the only pants in the world tougher than Levi's: Moleskins, (about $US90 a pair.) The best place in town for Aussie hats and clothing is the **R.A. Williams** ★★★ store off the Rundle Mall.

Another favorite haunt of Adelaide shoppers is the **Central Market**, behind the Hilton Hotel on Grote Street just west of Victoria Square. This is one of Australia's premier flea/produce markets. It's open Tuesday 7 a.m.–5:30 p.m.; Thursdays 11 a.m.–5:30 p.m.; Friday 7 a.m.–9 p.m.; and on Saturday from 7 a.m.–1 p.m. For Sunday market shopping, try the 300 or so stalls at the Adelaide Sunday Market, on East Terrace between Rundle and Grenfell streets; open 9 a.m.–4:30 p.m.

There are several shopping arcades in the downtown area, including the Link Renaissance Centre; the Southern Cross (between James Place and King William); the Regent Arcade off Rundle Mall; and the Adelaide Arcade, also off the mall. Melbourne Street in North Adelaide is the city's posh boutique area, with lots of clothing and accessories on view.

Where to Stay

Note: The South Australian Tourist Commission offices in Australia almost always have excellent package deals for hotels and resorts in Adelaide, the Adelaide Hills and the Barossa Valley. Worth a check.

Hyatt Regency Adelaide   A$200–1650   ★★★★

 North Terrace *(08) 8231-1234; FAX (08) 8238-2387.*
Doubles start around A$200; suites A$500–1650.
Part of the redevelopment of the city's old train station (which also houses the casino), the Hyatt has one of the best locations in town. Several restaurants, a nightclub, outdoor pool and views over the Torrens *probably* will become the premier hotel in Adelaide. The hotel also is home to **Shiki,** a Japanese teppanyaki restaurant. Well worth a try.

Ramada Grand Hotel   A$165–500   ★★★

 Mosley Square, Glenelg; *(08) 8376-1222; FAX (08) 8376-1111.*
Doubles from A$165–500.
Beachfront property, this hotel is not far from the end of the tram line and our favorite beach hotel in South Australia. Airy, yellow, wood lobby, with street lamp decor, cozy bars, nice views. It's close to a golf course and the racetrack. Two res-

taurants including the **Oz Rock Cafe**, which serves croc, emu and kangaroo. Two bars. Pool, sauna, gym.

Hilton International Adelaide   A$150–700   ★★★
233 Victoria Square; ☎ (08) 8217-0711; FAX (08) 80231-0158.
Doubles start at around A$150–300; suites A$360–700.
Located a fair walk from the shopping area, but site of one of the best hotel dining rooms in the city, the **Grange**, which boasts a huge wine cellar. Pool, sauna, two restaurants.

Terrace Inter-Continental   A$200–500   ★★★
150 North Terrace; ☎ (08) 8217-7552; FAX (08) 8231-7572.
Doubles from A$200–250; suites from A$275–500.
Near the Casino and close to Parliament House and King William Street, the hotel has three restaurants, a popular bar and grill called the **Fox and Hound**, a lounge and a nightclub, pool, sauna, gym.

Hindley Parkroyal   A$190–500   ★★★
65 Hindley Street; ☎ (08) 8231-5552; FAX (08) 8237-3800.
Doubles A$190; suits from A$220–500.
Heated pool, spa, sauna, gym, some cooking facilities, handicapped facilities, two nonsmoking floors.

Grosvenor Hotel   A$90–180   ★★
125 North Terrace; ☎ (08) 8407-8888; FAX (08) 8407-8866.
Doubles around A$90–130; suites A$180.
Long in tooth but comfy, with licensed restaurant and bar, gym, sauna, laundry facilities. Right across from the Casino.

West End All Suites Hotel   A$125–190   ★★
255 Hindley Street; ☎ (08) 8231-8333; FAX (08) 8231-4741.
One-bedroom units start at A$125; two-bedrooms from A$190.
An all-suite hotel, close to North Terrace and Lake Torrens. One- and two-bedroom apartments, restaurant, parking, spa, laundry facilities.

Thorngrove Manor   A$220–680   ★★★★
2 Glenside Lane, Stirling 55252; ☎ (08) 8339-6748; FAX (08) 8370-9950.
Located 20 minutes from the city center and 35 minutes from the airport, this luxury property is a member of the prestigious Small Luxury Hotels of the Words. It has earned a reputation as one of the finest lodges in Australia and is multi-towered with turrets and gables setting a Gothic mood. Guest and public areas are creatively decorated with antiques, canopy beds, bookcases and fireplaces, and all menus include premium food and wine. Numerous touring options can be arranged by the owners.

Earl of Zetland   A$65–95   ★
Corner of Gawler Place and Flinders Street; ☎ (08) 8223-5500; FAX (08) 8223-5243.
Doubles around A$65–95.
Close to the Town Hall, licensed restaurant, bar.

Barron Townhouse   A$95–200   ★★
Corner of Hindley and Morphett streets; ☎ (08) 8211-8255; FAX (08) 8231-1179.
Doubles from A$95–200 including breakfast.
Licensed restaurant, guests-only bar, pool and sauna, close to downtown.

Adelaide Travelodge   **A$65–125**   ★★

208 S. Terrace; ☎ (08) 8223-2744; FAX (08) 8224-0519.
Tower Wing doubles A$85–125; Parkview Wing doubles are $A65–100.
Next to the parks. Rooms in two separated wings. Restaurant and pool.

Festival Lodge   **A$80**   ★

140 North Terrace; ☎ (08) 8212-7877; FAX (08) 8211- 8137.
Doubles around A$80.
Opposite the casino; entrance on Bank Street. Restaurant, laundry.

Where to Eat

Grange, The   **$$**   ★★★

In the Hilton International, 233 Victoria Square; ☎ (08) 8217-0711.
Open for all three meals seven days.

Henry's Brasserie and Wine Bar   **$$**   ★★★

Ayers House, 288 North Terrace; ☎ (08) 8224-0666.
Breakfast Monday–Saturday; open seven days for lunch and dinner.
Located in the old stables and coachhouse on the Ayers estate (Ayers Rock fame).

Red Ochre Grill   **$$**   ★★

129 Gouger Street; ☎ (08) 8212-7266.
Open seven days lunch and dinner.
The place to go if you want to sample exotic Australian cuisine: kangaroo, water
buffalo, emu, witchetty grubs, other nasty stuff. Very popular, not just with tourists.
Outside dining area. Bouncy spot.

Cafe Piccante   **$$**   ★★

128 King William Road, Hyde Park; ☎ (08) 8272-7314.
Lunch and dinner seven days.
Courtyard dining in the summer, award-winning pasta. Good wine list using South
Australian products, available by the glass.

Near Adelaide

HMS Buffalo   **$$**   ★★

Patawalonga Boat Haven, Glenelg; ☎ (08) 8294-7000.
Lunch Tuesday–Friday-Sunday; dinner seven days.
In addition to being a replica of the first settlers' ship, the Buffalo is also a popular
restaurant. There are three dining rooms: the Governor Hindmarsh, seats 100;
Captain's Table, seats 35; and the First Mate's Cabin, seats 4-6 in style. The Buff
has a large cellar of excellent South Australian wines. Specialties include hot and
spicy Oysters Rio, chicken and Atlantic salmon wrapped in filo, or beef stuffed with
crayfish. One small caveat: the below-deck area carried a faint odor of stale cigarette
smoke. We dropped a star or two in response.

The Adelaide Hills

The Adelaide Hills, nestled to the east and southeast of the city center, are a combina-
tion of farms, small towns, parklands dotted with historic buildings, excellent places to
stay, pubs, restaurants and high vista spots to look back toward the gulf and the city below.

The best view in the hills is from the top of **Mt. Lofty**, about 2300 feet above sea level. There's a good road that winds all the way to the top. Near the summit is the **Mt. Lofty Botanic Gardens**. Also nearby is the **Cleland Conservation Park**, where you can get kissing-cousin close to koalas, roos, emus, wombats and anything else that happens to wander by. It's popular for picnics and is open daily from 9:30 a.m.–5 p.m. They feed the herds from 2 to 4 p.m. ☎ *(08) 8339-2572.*

While there are some good restaurants and hotels in Adelaide proper, some of our favorites are in the hills, maybe a half-hour or so from the city. One of the best eateries is the **Petaluma's Bridgewater Mill** ★ ★ ★ , *Mt. Barker Road, Bridgewater;* ☎ *(08) 8339-3422.* The restaurant is housed in a restored 1860s flour mill. The mill was built by John Dunne, a notorious teetotaler and now, ironically, owned by vintner Brian Croser. Like a lot of Aussie establishments, the Mill's cuisine is becoming more and more influenced by hints of Pacific Rim flavors. You either eat indoors or out. It has a cellar door for wine tasting, as well. Opens six days for lunch (closed Tuesdays), and seven days for dinner.

Bryan Shaw, an Adelaide lawyer, built a Tuscan-style villa in the Hills as a retreat and later decided to open it up as an elegant country lodge. He named it **Monte Bello** ★ ★ ★ , and it is, sitting on a ridge above a steep hillside covered with vines. Shaw's wife, Laura, is a world-class cook. (It also helps that Bryan loves wine, has a splendid cellar and is not reluctant to break out numerous bottles to encourage and edify his guests.) The Monte Bello experience is airy, Mediterranean, genteel and very laid back. When we last heard, however, Bryan had the place up for sale so we can't guarantee that things will stay the same.

Monte Bello is about a half-hour from downtown and less than an hour from the Barossa Valley. There are five double bedrooms. The master bedroom has a spa overlooking the valley. Rates start at A\$100-180 double, bed-and-breakfast. Add A\$30 per person for the four-course dinners. Lunch and picnics are also available. The Monte Bello is located on Harris Road near the village of Lenswood. ☎ *(08) 8389-8504 phone and fax.*

Not far away from Monte Bello in the village of Stirling is one of South Australia's more romantic places to stay, the **Thorngrove Country Manor** ★ ★ ★ ★ . Thorngrove, the creation of Ken and Nydia Lehmann, is a member of the prestigious Small Luxury Hotels of the World. The Multi-towered castlelike manor is classed as *Gothic Revival*, with turrets, gables, slate roof, dormer windows, stained glass and antique wood. Medieval tapestries, antiques by the score, gold chandeliers, canopied beds and modern amenities furnish for the manor's opulent rooms. All guest areas are highly individual, romantic and creatively furnished.

The facility is basically a bed and breakfast operation. Meals can be served in your room, or by prior arrangement, in a rococo, circular dining room. No kids under six allowed. Rates start around A\$220–780 a night double (dinner extra). The big draw at the manor is the *Tower Room suite*, complete with spiral staircase and a huge carved bed. Staying with Ken and Nydia, who are charming hosts, will be a real experience. *The manor is at 2 Glenside Lane in Stirling;* ☎ *(08) 8339-6748; FAX (08) 8370-9950.*

One of the major attractions in the Hills is the touristy Germanic village of **Hahndorf** ★ , where things are leather-panted and umlauted and you can nosh on wurst

Fielding
AUSTRALIA

AROUND ADELAIDE

In the space of a day you can stretch out on a sandy beach, visit fascinating museums, cruise winding roads in lush green hills or see some of Australia's rarest native animals.

Gorge Wildlife Park

Australia's largest privately owned collection of animals and birds both Australian and exotic.

Torrens Island

Port Adelaide

Morialta Conservation Park

In the Adelaide foothills, 10 minutes drive from the city, this park has extensive hiking trails and three waterfalls.

Adelaide Airport

Adelaide

Fort Glanville

Dating back to 1878, Australia's first fort presents re-creations of military life in the 19th century complete with cannon firings and rifle drills.

Gleneig

Cleland Conservation Park

Southeast of Adelaide, this scenic park of picturesque bushland houses a collection of native animals and birds.

Warrarong Sanctuary

Fourteen hectares of rehabilitated bush with more than 50,000 native plants and endangered species such as bettongs and potoroos.

Carrick Hill

Set in English style gardens in the Adelaide suburb of Springfield, the house contains a fascinating art collection while the 100 acre gardens offer spectacular views.

The World Thru Dolls Museum

Dolls from the 18th century to the present and dolls from every country are on display here along with historical information and fairy tale settings.

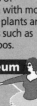

McLaren Vale

Barossa Valley

An hour's drive north are more than 50 wineries which produce a variety of culinary delights as well as wine. The Clare Valley, an hour farther north, is famous for its white grapes.

The River Murray

From Murray Bridge or Goolwa, you can take a half day or full day cruise on a paddle-wheeler or river cruiser.

STUART HIGHWAY

Great Victoria Desert

EYRE HIGHWAY

Port Augusta

Big Rocking Horse

The largest rocking horse in the world (18.3 meters high) has three observation platforms, a coffee house, toy factory and picnic area.

Adelaide

Hahndort

Murray Bridge

Kangaroo Island

Australia's third largest island is noted for its wildlife and natural landmarks. Seal Bay has a large colony of sea lions while Flinders Chase National Park is famous for Admiral's Arch and Remarkable Rocks.

Goolwa

Hahndorf

German Model Train Land features a miniature world of model trains and a colorful look at old and modern Germany recreated in one of Hahndorf's oldest buildings. The Antique Clock Museum nearby has the world's largest cuckoo clock.

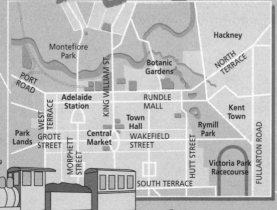

Hackney

Montefiore Park

NORTH TERRACE

Botanic Gardens

PORT ROAD

KING WILLIAM ST.

Adelaide Station

RUNDLE MALL

Kent Town

WEST TERRACE

Town Hall

Rymill Park

Park Lands

GROTE STREET

Central Market

WAKEFIELD STREET

HUTT STREET

FULLARTON ROAD

MORPHETT STREET

Victoria Park Racecourse

SOUTH TERRACE

and strudel. It's the oldest Germanic settlement in the country, and the locals milk that for every pfennig they can—here you will find, if you care, what is billed as the *world's largest cuckoo clock*. One of the main gathering spots is the **Old Mill Restaurant**, parts of which date to the 1850s. More lively is the **German Arms Hotel**, a rambling old heap where you can have a meal or sit outside and try one of the 10 locally produced lagers, an imported German beer or some South Australian wine. You can also try a sausage—and as former Sen. Lloyd Bentsen once noted, "I knew bratwurst, Senator, and you ain't even close." But the ambiance is OK, we guess. Unless you thrive on artificial quaint, you probably can avoid Hahndorf and never have a regret.

The Hills are also alive with small, "romantic" retreats, usually intimate cottages stuck in the woods or farmlands. If you like the genre, you might check out the **Apple Tree Cottage** and the **Gum Tree Cottage**, located in *Oakbank*, close to Hahndorf. Apple Tree, next to a lake, is a two-story, 1860s cottage with open fireplace. It has a kitchen and can sleep five. It sits in the middle of a 150-acre apple orchard. Gum Tree, less than a mile away, has two double bedrooms. It overlooks a lake. The cottages go for A$140 for a double on weekends or A$125 Monday through Thursday. They also can be rented by the week. *Information: Brenton and Gai Adcock, Box 100, Oakbank;* ☎ *(08) 8388-4193; FAX (08) 8388-4733.*

General information about the Adelaide Hills is available from the tourist information office at *64 Main Street in Hahndorf;* ☎ *(08) 388-1185.*

Wine Country

The Barossa Valley offers the charm of rolling hills, colorful vineyards, historic towns and quaint villages.

There are two major wine areas near Adelaide. The **Barossa Valley**, about 30 miles northeast of the city off the Sturt Highway (Highway 20) near Tanunda and Nuriootpa, is the premier **wine area** of the state and probably the country's finest. Nearby is the Clare Valley, an old wine district little known outside Australia, but judged by many wine experts to be a comer. In all, the two valleys boast more than 150 labels. Both offer that delicious mix of excellent restaurants, fine wines and elegant inns associated with the world's great wine areas. From time to time, the vintners get together with chefs from the valley and Adelaide and have gourmet weekends.

The Barossa was settled in the 1840s by German immigrants, and the area is full of Lutheran Churches and wineries with Germanic names. Almost 50 wineries are scattered on vineyards in the area, ranging in size from mom-and-pop outfits to huge producers such as **Orlando** and **Penfolds/Kaiser Stuhl**, the two largest in Australia. **Tanunda**, founded by German immigrants in the early 1840s, is the site of the biennial **Barossa Valley Vintage Festival** held every April in odd-numbered years.

The festival started in 1947 as a celebration to mark the crush, but over the years took on a life of its own and evolved into a week-long fair with heavy emphasis on Germanic and other European influences. The parade held as part of the festivities attracts more than 100,000 people, and the sit-down dinners held during the festival are three-course, four-hour affairs that are often booked two years in advance. The valley has become so popular, in fact, other festivals and events are planned annually so you don't have to wait for odd years to party in the Barossa. Information on the festival: **Barossa Music Festival**, *Box 123, Adelaide, South Australia 5001;* ☎ *(08) 8239-1990; FAX (08) 8239-0440.*

If you're in the area and want to take a guided tour of the wine areas, contact the South Australian tourist office in Adelaide. Expect to pay around A$50 or so for a one-day tour, which will include lunch and tastings. If you're around Adelaide in August, the vintners of the Barossa Valley usually hold a gourmet weekend (visiting chefs, tastings), and the Clare does the same thing in March or April. By yourself, you can get to the valley on special buses every day that run between Adelaide and the valley towns. The buses cost about A$5 one way.

The Barossa is not all that large, maybe 10 miles long. Among wineries worth a visit are **Seppelts**, another biggy, ☎ *(08) 8737-2613;* the very fashionable and increasingly popular **Wolf Blass**, ☎ *(08) 8562-1955;* and **Yalumba**, ☎ *(08) 8564-2423.* If you've never taken a winery tour, check the one at **Orlando Winery**, which will take you around and show you how to make wine Aussie style for about A$2. *Orlando, Barossa Valley Highway, Rowland Flat;* ☎ *(08) 8521-3111.* We are especially fond of **Bethany Wines**, located near Tanunda. The family-owned winery specializes in excellent table wines, including semillon and shiraz. ☎ *(08) 8563-2086.*

For general information about the area, contact the *Barossa Valley Visitors Central, 66 Murray Street, Tanunda;* open 9 a.m.–5 p.m. Monday–Friday, 10 a.m.–4 p.m. weekends. ☎ *(08) 8563-0600; toll free in Australia 1-(800) 812-662.* There is also an information office at *61 Murray Street in Gawler* ☎ *(08) 8522-6814.*

Where to Stay

Two of our favorite digs in all Australia are in the Barossa.

Lodge in Seppeltsfield, The — A$210–650 — ★★★★

☎ *(08) 8562-8277; FAX (08) 8562-8344.*
Rates, depending on days and meals, start at A$210 double for B&B; $310 for B&B and dinner. Weekend packages run around A$650 per couple with meals. The Lodge is closed Tuesdays and Wednesdays.

Run by Aaron Penley and Graham Butler, The Lodge is about as elegant and relaxed as a truly superb retreat can be. These guys are excellent chefs. They know wine, they are eloquent and they are everything that's ever been right with Australians. There are only four double rooms in the modern-style Lodge, which has a small dining room, sumptuous kitchen, open sitting room with fireplace, tennis court and pool. The lodge building, a former family home, is stone, and sits on three acres of gardens with a creek. Aaron and Graham advertise themselves as "setting a new standard," and they're right. The place is perfect, right down to the resident hound, Banjo, who plays nose soccer.

Landhaus — A$145 — ★★★★

In Bethany, near Tanunda. ☎ *(08) 8563-2191.*
The B&B room tariff goes for about A$145 (country breakfast, champagne).

The room—yes, that's room, singular—is nothing special. Elegant enough, with an outside spa and lace bedspread. It's billed as Australia's smallest motel, and it might well be. Forget that, however. You come to the Landhaus to eat, and waiting to take care of that basic need are Frans Kroese, who creates dishes so good you'll weep, and wife Vivien. The dining room seats only 12—the Landhaus is a tiny restored 1840s shepherd's cottage. The menu is fixed, but only after you discuss things with Frans— what's fresh, what does he feel like preparing, what's in season. The results are as good as any Michelin three-star anywhere. The man makes his own chocolate desserts that border on the obscene, but mostly his food is very Continental with a skew toward California/nouvelle sauces. Even if you don't stay at the Kroeses, plan on at least one elegant dinner there. Meals go for about A$80 for two, not counting wine.

Lawley Farm — A$120 — ★★

☎ *(08) 8563-2141; FAX same.*
Rates, including full breakfast, are about A$120 double.

Just outside Tanunda. Also worth a try and very much in the Barossa Valley tradition. Here the spirit is very agrarian, with excellent rooms situated in three 1850s farm buildings and a double-suite barn. Although antique, the facilities come with air conditioning, color TVs and fridges. Very comfy, not quite up to The Lodge.

Barossa Junction — A$90–140 — ★★

In Tanunda. ☎ *(08) 8563-3400; FAX (08) 8563-3660.*
The rooms range from about A$90 to A$140 double including breakfast.

Has rooms as well as fine food. Pool, spa, jogging track. At the southern entrance to the Barossa Valley is a place called Cockatoo Valley, near Lyndoch.

Miners Cottage — A$40–105 — ★★★

☎ *(08) 8524-6213; FAX (08) 8524-6650.*
The cottage goes for A$105 a night double; dinners are A$40 per person.

A romantic retreat so named because it's a 120-year-old stone cottage located in what were the Barossa gold fields. It sits in a quiet little valley with a stream and tall gum trees, within walking distance of a private swimming pool and barbecue area. The cottage has one bedroom with bath and comes with provisions for a light breakfast. Owner Brenda Gardiner, a fine cook, stands ready to whip up a three-course dinner or a picnic. The cottage is close to the more or less famous "Whispering Wall," actually a concrete dam at the Barossa Reservoir that has marvelous acoustic abilities.

The Clare Valley lies about 120 kilometers north of Adelaide between Auburn and the village of Clare. Wine production in the valley began in earnest in 1898 when a group of Adelaide businessmen started the Stanley Wine Co. in Clare to fill their cellars. In addition to the wineries, the Clare Valley also has some really good places to eat and stay. *Clare Valley Tourist Information Centre, Main North Road, Clare, open daily 10 a.m.–4 p.m.* *(08) 8 42-2131. Or try the office at St. Vincent Street in Auburn,* *(08) 8849-2208.*

Tatehams Restaurant and Guest House   A$110–120   ★★★

 (08) 8849-2030; FAX (08) 8849-2015.
Bed and breakfast rooms (which come with a free bottle of wine) are A$120 a night on weekends, A$110 during the week. Dinners are $60 per couple, not counting wine.
David Warner and Russell Beatty, the owners of Tatehams, restored this old building in Auburn to accommodate guests and also to offer fine dining. Kangaroo is a specialty at Tatehams. The à la carte menu changes once a month, and there is always a vegetarian entree. In addition to kangaroo, look for curried duck, smoked salmon and wonderful homemade ice cream. The boys also concoct hideously rich afters: "If you're going to have a dessert," says David, "have a real dessert."

Mintaro Mews   A$70–180   ★★★

 (08) 8843-9001; FAX (08) 8843-9002.
For an overnight B&B stay, with a four-course dinner, the tariff is between A$150 and A$180 double. Saturday nights are very popular, always crowded. A stay without dinner runs between A$70 and A$100 double a night.
Maybe the best filet of kangaroo you'll ever eat in Australia will be found here, a very comfy little inn/restaurant in the historic village of Mintaro, northeast of Auburn and not far from the famous Mintaro slate quarry, still in operation. The establishment is housed in a restored slate grain store and stables. In addition to the restaurant, there are 13 rooms (five with private baths) and an indoor pool and hot tub. The rooms have all sorts of nice touches such as heated towel racks, bathrobes, hair dryers, under floor heating and tea/coffee makings. Tennis courts are available.

The place is run by Paul and Ally Borland and Simon Burr. They put out some really marvelous food and love mixing with the guests after dinner. (Ask them about the care and eating of kangaroos.) The bar is on the honor system and the whole affair is very relaxed and low key.

Thorn Park Country House   A$105–285   ★★★

 (08) 8843-4304; FAX (08) 8843-4296.
B&B plus dinner is A$140 per person or A$105 per person without dinner; a weekend package (two-night minimum) is A$285 per person, which includes dinners Friday and Saturday, lunch Sunday and breakfasts.
Not to be confused with Thorngrove in the Adelaide Hills, it is a 130-year-old homestead in Sevenhill run by David Hay and Michael Speers. Their food is fantas-

tic—so good, in fact, they do very popular cooking schools. The house, a Mintaro slate dwelling dating to the 1850s, was restored in 1986. There are also rooms in a restored coach house near the main house. The property is close to about 20 wineries, and the owners will chauffeur you around. The view from the veranda of the house, looking through huge gum trees out over the property's 65 acres, is a delight. As for the food? Well, how does rack of lamb with a mild chili glaze served with couscous and vegetables grab you? Followed by a double fudge tart with strawberries in balsamic vinegar served with fresh cream? You get the idea.

What to See

If you're into Aussie trivia, or have an interest in classic cars, trucks and motorcycles, try the **National Motor Museum** ★ *in Birdwood, northeast of Adelaide.* Here you will find more than 300 old vehicles housed in an old mill. A main attraction is the black pursuit car Mel Gibson drove in the first "Mad Max" movie. Entrance fee A$8. ☎ *(08) 8668-5006; open daily 9 a.m.–5 p.m.*

On the same highway, further northeast from the museum, is the village of Springton, which is the location of a celebrated gourmet restaurant owned by the Henschke Winery, the **Cafe C** ★ ★ ★ ★. A speciality here is blackened kangaroo cooked in cabernet sauvignon on a bed of (hmmm) beets, or rack of lamb with mint and goat cheese crust. Very special place. It's open for lunch Friday-Monday and dinner Fridays and Saturday. ☎ *(08) 8568-2633.*

Wineries

The Clare Valley is probably most famous for its Rhine Rieslings, and the pioneer of that variety, and one of Australia's premier wine makers, is **Tim Knappstein** ★ ★, whose winery is in Clare. His fume blancs are award winners. Watch especially for wines that come from his Lenswood vineyard. The winery is open for tastings seven days; winery tours by appointment. ☎ *(08) 88422-600.*

The 1992 Hutt Creek sauvignon blanc and the 1991 Domaine chardonnay produced by **Leasingham Wineries** ★ ★ in Clare are a sure bet. It also makes a decent brandy and a fair shiraz. Open for tastings seven days. ☎ *(08) 8842-2555.*

Grosset Vines ★ ★ in Clare is a relatively new winery but has gained an increasingly wide reputation as the producer of excellent chardonnay, which the Clare Valley is becoming more and more associated with generally. The winery is open for tastings and sales only in September and October.

The view from **Pauletts Polish Hill River winery** ★ ★ is as fine as the wines produced here, especially the Rieslings and chardonnays. The winery also produces a pretty good sparkling wine and a good shiraz. It's open daily. ☎ *(08) 8843-4328.*

There are usually gourmet wine/food tours available in the Barossa, the Clare and the Adelaide Hills. These change constantly; for current offerings, check the South Australian tourism office in Los Angeles.

Beyond the Adelaide Area

Kangaroo Island is a wildlife paradise, a hiker's treasure, and wooded getaway with steep cliffs and great beaches.

Kangaroo Island

The Aussies have been trying to keep Kangaroo Island a secret. It's a wildlife paradise, a hiker's treasure, a wooded getaway with steep cliffs and great beaches. It also is home to about 4000 people, many of whom work small island farms or run charter fishing out fits. The island was discovered in 1803 by the indefatigable explorer Matthew Flinders, who chose to name it after the roos he and his men chowed on while they were there. It was first settled by convicts from Tasmania and served as a whaling base for Yankee skippers. It developed a nasty reputation as a hangout for low-life types who scrounged a living in the sealing trade. Today, most of the population lives in three settlements, **Kingscote**, **American River** and **Penneshaw**.

The island is basically limestone, which has been eroded into bluffs and has also formed large underground caves, one of which, **Kelly Hill Caves**, is open to the public. Among the large group of animals you'll run into are the Western gray kangaroo, a very large critter, indeed. Also hanging around are Australian sea lions, almost hunted to extinction and now found at several spots on the island. The sea lions, although under the protection of the government, are permitted to have visitors at the rookery at Seal Bay on the south coast. There is also a colony of New Zealand fur seals, also hunted to near extinction. Other furry things include wallabies, possums and bandicoots. Feathered inhabitants include fairy penguins and emus. At Emu Bay on the north coast of the island near Kingscote, scientists discovered the fossil of an ancient shrimp, something like 550 million years old. No big deal, except this is Australia, and the shrimp just happened to be the largest predator on earth in its day: the fossil remains show a beast that was more than six feet long.

A favorite spot for photographers is Remarkable Rocks at Kangaroo Island, where a pair of giant boulders balance on a cliff.

At the western tip of the island is **Flinders Chase National Park**, an area of dense forests and a perfect place to camp. A favorite spot for photographs is at a formation called the **Remarkable Rocks**, where a pair of giant boulders are balanced on the edge of a cliff. There are at least 60 species of orchids said to be growing in the park. Permits are required for camping. *Information: Flinders Chase National Park, 37 Dauncey Street, Kingscote 5223; ☎ (08) 8482-2381; FAX 8482-2531. There are annual passes available.*

There are several lodges and motels in Kingscote. One place to check for meals is **Sharpy's ★★**, Penneshaw not far from the ferry dock. For a licensed restaurant, try the Sorrento Resort. In American River, try the **Matthew Flinders Terraces ★★** or **Linnett's Island Club ★★**.

It's possible to do the island on a quick day trip with **Kendall Airlines**, which runs tours that includes full-day bus or four-wheel-drive treks. The flight takes about a half-hour from the Adelaide airport and costs about A$150 per person. *Kendall Airline Holidays, 33 King William Street, ☎ (08) 8231-9567.* Other airlines serving the island include **Emu Air, ☎ 1-(800) 182-353; Albatross ☎ (08) 8482-2296 in Kingscote;** and **Air Kangaroo Island**, the Qantas subsidiary, at ☎ *(08) 8211-8877; FAX (08) 8373-1930.* The half-hour flights will cost around A$70 one way.

You can also get to the island by boat aboard several car or passenger ferries. The major ferries are the **Kangaroo Island Sealink; Kangaroo Island Fast Ferries** and the **M.V. Valerie Jane**. Ferries leave either from the near-downtown area at Glenelg or from the tip of the Fleurieu Peninsula at Cape Jervis. Service is either to Kingscote or Penneshaw on the island. There is bus service from Adelaide to Cape Jervis, usually part of the ferry package. The Kangaroo Fast Ferries are high-speed craft that make the run from Glenelg to Kingscote; probably the easiest way to get to the island. Round-trip fares are about A\$65 per person. Daily departures are at 8 a.m. ☎ *(08) 8429-2688; FAX (08) 8429-3437.*

If you want to do the island in a big way, **AAT King's Australian Experience** has several good treks, including four-wheel drive tours and—shades of Alice Springs—a pair of week-long camel safaris. The motorized trip costs about A\$620 per person plus airfare. The camel trips run between A\$535 and A\$780. The company also has treks in the Flinders Ranges.

Any number of travel agencies in Adelaide can arrange tours to the island. As a general rule, the tours can be any combination of cruise and air transportation, and range from a day to a month if needed. A typical one-day fly/fly trips will run about are about A\$190; a fly/cruise one-day is about A\$165. Tours can also include accommodations and breakfasts.

A good bet is the **Kangaroo Island Complete Travel Service** at *27 Gresham Street in Adelaide* ☎ *(08) 8212-4550; FAX (08) 8231-1785.* The company offers a full range of tours and accommodations packages. Good folks, and they know the island well.

The Outback

Going north from Adelaide, you have two choices of highways, neither of which will suit city dwellers who hate wide open spaces. The Sturt Highway runs northeast across the Murray River basin to Muldara in Victoria, and the Stuart Highway starts its long, long journey to Darwin. Going south, the South Eastern Freeway runs through the Mt. Lofty Ranges where it splits to go south or east into Victoria. To go west, you run north to Port Augusta, then hang a left to catch the Eyre Highway, which heads toward the vast nothingness of Western Australia and the Nullarbor.

Captain Cook Cruises, which runs many tours in Sydney, also has paddlewheel service on the Murray River. The trips start at Mannum, about an hour northeast of Adelaide, and run to Morgan. The *Murray Princess,* for example, has a three-night cruise for about A\$300–A\$600 per person, depending on room class, which includes all meals and return bus to Adelaide. ☎ *1-(800) 894-843* toll free.

The farther north you go, the hotter and drier it becomes as the highways run through empty desert with no towns for what seems like years. Unless you have a lot of time or just love driving, you probably have no reason to go out in that stuff unless you're heading for the **Flinders Ranges**, one of the country's most beautiful—but barren—mountain ranges. The ranges, an extension of the Lofty Ranges near Adelaide, are sedimentary formations with some harder materials that have been buckled and twisted into jagged peaks, a real photographer's treat. One of the most popular spots is a large natural amphitheater, about 10 miles by four miles, called **Wilpena Pond**. The cup-shaped depression is surrounded by mountains and is home to big red kangaroos; their seldom-seen cousins, the yellow-footed rock wallaby, and numerous parrots and galahs. It's also a scientist's mecca because of pre-Cambrian fossil beds. The floor of the pound is an undulating plain with a few water courses and stands of pine. There are five marked trails in the area, including a 14-mile jaunt that takes you on a circuit to **Cooinda Camp** and back via 3800-foot-high **St. Mary's Peak**. There are also some much easier hikes.

There is only one **camping area** inside the pound, at Cooinda, about 11 kilometers from the park ranger quarters at the entrance. There is a commercial campground and motel at Wilpena, the **Wilpena Pound Holiday Resort** ★★, with a pool, doubles about A$85; ☎ *(08) 8232-5454; FAX (08) 8232-5280.* There are also accommodations available at Hawker, where the road to the national park turns off. The campground has no powered sites. About 20 kilometers south of Wilpena on the Hawker-Wilpena road is the **Rawnsley Caravan Park** with on-site units and powered sites. ☎ *(08) 8648-0030.*

There is regular bus service between Wilpena and Adelaide on **Stateliner buses**, which make the run in about seven hours and charge around A$30 one way. *For schedules and information,* ☎ *(08) 8212-1777.* A number of companies in Adelaide offer tours of variable length in the Flinders Ranges. **AAT King's Australian Experience** also has a variety of treks, from camel safaris to hiking trips. The camels will set you back around A$600 for a week; the hiking trips start around A$500. Information, ATS/Sprint. *For information about the Flinders Ranges, contact the ranger in charge, Flinders Ranges National Park,* ☎ *(08) 648-4244. For information about the nearby Gammon Ranges National Park* (the same formation, more remote) *contact the National Parks and Wildlife Service, Far North District Office, P.O. Box 34, Leigh Creek 5731;* ☎ *(08) 8675-2499, or the ranger in charge, Gammon Ranges National Park, Balcanoona, via Copley 5732;* ☎ *(08) 8648-4829.* Or try *Flinders Outback Tourism* in Adelaide, ☎ *(08) 8303-2346.*

If you drive beyond the two national parks up around Copley, the road mostly disappears and the next thing you know, you're on the Birdsville Track, the famous cattle drive route that heads up into the Northern Territory. If you go far enough—and only somebody with a desert fetish wants to try—you end up at Birdsville, site of the world's most out-of-the-way pub. The beer is frosty, of course.

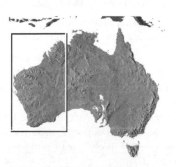

WESTERN AUSTRALIA

Fremantle is a port city with boardwalks, outdoor cafes and fun pubs.

Not a whole lot of Americans had ever heard of Perth or Fremantle, or even Western Australia for that matter, until January and February of 1987, when the cities hosted the America's Cup competitions. It was the Aussies, you will recall, who did what nobody else had ever been able to do—in 1983, they took the cup away from the United States for the first time in the 132 years the world's premier yachting contest had been in existence.

Hordes of curious yachting fans and tourists descended on the Perth area to see if the uppity Australians could hang onto the silver trophy (they didn't—the U.S. got it back), but in the process, a lot of visitors discovered what many people in Australia already knew. Perth is a friendly city, and Western Australia is, indeed, a land of Western hospitality.

You need a lot of time and a lot of interest to come to the Asian edge of Australia because it's a long, long way from the nerve centers of the country in Melbourne and Sydney. The nearest state capital to Perth—Adelaide—is 1700 miles away. Western Australia is a huge place. Almost one-third the whole continent of Australia. Four times the size of Texas. A coastline almost 8000 miles in length. Vast mineral deposits, mountains of iron, tons of gold, huge fields of diamonds, silver, nickel, lead and zinc. And, for most of its bulk, vast empty desert.

Within all that area live only 1.4 million people, most of them concentrated in the area around Perth, the capital. The coastal climate ranges from easygoing Mediterranean around the Swan River and Perth to mushy tropical in the north, where the state meets the Timor Sea. Along the long, long coast, there are small towns whose residents fish for lobster or work in the ports that ship Western Australia's ores to the world.

If you go to Perth expecting excitement, you'll be disappointed. It is nothing more than it has ever wanted to be: an easygoing, fairly laid-back city of a million plus, with life centered along the Swan River and its growing prosperity rooted in the minerals that lie beneath the state. Only a few miles in from the coast, you begin running into the beginning of huge deserts where paved roads are few and far between and people are about as common as rain.

In 1868, Western Australia was the last colony to abandon convict labor (the first settlers needed convicts because nobody was willing to go there to work), and the first years after its founding in the late 1820s were grim. When Australia was claimed by the English in 1788, they left out Western Australia, ending their interest at 129 degrees east, which just happened to be the meridian agreed to at the Treaty of Tordesillas in the 15th century when the pope split the world into two halves belonging to Spain and Portugal.

But the things that discouraged early settlers—the sheer vastness of the state and its often-amazing topography—are beginning to attract more and more people interested in experiencing what remains the most unspoiled part of Australia.

This is the land of the **Hamersley Range gorges**, hundreds of feet deep with pools in their depths. It is the land of the **Kimberleys**, often cited as Australia's last frontier, where saltwater crocodiles lurk in the shallows, and waterfalls tempt photographers. It is the land of the **Bungle Bungle**, a strange Salvador Dali landscape filled with rock formations out of a nightmare. It is a land becoming increasingly important as a wine-growing area, and a land that is becoming a water sports mecca, particularly along the Great Southern

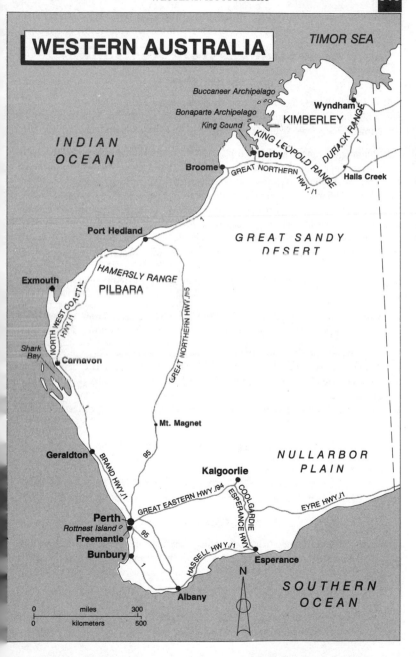

WESTERN AUSTRALIA

TIMOR SEA

Buccaneer Archipelago

Bonaparte Archipelago

Wyndham

King Sound

KIMBERLEY

KING LEOPOLD RANGE

DURACK RANGE

INDIAN
OCEAN

Derby

Broome

GREAT NORTHERN HWY. /1

Halls Creek

Port Hedland

GREAT SANDY
DESERT

Exmouth

HAMERSLY RANGE

PILBARA

NORTH WEST COASTAL HWY. /1

GREAT NORTHERN HWY. /95

Shark
Bay

Carnavon

Mt. Magnet

Geraldton

BRAND HWY. /1

95

NULLARBOR
PLAIN

Kalgoorlie

COOLGARDIE ESPERANCE HWY.

EYRE HWY. /1

GREAT EASTERN HWY. /94

Perth

Rottnest Island

Freemantle

95

HASSELL HWY. /1

1

Bunbury

Esperance

Albany

N

SOUTHERN
OCEAN

| 0 | miles | 300 |
| 0 | kilometers | 500 |

Ocean coast in the extreme south, where fishing is more a matter of how many you have the strength to throw back, not what you might catch.

Essential Western Australia

Getting There

It's a long haul from the eastern cities to Perth (several Asian capitals are a lot closer), almost like flying from Miami to San Francisco. **Ansett** and **Qantas Airlines** fly into the new terminal. Fares from Sydney are between A$400 and A$500 one way.

If you have the time, you can go from Sydney to Perth on the **Indian-Pacific**, one of the longest train trips in the world. It takes three days and goes across some of the most vacant real estate you'll ever see—Siberia without snow, one traveler described it. There is a stretch of 300 miles without a single curve, one of the longest straight stretches in railroad history. It's a popular excursion, so book well in advance. The cheapest fare without a pass is around A$300; sleepers go for around A$950 per person one way. Reservations during holidays are often needed a year ahead; in the high season, Sept.-March, at least a month in advance. In Perth, contact the *Interstate Booking Office, Westrail Travel Centre, City Rail Station, Wellington Street, Perth*; ☎ *(08) 9326-2159 or 2195*. There is also frequent service between Perth and the mining town of Kalgoorlie, eight hours, about A$50 one way.

 There is bus service from Adelaide and Darwin, both long hauls. From Adelaide, over the Eyre Highway, takes about 35 hours and costs around A$180 without a pass.

It's also possible to drive from the Northern Territory, either across country or down to Adelaide and over. From Darwin, it's 2700 miles, paved but desolate. The southern route, on the Eyre Highway through the desolate Nullarbor, has its own perils—it's subject to strange encounters. In 1988, a flying saucer swept over a family on the highway and turned the car's paint into dust. The Nullarbor area, by the way, is well named: Nullarbor; no trees.

Getting Around

There is bus service between Perth and Broome, a popular coastal city 1400 miles away, about 22 hours and about A$200 one way, as well as to inland cities. Interior flights are handled by Ansett WA; the fare to Broome is about A$350 one way.

Climate

Around Perth, the sunniest city in Australia, expect summer highs in the upper 80s, around 65°F in the winter. Farther north, it's more humid and hotter. Interior temperatures in the summer can get well above 100 in the summer and freezing at night in winter.

Time

The state is on Western Standard Time, two hours behind New South Wales. The area code for Western Australia is *(08)*.

Perth

Perth is the friendliest Aussie city.

We have been attacked by black swans only twice in our lives, once at a park in Queensland, once in Perth. The Queensland fowl was a nesting female, very territorial. The Perth attacks took place because the friends we were staying with were Australians, and being Australians, were full of mischief and wanted to see what would happen when the Yanks were suddenly surrounded by a near-riot of swans. They took us to a small park next to the aptly-named Swan River, gave us a handful of bread, and shoved us toward the water. In a nonce, friends, we were awash in swans—a sea of beaks and ocean of necks and wings, the Mormon Tabernacle Choir of honks. It was wonderful and we always remember Perth that way, up to our armpits in ravenous black swans.

It is truly a shame that Perth is so far from the normal tourist haunts of Australia because it is probably the most congenial of Aussie cities, the right size, the right weather, the right attitude toward life. It is very California in its approach to the world, both in climate and attitude. This is either good or bad, depending on how you view California. It is sunny, friendly and a lot more relaxed than most of the rest of the country. If Sydney and Melbourne are power dress, Perth and Fremantle are loafers and Levi's.

Perth is not on the coast but 12 miles up the Swan River from Fremantle, the seaport. The broad and lakelike Swan, unlike many urban Australia rivers, is blue. It was named by Dutch explorers who first sighted the black swans that nest on its banks. The city dads have managed to keep the river mostly pollution free, with industry being situated at Kwinana, on the coast south of the city. It is said that the city has the largest concentration of tycoons in Australia, mostly mining moguls, whose houses can be seen along the river's north shore. The Indian Ocean beaches on the coast are among the finest in the country, and the city, modern and easy to explore, is comfortable and friendly.

The heart of the city is the **Hay Street Mall**, which runs between William and Barrack streets. Shopping arcades, including the quaint **London Court**, branch off from the sides. The **business district**, whose skyline has a fair number of towers, sits back from the river banks, which are mostly gracious parks. In all, the city and environs claim to have 400 square miles of greenlands. In addition to the Swan, there is also the Canning River, which feeds into the Swan a bit south of town and adds a little watery luster to the southeast suburbs. Paralleling Hay Street is St. George's Terrace (which becomes Adelaide Terrace moving east), with such historic relics as **Government House** (1859), **St. George's Cathedral** (1880) and the **Supreme Court Gardens** (1829). At the western edge of St. George's Terrace is **Barracks Archway**, a small brick arch that is all that remains of a pensioners' barracks built on the spot in 1860. The arch was almost torn down for a development, but local furor won out and saved it.

Perth Sights

The **Old Perth Boys' School**, on the south side of St. George's Terrace, was built by convicts in 1854, a Gothic heap that makes you glad you never studied Greek and logic in its halls. Today, it's the headquarters of the western Australia branch of the National Trust. It's open 9 a.m.–5 p.m. Monday-Friday. *Information:* ☎ *(08) 9321-2754.* Another old school is **The Cloisters**, started in 1858 as a boys' secondary school and saved at the last tick from the wrecker's ball. Like many historic buildings in modern Australia, it now lives cheek by jowl with high-rise office buildings.

Government House, the official residence of the governor of Western Australia, looks like it was transplanted brick by brick from London. It stands next to St. George's Cathedral on St. George's Terrace, surrounded by some very nice gardens. When it was completed in 1864, riots were forecast—the A$30,000 cost was double the original estimate. *Information:* ☎ *(08) 9325-3222.*

On the Swan side of the residence is the **Old Court House**, one of the city's oldest surviving colonial structures, built in 1836. It now houses a collection of historical legal artifacts. *Information:* ☎ *(08) 9325-4787.*

East of Government House is the **Perth Concert Hall**, where opera and other musical performances are mounted. It's open weekdays, and there is a licensed restaurant and several bars. *Information:* ☎ *(08) 9325-9944.*

To the northeast of the city center is the **Western Australian Museum**, whose centerpiece is an old jail built in 1856. Along with the impressive collection of early Western

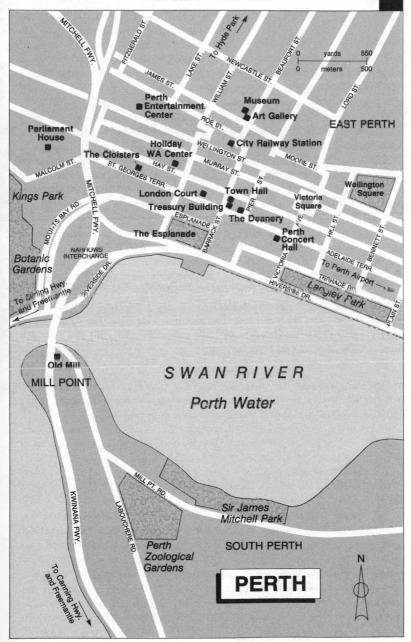

WESTERN AUSTRALIA

MITCHELL FWY.

FITZGERALD ST.

To Hyde Park

LAKE ST.

JAMES ST.

NEWCASTLE ST.

WILLIAM ST.

BEAUFORT ST.

LORD ST.

0   yards   550
0   meters   500

Perth
Entertainment
Center

Museum

Art Gallery

EAST PERTH

Parliament
House

ROE ST.

City Railway Station

Holiday
WA Center

WELLINGTON ST.

The Cloisters

MALCOLM ST.

HAY ST.

MURRAY ST.

MOORE ST.

ST. GEORGES TERR.

Kings Park

MITCHELL FWY.

MOUNTS BAY RD.

London Court

Town Hall

PIER ST.

Victoria
Square

Wellington
Square

HILL ST.

BENNETT ST.

Treasury Building

The Deanery

ESPLANADE

BARRACK ST.

The Esplanade

Perth
Concert
Hall

ADELAIDE TERR.

To Perth Airport

Botanic
Gardens

NARROWS
INTERCHANGE

VICTORIA AVE.

TERRACE RD.

Langley Park

PLAIN ST.

RIVERSIDE DR.

To Cirling Hwy.
and Freemantle

Old Mill

MILL POINT

SWAN RIVER

Perth Water

KWINANA FWY.

MILL PT. RD.

LABOUCHERE RD.

Sir James
Mitchell Park

SOUTH PERTH

Perth
Zoological
Gardens

To Canning Hwy.
and Freemantle

N

PERTH

Australian historical artifacts is a fine display on the life and times of the Aborigines who lived in the area. Another popular item is the Mundrabilla meteorite, one of the largest in the world. Western Australia seems to collect fallen space objects—it was in the state, remember, that the last remnants of the doomed American Skylab fell to earth in 1980. It was also the people of Perth who turned on every light they could find one night in 1962 when John Glenn made his historic orbital trip. The museum is open Mon.–Fri. 10:30 a.m.–5 p.m. and weekends 1–5 p.m. Free admission. *Information:* ☎ *(08) 9328-4411.*

The biggest park close to the city center is **Kings Park**, which is largely a chunk of bushland preserved for modern times. The park, almost 1000 acres in area, contains the Botanic Gardens, with displays of Western Australia wildflowers—a reminder that for all its desolation, the state has more types of wildflowers than any other place in Australia, by some estimates, as many as 7000 species. There are excellent views of the city and the Swan from a lookout tower, and if you hunger, there's a small restaurant and a fast-food kiosk. The park is up a hill east of St. George's Terrace, a fair walk. *Information:* ☎ *(08) 9321-4801.*

Perth, at least it is claimed, has the third-largest casino in the world, the Burswood, located east of the city center in Rivervale. It's part of a multi-million-dollar resort complex that includes a hotel, restaurant, nightclub, and an 18-hole golf course. There are 140 tables of one form or another where you can lose your shirt or break the bank. It's usually crowded. Open 24 hours. *Information:* ☎ *(08) 9362-7777.*

Finally, there is the **"Fremantle Doctor."** The doctor in this case—as all those hardy sailors discovered during the America's Cup—is a strong wind that often rises a little after noon and can rip your mizzen and tear your jib and generally make life at sea a trial. It does help cool off hot days in Perth, however.

Fremantle

The folks in Fremantle bet on the America's Cup outcome. They were hoping, oh, how they were hoping, that the America's Cup would stay put. When the hordes starting arriving in this small port town of 12,000, storefronts were painted, the glasses were polished, the cat was combed and, all in all, things got all gussied up. The Cup, of course, went away, but the benefits of its presence gave the town a shot of confidence that seems to be hanging on, despite the greatly reduced number of tourists who come down for a look. Because Fremantle is a port city, parts of it are Jersey-shore squalid, but the old, preserved parts of it are still enticing. Outdoor life is the way to go in Fremantle, with cafes along the old streets, pubs that brew their own beer, and boardwalks waiting for a stroll.

Amid the many historic buildings that have managed to survive developers' attacks is the **Round House**, the oldest building in Western Australia. It was built in 1831 as a place to house juvenile offenders and sits atop a hill overlooking the ocean and the port. Its displays are essentially penal in nature, including some preserved cells. The building, a 12-sided limestone hulk, is open for tours 10 a.m.–5 p.m. daily. *Information:* ☎ *(08) 9335-6422.*

One of the most impressive old buildings in Fremantle is the two-story **Western Australian Maritime Museum**, which houses some of the oldest historical artifacts in the country. The building was constructed in 1850 as a naval stores depot. Included in the displays is a reconstructed section of the Dutch merchantman Batavia, which sank off the coast in 1629. One of the real treasures is **Dirk Hartog's Plate**, a pewter plate left as a marker by a Dutch East India captain when he chanced by the Western Australian coast in 1616. The museum is open 10:30 a.m.–5 p.m. Mon.–Thur., 1–5 p.m. Fri.–Sun. *Information:* ☎ *(08) 9335-8211.*

For shopping maniacs, there are the **Fremantle Markets** at the corner of Henderson Street and South Terrace, where if you want it, you can probably find it among the 150 or so stalls. The markets are open Fri. 9 a.m.–9 p.m., 9–5 Sat., 11 a.m.–5 p.m. Sun.

Pub crawling in Fremantle is especially rewarding, particularly if you stop in at the **Sail and Anchor** on South Terrace and hoist a pint of the pub's own beer. The Sail and Anchor is housed in a building dating from the turn of the century. The house killer is a little brew called the Dog Bolter, supposedly so strong one will keel you over. It didn't. But they also serve a little number called Redback, named after the spider. Good suds. Also worth a call is the **Federal Hotel** across from the Town Hall, dating from the late 1880s. Or try the **Esplanade Plaza Hotel** ★ ★ ★, famous for gin slings and a good place to stay in its own right, probably the best in Fremantle. It's on Marine Terrace, with doubles starting around A$150. *Information:* ☎ *(08) 9430-4000.*

If you're curious, the **Fishing Boat Harbour**, opposite the Maritime Museum, is where the boats involved in the Cup battle were docked. Today, it's just a place for fish and chips and a beer, nothing left of the excitement but memories. The harbor does have one of the largest marinas in Australia, however.

In a huge building on the harbor, craftsmen built a full-size replica of the *Endeavor*, the ship Capt. James Cook used to explore New Zealand and Australia in 1769–70. The project was sponsored by Alan Bond, the mogul who was largely responsible for the successful Cup challenge. Bondy, as he's known, has fallen on grim days, going from billionaire to millionaire or something, and his vast empire was, at last report, crumbling. But the *Endeavor* made it to sea and when last heard of, was sailing off to re-create some of Cook's voyages.

There is regular bus and suburban train service to Fremantle from Perth; by road it's about 12 miles on either the Stirling or Canning highways.

Essential Perth

Information

For the Perth metropolitan area, as well as Western Australia in general, contact the *Western Australian Tourist Centre, Forrest Place (corner of Wellington Street). Open 8 a.m.–7 p.m. Monday–Thursday; 8 a.m.-9 p.m. Friday; 9 a.m.-5 p.m. weekends;* ☎ *(08) 9483-1111.*

Getting Around

Free transportation around the city center is provided on **Clipper** buses that run every 10 minutes Monday–Friday 7:30 a.m.–5:30 p.m.; Saturday 9–11:30 a.m. The city and suburbs are also served by bus, train and ferry systems. The main bus terminal is located on Wellington Street near Beaufort St. Buses run daily 6 a.m.–11 p.m. with reduced service on the weekends. Trains run to Fremantle and other suburban locations daily from 5:40 a.m.–11:30 p.m., reduced service on weekends. Suburban trains leave from the City

Station on Wellington; interstate trains and some buses run from the East Perth Railway Terminal. Ferries run daily between the Barracks Street jetty and the Mends Street jetty near the zoo in South Perth, 6:45 a.m.–7:15 p.m. The city also operates a bus from the domestic air terminal to downtown. The No. 338 buses run about every 40–50 minutes seven days, reduced service after 6 p.m. There is also a private bus serving most hotels that runs from both international and domestic terminals (they are five kilometers apart) and meets all flights. The fare is about $7. For information about all city transportation services, contact **Transperth**, *offices in the Wellington Street Central Bus Station*; ☎ *(08) 9221-1211*. Transperth offers a day pass that allows unlimited one-day travel on buses, ferries and trains for A$5.

A taxi ride in from the international terminal is about A$15; from the domestic terminal, about A$20. Major taxis are **Swan**, ☎ *(08) 9322-0111* and **Black and White**, ☎ *(08) 9328-8288*.

The Royal Automobile Club of Western Australia is at *228 Adelaide Terrace*; ☎ *(08) 9421-4444*. Emergency road service is available by calling ☎ *(08) 9325-0333*.

Fremantle has trams to take you on a guided tour of the city. They start every hour from the Fremantle Town Hall daily between 10 a.m. and 4 p.m. and depending on the tour, take between 45 minutes and an hour and a half. Prices range from A$6 to A$10. *Information:* ☎ *(08) 9339-8719*.

Telephone

The area code for the Perth area is (08). The main post office is at Forrest Place near Wellington Street across from the Perth Railway Station. *Information:* ☎ *(08) 9326-5211*.

Shopping

Normal shopping hours are 9 a.m.–5:30 p.m. Monday-Wednesday and Friday, 9 a.m.–9 p.m. Thursday, and 9 a.m.–noon Saturday.

Not surprisingly, given its economics, Perth is a major center for diamonds and opals. Western Australia's Argyle diamond mine is the largest in the world, producing millions of carats a year, mostly industrial diamonds, but also jewel-quality. Australian diamonds are noted for their interesting colors, champagne and cognac among them. There are several major stores around town where you can ogle the baubles, including **Quilpie Opals**, *68 St. George's Terrace*, ☎ *(08) 9321-8687*; **The Opal Centre**, *St. Martin's Arcade off London Court*, ☎ *(08) 9325-7931;* and **Swan Diamonds**, *London Court*, ☎ *(08) 9325-8166*.

As noted, the main shopping drag in town is the **Hay Street Mall**, but wandering through the arcades that you find scattered around is a treat, as well. **London Court**, built in 1937, is especially interesting. You decide: is the mock-Tudor decor quaint or just ticky-tacky? Perth has a fair share of jewelry stores where you can buy Western Australian diamonds, opals or stuff made from iron. For authentic Aboriginal art, check the **Aboriginal Art Gallery** at *242 St. George's Terrace*, a government-licensed store with controlled prices and a fair display of art works. The city's large department stores are found along Hay Street.

Where to Stay

Parmelia Hilton A$180–345 ★★★★

14 Mill Street; ☎ *(08) 9322-3622.*
Doubles from A$180; suites from A$285–345.
Downtown within walking distance of the Hay Street Mall. Three restaurants, three bars, pool, sauna, shops and lots of marble. Rooms with either river or city views.

Radisson Observation City A$200–2000 ★★★

The Esplanade, Scarborough; ☎ *(08) 9245-1000.*
Doubles from A$200–235; suites with spa and two or three bedrooms, A$300–2000.
Observation Club level rooms from A$300. Some weekend specials.
This complex sits on one of the best beaches in the Perth Area, about 10 miles outside town. Rooms are done in coral and turquoise, have balconies and ocean views. Four restaurants, three bars, two levels of shops, tennis court, pool, sauna, health center, bottle shop. Upper room levels are reserved for the Observation Club, with personal valets.

Burswood Resort Hotel A$160–600 ★★★★

Great Eastern Highway, Rivervale; ☎ *(08) 9362-7777.*
Doubles from A$160–250; suites with river view, A$600.
Multi-story pyramid on the shores of the Swan, probably the best views of the city around the area. The lobby atrium is almost big enough to have clouds. Three restaurants, two bars, pool, health facilities, tennis, bike hire, shuttle to city. Next to golf course.

Sheraton A$185–300 ▲ ▲ ▲

207 Adelaide Terrace; ☎ *(08) 9325-0501.*
Doubles from A$185–270; suites from A$300.
Large entrance with nice color themes, facing the Swan River. Two restaurants, two bars, disco, pool, sauna, handicapped facilities.

Hyatt Regency A$160–900 ★★

99 Adelaide Terrace; ☎ *(08) 9225-1234.*
Doubles from A$160–210; suites A$350–900.
Corner of Plain Street, formerly the Merlin, now an Asian-influence with huge atrium, shops, rooftop pool, sauna, tennis and squash courts, executive library, three restaurants.

Fremantle Esplanade A$160–310 ★★

Corner of Marine Terrace and Essex streets; ☎ *(08) 9430-4000; FAX (08) 9430-4539.*
Doubles from A$160–290; suites with harbor view and spa, A$310.
Refurbished and redecorated in 1989. On the beach. Pool, sauna, spa, parking, atrium garden restaurant, two bars and disco on the weekends.

Perth Parkroyal A$110–180 ★★

54 Terrace Road, Perth 6000; ☎ *(08) 9325-3811.*
Doubles start around A$110-180.
All 100 rooms overlook the Swan. Pool, spa, licensed restaurant and two bars.

Transit Inn A$160–195 ★★

37 Pier Street; ☎ *(08) 9325-7655.*
Doubles from A$160; suites from A$195.

Ruby's Restaurant, pool, sauna, parking, breakfast available.

Chateau Commodore   A$90   ★★

417 Hay Street, Perth 6000; ☎ *(08) 9325-0461.*
Doubles start around A$90.
Close to the mall, baronial motif. Pool, bar and karaoke restaurant.

Tradewinds   A$100–135   ★★

59 Canning Highway, Fremantle; ☎ *(08) 9339-8188.*
One-bedroom doubles A$100; two-bedroom A$135.
One- and two-bedroom units with cooking facilities. Restaurant/bar, pool, spa,
parking.

Where to Eat

Oyster Beds $$$ ★★

26 Riverside Road, East Fremantle; ☎ *(08) 9339-1611.*
Lunch and dinner seven days.
What Doyle's is to Sydney, this is to the Perth area. Established in 1932, it sits on
the Swan. Wide selection of seafood. Reservations necessary.

Hind Quarter, The $$

101 Canning Highway; ☎ *(08) 9367-4308.*
Dinner from 6:30 seven nights.
The oldest steakhouse in town (20 years). Char-grilled, grain-fed beef. Reservations
essential.

Verde's Brasserie on the Terrace $$ ★★

46 Marine Terrace; ☎ *(08) 9430-4000.*
Lunch and dinner seven days.
Esplanade Hotel. Delightful brasserie style food such as mushroom soup with cray-
fish served cappuccino style; linguini tossed with abalone, mushrooms and cream.
Fresh olive bread. Tasty, very tasty.

Han Palace $$

73-75 Bennett, East Perth; ☎ *(08) 9325-8883.*
Lunch and dinner seven days.
Cantonese cuisine. Nice decor with hand-painted murals, hand-crafted furniture,
indoor garden. Private rooms available. Parking.

Chunagon 46 $$

Mews Road, Fremantle; ☎ *(08) 9336-1000.*
Lunch and dinner Tuesday-Sunday, closed Monday; dinner only from 6 p.m. Saturday.
 Japanese steak and seafood. Teppanyaki room or à la carte.

Horsefeather $

Corner of William and Murray streets; ☎ *(08) 9481-1000.*
Open 7 a.m.–10:30 p.m. seven days.
Family restaurant, serving large juicy burgers, pasta, steaks, potato skins and full
breakfasts. Owned by the same folks who own the place next door, the **Moon and
Sixpence**, a traditional Brit pub. Pub grub, English ales on draft, entertainment
most nights. Open 11 a.m.–midnight Monday-Saturday; noon–9 p.m. Sunday.

Beyond Perth

Rottnest

It's good that Willem de Vlamingh spoke Dutch and not English. Otherwise one of the Perth area's favorite attractions would be called the Rat's Nest. But he did speak Dutch, so the island 10 miles offshore from Fremantle is called **Rottnest**, which doesn't sound quite as bad. De Vlamingh was given cause to name the island what he did because when he landed in 1696, he came across herds of little furry critters he just assumed were big rats. At first blush, that's just what a *quokka* looks like, a very large rat.

Well, quokkas really are some of Australia's friendliest marsupials—tame, spoiled rotten, and generally delightful—which draw thousands of visitors to the island every year. If you want to get technical, quokkas (the Aboriginal name) are also called short-tailed wallabies, *Setonix brachyurus.* They are an endangered species that also exist along some parts of the mainland coast.

But the island is much more than quokkas. There are good beaches, great hiking, and even hotels, motels, campgrounds and bars. It's where many Western Australians come to spend a week's vacation lazing around and feeding the quokkas, and it's often booked well in advance, especially on weekends.

The island is not very large, about seven miles long, three miles wide, and closed to automobile traffic. The only way to get around is by foot or rental bicycle or one of the buses that take visitors on tours of the island—get there early, on busy weekends, all the bikes are snapped up. The rental place is a short walk up from the island jetty, just behind the Hotel Rottnest; bikes go for about A$10 a day ☎ *(08) 9292-5043.* Bus tours cost A$10 and take two hours. Catch them at the visitors center. The island scenery is mixed, with cliffs, stunning white beaches, groves of pine and cypress, and crystal clear water. It was the site of the first settlement in Western Australia, in 1830, and later served as a prison for Aborigines until after the turn of the century. Many of the early colonial and prison buildings have been restored. In addition, as a treat for snorkelers and divers, there are at least a dozen shipwrecks scattered around the island. It's crisscrossed with trails and there are a number of salt-water lakes in the interior suitable for swimming. There is also a nine-hole golf course, horses for rent and boat rentals.

In addition to the quokkas, other animals you can look for on the island are several species of ducks, pheasant, peacocks, rock parrots, rainbow bee eaters, and osprey. Coral reefs near the island are home to many tropical fish as well as shrimp and crabs. Also around Rottnest you find huge spiny sea lobsters (they're called crayfish), the largest in Western Australia. There is a glass-bottomed boat for reef and shipwreck views. It leaves from the island jetty and costs about A$13. *The island's information office is in a kiosk at the jetty. Hours are 9 a.m.–5 p.m. Monday–Friday.*

A popular place to stay or hoist a beer is the **Rottnest Hotel** ★★, which dates from 1864 and was built as the summer residence for the governors of Western Australia. Rates at the hotel, often called the **Quokka Arms**, are around A$130–160 double, weekly rates available. *Information:* ☎ *(08) 9292-5011.* The upscale **Rottnest Resort Lodge** ★★★, once owned by the once very rich Alan Bond, has been remodeled and upgraded. It has a pool, and rooms range around A$90 to A$160 double. *Information,* ☎ *(08) 9292-5161.* For information about kitchenette units and tenting, contact the **Rottnest Island Authority**, *Rottnest Island 6161;* ☎ *(08) 9372-9727. Information and bookings are also available through the Western Australian tourist offices in Perth.*

The cheapest way to get to the island is to take the two-hour **ferry** from the Barrack Street Jetty in Perth (stops in Fremantle), which costs about A$45 for a round-trip fare. *Information: Boat Torque Cruise Ferries,* ☎ *(08) 9221-5844; fax (08) 9325-3717.* Air service to the island is available through Rottnest Airlines.

Wine Country

The wines of Western Australia, while not produced in the quantities of the nation's other areas, have an excellent reputation. Perth is lucky because most of the state's major wineries are only a short drive outside of town in an area called the **Swan Valley**. The vineyards are nestled around the towns of **Guildford** and **Midland**, and range in production from big operators such as Houghton's down to Mom-and-Pop shops.

Houghton's is set up for crowds, with picnic areas and tastings of its very popular white burgundy. It's open 10 a.m.–5 p.m. Mon.–Sat.; noon–5 p.m. Sun. *Information: Houghton's, Dale Road, Middle Swan 6056;* ☎ *(08) 9274-5100.*

Other wineries to check are **Sandalford**, riesling a specialty, open 10 a.m.–5 p.m. Mon.–Sat.; noon–3 p.m. Sun; *information, Sandalford, West Swan Road, Caversham 6055,* ☎ *(08) 9274-5922.* Or **Evans & Tate**, noted for its reds and a few whites, open 10 a.m.–5 p.m. Mon.–Sat.; noon–3 p.m. Sun. *Information, Evans & Tate Swan Street, Henley Brook 6055,* ☎ *(08) 9296-4329.* Excellent wine is also produced in the southwestern region of the state around Margaret River.

One nice way to get to the Swan River wineries is by boat. Among the boats that ply the river are the Miss Sandalford and the Lady Houghton, which go to the wineries they're named after. Both boats cost about A$45 for a full-day cruise, including lunch. *Information: Boat Torque Cruises, Barrack Street Jetty,* ☎ *(08) 9325-6033* or *(08) 9444-4686.*

Around Western Australia

Stirling Range National Park is home to 500 plant species, kangaroos, emus and hundreds of birds.

The **Pinnacles**, about 150 miles north of Perth on the Indian Ocean coast, are a weird collection of limestone fossils standing around like the remnants of some huge Druidic metropolis. The thousands of stone monuments sit in sand dunes and are found from pencil-lead thickness to huge pillars 15 feet high and seven feet wide. They are definitely worth the four-wheel-drive trip it takes to see them. The Pinnacles are the remains of ancient roots that were fossilized by rainwater leeching through mineral-laden topsoils. The formations are part of **Nambung National Park**, which is reached from the coastal highway. Camping is allowed; see the ranger on duty. The park, which also has a big supply of seabirds, is noted for its wildflower blooms in September and November. *Information: Nambung National Park, P.O. Box 62, Cervantes 6511;* ☎ *(08) 9652-047.*

The southwestern tip of the state, where the Indian Ocean meets the Southern Ocean, is the most fertile area of Western Australia, with cattle farms, orchards, and the vineyards of the Margaret River area. The **Rainbow Coast**, basically the Southern Ocean side of the area, is noted for sports fishing. At the extreme southwest edge, about 165 miles from Perth, is **Leeuwin-Naturaliste National Park**, which is famous for its forest of huge kauri trees which grow 200 feet high. The park also has a number of limestone caves, four of which are open for guided tours; there are others set aside for experienced cavers. The park sits on top of a granite ridge that runs for about 60

WESTERN AUSTRALIA

Fielding
WORLD WIDE

AUSTRALIA

THE GOLDEN WEST

Australia's largest state is more than three times the state of Texas and a land of wide open spaces, adventure and contrasts.

Kalbarri

The Murchison River estuary is a playground with beaches, skiing, swimming and fishing. The park is famous for its red granite rocks, wallabies, kangaroos and emus.

Ningaloo Reef/Exmouth

Hugging the shore for more than 200 miles, this reef offers excellent diving and snorkeling with more than 500 species of fish, whales, dolphins and sea turtles. More than 220 types of coral can also be viewed from glass bottom boats.

Monkey Mia Dolphins

Schools of dolphins come ashore to be fed and petted by visitors. Located near Denham, Monkey Mia can be reached by car or air from Perth, or by hovercraft from Carnarvon.

Rottnest Island

A 20 minute ferry ride from Perth, this island with rolling countryside is home to wildlife such as the rare quokka. Diving, snorkeling, bicycling and hiking are popular activities here.

Settlement
Settlement
Ferry to Perth

Bare Hill

Thomson B.

Lookout Hill

Oliver Hill

Conical Hill

Strickland Bay

Salmon Bay

Porpoise Bay

0   Kilometers   500

Margaret River

Located 174 miles south of Perth, this picturesque town is noted for its wineries, limestone caves, coastal scenery and world famous surfing.

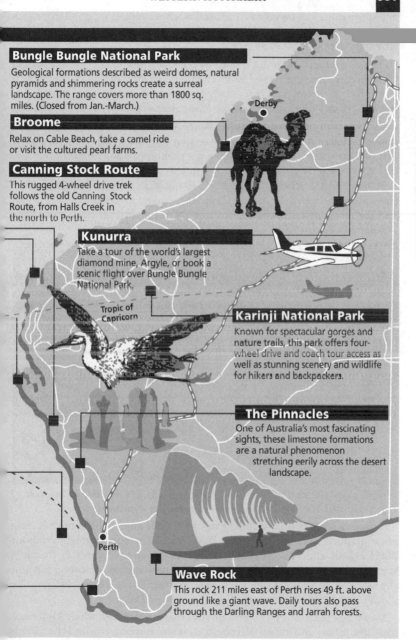

Bungle Bungle National Park

Geological formations described as weird domes, natural pyramids and shimmering rocks create a surreal landscape. The range covers more than 1800 sq. miles. (Closed from Jan.-March.)

Derby

Broome

Relax on Cable Beach, take a camel ride or visit the cultured pearl farms.

Canning Stock Route

This rugged 4-wheel drive trek follows the old Canning Stock Route, from Halls Creek in the north to Perth.

Kunurra

Take a tour of the world's largest diamond mine, Argyle, or book a scenic flight over Bungle Bungle National Park.

Tropic of Capricorn

Karinji National Park

Known for spectacular gorges and nature trails, this park offers four-wheel drive and coach tour access as well as stunning scenery and wildlife for hikers and backpackers.

The Pinnacles

One of Australia's most fascinating sights, these limestone formations are a natural phenomenon stretching eerily across the desert landscape.

Perth

Wave Rock

This rock 211 miles east of Perth rises 49 ft. above ground like a giant wave. Daily tours also pass through the Darling Ranges and Jarrah forests.

miles; the ridge can be hiked its entire length. Camping is permitted; check with rangers. *Information: Leeuwin-Naturaliste National Park, Post Office, Augusta 6290;* ☎ *(08) 9758-5182.*

The main settlement in the southwest is Albany, one of the oldest towns in Western Australia, which doubles its 20,000 population during the tourist season. It has air service from Perth, and a large fleet of sport fishing boats. *Information: Albany Tourist Bureau, Peels Place, Albany 6330;* ☎ *(08) 9841-1088.*

Not far north of Albany is **Stirling Range National Park**, which is the wildflower capital of Australia. The area has been a public preserve since the early part of this century, and its 290,000 acres are home to at least 500 plant species, 100 of which grow nowhere else in the world. The best time to go is September and October. It's also home to quokkas, western gray kangaroos, emus and 100 species of birds. Camping permits are required; sites about A\$3 for two people. *Information: Stirling Range National Park, Post Office, Amelup via Borden 6338;* ☎ *(08) 9827-9230.*

Hikers enjoy the natural wonder of Wave Rock, 211 miles(340km) east of Perth. The rock rises 49 ft.(15m) above ground like a giant wave.

Farther north, about 175 miles east of Perth, is one of the country's most photographed natural formations, **Wave Rock**. The rock formation, about 300 feet long and 50 feet high, looks like an ocean wave suddenly frozen in stone, and is the result of 2.7 million years of molding and coloring. It's near the wheat-country town of Hyden. *Information: Hyden Tourist Information Centre, Lynch Street, Hyden 6359;* ☎ *(08) 9880-5182.*

About 500 miles north of Perth on the coast is **Shark Bay**, where Dirk Hartog came ashore and left his plate behind. It also is where you find the famous

300 or so Monkey Mia bottlenose dolphins, wild but so used to humans that children can pet them standing in the surf. The dolphins are protected, and there are rangers around to help you shake flippers. Also in the Shark Bay area is the beginning of **Shell Beach**, a 60-mile stretch of coast composed of sea-shell deposits that are 30 feet deep. *Information: the Shark Bay Visitor and Travel Centre, Knight Terrace, Denham 6537;* ☎ *(08) 9948-1253.*

Boomtowns

The Western Australia Gold Rush of 1892 started at **Coolgardie**, and within four years, the town was the third-largest in the state with a population of around 15,000. There were almost 20 hotels on the main street, seven news-papers, and scads of expensive and impressive public buildings. Today, the town only has about 1000 population, one hotel, and scads of impressive buildings—now used as museums. Worth a stop is the **Goldfields Museum**, where there are displays of area history and gold field technology. Admission is A$2.50; hours are 9 a.m.–5 p.m. *Information: Coolgardie Tourist Bureau, Bayley Street;* ☎ *(08) 9026-6090.*

Kalgoorlie, not far away, is the site of the biggest strike of the whole rush. In 1893, an Irish prospector named Paddy Hannan hit gold on what was to become known as the **Golden Mile**, a square mile of land that has produced gold to the present day—70 percent of all the gold mined in Australia comes from here. Farther north is the tiny town of **Menzies**, once a boomtown and site of a mine managed in 1897 by a young American named Herbert Hoover.

The Pilbara

The richness of Western Australia's mineral deposits is starkly revealed in the Pilbara, a desolate swath of gorges and peaks that runs across the center of the state. Here you find mountains almost literally made of iron, part of geological formations that are among the oldest on earth. In the heart of the Pilbara is **Hammersley Ranges National Park**, almost 1000 miles north and east of Perth. The hardy visitors who travel to the park come because of its gorg-es, considered by many to be the most spectacular in Australia. The park has several camping areas, and there is a hotel, motel and caravan park at Witte-noom, just to the north of the park. *Information: Wittenoom Souvenirs and Tourist Shop, Sixth Ave., P.O. Box 24, Wittenoom 6752;* ☎ *(08) 9189-7011.*

There are at least a dozen major gorges in the system, many with cool pools of water at their bottoms, oases in a very harsh land. One of the most beau-tiful of the gorges, most of which can be reached on dirt roads in ordinary cars, is **Dales Gorge**. The gorge, 200 feet deep and 200 feet wide, runs for about 30 miles, but just under a kilometer is accessible. At the bottom, near a campsite, is a large pool, and nearby, a waterfall. Nearby **Hammersley Gorge** has a swimming hole, nestled among towering cliffs, and everywhere you find water, you find gum trees and wildlife. The park has many hiking trails, from easy to tough. There is an information display about 15 miles west of Wittenoom at the turnoff to Yampire Gorge, which takes you to Dales Gorge. *Information: Hammersley Range National Park,* ☎ *(08) 9189-8157, or the Department of Conservation and Management, P.O. Box 835, Karratha 6714;* ☎ *(08) 9186-8288.* Information about area tours, including Aboriginal activities and treks, is available from the visitors information center at Tom Price, just outside the national park to the east. Many of the Aboriginal tours last a week or longer.

Less primitive camping conditions and popular swimming areas are located at another Pilbara recreational area, **Millstream-Chichester National Park** about 90 miles in from the coast road near Roebourne. The park has water, toilets, swimming, barbecues, and a large collection of flying foxes. *Information:* ☎ *(08) 9184-5125. Lodging is available in Roebourne. Information: Roebourne Tourist Bureau, 173 Roe Street, Roebourne 6718;* ☎ *(08) 9182-1060.*

The Kimberleys

This is cattle country, gorge country, the land of the Fitzroy River, and the place you find the dramatic knobs and hummocks of the **Bungle Bungle Range**. It's a harsh land, where a short rainstorm can make travel impossible for days, and where the summer temperatures rise well into the 100s. Its northern location makes it subject to cyclones, and its tidal basins, estuaries, and mangrove swamps are home to saltwater crocodiles.

The main settlement in the area is the coastal city of **Broome**, which at the turn of the century was the largest pearl diving center in the world with more than 300 boats involved in the trade. The industry has shrunk considerably, and the boomtown years of the early 1900s are gone. But pearls remain big business in the port's many commercial beds of cultured pearls. It's history has been much influenced by Asia, as can be seen in its mixed race population and ethnic buildings. The town was bombed by the Japanese in 1942 and almost 100 people were killed, many of them refugees fleeing the Dutch East Indies. Broome's small population (about 6000) swells at least double in August or September every year during the **Shinju Matsuri**, or Festival of the Pearl. *Information about the town is available from the Broome Tourist Bureau, corner of Bagot Road and the Great Northern Highway, Broome 6725;* ☎ *(08) 9192-2222.*

A major chunk of the Kimberleys is composed of a huge, deep limestone formation, the remains of a gigantic coral reef. In places, where the river systems have cut through the old reef, there are immense gorges where flash floods five stories high can roar through after a rainstorm. About 220 miles northeast of Broome is **Windjana Gorge**, whose major feature is a 3.5-kilometer-long gorge cut through the Devonian limestone in some places to a depth of 300 feet. The gorge's permanent pools are home to freshwater crocodiles, and there are many examples of old Aboriginal art. The park is reached on a good dry-weather gravel road. Camping is available, and from April through October, rangers are stationed at the park.

The Bungle Bungle Range covers more than 1800 square miles.

The most popular of the gorge parks, however, is **Geikie Gorge National Park**, near the small village of Fitzroy Crossing. The nine-mile-long gorge averages about 100 feet in depth and its bottom is almost always wet with pools and river flows and supports a variety of wildlife including freshwater crocodiles. In parts, there is enough water for ranger-guided boat tours, usually available only after April when the annual Fitzroy floods have subsided. Camping is available at the park, and bush camping is allowed with permits. *Information: Ranger in charge, Geikie Gorge National Park, c/o Post Office, Fitzroy Crossing 6765;* ☎ *(08) 9191-5121.* There are two caravan parks, a lodge and a motel in Fitzroy Crossing. *Information: Derby Tourist Bureau, 1 Clarendon Street, Derby 6728;* ☎ *(08) 9191-1426.*

The newest national park in Western Australia is the **Bungle Bungle**, established in 1987 and already becoming popular because of its strange rock formations. The park has one of the most sensitive ecosystems in the country. The sandstone pillars are crisscrossed with thin growths of lichen, which protect the delicate sandstone from being dissolved by monsoon storms. The most-photographed spot, where the rock formations and vertical cliff faces are nothing less than spectacular, is at **Piccanninny Creek** at the southern edge of the park. One special plant found in the park is the huge fan palm.

Access to the park is being kept primitive because of its ecology, and the only way in is by four-wheel drive. Camping is allowed at designated campsites only, and the park is closed from January through March. *Information: Bungle Bungle National Park, Department of Conservation and Land Management, P.O. Box 242, Kununurra 6743;* ☎ *(08) 9168-0200.* **Accommodations** are available at **Hall's Creek**, about 100 miles south of the park, or at **Wyndham** or **Kununurra**, about the same distance north. *Information: Hall's Creek Tourism Centre, P.O. Box 21, Hall's Creek 6770,* on the Great Northern Highway, ☎ *(08) 9168-6262;* or from the *Kununurra Visitors Centre, Lot 75, Coolibah Drive, Kununurra 6743;* ☎ *(08) 9168-1177,* or *Wyndham Tourist Information Centre, O'Donnell Street, Wyndham Port 6741;* ☎ *(08) 9161-1054.*

Excursions to all the major national parks and attractions in Western Australia can be arranged through Western Australia tourism offices. **Feature Tours** has a one-day wildflower trip on Tuesday, Friday and Sunday between August and October for about A$70, including lunch; information ☎ *(08) 479-4131* at the Perth domestic airport. **Westrail Travel Centre** has a series of wildflower tours from three to six days. The three-day tour, including meals, accommodations, narration and wildflower guides, is about A$400; the six-day is about A$750. *Information: Westrail Travel Centre, City Rail Station (Wellington street);* ☎ *(08) 9326-2159.* A one-day tour to the Pinnacles with **Safari Treks**, including lunch and afternoon tea, is about A$80; information: ☎ *(08) 9322-2188.*

 In addition, **AAT King's Australian Experience** has a number of four-wheel-drive camping and hiking trips, ranging from overnights to two-week treks. They can be booked in the United States by calling either ☎ *(800) 353-4525 or (818) 700-2732.*

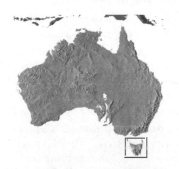

TASMANIA

Dove Lake at Cradle Mountain National Park is a peaceful place.

It seemed highly unlikely that one of the most tranquil settings in all Australia would become the scene of the most gruesome massacre in the country's history, but it happened. The soul of the whole country was horribly wrenched in April 1996 when a mentally ill man with a semiautomatic rifle killed 35 people in and around the Port Arthur settlement southeast of Hobart. Port Arthur, the site of one of the country's most infamous prisons in the 19th century, is almost holy ground to Australians, and a slaughter such as the April massacre left the whole country in shock. It would be much the same as a gunman opening fire at Arlington National Cemetery or the White House. The immediate result was laws being proposed all over Australia banning automatic weapons and pump shotguns. The long-term result will be that Port Arthur, the site of so much misery last century, will now always be associated with mass tragedy this century.

And that's a shame, because Port Arthur, like all of Tasmania, is clean, green and tranquil. Tasmania's landscape and climate are more New Zealand than Australia, with green pastures, lovely seacoasts, a small population and tons of sheep and deer. Plus, it has some of the best wineries in the country and a lifestyle that slows your heart rate down to sloth speed.

Besides, how can you not love a place that has produced two famous movie stars, one handsome, one ugly? Well, that's Tasmania, birthplace of Errol Flynn and the Tasmanian Devil. Flynn became famous playing Robin Hood and the field. The Devil became famous in Warner Bros. cartoons trying to make goulash out of Bugs Bunny.

These days, Tassie, as it's called, is still a mostly peaceful, pastoral place, with splendid mountains and gorgeous rivers, magnificent rain forests and preserved colonial villages. But once, this state was used as a name to frighten bad little children into being good. Back then, it was called Van Dieman's Land, and its worldwide reputation as a terrible penal colony was often warranted. Tasmania got many of the hard cases, the convicts who came to Australia because of a crime or mistake in England and who then did something wrong when they got to Australia, earning them double trouble. It is the prison past of Tasmania, especially the ruins of the Port Arthur prison, that attracts most tourists to this small island south of the mainland across the Bass Strait.

In Tasmania, you find that same sort of quiet resignation you observe in Hawaii now and then. Sure, Hawaii is part of the United States, but it's so far away that, if you're Hawaiian, you get the feeling nobody back in the continental U.S.A. knows you're alive. People feel the same way in Tasmania, sometimes bitter at what they see as disinterest or mockery on the part of all those clods up in Sydney and Canberra. But Tasmanians fight back as well as they can, referring to the mainland of Australia as "the northern island," and printing maps that show Tasmania as huge and the mainland just a dot. The island, at 25,000 square miles, roughly the size of Ireland, has a population of only around 450,000. It is the most decentralized state in Australia, with fewer than half the people living in Hobart, the capital. Other major population centers are Launceston, Devonport, and Burnie. Most of the people live in coastal areas. Almost the entire west coast area, because of the mountains and thick forests, is uninhabited. The state actually is a group of islands, including King and Flinders islands in the Bass Strait. Tasmania's wonderful forests and mountains have been a continuing battleground for conflict between the mining and lumber industries and the environmentalists for years, and the often angry, sometimes violent confrontations show no sign of receding. In the southwest corner are ugly examples of some of the

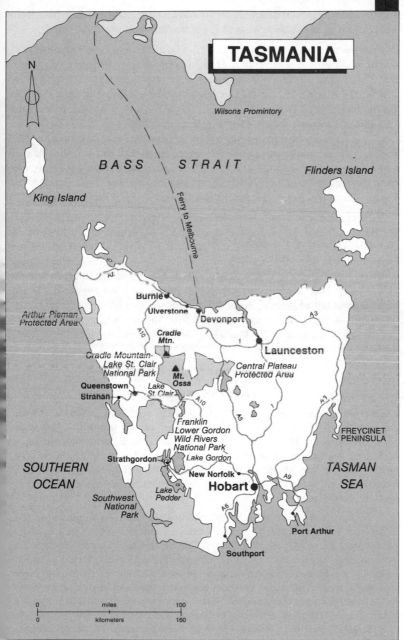

TASMANIA

N

Wilsons Promintory

BASS *STRAIT*

Flinders Island

King Island

Ferry to Melbourne

Arthur Pieman Protected Area

Burnie
Ulverstone
Devonport

A3

Cradle Mtn.

A10

1

Launceston

Cradle Mountain-Lake St. Clair National Park

Central Plateau Protected Area

▲ *Mt. Ossa*

Queenstown
Strahan

Lake St Clair

A10

A5

A3

Franklin Lower Gordon Wild Rivers National Park

1

FREYCINET PENINSULA

Strathgordon

Lake Gordon

SOUTHERN OCEAN

New Norfolk
Hobart

TASMAN SEA

Lake Pedder

A9

Southwest National Park

A6

Port Arthur

Southport

| 0 | miles | 100 |
| 0 | kilometers | 160 |

worst environmental damage in the whole country—whole mountains have disappeared so that industry could get at the minerals they contained.

If you spend a lot of time in Australia, your memories of it will usually be tinted red or brown because of the huge interior deserts and the dusty roads. But if you go to Tassie, your memories will always be green. Part of the reason for the island's lush and temperate climate is its location: smack dab in the Roaring 40s, 147 degrees east, 42 degrees south. Colonial Australians thought it was just like Mother England, and they built their farms and homes just as they had back home. Well, it's not that sort of green, English green. It's Tasmanian green, which is a special color all its own, the color of giant ferns and hardwoods and rare pines and bush so dense nobody can hack through it—some areas are unexplored to this day. If the loggers are kept under control, they might just stay that way.

Tasmania, like the other Australian states, is getting more and more into the wine business. There are six wine districts in Tassie, with a total of 35 wineries. These include: the Tamar Valley, the North Esk and Pipers River areas near Launceston; the Derwent Valley and Coal River Valley near Hobart, and the Huon Valley southwest of Hobart. Major varieties include chardonnays, pinot noirs and cabernets. (**Please see our section on Tassie wines later in this chapter.**) The state has even set up a licensing scheme with Tasmanian wines carrying appellation labels. Information is available from the **Vineyards Association of Tasmania,** *Box 214, Launceston 7250;* ☎ *(03) 6343-1313; FAX (03) 6343-0409.*

Essential Tasmania

Getting There

There are five airports in Tasmania, located at Launceston, Hobart, Wynyard, Devonport and Flinders Island. Service is provided by **Ansett, Aus-Air, Kendall** and **Qantas** airlines. The flying time from the mainland is around an hour either from Sydney or Melbourne, and high-season, one-way fares on Qantas and Ansett, the main carriers, are around A$300 Sydney-Hobart; around A$215 Melbourne-Hobart; and about A$275 Sydney-Launceston. Qantas and Air New Zealand provide service from Christchurch to Hobart; fares are about A$1000 round trip.

A very popular way to do the trip is on the **Spirit of Tasmania**, a passenger car ferry that makes 14.5-hour overnight trips between Melbourne and Devonport. The ferry leaves Melbourne at 6 p.m. Monday, Wednesday and Friday, arriving in Devonport at 8:30 the next morning. The return trip follows the same schedule on Tuesday, Thursday and Saturday. The ship has three dining rooms, pool and sauna, disco and several bar areas. In the main tourist season, December-March, one-way rooms range from hostel-type twin shares at A$120 per person up to doubles with private bathrooms for around A$280 per person; tickets include dinner and continental breakfast. If you take a car or RV with you, the charge is A$175 for vehicles under five meters in length and under 2.5 meters in height.

NOTE: there are no single cabins; doubles reserved for one person are charged at a rate for an adult and a half. Also note that as big as the ship is, the Bass Strait can get so stormy that the ride can be very unpleasant even with the ship's stabilizers. The ship can be booked at Tasmania travel offices in major Australian cities. The ship even has a **tourist information and reservations center**. It's located on E Deck and is open on sailing days from 3:30–9:30 p.m. and 7–9 a.m. For ship information and tour packages, call Spirit of Tasmania toll free in Australia at ☎ *(800) 81-1580; FAX (800) 63-6110.*

It's possible to get a package that will allow you to fly to Tasmania and return on the boat or vice versa. Also, you can choose to stop in Devonport or continue on by bus to Hobart. The bus fare, on **Redline Coaches**, is about A$30 one way; service also available to Launceston for about half the Devonport-Hobart fare. Bus service is available in Melbourne, as well. For A$4 per person, you can catch a bus at the Spencer Street Station that takes you to the ship's pier. The service leaves at 4 p.m. Monday, Wednesday and Friday, and returns from the pier to downtown at 9 a.m. Sunday, Wednesday and Friday.

Tasmania is very aware that it gets a lot of money from tourism, and it is one of the best states in Australia at providing options for visitors. **Tasmania travel bureaus**, working with the various airlines and car rental agencies, offer a bunch of packages leaving from either Sydney or Melbourne. There are so many plans available, in fact, there's no space here to list them all. The **Tasmanian Travel Centre** in Melbourne is at *256 Collins Street* ☎ *(03) 9206-7922; FAX (03) 9206-7947.* In Sydney, the office is at *149 King Street* ☎ *(02) 202-2022; FAX (02) 202-2055.* Once in Tasmania, almost every village and town has a visitor information office; just look for the big blue and yellow "I" signs. You should also check with **Aus-Air** offices in Melbourne or **Hertz** agencies around the country, which have good accommodations/car packages.

Tasmania has possibly the largest fleet of **rental campers** per capita in Australia, and caravaning is by far the most popular way of visiting the island. There are some really good deals available; it's not uncommon to be able to rent a campervan for about A$600–700 a week, including insurance, unlimited mileage and taxes. The RVs can be picked up in Hobart, at the Spirit of Tasmania dock in Devonport, or in Launceston. Check with **Autorent Hertz**, probably the best of the lot ☎ *(800) 030-500.* Note that some rental agencies require minimum rental periods. and there are sometimes age restrictions as well.

NOTE: On most rental cars, there are serious insurance conditions. In most cases, a flat rental is subject to a A$2000 deductible on damages. This can be reduced to A$200 deductible by paying a A$10–12 per day insurance fee. Rates for cars will be in the A$15–90 a day range, depending on type of car and length of rental. **NB:** Make sure if you are coming across on the Spirit of Tasmania you have reserved your car ahead; otherwise you'll discover every vehicle in Devonport is spoken for, even worse in holiday periods. The speed limit in built-up areas is 60 kph; on highways, the maximum, unless otherwise marked, is 110 kph. To drive in Tasmania, all you need is a valid U.S. or Canadian drivers license. Alcohol limits are.05, and there is random breath testing. *Information about RV parks is available from the Caravan and Holiday Parks Association of Tasmania, Launceston.* ☎ *(03) 6343-1313.*

If you simply want to fly over and take a short tour or two, that also is possible. There is no passenger train service in Tasmania, but there is regular **bus service** as well as tour buses. A full-day bus tour from Hobart to Port Arthur, for example, can go for as low as A$45 per person. **Redline Coaches** offers Tassie Passes ranging from seven to 30 days; the passes start at A$100. *Information: Redline Coaches, 9 Edward Street, Devonport,* ☎ *(03) 6424-5100; 199 Collins Street, Hobart,* ☎ *(03) 6231-3233, and 112 George Street, Launceston,* ☎ *(03) 6331-3233. Or call toll free* ☎ *(800) 030-033; FAX (03) 6234-9241.* **Air tours** from Hobart around the east coast and to the east coast wilderness areas will run around A$150-300 per person, depending on destination. Check with a Tasbureau office, or try these: **Tasmanian Aviation Centre**, Launceston airport ☎ *(03) 63 91-8330; FAX (03) 6391-8662;* **Wilderness Air**, the Esplanade, Strahan ☎ *(03) 6471-7280; FAX (03) 6471-7303;* **Par Avion** in Hobart; ☎ *(03) 6248-5390; FAX (03) 6248-5117; or Tasair,* Cambridge Aerodrome in Hobart, ☎ *(03) 6248-5088.*

Climate

Tasmania has four distinct seasons, from summer heat to winter cold, but it never gets as hot as the mainland. In fact, it's probably the most temperate of all Australia's states. Nights, even in the summer, can be cool, and the highlands are subject to rain-or snow-all year. Hobart, interestingly enough, is the second driest city in the country, after Adelaide.

Telephones

Tasmania, like every other state in Australia, has been busily revising its telephone codes the last few years, with little or no consistency between states. In Tasmania's case, all numbers are now eight digits, and the state area code is *(03)*, the same as Melbourne. Prefixes on the new numbers will tell you where you're calling— *62* in the Hobart area; *63* is Launceston, and *64* is the north and west of the state.

Time

Tasmania is on Eastern Standard Time, the same as Sydney and Melbourne. In the summer, (October-March) the state goes on daylight savings time. Bottle shops are open on Sundays in Tasmania, by the way.

Activities

As befits its rugged and undeveloped nature, Tasmania offers many outdoor activities, from whitewater sports to trout fishing, hiking to birdwatching. Some examples:

Whitewater

Some of the best fast water in the country is within 10 minutes from Launceston: the gorges of the South Esk River. The rapids on this stretch are in the Category 3-4+ range. A couple of companies offer trips: **Whitewater Experiences Tasmania** (W.E.T.) at *71A St. John Street in Launceston,* ☎ *(03) 6334-7999; or* **Wandering Albatross** *in Sandy Bay, a suburb of Hobart,* ☎ *(03) 6224-1577; FAX (03) 6236-9680. Look for prices around A$90-100 per person.* For really serious rafters, there are one- and two-week expeditions down the wild and woolly Franklin River, one of the great water thrills Down Under. Several companies offer trips starting in Launceston or Hobart. **Peregrine Adventures** in Hobart will guide you down the lower Franklin for about A$1000 per person for a week; an 11-day trip will run about $1950 per person. Information: ☎ *(03) 6225-*

0944; FAX (03) 6225-0946. Another good bet is **Rafting Tasmania**, with trips on all the major rafting rivers as well as sea kayaking. Prices for the Derwent one-day start around A$90; Franklin River trips are about the same as Peregrine. Information: ☎ *(03) 6227-9516, FAX and phone*.

Fishing

Tasmania, like any other place on the planet with a population of trout, proclaims that it has the best in the world. Right. Anyway, the mountain streams in the state are full of buff brown trout, plus you also have a shot at sea-run browns along the coasts. If you're a fly fisher, you won't find any better sport around, and compared to some other prime trout areas, the costs are low.

A 14-day license, for example, is about A$20; a one-day is only A$7. Rental equipment is available at fishing spots all over the state. Most inland waters open on the Saturday nearest to Oct. 1 and close the Sunday closest to April 30. A few of the better spots include **Arthur's Lake**, about 70 kilometers southwest of Launceston, great wild trout fly fishing; the **Macquarie River**, which flows north through the midlands, noted for hellacious mayfly hatches in October; **Lake Pedder**, part of a dubious hydroelectric project, which houses what are considered to be "modest sized" browns, only about 5 pounds; and **Great Lake**, located near Arthur's Lake, some 3000 feet up, said to be the largest natural freshwater lake in the country, full of rainbows as wells as browns. All the trout in Tasmania, by the way, came from a shipment of eggs sent to the island from England in 1864.

If you want a guided trout fishing trip, contact any member of the **Tasmanian Professional Trout Guides Association**. Look for rates for a one-day trip to run about A$125-$250 per person, which will usually include fishing equipment, meals, accommodations, licenses and wading equipment. If you really, really care about trout (or just happen to be in the neighborhood) check out the **Museum of Trout Fishing** at Plenty, on the Derwent northwest of Hobart. It's the site of the oldest fish hatchery in the Southern Hemisphere (they say), and was where those English fish eggs were placed when they arrived in Tasmania. The complex, known as **The Salmon Ponds**, is open daily from 9 a.m.–5 p.m. ☎ *(03) 6261-1614*. You can get meals or and a morning or afternoon tea at the Ponds Restaurant, open daily.

Flora

Tasmanians are garden crazy, as the number of flower and garden shows held each year will attest. In addition to the **Royal Tasmanian Botanical Gardens** in Hobart (see below), you will find rhododendron, tulip and orchid gardens all over the island. A couple of the best are the **Lapoinya Rhodo Garden**, about 40 kilometers from Burnie on the northwest coast, and the **Emu Valley Rhododendron Garden**, also near Burnie, with almost 10,000 plants.

September and October are the big flower months, with festivals such as the **Hobart Daffodil and Camelia Show**; the **Launceston Garden Festival**, the **Hobart Orchid Show**, the **New Norfolk Tulip Time** show, and the **Wynard Tulip Festival**. The **Royal Hobart Agricultural Show**, the equivalent of a state fair, is held every year at the end of October. Along with crops and agriculture shows, there are flower displays .

As for wildflowers, check with the Parks and Wildlife Service for exact bloom times. One of the best spots for spring blooms is Freycinet National Park on on the east coast, where spectacular displays of pilosa and orchids come out starting in September.

For general information about all things flowery in the island, contact **Blooming Tasmania**, *P.O. Box 973, Burnie, Tasmania.*

Parks

The state has more than a dozen national parks, most situated in the rugged rain forests of the west. Park fees are more than reasonable. A one-day vehicle pass, with up to eight passengers, is A$8, If you come to as park by bus, boat, bike or motorcycle, the fee is A$2.50 per person. Longer passes are available, as well. Any Tasmanian travel center will have information on the parks, or you can get further information by visiting the **Parks and Wildlife Service**, *134 Macquarie St. in Hobart,* ☎ *(03) 6233-6182 or (03) 6233-3865; FAX (03) 6233-3477.*

Wines

Chances are, unless you've been to Australia—and even then, maybe not—you've never tried Tasmanian wines. The reason is simple: the state's wineries are small, their production is limited and most Tassie wines (at least 75 percent of the production) are consumed in Tasmania. Between them, South Australia, New South Wales and Victoria produce more than 98 percent of all Australian wines. Tiny Tasmania produces just 0.5 percent of the country's total. Tasmanian wines are so good, however, that it's almost worth a trip to the island just to do some tasting. All of Tasmania's wineries are in a temperate microclimate ranging between 41 and 43 degrees south latitude. The result is wines that resemble European cool-weather vintages.

The main wine producing area is the *Tamar Valley* region, an area generally running from George Town on the Bass Strait to Launceston down the Tamar River. It also includes the *Pipers River* area east of the river. The drive down the main valley is quite scenic, either on the A7 (West Tamar Highway) or the A8 (East Tamar Highway.) Even better is to meander down the C728 on the west bank of the river. And it's a quite manageable exploration, only 60 kilometers or so from George Town to Launceston. To reach the Pipers River area, take the B82 east from George Town. In both areas, there will be signposts announcing that you're on the "Tasmanian Wine Route."

While many of the top Tasmanian wines are whites, the industry is seeing an increase in reds, especially cabernets and merlot blends. If you start your Tasmania visit in Hobart, a first good place to stop in is the Tasmanian Wine Centre in Battery Point. It has tastings representing a wide selection of Tasmanian wines by area, style, variety and vintage. It can also arrange winery tours, ship wines back home and arrange wine tasting lessons. The center is at *6 Montpelier Retreat, Battery Point.* ☎ *(03) 6224-0653; FAX (03) 6223-4591.*

The normal procedure at Tasmanian wine tastings is to charge a small amount (A$2-3) for the tasting, which is refunded if you decide to buy a bottle or two. The tasting hours listed are subject to change, so please check ahead. Among the wineries:

Tamar Valley

Marion's Vineyard is located in Deviot, not far from a local landmark, the Batman Bridge (not in honor of everybody's favorite comic book hero, but just a cable-stayed truss bridge.) Marion's is named after Cypriot-Australian Marion Semmens, who with American husband Mark started the winery in the early 1980s. Wines available include Muller thurgau, chardonnay, pinot gris and pinot noir. The couple is planning major expansions to the property, including an amphitheater, restaurant and a jetty on the Tamar. Open daily 10 a.m.–5 p.m. ☎ *(03) 6394-7434 phone and FAX.*

Strathlyn Wine Centre is at Rosevears and allows you to try the vintages of the Pipers Brook Vineyard without driving to Pipers Brook. The center is just a short drive north of Launceston, and includes a small restaurant offering cheese tastings and light lunches. Pipers Brook produces a range of wines including chardonnay, pinot noir, riesling, semillon, sauvignon blanc and cabernet merlot. The wine center and restaurant are open daily from 10 a.m.–5 p.m. ☎ *(03) 6330-2388 phone and FAX.*

Pipers River

Pipers Brook Vineyard is probably our favorite winery in Tasmania, producing really excellent whites under both the Pipers Brook and Ninth Island labels. The chardonnays are perfect, the sauvignon blancs not far behind. In addition to tastings, there is a self-guided tour of the winery. Light lunches are also available. The winery is located about eight kilometers east of Pipers River; look for the signs. It's open from 10 a.m.–4 p.m. Monday-Friday and 11 a.m.–5 p.m. November-April. ☎ *(03) 6382-7197; FAX (03) 6382-7226.*

Rochecombe Vineyard has a great label: a platypus, supposedly the portrait of a local beast that lives in a stream running through the vineyard property. The winery produces very good chardonnays, including some really impressive unoaked vintages. The reds tend to be light: pinot roses, pinot noirs. But the cabernet sauvignon was pretty good, too. The vineyard restaurant serves light lunches, or you can buy meat and other goodies and cook them yourself on the spot. Rochecombe is located at Pipers River about 25 kilometers east of George Town. It's open daily from 10 a.m.–5 p.m. ☎ *(03) 6382-7122; FAX (03) 6382-7231.*

Delamere Vineyard is a small operation close to Pipers Brook Vineyard, maybe eight kilometers from Pipers River. It specializes in pinot noir and chardonnays. The pinot noirs are worth a try; good flavor, nice and dry. It's open for tastings daily from 10 a.m.–5 p.m. ☎ *(03) 6382-7190; FAX (03) 6382-7250.*

Heemskerk Vineyard has some of the best cabernet sauvignons in Australia, meaning in the world. The 1993 vintage was exceptional (and all but gone.) The wines from the vineyard, located not far from Pipers Brook Vineyard, are consistently winning awards. It also produces some sparkling wines, chardonnays and pinot noirs. Hours are 10 a.m.–5 p.m. Monday-Friday; weekends also November-April. ☎ *(03) 6382-7133; FAX (03) 6382-7242.*

Dalrymple Vineyard sitting next to the Pipers Brook Winery was an instant success when it issued its first bottles in 1991. Awards piled in and everybody and her sister were trying to snap up the 1992 pinot noirs, a truly wonderful brew. Matter of fact, almost every vintage and variety produced has won some sort of an award. Hours are 10 a.m.–4 p.m. weekdays, 9 a.m.–5 p.m. weekends. ☎ *(03) 6331-3179 phone and FAX.*

Brook Eden Vineyard is a bit off the path, down the C818 from the B82, but worth the short (10 miles or so) drive. It specializes in boutique wines, producing some nice pinot noirs and chardonnays. Its open from 10 a.m.–5 p.m. weekends. ☎ *(03) 6395-6244 or (03) 6382-5137.*

Hobart and the South

The vineyards around the Hobart area are scattered about and not as easy to visit as the tight little clumps in the north. There are several worth a shot if you're in the neighborhood, including:

Moorilla Estate is a good stop even if you're not a wine person. It has a striking location on the Derwent River just 10 kilometers north of Hobart. The restaurant is first class, the wines excellent, and the whole package very suave and upscale. Moorilla is generally regarded as the granddaddy of the Tasmanian wine industry, with first plantings laid down in 1958. Again, whites are the more significant issues at Moorilla, with some exceptional chardonnays and decent rieslings. Reds include pinot noirs and cabernet sauvignon.

The menu at the restaurant, the Moorilla Estate, ★★★ is eclectic, with such offerings as scallops in an anchovy, dill, lemon butter sauce with seaweed noodles or pan-seared venison with a port glaze sauce. Lunches are nicely priced, with entrees in the A$15 range. It also has cheese tastings. You reach the winery by driving north from Hobart on the Brooker Highway (Highway 1) to Berriedale; it's well posted. Or you can go to the winery by boat from the Brooke Street Pier in Salamanca, a 45-minute trip. The restaurant and tasting room are open daily from 10 a.m.–5 p.m. ☎ *(03) 6249-2949; FAX (03) 6249-4093.*

Crosswinds Vineyard is an expanding facility located in the gentle pastoral area near Richmond, and a good stop during a tour of the National Trust villages. Less than a decade old, the winery produces chardonnays, pinot noir and champagnes. You reach the vineyard by going north on Highway 1 from Hobart to the Tea Tree turnoff, the C322. It's open daily from 10 a.m.–5 p.m. October-May and weekends 10 a.m.–5 p.m. the rest of the year. ☎ *(03) 6268-1091 phone and FAX.*

Orani Vineyard and **Palmara Vineyard** are two other wineries located in the same general area as Crosswinds. Orani is about four kilometers from Sorrell on the road to Port Arthur from Hobart. It offers pinot noir, chardonnay and riesling. It's open weekends and holidays from 9:30 a.m.–6:30 p.m. ☎ *(03) 6244-4121.* Palmara is a tiny winery on the main road in Richmond, specializing in cabernet sauvignon, pinot noir and chardonnay. It's open 10 a.m.–6 p.m. October-March and noon-4 p.m. the rest of the year. ☎ *(03) 6262-2462.*

The West

Not the best wine-producing area in the state, so wineries are virtually nonexistent. One definitely worth a stop, for the scenery alone, is the **Lake Barrington Estate** about 35 kilometers south of Devonport in the lake district. Champagne is on the menu here, as well as chardonnay, riesling and pinot noir. It's the perfect place to stop for lunch on the way to Cradle Mountain. It's located near West Kentish on the C141. Hours are 10 a.m.–5 p.m. weekends and holidays, November-April. ☎ *(03) 6491-1249; FAX (03) 6334-2892.*

Hobart

Of all Australia's capital cities, Hobart has probably best kept the look and feel of its colonial past. It sits in a wonderful location on the Derwent River, so wide at this point it creates a natural harbor as it meets the Tasman Sea on the island's southeast coast. After Sydney, Hobart was the second city founded in Australia. The British, agitated because of French interest in the area, decided in 1803 to stake out a claim to Van Dieman's Land, attempted settlements on the north coast, and explored the Derwent estuary. In February 1804, a colony was begun in a cove on the Derwent and named Hobart Town after the English secretary of state for colonies.

Behind the city is 4100-foot-high **Mt. Wellington**, often cloud-covered, sometimes snowy. It's well worth the drive up to the top of the mountain, but be prepared to be blown away—literally. It's very windy up there, and even in the summer, the peak is high enough up to give you a good chill. The mountain is also crossed with hiking trails, some of which go through some really nice fern forests. There is a glassed-in visitors lookout building on the lip of the mountain where you can see all the way to the Tasman Peninsula. To get there by car, take the A6 (Davey Street) south out of town to the B64 highway (also Davey Street) which becomes Huon Road. Then near Ferntree, look for the C616 and signs pointing you up the mountain.

Another spot to see the bay and the city is from the **Mount Nelson Signal Station** in Sandy Bay. The tower was built in 1811 as a way to announce the arrival of ships to the Derwent estuary. Today, the chief signalman's cottage is a restaurant offering lunch and morning and afternoon teas. There's also a gift shop and some bush walks. There is bus service to the site. Information ☎ *(03) 6223-3407.*

It is the combination of colonial buildings, the preserved waterfront with its seafaring spirit, and the agreeable climate that makes Hobart seem much more like a European coastal city than other Australian cities.

The **National Trust**, responsible for preserving historic buildings in Australia, has a full bag in Tasmania. Just in Hobart, there are several days' worth of touring involved to see everything—more than 90 buildings. The Trust's headquarters is at *39 Paterson Street, Launceston;* ☎ *(03) 6331-9077.* There is an office in Hobart (see below).

The most interesting sections of downtown are Salamanca Place and Battery Point. **Salamanca Place** is a cobbled street lined with Georgian sandstone warehouses and storerooms left over from the 1830s and 1840s when Hobart was one of the major whaling ports in the world. Today, the buildings are full of small shops, restaurants, pubs, and galleries. Included among the older buildings are **Sullivan's Cove**, a fashion shop housed in the street's oldest building (1833); the former **Stoppy's Waterfront Tavern**, now a sports bar set in a block of three buildings dating from 1840; and the **Salamanca Arts Centre**, a nest of small arts and crafts shops in a building erected in 1844. At *33 Salamanca Place* are the offices of the **National Trust**, which has a small gift store and information about the city's old buildings. *It's open 9:30 a.m.–5 p.m. Monday.–Friday and 9:30 a.m.–1 p.m. Saturday.* ☎ *(03) 6223-7371.* Every Saturday morning, Salamanca Place turns into a large open-air **flea market** with food stalls. Across from Salamanca Place in St. Davids Park is a statue honoring Abel Tasman, presented to the city by the Dutch government during the Australian bicentennial in 1988.

Battery Point, which lies on a hill above Salamanca Place, is named after a battery of guns set up to guard the port entrance in 1818. This is a wonderful old neighborhood, with 150-year-old houses, small restaurants and pubs, narrow streets and a village green. One of Battery Point's landmarks is **St. George's Church**, the so-called Mariner's Church, begun in 1836.

Not to be missed at Battery Point is the **Maritime Museum of Australia** on Secheron Road, which has materials relating to Tasmania's history dating back to the voyages of Abel Tasman. *The museum is open 1 p.m.–4:30 p.m. Monday–Friday.; 10 a.m.–4:30 p.m. Saturday., and 1 p.m.–4:30 p.m. Sunday; $2 admission charge.* ☎ *(03) 6223-5082.* The National Trust offers guided walking tours of Battery Point every Saturday at 9:30 a.m. The A$5 fee includes morning tea. Information ☎ *(03) 6223-7570.*

The major landmark in the city, much boasted of, is the **Wrest Point Casino and Hotel**, a tall white tower sitting on the shore at Sandy Bay south of Bat-

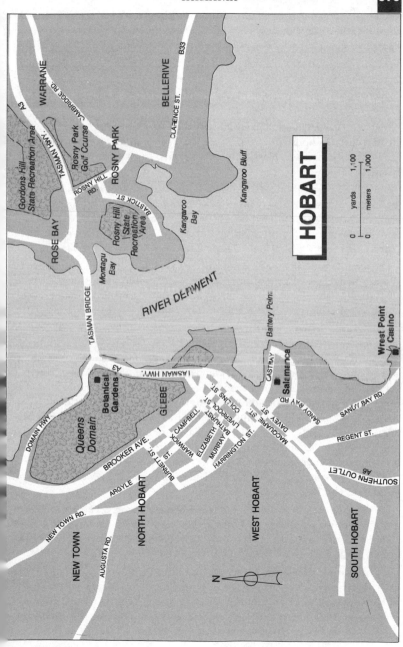

tery Point. Small by most gaming standards, it was the first casino in Australia and is still a popular spot.

Anglesea Barracks, on Davey Street back of the downtown area, is the headquarters of Australia's armed forces in Tasmania, and is the oldest military establishment in the country still in use. Its Georgian buildings have been restored. *Tours 11 a.m. Tuesday. Museum open 9:30 a.m.–3:30 p.m. Monday–Friday; free admission.* ☎ *(03) 6221-2260.*

One of the oldest buildings in Hobart is **Parliament House**, which started life as a customs house in 1840. There is a visitors gallery for viewing when the house is in session. Next to it is a very nice garden area that leads into Salamanca Place.

A good display of Aboriginal history is available at the **Tasmanian Museum and Art Gallery**, housed in new quarters at *40 Macquarie Street,* that include remnants of the city's oldest building, the **Commissariat Store**, built in 1808. The museum has a stuffed Tasmanian tiger and artworks dating back to the 18th century. *It's open daily 10 a.m.–5 p.m.; admission free.* ☎ *(03) 6223-1422.*

The **Royal Tasmanian Botanical Gardens** are small but mighty, with some really excellent displays of rare huon pines, cacti, tropical plants and an herb garden. The gardens sit on the Derwent north of downtown, and are well worth a look. *Hours are from 8 a.m. to dusk. Information:* ☎ *(03) 6234-6299.*

The **Cascade Brewery**, *140 Cascade Road,* home to Tasmania's best beer, is open for two-hour tours at 9:30 a.m. and 1 p.m. Monday–Friday; some additional tours in the summer. The tours require a fair amount of climbing and are not very handicapped friendly. Bookings necessary, A\$7 charge per person; A\$5 for seniors and students. ☎ *(03) 6224-1144.* Hobart is also home to Australia's only commercial whisky distillery. The first distillery in the city was built in the red light district in the 1820s; the new **Tasmania Distillery** is in the same area. Cellar door sales are available, and tours of the boozery and an accompanying museum are offered daily from 8:30 a.m.–6 p.m. in the summer; adults are A\$5. The company also sells jams, chocolates, mustards and other speciality foods. The distillery is at *2 Macquarie Street.* ☎ *(03) 6231-0588; FAX (03) 6231-0587.*

For the hungry, there are tours of the **Cadbury Chocolate Factory** in Claremont, a suburb northwest of Hobart. The tours are mornings and 1 p.m. Monday-Friday and cost A\$10 adults. Tickets for the tours must be purchased at the Tasmanian travel office on Davey Street.

It's impossible to visit Tasmania without meeting a devil, and your chance in the Hobart area is at the very good animal habitat at **Bonorong Park**, north of Hobart at the town of Brighton. The fastest way by car is to take Highway 1 (Brooker Street) north to Andrew Street to Tea Tree Road in Brighton, then south on Briggs Road to the park.

The facility has a big selection of Aussie critters, including koalas, emus, wombats, platypuses and kangaroos. When you pay for your ticket (A$6 adult), they give you a bag of corn to feed the animals. The kangaroos ignored us, the emus weren't hungry, and it's against the rules to feed the devils. Anyway, it's a good first introduction to Tasmanian wildlife, despite being overrun with loud and obnoxious peacocks. Information ☎ *(03) 6268-1184; FAX (03) 6268-1811.*

Essential Hobart

Information

The **Hobart Tasmanian Travel and Information Centre** is located at *80 Elizabeth Street,* ☎ *(03) 6230-8233; FAX (03) 6224-0289.* Hours are 8:30 a.m.–5:15 p.m. Mon.–Fri., 9 a.m.–4 p.m. weekends and holidays. The **Hobart Royal Automobile Club** office is located at the corner of Patrick and Murray streets; ☎ *(03) 6232-6300.*

Getting Around

There is regular service around Hobart and the suburbs on **Metropolitan Transit Trust buses**. *Information,* ☎ *(03) 6233 4223.* The Hobart airport is about 10 miles outside of town. There is bus service into town for about A$5, taxi fare runs about A$15. The **Redline bus** from the ferry dock in Devonport to Hobart is about A$30. There is Monday-Friday ferry service across the Derwent from the Brooke Street pier at Sullivans Cove in Hobart to the Bellerive Wharf on the east side of the river. It's a nice way to see the city from another angle, plus you can walk along Victoria Esplanade to Kangaroo Bluff, another site of historic batteries protecting the approaches to the city. The ferry crossing takes about 15 minutes and costs A$1.20 adults one way. The ferry is named the MV Emmalisa. ☎ *(03) 6225-5893.*

Tours

Walking tours, bus tours, chauffeured car tours, almost any kind of tour is available from Hobart. It's possible, for example, to do day or night tours of Port Arthur from Hobart for about A$50 per person, which usually includes a meal and entrance fees. Tours also go as far as Cradle Mountain and Launceston as well as East Coast resort areas. Some of the companies to contact are **Hobart & Intercity Coaches** (Gray Line), *4 Liverpool Street,* open seven days, ☎ *(03) 6234-4077, FAX (03) 6234-4408; toll free (008) 030-620;* **Tasmanian Wilderness Transport & Tours**, part of the Gray Line organization, also at *4 Liverpool Street,* same phone; and **TRC Tasmania**, *4/80 Elizabeth Street,* open seven days ☎ *(03) 6231-2200, FAX (03) 6234-9241; toll free (008) 030-033.* One interesting way to see the city is on a **Hobart Ghost Tour**, which has tours nightly during the summer leaving at 8 and 9:30 p.m. or at midnight for groups of 20 or more. The tours take you around to the historic parts of the city while guides fill you in on rascals, tramps, convicts, trollops and the other folks who made Hobart such a raunchy place last century. The tours are A$7 for adults. Tours leave from the corner of Campbell and Brisbane streets and can be booked through the travel and information center on Davey Street.

Events

Every year just after Christmas, a hardy bunch of yachties take off from the mainland on the sometimes perilous Sydney-to-Hobart and Melbourne-to-Hobart races across the Bass Strait. In conjunction with the races, Hobart puts on its best dress and presents the **"Taste of Tasmania,"** a week-long party featuring food, wine, operas, theater performances and arts displays. The festival, held at Princes Wharf Number One, culminates with ceremonies honoring the victorious yacht crews. Normal dates are Dec. 27-Jan. 4.

Post Office

The main post office is at the corner of Macquarie and Elizabeth Streets. ☎ *(03) 6220-7351.* The cost of a postcard back to the United States is A95 cents; about A$1 anywhere else in the world.

Shopping

Normal shopping hours in Hobart are 9 a.m.–6 p.m. Monday–Friday; some stores open until 9 p.m. Friday. The **American Express** office in Hobart is at *74A Liverpool Street* ☎ *(03) 6234-3711;* most of the city's banks are on Liverpool near Elizabeth Street.

The heart of downtown Hobart shopping is the **Cat and Fiddle Arcade** between Elizabeth and Murray streets, which has a number of shops. A great store in the Cat and Fiddle is **Naturally Tasmanian**, which has a good selection of food, wines, arts and crafts and clothing. The arcade leads into the **Elizabeth Street Mall**, the largest shopping area in the city. Look for shops offering items made from huon pine. You'll also find stores along Liverpool and Collins streets. Among good bets on Elizabeth Street is the **Tasmania Shop**, *108 Elizabeth Street*, which features the works of more than 100 Tassie crafts makers. You'll find wood carvings as well as high-quality woolen goods. If you really want to get into the wool, go to the **Sheepskin and Opal World** store at 35 Morrison Street just back of the ferry dock. The store carries kangaroo skin products, leather goods, Australian opals and hundreds of wool products. It's open Monday–Saturday from 9 a.m.–6 p.m. and Sunday from 11 a.m.–5 p.m. It offers overseas mailing service. For a good selection of Aussie western wear, such as Akubra hats and R.M. Williams moleskins, try **Country Comfort**, *104 Elizabeth Street*.

Where to Stay

Grand Chancellor   **A$175–300**   ★★★★

1 Davey Street; ☎ *(03) 6235-4535.*
Doubles start around A$175–240; suites from $A300.
Located at the city harbor, probably the best in town, with two bars, a cafe, and licensed restaurant. There is a health club and an indoor pool and sauna. Rooms come with a view of the harbor or Mt. Wellington.

Wrest Point Hotel Casino and Motor Inn   **A$100–340**   ★★★

410 Sandy Bay Road; ☎ *(03) 6225-0112; FAX (03) 6225-3909; toll free reservations (008) 030-611.*
Doubles at the casino hotel start around A$200; suites A$285–340. Motel-style rooms start at $A100 for doubles.
Four bars, a disco, the gaming tables, a nightclub, a revolving restaurant, Asian restaurant, a 24-hour coffee shop for light meals: in short, a rocking place to hang out.

The views are great, although the place is a bit out of town. It has a pool, sauna, gym, and tennis facilities. The casino is open every day except Good Friday and Christmas.

Salamanca Inn   A$180–240   ★★★

10 Gladstone Street; ☎ *(03) 6223-3300; FAX (03) 6223-7167.*
One-bedroom suites A$180; two-bedroom suites, $A200; apartments from A$220-240.
Great location within a half block of Salamanca Place with convenient parking garage. Suite and apartment accommodations, heated indoor pool and spa, restaurant and bar, guest laundry. Great choice for central touring. Probably our favorite hotel in Hobart; great service.

Lenna of Hobart   A$150–200   ★★★

20 Runnymede Street; ☎ *(03) 6232-3900; FAX (03) 6224-0112.*
Doubles start around A$150-200.
Ideally located for exploring Battery Point. The elegant main building, a National Trust site, is a restored 1880s mansion; other units are attached. Lenna also houses one of the best restaurants in Tasmania, **Alexander's**, ★★★★ **$$$** which specializes in Tassie foods served with a French flair. The seafood is marvelous. It's open daily from 6:30 p.m., and reservations are a must. ☎ *(03) 6234-4123.*

Westside   A$120–200   ★★★

156 Bathurst Street; ☎ *(03) 6232-6255; FAX (03) 6234-7884; toll free reservations (800) 030-003.*
Doubles start around A$120, suites from A$200.
The Westside is a very comfy Flag property a few blocks west of the harbor. It has two floors of nonsmoking rooms, plus some handicapped rooms. It has a couple of restaurants, including the laid back **Last Drop Steakhouse and Saloon** ★★★ **$$**. The other restaurant, the **Silver Skillet** ★★★ **$$**, specializes in game dishes.

Battery Point Guest House   A$85–100   ★★★

7 McGregor Street ☎ *(03) 6224-2111; FAX (03) 6224-3648.*
Doubles A$75–100.
One of the coziest nests in the city, an old two story house overlooking Battery Point. There are five rooms, one with spa, plus one room which is called the Empire Suite and is a replica of one of the staterooms on the ill-fated RMS Titanic. Nonsmoking facility. The building is the former coach house for the Lenna mansion.

Lodge on Elizabeth, The   A$100–140   ★★★

17-23 Regent Street, Sandy Bay ☎ *(03) 6223-3200; FAX (03) 6223-1126.*
Doubles $A100–140.
The lodge is a 1830s National Trust house, one of the oldest in the city. It's located a bit away from downtown, with eight rooms, including some with spas. There is laundry service, log fires and very nice breakfasts. If B&Bs are your thing, this is a good bet.

Regent Park   A$60–105   ★★★

249 Elizabeth Street ☎ *(03) 6231-3830; FAX (03) 6234-2566.*
Doubles A$60–105.
This double-tower facility overlooks Battery Point and the Derwent estuary, and has 28 two-bedroom apartments with guest laundry, mini-bars and microwaves. Four of the units are penthouse suites with balconies. It's close to the University of Tasmania.

Midcity Motor Inn   A$90   ★★

96 Bathurst; ☎ *(03) 6234-6333; FAX (03) 6231-0898.*
Doubles A$90.
Nothing glamorous, but centrally located about a half block from the Elizabeth Street Mall. Boxy building, ordinary furnishings. But it does have satellite TV, free parking and a guest laundry.

St. Ives Motel   A$100–115   ★★

67 St. Georges Terrace; ☎ *(03) 6224-1044; FAX (03) 6223-8774; toll free (008) 030-760.*
Doubles A$100–115.
Another Battery Point lodging. The multi-story facility has motel units and one- and two-bedroom apartments. Restaurant/bar, laundry, handicapped access.

Macquarie Motor Inn   A$80–90   ★★

167 Macquarie Street; ☎ *(03) 6234-4422; FAX (03) 6234-4273; toll free (008) 030-555.*
Doubles A$80–90.
Another unpretentious downtown hotel, located about two blocks from Salamanca Place. It does have a heated pool, sauna and spa, plus restaurant and bar.

Hobart Pacific Motor Inn   A$75–85   ★★

Kirby Court, West Hobart; ☎ *(03) 6234-6733; FAX (03) 6231-1197.*
Doubles start at A$75.
Cooking facilities, restaurant/bar, pool, great views, guest laundry. About two kilometers from the city center.

Backpacking   A$10

There are a number of backpacker facilities in Hobart. Probably the easiest to get to is **Transit Centre Backpackers**, which sits on top of the Redline Coach Terminal at 199 Collins Street downtown. In addition to sleeping facilities, it has bike hire, airport shuttle service and state-wide backpacking information. ☎ *(03) 6231-2400 phone and FAX.*

Where to Eat

Along **Liverpool Street** in the city center are a number of ethnic cafes and small restaurants, vegetarian hangouts, juice bars, coffee bars and pubs. It's a good strip, small but lively, not like Sydney but quite adequate anyway. Try the **Kara Cafe** *(119 Liverpool)* which has the best coffee in Tasmania, maybe in the South Pacific. If you're really hungry, try these:

Mures Upper Deck Restaurant $$$ ★★★

On Victoria dock near the Grand Chancellor; ☎ *(03) 6231-2121.*
Lunch and dinner seven days.
Actually a complex, with the restaurant on the top floor and a cafe on the ground floor. Used to be operated by the famous Muir family of fishmongers in Hobart, who got out of the restaurant business and moved to other quarters. Very popular spot for seafood; reservations at the Upper Deck necessary. The view over the harbor is dandy, and the best fish to try is one virtually unknown outside Tasmania, the stripey trumpeter. The street level cafe is nothing spectacular. The complex is open daily for lunch and dinner.

Dear Friends   **$$$**   ★★★

> 8 Brooke Street; ☎ (03) 6223-2646.
> Lunch Tuesday–Friday; dinner Monday–Saturday.

Housed in yet another old port building, antique surroundings. Known for Tasmanian game, seafood and lamb. Great list of virtually all Tassie wines.

Drunken Admiral   **$$$**   ★★★

> 17 Hunter Street (Old Wharf, near the Victoria Dock). ☎ (03) 6234-1903.
> Lunch Monday–Friday, December–January only; dinner seven days.

Housed in one of the oldest waterfront buildings in Hobart, and one of the most popular eateries in town. The decor is maritime with dashes of convict history. Menu features such goodies as the huge seafood platter named the **Sydney-Hobart**. Reservations a must.

Astor Grill   **$$**   ★★★

> 157 Macquarie Street; ☎ (03) 6234-3809.
> Lunch Monday–Friday; dinner Monday–Sunday.

The Astor has been popular in Hobart forever, mainly because the service and the chow are consistently good. Seafood is always top notch, but if you want to try a good Aussie steak, ask for the prime eye fillet pocketed with stilton cheese (and that's pronounced *fill-it*, remember.) Good wine list.

Sisco's   **$$$**   ★★★

> 121 Macquarie Street; ☎ (03) 6223-2059.
> Lunch Tuesday-Friday; dinner Tuesday-Saturday.

This place specializes in Spanish/Mediterranean fare, with tapas for lunch. Specialties of the house include stuffed squid, antipasto platters and *crema Catalonia* (creme caramel, topped with toffee.)

Ball and Chain, The   **$$**   ★★

> 87 Salamanca Place; ☎ (03) 6223-2655.
> Lunch Monday–Saturday; dinner from 7 p.m. seven days.

One of the bounciest spots in the area, housed in another old sandstone colonial building. The emphasis here is on charcoal-grilled steaks. Also Cajun-style trevalla or (oh, the shame of it all) wallaby sausages. Salad or hot vegetable bar. Good eats.

Beyond Hobart

The Tasman Peninsula

The location of Australia's most famous prison is no accident. It was placed on the Tasman Peninsula, about 60 miles southeast of Hobart, because the peninsula is attached to the mainland by a tiny isthmus called Eaglehawk Neck, making escape a very chancy and difficult endeavor. The neck is so narrow (about 100 yards wide) that it was once guarded by a single line of dogs to stop convicts from escaping across it. In addition, the authorities let it be known that the waters on either side of the isthmus were filled with deadly sharks—not true. There are a couple of motels, a B&B and a backpackers facility at the Neck. We recommend the **Lufra Holiday Hotel** ★★ which has units for about A$60 double including a continental breakfast; some handicapped units. ☎ (03) 6250-

3262. Contact the backpackers at ☎ *(03) 6250-3248*. There is also a dive shop—diving in the area is excellent, including kelp forests and the well-preserved wreck of the *S.S. Nord*. Contact the **Eaglehawk Dive Center** at ☎ *(03) 6250-3566*. (The main office is in Sorell, northeast of Hobart.)

The east coast of the Tasman Peninsula is sedimentary rock, mostly Permian sandstone, and constant wave action has created high cliffs and some spectacular blowhole-like formations. Three of the more notable are the **Tasman Arch**, **the Blowhole** and **Devil's Kitchen**, huge collapsed caves drilled through the rocks by wave surges. They are reached by taking a road from the Neck southwest to the ocean (it's clearly marked.) On the way to the coast, you will go through what is unofficially known as "Doo Town," a group of houses all with Doo names, such as "Much-a-Doo," X-Anadoo" and "Doo-Little." Yuck-yuck. Another popular spot is **Remarkable Cave**, a tube cut into the rocks that is dry at low tide and can be reached by a set of stairs. It's south of the prison.

As long as you're in the area, you might as well take advantage of your one sure chance to see a Tasmanian devil up close. About 10 kilometers south of Eaglehawk Neck (or 10 kilometers north of the prison) is the **Tasmanian Devil Park**. It's basically a wildlife rescue and treatment center. It was once possible to cuddle devils here, but strict new laws governing wildlife parks make that impossible now. It's against the law to take any normal animals from the wild, so all the beasts you see at the park are either orphaned or injured. One special thing at the park is a short movie taken of the last known Tasmanian tiger left alive in Australia, which died in captivity in the 1930s. There is a gift shop at the park office. Adults A$8. Open 9–5 daily ☎ *(03) 6250-3230; FAX (03) 6250-3406*.

A few miles farther south you'll see the black and white Tudor-style **Fox & Hounds Resort ★ ★**, with self-contained units and motel rooms. It has a pool, tennis court, bar, restaurant, guest laundry and a bottle shop. A small tourist train runs from the Fox & Hounds to the Bush Mill, next door. The resort is adding upscale lodging. Units run from A$90 to A$110 double. Or you can try a two-night package for A$140 per person that includes accommodation, two cooked breakfasts, two three-course menu fixe' meals, Ghost Tour tickets and Port Arthur one-day entry tickets. The resort is a couple of miles north of the Port Arthur entrance. ☎ *(03) 6250-2217; FAX (03) 6250-2590; toll free 1-(800) 635-840*.

Popular with the Aussies but a tad hokey for our tastes is the **Bush Mill**, which is a re-creation of a bush community in the 1800s, complete with a wood workshop, general store, bushman's camp, surveyors' tents, blacksmith shop and a hospital. It would be great for kids. As noted, it also has a small narrow-gauge train that runs back and forth to the Fox & Hounds. Meals and Devonshire teas are available at the coffee shop/restaurant. Bush Mill is open 9 a.m.–5 p.m. seven days. The train leaves the site hourly or so in the summer from 10 a.m. to 4:15 p.m. (July-August the park is open from 10 a.m.–4 p.m.) The fee is A$12 adults. ☎ *(03) 6250-2221 phone and FAX*.

Port Arthur

Enough time has passed since Port Arthur was abandoned—1877—that the old prison and its grounds have taken on the look of an ancient and crumbling Irish castle estate. The wide lawns and moss-covered bricks have gentled and softened what was once the most feared penal colony in the British Empire, although during its entire 50-year history, only 12,000 convicts passed through its gates, including 90 Americans. After it was closed, many of the buildings were damaged or removed because it reminded Victorian Australians of their sometimes shady roots. But over the years, preservationists finally won out and the old prison and the area around it have become one of the most popular tourist destinations in Australia (for Australians); most international visitors never make it to Tasmania, let alone Port Arthur.

As noted earlier, the park became the site of a horrible event in the spring of 1996 when a man carrying a semiautomatic rifle opened fire at several spots around the area and killed more than 30 people. The nation went into shock, and it will be many, many years before Port Arthur recovers. The prison area now will be remembered as the site of not only one of the cruelest prisons in modern history, but as the site of the worst mass murders in Australian history. The Broad Arrow Cafe, where many of the victims were killed as they sat eating lunch, has been closed and plans call for it to be razed and a memorial to be erected. *If you do visit Port Arthur, officials ask that you do not ask staff about the shootings. Tour guides refrain from mentioning the tragedy, as well.*

The prison was begun in 1830 as a sawing station to provide lumber, and then it was set aside for the penal system's worst prisoners. In the mid-1830s, a prison for juvenile male offenders was built, and not far away was a coal mine which had the worst working conditions in the whole prison colony. Port Arthur had a peak prison population of around 1200 convicts at one time, plus a military and civilian support force of around 1000. Between 1840 and 1853, most of the convicts sent from England went to Tasmania, requiring a larger and more permanent prison facility to be built. Its most infamous period was when it housed a "model prison," based on the quaint Victorian thought that isolation was better than physical abuse.

Prisoners were not allowed to speak, never saw one another, and spent their time in one-man isolation cells. (During exercise periods, they all wore masks.) Many prisoners went insane because of the isolation. After transportation to Tasmania was outlawed in 1853, the prison gradually became a sort of old folk's home for elderly prisoners, and also served as a mental asylum. Many of the buildings left standing after the prison was closed in 1877 were badly damaged by bushfires in 1895 and 1897. Whatever was left was finally saved in 1979 when Tasmania and the federal government set up a joint preservation project to excavate and restore the old prison. The result, of course, is why Port Arthur is such a big tourist attraction.

The first stop at Port Arthur should be at the **visitors center** and **museum**, where guided tours can be booked, information is available and there is an audiovisual program on the prison's history. Admission to the Port Arthur site is $13 per person; open 9 a.m.–5 p.m. daily. The tickets give free entry to the prison museum, a free tour of the Isle of the Dead and a 24-hour entry pass. The most popular building in the complex is the **penitentiary/grain mill** built to supply flour to the prison in 1844. The grist mill was powered by 24 convicts on a treadmill. It was enlarged into its present size in 1853, when it held about 600 prisoners.

The other always-photographed building is the **old church**, first started in 1836 and able to hold 1000 convicts and 200 officials. Nothing remains now but the shell; the church was the victim of the late-century bush fires, as was the grain mill. Much of it was built by teenaged prisoners.

Other structures on the site are an ornate, round **guard tower** (dating from 1836); the **commandant's house**, a timber and brick edifice with very nice gardens (1833); the **model prison** (1848), with its attached asylum (1867); the **hospital** (1842), and the **pauper's mess**, used to feed the elderly former prisoners (1864). In addition to the buildings in the main complex, there are excursions to the **Isle of the Dead**, a small island not far from the prison, which served as the settlement's graveyard. There are about 2000 graves on the island, mostly those of prisoners. The trip operates daily, costs about A$5, and can be booked at the visitor's center; the walking tour of the island takes about 45 minutes. There are also nightly "**ghost tours**," starting at 8:30 p.m. winters and 9:30 p.m. summer. Tickets are A$10 for adults and can be booked at the visitors center. We found them to be less than haunting, but the nightly tours do allow you to see parts of the park not open to day tours. ☎ *(03) 6250-2539.* One way to do the whole thing is to book a package through the **Port Arthur Motor Inn** ★ ★ the only accommodations within the park. ☎ *(03) 6250-2101; FAX (03) 6250-2417; toll free (008) 030-747.* For A$85 per person, you get a night's lodging, dinner, breakfast and the ghost tour. The package can be booked in Hobart at the tourist information center. The package does not include entry tickets to the Port Arthur site. *(All accommodations in the area offer packages that include lodging, meals and tickets for the Ghost Tours.)*

You can either take a leisurely drive to Port Arthur from Hobart (the A3 to Sorell, the A9 to Port Arthur) or join one of the many tours operating from Hobart. If you want more than a day trip, there are accommodations (including the aforementioned Port Arthur Motor Inn), a youth hostel, craft shop and cafe on the site. The youth hostel **(Roseview YHA)** has some very nice packages that include transportation form Hobart and entry tickets. One night stays are A$12 per person. ☎ *(03) 6250-2311.* The park has a nightly showing of the film based on Marcus Clarke's classic, *For the Term of His Natural Life*, a silent epic shot on the site in 1926. The cost is A$5, including tea; November-April. ☎ *(03) 6250-2242.* The **Frances Langford Tea Room** has light lunches, morning and afternoon teas and picnic packs. It's named for the wife of the first police officer stationed at Port Arthur. Open daily 10 a.m.–5 p.m. ☎ *(03) 6250-2562.* Park planners are hoping to open a new multi-million-dollar visitors center, complete with parking garage and interpretive center, by the end of 1997.

Our choice for accommodations at Port Arthur is the modern log cabins at **Port Arthur Holiday World** ★ ★ ★ at Stewart's Bay north of the park. The resort is reached going south by taking a left-hand turn just before a small grocery store—it's well marked. The Holiday World has one and two-bedroom self-contained units. One-bedroom cabins go for A$80 double from September-Dec. 24; A$90 from Dec. 25–Jan 31 and A$80 again from February through April 30. *Information:* ☎ *(03) 6250-2262; FAX (03) 6250-2513.* The facility has an excellent eatery, **Kelley's Restaurant** ★ ★ ★ ★ **$$$**, which specializes in Tasmanian seafood. Look for mussels in pesto sauce or Kelley's Katch, a mix of prawns and trevalleys in white sauce with mushrooms. The family owns its own mussel and oyster farm on the Tasman Peninsula. Reservations are a good idea. Open daily for lunch and dinner; no lunch in the winter on Mondays. ☎ *(03) 6250-2666; FAX (03) 6250-2736.*

Another choice is the **Port Arthur Holiday Villas** ★★ (it's a motel) just down the street from the Port Arthur Motor Inn. There are one- and two-bedroom units done up in knotty pine with full kitchens. It has a guest laundry and barbecue facilities. The one-bedroom units go for A$70–90 depending on season; two-bedrooms units are A$95-130. ☎ *(03) 6250-2239; FAX (03) 6250-2589;* toll free 1-(800) 815-775.

If you're in a camper, try for the **Port Arthur Caravan and Cabin Park**, about a mile from the prison down the same road as the Holiday World, which has very nice sites and facilities. When you check in, ask whoever's in charge if the wombats are still around. They're tame, cuddly, and very wombattish, and this will probably be the only time you'll get that close to a really tame one. Powered sites are A$13; cabins are A$45; dormitory spaces A$13 per person (very nice cooking facilities.) There is a good trail from the RV park to Port Arthur along the shore of Stewart's Bay; about 45 minutes to walk. ☎ *(03) 6250-2340; FAX (03) 6250-2509.*

If things are crowded at Port Arthur, you should head for **Nubeena**, a small settlement northwest of the park. There are several motels, a deli and a small cafe. Also close by is **White Beach**, one of the better beaches on the Tasman Peninsula. We recommend the **White Beach Holiday Villas**, which has four two-bedroom units with cooking facilities. The units go for A$55–65 double. ☎ *(03) 6250-2152; FAX (03) 6250-2578.*

For general information about the prison, contact the **Port Arthur Historic Site Management Authority**, *Clougha, Port Arthur 7182;* ☎ *(03) 6250-2363; FAX (03) 6250-2494.*

A good way to see all the highlights of the Port Arthur area is with the **Triple Pass** that allows entry into the prison, the Tasmanian Devil Park and the Bush Mill. The pass costs A$27.50 for adults, and can be purchased aboard the Spirit of Tasmania or at Tasmanian travel centers.

On the way back north up the Arthur Highway toward Hobart, just where the Forestier Peninsula meets the main island, you'll find a neat little pub, the **Dunalley Hotel** (in the wide spot of the same name.) It dates from 1886 and has great fish and chips, nice bar and a hearty kitchen. Well worth a pit stop if you are hungry.

The National Trust Villages

One of the things that makes wandering around rural Tasmania so charming is the small English-style towns and villages that dot the landscape, many dating from the first years of colonial settlement. Somehow, many of the old stone colonial and convict-constructed buildings have survived and are now protected by the National Trust. Among the most photogenic of all the villages are **Richmond** and **New Norfolk**, which are only a few miles outside Hobart, and **Ross**, south of Launceston.

The **oldest bridge** in Australia still in use is found at Richmond, a restored colonial village about 15 miles northwest of Hobart. The bridge (probably the most photographed site in Tasmania) was built in 1823 with convict labor. In the village itself are a number of historic buildings, including **St. John's**, the oldest Catholic church in Australia (1836), and the **Richmond Gaol**, which dates from 1825, but which saw most of its use for convicts in the 1840s. The gaol has cells and articles of punishment on view. Open daily 9 a.m.–5 p.m.; A$3 admission. One of the prisoners reportedly housed there was Izzy Solomons, a London brothel-keeper and fence who supposedly was the inspiration for Fagin in Dickens' *Oliver Twist*. ☎ *(03) 6260-2127*.

Another attraction worth a stop to history buffs is **Old Hobart Town**, a scale model of 1820s Hobart, built mostly from original plans. It's open daily 9:30 a.m.–5:30 p.m. Admission is A$5 adults. And because Aussies seem to be maze crazy, there's a wooden one available in Richmond (critics spurn it because it's not made of hedges.) Anyway, it's on Bridge street toward the south of town. It's open daily 10 a.m.–5 p.m.; admission A$3.50 for adults.

There are several good and historic hostelries in Richmond, including the **Richmond Arms Hotel** and the **Prospect House**. The Richmond Arms ★ ★ is a former stable dating from 1830. It can handle 16 guests; all rooms have private baths. There is a laundry and a continental breakfast is included. It has a dining room open daily for lunch and dinner; good country fare, meat and potatoes sort of place. Doubles are A$85. ☎ *(03) 6260-2109*. The Prospect House, ★ ★ ★ a bit more upscale, is a classy 1830 house sitting on a hill. In addition to good lodging, it has one of the better restaurants in Tasmania, $$$ a constant award winner set in a tasteful wood-paneled area. Trout, salmon and venison are specialties. Rooms are either serviced or self-contained, all with private bath. Dinner-breakfast packages are available. Doubles only start at A$100. ☎ *(03) 6260-2207*.

In good weather, the best place in town to sit outside and take the airs is in the garden of the **Richmond Wine Centre** $$, next to the Village Store on Bridge Street between Franklin and Percy streets. This is a great place to try local and regional Tasmanian wines, as well as some gourmet lunches (grilled salmon with fresh asparagus, fried trevalla with spicy sauce, etc.) Also decadent desserts. It's open 8 a.m.–5 p.m. daily.

New Norfolk lies on the Derwent about 25 miles northwest of Hobart, and is the hops-growing capital of Tasmania. It boasts the oldest church in Tasmania, **St. Matthew's**, an Anglican edifice. Other historic buildings include the **Old Colony Inn**, built as a hops shed in 1815 and used over the years as a school, gymnasium and barracks. You can tour the house for A$1.50 or simply chow down at the restaurant that serves meals all day and dinners on weekends. Also of interest is the **Oast House**, originally used to dry hops and now the home of a museum, art gallery and tea room. The museum claims to be the only hops museum in the Southern Hemisphere, and is open daily from 9:30 a.m.; A$3.50 adults. The tea room serves meals as well as Devonshire teas. Up the river 11 kilometers are the Salmon Ponds, home of all Tasmanian trout (see Fishing in the first part of this chapter.) New Norfolk is also a jet-boating center, where you can catch a ride on the Derwent. **Devil Jet** runs a 20-kilometer circuit on the river from the New Norfolk Esplanade next to the Bush Inn; the rides leave every half hour daily from 9 a.m.–4 p.m. Adults are A$40. Reservations recommended. ☎ *(03) 6261-3460; FAX (03) 6261-1743*.

Accommodations are available at the **Bush Inn**, which is on Montague Street next to the river, and the **Glen Derwent**, just off the Lyell Highway north of the river. The Bush

Inn ★★ claims to have the oldest bar license in Australia, dating from 1815. It has counter meals every day and dinners Monday-Saturday. It's a B&B with shared facilities for about 40 guests. Doubles start at A$50, which includes a cooked breakfast. ☎ *(03)* *6261-2011.* The Glen Derwent, ★★★ more upscale, was built by convicts in 1820. The house plus its outbuildings are National Trust sites. It sits on 15 acres of manicured grounds. Accommodations have private facilities, and there is a heated pool, croquet course and a garden breakfast room. Doubles start at A$90, which includes breakfast. ☎ *(03) 6261-3244; FAX (03) 6261-3770.*

Ross, 80 kilometers from Launceston, is one of the finest colonial villages in the country, and home to the most beautiful of the convict bridges in Tasmania, built in 1836 over the Macquarie River. Colonial officers were so impressed by the work they pardoned Daniel Herbert, the convict stonemason whose 186 carvings adorn the bridge. The town is almost too picturesque to handle, with some really excellent buildings including St. John's Anglican Church (1839); the Uniting Church (1885); the Methodist Sunday School (1827); Macquarie House and Store (1846), plus a whole bag of other structures. Our favorite place to get lunch and a beer is the **Man-O-Ross Hotel** (1835), which has a friendly bar and counter meals plus rooms.

The Man-O-Ross sits on the southwest corner of Bridge and Church streets and is known locally as *Temptation*. On the southeast corner is *Salvation* (the Roman Catholic Church, dating from 1920.) On the northeast corner is *Damnation*, where once stood the local gaol; and at the northwest corner is *Recreation*, site of the Town Hall.

Just down from St. John's Church is the Tasmanian Wool Centre, which has displays on the Tasmanian wool industry as well as woolen products for sale. The museum portion of the center is A$4 adults; the sales rooms are free entry. The center is open daily. ☎ *(03) 6381-5466; FAX (03) 6381-5407.*

In addition to the rooms at the Man-O-Ross (shared facilities, about A$50 double), accommodation is available in a number of cottages around town. They're private—you rent the whole cottage by yourself, and rates run from about A$90-115 double. Best bet is to contact Tim and Sue Johnson who operate **Historic Ross Cottages**, which includes three of the old buildings. ☎ *(03) 6381-5354; FAX (03) 6381-5408.*

The Huon Valley

About 40 kilometers southwest of Hobart is the mouth of the Huon River, which was discovered by the French in 1792. The river lies to the west of the D'Entrecasteaux Channel, named for the head of the French expedition, Admiral Bruni D'Entrecasteaux. The river was named for one of his captains, Huon Kermandec. The captain's name was later given to the stands of native trees found along the rivers in Tasmania: the huon pines. They are not really pines, but much sought-after and very slow-growing softwoods used in shipbuilding and furniture. The trees are now protected in Tasmania. There are small wood-turning galleries all over the area using huon pine and other native woods. Try the **Talune Woodturning and Wildlife Park** in Gardners Bay. (Carvings, plus devils, kangaroos, etc.) Open weekends throughout the year; closed weekdays June 7–Aug. 7. The area is reached by driving south from Cygnet, then taking a road (C627) that cuts over to Woodbridge and Kettering on the D'Entrecasteaux Channel. Gardners Bay is also the site of the **Hartzview Vineyard & Wine Centre**, which has a selection of wines from all over Tasmania as well as room for six guests. The colonial style guest house was built in 1988 and sits on 125 acres with a view of the mountains. Rates are A$110 double. ☎ *(03) 6295-1623 phone and FAX*. At The Deepings, reached by another east-bound road south of Cygnet (C626), is the **Deepings Woodturner**. The Deepings also has accommodations in two pine-decor houses with laundry facilities, barbecues and slate floors. Either B&B or you can cook your own. A small stream nearby supposedly is home to a platypus. Doubles are about A$90. ☎ *(03) 6295-1398; FAX (03) 6295-0498*.

The Huon Valley is a major apple-producing area, as well as a favorite vacation spot. The river itself is a popular jet boating venue. Several state and national parks are in the area and offer a good chance to see native rain forests and stands of old-growth trees. Among the parks is **The Esperance Forest & Heritage Complex**, located in the city of Geevston. The park, named after one of the French explorers' ships, has good trails, including several that take you into groves of really humongous swamp gums. One, called simply Big Tree, is 285 feet high and about 70 feet in circumference. Swamp gums are the tallest flowering plants in the world, often reaching more than 300 feet tall. The Esperance complex is also the trailhead for a strenuous hike out to the **Hartz Mountains National Park** and 4100-foot-high Mt. Hartz. The park can also be reached by driving. Near the end of the road coming from Geevston is the Waratah Lookout, which gives great views of the forests and ravines of the area. The rain forests in this part of Tasmania are mostly comprised of blackwood, sassafras, mrytles and celery-top pines.

At Woodbridge is one of our favorite spots to eat in the area, the **Woodbridge Hotel** ★ ★ ★ ★ $$. It serves great lunches and dinners. Do try the Tasmanian Platter, a selection of Tassie meats, cheeses and seafood, including quail, venison sausage, smoked salmon, marinated squid and mussels. Cheeses include King Island camembert. It's about A$30 each. The view is also great looking out over the channel. There is also accommodation ★ ★ for about A$90. A one-night stay with a three-course dinner, wine tasting and breakfast is about A$90 per person. ☎ *(03) 6267-4604*.

At Kettering, a few miles up the channel from Woodbridge, you can catch a ferry to **North Bruny Island**, which has nice beaches, hiking trails and fairy penquins. North and South Bruny islands are actually one island connected by a very narrow sand isthmus. You can take your car over for about A$20, passengers free; bikes are $A3 and foot passengers are free. The ride is about 15 minutes and lands at Roberts Point. Service is daily about nine times a day. ☎ *(03) 6233-5363*. There are many holiday rental units on both North and South Islands. If you like fish, drive down to Lunawanna on the South Island and try the smoked salmon or, would you believe, salmon burgers, at the **Smokehouse**. Or try a camel ride with **Camel Tracks**, located at the south end of the north island at the isthmus. Rides go for A$25 an hour, or half day with lunch, A$50, full day with lunch and morning/afternoon tea, about A$90; overnights A$70–120 a day. ☎ *(03) 6260-6335*.

At the mouth of the river is Huonville, the major apple center of the valley. Here the highway splits, running down the west bank of the river to Geevston or down the east bank to Cygnet and the ferry crossing to North Bruny Island. Near Cygnet is the **Talune Wildlife Park & Koala Gardens**, with the normal assortment of Tasmanian devils and other critters. It's open daily; adults A$5. If you're into apples in a big way, the place for you is at the **Huon Valley Apple & Heritage Museum** in Grove, about nine kilometers from Huonville toward Hobart. The museum has displays about apple farming as well as historical items from the 1800s. It's open daily from 9 a.m.–5 p.m. in the summer, 10 a.m.–4 p.m. in the winter, closed in July. Adults A$2.50. Also in the area is the **Huon Apple Visitor Information Centre** about four kilometers north of Huonville, open daily. ☎ *(03) 6264-1844*.

About 12 kilometers south of Hobart on the A6 at the village of Taroona is one of Tasmania's most famous landmarks, the **Shot Tower**, dating from 1870 and said to be the oldest remaining shot tower in the world. It was constructed of 8000 pieces of curved sandstone and stands about 185 feet overlooking the Derwent estuary. The tower has 287 steps. It's open daily from 9 a.m.–5 p.m.; admission is A$3. There is a museum, craft shop and small cafe serving Devonshire teas.

Launceston

Tasmania's second city, Launceston (pronounced LAWN-cess-tun), is also one of the oldest settlements in Australia. The city, which sits 40 miles from the ocean at the confluence of the north and south forks of the Esk River (which then becomes the Tamar River), was founded in 1805. It is named after a town in Cornwall. The city, with a population around 65,000, is the main settlement in the northern part of the island, which is largely rolling hills filled with sheep, cattle, crops and vistas that gave rise to the English-like image of the state.

In addition to being a major starting point for Tasmania tours, the city has a few attractions in its own right, including a bunch of **colonial buildings**, notably along St. John and George streets. In the countryside around the city are some of the finest preserved **colonial homesteads** in Australia, all under the care of the National Trust. One major attraction, a tad tacky and sometimes silly, is **Penny Royal World**, a re-creation of a 19th century industrial park, with a cannon factory, corn mill and several ships. It also has a restaurant, tavern, and gift shop. The site is open 9 a.m.–4:30 p.m. daily, admission about A$20. ☎ *(03) 6331-6699*.

Not far outside of town is **Cataract Gorge**, which has been a playground for the good people of the area almost since the city was founded. The South Esk River has cut a very sharp, deep gorge through the rocks, and a couple of natural dams have created large lakes where swimming and boating are popular. There is a suspension bridge at the first dam and also a number of hiking trails in the area. The most popular attraction at the gorge is a high, very high, **chairlift** that goes across the depths. The chairlift, they claim, has the longest single span of any lift in the world: 1010 feet. Hours are 9 a.m.–4:30 p.m. daily. The lift costs about A$3 per person ☎ *(03) 6331-5915*. In the park is the **Gorge Restaurant** ★ ★ $$ with seafood and game specialities, surrounded by a very nice park and gardens; open Tuesday–Sunday lunch and dinner. ☎ *(03) 6331-3330*.

The Launceston area is a major wool milling area, and the best tour is in one of the oldest, the **Waverley Woollen Mills** just outside of town off the A3 (Tasman Highway). The mill, which has a wide array of weavings, including jackets and skirts and some very nice rugs, was built in 1874 and has been producing goods ever since. Tours of the mill are offered every day 9 a.m.–4 p.m., and the showroom is open to 5 p.m. Tours are A$3 per person. There is a small **coffee shop** that serves Devonshire teas. Adjacent is the **National Automobile Museum of Tasmania**, where you can see some choice old cars; open 9 a.m.–5 p.m. daily, A$4 charge. Waverley also has an outlet at *81 Salamanca Place* in Hobart. *Information on the mill:* ☎ *(03) 6339-1106; FAX 6339-3537. Information for the museum,* ☎ *(03) 6339-3727.* Another woollen mill/factory outlet is the **Tamar Knitting Mills** on Hobart Road outside of town. Self-guided tours are offered, as well as a selection of products for sale. It's open 9 a.m.–5 p.m. Monday–Friday and 9 a.m.–4 p.m. weekends and most holidays. ☎ *(03) 6344-8255; FAX (03) 6344-5070.* A unique place to visit is the **Old Umbrella Shop** at *60 George Street* downtown. It's built entirely of Tasmanian blackwood and is much the same as it was when it was built in the 1860s. The **National Trust** store has a display of antique umbrellas as well as a variety of Tasmanian products. It's open from 9 a.m.–5 p.m. Monday–Friday and 9 a.m.–noon Saturdays.

The Tasmania Travel and Information Centre is at the corner of *St. John and Paterson Streets;* ☎ *6336-3122. The RAC office is at the corner of York and George streets;* ☎ *(03) 6331-3166.*

Where to Stay

Country Club Casino   **A$200–390**   ★★★★

Country Club Avenue, Prospect Vale; ☎ *(03) 6344-8855; FAX (03) 6343-1880.*
Doubles start around A$200; suites from A$300–390.

About four miles outside of the city, with casino, golf course, licensed restaurant, coffee shop, three bars and sports facilities. Health center with spa, squash courts, tennis, indoor pool, sauna and gym. Business center.

Novotel   **A$120–400**   ★★★★

29 Cameron Street; ☎ *(03) 6334-3434; FAX (03) 6331-7347.*
Doubles start around A$120; suites from A$200–400.

Arcade shopping, two bars with live entertainment, restaurant, suites with spa baths, garage parking, business center. Some smoke-free rooms.

Elphin Gardens   **A$110–140**   ★★★★

47-49 Elphin Road; ☎ *(03) 6334-5988; FAX (03) 6334-5588.*
Doubles starting around A$110, two-bedroom units about A$140.

These are very nice digs, indeed, located near the racetrack on the road that heads toward the East Coast. Spacious rooms done in beiges with large bathrooms, balconies, covered parking, complete kitchens, mini-bars. The decor is very 1930-ish; all in all, a great choice of accommodations.

O'Hara's Resort Hotel   **A$100**   ★★★

10 Casino Rise near the Launceston Casino; ☎ *(03) 6343-1744; FAX (03) 6344-9943.*
Doubles starting around A$120.

The resort is in the Prospect Vale area southeast of town, handy if you want to visit the casino. The name is part of an effort to Irish up the place, so naturally the restaurant is named Scarlett's. (But it has nothing to do with *Gone With the Wind*, being based instead on the romance of a felon named Mike O'Hara and his lady, Scarlett O'Brien.) The rooms are in detached brick units. There is a spa and pool, tennis courts, guest laundry and same-day dry cleaning service.

Penny Royal Motel   **A$120**   ★★★

145 Paterson Street; ☎ (03) 6331-6699; FAX (03) 6331-1632; toll free (008) 060-954. Doubles starting around A$120.

The area is classified by the National Trust. There are actually three motels on the theme park site, including the Watermill, a reconstructed 1825 stone building, and the Penny Royal Village, which has units with two to four bedrooms. There is a restaurant and laundry.

Colonial Motor Inn   **A$115–150**   ★★

Corner George and Elizabeth streets; ☎ (03) 6331-6588; FAX (03) 6334-2765. Doubles start around A$115 suites A$150.

Another National Trust building, this one built in 1847 as a grammar school. It's Australia's oldest public school building. Licensed restaurant.

Great Northern Hotel   **A$100–180**   ★★

3 Earl Street; ☎ (03) 6331-9999; FAX (03) 6331-3712; toll free (008) 030-567. Doubles start around A$100; suites from A$180.

Two restaurants and the **No. 11 Tram Car Lounge**, which has an old tram on display.

Where to Eat

Shrimps   **$$$**   ★★★

72 George Street; ☎ (03) 6334-0581; FAX (03) 6334-3764.

Seafood served in a National Trust building. The businessman's hangout for lunch and considered by many to be the best seafood place in the area. Great sauces, wicked desserts. Dinner Monday–Saturday, lunch Monday–Friday.

Balleys   **$$$**   ★★★★

150 George Street, ☎ (03) 6334-2343.

Housed in an 1834 National Trust building. Seafood, pasta, Tassie beef. BYO. Really good food. Lunch Wednesday–Friday; dinner Tuesday–Saturday.

Pierre's Cafe Bar Restaurant   **$$**   ★★★

88 George Street; ☎ (03) 6331-6835

Very European in style, tasty blackboard specials; serves everything from burgers to French haute cuisine. Try the chicken livers in Worchestershire sauce. Licensed. Open six days from 11 a.m. Closed Sundays.

Fee and Me   **$$$**   ★★★

190 Charles Street; ☎ (03) 6331-3195.

Consistent award winner, nestled in one of the city's most distinguished National Trust homes, Morton House. Eclectic menu, with venison and Thai selections. Excellent Tassie wine list. Dinner Monday–Saturday. Closed Sunday.

The East Coast

One of the most popular recreational areas in Tasmania for Australians is the east coast, which has some very fine white beaches, outstanding scenery and several small and delightful resort communities. The area is virtually unknown to international visitors, who tend to spend all their time either in Hobart, Port Arthur or the rugged west. In many cases, knowledgable visitors driving around the island plan out a circle trip starting from the Devonport/Launceston area, passing down the East Coast to Port Arthur, then to Hobart, then to the western wilderness areas or the central mountains and the west coast. It can be done in a few days if you're in a hurry, but a week is better, particularly when you remember most fly/drive or sea/drive packages are priced for a week.

On the way to the coast on the A3, you will pass a couple of small forest parks, and if you're lucky, take a detour to feed a big pig a warm beer. To the east of Scottsdale about 20 kilometers is **Myrtle Grove Forest Preserve** with a nice walking trail, and better, on what is called the Weldborough Pass northwest of St. Helens, is the **Weldborough Pass Rainforest Walk**, well worth a stop to see, if nothing else, Grandfather and Grandma Mrytle on an interpretive walk. The pig in question is found near St. Columba Falls at a wayside stop called the **Pub in the Paddock** (more formally known as the St. Columba Falls Hotel, dating back more than a century and a half.) Piggy Boo, a nine-year-old hog, will come running when you bang a stick on a piece of metal and for A50 cents, you can give her a bottle of beer dregs from the pub. The pub has counter meals and teas daily, and there are backpacking accommodations (A$10 per person including breakfast) and RV sites. ☎ *(03) 6373-6121.* The park preserve and the 300-foot-high falls with nice paths and rain forest scenery is about five kilometers from the pub on a partially unpaved road. You get to the pub and the park by taking Highway 428 to Pyengana (about 30 kilometers northwest of St. Helens.) On the way to the pub, you pass the **Pyengana Cheese Factory**, which has tastings of old-fashioned cheddar and views of the cheese-making process. It's open daily from 8:30 a.m.–6:30 p.m. ☎ *(03) 6373-6157.*

The main East Coast resorts are **St. Helens**, **Bicheno, Swansea** and **Orford**, situated on what the locals call the Sun Coast. It's very Mediterranean in climate, with rocky headlands overlooking the deep blue of the Tasman Sea. In addition to beaches and sports fishing, the towns are also major commercial fishing and lobstering centers. You'll find a good range of accommodations in all four.

To reach the coast from Launceston, take either the Midland Highway (Hwy. 1) or the Tasman Highway (the A3.) It's about 90 to 100 miles to the coast.

St. Helens

St. Helens started life as a whaling port last century, and later became a major tin shipping center. It earns most of its bread these days as a tourist center, but is also famous for its crayfish (as is most of the whole coast.) Trying to get one to take home to the RV or your cabin and cook can be a bit tough, however, because most of the catch is exported out of the country. When the season is on, expect to pay about A$30 for a one-pound cray.

The St. Helens area is full of state parks and coastal preserves, including Humbug Point State Recreation Area, Bay of Fires Coastal Reserve and St. Helens Point State Recreation Area. The parks are popular hiking and bird-watching areas, full of cockatoos, wattlebirds, honeyeaters and many species of seabirds, including ospreys, gannets, petrels and albatross. A good spot for a picnic lunch is **Burns Bay** at St. Helens Point; great dune walking. To reach the point, take the main highway southeast of town to the St. Helens Point Road. It's about 10 kilometers from the main highway to the beaches.

Information about the tin mining history of the area is located in the **St. Helens History Room**, which also offers guided tours to some of the old mines. The museum is open Monday-Friday from 9 a.m.–4 p.m.; admission is A$3.

St. Helens is also home to one of our favorite little fish shops, **Ripples**. During the crayfish season, Ripples will serve up gourmet packs which include half a cray, salad, oysters and prawns for A$20–25, depending on how big the crayfish is. The shop is located on the Esplanade and is open seven days from November-May, and weekdays and Saturday mornings the rest of the year. *(03) 6376-1000.*

Where to Stay

Bayside Inn   **A$60**   ★★

2 Cecilia Street; *(03) 6376-1466; FAX (03) 6376-1657.*
Motel units start at A$60 for two.
Overlooking Georges Bay and the Esplanade, short walk to the beach. Standard motel rooms and two-bedroom units, heated pool, nice views and home of the best cooking ★★ in town $$. Counter meals as well as dinner, featuring steaks, roasts and seafood. Lunch from noon–2 p.m.; dinner Monday–Thursday 6–8 p.m.; Friday–Saturday 6–8:30 p.m. and Sunday 5:30–7:30 p.m.

Anchor Wheel Motel & Restaurant   **A$50–60**   ★★

59-61 Tully Street; ☎ *(03) 6376-1358; FAX (03) 6376-2009.*
Motel units start at A$50 for two.
On the Tasman Highway coming into town from the northwest. Room service breakfasts available. The restaurant specializes in steaks and seafood. It's open for dinner from 6 p.m. Monday–Saturday.

An alternative to the motel scene, and one found all along the coast, are self-contained cottages. Among the choices in St. Helens are the **Queechy St. Helens**, close to the town center, and two beach-area facilities, **Cockle Cove** and **Binalong Bay Cottages**. Queechy ★★, the less pretentious of the trio, has cottages which sleep up to four, equipped with stoves and microwaves, laundry, electric blankets and all linens. The units run from A$50–65 double. ☎ *(03) 6376-1321; FAX 6376-1652.* **Binalong Bay Cottages**, ★★ situated on the bay of that name northeast of town, has units with verandahs and modern trimmings. The ambiance is more suburban than beach, with a road between you and the

view. The units have barbecue and laundry facilities. ☎ *(03) 6376-8262 phone and FAX.*
And out toward St. Helens Point are the **Cockle Cove Cottages ★★** with queen-sized
beds, linen supply and cooked breakfasts if ordered. ☎ *(03) 6376-3036; FAX (03) 6376-
3226.*

A bit farther down the road from St. Helens is the small hamlet of Beaumaris, the
home of a very nice B&B, **Bensons ★★★**. It's located in a rambling white house close
to the shore, and all rooms have private bath; the whole house is smoke free. Doubles are
$A90-100; dinners can be arranged.

South of Beaumaris near Falmouth, the road splits, with the Tasman Highway hugging the coast and heading south to Bicheno and the Esk Main Road (A4) heading back
west. If you want a real treat, take the A4 over a pass to St. Marys, and from there take
the Elephant Pass road back to the coast. At the top of the pass is one of the more delightful places to snack on the East Coast, the **Mount Elephant Pancake Barn ★★★**,
which, as the name suggests, is a pancake place. Except these are pancakes à la France,
meaning wonderfully tasteful crepes. It's open daily from 8 a.m.–6 p.m.

Bicheno

The city proclaims itself to be the "Sun Capital of Tasmania," and who are
we to quibble. The coastline is lovely, the beaches first-rate, the seafood excellent and the weather balmy—in the summer. Like St. Helens, Bicheno
started out as a whaling village. It was originally called Waubs Harbour,
named after a local Aboriginal woman, Waubedebar. The city was named
later to honor James Ebenezer Bicheno, a colonial secretary.

In addition to a heavy tourist industry, the city is home to a small fleet of
crayfish boats, abalone divers and several oyster farms. A short distance off
the city jetty near **Governors Island** is an excellent marine reserve. The waters
around Bicheno are full of sponges, kelp forests and huge granite formations
with caves. The Bicheno Dive Centre downtown has a variety of dive trips
available. If you have your own equipment, there's a A$6 per tank fill charge
plus A$25 for a boat space (generally two dives per trip.) The kelp forests are
about 70 feet at the deepest; the huge sponge gardens at The Hairy Wall
bottom out at about 150 feet. ☎ *(03) 6375-1138.*

Bicheno is famous for its fairy penguins, which are probably best seen on a
tour with **Bicheno Penguin and Adventure Tours** on Foster Street. The nightly
trips to the bird rookeries are A$7.50 for adults and include transport from
your accommodations. The trips run from September to February and April
to July. The company also has bicycle tours, mountain bike hire, fishing
trips, bushwalking and guided camping trips. Trips can be arranged through
any Tas Travel Centre or in Bicheno. ☎ *(03) 6375-1333 phone and FAX;
after hours (03) 6375-1356.*

One of the more popular tourist attractions in town is the **Blow Hole**, along-
side of which is a huge precariously balanced chunk of granite known as the

Barossa Valley is the premier wine region in Australia.

Lasseter Highway offers great views of Uluru (Ayers Rock).

Lone Pine Sanctuary outside Brisbane is a haven for koalas.

Kakadu National Park is home to 250 bird species.

Cradle Mountain Lake, St. Clair Park, Tasmania offers spectacular scenery.

Bungle Bungle National Park is popular for its strange rock formations.

Rocking Rock, all 80 tons of it swaying in the waves. There's a walking path that follows the city shoreline and passes the Blowhole and other attractions.

North of town about three kilometers is the turnoff to Tasmania's newest outdoor reserve, **Douglas-Apsley National Park**, which has a range of hiking trails from 10 minutes to a few days, and is home to some endangered Tasmanian plants and animals. The road in from the main highway is about seven kilometers long, ending at a parking lot. Nearby is the Apsley Waterhole, a deep and photogenic spot on the Apsley River. The hike to the pool is wheelchair accessible. The pool is home to the very rare Tasmanian grayling. Entry to the park is A$8 a car.

Close to the park entrance is another spot to check on Tasmanian devils, emus, kangaroos et al, the **East Coast Birdlife and Animal Park ★ ★**. The animals are all free ranging, and include Australia's most obnoxious bird, the native hen. The hens will chase you like demented dogs trying to steal bird seed. Among the stars of the animal park are Minnie the Tasmanian devil and her two brothers. The trio was orphaned when their mother was run over by a car. They were saved by the new park owners and hand fed until they reached maturity. Also hanging around looking for freebies is Charlie the Emu, a 13-year veteran of the corn-stealing scene.

Among other birds in the facility's aviary are golden pheasant, Yankee turkeys, Indian ring necked parrots, rosellas and galahs. The park is open daily from 9:30 a.m.–5 p.m. Tickets are A$6.50 for adults.

The Bicheno information center is housed in a small building next to the Bicheno Cabin and Tourist Park at the corner of Foster (Tasman Highway) and Champ streets. ☎ *(03) 6375-1333*.

Where to Stay

Diamond Island Resort   A$80–120   ★ ★ ★

69 Tasman Highway; ☎ *(03) 6375-1161; FAX (03) 6375-1349; toll free 1-(800) 030-299.*
Doubles start around A$80.
Located on a curve just as you come into town, next to a penguin rookery (free tours) and a sandy beach. Spacious seven-acre grounds with heated pool, tennis and a game room. Standard motel rooms and 15-self-contained units, some units with spas. Laundry facilities. The restaurant ★ ★ ★ is one of the best in the area, **$$** specializing in game and seafood.

Silver Sands Resort   A$60–70   ★ ★

Burgess Street at Peggys Point; ☎ *(03) 6375-1266; FAX (03) 6375-1168.*
Doubles start around A$60.
Located on a beach right downtown; most units have an ocean view. Pool, game room, cozy log-fire restaurant. Laundry and dry cleaning service. Off-season rates available. Two-day packages available for A$200 that includes accommodation and meals.

Bicheno Hideaway   **A$75**   ★★★

> *87 Harveys Farm Road;* ☎ *(03) 6375-1312 phone and FAX.*
> *Doubles start around A$75, less for extended stays.*

Romantic, solitary getaway in one of three quanset-hut type units perched on a chunk of bush next to the ocean. It's about three kilometers south of town off the main highway. A real treasure, run by a retired German-Slovenian couple. The well-equipped units are perfect for a couple. Good hikes, snorkeling and fishing, plus a selection of local wildlife wandering around including wallabies and possums. Laundry available. Our favorite on the East Coast.

Bicheno Holiday Village   **A$110**   ★★

> *The Esplanade, downtown;* ☎ *(03) 6375-1171.*
> *Doubles start around A$110.*

Scandinavian decor A-frame villas, with private bath and washing machines. It's a large complex of 20 units with ocean views and a heated pool. Dinners are available to the public, specializing in char-grills and seafood. Units vary in size, with some handling up to a dozen guests.

In addition to the resort restaurants, you can also try either the Sea Life Centre, Waubs Bay House or the village deli. The **Sea Life Centre ★★**, across from the dive shop on the Tasman Highway, specializes (naturally) in seafood $$, and also has an aquarium full of local critters (A$4.50 to see them.) **Waubs ★★**, also a seafood place $$, is famed for its scallop pies and crayfish in season; Wednesday night specials. Finally, the **Bicheno General Store** (a.k.a. Sam's), is a surprising little place with some excellent deli preparations and a well-stocked wine cellar. Perfect for a lunch or some goodies to take to the cabin or RV and cook.

Freycinet National Park

About 10 kilometers south of Bicheno is a turnoff to **Freycinet National Park** which probably has the best drop-dead coastal scenery in Tasmania, if not in the whole country. The park takes up the south end of the Freycinet Peninsula, which juts southeasterly into the Tasman Sea. And in addition to the scenic spots, there are ample opportunities to hike, swim and stay in some very nice digs. The name is French, *pronounced FRAY-sin-ay*, so-named by French explorers who passed by in 1802. The main features of the park are its red granite cliffs, including a range called **The Hazards**, and many white-sand beaches, hiking trails and wildlife. It's not unusual at all to run into very friendly Bennett's wallabies on a hike, and there are some major bird breeding grounds in the area, including those of the black swan and fairy penguins. The park is also home to wombats, devils, echidnas and possums. There are also about 70 species of ground orchids in the park.

Information

The main park entrance and visitor center is just past Coles Bay, about 30 kilometers south of the turn-off from the Tasman Highway. The park office is open daily until noon; all day in the summer. There is also an information board about park activities posted outside the general store in Coles Bay. Information about the park is available from the **Parks**

and Wildlife Service at *134 Macquarie Street* in Hobart, or by calling the park headquarters at ☎ *(03) 6257-0107*.

Activities

The hikes at Freycinet can be short and simple or long and rugged. If you've a mind to see some black swans en masse, there are several areas around the park, including **Moulting Lagoon** and **Saltwater Lagoon**. Moulting Lagoon is the major breeding ground for the swans, and is situated close to the main road through the park. Saltwater Lagoon is near the so called **Friendly Beaches**, a long sweep of dunes and tidal pools along the east coast of the peninsula. You get to the beaches—well worth the time—by taking a gravel road well marked off the Coles Bay main road. Take a lot of film.

One of the very best hikes in the whole park is a 2.5-hour, fairly easy trek up over the spine of the mountains to **Wineglass Bay**, which is simply stunning. The trail is a self-guided nature tour. It's also possible to hike to the top of the Hazards. The best long trek is probably the three- or four-hour round trip to the summit of **Mt. Amos**. The trailhead begins at the Parsons Cove parking lot (also the start of the Wineglass Bay hike.) The trail to the top of Mt. Amos is fairly strenuous, but the view is worth the work. The park rangers suggest you wear "robust" hiking boots. They also ask that you register before taking any hikes. During the summer, rangers offer daily walks, talks and slide shows at various locations in the park.

The diving around the park is generally good, especially at **Sleepy Bay** off the Cape Tourville Road, and for amateur snorkelers, **Honeymoon Bay**, well sheltered on the west coast of the peninsula. If you try the drive out to Cape Tourville, check with the rental company first—the road is unpaved and rugged in spots. At the end of the short (4.5 miles) road is a lighthouse, plus the usual incredible scenery.

The main center of activity in the park is Coles Bay, which has accommodations, supplies and a couple of restaurants. The best place to stay is the new and fairly upscale **Freycinet Lodge ★ ★ ★**. There are no rooms in the main lodge itself. Rather, there are about 40 cabins sited in secluded spots around native bush, connected to the lodge by timbered walkways. Units are either one- or two-bedrooms; handicapped rooms available. Some of the one-bedroom cabins have spas. All cabins have private balconies, and units come without telephones, radios or television sets. Double cabins without spas are A$130 with spas, A$160. Two-bedroom cabins are A$175. Cooking facilities in the cabins are optional, and are an extra A$20 a night. The lodge has a wide range of activities available, including cruises, 4-wheel-drive treks, penguin rookery tours, guided hikes, scuba classes and rock climbing. The lodge also has a restaurant $$$ with a great view and a good selection of steak, seafood and wines. ☎ *(03) 6257-0101; FAX (03) 6257-0278*.

About the only other spot in the area to eat is the **Captain's Table Restaurant and Takeaway ★ ★** across from the Coles Bay post office $$. It's open daily for lunch and dinner and specializes in seafood and steaks.

Other area accommodation includes **Coles Bay Holiday Villas** and the **Iluka Holiday Centre**. The Holiday Villas ★ ★ are located on beachfront acreage. The units have fireplaces, sundecks and barbecues. There are two tennis courts. Minimum stay requirements might apply. Two-bedroom units are A$95 for the first two nights, A$55 thereafter. During high season (December-February) rates are A$120–136. ☎ *(03) 6257-0102.* The Iluka Centre ★★ features knotty pine cabins plus on-site RVs, tent sites and a market, tavern and bakery. The cabins are A$45–50 double. Tent sites are A$10; on-site RVs are A$30 double, and powered RV sites are A$12. ☎ *(03) 6257-0115; FAX (03) 6257-0384.*

The best place to put your RV is at the **Freycinet Camping Ground** at Richardsons Beach. Tent sites are A$8; RV sites are A$10. Barbecues facilities, tons of wildlife, scenery, close to town. ☎ *(03) 6257-0107.*

Swansea

Swansea is an historical rural community sitting on Oyster Bay, full of old Georgian houses and other historical buildings. One of the big history draws is a restored mill (1885) that was used to crush black wattle bark, used in the tanning industry. The mill is part of the **Swansea Bark Mill and Tourist Centre**, which also includes the Swansea Wine and Wool Centre. The wine and wool centre has woolen goods for sale and wine tasting (A$2 per person.) It's open daily from 9 a.m.–5 p.m. The bark mill and its museum are open daily 9 a.m.–5 p.m.; A$5 admission charge.

During the first week in November, the city stages the **Great Oyster Bay Festival**. The main street is closed off and is full of crafts, art and food stalls. There is normally wine tasting, a concert or two and entertainment. One recent delight was a stall offering pigs and emus roasted over a fire.

Swansea has a couple of elegant old houses offering accommodations: Meredith House (1850s) and Redcliffe House (1835.)

Meredith House has sweeping views of Oyster Bay and is filled with antiques and red cedar furnishings. Full breakfasts are served and dinners are available by arrangement. There are laundry facilities. Rooms include a suite with private bath and several queen-bed units. Smoke free house. Doubles are A$110-130; packages are available. ☎ *(03) 6257-8119; FAX (03) 6257-8123; toll free 1-(800) 65-8880.*

Redcliffe House ★★★ is a classic Aussie beauty, all yellow clapboard and verandahs, a picture of how the quality lived in the beginning of the nation's history. It sits on the banks of the Meredith River which feeds into Oyster Bay. There are suites with private bath and also sleeping rooms. Smoke free house. The tariff includes a cooked breakfast; dinners available on request. Doubles are A$85–95; packages available. ☎ *(03) 6257-8557; FAX (03) 6257-8667.*

Where to Eat

Fiddlers   **$$$**   ★★★

1 Waterloo Road; ☎ *(03) 6257-8564.*

Housed in the historic Schouten House, an 1846 Georgian building, with an emphasis on white linen dining. (You should probably wear a tie.) The food is sort of California cuisine, with a dependence on seafood and local vegetables. Dinner seven days; lunch by arrangement.

Kabuki by the Sea   **$$**   ★★★

12 miles south of town on the Tasman Highway; ☎ *(03) 6257-8588.*

Tasmanian seafood and produce, often with a Japanese flair. Tremendous view
overlooking the Tasman Sea. Dinner Tuesday–Saturday from December–April;
weekends in the off season. Lunch and Devonshire teas all year.

Shy Albatross   **$$**   ★★

10 Franklin Street; ☎ *(03) 6257-8110, phone and FAX.*

Casual and relaxed Mediterranean/Italian place, with extensive wine list and daily
specials. Dinner Tuesday–Sunday.

Orford

Orford is the gateway to a popular ocean vacation spot, **Maria Island**. The
city sits on the banks of the Prosser River, which upstream forms a scenic
gorge. The sandstone hills near town have been used in the construction of
many Australian buildings, including the Law Courts in Melbourne. Maria
Island was a penal settlement that actually predates Port Arthur. It once
housed more than 700 men, and was closed in 1851. Some of the old prison
buildings at Darlington on the island have been converted into hostel bunk-
houses. The island is also filled with animals, including Cape Berren geese,
wallabies and pademelons. A trail from Darlington will take you to the so
called Fossil Cliffs, and another trail goes to the lovely Painted Cliffs, which
are iron-oxide stained sandstone. There are no shops on the island; if you go,
take a lunch. The ferry from Orford to the island runs at 10:30 a.m., 1 p.m.
and 3:30 p.m. daily, and returns from the island at 11 a.m., 1:30 p.m. and 4
p.m. During the summer (Dec. 26-April) there is an additional departure
from Orford at 9 a.m. The ferry dock in Orford is located at the Eastcoaster
Resort. The fare for a day trip is A$16 round trip ☎ *(03) 6257-1589.*

Where to Stay

Eastcoaster Resort   A$90–140   ★★

Six kilometers north of downtown on Spring Bay; ☎ *(03) 6257-1172; FAX (03) 6257-1564.*
Motel units start at A$90 for two.

The resort has a variety of accommodations, ranging from basic motel units to
detached cabins. It has a seafood restaurant, RV sites and a tavern. There are also an
indoor heated pool and outdoor unheated pool, squash courts, jogging track, charter boats and bike rentals.

Spring Beach Holiday Villas   A$85   ★★

Located at Spring Beach, five kilometers south of town; ☎ *(03) 6257-1440; FAX (03)*
6223-7797.

Motel units start at A$85 for two.

The facility has isolated two-bedroom units complete with washing machines, electric blankets, full kitchens, plus a tennis court, putting course and wood heaters.
The view toward Maria Island is splendid.

Orford Riverside Villas   **A$75**   ★ ★

Old Convict Road in town; ☎ *(03) 6257-1655; FAX (03) 6223-1677; toll free 1-(800) 817-533.*

Motel units start at A$75 for two.

The one- and two-bedroom units sit on the Prosser River and have private spas. The units come with full kitchens, barbecue equipment and private jetties.

Blue Waters Motor Inn   **A$45–50**   ★ ★

Tasman Highway in town; ☎ *(03) 6257-1102; FAX (03) 6223-1621.*

Motel units start at A$45 for two.

The motel has a restaurant/bar and also serves counter meals. There is tennis court and the facility is close to the beach.

The West

The Cradle Mountain Overland Track in Tasmania is a strenuous 50-mile (80 km) bushwalk.

The true glories of Tasmania, at least to us, are the rain forests and dense vegetation of the western half of the island. From Hobart, take the A10 to the Queenstown-Strahan area, which is the heart of the Gordon River headwaters country. There are several magnificent national parks in the area, the **Cradle Mountain-Lake St. Clair National Park** and the **Franklin and Lower Gordon Wild Rivers National Park**. These parks are for the outdoor-minded, with whitewater sports, excellent brown trout fishing, mountain climbing and hiking.

Cradle Mountain

The Cradle Mountain-Lake St. Clair park is large, with park headquarters for Cradle Mountain at Cradle Mountain Village about 145 kilometers southwest of Devonport. Headquarters for the Lake St. Clair portion of the park is at Cynthia Bay near Derwent Bridge on the Lyell Highway (A10), about 80 kilometers east of Queenstown. Bus service from the Devonport ship terminal is available for about A\$55 round trip person. The two sections of the park together stretch about 80 kilometers, and for the fit and hardy, there awaits what is probably the best hiking trail in Tasmania and one of the most popular in all Australia, the 50-mile-long **Overland Track**, which has huts along the way from Cradle Mountain to Cynthia Bay. It passes along some simply delicious scenery and costs \$10 per hiker. It's normally done in about a week, and all hikers must register with the park rangers. The rangers, in fact, request that you register even if you're planning a short hike.

If you want to do serious hikes in the area, try the trips offered by **Craclair Tours** in Devonport. The one-week Overland Track experience, for example, runs around A\$935 per person, including all gear (you bring only your boots and personal gear. And the guides prepare the meals.) The price is slightly higher during the Christmas-New Year's holidays. Hiking trips with accommodations in cabins are about A\$420. ☎ *(03) 6424-7833; FAX (03) 6424-9215*

There are some excellent and fairly easy walks around Cradle Mountain. One of the best is the circular route that goes around Lake Dove about 7.5 kilometers from the village. If the weather cooperates, the scenery on the hike will be some of the best you'll see in Tasmania. A really good place for a photo stop or a lunch is a rocky outcrop about a half-mile from the parking lot (go southeast) at **Suicide Rock**. And a really nice, but strenuous climb, is on the other side of the lake where the trail from the main trail juts up to a saddle and a place called **Marion's Lookout**. Drop dead scenery. Cradle Mountain itself rises to about 5000 feet and is a favorite target for hikers and climbers—but it's a long and often strenuous trek. **Lake St. Clair** proves that once upon a time, Tasmania had glaciers—it's the deepest lake in Australia, something like 700 feet down. The whole region is alpine and semi-alpine, and subject to sudden and dramatic changes in weather. The wildlife is unavoidable, especially the ever-present Bennett's wallabies, who apparently were born to mooch food. Rangers are now actively discouraging visitors from feeding the wallabies because they have developed diseases and many are too dependent on humans for food.

The visitors center at Cradle Mountain is well-stocked with maps, books and displays, and right behind the office is a handicapped-friendly boardwalked trail through the rain forest to Pencil Pine Falls. There is unleaded gasoline available at the Cradle Mountain Roadhouse and also the Cradle Mountain Lodge. The center is open daily from 8 a.m.–5 p.m. ☎ *(03) 6492-1133.*

The nicest way to spend a few days in the Cradle Mountain portion of the park is to stay at the **Cradle Mountain Lodge** ★★★★, a famous and cozy inn with rustic, elegant cabins in the woods, complete with wood fireplaces, super hot water showers and resident swarms of possums and pademelons who come calling for goodies at night. There is, in fact, a mass possum feeding at the main door of the lodge every night. The lodge provides boxes of fruit for guests to feed to the critters, and it looks like a stampede. Exercise care: possums have nasty teeth and very sharp claws. The cabins have small but usable kitchens, or you can choose to sup at the lodge, which is very good but expensive (about A$100 for a two-course dinner for two with a bottle of wine.) The wine selection is extensive (about 110 kinds) and you get to pick your own from the lodge's cellar. The lodge also has a pub where counter meals are available; comfy, nice view. There is also a small store that sells booze, food and supplies. It also rents fly rods for those who want to try their hand at a trout in the small pond near the lodge. Don't bother; the equipment is in bad shape. It's a P&O lodge, owned by the same organization that operates Heron Island on the Great Barrier Reef and Silky Oaks in northern Queensland. Doubles start around A$135-190. There are also three rooms in the main lodge with shared bath, for about A$85 double. Bus transfer from Launceston is A$65 round trip; from the Devonport Ferry Terminal, A$55. ☎ *(03) 6492-1303; FAX (03) 6492-1309. Reservation information in the U.S. and Canada:* ☎ *(800) 225-9849.*

The Rugged Southwest

It's a long way around to get to the Lake St. Clair portion of the park, with the fastest route doubling back to Devonport, where you pick up the Murchison Highway (A10). After passing the paddock country southwest of Devonport, the highway starts into the wilderness areas of the western half of the state. At Queenstown, the highway splits, with the A10 continuing toward Lake St. Clair and Hobart, and the B24 running to Strahan on the West Coast.

Queenstown

Queenstown, if you are of the conservationist bent, will make you scream. The whole area has been mined to death, and the town, which sits next to a working mine, has all the allure of a dead carp. Underneath all those forests are mountains rich in minerals, and virtually unregulated mining has created a shameful moonscape. It's worth a trip here just as a reminder of what the world will be like if nobody cares. The hydroelectric folks are still at, as well, with the new dam on the King River creating Lake Burbury, stalked with trout and waiting for tourists to come.

Should you care, there are tours available of the Mt. Lyell open pit mine. During the hour and a half tour, guides describe reforestation projects, mine operations and give details about what the tour brochures proudly describe as "our famous lunar landscape." Tours start from the Western Arts & Crafts Centre on Driffield Street. Tickets are A$10 per person. Or you can see where the mountain went by looking at the historic photos at the Galley Museum at the corner of Driffield and Sticht streets. It's open weekdays from 10 a.m.–12:30 p.m. and 1:30–4:30 p.m., and from 1:30–4:30 p.m. weekends. There's a chairlift in town for panoramic views of the city, but you get the same vistas on the highway heading to Strahan.

There are a couple of places to stay in Queenstown including the Commercial Hotel ★ ★ on Driffield Street, which has a restaurant with counter meals and dinners; doubles about A$60. ☎ *(03) 6471-1511; FAX (03) 64/1-1826.* Or the slightly more upscale **Silver Hills Motor Inn** ★ ★ on Penghana Road, which has probably the best restaurant in town. Doubles are A$75. ☎ *(03) 6471-1755.*

Past Queenstown about 35 kilometers is the bayside village of **Strahan** (pronounced strawn), the gateway to the **Gordon River** and **Macquarie Harbour**. Both the river and the harbour are examples of all that was bad in Australian history.

After Hobart was established in the early 1800s, it became obvious that civilized society was no place for really hard-rock bad guys, so the colonial officials looked around for another place to stash them. The first place they tried, before Port Arthur, was Macquarie Harbour, the huge estuary of the Gordon River on the extreme west coast of Tasmania. There was a capitalistic rationale behind all this effort, as well, because the area was rich in huon pine and coal. The pine, now very rare, was an exceptionally fine ship-building material. It's very dense, easy to work and was highly valued by shipwrights supplying colonial and Royal Navy vessels. Some of the survivors are estimated to be 3000 years old.

Convicts were brought to mine the coal and fell the pines, and they were forced to live at one of the worst prison facilities in Australia, **Sarah Island**, which sits near the mouth of the Gordon. The island has no natural water, so supplies were brought in every day, and the living conditions were often ghastly. The island was eventually abandoned in 1834, and the convicts were sent to Port Arthur. Some parts of the buildings from the prison still stand and can be seen on a Gordon River cruise.

The river itself is the site of one of Australia's most famous environmental battles. The Tasmanian government decided to dam the Franklin River, which feeds into the Gordon, for hydroelectric power to provide jobs for the West Coast. Many people, feeling the dam would destroy some of the best whitewater in the state and lead to destruction of the west's primitive beauty, started an eight-year campaign that not only stopped the project, but also toppled the state government in the process. At one point, the Gordon, not far from where the Franklin flows in, was blockaded by protestors in rubber boats who stopped heavy machinery from being moved to a construction site. In the end, the conservationists won out, and the site of the blockade is a favorite stop for tour boats.

Strahan

At Strahan, you can catch a half-day or full-day cruise that will take you up the Gordon, out to the headlands where Macquarie Harbour begins, and stop at Sarah Island. The company, **Gordon River Cruises**, operates boats with guides and offer soft drinks and light meals for sale. Advance bookings are usually necessary. Half-day tours are about A$45 per person; full-day about A$60. The half-day cruises depart at 9 a.m., return at 1:45 p.m. Full-day cruises, available from Nov. 1–April 30, depart at 9 a.m. and return at 3 p.m. ☎ *(03) 6471-7187; FAX (03) 6471-7317.*

If you have time and want to see the devastating effects of 100 years of mining on a once-pristine river, try one of the jet boat trips from Strahan up the nearby King River with **Wild Rivers Jet**. The 50-minute trips leave daily from the Strahan Wharf between 9 a.m. and 5 p.m. Tickets are A$35 per person. ☎ *(03) 6471-7174; FAX (03) 6471-7431.*

Try to stop in at the **Strahan Wharf Centre**, an information and exhibit building, with great displays of local history, including Sarah Island, the huon pine story and the Gordon River Battle, plus Aboriginal history. You can also book tours and accommodations, plus pick up reams of tourism information. The self-guided tour through the displays is really worth the A$4.50 per person charge. As these things go, it's well done. The center is open from 10 a.m.–6 p.m. in the winter, 10 a.m.–8 p.m. in the summer. ☎ *(03) 6471-7488; FAX (03) 6471-7461.*

The village really seems like something you'd find along the coast of Maine, with a very oceany feeling and several nice places to stay and eat; all in all, a great place to haul in and chill for a couple of days.

A good bet for a night's rest in town is the **Strahan Motor Inn Street** ★★★, perched up on Jolly Street overlooking Macquarie Harbour. All units are ground floor; some suites have spas. The house restaurant is pretty good, and they'll pack a picnic lunch for you, which is a good way to reduce the hassle on a Gordon River cruise. Doubles start around $A100; suites A$120–130. ☎ *(03) 6471-7160; FAX (03) 6471-7372.*

Another good choice downtown are the rather quaint apartments and units at the **Strahan Village Cottages and Terrace** ★★★ on the Esplanade. The new Victorian-style units go for A$95-130 double and are within a stone's throw of the wharf. ☎ *(03) 6471-7191; FAX (03) 6471-7389.* There are also a bunch of small, self-contained places to stay along the harbor on the Esplanade toward Regatta Point.

However, the best place in the area, and one of the premier hotels in Tasmania, is the **Franklin Manor**, ★ ★ ★ ★ a rambling old wood mansion built in 1896. Remodeled and gussied up, the elegant old heap has 14 rooms, all with private bath (five with spas), plus outside cottage rooms. There are three dining rooms, a vast underground wine cellar and two lounges with open fire. The bar and wine cellar are operated on the honor system, and dinners are available with prior arrangement. They're superb, with selections of ocean trout, free range poultry and great lamb. Dinners will run about A$40, not counting wine. A caveat: the owner has been threatening off and on for the last few years to close the manor down, so check ahead. If it's open, it's a great experience. Doubles are A$130–155. ☎ *(03) 6471-7311; FAX (03) 6471-7267.*

The best place in town for a relaxed, country-style meal is **Hamer's Hotel Grill and Cafe** ★ ★ ★ which serves large portions of pub fare as well as fish offerings. We especially liked the fish basket made with fresh salmon, and the warm chicken salad was good, too. As befits a good Tassie eatery, it has a great wine selection. Breakfasts are 7:30–9 a.m.; lunch noon–2:30 p.m. and dinner 5:30–8:30 p.m. The cafe is right across from the city wharf. ☎ *(03) 6471-7191; FAX (03) 6471-7380.*

One source for whitewater rafting or camping treks in the central mountains is **ATT King's Australian Experience**, which offers a wide variety of Tasmania trips including week-long Franklin River excursions, Cradle Mountain bushwalking, kayaking, and four-wheel drive expeditions. *For information and bookings,* ☎ *(800) 423-2880 USA.*

Lake St. Clair

Back on the main highway toward Hobart, it's about 80 kilometers from the Strahan turnoff to Derwent Bridge, where you catch the Lake St. Clair road into the south end of the park. By most Tasmanian national park standards, the settlement at Cynthia Bay on the lake is booming. A sparkling new visitors center has opened, containing a trout fishing shop, general store, restaurant, interpretation center and the park headquarters offices. The view from the restaurant is wonderful, looking through a window that rises about 25 feet. When the weather's decent, you can dine on an outside deck.

The Overland Track ends here, and it's an easy hike along the west shore of the lake just so you brag that you were on the Track. Or there's a longer and more strenuous trek to the top of Mt. Rufus, with great views of the lake and in the distance, Mounts Ida and Olympus. A favorite trail is out to a place called Watersmeet, where the Hugel and Cuvier rivers join, about an hour round-trip. This is a great rain forest walk.

If you want to see the lake up close, take one of the ferries that run from Cynthia Bay to the far north end of the lake at Narcissus Bay. The ferries leave at 9:30 a.m., noon and 3 p.m. The round trip fare is A$20 per person and can be booked through Lakeside St. Clair Wilderness Holidays, which also has a range of accommodations at the lake. Top of the list are alpine-style lodges ★★ which run about $110 double. Also available are bunkhouse units and camping and RV sites. These units are likely to be booked well in advance during the summer. ☎ *(03) 6289-1137; FAX (03) 6289-1250.* Park information: ☎ *(03) 6289-1172.*

Accommodation and food is also available at Derwent Bridge. The main digs are at the **Derwent Bridge Wilderness Hotel** ★★, which has one of the biggest lounges in the state with a huge fireplace. The range of rooms runs from family rooms to cabins. Rates run about A$65 double for the main rooms. The restaurant serves large and adequate family-style meals. ☎ *(03) 6289-1144; FAX (03) 6289-1173.*

GLOSSARY

Although English is the official language of Australia, most residents speak a variety known as "Strine" (Australian). Besides having their own words and expressions they also pronounce some words differently. For example: towel is pronounced *tawl* and mate is *mite*. Aussies is spoken as *Ozzies*. Another common modification is to shorten words by replacing some letters with "y" or "i.e." (e.g. brekkie for breakfast, telly for television). Nouns and people's names are often followed by an "o," such as "journo" for journalists or "Jacko." You may also expect to see British spellings of certain words (e.g. harbour, practise, civilisation).

AUSTRALIAN TRANSLATIONS

Strine	English
Drinking & Eating	
amber fluid	beer
barbie	barbecue (BBQ)
billy	tin container used to boil tea in the bush
biscuit	cookie
boozer	pub
bottle	750 ml bottle of beer
bottle shop	liquor shop
bottlo	bottle shop
bush tucker	food found in the Outback
cackle-berries	eggs; also 'hen-fruit', 'chook-nuts' and 'bum-nuts'
camp oven	large, cast-iron pot with lid, used for cooking on an open fire
cask	wine box (an Australian invention)

AUSTRALIAN TRANSLATIONS

Strine	English
Chiko roll	Australian junk food
chook	chicken
chips	French fries
counter meal, countery	pub meal
cuppa	tea or coffee
cut lunch	sandwiches
damper	bush bread made from flour and water and cooked in a *camp oven*
Darwin stubby	two-liter bottle of beer sold to tourists in Darwin
dead horse	tomato sauce
deli	delicatessen, milk bar in Southern Australia
Esky	trademark name for a portable ice box for keeping beer etc. cold
flake	shark meat, used in fish and chips
floater	meat pie floating in pea soup
grog	general term for alcohol
icy-pole	frozen lolly water or ice cream on a stick
jaffle	sealed toasted sandwich
lamington	square of sponge cake covered in chocolate icing and coconut
lemonade	Australian Seven-Up
lollies	sweets, candy
lolly water	soft drink made from syrup and water
middy	285 ml beer glass (New South Wales)
milk bar	general store
mystery-bags	sausages
on the piss	drinking alcohol
pavlova	Australian meringue and cream dessert, named for the Russian ballerina Anna Pavlova
piss	beer
piss turn	boozy party
pissed	drunk

GLOSSARY

AUSTRALIAN TRANSLATIONS

Strine	English
plonk	cheap wine
pot	285 ml glass of beer (Victoria, Queensland)
rat's coffin	meat pie of questionable quality
sanger	sandwich
scallops	fried potato cakes (Queensland), shellfish (elsewhere)
schooner	a 425 ml beer glass in New South Wales, or a 285 ml glass in South Australia (where a 425 ml glass is called a 'pint')
serviette	napkin
session	long period of heavy drinking
shanty	pub, usually unlicensed
shout	buy round of drinks (as in 'it's your shout')
slab	package with four six-packs of *tinnies* or *stubbies*, usually covered in plastic on a cardboard base; called a 'carton' when packaged in a box (Victoria)
smoke-oh	tea break
snag	sausage
stubby	small bottle of beer
takeaway	fast food, or a shop that sells it
tea	evening meal
technicolor yawn	vomiting
thirst you could paint a picture of	craving for lots of foaming, ice-cold, nut-brown ale
tinny	can of beer; also a small, aluminum fishing dinghy (Northern Territory)
tucker	food
two-pot screamer	person unable to hold their drink
wobbly boot	drunk
yabby, yabbie	small freshwater crayfish

Aboriginal Terms

abo	derogatory term for "Aborigine," best avoided
boomerang	a curved flat wooden instrument used by Aborigines for hunting
dijeridu (also didgeridoo)	cylindrical wooden musical instrument played by Aboriginal men

GLOSSARY

AUSTRALIAN TRANSLATIONS

Strine	English
dilly bag	Aboriginal woven-grass carrying bag
gibber	Aboriginal word for stone or boulder; gibber plain—stony desert
humpy	Aboriginal bark hut
Koori	Aborigine (mostly south of the Murray River)
Murri	Aborigine (mostly in Queensland)
nulla-nulla	wooden club used by Aborigines
waddy	wooden club used by Aborigines
woomera	stick used by Aborigines for throwing spears
yakka	work (from an Aboriginal language)

Transportation

bikies	motorcyclists
bitumen	surfaced road
bonnet	hood of a car
boot	trunk of a car
bowser	fuel pump at a service station (named after the U.S. inventor S.F. Bowser)
bull bar	outsize front bumper on car or truck used as a barrier against animals on the road
chuck a U-ey	do a U-turn
dink	carry a second person on a bicycle or horse
donk	car or boat engine
duco	car paint
FJ	most revered Holden car
HQ	second most revered Australian car
rego	registration, as in 'car rego'
road train	*semi-trailer*-trailer-trailer
sealed road	surfaced road
semi-trailer	articulated truck
shitbox	neglected, worn-out, useless vehicle
surfaced road	tarred road
taxi rank	taxi stand
Troopie	Toyota Landcruiser Troopcarrier

AUSTRALIAN TRANSLATIONS

Strine	English
trucky	truck driver
tucker bag	kanpsack or backpack used by hobos or hitchhikers
ute	utility, pick-up truck
wagon	station wagon, estate car

Flora and Fauna

barra	barramundi (prized fish of the north)
blowies	blow flies, bluebottles
boomer	very big, a particularly large male kangaroo
brumby	wild horse
bug (Moreton Bay bug)	a small crab
bungarra	any large (1.5 meter-plus) goanna, but specifically an Aboriginal name for Gould's goanna, prized as food
gidgee	a type of small acacia
joey	young kangaroo or wallaby
jumbuck	sheep
mallee	low, shrubby, multi-stemmed eucalypt; also 'the mallee' — the bush
March fly	horsefly, gadfly
mozzies	mosquitoes
mulga	arid-zone acacia; the bush, away from civilization
pad	animal track
scrub	stunted trees and bushes in a dry area; a remote, uninhabited area
sea wasp	deadly box jellyfish
stinger	box jellyfish
woolly rocks	sheep
yowie	Australia's yeti or bigfoot (also known as a bunyip)

What People Are Called

ankle-biter	small child, tacker, rug rat
banana bender	resident of Queensland
battler	hard trier, struggler
bloke	man

AUSTRALIAN TRANSLATIONS

Strine	English
bludger	lazy person, one who won't work
bluey	swag, or nickname for a red-haired person
bruss	brother, mate (used by central Australian Aborigines)
bushranger	Australia's equivalent of the outlaws of the American Wild West (some goodies, some baddies)
cobber	mate (archaic)
crow eater	resident of South Australia
dag, daggy	dirty lump of wool at back end of a sheep, or an affectionate or mildly derogatory term for a socially clumsy person
digger	Australian or New Zealand soldier or veteran (originally, a miner); also a generic form of address assuming respect, mainly used for soldiers/veterans but sometimes also between friends
dill	idiot
drongo	stupid or worthless person
galah	noisy parrot, thus noisy idiot
game	brave (as in 'game as Ned Kelly')
hoon	idiot, hooligan, yahoo
kiwi	New Zealander
knocker	one who knocks
lair	layabout, ruffian
lairising	acting like a lair
larrikin	a bit like a lair; rascal
mate	general term of familiarity, whether you know the person or not
ocker	an unsophisticated or boorish Australian
off-sider	assistant or partner
pal	mate
pom	English person (almost always "bloody pom")
push	group or gang of people, such as shearers
ratbag	friendly term of abuse
sandgroper	resident of Western Australia
septic tanks	(also 'septics') rhyming slang for Yanks
sheila	woman, sometimes derogatory

GLOSSARY

AUSTRALIAN TRANSLATIONS

Strine	English
sport	mate
squattocracy	Australian 'old money' folk, who made it by grabbing the land first
stickybeak	nosy person
surfies	surfing fanatics
swaggie, swagman	itinerant worker carrying his possessions in a *swag*
tacker	small child, *ankle-biter*
tall poppies	achievers (*knockers* like to cut them down)
Taswegian	resident of Tasmania
terrorist	tourist
wowser	spoilsport, prude
yahoo	noisy and unruly person
youse	plural of you
yobbo	awkward, aggressive person

Professions, Occupations & Related Terms

award wage	minimum pay rate
booze bus	police van used for random breath testing for alcohol
cocky	small-scale farmer
cop, copper	policeperson (not uniquely strine but very common nevertheless); see *walloper*
cow cocky	small-scale cattle farmer
divvy van	police divisional van
garbo	person who collects your garbage
grazier	large-scale sheep or cattle farmer
homestead	the residence of a *station* owner or manager
jackaroo	young male trainee on a *station* (farm)
jillaroo	young female trainee on a *station*
journo	journalist
lock-up	*watch house*
milko	milkman
mob	a herd of cattle or flock of sheep while *droving;* any bunch of people
muster	round up livestock

AUSTRALIAN TRANSLATIONS

Strine	English
outstation	an outlying *station* separate from the main one on a large property
paddock	a fenced area of land, usually intended for livestock
pastoralist	large-scale *grazier*
postie	mailman
salvo	member of the Salvation Army
sickie	day off work ill (or malingering)
squatter	pioneer farmer who occupied land as a tenant of the government
station	large farm
walloper	policeperson (from 'wallop' to hit something with a stick)
watch house	temporary prison at a police station
wharfie	dockworker

Geographical Terms & Landmarks

back o'Bourke	back of beyond, middle of nowhere
backblocks	*bush* or other remote area far from the city
banker	a river almost overflowing its banks (as in 'the Cooper is running a banker')
billabong	water hole in dried up riverbed
black stump	where the *back o' Bourke* begins
blaze	(a blaze in a tree) a mark in a tree trunk made by cutting away bark, indicating a path or reference point; also 'to blaze'
Bullamakanka	imaginary place even beyond the back o' Bourke, way beyond the black stump
bull dust	fine and sometimes deep dust on outback roads, often hiding deep holes and ruts that you normally wouldn't drive into; also bullshit
bunyip	mythical bush spirit said to inhabit Australia's swamps
bush	country, anywhere away from the city; *scrub*
bush (ie go bush)	go back to the land
bushbash	to force your way through pathless bush
culvert	channel or pipe under road for rainwater drainage
Dog Fence	the world's longest fence, erected to keep dingoes out of southeastern Australia

AUSTRALIAN TRANSLATIONS

Strine	English
donga	small portable hut; also the bush
down south	the rest of Australia, viewed from the Northern Territory or anywhere north of Brisbane
Dry, the	the dry season in the north
Eastern states	the rest of Australia viewed from Western Australia
Green, the	term used in the Kimberley for the wet season
Hughie	the god of rain and surf ('Send her down, Hughie!', 'You'll answer to Hughie!'); or God in general ('It's Hughie's way')
jump-up	escarpment
mud map	map drawn on the ground with a stick, or any rough hand-drawn map
never-never	a place more remote than back o' Bourke
north island	mainland Australia, viewed from Tasmania
northern summer	summer in the northern hemisphere
Outback	remote part of the bush, back o' Bourke
seismic line	shotline
shotline	straight trail through the bush, often kilometers long and leading nowhere
table drain	rainwater run-off area, usually quite deep and wide, along the side of a road
Tip, the	the top of Cape York
Top, the	the top of Cape York
Top End	northern part of the Northern Territory
up north	New South Wales and Queensland when viewed from Victoria
washaway	washout; heavy erosion caused by running water across road or track
Wet (ie the Wet)	rainy season in the north
willy-willy	whirlwind, dust storm

Clothing

bathers	swimming costume (Victoria)
brolly	umbrella
clobber	clothes
cozzie	swimming costume (New South Wales)

AUSTRALIAN TRANSLATIONS

Strine	English
daks	trousers
jocks	men's underpants
jumper	a sweater
sandshoes	sneakers
singlet	sleeveless shirt
togs	swimming costume (Queensland, Victoria)

Expressions & Miscellaneous Terms

arvo	afternoon
avagoyermug	traditional rallying call, especially at cricket matches
bail out	leave
bail up	hold up, rob, earbash
barrack	cheer on team at sporting event, support (as in 'who do you barrack for?')
beaut, beauty, bewdie	great, fantastic
big bikkies	a lot of money, expensive
big mobs	a large amount, heaps
blue (ie have a blue)	to have an argument
bonzer	great, ripper
Buckley's, Buckley's chance	no chance at all
bunfight	a quarrel over a silly issue or one that gets blown out of proportion
burl	have a try (as in 'give it a burl')
BYO	Bring Your Own (booze to a restaurant, meat to a barbecue, etc.)
caaarn!	come on, traditional rallying call, especially at football games, as in 'Caaarn the Blues!'
camp draft	Australian rodeo, testing horse rider's skills in separating cattle or sheep from a herd or flock
chocka	completely full (from 'chock-a-block')
chunder	vomit
come good	turn out all right
compo	compensation such as workers' compensation
cooee	shouting distance, close (to be within cooee of...)

AUSTRALIAN TRANSLATIONS

Strine	English
crook	ill, badly constructed, inferior
cut snake	see *mad as a...*
dinkum, fair dinkum	honest, genuine
dinky-di	the real thing
dob in	to tell on someone
don't come the raw prawn	don't try and fool me
droving	moving livestock a great distance
duffing	stealing cattle (literally: altering the brand on the 'duff', or rump)
dunny	outdoor lavatory
earbash	talk incessantly
fair crack of the whip!	fair go!
fair go!	give us a break
feeding the ants	dead out in the bush
flat out	busy
flog	steal; sell; whip
fluke	undeserved good luck
fossick	hunt for gems or semiprecious stones
from arsehole to breakfast	all over the place
furphy	a misleading statement, rumor or fictitious story
gander	look (as in 'have a gander')
g'day	good day, traditional Australian greeting
give it away	give up
good on ya	well done
grouse	very good, unreal
happy as a bastard on Father's Day	depressed or sad
how are ya?	standard greeting, expected answer 'good, thanks, how are you?'
how ya goin'?	*how are ya?*
jumped-up	arrogant, full of self-importance
knackered	exhausted, very tired

AUSTRALIAN TRANSLATIONS

Strine	English
knock	criticize
lay-by	lay away (put a deposit on an article so the shop will hold it for you)
loo	toilet
lurk	a scheme
mad as a cut snake	insane, crazy; also insane with anger
manchester	household linen
Matilda	swag
no-hoper	hopeless case
no worries	she'll be right, that's OK
ocky strap	octopus strap: elastic strap with hooks for tying down gear
off like a bride's nightie	leaving in a hurry
O-S	overseas (as in 'he's gone O-S')
OYO	own your own (flat or apartment)
Oz	Australia
perve	to gaze with lust
pineapple, rough end of	sharp end of a stick
pissed off	annoyed
pocamelo	camel polo
pokies	poker machines, found in clubs, mainly in New South Wales
pommy's towel	a notoriously dry object ('the Simpson Desert is as dry as a pommy's towel')
possie	advantageous position
quid	literally: a pound. A common term in the bush for an unspecified amount of money, as in 'can you lend me a quid?'
ratshit (R.S.)	lousy
rapt	delighted, enraptured
razoo	a coin of very little value, a subdivision of a rupee ('he spent every last razoo').
reckon!	you bet!, absolutely!
ridgy-didge	original, genuine
ripper	good (also 'little ripper')

AUSTRALIAN TRANSLATIONS

Strine	English
root	have sexual intercourse
rooted	tired
ropable	very bad-tempered or angry
rubbish (is to rubbish)	deride, tease
see you in the soup	see you around
shellacking	comprehensive defeat
she'll be right	*no worries*, it'll be OK
shonky	unreliable
shoot through	leave in a hurry
skint	the state of being *quidless*
sleep-out	a covered verandah or shed, usually fairly open
sling off	criticize
spunky	good looking, attractive (as in 'what a spunk')
squiz	a look (as in 'take a squiz')
stick, sharp end of	the worse deal
stoush	fist fight, brawl
stretcher	camp bed
strides	*daks*
strine	Australian slang
sunbake	sunbathe (get a tan)
super	superannuation (contributory pension)
swag	canvas-covered bed roll used in the outback; also a large amount
ta	thanks
thingo	thing, whatchamacalit, thingamajig
too right!	absolutely!
true blue	*dinkum*
two-up	traditional heads/tails gambling game
uni	university
wag (ie to wag)	to skip school or work
walkabout	lengthy walk away from it all
wallaby track (on the)	to wander from place to place seeking work (archaic)

AUSTRALIAN TRANSLATIONS

Strine	English
waltzing Matilda	to wander with one's *swag* seeking work or a place to settle down (from the song)
whinge	complain, moan
weatherboard house	wooden house clad with long, narrow planks
woof wood	petrol used to start a fire
wobbly	disturbing, unpredictable behavior (as in 'throw a wobbly')
yonks	ages; a long time

HOTEL INDEX

A

Acacia Court, *207*
Adelaide Travelodge, *328*
Albert Park Motor Inn, *182*
Alice Springs Pacific Resort, *282*
Alice Tourist Apartments, *283*
All Seasons Sunshine Tower, *207*
Ana, *118*
Anchor Wheel Motel & Restaurant, *393*
Anchorage Village Beach Resort, *178*
Aquarius on the Beach, *198*
Astoria City Travel Inn, *308*
Atrium Hotel Darwin, *262*
Ayers Rock Campground, *290*

B

Backpacking, *380*
Barossa Junction, *334*
Barron Townhouse, *327*
Battery Point Guest House, *379*
Bayside Inn, *393*
Beaufort Hotel, The, *262*
Bellevue Hotel, *182*
Bicheno Hideaway, *396*
Bicheno Holiday Village, *396*
Blue Waters Motor Inn, *400*
Brisbane City Travelodge, *181*
Brisbane Parkroyal, *182*
Burswood Resort Hotel, *351*

C

Cairns Colonial Club Resort, *206*
Cairns International, *206*
Canberra International, *161*
Canberra Travelodge, *160*
Capital Parkroyal, *160*
Casaurina, *149*
Centra Melbourne on the Yarra, *307*
Chancellor on the Park, *183*
Chateau Commodore, *352*
City Gardens, *263*

Colonial Motor Inn, *391*
Convent Peppertree, The, *148*
Country Club Casino, *390*
Country Comfort Inn, The, *148*
Country Comfort Old Melbourne Hotel, *307*

D

Darwin Transit, *263*
Darwin Travel Lodge, *262*
Desert Gardens Hotel, *290*
Desert Palms Resort, *282*
Diamond Beach Hotel/Casino, *262*
Diamond Island Resort, *395*

E

Earl of Zetland, *327*
Eastcoaster Resort, *399*
Elkira Motel, *282*
Elphin Gardens, *390*
Emu Walk Apartments, *290*

F

Festival Lodge, *328*
Fremantle Esplanade, *351*
Frontier Darwin Hotel, *262*
Frontier Oasis Resort, *282*
Furama Hotel Sydney (formerly the Metro Inn), *122*

G

Gazebo Hotel Court, *121*
Gazebo, The, *182*
Grand Chancellor, *378*
Grand Hyatt on Collins, *306*
Great Northern Hotel, *391*
Grosvenor Hotel, *327*

H

Harbour Rocks Hotel, *119*
Harbourside Quality Inn, *206*
Heritage, The (a Beaufort Hotel), *181*

Hilton International Adelaide, *327*
Hilton International Brisbane, *181*
Hilton International, *205*
Hilton on the Park, *306*
Hindley Parkroyal, *327*
Hobart Pacific Motor Inn, *380*
Holiday Inn Cairns, *207*
Holiday Inn Menzies, *121*
Hotel Inter-Continental Sydney, *120*
Hotel Nikko, *122*
Hunter Country Lodge and Restaurant, *148*
Hunter Resort, The, *148*
Hyatt Hotel Canberra, *160*
Hyatt Kingsgate, *121*
Hyatt Regency Adelaide, *326*
Hyatt Regency, *351*

K

Kirkton Park Country Hotel, *148*
KOA and Malak Caravan Park, *263*

L

Lakeside International, *160*
Landhaus, *334*
Landmark, *121*
Lasseters Hotel Casino, *282*
Lawley Farm, *334*
Le Meridien, *306*
Lenna of Hobart, *379*
Lennons Hotel Brisbane, *182*
Lodge in Seppeltsfield, The, *334*
Lodge on Elizabeth, The, *379*

M

Macquarie Motor Inn, *380*
Magnolia Court Boutique Hotel, *307*
Manly Ocean Royal, *123*
Manly Pacific Parkroyal, *123*

RESTAURANT INDEX

INDEX

Order Your Guide to Travel and Adventure

Title	Price	Title	Price
Fielding's Alaska Cruises and the Inside Passage	$18.95	Fielding's Indiana Jones Adventure and Survival Guide™	$15.95
Fielding's America West	$19.95	Fielding's Italy	$18.95
Fielding's Asia's Top Dive Sites	$19.95	Fielding's Kenya	$19.95
Fielding's Australia	$18.95	Fielding's Las Vegas Agenda	$16.95
Fielding's Bahamas	$16.95	Fielding's London Agenda	$14.95
Fielding's Baja California	$18.95	Fielding's Los Angeles	$16.95
Fielding's Bermuda	$16.95	Fielding's Mexico	$18.95
Fielding's Best and Worst	$19.95	Fielding's New Orleans Agenda	$16.95
Fielding's Birding Indonesia	$19.95	Fielding's New York Agenda	$16.95
Fielding's Borneo	$18.95	Fielding's New Zealand	$17.95
Fielding's Budget Europe	$18.95	Fielding's Paradors, Pousadas and Charming Villages of Spain and Portugal	$18.95
Fielding's Caribbean	$19.95	Fielding's Paris Agenda	$14.95
Fielding's Caribbean Cruises	$18.95	Fielding's Portugal	$16.95
Fielding's Caribbean on a Budget	$18.95	Fielding's Rome Agenda	$16.95
Fielding's Diving Australia	$19.95	Fielding's San Diego Agenda	$14.95
Fielding's Diving Indonesia	$19.95	Fielding's Southeast Asia	$18.95
Fielding's Eastern Caribbean	$17.95	Fielding's Southern California Theme Parks	$18.95
Fielding's England including Ireland, Scotland and Wales	$18.95	Fielding's Southern Vietnam on Two Wheels	$15.95
Fielding's Europe	$19.95	Fielding's Spain	$18.95
Fielding's Europe 50th Anniversary	$24.95	Fielding's Surfing Australia	$19.95
Fielding's European Cruises	$18.95	Fielding's Surfing Indonesia	$19.95
Fielding's Far East	$18.95	Fielding's Sydney Agenda	$16.95
Fielding's France	$18.95	Fielding's Thailand, Cambodia, Laos and Myanmar	$18.95
Fielding's France: Loire Valley, Burgundy and the Best of French Culture	$16.95	Fielding's Travel Tool™	$15.95
Fielding's France: Normandy & Brittany	$16.95	Fielding's Vietnam including Cambodia and Laos	$19.95
Fielding's France: Provence and the Mediterranean	$16.95	Fielding's Walt Disney World and Orlando Area Theme Parks	$18.95
Fielding's Freewheelin' USA	$18.95	Fielding's Western Caribbean	$18.95
Fielding's Hawaii	$18.95	Fielding's The World's Most Dangerous Places™	$21.95
Fielding's Hot Spots: Travel in Harm's Way	$15.95	Fielding's Worldwide Cruises	$21.95

To place an order: call toll-free 1-800-FW-2-GUIDE
(VISA, MasterCard and American Express accepted)
or send your check or money order to:
Fielding Worldwide, Inc., 308 S. Catalina Avenue, Redondo Beach, CA 90277
http://www.fieldingtravel.com
Add $4.00 per book for shipping & handling (sorry, no COD's), allow 2–6 weeks for delivery

International Conversions

TEMPERATURE

To convert °F to °C, subtract 32 and divide by 1.8. To convert °C to °F, multiply by 1.8 and add 32.

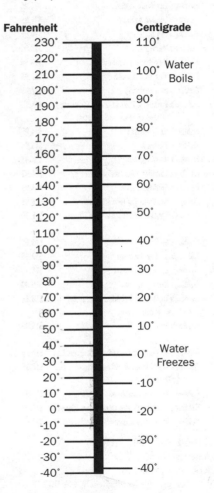

Fahrenheit	Centigrade	
230°	110°	
220°	100°	Water Boils
210°	100°	
200°	90°	
190°	90°	
180°	80°	
170°	80°	
160°	70°	
150°	60°	
140°	60°	
130°	50°	
120°	50°	
110°	40°	
100°	40°	
90°	30°	
80°	30°	
70°	20°	
60°	20°	
50°	10°	
40°	0°	Water Freezes
30°	0°	
20°	-10°	
10°	-10°	
0°	-20°	
-10°	-20°	
-20°	-30°	
-30°	-30°	
-40°	-40°	

WEIGHTS & MEASURES

LENGTH		
1 km	=	0.62 miles
1 mile	=	1.609 km
1 meter	=	1.0936 yards
1 meter	=	3.28 feet
1 yard	=	0.9144 meters
1 yard	=	3 feet
1 foot	=	30.48 centimeters
1 centimeter	=	0.39 inch
1 inch	=	2.54 centimeters

AREA		
1 square km	=	0.3861 square miles
1 square mile	=	2.590 square km
1 hectare	=	2.47 acres
1 acre	=	0.405 hectare

VOLUME		
1 cubic meter	=	1.307 cubic yards
1 cubic yard	=	0.765 cubic meter
1 cubic yard	=	27 cubic feet
1 cubic foot	=	0.028 cubic meter
1 cubic centimeter	=	0.061 cubic inch
1 cubic inch	=	16.387 cubic centimeters

CAPACITY		
1 gallon	=	3.785 liters
1 quart	=	0.94635 liters
1 liter	=	1.057 quarts
1 pint	=	473 milliliters
1 fluid ounce	=	29.573 milliliters

MASS and WEIGHT		
1 metric ton	=	1.102 short tons
1 metric ton	=	1000 kilograms
1 short ton	=	.90718 metric ton
1 long ton	=	1.016 metric tons
1 long ton	=	2240 pounds
1 pound	=	0.4536 kilograms
1 kilogram	=	2.2046 pounds
1 ounce	=	28.35 grams
1 gram	=	0.035 ounce
1 milligram	=	0.015 grain

cm 0 1 2 3 4 5 6 7 8 9 10

Inch 0 1 2 3 4